Artists & Agents

Performance Art and Secret Services

Kata Krasznahorkai,
Sylvia Sasse (Eds.)

Spector Books

in the context of the exhibition *Artists & Agents: Performance Art and Secret Services*, curated by Inke Arns (HMKV), Kata Krasznahorkai (University of Zurich) and Sylvia Sasse (University of Zurich).

Kata Krasznahorkai, Sylvia Sasse
Artists & Agents
Performance Art and Secret Services
2019
1

European Research Council

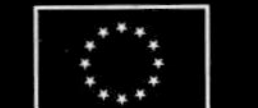

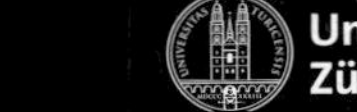

HMKV Hartware MedienKunstVerein

Subversion belongs to no one. It can come from artists who outwit the state, or from secret services who infiltrate the art scene on behalf of the state. But what happens when both sides meet?

Since the gradual opening of the secret service archives in Eastern Europe and the fiches in Switzerland, as well as increasing access to individual files in the USA, we know how art and artists have become the target of observation and disinformation. In Eastern Europe, the secret police were particularly afraid of happenings, performance art, and action art, and therefore documented them particularly intensively while also trying to manipulate them with counteractions. In *Artists & Agents*, we show the "disruptive" creativity of secret police work, the interaction between artistic and secret service actions, as well as the relevance of research in secret service archives for art and cultural history. However, we will also show how artists work with the potential observation of the informers, and how they deal critically with secret service documents and missions today.

Artists & Agents

Performance Art
and Secret Services

EDITED BY:
Kata Krasznahorkai,
Sylvia Sasse

GRAPHIC DESIGN:
Malin Gewinner

TYPEFACES:
Kolektiv Book (Ondrej Bachor),
Vevey (Clemens Piontek),
Diatype Pre (Dinamo),
Monument Grotesk (Dinamo)

LITHOGRAPHY:
Ralf Lenk, ScanColor Leipzig

TRANSLATION:
Brian Alkire,
Gwen Jones,
David Riff,
Olga Stefan,
Dagmar Wallace-Tarry

COPYEDITING/
PROOFREADING:
Victoria Nebolsin

PRINTING AND BINDING:
Druckhaus Sportflieger,
Berlin

PUBLISHED BY

Spector Books
Harkortstraße 10
04107 Leipzig
www.spectorbooks.com

DISTRIBUTION:
Germany, Austria:
GVA, Gemeinsame
Verlagsauslieferung
Göttingen GmbH & Co. KG,
www.gva-verlage.de
Switzerland: AVA
Verlagsauslieferung AG,
www.ava.ch
France, Belgium: Interart
Paris, www.interart.fr
UK: Central Books Ltd,
www.centralbooks.com
USA, Canada, Central and
South America, Africa:
ARTBOOK | D.A.P.,
www.artbook.com
Japan: twelvebooks,
www.twelve-books.com
South Korea:
The Book Society,
www.thebooksociety.org
Australia, New Zealand:
Perimeter Distribution,
perimeterdistribution.com

The German edition
of this publication
entitled *Artists and
Agents—Performacekunst
und Geheimdienste* has
been published by
Spector Books in 2019
with the
ISBN 978-3-95905-313-6

Printed in Germany

ISBN 978-3-95905-333-4

This publication was first released in German in the context of the exhibition "Artists & Agents—Performance Art and Secret Services," October 25, 2019–March 22, 2020 at HMKV (Hartware MedienKunstVerein), Dortmund.

Curated by Inke Arns (HMKV), Kata Krasznahorkai (University of Zurich), and Sylvia Sasse (University of Zurich).

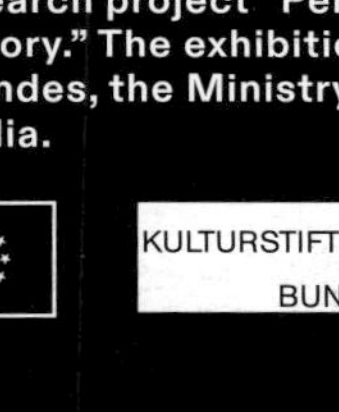

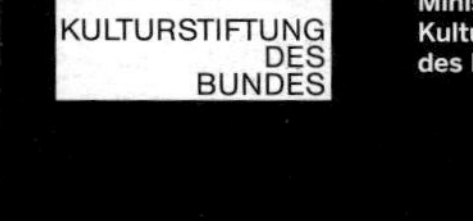

The publication is funded by the European Research Council (ERC) in the framework of the research project "Performance Art in Eastern Europe 1950–1990: History and Theory." The exhibition was additionally supported by the Kulturstiftung des Bundes, the Ministry of Culture and Science of the State of North Rhine-Westphalia.

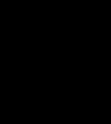

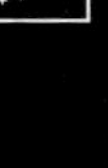

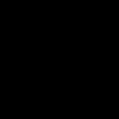

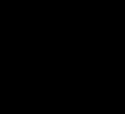

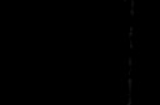

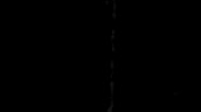

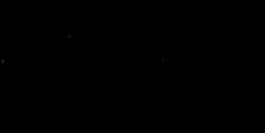

Archives and Agents

Theories

Documentations

Interactions and Counteractions

Counter-surveillance

Measures and "Decompositions"

Re-reading, Re-enactment, Re-construction

Archive Appropriation

Annex

Surveillance and “Decomposition”

An Introduction

Kata Krasznahorkai, Sylvia Sasse

Subversion belongs to no one. It can be performed by artists trying to outsmart the state or by secret police who are ordered by the state to infiltrate the art scene. But what happens when both sides encounter each other? Such collisions are the subject of this book. We know a great deal about subversion and criticism in the arts, yet little about the strategies that the secret police used—and continue to use—to spread disinformation about art, through the medium of art itself.

The causes of this disinformation and surveillance can vary greatly, though generally, they concern the attempt to surveil, prevent, disrupt, and destroy art that appears aesthetically risky. These efforts discredit, pathologize, and in the worst cases, even criminalize subversive artists. And so it happens that secret police agents interfere in performances, become photo models themselves, and even plan and carry out their own art actions, sometimes against a planned performance and sometimes as members of artist groups. At first glance, this might sound somewhat fantastic. However, after reading thousands of pages of secret police reports written between 1950 and 1990 in Eastern Europe's former socialist states, it became evident that the artists were confronting what went beyond the secret police's abstract force and concrete threats. In fact, informants intervened in the art scene itself, as well as in the processes of artistic creation, through shockingly ingenious methods. Secret police services themselves documented these interventions in meticulous detail: producing “Who's-Who” summaries, writing operational plans, inventing “decomposition measures,” planting informants, destroying works of art, stopping exhibitions, introducing happening prevention, and inviting artists to “discussions.”

Was This Only the Case in Eastern Europe?

We do not know if what we read about in the files only happened in Eastern Europe. Secret police documents are, by nature, not easily accessible. As a rule, this knowledge isn't public. As early as 1967, it was discovered that the Central Intelligence Agency had attempted to influence international art and intellectual scenes. The CIA financed the "Congress for Cultural Freedom," an organization founded in Berlin in 1950 with the purpose of creating propaganda directed against the communist East. The extent to which the United States surveilled the domestic art industry via the Federal Bureau of Investigation remains, however, unknown.[1] With the collapse of Eastern Europe's former party dictatorships in 1989, we encountered a historically unique situation. Gradually, the materials of the former state security services have become open to personal and scholarly research. The only exceptions are Russia and Yugoslavia (excluding Slovenia), where accessing the files is still not possible. In all other Eastern European countries, however, it is now possible to gain a comprehensive overview of secret police (domestic) and intelligence service (foreign) operations. This inevitably leads to an imbalance of knowledge about secret service practices in dictatorships as opposed to democracies. Subsequently, Eastern Europe is primarily the *site* of research rather than its exclusive *subject*. We could say that the materials from Eastern European secret police **archives** allow us to imagine the practices which have been and are still used worldwide, with variating degrees of how they have been directed towards a country's own population as well as towards the art world. Nevertheless, the newly discovered material cannot simply be applied to different political situations. When researching Eastern Europe's open archives, we are confronting secret police operations in autocratic systems that classified underground artists as aesthetic and political "**hostile-negative** elements," thus persecuting them as such. Research in Switzerland has shown, however, that critical or leftist artists have also been subject to **surveillance** in a democratic society. Between 1900 and 1990, Switzerland compiled over nine hundred thousand state security files called "**Fichen**" (compared to the forty-one million index cards and one hundred eleven kilometers of files in the GDR), which were made accessible in 1990 after the so-called **Fiche Scandal** that exposed the **surveillance**. Even members of the Dadaist movement—Hugo Ball, Emmy Hennings, and Tristan Tzara—were placed under **surveillance** in Switzerland in 1919 on suspicion of "propagating" "revolutionary ideas"; in Zurich, Dada was suspected of being a "Bolshevik enterprise."[2] This is the fear that finds expression in the Swiss Fichen—and presumably not only there. While the GDR labeled its critics as "hostile-negative elements" in Switzerland, it was the "anarchists," "militants," "extremists," and "socialists" who were placed under surveillance and imagined to be potential enemies.[3] This fear continues even in contemporary rhetoric, e.g. when it was revealed in 2018 that the German Center for Political Beauty (*Zentrum für Politische Schönheit*) was being investigated on suspicion of "forming a criminal organization." Paragraph 129 of the German Criminal Code is considered the "snooping paragraph." Under its jurisdiction, investigative authorities are authorized to take invasive measures, such as reading mail, phone-tapping, long-term surveillance, the use of informants, clandestine investigators, dragnet operations, and "major eavesdropping."

Actions Against Action Art

Even if dictatorships are often portrayed as perfect systems of surveillance in the films and dystopias of popular culture, keyword "Big Brother," it was always only a starting point for what state security services in Eastern Europe called "decomposition." "Decomposition"[4] is a word stemming from the Russian *razlozheniye* that indicates the psychological and physical destruction of persons, groups, and objects. The art scene and the conditions of underground artistic production were also subject to "decomposition" in most socialist countries. Reading about these practices remains disturbing, even thirty years after the fall of the Iron Curtain. They reveal the performative aspect of the secret police—a factor that manifests in its actions and interactions with artists. It is this aspect that interests us here, particularly with regards to its uncanny, destructive creativity. During our research, we were continually asking ourselves where the handling agents got their ludicrous ideas for the interventions, counteractions, and subversions that they used to unsettle the art scene, discredit individuals, and even "create" "art" themselves—e.g. anti-Stasi poems. These actions were creations so similar to artistic actions as to be almost indistinguishable, such as in cases of mimicry or "fake actions."

It is no surprise that the secret police's preference for actions aroused a special interest in a specific genre, at least in Eastern Europe: performances, happenings, and action art. Their interest was piqued not only because performance art originated in the reviled avant-garde movement and bourgeois West, but also because these actions could not immediately be recognized for what they were. They spurred suspicion because the secret police didn't understand what exactly was happening in these actions and were afraid of their unpredictability and influence, i.e. that they could produce an equally uncontrollable public sphere or be interpreted as "demonstrations." For this reason, action art was often not just kept under **surveillance**, but prevented from happening or frequently disturbed—especially with counteractions. In some cases, this led to actual competition between artistic actions and secret police actions.

If we wanted to write a sequel to Michel Foucault's famous *Discipline and Punish* in Cold-War-era Eastern Europe, we could easily call it *Discipline and Disrupt*, drawing attention to precisely the aspect that must remain hidden and that was meant to be preventive: "**decomposition**." "**Decomposition**" is a covert, theatrical punishment outside the bounds of the law. It refers to a clandestine state or secret police actions that violate the state's own laws and constitution in the name of the law. Foucault spoke of a punishment process becoming more discreet, as well as of a soberness of discipline that had replaced the previous theater of punishment. His observation that punishment disappeared from public view over the course of history, becoming increasingly subtle and insidious in the process, can be supplemented by the thesis that during the Cold War, theater again became subject to illegal sanction. However, this was a sanction that was forced to remain covert. Seriously taking the practice of "**decomposition**" as a disciplinary practice would require supplementing Foucault's thesis with another claim: that autocratic systems (at least) introduce discreet yet performative, disciplinary actions which do not reveal themselves as such.

Is This Not All Just a Thing of the Past?

This book and its accompanying exhibition are being put together in 2019, thirty years after the end of the Cold War and about twenty years after the opening of secret police **archives** in most Eastern European countries. So far, the knowledge acquired from these **archives** has remained stuck in the discourse of reappraisal and has only occasionally, and in isolated instances, become part of debates in scholarly studies of art, literature, and theater. This is unfortunate, considering the fact that we've entered the era of the Mueller Report and "Ibiza-gate," i.e. a period of learning how clandestine practices still shape and alter social and political reality. Even interaction with the **archives** itself is not free of political interests and a naïve faith in its **sources**. The Julia Kristeva case reminded us again that the reading and interpretation of state security files is a challenging task. These files do not reflect facts; they were made as an attempt to *produce* them.

And in art? After sixteen months of **observation**, the investigation of the Center for Political Beauty concerning "suspicion of forming a criminal organization" was dropped, but we do not know whether the artist collective was also placed under **surveillance** by the German Federal Office for the Protection of the Constitution (*Bundesverfassungsschutz*). In Russia and Serbia, exhibitions are frequently disrupted under the pretext of bomb threats or broken water pipes—all actions that are familiar from the secret police files. The Hungarian state propaganda compiles "blacklists" with the names of writers and artists who allegedly act against the Hungarian people and who are allegedly financed "by the West." This reactivates the secret police narrative that criticism can *only* emerge from and be paid for by the "West," foremost by George Soros.[5] We can currently observe how this secret service narrative has migrated from the era of genuine socialism into nationalist, right-wing populist discourse. The practices of the secret services have thus arrived in nationalist circles, and it is these circles that are "exposed" in their practice of similar methods. One such example is the 2019 "Strache-video," which cost the far-right Freedom Party of Austria (*Freiheitilche Partei Österreichs*, FPÖ) their participation in the governing coalition. The production of **kompromat** is a contemporary political praxis—but not only that. Do you remember the case of Pyotr Verzilov? During the 2018 FIFA World Cup final between France and Croatia, Verzilov ran onto the field with his colleagues from Pussy Riot[6] to protest for the release of the Ukrainian director Oleg Sentsov. Barely two months later, on September 11, 2018, Verzilov came home from a court hearing, began to feel ill, and lay down in bed. When he woke up, he could no longer see properly, and soon, could no longer speak either. As more time passed, he could hardly even walk. Initially, he went to a Moscow hospital's poison control center, before being flown on a private helicopter to Berlin's Charité hospital two days later. There, physicians confirmed that he had been poisoned.

In the German opinion columns on the case, there were some who made a stir about the events being Western anti-Putin propaganda, or who asserted that Verzilov was being paid by George Soros, an explanation for why he was able to be flown to Germany. Or, to cite the commentator "John S.": "If you're drunk and eat a three-week-old fish, it's a great idea to give Putin as the cause, so your insurance keeps on paying. But in all seriousness, maybe we should take a closer look at the uncommon consumption of uncommon substances in these 'artist's' guilds."

These two patterns recurred repeatedly in the opinion columns: first of all, they claimed the story was invented, that it was a cock-and-bull story created by the lying Western press and that Verzilov had staged the whole thing using the financial support of Soros (a frequent name in these sorts of circumstances) in order to damage Putin. Second, they made the familiar assertion that artists like to claim that they have been poisoned when they've simply overdosed on drugs. And, the claim continues, it is exactly those artists that the Western press gives endless attention to with the purpose—in this case—of painting Russia in a false light.

Negative Inclusion

We owe our ability to examine the Stasi records, in Germany at least, to those who were themselves subjects of **surveillance**. In the GDR, dissident activists in Erfurt, including artist Gabriele Stötzer, occupied the local Stasi headquarters in a concentrated action on December 4, 1989. On January 15, 1990, the headquarters in Berlin were also finally occupied. The massive destruction and disordering of files was thus able to be stopped, and shredded paper scraps were salvaged. File destruction took place not only in the GDR, but also in all other former socialist states, where it continued to take place for much longer beyond 1990. In Hungary, for example, the "Underground" file, approximately four hundred pages long, was destroyed.[7] In Russia, the destruction of important files was particularly dramatic. As Arseny Roginsky and Nikita Okhotin summarized at a 1993 symposium on "State Security Services and Literature," the total destruction of all files concerning **unofficial informants** was ordered during the fall of 1990; in 1991, numerous files of victims, "among them many writers,"[8] were destroyed.

Former secret service **archives** are not like those that Michel de Certeau describes in "The Space of the Archive and the Perversion of Time"—**archives** which set something aside, organize what already exists, or define something as a **source**.[9] Instead, this kind of **archive** collects that which only came into existence *through* an agency in the first place—in this case, the secret police. There is no preexisting archivable material: instead, there is a demand to produce material, specifically about those who are to be registered and documented as potential enemies of society. The act of making and producing, including the production of persons as enemies, precedes the act of archiving. The "institutive and conservative" function of the **archive**, as described by Derrida in *Archive Fever*,[10] shifts solely to its institutive role in the case of secret service files. That which is preserved is that which itself has been produced for the sole purpose of existing. "Production" here does not mean what it usually does in the **archive** science of cultural studies, i.e. the archival events of copying, printing, binding, and classification, but rather, points to the fundamental generation of the material to be collected: the creation of the **source**. Interestingly, it is an artist, György Galántai, who makes a connection to precisely this active function, naming his **archive** "Active Archive." In contrast to traditional **archives**, Galántai, as he writes in a manifesto,[11] not only collects preexisting material but, in certain cases, also produces the very material which is to be collected. The real, ironic parallel to the secret service **archives** is not coincidental. It is Galántai who was the first artist in Hungary—and not only in Hungary—to make his secret police files public in this "Active Archive," and thus stimulated artistic and scholarly research into these files far beyond his native Hungary.

In the case of secret service documents, the cultural technology of archiving has the function of producing a secret, nonpublic memory of political and artistic deviation.[12] Secret service **archives** are thus not what Foucault described in *The Archeology of Knowledge* as "first the law of what can be said, the system that governs the appearance of statements as unique events."[13] Instead, secret service **archives** function according to the law of what *cannot* be said—both regarding stored objects (the socially deviant, the nonconformists) as well as with respect to the cultural technology of **observation**, documentation, storage, encoding, registering, and archiving. It is the **archive** and the act of archiving itself which must be concealed, and the contents of the **archive** must be partially enciphered so that they cannot be read without the code, the lexicon, and insider knowledge. This means, absurdly, that the analysis of Stasi documents required the assistance of former Stasi **agents**, who ensured both access to and legibility of the files.

This does not fundamentally concern a process of inclusion and exclusion, of the discernment of what a society considers worth preserving, but rather explores a form of "negative inclusion."[14] In the **archive**, we can find (in this case) exactly the point of entry that is not intended to be part of public memory—e.g. the false "documentation" of nonconformist literature and art generated through continual surveillance. The "documents" produced serve the exact purpose of justifying the performance of the archive—its negative inclusion.

"But there's nothing there, there's nothing in there"

During our research, we repeatedly heard the sentence: "but there's nothing there, there's nothing in there. And even if there is, it's only banal." In the introduction to his book *Stasi Konkret* (*Stasi Concretely*), the historian Ilko-Sascha Kowalczuk writes that historians of the era repeatedly assert that material from the catalogues of state security services is "boring."[15] In Hungary, György Gyarmati—long-time director (2003–17) of the ÁBTL archive—himself downplayed the relevance and significance of the documents collected in the **archive**, using the same motto of "there's nothing there."[16]

We are glad that we chose not to follow this advice. We often even wished that the "**operative measures**" were *more* banal, like in cases involving the systematic destruction of artists. And even the most banal reports reveal the logic of secret police work, which falls fully in line with Hannah Arendt's thoughts on the "banality of evil" as here too, we are dealing with narrow-minded bureaucrats and their ideas about art and artists. This is particularly apparent in the files of the Czechoslovakian secret police, who now and again placed Milan Knížák and Marie Saudková under **surveillance**. The investigation reports contain highly detailed accounts of their daily lives—the opening of a window, shopping purchases, walking into the studio—while also specifying the time and describing their clothes. But they also document the disproportionate amount of effort that went into collecting these everyday details: an average of seven **informants** was simultaneously deployed to observe both the artists; the newest and most expensive automobiles were used for "discreet" **observation**, with telescopes pointing from the cars; the **informants** began to need more space in their reports for the recording of unrelated activities. They would describe their disguises (the clothing concepts of each individual **informant**) and paint cards indicating the locations of the **surveillance** vehicles around Knížák's studio. In this case, the reports reveal their own self-referentiality, and refer more to their own work than to whatever they had observed. In this case, the phrase "there's nothing there" would need to show how much manpower, time, and money was used to report about "nothing," a practice that Max Frisch also described in a commentary on his own files in Switzerland. With reference to the secret police, however, this "nothing" is a direct component of practicing self-preservation and self-reference. It's a system which constantly invents its other, its enemies, and its threats—and it does so to remain in existence. Our interview with Hristo Hristov, a specialist in research of the Bulgarian **archives**, shows that the contents of the **archives** are not "nothing" and can even be dangerous. Ironically, it is his research on secret police activity that is now being suppressed with the secret police's old methods.

*

We would like to express our gratitude to a number of different people who helped us during our research and analysis of our material. First of all, we would like to thank the archivists, without whom none of our research into former secret service archives would have been possible: Tamás Szőnyei (ÁBTL), Gudrun Krauss (BStU), Tadej Cankar (Ministrstvo za kulturo Arhiv Republike Slovenije), Peter Mikle (Archív Ústavu pamäti národa vBratislavě, Bratislava), Jaroslav Vaňous (Archiv bezpečnostních složek, Prague), Grzegorz Perzyński (IPN, Warsaw) and the Robert Havemann Gesellschaft (Christoph Ochs, Rebecca Garcia, Frank Ebert), the archive of the Forschungsstelle Osteuropa in Bremen (Maria Klassen), the GZSI (National Center for Contemporary Art, Mariya Chuykova), the editors of the journal *Iskusstvo*, as well as Gabriele Stötzer, Kurt Buchwald, Tamás St.Turba (NETRAF-agent), Béla Révész, Thomas Ranft, Gunar Barthel, Dov Bar-Gera, Vladimir Sychev, and Alya Tesis, who provided us with works from their own private archives. We thank Mariya Chuykova, Nikolay Yerofeyev, and Yuri Albert for their useful guidance. We would also like to thank Sandra Frimmel, Tomáš Glanc, Alexia Panagiotidis, Anja-Rebecca Römisch, and Liliana Gómez for their research assistance and cooperation. We worked especially closely with our translators, whom we owe a special thanks: Brian Alkire, Alexandru Bulucz, Karl Hoffmann, Sabine Hofmann, Gwen Jones, Kristina Kallert, Anne Krier, David Riff, Nina Seiler, Olga Stefan, Monika Stekowski, Tímea Tankó, and Dagmar Wallace-Tarry.

Special thanks are owed to Malin Gewinner, the book designer, to Victoria Nebolsin for copyediting and proofreading, and to Jan Wenzel of *Spector Books* for the wonderful collaboration. We would like to thank Inke Arns, cocurator of the eponymous exhibition at the HMKV Dortmund and who wrote many of the work descriptions in the book, as well as the staff of the HMKV for their inspiration, ideas, communication, and discussion of the texts.

Translated from German by Brian Alkire

Endnotes

1 "Parapolitics: Cultural Freedom and the Cold War. Haus der Kulturen der Welt, Berlin," https://www.hkw.de/en/programm/projekte/2017/parapolitics/parapolitics_start.php (accessed October 19, 2020).

2 Guido Koller, "Unter Beobachtung," *Neue Zürcher Zeitung*, February 10, 2016, https://www.nzz.ch/feuilleton/100-jahre-dada/100-jahre-dada-unter-beobachtung-ld.5195 (accessed October 19, 2020).

3 See Christof Nüssli/Christoph Oeschger (eds.): *Nikolaus Rosza, N. Rosza, Niklaus Rosza, Miklos Rosza, Robert (Miklos) Nikolaus Rosza, Rosza, K. Rosza, Rochat, Klaus Schmidt, Klaus Schmid, Nikolaus Rozsa, Niklaus Rozsa, Klaus Rozsa, Miklos Rozsa, Miklos (Klaus) Rozsa, Robert Nikolaus Rozsa, Rozsa, K.Rozsa, M. Rozsa, Miklós Klaus Rózsa*, (Leipzig/Zurich: Spector Books, 2014).

4 "Decomposition" invokes biological semantics in Russian; it means the psychical destruction of opposition members and the class enemy (subversion of the enemy). The term was already used by Lenin in order to describe the state of capitalism as a rotten state. The same meaning was used for the opposition, the critics, etc. To "decompose" them means to make their decay visible. In this sense, the term describes both a state of affairs and the central measure used by the secret services and state security to destroy the enemy.

5 George Soros is an American philanthropist and investor of Hungarian origin. He has been supporting democratic causes for the last thirty years, particularly in Eastern Europe. His organization, the Open Society Foundation, supports democracy and human rights in one hundred countries. Soros is the main target of the current right-wing Hungarian government's campaign against migration, democratic values, and European standards in political and cultural policies. The government identifies him as the head of an "anti-Hungarian worldwide conspiracy."

6 Sylvia Sasse, "'Der Milizionär kommt ins Spiel' – Wie Pussy Riot den Dichter Dmitrij Prigov zitieren und das Politische poetisch wird", *Geschichte der Gegenwart*, July 22, 2018, https://geschichtedergegenwart.ch/der-milizionaer-kommt-ins-spiel-wie-pussy-riot-den-dichter-dmitrij-prigov-zitieren-und-das-politische-poetisch-wird/ (accessed October 19, 2020).

7 The three volumes of the "Underground" files, originally opened under number Cs-771 under suspicion of agitation and archived

on October 14, 1976 under number O-16097, consisted of 225, 263, and 29 pages. The files, however, no longer exist—they were shredded in 1989, as we know from page 17 of an untitled object registry: ÁBTL, 3.1.5. (O-Register) 15860-19897. We will thus not be able to review the corresponding reports of the secret agent "Pécsi Zoltán", nor of any other **informants**. The fact that the files were shredded twenty-three years after their archiving points with the intention of destroying the information specified therein.

8 Arseny Roginsky and Nikita Okhotin, "Archivquellen zum Thema KGB und Literatur," in *Stasi, KGB und Literatur. Beiträge und Erfahrungen aus Russland und Deutschland* (Cologne: Heinrich-Böll-Stiftung, 1993), 135. In Roginsky/Okhotin, it also becomes clear that only one person initially had access to the 1930s dossiers—Vitaly Shentalinsky, who published the results in a narrative and rather unscholarly form: Vitaly Shentalinsky, *Arrested Voices: Resurrecting the Disappeared Voices of the Soviet Regime* (New York: Free Press, 1996). Also from this time period: the file-reading scene of Vladimir Voinovich, *Delo № 34840 (Case № 34840)* (Moscow, 1994).

9 Michel de Certeau, "L'espace de l'archive ou la perversion du temps," *Traverses. Revue du Centre de Création Industrielle*, no. 36 (1986): 4–6.

10 Jacques Derrida, "Archive Fever: A Freudian Impression," trans. by Eric Prenowitz, *Diacritics* 25, no. 2 (Summer 1995): 12, http://artsites.ucsc.edu/sdaniel/230/derrida_archivefever.pdf

11 György Galántai, "Active Archive 1979–2003," in *Artpool—The Experimental Art Archive of East-Central Europe: History of an active archive for producing, networking, curating, and researching art since 1970*, ed. by György Galántai and Júlia Klaniczay (Budapest: Artpool Art Research Center, 2013): 15.

12 An overview of the **archive** can be found in the glossary. On comparative research: Dagmar Unverhau and Roland Lucht, *Lustration, Aktenöffnung, demokratischer Umbruch in Polen, Tschechien, der Slowakei und Ungarn* (Münster: LIT Verlag, 2005).

13 Michel Foucault, "The Historical *a priori* and the Archive," in *Archaeology of Knowledge and the Discourse on Language*, trans. A.M. Sheridan Smith (New York: Pantheon, 1972), 145.

14 On the question of how the institutions of modernity engage in negative inclusion through **archives**, e.g. through court hearings against marginalized people, see Foucault, "The Life of Infamous Men," in *Power, Truth, Strategy*. We thank Anne Krier for the tip.

15 Ilko-Sascha Kowalczuk, *Stasi Konkret. Überwachung und Repression in der DDR* (Munich: Beck C.H., 2013), 16.

16 Gyarmati György, *Kísértő közelmúlt – avagy a rendszerváltás egyik deficitje* (Budapest: L'Harmattan - Líceum, 2011). Krisztián Ungváry referred to this lack of reflective access to the archive catalogues on Gyarmati's part: Krisztián Ungváry, "Források és alulértékelésük," in *Az ügynök arcai*, ed. by Sándor Horváth (Budapest: Libri Publishing Hungary, 2014), 89–106. See also: Ungváry, *A szembenézés hiánya. Felelősségre vonás, iratnyilvánosság és átvilágítás Magyarországon 1990–2017*).

Exhibition:

Artists & Agents Performance Art and Secret Services

The international group exhibition *Artists &* Agents—*Performance Art and Secret Services* focuses on the interaction between secret services and performance art—an art form that was considered particularly dangerous by the secret services of the Socialist countries in Eastern Europe. Accessible archives today exist almost exclusively in Eastern Europe and reveal the "disruption" and "liquidation" of dissident artists by state security services. For this, however, some of the agents had to become "performance artists" themselves. Artists & Agents presents examples of artistic subversion and secret service infiltration, some of which have never been shown before. Recent works show that the issue of the increasing use of secret service methods in today's politics and everyday life is highly topical.

The exhibition features works by artists from Bulgaria, Chile, Croatia, the Czech Republic, Germany, Hungary, Poland, Romania, Russia, and the USA.

An exhibition by HMKV (Hartware MedienKunstVerein), Dortmund in cooperation with the Slavic Department of the University of Zurich, October 26, 2019 –April 19, 2020, Dortmunder U.

+++ Awarded as "Exhibition of the Year 2020" by the German section of the International Art Critics Association, AICA .

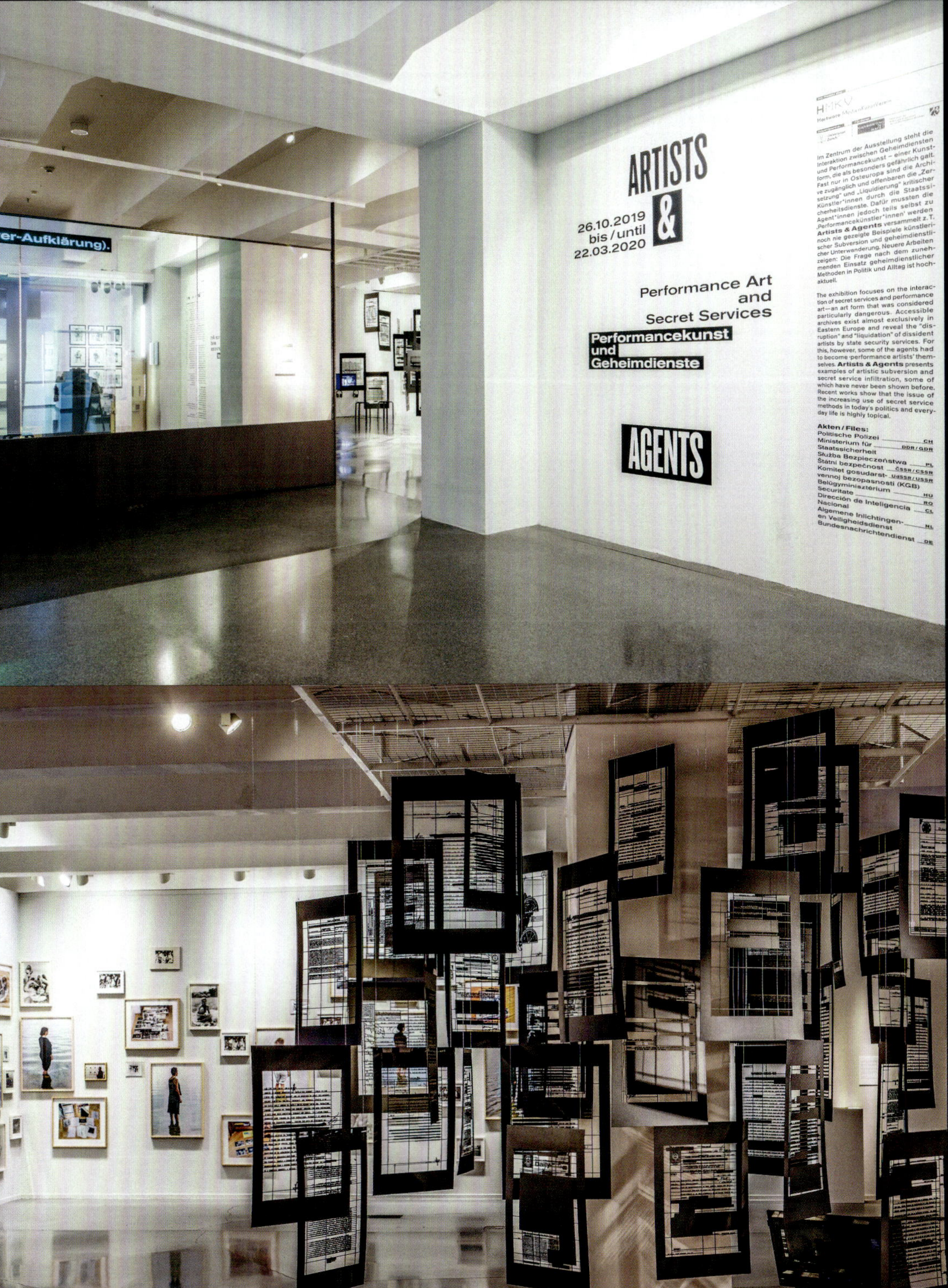

I. Arns, S. Sasse, K. Krasznahorkai, Exhibition

HMKV Hartware MedienKunstVerein, Dortmund in cooperation with the Slavic Department of the University of Zurich, October 26, 2019 – April 19

2019 –2020

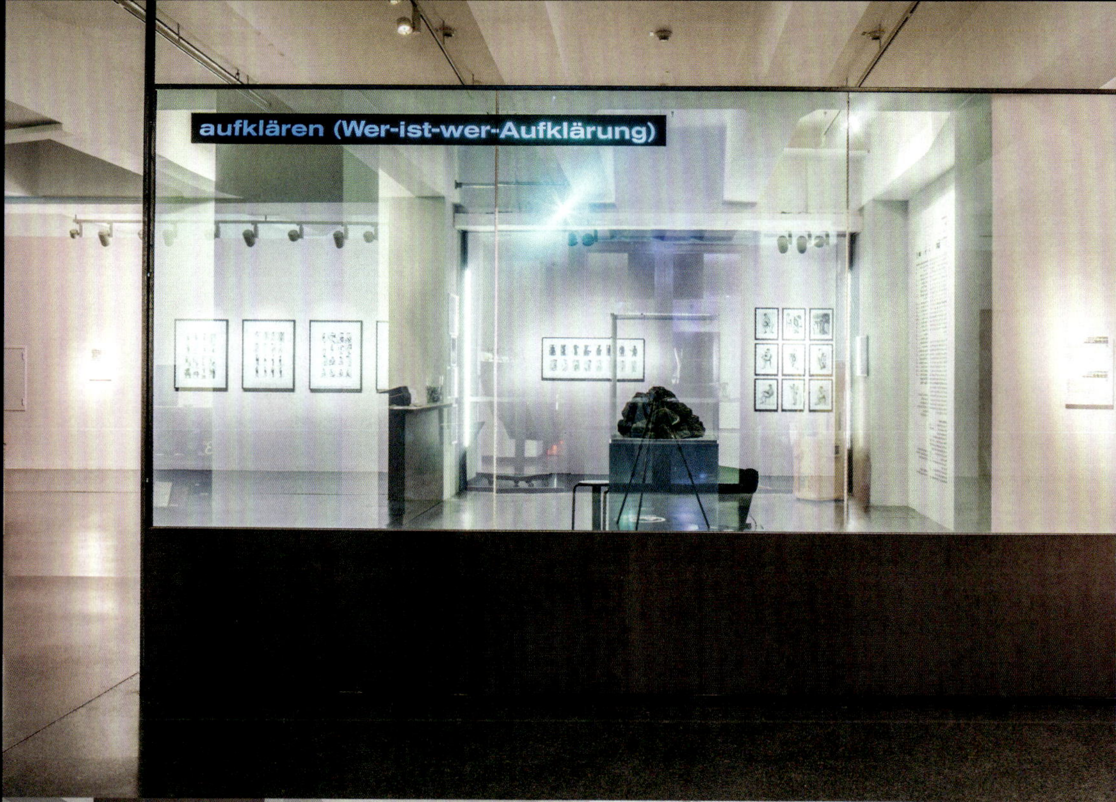

aufklären (Wer-ist-wer-Aufklärung)

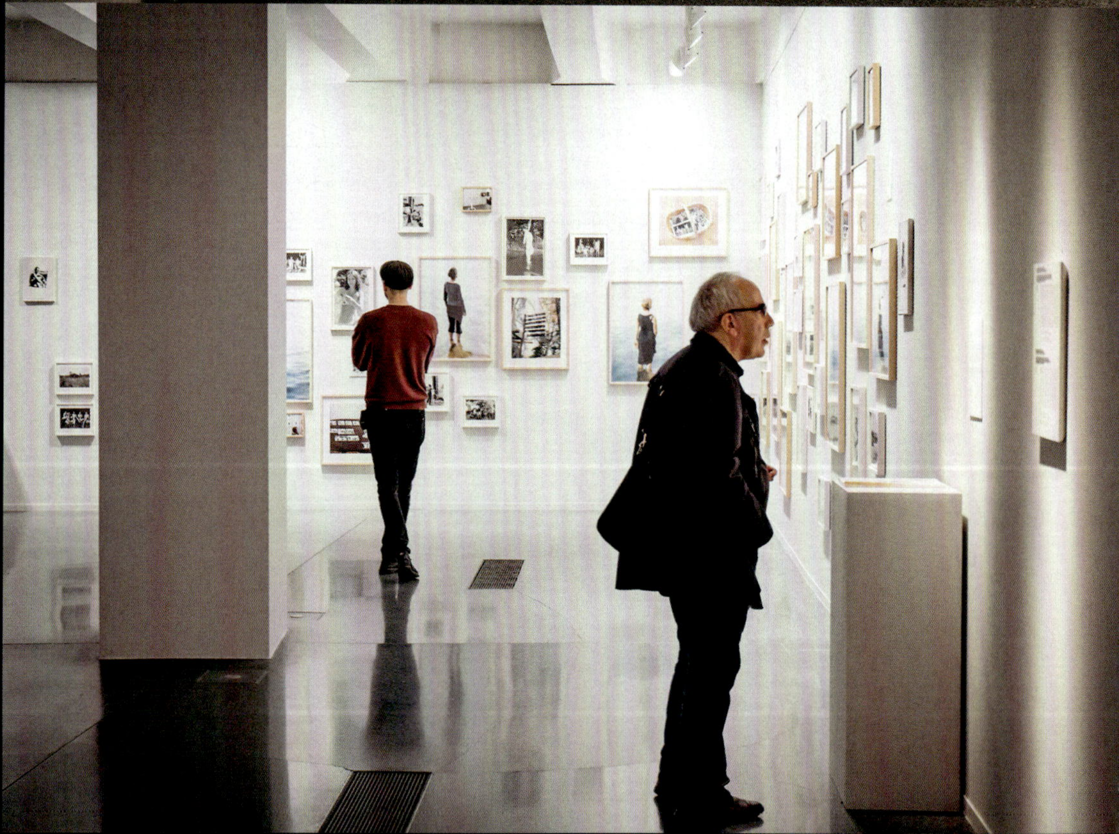

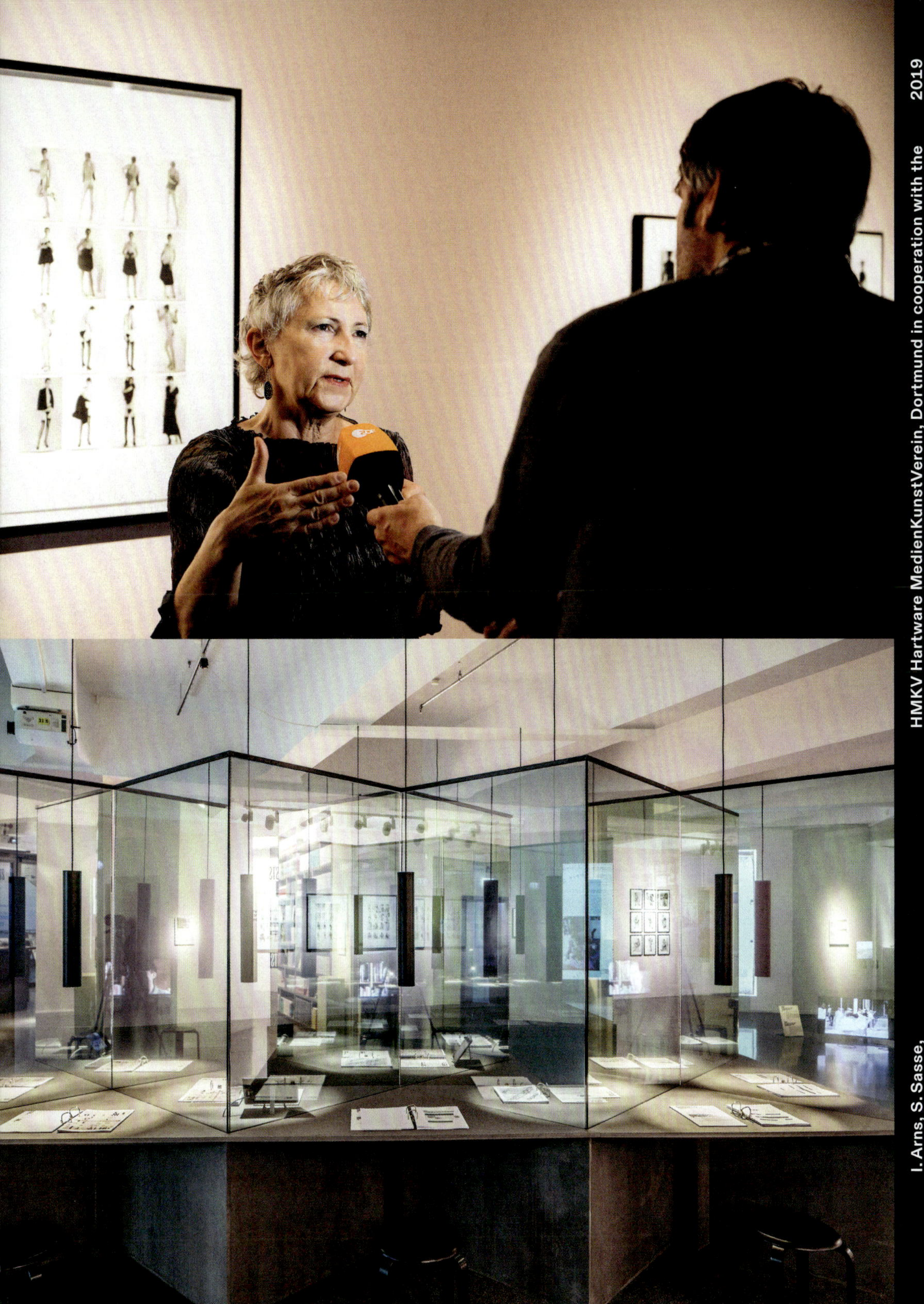

HMKV Hartware MedienKunstVerein, Dortmund in cooperation with the Slavic Department of the University of Zurich, October 26, 2019 – April 19

Archives and Agents

2019

Archives and Agents

27

Operative Knowledge: Secret Police Archives as Art Archives?[1]

Kata Krasznahorkai

"... subjugation by the logic of a confused world, in other words when participants give up their illusory rights, which they believe can influence chance, and admit the fact of their absolute defenselessness right up until their own physical destruction."[2] This is how, in 1966, an informant for Hungarian state security quoted Allen Ginsberg of all people. The year before, Ginsberg had taken a tour of Poland, Czechoslovakia, and Russia. He was used to being cited in a wide variety of contexts, but it would have amazed even him to know that this quote was used by a Hungarian state security officer to define the intentions of happenings as a new artistic phenomenon. The state security urgently needed a definition: the first Hungarian happening had all but thrown them into panic. This happening, entitled *The Lunch (In Memoriam Batu Khan)*,[3] was illegally organized by Tamás Szentjóby and Gábor Altorjay on June 25, 1966 in Budapest. It was held in a private basement for about fifty to sixty people. In other words, the state security's panic was focused on a handful of artists that were barely in their mid-twenties. To take action against the happening, in its existence as a phenomenon, they needed information about the genre that was as precise as possible.

Informant Knowledge

But what did the informants report about the happening and who were these informants? In the case of the first Hungarian happening, we have three reports from informants "Mészáros," "Hajdu," and "László," who were independently reporting on the basis of an "inner conspiracy."[4] The reports claim to list the names and employment of the participants, as well as those who were invited but failed to show up, and even those that showed up late. They report that there was a cover fee, and that invitation cards were printed and sent to the *crème de la crème* of contemporary Hungarian intellectuals, including Sándor Weöres and János Pilinszky.

(Neither poet showed up according to one **informant**.) The reports also document the course of events that evening, albeit in differing versions, as well as the audience's reaction and the response of the press. Supposedly, photographers and even a cameraman were present, and we are told of months of preparation, especially with regards to the difficulty of finding a location. The reports are detailed and fact-oriented, but fundamentally, they are unreliable. Regarding the first happening, we don't know anything concrete that might correlate with real facts or artistic intentions. What we do know with certainty, however, is that state security became aware of the danger happenings presented even *before* the first event was organized, and so sent three **informants** to document what they saw and heard in that basement. From these reports, in addition to the reports on operative procedures and **decomposition** measures, we can reconstruct how Hungarian state security categorized happenings and performances as activities that are hostile to the state, even though some appeared in official media and sometimes even in public locations. We can also reconstruct how performances and happenings were documented and manipulated from the state security's perspective via the surveillance and "**handling**" of the artists, as well as how interaction between state security and artists occurred.

The "counteractions" of state security came into effect simultaneously with the first happening. With it, began Hungary's decade-long **surveillance** and "**decomposition**" of the happening scene, which lasted until Szentjóby's forced emigration in 1975. The files bear witness to the fear of this artistic genre and the attempt to restrain it through numerous **active measures**. Because happenings and performance art were something like a blind spot, i.e. a source of uncertainty, state security needed to acquire as detailed material as possible about the actions and their "theory."

Happenings as a State Enemy

Interest in happenings was triggered—paradoxically—by an article in an official journal where the "happening" was first mentioned. The article was written by author Mária Ember and appeared in the state-sanctioned journal *Film, Színház, Muzsika* in 1966, titled "Happening and antihappening"[5] *(Happening és antihappening)*. In it, she expresses outrage regarding the happenings of Salvador Dalí, Robert Rauschenberg, and Joseph Beuys. In a sarcastic and ironic tone, Ember intended to describe the absurdity and ludicrousness of happenings in the United States and Western Europe, but instead she inadvertently initiated the Hungarian happening movement. It was this article that initially gave Szentjóby and Altorjay the impetus to organize the first iteration a month later.

In the case of this first happening, the **informants** took five days after the event to deliver not just a detailed description, but a full analysis of the genre from a political, social, and philosophical perspective. According to one report, the form of the happening existed "philosophically in the pronouncement of nihilism, darkness, and the irrational."[6] It states that it was initiated by Filippo Tommaso Marinetti, Salvador Dalí, and Kurt Schwitters, being transported to the US by László Moholy-Nagy. In the US, the happening led "in its end stages to a series of violent acts, mass drug consumption, and open confrontation with police."[7] This "open confrontation with police" and the classification of happenings as an act of violence could not be demonstrated, however, on the basis of the first happening in Hungary. Here, it was a rooster in one of the reports (or a cat in another) that might be interpreted as the single ailing victim of imperialistic decadence. For the duration of the presentation, the rooster was fastened to a red pot and crowed wildly, as if it wanted to outdo Krzysztof Penderecki's composition *Threnody to the Victims of Hiroshima* (or, as another report wrongly claims, Karlheinz Stockhausen's *Sieg*). As the fourth protagonist of a chaotic Dada-Fluxus overkill, rampaging on parallel levels and systematically destroying the equipment, the rooster entered into the history of the Hungarian happening-performance-Fluxus scene. The audience remained, according to the report, largely untouched, apart from a few pillow feathers, and generally responded positively to what they had seen. Even state security did not want to seem too conservative. According to interrogation protocols from 1972, when Szentjóby—under the code name "Schwitters" in the files—was asked why he did not attempt to perform his activities in a legal context, he supposedly replied that the authorities had denied his request on the grounds that "happenings are old-fashioned"[8]: that they had already been out of fashion for thirty(!) years in the West and were thus "opposed to progress."[9] Despite his allegedly "old-fashioned" activities, Szentjóby was classified by state security as dangerous enough to warrant a decade of **observation** by an average of six **agents**.

By 1969, three years after the first happening, the state had already come to consider happenings as an "instrument of rebellion of western youth which is generally opposed to any kind of society,"[10] according to a report entitled "On the Social Impact of Happenings" (*A happening társadalmi hatásáról*). This was written by one of the most well-versed authorities on the scene, working under the code name "László" and delivering analyses to state security. Even in socialist countries, "its content lies in anti-social tendencies, even if it is not openly propagated ... it manifests itself primarily in attitudes and mindsets rather than on a political level."[11] The ultimate goal of these secret police efforts was to decode these "attitudes and mindsets" and to know "all and everything" about the subversive art scene. State security was not primarily interested in understanding art theory, but they knew how to arrive at this knowledge: by planting well-connected, intellectual **agents** who could make sense of what they were seeing and usefully summarize it for "operative knowledge." Subsequently, they would themselves "theorize" what they were seeing. The effect of this—and not only in Hungary—was that people were hired who were themselves part of the scene and thus, were in a position not just to document the performances, but also to participate as performers and audience members. In an order from the interior ministry in 1979, we read that "specially-qualified persons suited to in-depth discoveries"[12] needed to infiltrate "hostile elements on a cultural level."[13] This concerned a "transfer of knowledge" where the **informant** played the crucial role of transforming what had been seen and heard. The **informants** "tapped into" the artists, in a certain sense, with the goal of having them personally provide arguments for classifying their actions as hostile. The "transfer of knowledge" also functioned in the reverse direction, as the **informant** reports always mirrored the expectations of whoever had assigned the task. They would mold the seen and heard into whatever the other side expected.

Despite its relative invisibility and lack of analytical reception in the art world—both official and unofficial, even after 1989—the happenings of the 1960s and 1970s were watched, disrupted, and in this way, documented with an obsessive, paranoid intensity. There are several possible reasons for this. First of all, happenings and performances were genres of art that were invisible to state security: both in the literal sense of the word, as they generally did not take place in public museums, galleries, or theaters, as well as in a more figurative sense, as they did not fit into the prevailing "understanding of art" and so, were not recognizable as an art "product" (neither as painting nor as sculpture nor as theater). Furthermore, happenings were classified as even "more dangerous" as they created a sense of community and were akin to public gatherings,[14] thus causing unpredictable public reactions. Nothing was more disturbing to state security than seemingly spontaneous artistic actions in public spaces.

The Informant Between the Underground and the State

Hungarian state security records tell us about more than just the history of the state security's perspective on happenings. The genre of "apartment theater," which has numerous features in common with happenings, did not escape the attention of the surveillance authorities and their urgent interest in new genres of art. The development of the group surrounding Péter Halász—especially those who would later enter into the history of theater with Squat Theater in New York—would hardly have been imaginable without the "contribution" of state security, which occurred before the entire troupe's expulsion from Hungary in 1976.

The main argument against Halász and his theater group, the one which would ultimately lead to their expulsion, was the accusation of obscenity. No other argument was well-founded enough for legal prosecution. However, in the fifteen-page report from 1974 that analyzes the ensemble's early pieces, the informant "Pécsi Zoltán"[15] downplays their alleged obscenity, describing it as a "special effect."[16] This might be an attempt to tone down the accusation, because although, as he writes, "some western artists defined the sexual act as such as art ... and there have doubtless been examples of group sex in Hungary, although I have never seen proof of this with my own eyes, no sexual acts take place in the ensemble's pieces, and I am firmly convinced that none of the members would be able to perform such a thing in public."[17]

"Pécsi Zoltán" knew quite well, however, that nudity was a "stylistic tool" of happenings and performances. He read in detail about the international art scene and reported, for example, about the biannual Théâtre du Monde Festival in Nancy, to which Halász and his theater group were invited in 1971. The Hungarian authorities did nothing to prevent their acceptance, while at the same time, Szentjóby was forbidden to travel to the Paris Triennale. The night before his departure, Halász asked his group not to emigrate yet. At the time, he himself did not want to leave Hungary. He had a legal, authorized theater group which had rented the Kassák House Studio (*Kassák Ház Studió*) and was allowed to perform their pieces in public.

One of the report's more alarming passages is a description of how the state-supported avant-garde theater was criminalized, a criminalization which in turn stimulated the theater and made an essential contribution to its aesthetic radicalization. But it is precisely this gray area that cannot be objectively illuminated from the memoirs of the members and friends of the group, as this criminalization was retrospectively reinterpreted into a badge of honor and even seen as a prerequisite for any kind of avant-garde activity.

"Pécsi Zoltán" writes a completely different story about this criminalization, however. According to the informant, Halász tried to keep everything legal: "The members of the group were unable to deal with the fact of their criminalization for a surprisingly long time. The group was not at all saturated with some kind of illegal, oppositional 'underground' ideology; the state of illegality found them completely unprepared ... and caused deep despair in many of them. Only after a long period of time ... did this illegal status become firmly established."[18] He adds another comment to these statements: through his contacts to high-ranking officials, Halász had attempted to secure a legal option for the performances. However, his efforts remained fruitless and ultimately his grandmother offered to let the group perform in her apartment. The genre of apartment theater, which would later become famous in New York as Squat Theater, thus partially owes its radicality of blurring art and life into one absurd theatre piece to these operative measures.

Both the content and the style of these meticulous analyses, carried out by state security over years, allow us to conclude that "Pécsi Zoltán" was an educated person who obviously delivered his texts with enjoyment. This informant is also one of the few whose identity was discovered after 1990: the informant was László Algol, who belonged to the inner circle of the relatively —as he describes it—exclusive Halász group. For a time, he composed texts for them and even acted in several pieces. He was the author of his own performance about the schizophrenia of his personalities as an artist, scientist, and agent in *The Chemistry Engineer and The Construction Manager. The Person(ality) of the Three (An Approximation Exercise)* (1973). However, the fluidity between the artist and the agent in this performance only became clear nearly twenty years later. This highly intelligent man, who spent most of his time occupied with cybernetics and psycholinguistics, lived on radio-quiz-show winnings and also wrote mystical poems. At the time, he was hardly able to publish and lived out his passion in writing informant reports. "Pécsi Zoltán" was one of the authorities' most important sources, as he was intellectually capable of translating the artists' knowledge into the state security's system of operative knowledge.

Algol, alias "Pécsi Zoltán," now lives in New Zealand and teaches psychology there under the name Professor Gusztáv M. Hábermann.[19] In a letter of apology to his former theater friends, he admits that he was an informant based on conviction. He thought he could establish new communication channels between the authorities and independent young artists, as well as resolve their mutual misunderstandings and thus be of use for the new artistic initiatives. The informant-performer, who saw himself as a connecting link between the state and performance art, used his knowledge of both systems to clear up "misunderstandings" between the two. He has, since the opening of the archives in the 1990s, become a standard trope—a figure of legitimation—in secret service research.

Secret Police Archives as Art Archives?

Gabriella Unger's study "Counterculture and State Security" (*Ellenkultúra és állambiztonság*)[20] reports on how in Hungary, a total of nine hundred people from the cultural sector were placed under surveillance between 1973 and 1977. Together with their contacts, this amounted to about sixteen to eighteen hundred people, most of whom were no older than their late twenties. There are thus detailed descriptions not only of famous protagonists of the art scene, like Tamás Szentjóby and Péter Halász, but also of forgotten artists and initiatives of youth culture. These descriptions portray not only the routes of communication within the various scenes, but also their contacts with the West.

We have this fear of art, a "platonic fear of culture," and youth to "thank" for the availability of descriptions and photographs of performances—sometimes even several of the same event, which were composed independently for the most part (if not usually in the style of "Pécsi Zoltán"). There the "reaction" as a "counteraction" by the state can also be reconstructed parallel to the artistic action. These photographs—which are no more "factual" or reflective of reality than the written documents—supplement artistic photographic documentation with state security's parallel view of the same event. In some cases, secret police photographs are the only available photographic documentation. In other words: of all things, informant photographs are sometimes the only visual evidence we have of performances and happenings. This evidence, with the opening up of state security archives in Eastern Europe, needs to be rehistoricized and analyzed apart from the "operative knowledge" they transmit. These reports and photographs by state security agents can only be useful as a source for research if their system and language are decoded, their statements critically questioned, and individual events systematically examined and analyzed with a critical view of the sources.

Of the interpretation of state security files, Cristina Vatulescu writes that "the secret police has its own way of doing things with words"[21]—and with images, we might add. Intentional disinformation and conscious misinterpretation make it impossible to use these documents as a reliable source for a purely art-historical analysis. The opportunities offered by the opening of the archives are not so much in the reconstruction of performances and happenings, even though new, previously unknown performances and artists come into art history's view. They are more prevalent in reconstructing the state's perspective based on its "operative knowledge" of artistic procedures and genres, of the state security's strategic methods and their interaction with artistic actions.

Secret police archives can thus—taking into account the fictionality of the files—be fully understood as art archives, but only if we ask the right questions. Research into documents about the art scene has already begun in most Eastern European states. Self-reflective research that historicizes the mindsets and techniques of suppression by state security prevents the dominance of a narrative and canon that's been shaped by the secret police. It enables an understanding of how dictatorships spread disinformation about artists and genres of art, both creatively and intentionally. This last aspect is particularly relevant today, thirty years after the end of the Cold War, with a new wave of disinformation about subversive art and artists which follows the old, familiar practices—and this occurs not only in Eastern Europe.

Translated from German by Brian Alkire

Endnotes

1 Parts of this article have been published in Kata Krasznahorkai, "Wie Spitzel unser Wissen über Kunst vermehren," *Frankfurter Allgemeine Zeitung*, January 7, 2012.

2 "A zavaros világ logikájának való alávetettség, vagyis a résztvevők lemondanak arról az illuzórikus jogukról, hogy a véletlen felett befolyást gyakoroljanak, és beismerik tökéletes kiszolgáltatottságuk tényét egész a fizikai megsemmisülésig." "Mészáros" in the "On the Happening" report, Budapest, July 1, 1966, ÁBTL–V–156455, 55. All translations from Hungarian are by Gwen Jones and Kata Krasznahorkai in cooperation with Brian Alkire.

3 Tamás Szentjóby and Gábor Altorjay, *The Lunch (In Memoriam Batu Khan), Happening Budapest H 1966*, June 25, 1966, Budapest: Hegyalja Street, 20/b. In cooperation with Miklós Jankovics and István Varannai, with assistance from Enikő Balla, Miklós Erdély, and Csaba Koncz. See detailed analysis of the happening and its artistic and cultural historical context as well as the relation to informant reports in Kürti, "A szabadság anti-esztétikája. Az első magyarországi happening" ("The Anti-Aesthetics of Freedom: The First Hungarian Happening"). (http://exindex.hu/index.php?l=hu&page=3&id=967 [26.3.2019]) After almost fifty years of silence on the subject, recent research has recognized the first Hungarian happening as one of the most significant events in the history of art of the 1960s and 70s. See St.Turba, *Az ebéd. (In memoriam Batu kán), Happening Budapest H 1966 / The Lunch (In Memoriam Batu Khan), Happening Budapest H 1966*; St.Turba, FIKA. *Fiatal Művészek Klubja. Interjú St.Auby Tamással* / BOGEY. *The Young Artists' Club. An interview with Tamás St.Auby.*

4 "Mészáros," "On the Happening" report, Budapest, July 1, 1966, ÁBTL–V–156455, 55–58; "Hajdu," Budapest, August 4, 1966, ÁBTL–V–156455, 59–60; "László," Budapest, July 22, 1966, "On the First Happening Party," ÁBTL–V–156455, p. 53f.

5 Mária Ember, "Happening és antihappening," in *Film, Színház, Muzsika*, October 13, 1966, 18.

6 "Mészáros," "On the Happening" report, Budapest, July 1, 1966, ÁBTL–V–156455, 56.

7 Ibid.

8 Report [anonymized] on the interrogation of Tamás Szentjóby, February 14, 1967, ÁBTL–V–156455, 14.

9 Ibid.

10 "László," Report "On the Social Impact of Happenings," Budapest, April 11, 1969 and April 28, 1969, ÁBTL–V–156455, 177–79.

11 Ibid.

12 This order by the Ministry of the Interior, labelled 0022/1970, has been analyzed in detail by Edit Sasvári and Tamás Szőnyei. See Sasvári, "*A balatonboglári kápolnatárlatok kultúrpolitikai háttere*" ("The Cultural-Political Background of Chapel Exhibitions in Balatonboglár") and Szőnyei, *Nyilván tartottak. Titkos szolgák a magyar rock körül 1960–1990* (*Registered. Secret Agents in the Hungarian Rock Scene, 1960–1990*).

13 Ibid.

14 In Russia in 1966, for example, the laws regarding freedom of assembly were tightened, resulting in public actions and gatherings that could always be interpreted as mobs. Thus, paragraphs 190/1 and 190/3 were added to the criminal code where the "organization of group actions which disturb public peace, traffic, etc." could be punished with a year's imprisonment or a fine of up to 100 rubles.

15 For more on "Pécsi Zoltán," see the article by Aniko Szucs and Tamás Szőnyei in this volume.

16 "Pécsi Zoltán," report on the "Changes in the Activities of the Ensemble between 1969 and 1973," Budapest, January 10, 1974; Report on "The Activities of Péter Halász and His Group," November 20, 1973, ÁBTL–O–16268/1, 238–52.

17 Ibid.

18 Ibid.

19 See the article by Aniko Szucs and Tamás Szőnyei in this volume.

20 Gabriella Unger, "Ellenkultúra és állambiztonság," *Trezor* 3 (2003): 165–88, http://www.abtl.hu/html/hu/iratok/unger_ellenkultura.html.

21 Cristina Vatulescu, *Police Aesthetics: Literature, Film, and Secret Police in Soviet Times* (Stanford: Stanford University Press, 2010), 35.

Dangerous Research:

Ilijana Kamenova (IK) and Sylvia Sasse (SS) in Conversation with Hristo Hristov (HH)

IK: For years, you have been conducting research in the Bulgarian secret police archives (COMDOS, Dossier Committee) and have written a number of books about the domestic and international "decomposition" of writers by the secret services and secret police, including about the writer Georgi Markov and the use of secret service techniques against Bulgarian emigrants. First, a question about the archival records in Sofia: how much material was preserved in Bulgaria? Since when has the material been accessible to researchers?

HH: In the first years following the collapse of the dictatorship, several unsuccessful attempts were made, including through legislation, to open up the files of the former state security apparatus and related parties. Only in 2006 was a law finally passed regarding access to the records of the archive, a law which is still in effect. An independent commission was selected with three primary duties. First of all, it was tasked with bringing together all of the institutional archives of the former dictatorship into one location through the construction of a central archive. This archive was opened in 2011 and is the most modern archive building in Eastern Europe. Presently, there are more than four million documents, or about fourteen kilometers of files, from state security and the secret services of the Bulgarian People's Army, as well as numerous videos and over 2.5 million file covers. In 1990—the year the Communist Party and state security began to fear the beginnings of democracy—approximately forty-two percent of the agent files were secretly destroyed, primarily incriminating material. These materials were destroyed to prevent the reconstruction of how agents and informants denounced others. Secondly, the law requires the commission to check whether potential public employees and people in leadership positions, starting from November 10, 1989, were active in state security and to publicly disclose this information.

The commission, which has now been active for twelve years, has so far uncovered approximately thirteen thousand former agents. This lustration helps us to illustrate the enormous influence of the former repressive apparatus on the political situation in Bulgaria and its transition to democracy after 1990. Thirdly, the commission is legally required to secure the massive archive while guaranteeing access to those affected as well as enabling access for research purposes. This access has been in place since 2007, since which a series of studies have been carried out in Bulgaria.

SS: We are especially interested in the surveillance, "documentation," and "decomposition" of the art scene in Eastern Europe, and above all, in the underground art scene. We conducted research in particular in the archives of the GDR, in Hungary, the Czech Republic, and Poland. The differences are immense. The active and often highly creative "decomposition" of the artistic underground was especially massive in the GDR. Which artists and genres were especially subject to surveillance and "handling" in Bulgaria?

HH: What you call the artistic underground goes by the name *inteligencija* in the Bulgarian research literature. After the establishment of the Communist regime in Bulgaria on September 9, 1944, the repressive apparatus of the Bulgarian Communist Party began to persecute the *inteligencija* with the state security's help. As a first step, in 1945, a series of writers and journalists were sentenced in fabricated political court proceedings. They were also prohibited from printing and publishing and were excluded from their respective artistic associations. This led to a rise in fear among artists, although we do have to point out that a large part of the artistic intelligentsia was bought off by the regime through a series of privileges. Party offices for the various organizations—associations of writers, artists, musicians, actors, journalists—were established with members of the Communist Party, who also informed state security whether the party line was being held in creative matters.

During the entire period from 1944 to 1989, there existed a structure of surveillance and denunciation, with the goal of achieving as much control as possible over artists. In some cases, the DS (*Dăržavna sigurnost*, Committee for State Security) achieved their goal; in others, they did not. The DS archives contain a vast amount of material, demonstrating the methods and means the BCP (Bulgarian Communist Party) attempted to use to implement control.

Apart from conducting research into these types of archival documents, I have published them on my website, desebg.com, which I have been maintaining for the last eight years. There you can find a document with my commentary on how the forced exile of Alexander Solzhenitsyn from the USSR in 1974 was discussed in Bulgaria, as well as discussion surrounding the composition of *The Gulag Archipelago* (1973).[1] Apart from that, in my documentary studies, I have extensively researched the forgotten influence of the Communist Party and the DS on the Bulgarian intellectual elite. I detail this in my book, *Kill the Wanderer*, written in response to the murder of writer Georgi Markov.

SS: After the exile of Solzhenitsyn, the DS feared that Bulgarian writers, artists, and youth might start to resist the Communist Party. Did they take any concrete measures in this regard?

HH: Yes, state security feared the influence of Solzhenitsyn on the Bulgarian intelligentsia, which is why they monitored conversations and commentary among intellectuals in Bulgaria. This also had an impact on the younger generation, who learned about Solzhenitsyn's exile from the USSR and the scandal's development via banned Western radio broadcasts. The most famous and relevant scandal in Bulgaria, which occurred in connection with Solzhenitsyn and his work, was the refusal of five Bulgarian writers—Radius Ralin, Valeri Petrov, Marco Ganchev, Blagoy Dimitrov, Hristo Ganev and Gosho Goshev—to sign a declaration by the Bulgarian Writers Association in February 1974. The declaration criticized and denounced Solzhenitsyn for the publication of his novel *The Gulag Archipelago*. Due to this refusal to sign the statement, the five writers were barred from the Writers Association and the Communist Party, and their texts were not published again for a significant period of time.

SS: For us, it was important to understand that the actual work of the secret police did not consist in **surveillance** but rather in the "**handling**" of the art scene, i.e. in its "**decomposition**." We are interested above all in what we call "**performative censorship**," which is not the prohibition of art but rather its actionistic interruption and prevention (broken water pipes, fake invitation cards with wrong dates, apartment fires, break-ins, planting **informants** in artistic actions). Was this also a phenomenon in Bulgaria? What measures were used in Bulgaria to disrupt underground art?

HH: State security in Bulgaria used various methods and means to control the intelligentsia between 1944 and 1989. The DS also used a method they called "**decomposition**" (*razlaganie*). In practice, this meant actions which hindered the leading figures of the artistic elite from gathering together; their intention was to prevent them from becoming strong as a group and thus becoming attractive to others. Apart from this, the most effective method the DS used was surveillance via the "apparatus." By means of dozens of agents assigned to different tasks, state security was gathering daily information about what writers and artists were thinking and how they were unofficially communicating. In this way they learned, for example, about the organization of secret events in the apartments of artists, about performances which were not permitted in public. Through the use of technology (tapping telephones and continual monitoring of correspondence), total control was exercised over certain artists who were actively "dangerous" in the eyes of the regime. One example is the case of the writer Radoy Ralin, the author of a series of epigrams making fun of the regime. State security handled him under the pseudonym "B" ("*Kozel*"), continually tapping his telephone and monitoring all of his correspondence, even though he was already prohibited from publishing. State security also confiscated the personal archives of artists. This happened in 1988 to the writer Peter Manolov, for example, who at the time was also secretary of the recently founded Independent Association for the Defense of Human Rights in Bulgaria. His archive was confiscated, and he was arrested. However, he began a hunger strike with the aim of getting the confiscated material back—an event publicized abroad by Radio Free Europe/Radio Liberty.

SS: What differences can be seen between the "handling" and surveillance of artists remaining in Bulgaria and those abroad (in emigration)?

HH: The difference was basically just that it was much easier for the Communist regime to keep artists, and people in general, under surveillance in Bulgaria. In general, Bulgarians abroad who were critical of the regime were grouped together under the umbrella term "hostile emigration," regardless of whether the person was a journalist, a writer, or something else. Because of difficult access to these people, the Bulgarian Communist Party allowed state security to use more extreme methods, so-called active measures (*ostriye meropreyatiya*), which in the operative language of state security included murder, kidnapping, and sabotage. One case of this was the attempted kidnapping of writer Dimitar Inkjov in Austria: Inkjov worked in the Bulgarian section of Radio Free Europe in West Germany in the 1970s. Then in 1974, the successful kidnapping of Bulgarian exile Boris Arsov in Denmark, who was brought back to Bulgaria and murdered there. There was also the assassination of writer Georgi Markov in London in 1978. Markov broke the taboo against speaking about the General

Secretary of the Bulgarian Communist Party, Todor Zhivkov. From archival documentation, we learn that state security defined him as a personal ideological enemy of the Communist Party in Bulgaria because he had delivered tips for resistance against the regime to the intelligentsia via Radio Free Europe.

IK: You wrote a book about the umbrella assassination of Georgi Markov on September 7, 1978 on the Waterloo Bridge in London. What surprised you most during your study of the files?

HH: I dedicated six years of my life to working on this case. Because at the beginning of the 1990s, the period of political transformation, there was a myth that almost all materials by and about Markov had been destroyed. And it was true that state security had destroyed two operative dossiers on Markov with a total of ten volumes of file material. That was the greatest obstacle during my research and investigation into the question of who had ordered and executed the political assassination. I was most amazed by the fear [that] the recently collapsed Communist regime still had of Georgi Markov, even though he was no longer alive.

Through numerous new "active measures" undertaken after 1989, primarily by agents of state security in the media, the Communist regime killed Georgi Markov a second time—by killing his name, which symbolized resistance to the Communist dictatorship in Bulgaria. An unbelievable amount of filth was spread about him, and now that the files in Bulgaria are accessible, it is obvious that all of the people who took part in this second, moral murder were agents of state security, the same people who killed him physically, following the whims of the vengeful and vain party chairman Zhivkov.

The other thing that amazed me was the lack of political will on the part of all Bulgarian presidents and prime ministers in Bulgaria after 1989. They did nothing to expose political murder and did not request the corresponding political material from the Kremlin's KGB archives, as Sweden did for example, in the case of diplomat Raoul Wallenberg who was kidnapped and brought to Moscow in 1945, or as the United States did in the case of Oggings,[2] or Poland with the mass murder of Polish officers in Katyn.

SS: You also recently spoke about the contents of Julia Kristeva's files. The international press had condemned Kristeva before even reading the files. You drew attention to a fundamental problem, namely that we cannot read secret police dossiers as objective sources, as factual documents. What is your assessment of the Julia Kristeva files? And how "fictional" are these kinds of files in general? The Russian writer Vladimir Voynovich wrote ironically of a kind of "inner disinformation" where it becomes clear how informants and agents tell lies "upwards," portray their activities and those of the people being surveyed in an exaggerated manner, in order to make a career for themselves or simply to meet a quota. [He writes,] "I always knew that one of the key phenomena of the Soviet system was that those below lied to those above and those above to those below and that they both expected lies from each other."

HH: The disclosure that Julia Kristeva was an associate of state security occurred in March of 2018 by means of the Dossier Committee. This happened when persons who had held or were holding leadership positions at various publications were being reviewed, including literary journals and magazines. She was reviewed as one of the editors of *The Literary Magazine* (*Literaturen Vestnik*). The revelation of her collaboration shocked many people and triggered intense polemical debate in our country. Some intellectuals who were close to her defended her with arguments that were, in my opinion, lacking in objectivity. Others have even portrayed her as a victim of state security, which I do not agree with either. On my website, I published a detailed analysis which has been reprinted again and again, including abroad. The main question in my analysis is how we interact with the files of the DS and whether we have learned to read them objectively thirty years after the collapse of the regime. Julia Kristeva's defenders claim that there are no denunciating reports contained in her files, which she herself composed, and that she was thus not a DS collaborator. I say, on the other hand, that that cannot be an argument and compared this with the case of the files of Georgi Parvanov, the former president of Bulgaria and former head of the BSP (Bulgarian Socialist Party, 2002–2012), a successor to the Communist Party. His files also did not contain anything which he himself composed. But when his collaboration with the DS was announced by the commission, no one used this argument to defend him. That means that we cannot say that some agents and/or informants are "good" and others "bad" on the basis of their political orientation, just because we know them or sympathize with them. That is not an objective reading of the files. An objective reading begins for us, the researchers, with the question of whether a dossier is complete or whether we find inconsistencies in it which point to an illegal cleansing of them by the Bulgarian Communist Party and the DS after 1989, something which happened to forty-two percent of the dossiers of the secret service apparatus. And I justifiably pointed out the fact that Julia Kristeva's dossier was one of these scrubbed files. It is of no significance whether the documents contained in this file are reliable as sources of information but rather, whether this information is complete. In Kristeva's dossier, there is a series of anomalies and contradictions which indicate to anyone seriously engaged in the investigation of the archives of totalitarian communist state security services that the dossier was cleansed. Which materials were removed during a cleansing of this kind? As a rule, those which compromised the relevant agents. I want to be clear here that this is not a matter of falsified documents which Kristeva could have compromised in their original form. It is, rather, a matter of an incomplete dossier missing certain materials which would otherwise be necessary for collaboration according to the state security's own requirements, which were described in the top-secret instructions for operative reports. The operative report was the central document of the DS for the generation, processing, and storage of the huge flow of data which emerged over the course of forty-five years. We need to recognize that these rules were set in stone for operative agents. I also drew a parallel between Julia Kristeva and her code name "SABINA," and Georgi Markov and his code name "SKITNIK" ("Picker"). State security almost always gave their agents personal, human names, while they chose descriptive pseudonyms for the people that they were "handling," their victims. "SABINA" never officially broke with the communist regime and she also never criticized it publicly, while "SKITNIK" not only broke with the BCP (Bulgarian Communist Party), he also massively criticized the regime on Western radio broadcasts, which he ultimately paid for with his life. The differences in the lives of two intellectuals can thus be immense. At the same time, I am of the opinion that the reading and interpretation of state security collaborator files has to serve the purpose of learning what happened; the point is not to pass judgment, even though there are people in Bulgaria who gladly play the role of a judge in order to demand moral "justice." No one should judge Julia Kristeva for maintaining contact with state security after remaining in France, for answering their phone calls, meeting with them, and exchanging opinions. Everyone must make that decision for themselves.

IK: We read that you yourself have received threats due to your research. Where are these threats coming from?

HH: You are asking me something which I would prefer not to speak about publicly. For one, because my work as an investigative journalist comes with a number of risks that I assumed [already] when I began serious journalistic investigation two decades ago. Secondly, because the attacks against me also affect my family. I can only point to the fact that, immediately after I began my first investigations in the archive of the DS on the case of Georgi Markov's assassination, the apartment I was living in at the time was broken into; this was followed by a robbery where my computer was stolen (which I had bought on credit). There then followed two more robberies—always after my publications about the Markov case. The goal was presumably to ruin me psychologically and financially. Then, after the first robbery, I said to myself that if I show fear now, the people who wanted to stop my research would have achieved their goal. I would have been forced to give up my career. But I didn't do that. Then, in 2006, when the still-valid law about the disclosure of the files was adopted, I was anonymously threatened with a bomb attack if I did not stop appearing in public.

In 2012, someone attempted to compromise and hack my website after a major journalistic investigation about a robbery carried out by state security. It concerned the theft of the 1985 original of Paisius of Hilendar's *Istoriya Slavyanobo lgarskaya* (Slavic-Bulgarian History) from the Bulgarian monastery of St. George the Zograf, one of the twenty monasteries of the Mount Athos republic.

There were then other anonymous assassination threats and the tires on my wife's car were slashed three times (I myself don't have a driver's license and don't own a car), the last time being in January of 2019. One time they slashed all four tires of the car. I called the police after every attack. When I received a death threat in 2013, there were several public personalities who defended me and publicly demanded law enforcement to find out who was making these threats, but the police failed to do this. I still receive these anonymous threats to this day, as there are still people who do not want us to investigate the Communist regime and its collaborators. These opponents probably see in me a person who, through my journalistic investigations and publications on the website desebg.com, is doing exactly that which they want to avoid at any cost. For this reason, my family and I have become an object of their attacks.

Translated from German by Brian Alkire

Endnotes

1 https://desebg.com/2011-01-13-09-25-08/3979-2019-05-24-12-49-12.

2 The third case concerns Isaiah Oggings (also known as Ysai or Cy), he was an American-born communist and spy for the Soviet secret police. After working in Europe and the Far East, Oggins was arrested, served eight years in the Gulag detention system, and was summarily executed on the orders of Joseph Stalin. In 1992, at the insistence of the United States, President Boris Yeltsin presented a list of Americans who died in the Soviet Union during the Second World War as well as during the Cold War. The list included Isaiah Oggings.

Real “Network”

Virtual Folder: A Reconstruction of “Pécsi Zoltán’s” Hidden Work Dossier

Tamás Szőnyei

For fifteen years, one of the most knowledgeable figures of the Hungarian nonconformist art scene has been an informant for the secret police, yet his own dossier has not yet come to light. Just as archaeologists reconstruct animal skeletons from scattered bone fragments, so can we attempt to collate the dossier documenting the activities of the secret informant[1] code-named “Pécsi Zoltán.”

At present, the Historical Archives of the Hungarian State Security (ÁBTL) hold 13,341 work dossiers (W-dossiers) containing reports from a smaller number of networked individuals (agents, informants, secret representatives, and employees), many of whom produced long, multivolume series over years, even decades, while the others’ informant dossiers ran to only about a dozen pages. However, these 13,341 dossiers represent only a third of the total files mentioned in the eight-volume work registry (W-registry) in the ÁBTL, which records the filing of 42,333 dossiers between 1957 and 1989. The dossiers were entered in the W-registry only after they had been closed and were allotted a W-number according to this chronological sequence, one which also determines their archival classification.

Unfortunately, since there are no work registries available from the pre-1957 period, we do not know how many networked individuals’ reports were filed during this time. Regarding the post-1957 period, the only clue to the difference between the 13,341 dossiers and the 42,333 documents recorded in the registries—that is, the fate of 28,922 dossiers—is the “DESTROYED” (MEGSEMMISÍTVE) stamp in the remaining register, usually with a date.

In most cases, we can only guess what the destroyed files contained. We might assume that from a state security point of view, the files were full of worthless, irrelevant reports, which after a certain point of time—about eight to ten years—were no longer needed. However, particularly in the 1989 case of destroyed files, we might suspect that it was not standard procedure that led them to the shredder, but rather, operational interests: the intention to cover their tracks. We might believe that the files contained extremely valuable and sensitive information, and as the change of the political system approached, it was judged that in the interests of the state security apparatus and their secret **collaborators**, it was better for them to remain hidden and not end up in the hands of "unauthorized" individuals. It is no accident that recommendations were made in November and December 1989 by the Interior Ministry's III/III Division—which dealt with homeland domestic intelligence—to revise the state security operative records system because of the "change in society's political state of affairs together with the operational situation."[2] These recommendations included the review of W-dossiers and, in certain cases, their destruction as well.

In other words, we can probably give up the idea of knowing anything about the almost twenty-nine thousand **informant** work dossiers. Researchers may glean some consolation and hope from the fact that some of the reports were prepared with numerous copies. Handwritten drafts were often typed up, and if a **networked** individual gave an oral account, the handler would later record this, usually on a typewriter. Multiple copies of reports were prepared in case of covert investigations: they formed part of the secret **surveillance** of an individual or group. In such cases, one copy was attached to the **networked** individual's work dossier, and the other to the object dossier (O-dossier) of the individual(s) under **surveillance**. The ÁBTL holds about twenty thousand such O-dossiers, which provide us with an opportunity to not only excavate the subject at hand, but to also put together a fragmented picture of the contents of certain missing W-dossiers.

An excellent example is the case of the secret **informant** codenamed "Pécsi Zoltán." Naturally, "Pécsi Zoltán" also had a W-dossier. This is evident from the page numbers written at the top of the pages, often deleted or changed (referring to the location of copies or the reorganization of a dossier), or from the lines at the bottom of the page. These show the quantity of typed copies, refer to the other dossiers the reports were filed in, and indicate where they were forwarded to (which department and/or officer). However, this W-dossier itself is not in the ÁBTL. Luckily, the supposition that the W-dossier was not in fact filled with worthless material is supported by the object dossiers, to which reports or extracts from reports were attached, mostly as copies.

We do not know the registry number of “Pécsi Zoltán’s” W-dossier; there is no trace of it in any of the W-registries. This is presumably because thirteen years after his recruitment in 1973, his cooperation with the state security apparatus was upgraded to a higher level than before. On January 28, 1986, still under the code name “Pécsi Zoltán,” he provided a secret detailed report on a meeting of the István Örley circle.[3] Incidentally, this document was probably written on an electronic typewriter in italics, an atypical choice, and signed by hand using the code name. On April 20th of the same year, he was reporting, in his role as Captain “E/20,”[4] on the launch of an anthology entitled *Poetry The Next Day* (*Költészet másnapja*). His report from November 5, 1987, also in italics, is the only document hand-signed with his code number. He had been promoted from a member of state security’s “external” **network** to a member of the official permanent staff, a strictly confidential staff member, which is to say that he had been awarded the rank of SZT Officer (SZT or *Szigorúan Titkos*, Hungarian for “Strictly Confidential”). SZT Officers received their employment and civil (hence: cover) jobs from the Interior Ministry. The ministry also paid their salaries and arranged their cover pension.

We might assume that after this promotion, the W-dossier containing reports by the **informant** code-named “Pécsi Zoltán” continued with records by police captain “E/20,” but we are presently unable to confirm this. We do not know whether separate dossiers were used to store his reports, or whether they were attached to the several cases in question. Insofar as they were used, did registers exist for filing them, similar to the W-dossiers? Logic would seem to indicate that SZT Officer reports had to be preserved, and that when their dossiers were closed, their filing had to be recorded, but we do not know how any of this actually happened. Nor do we know how Captain E/20’s undercover activities came to an end. His last known report is from November 1987. While the ÁBTL holds personnel materials on SZT Officers, his documents are not among them: they do not appear anywhere in the microfilm, paper, or magnetic tape of the **archive**’s accessible materials. Alongside the unknown circumstances of his recruitment, the question also remains whether he continued to work during the political transition years of 1989 and 1990. If so, which cases was he assigned to, and whom did he inform on? Ultimately, the secret police did not destroy the documentation entirely, but neither did they preserve it or make it available for research.

This is exactly why we're left with gaps of information. What is certain is that while "Pécsi Zoltán" went from being an undercover agent to an undercover police captain code-named "E/20," from among his handling officers (and later colleagues), most of his reports were received by Tibor Horváth, who was promoted from second lieutenant to major. In addition, first lieutenant Vilmos Mályi had dealings with "P. Z." in 1973, as did József Horváth in 1974–76 and second lieutenant Gyula L. Kékesdi in 1978–79. All three served in the Interior Ministry's Department III/III-4, the section within Division III/III devoted to the cultural affairs that dealt with "countering domestic reactionary forces." This secret cooperation lasted for at least fourteen years: from 1973 to 1987, an exceptionally eventful period of political and cultural life that provoked constant counterintelligence in the cultural sphere. A total of 101 reports remain from this period, sporadically distributed. For example, there is not a single report from 1977, and only one report from 1985, while the busiest years were 1974 and 1984, which prompted, respectively, fifteen reports and fourteen meetings, as well as eleven reports and ten meetings between the undercover agent and his handling officer. "Pécsi Zoltán" often provided information on other subjects at the meetings, information which was sometimes recorded separately, hence the difference between the number of reports and the number of meetings (there are also reports that can be read in summary or detailed form).

These meetings occasionally took place in public places, but more often at "K and T flats." K stood for *konspirált* (conspired), an apartment maintained by the security services specifically for this purpose, while T stood for *találkozási* (for meetings) apartment, whose occupant authorized its use by the security services according to a predetermined system.[5] Wherever these meetings took place, the tranquil environment allowed for a careful discussion of the details. "Pécsi Zoltán's" reports were, at times, over ten pages in length. He presumably wrote his reports at home on a typewriter (there are no handwritten texts in the files), but in some cases, he recorded dictations on a cassette, a transcript of which ended up in the dossier.

In the second half of the 1960s, a generation of young artists grew up and started to become active. This was a generation that could not and did not want to conform to the frameworks defined by socialist cultural policy. Uninspired by ideals dictated from above, they hated the walls erected by the party-state, which they clashed with at every step. "Be forbidden" was the slogan coined by Tamás Szentjóby for creative types who defied restrictions and wanted to enjoy civic and artistic freedom.

In the second half of the 1970s, Szentjóby chose to emigrate to the West, as did Péter Halász and István Bálint (whose apartment theater company, Kassák Ház Stúdió, was banned from performing publicly in Hungary), Gergely Molnár and László Najmányi (members of the art-punk band Spions), as well as the social scientists Ágnes Heller and Iván Szelényi (both of whom were also prevented from carrying out their academic work). Others, however, stayed in Hungary, including Miklós Erdély (active in the fine arts, literature, and film), visual artist György Galántai (who organized exhibitions without official approval and published an arts samizdat)[6] and art historian and organizer László Beke.

It was within this "unofficial," "neo-avant-garde," "underground" artistic and intellectual sphere that the young informer code-named "Pécsi Zoltán" moved comfortably. A graduate in psychology and English he stated in the first sentence of his report from November 20, 1973, that as an author he used the name László Algol because of his interest in cybernetics. This is the name under which he had been known in Péter Halász's circle since 1972, whose surveillance he also undertook. In effect, the statement in the report disclosed his identity beyond all doubt. Behind the artist name and code name, there is a third name: his birth name, Gusztáv M. Hábermann. This third identity was first revealed in 2003 by György Galántai in his personal memoirs and documentation, as well as in an essay based on archival research by the art historian Edit Sasvári, published in a volume exploring the Balatonboglár Chapel Studio exhibitions.[7] Hábermann's "unmasking" was connected to his surveillance of Galántai. This is why, during a 2005 online interview with a journalist, Hábermann asked for forgiveness primarily from Galántai, and also "everyone else." He apologized from New Zealand, where he was living and teaching at a university.[8]

The 101 reports are currently available in the following ten dossiers, covering five far-reaching cases. We arranged them chronologically in the virtual filing cabinet:

- 3.1.5. O-16268/1, 2, 3 "Horgászok" ("Fishermen")[9]: surveillance of Péter Halász and his theater group between 1973–76

- 3.1.5. O-17740 "Alapítók" ("Founders"): surveillance of attempts by Veronika Csillag and Balázs Györe to start a publication in 1978–79

- 3.1.5. O-19618/1, 2, 3 "Festő" ("Painter"): surveillance of György Galántai's activities aimed at creating an alternative art scene between 1980–87

- 3.1.5. O-19619/11, 14 "Lidi": Thirteen volumes of surveillance reports about György Krassó's oppositional activities and private life from 1963 to the end of 1985, focusing on the period 1984–85

- 3.1.5. O-19764/4 "Persons (and their connections) carrying out hostile, subversive activities within the youth circle of the so-called Flying University": the period 1983–84 from the five-volume series covering the period 1980–86

Reports by "Pécsi Zoltán" and "E/20" were used not only in the cases referred to in these dossiers' names, but in other fields too. According to the stipulations of the official cultural policy of the "Three Ts,"[10] most of the artists belonged to the banned or tolerated categories, and thus did not restrict themselves to a single artistic direction, showing their talents in several fields (e.g. literature, film, photography, visual arts, theater, music). Therefore, their own **networks** extended beyond the arts scene: they made contact "downwards" with university and college students receptive to novelties and radical ideas, as well as "upwards" with researchers and teachers in various social sciences. All this meant a move out of art and culture and into the political sphere, the so-called democratic opposition, referred to in Party and Interior Ministry documents as "hostile individuals in opposition."

"Pécsi Zoltán" was first deployed in the case code-named "Fishermen," but his reports were almost immediately used in the case code-named "Underground" as well.[11] This was a fairly precise name for the scene: in contrast to state-supported artists, they instead chose to take on the risk and excitement of "being underground." They dared to establish a journal called *Szétfolyóirat*[12] without a permit—that is, without Party control—and organize unpredictable happenings, theater performances, and exhibitions curated from an official panel and without a permit. "Pécsi Zoltán" was also assigned to other cases than the underground art scene, or at least, there was evidence of other planned assignments.

One of these was the investigation regarding incitement charges of the writer György Konrád and the sociologist Iván Szelényi, who had organized the smuggling of their book, *Intellectuals on the Road to Class Power* (*Az értelmiség útja az osztályhatalomig*), to the West for publication. The subjects were code-named "The Pushy Types" (the dossier for this case, O-19103, was destroyed, but the investigation material remained: V-160493). The secret police gave similar tell-tale names to "People Waiting" (János Kis, György Bence, Ferenc Kőszeg, and others), "Beggars" (including target Ottilia Solt, who was given the code name "Know-it-all," and her friends Gábor Havas, András W. Nagy, and others), "Amateurs" (a group of political artists in opposition called Inconnu), "Rotters" (the rock band Beatrice), "The Six" (the literary group called *Fölöspéldány*, Hungarian for "extra copy," who worked with Beatrice for a while), or the neutral-sounding "The One with the Studio" (the target of this undercover investigation was András Bán, an art historian who supported "problematic" artists).

All of these people—and many more—were featured in "Pécsi Zoltán's" reports. Paradoxically, his useful work for the security services also functions today as a unique **source**, one that records countless important facts and data that can confirm existing information or supply missing data. If we are to judge his activities on a moral basis, we should grant him this one thing in his favor. On the basis of the documents available, he confined himself to politically and aesthetically relevant issues. "P. Z." rarely shared information that we would need to anonymize today due to their sensitive nature as determined by law, even though over the course of fifteen years, he must have acquired information on his acquaintances' sex lives, health, or addictions. He conveyed information on his acquaintances' health in an objective fashion, and never spoke of sex, even though he often wrote about the "obscenity" of several works or performances he described and analyzed in his reports.

The virtual W-dossier of undercover **informant** "Pécsi Zoltán" and the identical police captain "E/20" contains 101 reports over 420 pages. A detailed analysis of all this material would exceed the scope of this text, but it is certainly worth mentioning that while the documents contain their own cultural and historical value for posterity, at the time of their creation, they represented supremely effective assistance to the secret police's work. It is no accident that in his evaluation on April 23, 1980, Captain Tibor Horváth wrote that "Pécsi Zoltán" had "provided much information of operational value."[13]

Appendix

An accurately maintained state security dossier—and far from all dossiers were like this—contains an index of names and a table of contents. We have recreated these for "Pécsi Zoltán's" virtual W-dossier, but emphasize once again, that these are based only on the papers we are aware of to date, and thus cannot be regarded as complete. The same applies to the whole reconstructed W-dossier. We have no files from 1977, and although "P. Z." was instructed in August 1980 to attend the funeral of performer and writer Tibor Hajas, no report on this event can be found in any of the documents available to date. (It may come to light sometime in the future, though presently, we do not know for certain whether he wrote about it or not.) Ultimately, we cannot compile a complete inventory based on what is "missing."

Although not contained physically in the virtual W-dossier, two further items that are relevant in terms of content belong to it: a Daily Operative Information Bulletin (NOIJ) prepared for the Minister of Internal Affairs, and a Special Bulletin for the political leadership. Both were written on the basis of one of "Pécsi Zoltán's" exhaustive reports from January 1984 on the exhibition organized by György Galántai: *Hungary Can Be Yours/International Hungary* (*Magyarország a tiéd lehet/ Nemzetközi Magyarország*) at the Young Artists' Club,[14] which had to be closed down three days after its opening.

Contents

Meetings listed by date (the date of writing the report was usually later), and in brackets, the dossier where they can be found.

1973 – six meetings, eight reports

November 20:
Activities of Péter Halász and his group (in two parts) ("Fishermen"/1)

November 20:
The *Szétfolyóirat* ("Fishermen"/2)

November 26:
Péter Halász's group and Balatonboglár ("Fishermen"/1)

December 3:
The *Szétfolyóirat* ("Fishermen"/2)

December 3:
The Halász group (conflicts with local residents) ("Fishermen"/2)

December 3:
Mrs. Péterné Nádori, née Emőke Dobos, relationship to Halász et al. ("Fishermen"/2)

December 10: Béla Hap and the *Szétfolyóirat* ("Fishermen"/2)

December 10:
Halász et al., trip to Wroclaw ("Fishermen"/2)

December 19:
Halász et al., trip to Wroclaw ("Fishermen"/2)

December 20:
Péter Halász ("Fishermen"/2)

1974 – fourteen meetings, fifteen reports

January 7:
Béla Hap ("Fishermen"/2)

January 24:
Béla Hap and the *Szétfolyóirat* (two copies, differing typed versions; "Fishermen"/2)

January 24:
György Galántai (two copies, differing typed versions; "Fishermen"/2)

February 7:
György Galántai and the *Népszabadság* article ("Fishermen"/2)

February 18:
Péter Halász et al. ("Fishermen"/2)

March 4:
Péter Halász et al. ("Fishermen"/2)

March 14:
Péter Halász et al., György Galántai, Béla Hap ("Fishermen"/2)

April 16:
Halász et al., Béla Hap, Gergely Molnár ("Fishermen"/2)

April 30:
Performance entitled "The Child Killer of Bethlehem" ("Fishermen"/2)

May 4:
Péter Halász et al. ("Fishermen"/2)

June 11:
Péter Halász et al., Júlia Vajda ("Fishermen"/2)

July 4:
Péter Halász et al., Júlia Vajda's exhibition ("Fishermen"/2)

July 16:
Péter Halász et al. ("Fishermen"/2)

October 8:
New piece by Péter Halász et al. ("Fishermen"/2)

December 3:
Young Artists' Club (*Fiatal Művészek Klubja*, often referred to as "FMK") ("Fishermen"/2)

1975 – ten meetings, ten reports

January 14:
György Galántai ("Fishermen"/2)

January 24: Péter Halász et al. ("Fishermen"/2)

February 18:
Gergely Molnár, Ferenc Temesi ("Fishermen"/2)

March 4:
Péter Halász et al. ("Fishermen"/2)

May 9:
Péter Halász et al. ("Fishermen"/2)

June 27:
Performance "The Three Sisters," film plan ("Fishermen"/2)

July 25:
Péter Halász et al., Ádám Tábor, Gergely Molnár ("Fishermen"/2)

October 10:
On the acquaintances of Halász et al. ("Fishermen"/2)

October 24:
Plans of Péter Halász et al. to emigrate ("Fishermen"/2)

November 18:
Halász et al., György Galántai, Sándor Simon ("Fishermen"/2)

1976 – four meetings, four reports

January 6:
Halász et al., Gergely Molnár, Ganz-MÁVAG Cultural Centre ("Fishermen"/3)

April 9:
Gergely Molnár ("Fishermen"/3)

July 13:
Gergely Molnár, Miklós Kovács ("Fishermen"/3)

September 30:
G. Molnár, M. Kovács, Western affairs of Halász et al. (two extracts, probably the same report, "Fishermen"/3)

1977

We already know that no reports from this year can be found in the O-dossiers, even though the subjects of P. Z.'s surveillance were particularly busy. They organized events, performances, and exhibitions at the Ganz-MÁVAG Cultural Centre, the Young Artists' Club, the Mini Gallery in Újpest or the Bercsényi Club, about which "Pécsi Zoltán" reported the year before and the year after.

1978 – nine meetings, nine reports

March 14:
Spions concert, publication plans of Györe et al. and the Napló ("Founders")

April 10:
Publication plans of Balázs Györe and Veronika Csillag ("Founders")

May 9:
Publication plans of Balázs Györe and Veronika Csillag ("Founders")

June 13:
Defection of Spions members, Györe et al., the Profil ("Founders")

July 10:
Defection of Gergely Molnár, Györe et al. ("Founders")

July 25:
Publication plans of Balázs Györe et al. ("Founders")

October 17: Veronika Csillag and the planned journal ("Founders")

November 9: Veronika Csillag and the planned journal ("Founders")

November 20:
Veronika Csillag and the planned journal ("Founders")

1979 – two meetings, two reports

No date:
V. Csillag and Miklós Szabó's apartment seminar ("Founders")

August 13:
Concert by Beatrice and Fölöspéldány, Györe et al. newspaper plans become book plans, Galántai's mail-art activity ("Founders")

1980 – eight meetings, eight reports

March 27:
György Galántai's exhibition ("Painter"/1)

April 1:
Planned museum of the contemporary Hungarian avantgarde; Artpool ("Painter"/1)

April 21:
György Galántai and the Artpool ("Painter"/1)

June 3:
Joint work by György Galántai and Achile Cavellini ("Painter"/1)

July 29:
Galántai and Cavellini, mail art, Artpool ("Painter"/1)

August 5:
Cavellini's work ("Painter"/1)

November 18:
György Galántai on the SZETA (Fund for Supporting the Poor) charity auction ("Painter"/1)

December 16:
György Galántai on the Artpool arts archive ("Painter"/1)

1981 – six meetings, six reports

May 12:
On Galántai's plans and connections e.g. with Inconnu, L. Rajk ("Painter"/1)

July 14:
On György Galántai's works in progress ("Painter"/1)

August 26:
On the mail-art exhibition *Art and the Post Office* ("Painter"/1)

November 3:
The Velem symposium and Galántai's Swiss visitor ("Painter"/1)

November 24:
Lecture by the Swiss artist; the *Tower* exhibition ("Painter"/1)

December 1:
György Galántai's planned stamp exhibition ("Painter"/1)

1982 – seven meetings, ten reports

January 26:
SZETA; Galántai's planning application for the art stamps ("Painter"/1)

February 9:
Zsuzsa Simon's apartment gallery ("Painter"/1)

February 9:
György Galántai’s planned exhibition of art stamps and seals (“Painter”/1)

March 2:
György Galántai’s exhibition of seals in the FMK (“Painter”/1)

April 7:
Work by Inconnu at the Mini Gallery art book exhibition (“Painter”/1)

April 7:
Exhibition of art stamps organized by Galántai at the Fészek Club (“Painter”/1)

May 24:
Galántai on his stamps and soundwork, the Xertox Group exhibition (“Painter”/1)

May 24:
The Xertox Group exhibition closes (“Painter”/1)

September 21:
World Art Post catalog, Galántai et al. trip to the West (“Painter”/2)

October 13:
György Galántai’s plans (“Painter”/2)

1983 – eight meetings, nine reports

January 3:
Galántai’s Stamp Film, planned arts journal (“Painter”/2)

January 13:
Zsuzsa Simon and Zsigmond Károlyi’s workshop-gallery (“Painter”/2)

February 8:
TGM’s (Tamás Gáspár Miklós) cancelled his talk at the FMK, SZETA, Artpool Letter (“Painter”/2)

March 11:
Where the Galántai Artpool Letter was printed (“Painter”/2)

June 17:
Demszky on the Free University, Imre Nagy memorial evening (“Flying Uni.”/4)

August 31:
Analysis of the arts samizdat *Artpool Letter* (“Painter”/2)

August 31:
Galántai exhibition (Liget Gallery), Tamás Papp’s planned Squat-documentary (“Painter”/2)

September 19:
Performance in the Lajos Vajda Studio, Galántai sells AL (Artpool Letter) (“Painter”/2)

September 28:
László Lugosi Lugo's photo action on Mayakovsky St. ("Painter"/2)

1984 – ten meetings, eleven (with an additional two) reports

January 30:
Hungary Can Be Yours exhibition at the FMK ("Painter"/2); on this basis, a Daily Operative Information report was prepared to inform the Interior Minister, as well as a "Specialist Distribution" report for György Aczél and other political leaders. See appendix for more details.

January 30:
Brief summary of the previous report ("Painter"/3)

February 15:
On the measures against the Monday University on the basis of Haraszti ("Flying Uni."/4)

June 26:
SZETA seminar on poverty at Ottilia Solt's apartment ("Painter"/3)

July 10:
Júlia Klaniczay on an Austrian artists' meeting ("Painter"/2)

July 10:
Ádám Tábor on the Lélegzet evenings, the Squat Theater of Halász et al. ("Painter"/2)

September 19: The Rainer Maria Rilke Society and its festival ("Painter"/3)

October 17:
Galántai rebuilds his basement, turns to the Soros Foundation ("Painter"/3)

November 9:
SZETA seminar on Gypsies in Ottilia Solt's apartment ("Lidi"/11)

November 11:
Galántai on the Plánum festival and his (photo)copying problems ("Painter"/3; the second page of the report is missing, and a page from a different piece of paper is attached in its place)

December 3:
Inconnu exhibition, Gy. Krassó in the Artéria apartment gallery ("Lidi"/11)

December 3:
Inconnu exhibition, Gy. Krassó in the Artéria apartment gallery ("Lidi"/11; long version)

December 5:
SZETA seminar on workforce at Ottila Solt's apartment ("Lidi"/11)

1985 – one meeting, one report

October 7:
Polish political cartoons in the Inconnu Artéria gallery ("Lidi"/13)

1986 – four meetings, four reports

January 28:
Meeting of the Örley circle in the Corso restaurant ("Painter"/3)

April 23: Launch of the anthology entitled *Poetry the Next Day* ("Painter"/3)

June 3:
György Galántai's mail art call and plans ("Painter"/3)

July:
Individeo, Monteverdi Wrestling Circle[15] (Theater led by András Jeles), Péter Forgács ("Painter"/3)

1987 – one meeting, two reports

November 6:
Hungarian Workshop evening at the FMK ("Painter"/3, unsigned)

November 6:
Galántai on the closure of Artpool Letters, his new plans ("Painter"/3, signed by hand)

Persons mentioned in the reports

A

Adamis, Béla
Ajtony, Árpád
Albert ...
Algol, László = "Pécsi Zoltán"
Ambrus, Péter (László)
Andropov, Yuri
Aranyi, László
Ascher, Tamás

B

Bába, Iván
Bácskai, Dóra
Bak, Imre
[Man resembling] Balaskó, Jenő
Balla (male)
[Wife of] Bálint, Endre
Bálint, István
Bálint, István and his wife
Bán, András
Bánki, Dezső
Baranyay, András
Barna, Judit
Bernstein, Sandra
Bidner, Michael
Biermann, Wolf
Bikácsy, Gergely
Buchmüller, Éva
Bujdosó, Alpár
Beuys, Joseph
Beke, László
Bence, György
Bereczky, Lóránd
Bika, Júlia
Birkás, Ákos
Bíró, Dániel
Bíró, József
Bíró, Yvette
Bodánszky, György
Bódy, Gábor
Bogád, Antal
Bojti, János
Bokros, Péter
Böröcz, András
Breznyik, Péter

C

Can (Dzsan), Togay
Cavellini, Guglielmo Achile
Ceaucescu, Nicolae
Chernenko, Konstantin
Clementi, Pierre
Csáji, Attila
Csalog, Zsolt
Csányi, M (?)
Császár, István
Csécsei, Mihály
Csillag, Ádám
Csillag, Veronika

D

Dávid, Edit
Demszky, Gábor
Dobos, Emőke
Dobos, Gábor
Donáth, Péter
Duray, Miklós

E

Ék, Sándor
Endreffy, Zoltán
Endrődi Szabó, Ernő
ef Zámbó, István
Eörsi, István
Erdély, Miklós
Erdey, István
Erdős, Péter
Esterházy, Péter

F

Farkas, Tamás
fe Lugossy, László
Ferge, Zsuzsa
Filliou, Robert
Fitz, Péter
Fodor, Tamás
Forgács, Péter
Földényi, F. László
Frank, Peter
Fridnach, Kenth (?)

G

Gá(g)yor, Tibor
Galántai, György
Garaczi, László
Géher, István
Gion, Nándor
Gondos, Béla
Gosztola, Gábor
Groh, Klaus
Grósz, Károly
Grunwalski, Ferenc
Györe, Balázs
Györe, Pál
Győri, Péter

H

Haász, István
Hajas, Tibor
Halász, András
Halász, Péter
Hamvas, Béla
Hankiss, Elemér
Hap, Béla and his wife
Haraszti, Miklós
Havas, Gábor
Háy, Ágnes
Hegedüs, László

Hegedüs, Péter
Hegedűs, Tamás
Hegyi, Lóránd
Hekerle, László
Hodosán, Róza
Hofi, Géza
Horgas, Béla
Hudák, János

I

Isztray, Botond
Iványi, Gábor

J

Jancsó, Miklós
Jaruzelski, Wojciech
Jávor, István
Jonge, Ko de
Jovánovics, György
Juhász, Pál

K

Kaczián, Lóránd
Kakuk, Tamás
Kántor, István (Monty Cantsin)
Kapitány, Éva
Karátson, Gábor
Kardos, László
Károlyi, Zsigmond
Katona, János Tamás
Kemenczky, Judit
Kemény, István
Kemény, Katalin
Kenedi, János
Kennedy, Tom
Kéri, Ádám
Kertesi, Gábor
Keserű, Ilona
Király, Béla
Kis, János
Kistamás, László
Klaniczay, Júlia
Klaniczay, Gábor
Klaniczay, Tibor
Kodolányi, Gyula
Konrád, György
Koós, Anna
Koós, Éva
Koós, Péter
Kornis (Kertész), Mihály
Kovács, András
Kovács, Miklós
Kováts, Albert
Kozák, Gyula
Kőbányai, János
Körber, Ágnes
Kőrössi, P. József
Kőszeg, Ferenc
Krassó, György
Krokovay, Zsolt
Kukorelly, Endre
Kurtág, György
Kurtág Junior, György

L

Laborcz, Mónika
Ladányi, János
Lajtai, Péter
Lakos, István
Laurenczi, Ágnes
Leary, Timothy
Léderer, Pál
Legéndy, Péter
Lengyel, András
Lengyel, Gabriella
Levendel, Júlia
Ludassy, Mária
Lukács, Mária

M

Major, János
Widow of Maléter, Pál
Malina, János
Mányoki, Endre
Márta, István
Márton, János
Matern, Éva
Maurer, Dóra
Mészáros, István
Mészöly, Miklós
Mezei, Ottó
Miklóssy, Endre
Minkoff
Mledk, Meda
Molnár, Gergely
Molnár, Tamás
Müller, Péter

N

Nádas, Péter
Nádori, Péter
Nagy, Imre
Nagy, W. András
Nagy, Bálint
Nagy, Jenő
Najmányi, László
Nyíri, Kristóf

O

Oláh, Andor
Oláh, Mátyás and his wife
Oravecz, Imre
Örsi, Katalin

P

Pácser, Attila
Pálinkás Szüts, Róbert
Pap, Mária
Papp, Tamás
Papp, Tibor
Péntek, Imre
Petőcz, András
Petri, György
Philippe, Gerard
Pilinszky, János

Pochitti, Gian Carlo
Pope John Paul II
Popieluszko, Jerzy
Prutkay, Péter
Puskás

R

Rácz, Péter
Rajk Junior, László
Rákosi, Mátyás
Rauzer, Péter
Reszler, Ernesztin
Rilke, Rainer Maria
Révész, László
Réz, Pál
Ruszt, József

S

Sacharov, Andrey
Sántha, Ágnes
Simon, Sándor
Simon, Zsuzsa
Solt, Ottilia
Somogyi, Győző
Somogyi, József
Soros, György
Stalin, Josef
Surányi, László
Swierkiewicz, Róbert

SZ

Szabó, Miklós
Szalai, Júlia
Szántó, Tamás
Szegő, István
Szelényi, Iván
Szemadám, György
Szendrei, Éva
Szent-Iványi, István
Szentjóby Tamás
Szerb, János
Szilágyi, Ákos
Szilágyi, Sándor
Szirtes, János
Szkárosi, Endre
Szőcs, Géza
Sztáray, Zoltán
Szabó, Miklós
Szalai, Júlia
Szántó, Tamás
Szegő, István
Szelényi, Iván
Szemadám, György
Szendrei, Éva
Szent-Iványi, István
(Name redacted)
Szerb, János
Szilágyi, Ákos
Szilágyi, Sándor
Szirtes, János
Szkárosi, Endre
Szőcs, Géza
Sztáray, Zoltán

T

Tábor, Ádám
Tábor, Eszter
Tamás, Gáspár Miklós
Temesi, Ferenc
Togay, Can
Tokaji, András
Tót, Endre
Tóth, Dezső
Tóth, Eszter
Tóth, Gábor
Tóth, Judit

U

Ungváry, Rudolf

V

Vajda, György
Vajda, Júlia
Varga, Vera
Vargha, János
Vásárhelyi, Júlia
Vekerdi, Tamás
Vető, János
Vitányi, Iván

W

Wahorn, András
Walęsa, Lech
Wehner, Tibor
Wessely, Anna
Wilheim, András

Z

Záborszky, Károly
Zrínyifalvi, Gábor
Zsigmond, Attila
..., Andrea

Translated from Hungarian by Gwen Jones

Endnotes

1 For the meaning of the various terms used by the Hungarian secret police, see the glossary.

2 ÁBTL 1.11.1. 45–146/2/1989 (Recommendation on the review of the state security operative records system; recommendation to issue deputy ministerial measures).

3 István Örley was a talented young writer who died during the bombing of Budapest in 1945, and therefore had nothing to do with the Sovietization of the literary scene after the Communist takeover. Örley was revived in the 1980s by writers who formed an autonomous circle under his name, thus expressing their independence from the one-party rule that was forced upon the official institutions of literary life.

4 The system of issuing code numbers to strictly confidential staff officers was not uniform: the use of quotation marks was occasional, thus we can find "E/Twenty," "E/No. 20," and "E/20."

5 "Pécsi Zoltán" met with his leading officers in a K apartment (Budapest, XIV district, Fogarasi út 29/b), which operated under the code name "Fogas." He also met in the K apartment (Budapest, XIV district, Ungvár u. 24/b) code-named "Pongrácz" or "Pongrác," as well as the T apartments "Pilóta" and "Zuglói." The latter cannot be clearly assigned. In the documents of the ÁBTL there is an apartment with the code name "Pilóta," but a K-apartment, not a T-apartment. There is a T-apartment with the code name "Zugló," but none with the code name "Zuglói."

6 Samizdat (from Russian) means self-publishing and refers to underground publication practices.

7 Júlia Klaniczay and Edit Sasvári, eds., *Törvénytelen avantgárd – Galántai György balatonboglári kápolnaműterme 1970–1973* (*Illegal Avant-Garde: The Chapel Studio of György Galántai in Balatonboglár 1970–1973*) (Budapest: Balassi-Artpool, 2003), 83. The fourth name gleaned from the "Painter" dossier, "E/20," was published online in 2011 on a list of SZT officers (szigoruantitkos.hu).

8 Johanna Rácz, "*Nem hajlandó magyarul beszélni Galántai György besúgója*" ("György Galántai's informer is not willing to speak Hungarian"), *Index*, March 22, 2005, http://index.hu/politika/belfold/galant03xx/.

9 These code names, just like those used by the Stasi, are mostly aptronyms: "Horgászok" ("fisherman"), for example, is an allusion to the surname of Péter Halász, which means fisherman.

10 In Hungarian, the three Ts stand for *tiltott, tűrt, támogatott*, meaning "banned, tolerated, and supported."

11 The dossier "Underground" was opened in May 1971. Its opening number (Cs-771) referred to the fact that a group of people (in Hungarian, their name was *csoport*, hence the Cs) was put under surveillance. The dossier was closed and entered into the object registry on October 14, 1976 with the number O–16097. It contained three volumes with 225, 263, and 29 pages. None of them are available. According to a note on page seventeen in the O-registry, they were shredded in 1989. This happened during the political transition, twenty-three years after their closure, which clearly points to the intention of destroying the valuable information they contained.

12 The title *Szétfolyóirat* is a pun on several words including *folyó* ("river" in Hungarian). It refers to a periodical whose copies are all different from both the original and each other, just like the different branches of a river forming a delta with the sea. The idea of *Szétfolyóirat* was that those who had confidentially received a typewritten copy had to act as contributing editors when forwarding it to someone else. They did this by copying the larger part and adding his or her own new content to it. In fact, only a few different copies were made this way, so it did not become the wide river delta it was meant to be.

13 "Painter" report, ÁBTL, 3.1.5.–O–19618/1, 106.

14 Translator's note: This is the name of a venue that played a major role in the alternative art and culture scene during the years 1960–1989, also known as Fiatal Művészek Klubja (FMK, Club of Young Artists).

15 Translator's note: Monteverdi Birkózókör (Monteverdis Wrestling Circle) is the name of the avant-garde theater troupe founded by András Jeles in 1985.

The Disidentifying Artist/**Agent**:

A Close Reading of the Hungarian **Informant** "Pécsi Zoltán's" Early files

Aniko Szucs

In early 1972, a tall, lanky, bearded young man joined the Kassák Ház Stúdió, a Hungarian neo-avant-garde theater troupe led by performance artist and theater director Péter Halász.[1] The newcomer, barely twenty-two years old and a double-major in English and Psychology, introduced himself as "László Algol":

LA: In the group, they primarily knew me as [name redacted]. I told them of this name, because at my former work place, [location redacted], where I continued to work for a couple of months, this was kind of a nickname they used because of my interest in cybernetics. When I joined the group, it seemed to me, I did not know what it was all about, therefore it made more sense to introduce myself this way. However, as it happened, through some connection, they also learned that was not what I was called in reality, and for this reason, a month or three weeks later they asked what my real name was: [name redacted]? Péter Lajtai asked, was I called [name redacted], or was [name redacted] the real one?[2]

This testimonial was the opening of a ritual act dated to November 20, 1973, through which Hungarian citizen Gusztáv M. Hábermann officially assumed his third alias: the code name "Pécsi Zoltán." He signed the **informant** report under this name, presumably his first.[3] From this moment on, Gusztáv M. Hábermann had three different personas: the sociolinguist-psychologist researcher, the avant-garde artist and community member, and the **informant**.[4] This timid and lanky hippie, as many described him, became one of the most prolific and studious **informants** in the Hungarian cultural sphere, feeding information to state security regarding the underground art scene between 1973 and 1987.[5]

In this essay, I propose to study the files as "performances of the self," as theorized by social psychologist Erving Goffman. Through a close reading of the reports, I seek to better understand how one individual negotiated and navigated the contradictory roles of astute scientist, underground artist, and ideologically committed collaborator. My primary interest lies in the files themselves: how the texts construct, perform, or simply reflect on these three different personas.

Building on the performance studies scholar José Muñoz's theory of disidentification, I also examine if we may locate instances in the reports where the informant attempts to counter or disidentify with the ideological lens through which he surveils the underground community. Disidentification is a performative act and, as such, is constituted of repetitious performances. This angle of inquiry thus allows me to study if and how the enduring performance of a role, whether of the artist-critic or the collaborator-ideologue, may reframe one's (perception of) reality.

My research is limited to the analysis of informant reports and the conclusions in my paper are thus equally constrained. For this reason, I primarily consider this an experiment in methodology: what semiotic, syntactic, and perhaps psychoanalytical markers in the text allow us to better understand the complex roles and underlying experiences of informants, who, as insiders of intimate and close-knit communities, were also interpellated into the role of surveilling, and thereby betraying, the very communities to which they belonged.

Becoming "Pécsi Zoltán"

Researcher-archivist Tamás Szőnyei at the Historical Archives of the Hungarian State Security (ÁBTL) has established that the archive has, to date, identified 101 reports authored by "Pécsi Zoltán." These reports focus on five different so-called operative processes: the files on Halász and his theater company's performances (under the code name "Fishermen") belong to the early stage of "Pécsi Zoltán's" career with state security.[6] Szőnyei has carefully and innovatively reconstructed the "hidden" work dossierof this agent.[7]

"Pécsi Zoltán" is one of the most-discussed former informants of the Hungarian art scene in the context of current research on Hungarian state security. There are three reasons for this: first, his were some of the first informant reports that any interested person could access and read, as the C³-Center for Culture and Communication Foundation made a selection publicly accessible via their website as early as 1998.[8] Second, dissident movements, whose activities often overlapped with the underground artists' work in the late 1970s and 80s, received much attention after the political transition: both because their actions may have directly or indirectly contributed to the collapse of communism and because many members of the former dissident movement became politicians. At the same time, a number of formerly underground artists entered the official art scene, making the Hungarian public eager to learn about these histories.[9] Third, the **informants** in the illegal art scene gained much attention because of their conspicuously contradictory positions in the oppressive communist regime: they were simultaneously trusted insiders of a close-knit underground community *and* often reliable **collaborators** of the state security **network**.

The astonishment over Algol's duplicity was articulated by many artists, including Anna Koós, former member of the Kassák Ház Stúdió, and wife of Péter Halász in the 1970s and early 80s:

AK: It was a curious experience to learn that someone, who was one of us, would become an informant, unless he was already one. ... Algol was a university student and to this day I don't understand why he agreed to collaborate. He hung out with us a lot. If we asked him to participate in a play, he joined; if it was mentioned that we were editing an issue of *Szétfolyóirat*, he submitted a poem too. At the same time, he was reporting on all of us.[10]

While there is no confirmed information[11] on why Gusztáv M. Hábermann joined state security, some **gossip** and speculation has circulated in Hungarian artistic and intellectual circles since his **files** were made public. One of his former victims, performance artist László Najmányi, wrote that he "heard accounts according to which Hábermann was caught stealing precious LPs at the Rózsavölgyi Music Store, where he worked in the 1970s, and he was blackmailed. Others thought that he could be blackmailed because of his alleged homosexuality."[12] Hábermann himself, when journalist Johanna Rácz exposed his state security past in 2005, sent the following explanation in an apologetic email to György Galántai:

GH: 30 years ago, I believed that what I was trying to do could help us to find a way to each other, to reach a détente. I was hoping that analysing my actions, sharing, discussing and bringing arguments could in some way build a bridge between us, and reduce antagonism and tension. I hoped that opponents could gradually approach each other, in the long term. (?) That the extremum can be prevented and the conflict muted. I can see now that viewed from the present, this approach of mine was naïve and/or mistaken. Some will simply call it a mere illusion. (?)[13]

José Muñoz introduced the term "disidentification" in his seminal study of queer identificatory practices and performance. Building on Michel Pêcheux's theory, he argued that in an ideological state apparatus, individuals have to choose between either identifying or counteridentifying with the dominant ideology. The danger of such reductionist schema, both Pêcheux and Muñoz claim, is that "such a system installs a structure that validates the dominant ideology by reinforcing its dominance through the controlled symmetry of 'counterdomination.'"[14] For this reason, theorists offer a third mode of identification, "one that neither opts to assimilate within such a structure nor strictly opposes it; rather, disidentification is a strategy that works on and against dominant ideology."[15] As such, it "tries to transform a cultural logic from within."[16] Hábermann's hope—or excuse—that his "mediation" would have increased understanding and tolerance suggests that the former informant, as he recalls today, was trying to find a disidentificatory position, a successful strategy that would indeed have allowed him to "transform the cultural logic from within."

Building on the work of performance theorists, I propose to perceive the three personas that Gusztáv M. Hábermann embodied in the 1970s as three distinctive, though increasingly overlapping, "performances of the self," as described in the canonical *The Presentation of the Self in Everyday Life*, written by Canadian American social psychologist Erving Goffman:

EG: When an individual plays a part he implicitly requests his observers to take seriously the impression that is fostered before them. They are asked to believe that the character they see actually possesses the attributes he appears to possess, that the task he performs will have the consequences that are implicitly claimed for it, and that, in general, matters are what they appear to be. In line with this, there is the popular view that the individual offers his *performance* and puts on his show 'for the benefit of other people.'[17]

In other words, Goffman argues that one always performs their "self," and devotes his research to exploring the ways in which one manages the impression they make in the "front," while "assuming that there may be another region—a 'back region' or 'back stage'—where the suppressed facts make an appearance," and "where the impression fostered by the performance is knowingly contradicted as a matter of course."[18] In the spirit of Goffman's analysis of performance and frame, I read the reports as Goffmanian performances. This framing of the files should remind the readers of the invisible—unknown and unknowable—"back stages," where suppressed facts, experiences, and drives could complicate and contradict the superficial interpretation of the documents and allow for the performative act of disidentification.

By offering a close reading of "Pécsi Zoltán's" early reports, which specifically focused on Péter Halász and his company in 1973 and 1974, I seek to locate traces of the Goffmanian "back region" while asking: do the reports, as performances in and to the "front," reveal contradicting or contradictory underlying identities? Can these texts help us to understand in the present how a committed member of the neo-avant-garde could become, or perhaps always was, a committed member of the network?

Attempts at Disidentification

The opening of "Pécsi Zoltán's" first informant report, as quoted in the introduction of this essay, reads as anything but performance. Introducing himself at the beginning of his narrative, and reinserting his two known names again and again—a total of five times within these first two paragraphs—may suggest an almost overzealous enthusiasm for owning the authorship of the account that follows. In this first report, "Pécsi Zoltán" also takes it upon himself to articulate his own relationship to the members, the aesthetics, and the performance practices of the company of Péter Halász. He recalls:

PZ: Until August 1972, I attended a few rehearsals and performances, but I did not want to join any performances. The first time this opportunity came up was when Halász did not have enough people while he was rehearsing the play "Kurcz Rudolf" written by Lajtai, and asked if I wanted to take a role. I was hesitant, but after a while I thought that I would give it a try, and that's how I got into the performances. This is how I got closer to the events that were happening in the group. In the beginning the group didn't really affect me, the first important effect happened while camping in Surány in August 1972, when Péter Lajtai asked me to discuss one of my texts that I had already presented to the group. This was quite a vague, lyrical, and kind of religious poem, and then later I participated in resolving technical issues surrounding the performances.[19]

Soon after this, however, "Pécsi Zoltán" distanced himself from the group:

PZ: ... for a few weeks I did not even show up at any rehearsals or performances, in reality they had to find me at the university, because from the beginning of 1973 a number of elements in the performances started to disgust me. The obscene elements repulsed me, but I could not judge the dangerous, harmful, or negative affect of these [elements] in their totality ... I realized that everything that I did in this group is not compatible with my convictions, my work, my objectives, my worldview, the work I do at the university.[20]

For this reason, the young man came to the conclusion, and announced on September 25, 1973, that he would quit the group,[21] breaking off all his personal relationships.

PZ: With this, the [name redacted] name also ended, although let me briefly note here that—except for the first month—from February 1972, it was clear to everyone what my real name was, and they only used Algol as a nickname.[22]

The birth of "Pécsi Zoltán" was supposed to mean the symbolic death of [name redacted], at least according to the agent's own narrative.[23]In an Austinian performative gesture,[24] he reassumed his civilian name, and the persona who had aspired to become an avant-garde artist and mingle with the underground community seemingly receded. However, the relationship between these two personas is defined by an ontological interdependence: one cannot—or is not allowed to—exist without the other. Despite the intention of the author of this testimonial, who is, after all, Hábermann, to kill Algol off, László Algol very much needed to stay alive and thrive as an underground artist and activist in order for "Pécsi Zoltán" to succeed as a newly-recruited informant of the network.[25]

The opening of this first secret police report reads as an anxious performance of the "good citizen." Even though the report's topic is Halász and his company, the informant is eager to distance himself from everything that the group represents. He emphasizes that the artists' activities and aesthetics are incompatible with all aspects of his—the good citizen's—life: with his respectful work at the university, his career goals, and the views with which he conducts his life. Nevertheless, these are merely the first paragraphs of a nineteen-page-long report, and what follows is "Pécsi Zoltán's" insightful analysis of the work of Péter Halász and his company. In this section, the alleged repulsion that prompted his alienation from the artists disappears from the narrative; what follows instead is an extremely detailed and insightful political and semiotic analysis of the Kassák Ház Stúdió performances.

With respect to the politics in Halász's performances, for instance, "Pécsi Zoltán" writes: "One can say that the political meaning only manifested itself indirectly, if at all. Halász thoughtfully strived to not make any overt political comments."[26] On Péter Breznyik's work he comments:

PZ: In one of his untitled pieces, we could hardly identify the man in a military uniform as a Soviet soldier, despite the fact that the man was reading excerpts of a Soviet writer's novel in the play. It is possible that, based on this, some members of the audience associated this figure with a Soviet soldier. At the same time, the character had no value in the overall structure of the play, and the play therefore did not make any commentary with respect to this character.[27]

Kata Krasznahorkai points out in her comprehensive analysis of "Pécsi Zoltán's" second expansive report—a fifteen-page long summary written in January 1974, entitled "Changes in the Ensemble's Activities from 1963 to 1973"—that "Pécsi Zoltán" was even "soften[ing] the accusations" of obscenity and violence.[28] "He interpreted the elements of public obscenity as 'special effects' in the performances, which the group only employed 'externally' to catch the audience's attention. Even though," and here Krasznahorkai quotes the report,

> Some artists from the West defined the sex act per se as art ... and substitute group sex for their pieces ... and there were doubtless instances of group sex in Hungary—although I never witnessed the fact with my own eyes ... no sex act ever occurred in the ensemble pieces and I am completely convinced that none of the actors in the group could have performed such an act in public.[29]

"'Pécsi Zoltán' seriously questioned whether the simple imitation of obscene acts can be defined as obscenity," concludes Krasznahorkai, "attempting thus to counter an accusation that was obviously known to him and [was] the authorities' pet issue."[30]

I assert that in these early informant reports we may find multiple traces of the author's attempts to disidentify both with the informant role and the ideological lens of state surveillance: embedded within the jargon and the semiotics of the oppressive ideological language, "Pécsi Zoltán" presents a reading of Péter Halász's performances that differs both from the ways in which the repressive state apparatus and the group itself would perceive, describe, and conceptualize them. In this way, after cautiously distancing himself from the artists, he offers a seemingly objective analysis of the artworks.

The relative objectivity with which "Pécsi Zoltán" describes the performances may also be interpreted as a disidentifying act. In his first two extensive accounts about the works and aesthetics of Halász's theater, there are a number of instances of the informant using straightforward descriptions that refrain from interpreting or evaluating the performances within the state security's ideological framework. A lesser-known example is from a report that "Pécsi Zoltán" gave on December 19, 1973 regarding a performance that Halász's troupe held at the International Theater Festival in Wrocław a few months earlier.

PZ: The piece has not been performed in Hungary yet in the form in which it was done [in Wrocław]. The parts it consisted of though were all taken from already-existing pieces, such as the "King Kong" and the untitled performance that they simultaneously showed in Balatonboglár, which was called "Bird" within the group. Péter Breznyik, from King Kong, took the wrist-cutting scene (in which he cut his wrist), as well as the castration scene, which was staged very similarly to how it had been in "King Kong" (attaching and tearing off artificial genitalia). From the play titled "Bird," a bird-dance was taken, in which basically a man (played by Halász) mimes a bird-dance, jumping around a half-naked man with open arms who is lying on the floor. The bodies did not touch, even though in its original (Boglár) version, there were multiple symbolic gestures hinting at the approximation of the two men.[31]

A certain dispassionate and nonchalant tone marks the descriptions of these performances; it may seem that "Pécsi Zoltán" is making an effort to take the edges off the provocative and subversive aesthetic choices. In this report, due to the dubious grammatical structure and verb tense, the reader may not even be able to decide if Breznyik actually performed the ultimate subversive act: the cutting of his flesh. Then, later on, in another report that "Pécsi Zoltán" penned in early October 1974 describing a performance in the apartment theater, he makes an effort to clarify that the "scene merely hinted at the wrist-cutting act without actually doing it."[32] He also describes the setting of this performance, "a square-shaped house in the center of the room built of furniture," which has windows through which the audience can "observe the well-lit, condensed inner space with thousands of small objects. ..." The central idea, argued "Pécsi Zoltán," interrogated "the working of the theater itself, as well as the characteristics of the actors performing in it."[33] The lieutenant officer reading the report, Vilmos Maghi (?), jovially and forgivingly commented in the margins: "The informant attempts to analyze Halász's confusing plays as a critic would, but fails to find any politics so to speak."[34] On this occasion, "Pécsi Zoltán" may perform the role of the critic, and his extensive knowledge of the history and theory of performance art may present his perception of the artworks as such. At the same time, we may generally observe that in these early reports, "Pécsi Zoltán" often refrains from using a critical voice; with this performance of distance and objectivity he seems to attempt to tone down the edgy performances.[35] He positions himself as an unconcerned outsider who does not care to be affected by the performance in any way.

Remaining quiet about certain aspects of the events the informant reports on is another performative choice that may allow the informant to disidentify with the ideological lens of surveillance. At the same time, identifying the silences and erasures in a state security report today may prove to be an impossible task. Only the juxtaposition of the files with other historiographical records, such as oral testimonies and other archival records, might expose what could be missing from the informant's report.

What is undoubtedly missing from "Pécsi Zoltán's" accounts of the artistic and communal events that took place in Péter Halász's apartment is a description of the embodied, affective experience of participating in such a secretive, subcultural event. Those who attended these evenings were undoubtedly members of a select group of insiders, which, inevitably, included the informant(s) too. In a 1991 special issue of the Hungarian periodical *Színház* ("Theater"), which is dedicated to Péter Halász and celebrates his homecoming from the United States[36], many members of the 1970s underground art scene recalled the freedom they felt as they entered and participated in apartment theater. They described a euphoric and utopian togetherness. For instance, the late drama theorist and dramaturge Géza Fodor recalled the diverse crowd that gathered on Dohány Street at Halász's apartment theater: "it attracted people of the most diverse worldviews, and people without worldviews, from philosophers, to scientists, to artists and bluestockings; the only thing that united us, rather harmoniously, was that we all hated the system and what happened here was outside of it; the sense of togetherness was very much sensible."[37] Visual artist El Kazovszky recalled: "Even getting in was exciting! Your 'entry ticket' created a collaborator out of you. ... It started with the invitation and as you entered the building approaching the door slowly with the others."[38]

While one of the top officers of Hungarian state security assessed that the performances on Dohány Street could "give back total freedom and spontaneity to the individual, to the body, to the word and to the act,"[39] "Pécsi Zoltán" provides much less visceral and interesting descriptions of these events. This is a third indication of the disidentificatory efforts that one may note in his early reports: despite the fact that the informant participated in these occasionally intoxicating and liberating embodied and communal experiences, his descriptions of the underground events are surprisingly affectless and disembodied. He enumerates how many people participated: "The number of audience members at the performances in Halász's apartment were around 15–25 ... but it even occurred that no one showed up, or only four to five audience members watched the performance. In such cases, the audience outnumbered the performers."[40] He also mentions that "the new production series didn't move a big crowd either, there were quite a few familiar faces, we could say that artists were performing to artists."[41] These reports show the ways in which informants transform an affective experience into a discursive framework. It is also notable that in these descriptions the most celebrated aspects of the performance-event, the sense of togetherness, the joy of provocation, the intrigue of secrecy, and, yes, that ephemeral feeling of freedom—all of which are often recalled in oral histories by former attendees—are either completely lost on or disproportionately belittled by the informant.

The conspicuous discordances between the recollections of the nostalgic underground artist community in 1991 and the informant reports of the apartment-theater performances leave the readers to wonder: was the informant performing while he presented himself as a seemingly—as others recall—engaged and engaging member of the intimate subcultural community, or was he performing to the network in his accounts? The research question that has driven this investigation is a conundrum that, with our limited knowledge in the present, cannot be resolved. "Pécsi Zoltán's" early reports show efforts to performatively negotiate the oppressive, ideological lens of state surveillance with the once-underground artist's lingering commitment to his own autonomous taste and thoughts. Even so, these early, traceable attempts of disidentification will disappear from the records of his communication with the state. As the files reveal, his precarious "performance of the self" among his artist friends will soon turn into a pretense, while the regular, repetitive, and ritualistic act of informing will transform the hailed subject[42] once and for all. The performance towards the state security network will increasingly become a performative act, one that repeatedly reinforces the position of the informant within the oppressive state apparatus, thereby constituting a different reality than the one the disidentifying informant-subject was striving for.

The early reports I discussed in this essay highlight misrepresentations and silences that could be read as the informant's attempts to perform the role of an unaffected and unemotional critic, whose point of view differed from both state security and the underground art scene. It is also important to note how quickly "Pécsi Zoltán" internalized the ideological lens and especially the methods the secret service used to infiltrate close-knit communities and manipulate individuals' trust and generosity. He abused the "radical care"[43] that tied this intimate group together by taking advantage of his established friendships and pretending to be a caring ally—one who organized countryside excursions,[44] offered to teach Japanese lessons,[45] and listened empathetically—only to, as he himself states, collect information for the repressive state apparatus.

This essay focused on the first few reports that are attributed to the informant "Pécsi Zoltán." However, a similar close reading of reports that followed these earliest pieces, some written as early as the summer of 1974 and others as late as the winter of 1987, would have engendered a very different analysis. The 101 reports in their totality suggest that disidentification is merely a liminal phase in the rite of passage of becoming a committed collaborator in the state security network. Reading the files one after the other, one may witness the personas of both the good civilian and the artist/art critic gradually disappear. What remains—at least within the two-dimensionality of the documents—is an informant whose mode of existence and sense of being are defined by his commitment to the repressive state apparatus and its all-pervasive ideology.

Endnotes

1 Péter Halász (1943–2006) formed the Kassák Ház Stúdió in Budapest in 1969. Their experimental performances soon gained popularity in both the Hungarian underground and the European neo-avant-garde scene, participating at festivals such as the World Theater Festival in Nancy, France and the Open Theater Festival in Wrocław, Poland. By 1972, their productions were banned, and they could only perform in the private apartment of Halász's grandmother. The illegality and permanent surveillance left no other choice for the company but to leave Hungary; in early 1976, they left for a year-long European tour with an "emigrant passport." A year later, the company settled in the Chelsea neighborhood of New York City, where Halász founded the Squat Theater.

2 "Pécsi Zoltán," "Jelentés" Report, ÁBTL Dossier 3.1.5.-O-16268/1, November 20, 1973, 259.

3 Some would, perhaps rightfully so, argue, that the ritual of becoming an informant started with the Austinian speech-act of "naming" during the informant's signing of the recruitment contract and subsequent alias assignment. However, there were a number of recruited individuals, who—under duress and the interrogators' coercion—signed the contract, but never wrote any reports. Therefore, the first few reports are equally important, as the repeated performative acts of reporting and signing allow for informants to assume their new identities.

4 It was György Galántai who first identified and outlined these three personalities in the seminal book, *Törvénytelen avantgárd* (*Illegal Avant-Garde*), and explored how they might have interplayed or how together, they might have constituted *The Personality of the Three*. This is a reference to Algol's own performance work at Balatonboglár, conspicuously titled as *The Personality of the Three*—a personality that is a mystical synthesis of the scientist, the artist, and the politician. Galántai, however, concludes that already the early reports on Péter Halászhow show that: "the three personalities [of 'Pécsi Zoltán'] were in no connection with each other, there was no crossing [between them], they were separate." Júlia Klaniczay and Edit Sasvári, *Törvénytelen avantgárd. Galántai Görgy balatonboglári kápolnaműterme 1970–1973* (*Illegal Avant-Garde:. György Galántais Chapel Studio Atelier in Balatonboglár, 1970–1973*) (Budapest: Artpool Art Research Center, 2003), 83.

5 The informant reports written by "Pécsi Zoltán" that the Historical Archives of the Hungarian State Security has excavated thus far date between 1973 and 1987. However, there is a possibility that there are/were also documents from 1988–1989 that either got destroyed or that researchers have not discovered yet.

6 Tamás Szőnyei, "Valódi hálózat—virtuális iratgyűjtő 'Pécsi Zoltán' lappangó Munka-dossziéjának rekonstrukciója," (Budapest, 2019), p. 4. See also in this volume: "Real Network, Virtual File: A Reconstruction of 'Pécsi Zoltán's' Hidden Work Dossier."

7 Ibid.

8 The two lead researchers on this project, Dániel Erdély and Miklós Peternák, were heavily criticized by the underground artist community, as well as by historians and archivists, for their premature decision to make the documents public. In 1998, only two years after the Historical Office (Történeti Hivatal)—the predecessor of the Historical Archives—opened, historians and archivists were in close collaboration with lawmakers to continue exploring the moral implications and necessary legal regulations for ensuring the ethical use of these confidential and subject-matter-sensitive documents.

9 However, it is important to note that Algol himself lost contact with the dissident and artist community in the late 1980s and was virtually unknown to wider audiences until 2005, when Johanna Rácz published her article focusing on the informant. At the same time, "Pécsi Zoltán's" reports garnered great attention for their detailed descriptions of the Kassák Ház Stúdió's performances and the underground exhibitions that György Galántai organized. Johanna Rácz, "*Nem hajlandó magyarul beszélni Galántai György besúgója*" ("Galántai György's informant refuses to speak Hungarian"), *Index*, March 22, 2005. https://index.hu/belfold/galant03xx/.

The public first learned of "Pécsi Zoltán's" informing activity through the *Hungary Can Be Yours!* (*Magyarország tied lehet!*) exhibition that took place in the Central Gallery in 2001. Later, researchers could also access many of "Pécsi Zoltán's" reports online. Visual artist and curator György Galántai made all the state security reports and documents on him—authored by "Pécsi Zoltán" as well as by other informants—available on his website: http://www.galantai.hu/festo/.

10 Pál Várnai, "*Beszélgetés Koós Annával, a 'lakásszínház' társalapítójával*" ("Conversation with Anna Koós, the founder of the 'apartment theater'"), *Szombat*, July 22, 2010, https://www.szombat.org/politika/4041-akkor-is-tortent-valami-ha-csak-a-labunkat-logattuk.

11 In the Historical Archives of the Hungarian State Security, the dossiers that might contain information regarding recruitment are the files marked as "B" (*Beszervezés*, "recruitment") and "M" (*Munka*, "work"). However, in "Pécsi Zoltán's" case, both folders are missing.

12 László Najmányi, "*Spions. 6. Rész*" ("Spions: Part 6"), *Balkon* 6 (2010): 24.

13 Gusztáv M. Hábermann, "*György Galántai urnak*" ("To Mr. György Galántai"), accessed April 6, 2019, http://www.galantai.hu/dokumentum/PecsiZoltan.html.

14 José Esteban Muñoz, *Disidentifications: Queers of Color and the Performance of Politics* (Minneapolis: University of Minnesota Press, 1999), 11.

15 Ibid.

16 Ibid.

17 Erving Goffman, *The Presentation of Self in Everyday Life* (Woodstock: Overlook Press, 1973), 17.

18 Ibid., 112.

19 "Pécsi Zoltán," "Jelentés" Report, ÁBTL Dossier 3.1.5. –O–16268/1, November 20, 1973, 259.

20 Ibid., 260.

21 "Pécsi Zoltán" gave his first report on November 20, 1973, so this may also have been the time when the state security network approached him and initiated the recruitment process.

22 "Pécsi Zoltán," "Jelentés" Report, ÁBTL Dossier 3.1.5. –O–16268/1, November 20, 1973, 260.

23 Since this essay only focuses on the early reports of "Pécsi Zoltán," I write little about the ways in which the reports present and/or perform the role of "good civilian." From the mid-1970s however, the informant regularly mentions his civilian job in the reports, as he utilizes his connections and research projects to convert "bad subjects" by offering them work and introducing them to the university world. On the contrary, the reference to Hábermann's civilian life more or less disappears from the documents later on. By 1978, he even stops giving accounts in first person. Instead, every report now opens with "my acquaintance," describing what activities the informant had participated in and observed as part of his work within the network.

24 The act of "naming" is one of the main examples that linguist J. L. Austin uses as he lays down the foundation of his speech-act theory and provides definitions for the group of "performative" verbs. His emphasis is that by giving and/or assuming a name, a

new person—or, in the language of psychoanalytical theory, a new subject—comes into being.

25 A reverse logic would suggest here that the annihilation of "László Algol" would also have led to the end of "Pécsi Zoltán," but for some reason—and the readers of these files may never know why—this did not seem to be an option for Hábermann.

26 "Pécsi Zoltán," "Jelentés" Report, ÁBTL Dossier 3.1.5. -O-16268/1, November 20, 1973, 263.

27 Ibid., 264.

28 Kata Krasznahorkai, "Heightened Alert: The Underground Art Scene in the Sights of the Secret Police—Surveillance Files as a Resource for Research into Artists' Activities in the Underground of the 1960s and 1970s," in *Art Beyond Borders: Artistic Exchange in Communist Europe 1945–1990*, eds. Jerome Bazin, Pascal Duborg Glatigny, and Piotr Piotrowski (Budapest: Central European University Press, 2016), 131.

29 Ibid., 131.

30 Ibid., 131.

31 "Pécsi Zoltán," "Jelentés" Report, ÁBTL Dossier 3.1.5.–O–16268/2, December 19, 1973, 47.

32 "Pécsi Zoltán," "Jelentés" Report, ÁBTL Dossier 3.1.5.–O–16268/1–2, October 8, 1974, 158.

33 Ibid., 157.

34 Ibid., 159.

35 After the opening of the Historical Archives, many recognized the value of these state security documents. First, dissident writer István Eörsi reminded his readers: "Let's not forget: these all are the irreplaceable and estimable documents regarding the methodologies of the Kádár era, which almost exclusively preserved an oppressed and humiliated, but extremely significant, movement of the period's artistic scene and intellectual life." István Eörsi, "*Abesúgójelentés*" ("Informant Report"), *Élet és Irodalom* 46, no. 47 (2002). https://www.es.hu/cikk/2002-11-25/eorsi-istvan/a-besugojelentes.html.
In an interview, Péter Halász also acknowledged, if somewhat ironically, the documentary value of "Pécsi Zoltán's" work: "'Pécsi Zoltán,' or László Algol, wrote quite accurate reports," he said. "He was an excellent poet, a serious brain, and I am not angry at him at all, because he saved me from the task of documenting my own life. I do not need to mess around with historiography now; if someone wants to do something with my life, then they can find everything about me, with no missing pieces, in the reports he wrote. Other than this, of course I despise snitching."

Zoltán Trencsényi, "*Szalámiszeletelés. Interjú Halász Péterrel*" ("Slicing the Salami: Interview with Péter Halász"), *Népszabadság*, November 13, 2004. http://nol.hu/archivum/archiv-339789-157215.

36 In 1991, Halász returned to Hungary and directed performances at prestigious art theaters, including the Katona József Theater, the New Theater (Új Színház), and the National Theater of Budapest. He also taught at the University of Theater and Film of Budapest, and for a while, he and András Jeles—another neo-avant-garde theater and film director—ran the City Theater (*Városi Színház*) together.

37 Géza Fodor, "*A Halász*" ("The Halász"), *Színház* 24, no.10–11 (1991): 20.

38 El Kazovszky, "*Az éles élet*" ("The Sharp Life"), *Színház*, 24, no.10–11 (1991): 39

39 "Pécsi Zoltán," "Jelentés" Report, ÁBTL Dossier 3.1.5. -O-16268/2, March 4, 1974.

40 "Pécsi Zoltán," "Jelentés" Report, ÁBTL Dossier 3.1.5. -O-16268/1, November 20, 1973, 248.

41 Ibid.

42 Applying the analytical frame of Louis Althusser's interpellation theory in this context, the informant is hailed into collaboration through the completion of the recruitment process.

43 The concept of "radical care" builds on Derrida's "unconditional hospitality" and asserts, as Harry Josephine Giles eloquently proposes, that "in a political situation in which care is both exceptionally necessary and exceptionally underprovided, acts of care begin to look politically radical. To care is to act against the grain of the social and economic [and in the context of communism also ideological—A. S.] orthodoxy: to advocate care is ... to advocate a kind of political rupture." In other words, radical care relies on selflessness and generosity; it is an existential mode of togetherness for communities striving to survive. The state security reports of the 1970s reveal a variety of such performative acts of radical care: sharing work and incomes (illegally), offering shelter and protection against state surveillance, and, most relevant in this context, becoming a trusting and intimate community. This definition of "radical care" is imbued by the conceptualizations of a number of theorists, including Harry Josephine Giles, Faranak Miraftab, and Jane Turner, as well as Patrick Campbell. Patrick Campbell and Jane Turner, "Radical Care: Performative Generosity and Generativity in Third Theater," in *Performance Research* 23, vol. 6: 58–64; Harry Josephine

Giles, “Shock and Care: An Essay About Art, Politics and Responsibility,” April 24, 2016. https://harrygiles.org/2016/04/24/shock-and-care/; Faranab Miraftab, “Radical Care as Transformative Solidarity,” filmed September 2017 at University of Illinois at Urbana-Champaign, video, 14:55, https://www.youtube.com/watch?v=1AtrK2d5Qhk.

44 According to his friends, he regularly organized excursions for the dissident underground community. He notes in a report from February 1974: “Despite the short notice and the several months of distance from the company, the turnout was great, which indicates Halász and the group members’ trust towards me. At the same time, there was no discussion of any topics relating to the performances, not even in the longer conversations. Overall, this meeting gave an occasion to re-initiate my relationship with the group.” “Pécsi Zoltán,” “Jelentés” Report, ÁBTL Dossier 3.1.5. –O–16268/2, March 4, 1974, 105.

45 Soon after his recruitment, “Pécsi Zoltán” offered to teach Péter Halász’s wife, Anna Koós, Japanese. In his account to the state security, he explained: “Considering that it was in my interest to establish a relationship that would allow me to regularly gather information about the work of the group, I offered that until September 1974 I would provide temporary classes (a language course) for Halász’s wife. My explanation for this was that in the second semester of the 1973/74 academic year no beginner course was offered. ... We agreed that the first class would be on March 5, 1974. ... The aforementioned events suggest that after the February 16 excursion, Halász trusts me more and he has no intention to prevent me from occasionally joining the rehearsals ...” Postscript: “Halász even offered that he would leave the written rehearsal schedule as a message at the university. I declined, arguing that ‘the message’ could land in untrusted hands.” “Pécsi Zoltán,” “Jelentés” Report, ÁBTL Dossier 3.1.5. –O–16268/2, February 18, 1974, 111.

László Algol / **Informant** "Pécsi Zoltán"

The Chemistry Engineer and the Construction Manager. The Person(ality) of the Three (An Approximation Exercise)

The man with the long hair and blue shirt introduced himself as László Algol to other fellow artists. His real name, however, was Gusztáv Hábermann, and Hábermann/Algol worked for the Hungarian state security under the code name "Pécsi Zoltán," ultimately as a full-time officer. In his performance *The Chemistry Engineer and the Construction Manager. The Person(ality) of the Three (An Approximation Exercise)* (*A vegyészmérnök és az építésvezető. A hármság személyisége [approximációs gyakorlat]*), he confronted these three identities during the night of August 12, 1973 in Balatonboglár. He sits like a guru in the audience, draws a circle, paints a net of threads that is fixed on three pine trees white, and reads his texts about the three identities through out the performance from 6:30 p.m. to the next morning about the three identities. With this triple identity, he wrote 101 reports about the art scene over the course of 14 years. None of the audience members, knew that they were literally being trapped in the net of state security. Nor had other artists in Hungary even the slightest suspicion that this man, would turn out to be one of the most valuable informants for the state security. After 1999, Galántai opened his files to the public and unmasked Algol-Hábermann-Pécsi. A journalist published an article about this unmasking in 2005, which caused a shock effect for the Hungarian art scene. Today, Hábermann lives in New Zealand, where he teaches psycholinguistics at a university. Following a letter in which Galántai asked him to clarify his position, he answered with a blanket letter of apology to the artists he reported on and claimed that he was acting as a bridge between the state and artists.(K)

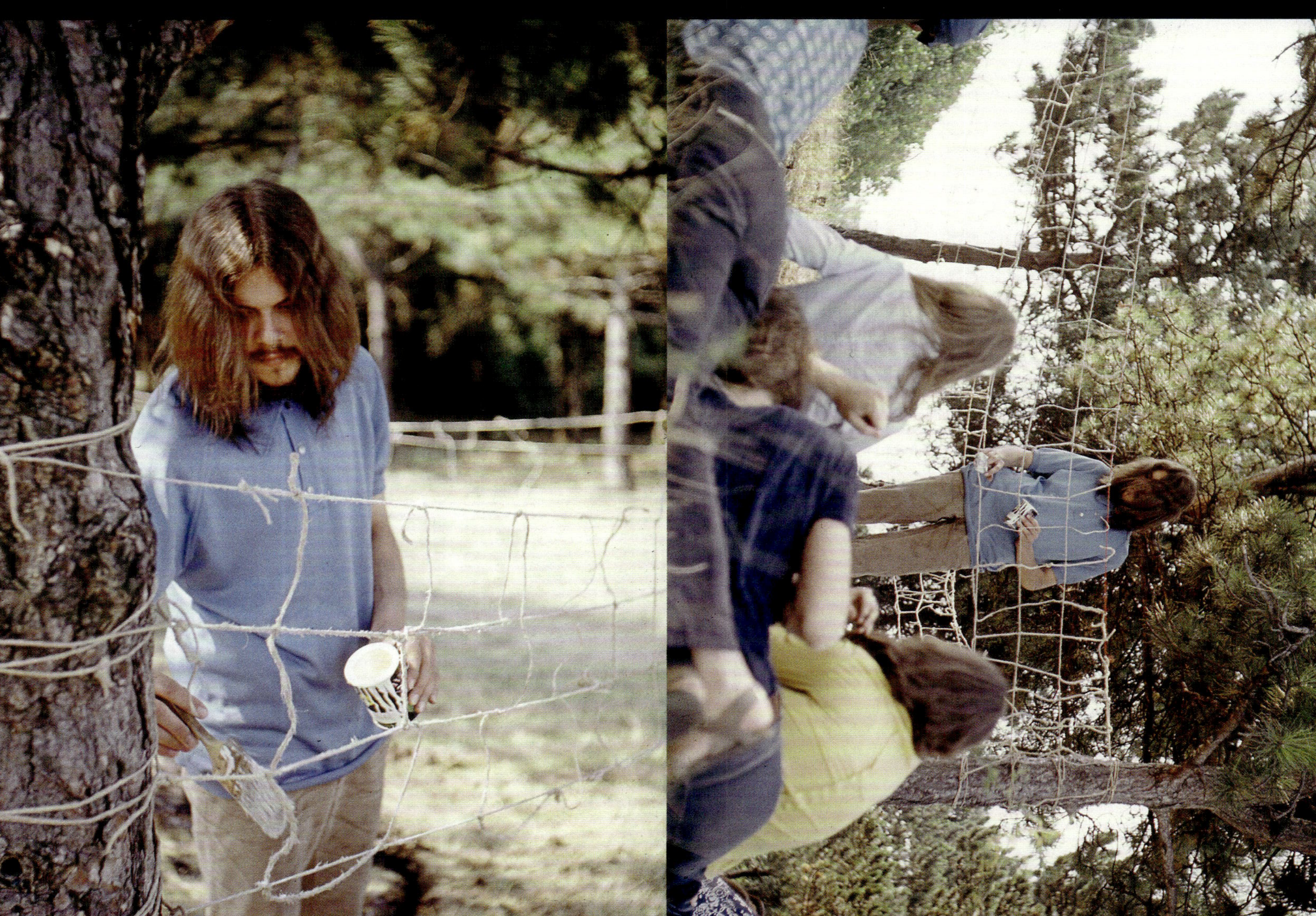

Four color photographs, Courtesy of Artpool Art Research Center / Museum

Kosiński Quotes

Jill Magid

In 2005, Jill Magid was tasked by the Dutch Intelligence Service (*Algemene Inlichtingen-en Veiligheidsdienst*–AIVD) with producing a work that would give "a human face" to the AIVD. Over the course of three years, the artist met with eighteen employees of the agency. Because recording devices were prohibited during these meetings, Magid took handwritten notes. These became the basis of a report which blended the individual statements into a collective persona which Magid referred to as "the Organization." "The transformation of an artist into an agent began," Magid writes. Her model was a literary figure named Tarden from Jerzy Kosiński's novel *Cockpit* (1975), which she read parallel to her research. The *Kosiński Quotes* are passages from *Cockpit* that Magid "redacted" in the way commonly used by intelligence services—but instead of using black to redact, she used yellow. She did this to emphasize that which remains secret. Magid's report developed into a novel with the title *Becoming Tarden*—which could only, however, be published after significant redaction by Dutch intelligence. **(K/A)**

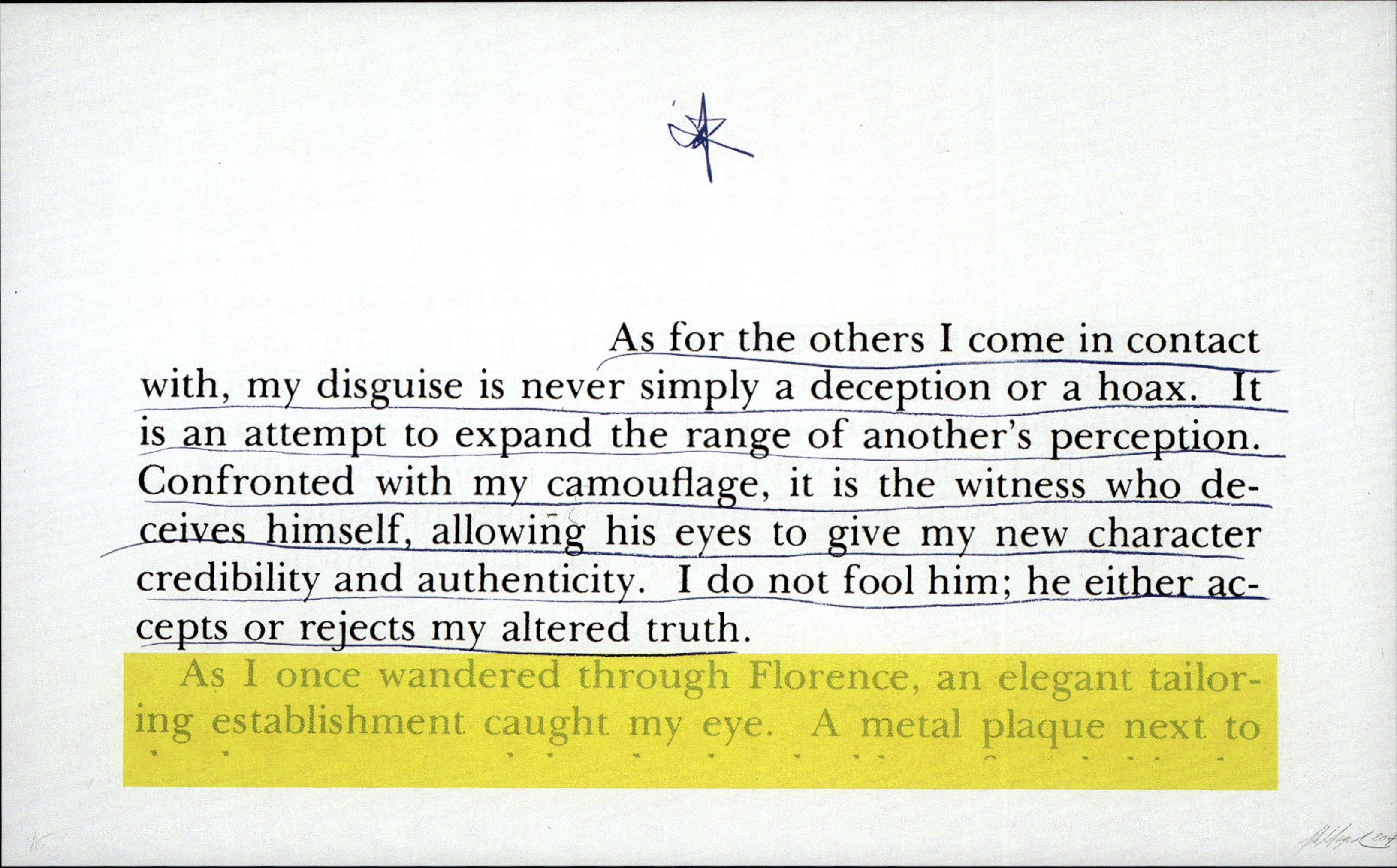

As for the others I come in contact with, my disguise is never simply a deception or a hoax. It is an attempt to expand the range of another's perception. Confronted with my camouflage, it is the witness who deceives himself, allowing his eyes to give my new character credibility and authenticity. I do not fool him; he either accepts or rejects my altered truth.

As I once wandered through Florence, an elegant tailoring establishment caught my eye. A metal plaque next to

Disguise, colored screen print on Rives BFK paper, 69.9 × 111.8 cm, Courtesy of LABOR Art Gallery, Mexico City

Vaulting, colored screen print on Rives BFK paper, 69.9 × 111.8 cm, Courtesy of LABOR Art Gallery, Mexico City 2007

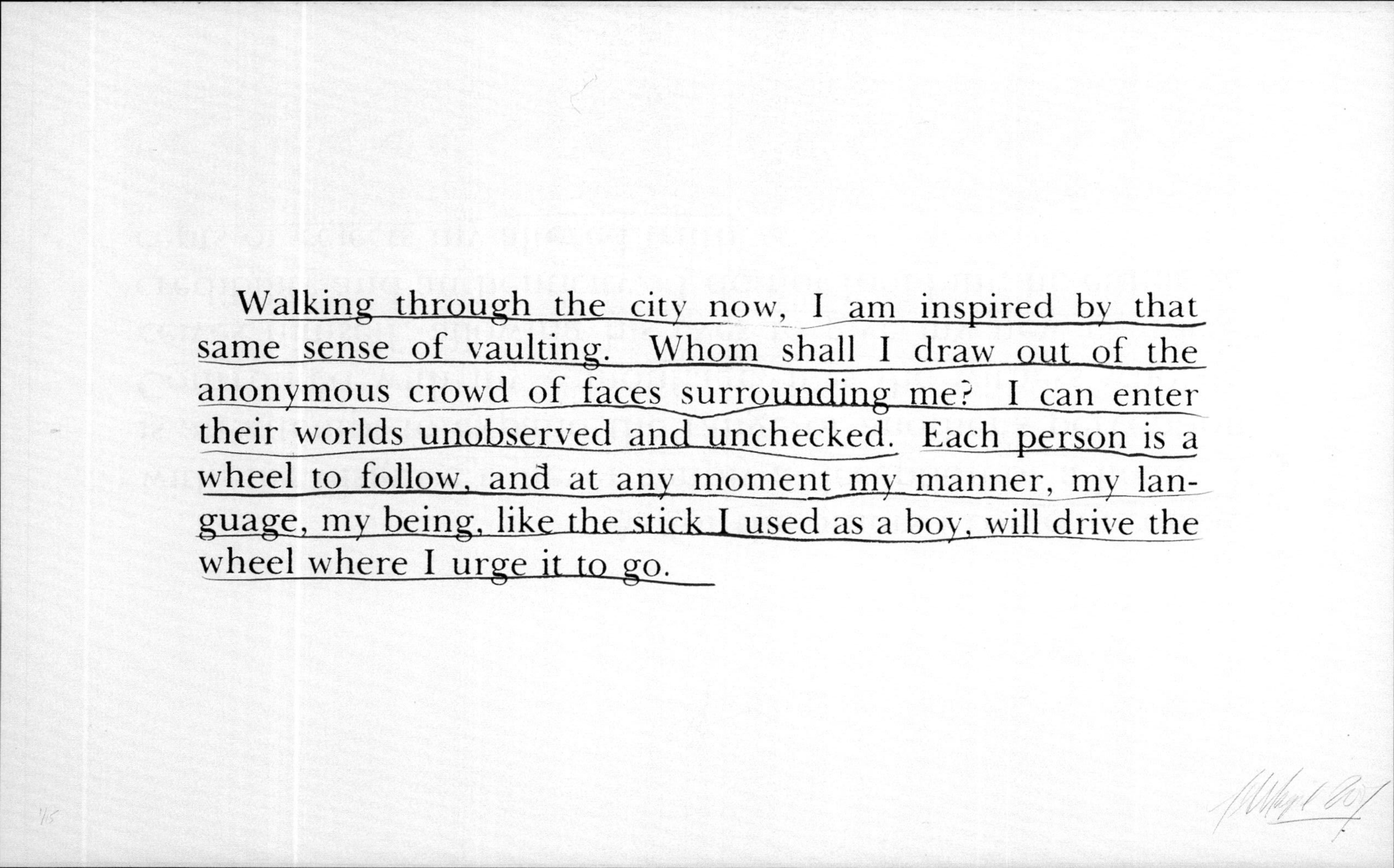

Walking through the city now, I am inspired by that same sense of vaulting. Whom shall I draw out of the anonymous crowd of faces surrounding me? I can enter their worlds unobserved and unchecked. Each person is a wheel to follow, and at any moment my manner, my language, my being, like the stick I used as a boy, will drive the wheel where I urge it to go.

friend for advice, without even realizing that she was ad-
mitting she'd been sleeping with another man.

My sensitivity to the slightest change in my environment, and my craving for unusual psychological pressure have made me aware how little other people are aware of their surroundings, how little they know of themselves and how little they notice me.

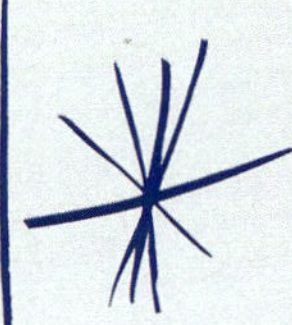

Once, I attended a party given by a wealthy businessman who had rented paintings from a small, private museum to impress his guests. When the guests arrived, they were

My Sensitivity, colored screen print on Rives BFK paper, 69.9 × 111.8 cm, Courtesy of LABOR Art Gallery, Mexico City 2007

Intelexit is a subsidiary organization of Peng Collective.
With support and contributions by: Tatiana Bazzichelli, Bewegungsstiftung.de, Brandon Bryant, Nighat Dad, Pia Eisenträger, Emily Jeffries, Ben Korta, Alisa Tretau, Yehudit Yinhar, Jeremie Zimmermann, The Centre for Investigative Journalism, Intelexit, Anonymous himself/herself, and many anonymous spies.

Intelexit

Peng! Collective

The self-described "world's first exit programme for members of secret services," the Berlin-based Peng! Collective, attracted international media attention in the autumn of 2015 with *Intelexit—Exit to Democracy*. In the context of the campaign, which is uncoincidentally reminiscent of the EXIT breakaway program for neo-Nazis, the Peng! Collective called for employees to leave the surveillance apparatus using poster walls in front of the U.S. National Security Agency, the German Federal Intelligence Agency, and the U.K. Government Communications headquarters. They also dropped flyers over the NSA military data center in Darmstadt with the help of a drone and provided an encoded information and consultation infrastructure for those affected (Call-a-Spy). The short advertising video, published on YouTube, collects statements from former secret service employees, such as Thomas Drake, who was a whistleblower eleven years before Edward Snowden. In 2002, he published secret information on Project Trailblazer, which was to serve the purpose of comprehensive, global surveillance by the NSA. However, Walter Eichner, the "former Stasi Officer" is a fictional figure probably based on Klaus Eichner, an MfS officer who specialized in counterintelligence and after 1990, published information about the intertwined relations between the GDR and Western intelligence services. The video encourages secret service employees to turn their backs on the services: "Be smart. Exit intelligence now." (A)

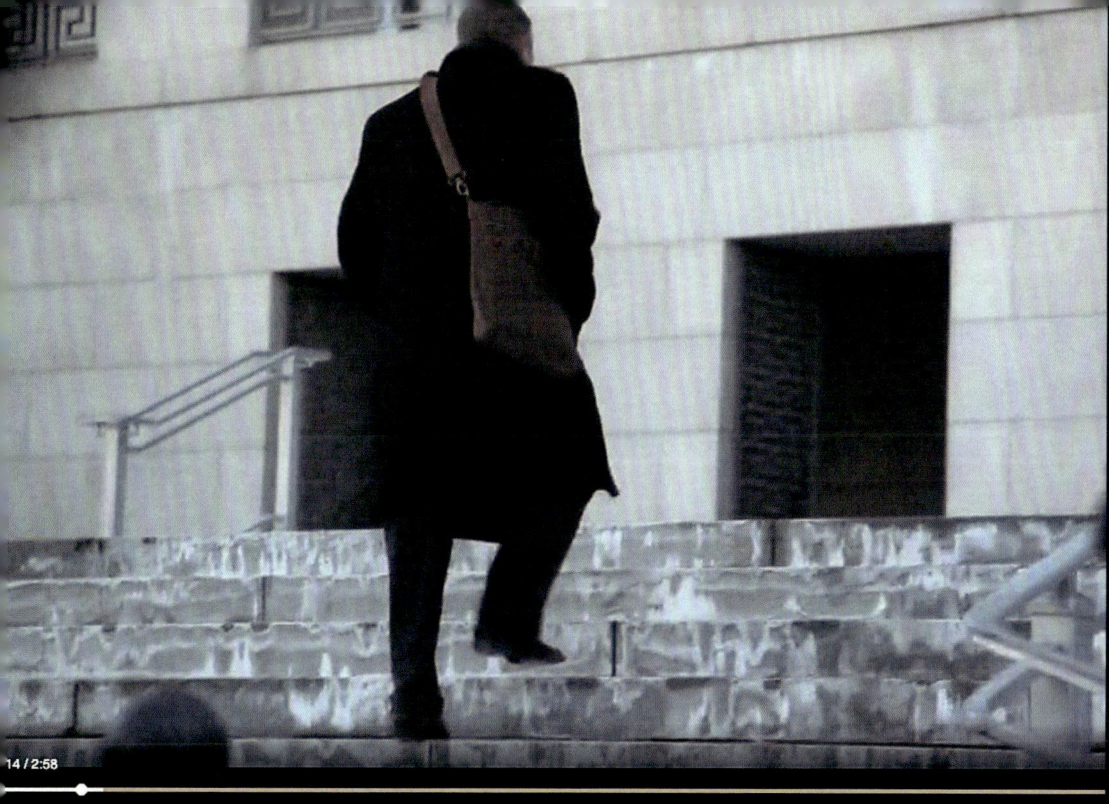

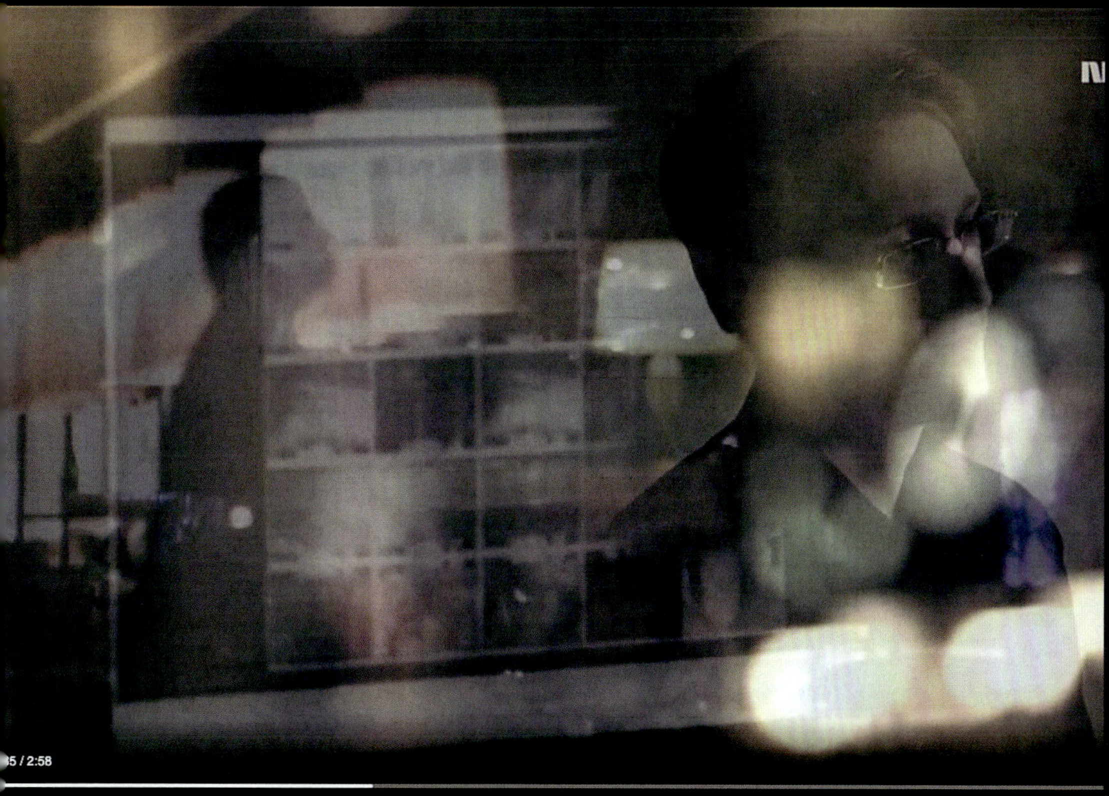

Peng! Collective

Archives and Agents

Video, 2:58 min., Courtesy of GNU Free Documentation License v 1.3

2015

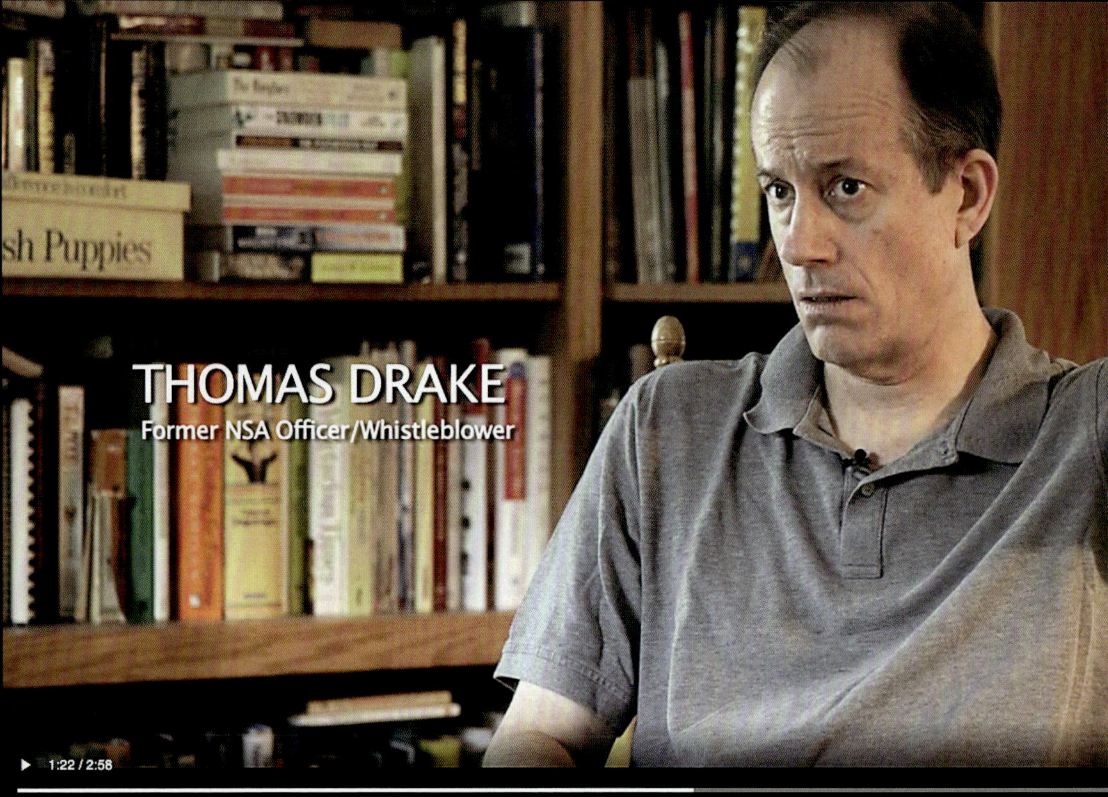

THOMAS DRAKE
Former NSA Officer/Whistleblower
1:22 / 2:58

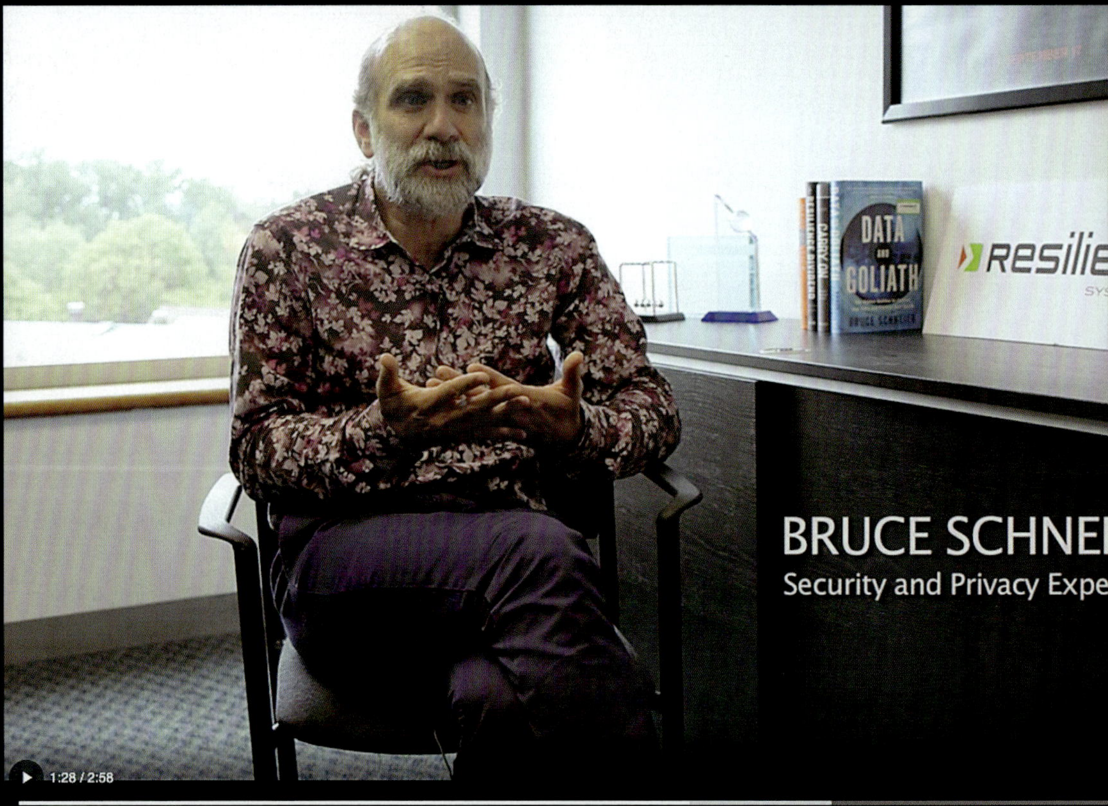

BRUCE SCHNE
Security and Privacy Expe
DATA AND GOLIATH
BRUCE SCHNEIER
Resilie

1:28 / 2:58

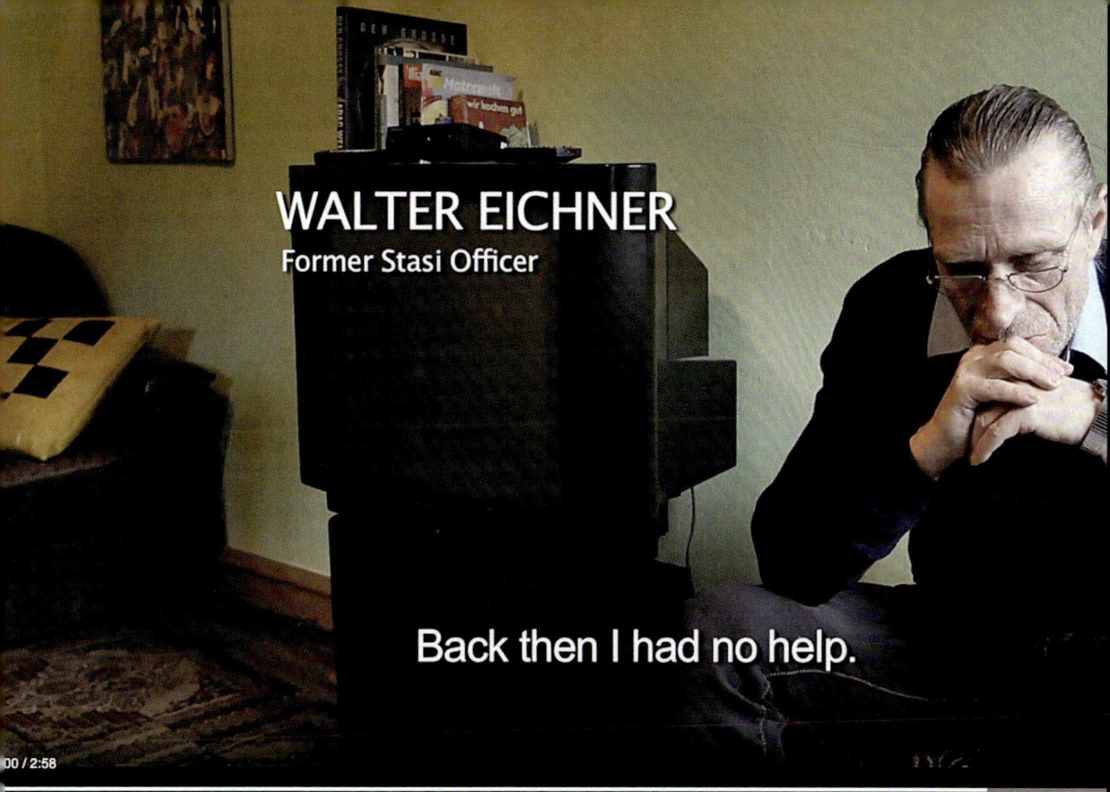

WALTER EICHNER
Former Stasi Officer

Back then I had no help.

00 / 2:58

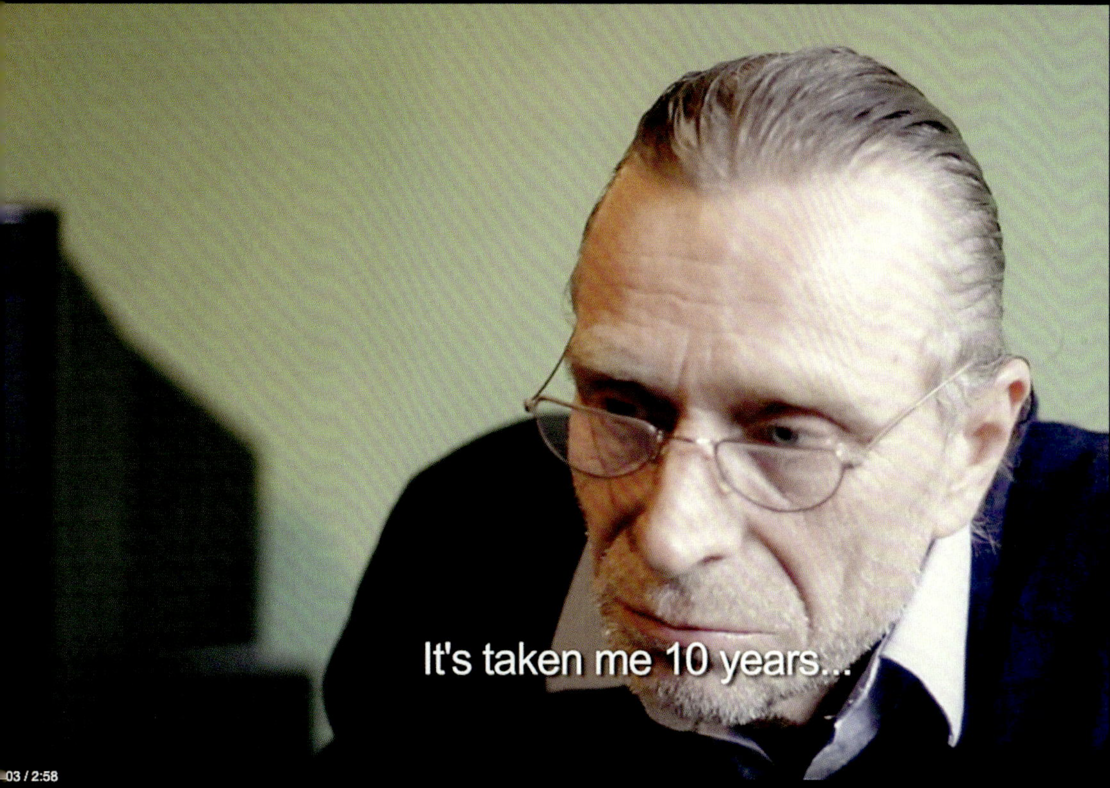

It's taken me 10 years...

03 / 2:58

Video, 2:58 min, Courtesy of GNU Free Documentation License v.1.2 2015

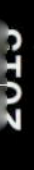

to realize what I'm responsible for.

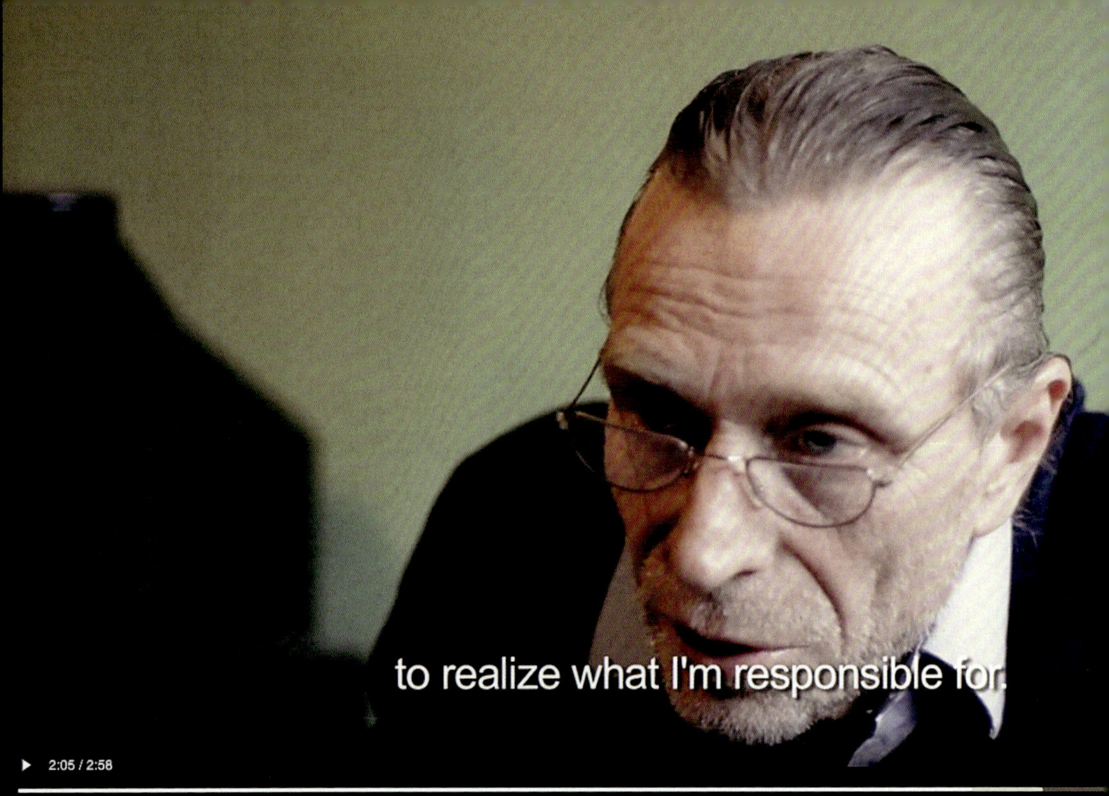

2:05 / 2:58

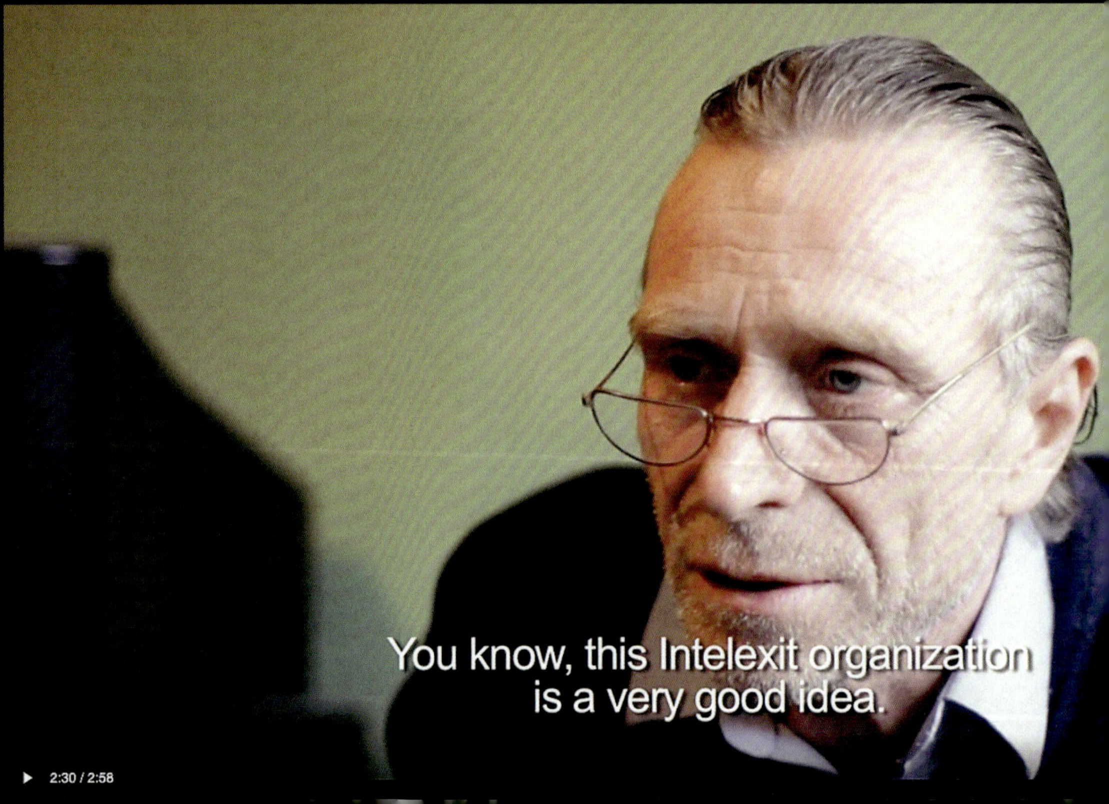

You know, this Intelexit organization
is a very good idea.

2:30 / 2:58

“Theories”

"Decompositional" Theory:

Hungarian State Security and the "Theory" of Happenings

Kata Krasznahorkai

In the files of Hungarian state security, we find not only documentation of happenings and performances but also intense discussion about the question of what happenings and performances actually *are*. These attempts at definition fundamentally served the purpose of prevention—a "happening prevention," which we also encounter in the Polish files surrounding the Orange Alternative. By examining the texts in official newspapers, informant reports, the state security's internal reports, as well as in attempts to define happenings, we can detect the effort exerted towards the ideological justification for classifying happenings as a danger to socialist society. Incidentally, this also provides justification for the enormous amount of labor that state security put into the surveillance and "operative handling" of the art sphere. On the other hand, this "theorization" was also conceived of as an aid for the informants, one which allowed them to recognize when and why surveillance and reporting was necessary.

The "theory" of happenings in the files

So what did state security understand by the term "happening"? In Hungary, the term first appears in the context of an article titled "Happening and Antihappening" ("*Happening és antihappening*") by Mária Ember in the state-run magazine *Film, Színház, Muzsika*.[1] In a sarcastic, ironic tone, the author intended to describe the absurdity and ludicrousness of happenings in the United States and Western Europe; however, she unintentionally gave inspiration to Hungarian artists. It was also this article (among other inspirations) that provided the initial impetus for

Tamás Szentjóby[2] and Gábor Altorjay to organize the first Hungarian happening a month later, *The Lunch (In Memoriam Batu Khan)*.[3] This was followed by numerous other happenings until Szentjóby's emigration in 1975.[4] Szentjóby, initiator and author of the happening, was aware of the explosiveness of this genre, already naming it the "atom bomb of the culture" in 1966.[5]

Three informants were immediately tasked with reporting on the first happening, a sign that state security perceived it as a source of danger even before it was organized. Before describing the happening's content, a report from July 1, 1966, written by the informant "Mészáros," started with the genre's supposed historical context—a completely fictional "context" that had nothing to do with the actual history of the happening:

> Before I get to an account of the facts, I should note that this concept is well known in certain circles, and thus the role of chance is more or less excluded. I must admit this at the outset because the entire background and spirit of this social phenomenon is such a fundamentally determined thing that its aim to exclude all doubt and even its forms of appearance are not always explicit. The happening—although not under this name—has a rather long past, beginning with the gatherings of avant-gardist movements (e.g. Dadaism) in the thirties and ending with the activities of the school's direct founding father, Salvadore [*sic*] Dalí, which were an institutionalized variant of this pastime. Salvadore Dalí mostly invented this form of "entertainment" for business reasons, as ornamentation for his works, and of course aimed at the propaganda around his person. It first became institutionalized in America. Happenings took place under this name and spread in Los Angeles, Greenwich Village, and other beatnik and hipster centers. Alan [*sic*] Ginsberg defined the aim of the happening as: "subjugation by the logic of a confused world, in other words when participants give up their illusory rights, which they believe can influence chance, and admit the fact of their absolute defenselessness right up until their own physical destruction."

With this pseudo-(art-)historical contextualization, the informant locates the happening in the "enemy" block of the Cold War and, by excluding the possibility of "coincidence," ascribes a kind of malice to the genre's emergence in Hungary.[6] In addition, he characterizes the happening as a "crisis phenomenon, an *enfant terrible*" and as a "tool of a kind of exaggerated decadence," "nihilism," and a "desire for shock," all of which are typical descriptions of "bourgeois art" in Eastern Europe during the

Cold War.[7] In America, the informant claims, the happening even led to a wave of violence, drug consumption, and direct confrontation with the police. In the report's evaluation section, the police lieutenant writes that the report is "valuable from an operative standpoint" because it "reflects a new phenomenon in youth circles in Hungary which is beginning to spread through Western influence."[8]

The second agent "Hajdu"[9] submitted his report one month after Mészáros's, typed on August 4, 1966. He describes the difficulties the artists face in finding a location for the happening, complains about the bad weather, as well as the fact that he thought that the event was not going to take place at all. That is why he did not attend it. Nevertheless, he claims to know who was present and writes that "Dr. László Végh[10] was so thrilled by the happening that he decided to organize an anti-happening."[11] Neither of the first two informants knew that a third informant was present and had reported on the same happening: "László," on July 22, 1966.[12] This informant was not commanded to make a report (like "Mészáros,") but, rather, reported independently of his duties. After listing the prominent names of the Budapest intellectual elites who had been invited, he described the meaning and goal of the happening: "Essentially, viewers could witness new, shocking, never-before-seen spectacles. The whole phenomenon was analogous to going to church or the theatre, in which the important thing is the shared experience. /*two lines redacted*/ The 'happening' is a regular form of entertainment in the West and has also been popular for years in Poland."[13] Furthermore, he conceives of the happening in the West (but "for years in Poland, too") as a form of entertainment. According to a rumor, György Aczél, the Vice Minister of Culture, was also engaged with this topic and supposedly did not like it at all.

In his evaluation, the chief of police wrote that the report "describes a new direction in events in Hungary. ... Shortly after this, we can report the attendance of intellectuals—writers, artists, etc. and young people."[14]

The three reports were compared and, in 1967,[15] forwarded in summarized form to the Ministry of the Interior.[16] In the comments on this summary, we read that the state security's work was aimed at "uncovering the goal of the happening and those who are organizing it."[17] But it was already clear at this point that no infiltration of the political system was to be expected from the happening. Nevertheless, they continued pursuing the strategy of conducting surveillance in this area and reviewing the possibility of criminal proceedings.[18]

After 1968, the state security's sense of alertness in surveilling the cultural scene increased substantially, a result of revising the state security's working methods and strategies following the Prague Spring. After a meeting of the Central Committee in November 1969, a decree by the Ministry of the Interior demanded more "courage" in interactions with "hostile activities" from the ranks of culture; the "initial feebleness" should be overcome, the **network** of **informants** expanded, the limits of cultural criminal offenses broadened, and the introduction of criminal proceedings facilitated.[19]

The state security's subversive operative practices—which, in the cultural sphere, were concentrated more and more on the happening between 1966 and 1978—were planned to deliver evidence against happeners by means of "theory," ideology, and ethics. This could only be successfully achieved if **collaborators** were well-versed enough in ethics and politics to be able to reliably deliver such information. State security recognized that the existing **informant network** in the mid-sixties was unsuited and insufficiently trained for this, subsequently seeking to recruit more and more "qualified" **informants** from the art scene.

On March 25, 1968, the **agent** "Kurucz Tibor" (by day a popular disc jockey of the Kádár era) reported on a happening in the Utasellátó Club[20] in the context of the file on economics student István Poór, who wanted to open a music club. Poór did not have much to do with happenings, but in order to prosecute him, his connections to the happening scene provided a good cause for considerably intensifying his **surveillance**.[21] Previously, state security only noted "rabble-rousing" comments among his circle of friends, but now it was public performances of this "hostile" art genre which made him even more suspicious:

> Although a talk about the hippies was announced in the Utasellátó Club, Poór, due to illness, said nothing about what kind of talk it would be and who would be giving it, but then, by the third time I was with him, he told me that Miklós Erdély, the number one happening author, would be giving a talk. First, they would play a tape of the radio play he had presented in the University Club, then there would be a debate led by Poór, who was the editor of a radio program for young people. Then there would be a "happening"—improvised, of course.[22]

This sarcastic attitude towards the happening as a result of its supposedly improvised presentation would be repeated in reports and serve as an identifying feature of the happening genre, even though the happening, as described by Szentjóby in an interview in 2006, was characterized as planned and choreographed and thus explicitly *not* improvised: "The planned, artificial event is the Happening. The planned modifies the spontaneous more radically than the other way around."[23] We nevertheless read again and again in the reports of the "improvised" character of the happenings, which is probably based on intentionally falsified informant statements. "Fung," for example, reports of an alleged statement by Poór in which he claims that "a really good 'happening' is one which is not at all organized but simply happens automatically."[24] In the same file, we read that "Fung's" reports on the happenings led to the crystallization of the following picture for state security:

> The "happening" is a harmful, anti-progressive phenomenon for the political development of youth, a phenomenon which is in service of the imperialistic politics of softening. From a philosophical point of view, it signifies the promulgation of nihilism, irrationalism, and the negation of healthy human action.[25]

At the end of the report, there is a handwritten note by the informant "Kurucz Tibor"[26] addressed to his commanding officer. From it, we can get a sense of the "routes" of informant reports in the state security's labyrinth. Police lieutenant Ferenc Kovács calls upon the commanding officer to prepare an action plan against happenings on the basis of reports prepared by several informants. "Happening" had meanwhile become a catch-all term for every possible kind of subversive public event, such as readings or even concerts:

> Comrade Bándi! It seems that "Kurucz" was also positively engaged in the monitoring of the "happening" line. He confirms "Fung's" data. The data received thus far needs to be summarized. At the same time, make a recommendation for how the "happening"-like programs can be prevented.[27]

Only a couple of months later, in November 1968, we again find a new "theoretical" contextualization of the happening in one of the Ministry of the Interior's[28] "records" about Poór: according to this record, it is "a harmful, regressive phenomenon for the ideological, political development of youth, a phenomenon in service of the imperialistic politics of undermining."[29] The "philosophical" judgments of the informants about the first happening in 1966 cited at the beginning are taken over here almost word for word when we read: "With respect to the philosophical dimension, it is the propagation of nihilism and irrationalism, the negation of healthy human activities."[30]

On December 20, 1968, a report by two police lieutenant colonels confirms that "on the basis of the confirmed data of the Ministry of the Interior, Section III/III/2, a decomposition measure was undertaken."[31] The happening is turned into a "semi-artistic western ideological orientation designed to subvert [the socialist system—K.K.]."[32] And further: "The basic idea arises from the irrational conclusion that nothing in the world or in a society can be grasped with logic. The triggers of acts are unknowable to human beings and the effects of these acts unpredictable. Thus, the most appropriate human act (the happening) is the meaningless, disjointed succession of acts. According to this understanding, the consciousness of human beings is limited, their actions determined by advertising which attempts to shock humans into attention and drive them to individual acts."[33]

At the end of the report, it is concluded that "the effects of the disruptive measures monitored via operational methods have so far been satisfactory."[34]

Due to the alleged critique of consumerism and capitalism in the "theory" explained in this report (e.g. the critique of the effect of advertising), the happening and its anticapitalist theoretical background should not have actually presented a problem for the socialist system—if not for issues like "irrationality" and "nihilism," its unpredictability, the rejection of logic or the production and development of a new public sphere.

State security was also interested in debate within the happening scene, with the intention of using it for the development of their own operational subversion. "Fung," who studied anthropology, seems to have integrated himself well into the happening scene, as he reported of an argument between István Poór, Miklós Erdély, and, allegedly, Tamás Szentjóby.[35] According to the report, Poór was unwilling to organize new happenings due to different understandings of the happening's definition. Much more likely, however, is that his decision was a consequence of a decomposition plan. The police had sent him a warning, tapped his phone, and placed him under surveillance—all without any relevant cause. In the evaluation of the measures, we read: "individual members of the society [surrounding Poór] have made statements to the effect that it would be best to avoid contact, so as not to trigger a series of police actions, or the decomposition of their university studies by the relevant authorities."[36]

Measure Plan Against Happenings

The nine-page "Summary Report and Measure Plan," dated May 11, 1968, shows where individual informant reports and "records" arrived and how their theoretical evaluations were realized in concrete actions. This report was composed only three days after "Fung's" and before the "record" of the successful "decomposition."[37] This report contains descriptions by a total of six informants regarding the four happenings which were known to have happened up to that point. Theorization and historical background feature as early as the first paragraph—created solely for state security's point of view. The previously cited informant reports on the first happening are referenced almost word for word, as are those about Poór. In the introduction to the measure plan, we read:

> In light of the above it can be established that the spread of happenings is harmful to young people's intellectual and political development, anti-progress, and a phenomenon that promotes imperialist circles' politics of rebellion.[38]

This justification is repeated like a mantra in reports, records, and here in the measure plan.

Highly specific measures are developed on this "theoretical" basis: the relevant functionaries are informed; no more venue permits are to be issued for happenings in the future; the correspondence of the "happeners" is to be monitored, this information being forwarded to the passport authorities; and the "KISZ administration[39] and party leadership in humanities departments of the ELTE should be preventatively" informed. Even the theoretical dispute between Tibor Hajas [alias Tibor Frankl] and Tamás Szentjóby was used as a "decomposition measure":

> A measure plan to be taken must be worked out to disrupt the happening movement. According to our knowledge to date, the conflict of principles on the question of happenings between Tibor Frankl and Tamás Szentjóby could easily be exploited to this end.[40]

They planned a special measure for Szentjóby:

> The main leaders of the happenings must be warned to desist from their planned performances in the future. Special attention must be paid to Tamás Szentjóby, who is the most active in this field. Szentjóby's attention must be drawn to the fact that if he is not willing to desist from organizing happening performances in the future, then we will recommend that he be treated in a closed psychiatric institution.[41]

An evaluation of the measure plan in November 1968, as well as the cited "record" of December 20, 1968, show that the measures seemed to have worked—but also that antihappening measures were far from finished.

Happenings as a Danger to Society

The reports of informant "László,"[42] who was revealed to be the writer Gyula Lugossy after the end of communism, were particularly useful to state security. He was one of the most talented and well-versed informants in the cultural sphere, especially when it came to the potential dangers of happenings. On April 28, 1969, "László" composed a summary report entitled "On the Social Impact of Happenings" ("*A happening társadalmi hatásáról*").[43] "László" was even sent to Poland and Czechoslovakia to report on the happening scene there. In his report, he also begins by sketching the happening's historical and theoretical context. But even this well-educated informant wrote of a "theory" tailored to fit state security which he thought could be "helpful" to them:

> Happening events spread in the West after the Second World War. Their basic principle is rebellion against social conditioning, conventions, and common attitudes. During certain shows, manmade articles are used in an unorthodox manner. By this means, they attempt to act on people's instincts for destruction, upheaval, and desire for novelty. The happening is one of the means of such western youth rebellion, and is usually directed against all forms of society; thus, in terms of its fundamental idea and practice, it shows a close affinity to anarchist endeavors.[44]

Even at the beginning of the report it is clear that "László" wants to offer a basis for state security's course of action against the art genre by situating it in the context of "rebellion" and "anarchy." It was thus not sufficient for officers to repeatedly confirm on the basis of informant reports that happenings were not at all political—the operative measures were not stopped (in contrast to Poland, where proceedings were stopped when the content was not political). "László" writes specifically of happenings in a socialist context:

> Naturally, happenings organized in socialist countries are also hostile to society; even if this is not openly propagated, it is still the case. Yet it is also true that this hostility to society is materialized not primarily in political terms, but in lifestyles and ways of thinking. It proclaims the absolute right and freedom of the individual to self-expression and conflict with everything, even when this approaches pointless vulgarity, or indeed directly borders on brutality.[45]

Here, the double argument of "László" becomes clear: on the one hand, he makes a charge against artists—but only morally, not politically. In the report, he then addresses individual protagonists, and characterizes them on the basis of moralistic (and tendentious) principles as alcoholic, homeless bums:

> Some of the happenings he organized over the past three years have been good in terms of camp formation, one can speak of the far-reaching consequences of their great impact. Those present experienced them as new endeavors hitherto unknown in Hungary. The conditions necessary for these to become mass phenomena in Hungary do not exist in Hungary as they do in the West; in my opinion the mass of youth would be unimpressed even if they organized them every week. Their participants and supporters come from a narrow stratum of younger intellectual university students, those who are always present at Dr. Végh and Pál Petrigella's apartment and on other occasions too, if something "new" and "exceptional" is taking place.[46]

"László" does emphasize that debates about the happening and its consequences took place, but he immediately relativizes its significance for society by describing it as a niche phenomenon of young intellectuals and as an attempt to transfer a Western phenomenon into Hungarian society:

> Although their aim is primarily to entertain themselves, and to attract attention, the experiment is by no means a threat to those irrational tendencies that exhort a large part of western youth towards mindless rebellion against every existing order, institution and custom. Naturally, everything that is wholly alien to socialist society. This is also proved by the fact that so far, [name redacted] has only managed to secure premises for their events by cheating and misleading people.[47]

In the evaluation, the Captain concludes by summarizing: "The happening organizers use deception to secure more opportunities for their shows. Their activation demands that **measures** be carried out for their urgent **decomposition**."[48] Hungarian state security wanted to "disrupt" happenings "as quickly as possible" even though both the **informant** reports and the summary reports repeatedly emphasize that the happening has no explicit political content or goals. Poland, in contrast, chose another route, closing the "operative file" if there was a lack of evidence for antipolitical behavior.[49]

The Hungarian state's disproportionate, "platonic" fear of happenings was based on the happening's theoretical indefinability on the one hand and, on the other, on its supposed Western origins. To a certain extent, happenings took place in a no-man's-land between state security's fear of Western influence and the artists' desire for freedom. They filled a blank spot in the art of an established socialism, a spot which was to be filled with the help of "theory."

State security's interest in precisely this term also had a direct impact on its use in the art sphere. In response, artists used alternative definitions, camouflaging the terminology of happenings and—according to state security—referring to them as "Op Art" or "Pop Art" or, in the case of the GDR, as "Pleinairs" to put the secret police on the wrong track. The artists did not know, however, that the secret police were also well-informed about these camouflaged terms. In this way, the terminological camouflage backfired, as the investigation and surveillance of happenings expanded even more:

> During the meeting, to supplement the report, the informant also told of how the police, according to Poór, had recently sprung upon the word "happening." Even merely hearing the word "happening" irritated police officers, which is why "happening" needed to be replaced in the future with either "Op Art," "Pop Art," or another word. Because police are idiots who understand nothing about art and won't even notice it.[50]

The specific language used in the reports originated from reviews, which were also collected in the files. Alongside "László's" evaluation of the social effects of the happening, for example, we find László Kamondy's three-page review of *The Lunch* in the journal *Tükör*,[51] as well as an article about happenings in the largest daily newspaper *Népszabadság*[52] and a press review from German newspapers translated into Hungarian about the happening with the title "The Predecessor of the Happening: Kurt Schwitters Died Twenty Years Ago ("*A happening előfutára. Húsz évvel ezelőtt halt meg Kurt Schwitters*"). In this review, certain passages are underlined by hand, e.g. "Marinetti's Futurists and the Dadaists are supposed to be the true forerunners of today's Op-Pop and Cop [*sic*]? Time has definitely proven this true. They are the forefathers of the happening and Polit-Pop..."[53] The "theory" about Schwitters's or Dali's roles as "forerunners" of the happening as well as the recurring references to Dadaism and Futurism were intended, two years after the first happening, *The Lunch*, to ensure "art historical" verification in the files. It is thus no surprise that the "operative case file" created for Szentjóby received the cover name "Schwitters."

The meticulousness of the collected materials also shows that the exact definition of the happening was of fundamental significance and was pursued simultaneously by both artists and official cultural politics. In this way, the happening as a term and genre became contested territory which, for the state, stood in for "hostile" artists while becoming a territory for artistic freedom for the artists.

Tamás Szentjóby and Gábor Altorjay answered the question of the happening's actual goal in a 1966 interview, conducted after *The Lunch*:[54] "taking over power."[55] State security, however, did not understand the irony, and neither did they have a sense for artistic exaggeration. One of the greatest failings of the secret police was that they were manically focused on certain words without being able to recognize the actual threat—including its theoretical and ideological side. And so, they pursued a term like "happening" for years, shaping the word to the present day. They turned it into a taboo term, which is still, to this day, impugned by official authorities.

That state security's "theorization" of the happening bore consequences beyond their own intended goals can be seen in two specific effects. In 1979, the happening made an appearance in the syllabus of a two-semester course about postwar art at the Budapest Academy of Arts.[56] This occurred at a moment when happenings were no longer the dominant name for live actions—the term "performance" had widely replaced happenings in art (and in the files). The appearance of the term "happening" in the 1980s testifies to its political domestication. Starting in the 1960s, the definition of the happening as an enemy of the state began to appear in the files of the secret police: it played a part in the ever-decreasing use of the word in official discourse, while other terms for presence-based art forms, such as "performance," sprouted. If we take these dynamics into account, it becomes clear why Szentjóby, who paved the way for happenings in Hungary, is to this day vehemently opposed to the term "performance," seeing it as a form of "degeneration" of the happening.

In Poland, on the other hand, the term "happening" remained an explosive topic for state security until the late 1980s. In 1988, for example, in a secret report entitled "Alternative Youth Movements" ("*Młodzieżowe Ruchy Alternatywne*"),[57] Dr. Marek Zieliński defined the happening as a "street festival" accompanied by "a march on a pre-determined route."[58] Zieliński refers to the happenings of the Orange Alternative as a "representative point of reference"[59] for the genesis of alternative movements. Happenings were perceived as a form of dissatisfaction and youth rebellion against the socialist system: "this form of demonstrating your dissatisfaction, rebellion, and simultaneously your autonomy is described as a free, spontaneous, and independent art."[60] Zieliński cites a journalist who portrays these happenings and their initiator Waldemar Fydrych as a true mass phenomenon in the alternative scene: "In the fighting groups, we never met anyone who was not fascinated by the happening or didn't like its author."[61] He gives the movement an eminently important role, which gained even more popularity and influence in oppositional circles during 1988. It seems even more threatening to him that alternative movements were "activated" after 1987—e.g. the happenings of the Orange Alternative—*Away with the Truncheons, away with the Heat* (*Precz z [u]pałami*, 1987), or in *Day of the Secret Agent* (*Dzień Tajniaka*, 1988), where a five-meter tall model of a flower was placed in the center of Wrocław and was "dedicated to all working in the departments" (*bezimiennym pracownikom resortu*). Banner inscriptions appeared like "Youth of Wrocław, thank Miliz and SB [the political names of state security] for a smile and humor" (*Młodzież Wrocławia dziękuje milicij i za uśmiech i humor*) or "let them become '100 years old' (*spiewano pracownikom resortu '100 lat'*)."[62] Because or in spite of the explicit political content of the happenings, the participants insisted in an interview with the British Broadcasting Corporation, following the arrest of Fydrych, that happenings should not be reduced exclusively and one-dimensionally to their political content—thus only being taken as a political act, which Zieliński also cites in his report: "Reducing the idea of the happening to a one-dimensional political demonstration must be considered tendentious."[63] Zieliński refused to consider happenings as an artistic position, however. "Spontaneous artistic activities" were in his view nothing more than street riots, but he describes them consistently as "major street actions" (*ważniejsze akcje uliczne*). Zieliński does not judge these actions to be spontaneous artistic acts but rather precisely planned "political demonstrations" (*manifestacje polityczne*).

Hungary's case shows the legitimization attempts of a small number of well-versed, knowledgeable informants who composed "art historical" reports in the innermost circle of artists, declaring these reports to be "aids to reconciliation and mutual understanding" between artists and state security (a typical self-justification of informants before and after 1989). We can only read this self-justification as a fatal error and/

or a conscious playing down of its intentions. In Poland too, educated art historians who thought they could build a "bridge" with the help of theoretical evaluations were acquired by state security. But the attempt to "theorize" could also be directed towards the informants themselves. After completing their work, they were themselves often privately and professionally destroyed—as Łukasz Ronduda shows in his article about Jerzy Ludwinski.[64] Though there are also counterexamples, like the case of Hungarian informant "Pécsi Zoltán," who, after thirteen years of intensive and "profound" reports about the underground scene, was promoted as an officer. He did not have to deal with any repercussions after 1989 for his engagement as a "mediator."[65]

The reports about happenings did not at all lead to a "reconciliation," however. Instead, they were used to justify the surveillance and destruction of the art scene. The attempts of state security to categorize the happening in terms of "art history" was in no way harmless. Quite the opposite: "theory" based on "art history" itself became a dangerous instrument for the development of suitable decomposition measures—not only against the genre, but above all against the artists themselves.

Translated from German by Brian Alkire

Endnotes

1 Maria Ember, "Happening és antihappening" ("Happening and Antihappening"), *Film, Színház, Muzsika.* October 19, 1966, 18.

2 Because Tamás Szentjóby has been using numerous variations of his name for decades, here I am using the spelling which appears in historical documents and citations. The most commonly used form is by now Tamás St.Auby.

3 Zsuzsa László and Tamás St.Turba, eds., *The Lunch (In Memoriam Batu Khan) Happening Budapest H 1966* (Budapest: transit.hu, 2011), 18.

4 For more on the influences and conditions of the first Hungarian happening, see Kürti, *A szabadság anti-esztétikája. Az első magyarországi happening* (*The Anti-Aesthetics of Freedom: The First Hungarian Happening*), in: *exindex*, http://exindex.hu/index.php?l=hu&page=3&id=967 (October 10, 2018).

5 Tamás St.Turba, ed., FIKA. *Fiatal Művészek Klubja. Interjú St.Auby Tamással (*BOGEY. *The Young Artists' Club. An interview with Tamás St.Auby)* (Budapest: Ludwig Múzeum Kortárs Művészeti Múzeum, 2013), p. 27.

6 "Mészáros T.", "Jelentés" (Report), 1.7.1966, 3.1.9.–V–156455, 55.

7 "Mészáros T.", "Jelentés" (Report), 1.7.1966, 3.1.9.–V–156455, 55.

8 Ibid., p. 57.

9 "Hajdu," "Jelentés" ("Report"), ÁBTL 3.1.2–M–34608/1, 1966, 297; ÁBTL 3.1.9–V–156455, 1966, 59. Translated from Hungarian by Gwen Jones.

10 Dr. László Végh was a radiologist and composer. From the early 1960s, Végh was a central figure of the Hungarian artistic underground, primarily in the area of electronic music. From 1951–1962, however, he became an employee of Hungarian state security after he was arrested in 1951 and forced into collaboration. For more on Végh and his circle, see: Emese Kürti, *Glissando és húrtépés. Kortárs zene és és neoavantgárd művészet az underground magánterekben 1958–1970.*

11 "Hajdu," "Jelentés" ("Report"), ÁBTL 3.1.9.–V–156455, October 4, 1966, 60.

12 "László," "Jelentés" ("Report"), ÁBTL 3.1.9.–V–156455, July 22, 1966, 53. Translated by Gwen Jones.

13 Ibid.

14 Ibid., p. 54.

15 Cf. "Summary Report," Budapest, March 7, 1967, ÁBTL–V–156455.

16 Belügyminisztérium, III/III. Főcsoportfőnökség, 2/b alosztály

(Ministry of Interior, Section III/III. Subsection 2/b). Among state security units, III/I (Foreign Intelligence Service), III/II (Counter-espionage) and III/IV (Countermilitary), section III/III was tasked with interior counterintelligence, which also included cultural matters. Subsection 4 was actually tasked with cultural surveillance, but here it is subsection 2 that is responsible for the surveillance of youth.

17 "Summary Report," ÁBTL–V–156455, March 7, 1967, 37.

18 Ibid.

19 This order from the Interior Ministry, labelled 0022/1970, is analyzed in depth by Edit Sasvári and Tamás Szőnyi. Cf. Edit Sasvári, "*A balatonboglári kápolnatárlatok kultúrpolitikai háttere*" ("The Cultural-Political Background of Chapel Exhibitions in Balatonboglár"); Klaniczay and Sasvári, eds., *Törvénytelen avantgárd. Galántai Görgy balatonboglári kápolnaműterme 1970–1973* (*Illegal Avant-garde: György Galántai's Chapel Workshop in Balatonboglár 1970–1973*); and Szőnyei, *Nyilván tartottak. Titkos szolgák a magyar rock körül 1960–1990* (*Registered: Secret Agents in the Hungarian Rock Scene 1960–1990*).

20 "Kurucz Tibor," "Jelentés" ("Report"), ÁBTL 3.1.5. –O–15636, March 25, 1968, 55. On February 20, 1968, in the Utasellátó club on Arany János Street, István Poór organized an evening with the title "Hidden Parameters." There was a talk by Miklós Erdély and a happening by Tamás Szentjóby. For a summary report and action plan, dated May 30, 1968, see: http://www.c3.hu/collection/tilos/krono.html.

21 See Szőnyei, *Nyilván tartottak. Titkos szolgák a magyar rock körül 1960–1990*, 240–41.

22 "Kurucz Tibor," "Jelentés" ("Report"), ÁBTL 3.1.5. –O–15636, March 25, 1968, 54.

23 Tamás Szentóby, "Már csak azért is, mert vannak spontán és vannak tervezett események. A tervezett, mesterséges esemény a Happening. A tervezett radikálisabban módosítja a spontánt, mint fordítva," in FIKA. *Fiatal Művészek Klubja. Interjú St. Auby Tamással (*BOGEY. *The Young Artists' Club: An interview with Tamás St. Auby)*, ed. St. Turba, trans. Katalin Orbán, (Budapest:Ludwig Múzeum Kortárs Művészeti Múzeum, 2013), p. 30. Translated from Hungarian by Katalin Orbán.

24 "Fung György," "Jelentés" ("Report"), ÁBTL 3.1.5. –O–15636, May 9, 1968, 60. Translated from Hungarian by Brian Alkire and Kata Krasznahorkai.

25 Ibid., p. 104.

26 "Kurucz Tibor," "Jelentés" ("Report"), ÁBTL 3.1.5. –O–15636, March 25, 1968, 54–56. Translated from Hungarian by Brian Alkire and Kata Krasznahorkai.

27 Ibid., also cited in Szőnyei, *Nyilván tartottak*, p. 243.

28 Record, Ministry of Interior Affairs, ÁBTL 3.1.5. –O–15636, November 14, 1968, 104–05. Translated from Hungarian by Brian Alkire and Kata Krasznahorkai.

29 Ibid.

30 Ibid., p. 105.

31 Report, Dr. Gábor Bruzsa Lieutenant Col. and Dr. László Turányi Lieutenant Col., December 20, 1968, ÁBTL 3.1.5. –O–15636, p. 134. Translated from Hungarian by Brian Alkire and Kata Krasznahorkai.

32 Dr. Gábor Bruzsa, Lieutnant Col., and Dr. László Turányi, Lieutnant Col., Report, ÁBTL 3.1.5. –O–15636, December 20, 1968, 132–34.

33 Ibid., p. 133.

34 Ibid., p. 134.

35 "Fung György," "Jelentés" ("Report"), ÁBTL 3.1.5. –O–15636, May 9, 1968, 60.

36 Dr. Gábor Bruzsa, Lieutnant Col., and Dr. László Turányi, Lieutnant Col., Report, ÁBTL 3.1.5. –O–15636, December 20, 1968, 134.

37 "Summary Report and Measure Plan, Case File 'Schwitters,'" ÁBTL–3.1.9.–V–156455, May 11, 1968, 127–35. In this version, released by the ÁBTL Archive and not originating in the case file "Schwitters" itself, the passages pertaining to Tamás Szentjóby have been anonymized. In this version, they were placed online in 1996 without Szentjóby's approval in the framework of the "Schwitters" case, i.e. before the current regulations of the ÁBTL Archive. The names of the secret police officers and agents have been redacted. This shows how variously the release and publication can take place, depending on who makes files public and when. Translated from Hungarian by Gwen Jones.

38 "Summary Report and Measure Plan, Case File 'Schwitters,'" ÁBTL–3.1.9.–V–156455, May 11, 1968, 127–35. Translated from Hungarian by Gwen Jones.

39 *Kommunista Ifjúsági Szövetség* (KISZ), Communist Youth Organization, was the Hungarian equivalent of the Free German Youth (FDJ).

40 http://www.c3.hu/collection/tilos/111.html. Translated from Hungarian by Gwen Jones.

41 Ibid.

42 In the case of this report, like with the cited "Summary Report," there are two sources for accessing the report (with different redactional practices): two pages of the report are on the website of the C³—Center for Culture and Communication, http://www.c3.hu/collection/tilos/docs.html (accessed May 28, 2018), and the entire report is in the ÁBTL Archive under the signature ÁBTL 3.1.9-V-156455, pp.177–79. In the 1970s, there were several agents with the cover name "László." See Szőnyei, *Nyilván tartottak*, 246 and 628. Another "László" reported about the *Nalaja Happening* in Szentendre in 1971, see ibid., 627–628. The informant "László" had already befriended Tamás Szentjóby and traveled with him to Poland in 1967, allegedly to see a happening by Tadeusz Kantor. However, "László" hindered Szentjóby from escaping to Sweden via Poland. Afterwards, Szentjóby was unable to even get a passport for travel to the "brother countries."

43 "László," "Jelentés" ("Report"), ÁBTL 3.1.9-V-156455, April 11, 1969, 177–79. Translated from Hungarian by Gwen Jones.

44 "László," "Jelentés" ("Report"), http://www.c3.hu/collection/tilos/111.html, (accessed May 28, 2019). Translated from Hungarian by Gwen Jones

45 Ibid.

46 Ibid.

47 Ibid.

48 Ibid.

49 Cf. Ronduda, "Neo-avant-garde Movement in the Security Service Files," 34–97.

50 "Fung György", "Jelentes" ("Report"), May 6, 1968, ÁBTL 3.1.5.-O-15636, pp.58–59, and the same report in "Fung's" register of work: "Fung György", ÁBTL, M-33528, pp.270–71. Translated from Hungarian by Brian Alkire and Kata Krasznahorkai.

51 László Kamondy, "*Ebéd in memoriam Batu kán. Meditáció az első Happeningről*" ("The Lunch—In memoriam Batu Khan: *Meditation on the First Happening*"), *Tükör*, November 13, 1966, 11–13.

52 Tamás Koltai, *Happening úton-útfélen* (*Happening at Every Turn*), *Népszabadság*, July 17, 1968.

53 *Sajtószemle erdetei német újságokból* (*Press Reviews from German Newspapers*), April 29, 1968, Hamburg C21594, in ÁBTL 3.1.9. V-156455, 271–72.

54 Tamás Szentjóby and Gábor Altorjay, *The Lunch (In Memoriam Batu Khan), Happening Budapest H 1966*, June 25, 1966, Hegyalja street 20/b, Budapest. In cooperation with Miklós Jankovics and István

Varannai with the help of Enikő Balla, Miklós Erdély, and Csaba Koncz. See also St. Turba and Zsuzsa, eds., *Az ebéd.(In memoriam Batu kán), Happening Budapest H 1966 / The Lunch (In Memoriam Batu Khan), Happening Budapest H 1966.*

55 Gábor Altorjay, "Az ebéd. (In memoriam Batu kán)" ("The Lunch. In Memoriam Batu Khan"), in *A magyar neoavantgárd elsõ generációja 1965–1972 (The First Generation of the Hungarian Neo-Avant-Garde, 1965–1972)* (Szombathely: Szombathelyi Képtár Museum, 1998), 14.

56 I thank Noémi Fórián Szabó for this tip. She found the relevant documents in the Academy of Arts archives where Hedvig Dvorszky describes her teaching plan (September 1979) as well as the presidium's meeting documents (October 5, 1979), which approved these plans.

57 Capt. Dr. Marek Zieliński, "Youth Alternative Movements—Evaluation, Conclusions and Prognosis," Report, September 20, 1988, Warsaw, National Military Service, internal doc. 220/88, http://www.orangealternativemuseum.pl/#captain-zielinskis-report.

58 Ibid., "They appear first of all in the form of a happening, so most often street parties accompanied by a march on a given track."

59 Ibid., "representative points of reference."

60 Ibid., "This form of demonstrating your dissatisfaction, rebellion, and at the same time your autonomy, is described as free, spontaneous, and independent art. Its founder and organizer explains the usefulness of happenings."

61 Ibid., "Among the fighting groups we have not met anybody who wouldn't be fascinated with happenings and who wouldn't like their author."

62 English translation is from the website. The description and slogans cited by Capt. Zieliński after A. Grabowska, "Who is afraid of toilet paper," Radio Free Europe, March 10, 1988, in: Capt. Dr. Marek Zieliński, "Youth Alternative Movements—Evaluation, Conclusions and Prognosis," Report, 20 September, 1988, Warsaw, National Military Service, internal doc. 220/88, http://www.orangealternativemuseum.pl/#captain-zielinskis-report.

63 Ibid., "Limiting the idea of happening to [the] one dimensional form of a political demonstration should be considered tendentious."

64 Cf. Ronduda, "Neo-avant-garde Movement in the Security Service Files," 87–94.

65 See Szőnyei, "Real Network, Virtual Folder: A Reconstruction of "Zoltán Pécsi's" Hidden Work Dossier," in this volume.

Action Art, Happening Definitions

BM, SB, MfS, StB

The Eastern European secret services feared genres such as action art and happenings. They classified them as Western, neo-avant-garde, decadent, bourgeois, and thus, antisocialist. In order to get a grip on the performative genres, they tried to find definitions and art historical derivations; they also read “Western” theory. Once a definition had been found, it appeared—as in the GDR—in very different documents with always the same wording: “The essential content of ‘action art’ is that decadent artistic structures are produced and then destroyed, and these sequences of movements are documented.” In Hungary and Poland, it was less action art than happenings that caused concern: “Happening is one of the means by which the youth of the West revolts against the existing. It is directed against every kind of society and is closely related to anarchist aspirations in its basic idea and also in practice. ... Of course, happenings that are organized in socialist countries are also directed against society, even if this is not openly stated.” Happenings were regarded as political events that cause unrest: “What good are the so-called happenings to student culture if they are in fact street riots and foolishness?” The different texts, with all their funny mistakes (“Hoppenings” and “Boys” [Beuys] as inventor of the genre), show how seriously the state security tried to prevent happenings and actions, classifying the genre itself as dangerous. (S)

BM. III. Head Directorate
III. Dir. Subdivision 2/b

Strictly confidential!

Erhalten von: Informant «László»
Received: Antal Tóvölgyi Pol. Lt.-Col
Tóvölgyi Oberstleutnant
Date: April 11, 1969
Subject: On the Social Impact of Happenings

R e p o r t

Budapest, April 28, 1969
Agent "László" reports

Happening events spread in the West after the Second World War. Their basic principle is rebellion against social conditioning, conventions, and common attitudes. During certain shows, man-made objects are used in an unorthodox manner. By this means, they attempt to act on people's instincts for destruction, upheaval, and desire for novelty. The happening is one of the means of Western youth rebellion and is usually directed against all kinds of society; thus, in terms of its fundamental idea and practice, it shows a close affinity with anarchist endeavors.

Naturally, happenings organized in socialist countries are also hostile to society; even if this is not openly propagated, it is still the case. Yet it is also true that this hostility to society is materialized not primarily in political terms, but in lifestyles and ways of thinking. It proclaims the absolute right and freedom of the individual to self-expression and conflict with everything, even when this approaches pointless vulgarity, or indeed directly borders on brutality.

The happening therefore originally serves such aims and materializes with various modifications by individual representatives of these endeavors.

85

BM.III.Főcsoportfőnökség.
III.Csfség.2/b.alosztály.

Szigoruan titkos!

Pálinkás el.

Adta:"László" fn.ü.
Vette:Tóvölgyi Antal r.alez
Idő: 1969.április hó.11.
Tárgy:A Happening társadalmi hatásá-ról

Jelentés.
Budapest,1969.április hó.28.

"László" ü.jelenti.

A happening rendezvények Nyugaton a második Világháboru után terjedtek el. Alapelvük a társadalmi beidegzések, konvenciák, megszokott látásmódok elleni lázadás. A müsorok egyes számaiban ember által alkotott tárgyakat a megszokottnál eltérő módon használnak fel. Ezáltal az ember romboló, felforgató, ujat akaró ösztöneire igyekeznek hatni. A happening e nyugati fiatalság lázadásainak egyik eszköze,és általában mindenfajta társadalom ellen irányul; igy alapgondolatában, gyakorlatában szoros sokaságot mutat az anarchista törekvésekkel.

Természetes, hogy szocialista országban rendezett happeningnek is a társadalomellenesség a tartalma, még ha ezt nyiltan nem is propagálják, akkor is. Igaz azonban az is,hogy a társadalomellenesség nem elsorban politikai szakon, hanem életfelfogásban,gondolkodásmódban jelentkezik. Az egyén korlátlan jogát és szabadságát hirdeti az önkifejezésre és mindennel való szembekerülésre még akkor is, ha eközben az értelmetlenség közönségesség, söt egyenesen a brutálitás határát surolják.

A happening eredendően tehát olyan célokat szolgál, más-más módosulásokkal jelentkezik azonba n az egyes törekvések képviselőinél.

ÁBTL -3.1.9. - V - 156455 /177

./.

Source: ÁBTL 3.1.9. –V–156455, 177–79, http://www.c3.hu/collection/tilos/85.html. Source of the italics: TH V-156455 ("László") 84–95.

In the case of Tamás Szentjoby [*sic*], Miklós Erdélyi [*sic*], and Miklós Urbán, this is not a matter of conscious principled concepts, but rather indicates these individuals' whims, conspicuousness, and the expression of their burnt-out inner worlds. All three declare themselves to be artists: Szentjoby [*sic*] and Urbán primarily write poems, while Erdély writes prose and essays. They approach the happening from this perspective too, calling it a "new genre" and taking artistic impact as their primary aim, while refraining from making any kind of ideological statement.

It is a different matter that [in] the shows they organize, they involuntarily express certain ideological content, content which, even if it is not outrageously hostile to society [misspelled in original], is certainly offensive and goes against [misspelled in original] commonly accepted and customary public taste. Szentjoby [*sic*] is the most active individual, he regards the organization of happenings as the sole point and pleasure of his life. ["Berettyó," a nonsense place indication is in the original out of the context the sentence here.] At the same time, since his life is one of sheer boredom, [he] cannot immerse himself in work, human relationships, or emotions, and fills his days from morning to night with idleness, while at the same time blaming the world around him for the emptiness of his life.

I know Miklós Erdély less well. What I do know about him is that of these three individuals, he is the most cultured, the most mature for his age, and is also interested in questions of aesthetics. He wrote a long essay about "prop-art" [*sic*], which Gyula Ortutay did not ultimately allow to be published in *Valóság* [*Reality*]. He is a drinker, and although he has a family and children, he often employs this cynical, decadent intellectual pose, and also takes part as a participant in some happening shows. He clearly rejects everything that the country's cultural policy offers for society; and together with Szentjoby [*sic*] and Urbán, they only respect certain decadent products of Western culture, and do so with a certain superiority and pride, while hating everyone else for their stupidity. Szentjoby [*sic*], for example, often makes insulting remarks about contemporary Hungarian artists and writers, judging not merely their aesthetic conservatism, but holding socialist art to be something ridiculous and stupid.

Miklós Urbán's thoughts and statements stem from his lifestyle. He lives on a few hundred forints a month, which he earns from books reviews, and, more recently, painting tapestries. He has been tramping around without an apartment for years and currently lives in a sublet, spending his days in the Hungária Coffee House; he lives in the center of the city as if he were an island-dweller or a savage. Outside of society, just like Szentjóby, he believes fanatically in happenings and anarchist artistic trends; but his more serious, cultured, objective, but his unfortunate lifestyle, however, excludes him from other people's company, and thus he cannot respond to healthy influences.

Some of the happenings organized over the past three years have been good in terms of camp formation, one can speak of the far-reaching consequences of their great impact. Those present experienced them as new endeavors hitherto unknown in Hungary. The preconditions necessary for these to become mass phenomena in Hungary do not exist as they do in the West; in my opinion the mass of youth would be unimpressed even if they organized them every week. Their participants and supporters come from a narrow stratum of younger intellectual university students, those who are always present at Dr.Végh and Pál Petrigella's apartment and on other occasions too, if something "new" and "exceptional" is taking place.

The happenings initiated by Szentjoby [*sic*] et al. do not therefore grow organically out of our contemporary social reality.

86

Erdély Miklóst kevésbé ismerem. Tudom róla, hogy e három személy közül a legmüveltebb, már koránál fogva is a legérettebb, aki esztétikai kérdésekkel is foglalkozik. A "prop-art" ról hosszu tanulmányt irt, amelyet végül is Ortutay Gyula nem engedett közölni "Valóságban." Iszákos ember, s bár családja, gyermekei vannak, gyakran használja e cinikus, dekadens értelemségi pózokat, és az egyes happening müsorokba szereplőként is résztvesz. Nyilvánvalóan elutasitja mindazt, amit az ország kulturpolitikája a társadalomnak kinál;

Urbán Miklós gondolatai, megnyilvánulásai, életmódjáról fakadnak. Havi néhányszáz forintból él, amelyet könyvismertetéssel, ujabban goblein festéssel keres. Évekig lakás nélkül csavargott, jelenleg albérletben él, napjait a Hungária Kávéházban tölti; a város közepén él, de ugy, mint egy szigetlakó, vagy egy vadember.

Az elmult három év folyamán rendezett néhány happening jó volt arra, hogy tábora alakuljon ki, nagy hatásáról mélyreható következményeiről lehessen beszélni. A megjelentek ugy fogadták mint uj, Magyarországon eddig még ismeretlen kezdeményezést. Nincsenek meg az előfeltételek arra, hogy olyan tömegjelenséggé váljon nálunk, mint Nyugaton; szerintem a fiatalság tömegére akkor is hatástalan lenne, ha hetente rendeznének. Résztvevői, szinpatizánsai egy szük fiatalabb értelmiségi egyetemista rétegből kerülnek ki, azokból akik Végh doktor, Petrigella Pál lakásán és más alkalmakkor mindig is jelen vannak, ha "uj" "rendkivüli" dologról van szó.

A happeningek tehát nem szervesen nőnek ki a mai társadalmi valóságunkból. Hanem arról

./.

But this concerns their attempt to transplant a western phenomenon in our country. Although their aim is primarily to entertain themselves, and to attract attention, the experiment is by no means a threat to those irrational tendencies that exhort a large part of western youth towards mindless rebellion against every existing order, institution, and custom. Naturally, everything that is wholly alien to socialist society. This is also proved by the fact that so far, [name redacted] has only managed to secure premises for their events by cheating and misleading people. Most recently for example, the happening held at the Pesterzsébet Cultural House was interrupted at the direction of the cultural center, and Tamás Nádor, the leader of the literary group, stated that what is happening here is not art but troublemaking.

"László"

Evaluation:
The happening organizers use deception to secure more opportunities for their shows. Their activation demands that measures be carried out for their urgent decomposition.

Measure:
Prepare controlplan, alert.

Instruction:
1./ [redacted][1] to establish who plays such a role in the organization of these events.
2./ To endeavor to learn the time and place of events in advance and inform us under the term exceptional case by telephone. To take part in every event and precisely record everything that happens there.
3./ To report on who their Czechoslovak, Polish, and Austrian contacts are, how active these contacts are, what kinds of help they receive, primarily via their Polish and Austrian contacts.

[signature]
Pol. Lt.-Col. Antal Tóvölgyi

No. Copies:	3
Received:	"M" d. [...]
Registrationno.:	2/7-673

Translated from Hungarian by Gwen Jones

Endnotes
1 Translator's note: /redacted/ means that the relevant passage on the basis of §25/G of Act XXIII. of 1994 was anonymized.

87

- 3 -

van szó, hogy megkisérelnek egy nyugati jelenséget hozzánk átültetni. Bár céljuk elsősorban önmaguk szórakoztatása, a feltünéskeltés, a kisérlet korántsem veszélyeztető kifejezője azoknak, irracionális tendenciáknak, amelyek a nyugati világ fiataljainak jórészét esztelen lázadásra buzditják minden fennálló rend, intézmény szokás ellen. Természetes, hogy minden a szocialista társadalomtól merőben idegen. Ezt az is bizonyitja, hogy eddig csak csalással és emberek félrevezetésével sikerült helyiséget szerezniük rendezvényeik számára. Legutóbb például, a Pesterzsébeti Kulturotthonban tartott happeninget egy idő mulva félbeszakitotta a kulturház igazgatója és Nádor Tamás az irodalmi csoport vezetője kijelentette, hogy ami itt történik az nem müvészet, hanem zavarkeltés.

"László"

Értékelés:

Happening szervezői szélhámosság utján mini több lehetőséget teremt a bemutatóik számára. Aktivizálódásuk megköveteli a mind sürgősebb bomlasztásukat teendő intézkedések megtételét.

Intézkedés:

Ellenőrzési tervet kidolgozni, jelzésben.

Utasitás:

1./ Állapitsa meg, akinek ilyen szerepe van a rendezvények szervezésében.

2./ A rendezvények idejét, helyét igyekezzen előre megtudni és rendkivüli esetként jelentse telefonon. Minden rendezvényen vegyen részt, s az ott történteket pontosan regisztrálja.

3./ Jelentse, hogy kik a Csehszlovák, Lengyel és Ausztriai kapcsolatuk, ezek a kapcsolatuk mennyire aktivak, milyen segitséget kapnak elsősorban Lengyel és osztrák kapcsolatainkon keresztül.

/: Tövölgyi Antal r. alez. :/

Készült: 3 pél.
Kapja: "M" d. jelzés papka.
tájékozt.
nyt.sz. 2/7-673

ÁBTL -3.1.9. - V - 156455 /179

123 «László» "Theories" 1969 Source: ÁBTL 3.1.9. –V–156455, 177–79, http://www.c3.hu/collection/tilos/85.html. Source of the italics: TH V-156455 ("László") 84–95.

225

September 20, 1988, Warsaw –
Report of Capt. Marek Zieliński on Alternative Youth Movements in Poland in the 1980s
National Military Service Internal Doc.220/88
Top Secret
Art no.000108
Author: Capt. Dr. Marek Zieliński

Alternative Youth Movements
evaluation, conclusions, and prognosis

5.1 Inspirations for programs of the opposition alternative movements

…

To interpret the programmatic framework of alternative movements, the form of activity is of essential importance. They appear first of all in the form of a **happening**, (bold in the original) so most often street parties accompanied by a march along a given route. The organization of most important happenings is presented in the calendar (point 6).[1] This form of demonstrating your dissatisfaction, your rebellion, and at the same time your autonomy, is described as free, spontaneous, and independent art.[2] Its founder and organizer explains the usefulness of happenings: "People want to have fun, express their individual and collective spirit. In Wrocław, there is no place open where you can have fun. Actions of Orange Alternative are a strict reflection of the situation in the country. So far, our need to have fun to meet in groups was being consequently limited."[3] Talking to the editor of the weekly *Mazowsze*, Fydrych says: "Everybody likes the moments when you jump out of the political borders. And this seems just as important to Wrocław as Grotowski was.[4] …

Everybody helps, anyway we are cheap, all last year cost only 175 thousand."[5] And the authors of the article add: "Among the fighting groups we have not met anybody who wouldn't be fascinated by happenings and who wouldn't like their author."[6] It is difficult to find any more enthusiastic evaluations.

…

5.2
The genesis, basic types and creativity of alternative opposition movements

In describing the genesis of this group of alternative movements, the essential point of reference will be the activity of Waldemar Fydrych and the Wrocław-based group founded by him, Orange Alternative.

While still a student at the University of Wrocław in 1980, and later during student strikes in 1981 and martial law afterwards, W[aldemar] Fydrych organized various actions articulating the so-called spontaneous rebellion of academic youth. This was expressed through actions like the painting of dwarfs and flower emblems on the walls of buildings in Wrocław. However, these actions were not organized were of local importance.

It was only in 1987 that alternative movements became clearly activated. The first serious action was a celebration of International Children's Day on June 1, when Orange Alternative organized a happening with the participants disguised as dwarfs. They shouted various slogans like: "Long live and flourish socialist surrealism!" As a "last chance," … the reform[ed] Santa Claus appeared.

In Wrocław in the summer of 1987, a group of fourteen young people dressed in white t-shirts. On each of the t-shirts was a letter. Standing in a row so they were composing a slogan: "Down with the heat!" (*Precz z upałami*). When one of them with the letter "u" occasionally knelt down to fasten his shoelaces, the slogan changed to "Down with the batons!" (*Precz z pałami*).The next happenings in 1987 were: on September 1, an antifascist protest; on October 7—the anniversary of the founding of the militia (MO) and state security (SB)—there appeared in the center of Wrocław, a huge five-meter-high cardboard flower dedicated to "All those nameless workers of the apparatus" and the painted slogans like "The Youth of Wrocław would like to thank the militia and the SB for a smile and humor" and sang for the employees of the departments: "Let them live 100 years" handing over flowers to them.[7] On the Day of the Polish People's Army, October 12, the happenings were organized according to the mottoes: *Melon in Mayonnaise* and *The Warsaw Pact is the Avant-garde of Peace*. On the eve of the anniversary of the October Revolution, November 7, they organized a "red" protest, with the participants (people and animals) dressed in red scarves, red bows, and *budenovkas* with red stars. They carried bayonets on sticks and baguettes dipped in ketchup. A day before the referendum, on October 29, a banner was exposed during the street happening saying: "Wrocław –the city of 200% attendance" revealed. In the autumn of 1987, members of Orange Alternative handed out leaflets entitled: "Who's afraid of toilet paper?" where they asked: "Do you think that using toilet paper may deepen socialism?" or "Is toilet paper the ally or enemy of the global revolution?"

In 1988, the activities of Orange Alternative began to significantly gain in momentum. They began to organize happenings and other actions more and more often (leaflet distribution, wall painting with slogans, small gatherings in front of public buildings, etc.). The shortened descriptions in their calendar testify, generally speaking, to the growing dynamism and obstinacy of the movement's animators and its huge popularity, especially in opposition circles. This was proven by a broad protest action started in defense of Waldemar Fydrych, who was arrested on March 8, 1988, and was sentenced by the misdemeanor council to two years imprisonment for disrupting public order.[8] Fydrych was supported and defended by members of the "Freedom and Peace" Movement, the so-called Local Laborers' Committee of the Polish Socialist Party, the Regional executive Committee of Solidarność, and the Independent Student Association at the University of Warsaw. They started petitions to request the release of Fydrych from prison. In a special announcement, the activists of Solidarność in Wrocław claimed that the activity of Orange Alternative is "the antidote to the gray, sad reality of our country, and the sentence is a provocation reminiscent of the events of 1968."[9] Fydrych was also strongly supported by, among others, fifty intellectuals, including: Artur Międzyrzecki, Kazimierz Dziewanowski, Halina Mikołajska, Jacek Kuroń, Marian Brandys, Andrzej Wajda, and Krystyna Zachwatowicz.[10] Of course there were comments from the members of Orange Alternative, who stated on February 22, 1988: "All reports presenting artistic activities of Orange Alternative as political ones are considered untrue by the movement. ... The feature of art is its ambiguity. ... Limiting the idea of the happening to a one-dimensional form of political demonstration should be considered tendentious."[11] The description of the so-called artistic activity of Orange Alternative are presented in the above-mentioned holiday-calendar.

The Student Committee of the University of Wrocław took a strange position on the sentencing of W[aldemar] Fydrych. The statement of the council was made "with regret": "We are of the opinion that somebody is trying to impose a more-than-artistic character, which they do not have, to the actions of Orange Alternative and its leader Waldemar Fydrych, the actions are purely subcultural artistic events."

Later they praise the "creative" activity of Fydrych and the Orange Alternative movement as "strongly rooted in the student culture stream." They write: "It introduces – as we read – a healthy irony, a fun, critical approach to the highly systematic ordinary reality in the life of the citizens of our town." In its conclusion, the Student Committee interpreted the sentence against Waldemar Fydrych as a "non-legitimate attack on artistic activity." Indeed, when you read such an irresponsible document, it is difficult to comment upon it.

I wonder if the members of the Student Committee would consider offensive shouting against leading committee-members of the government and the party "spontaneous artistic activity," or the puppet in green clothing and dark shades,[12] carried so proudly during one of the happenings? In what way is student culture enriched by these so-called happenings, which are in fact street riots and tomfoolery? ...

The questions are many, but the problem remains. And maybe the Student Committee, alienated from student society, is trying to charm their environment in order to gain sympathy? If this is truly the case, it is a very poor way of earning support and sympathy.

As I have mentioned before, the most active period of Orange Alternative activity is to be the first half of 1988. Just as a reminder: from June 1 to December 31, 1987, as many as nine happenings were organized in Wrocław, and in the first half of 1988, [there were] ten of them. Altogether this year in Wrocław, Warsaw, Sopot, Lublin, Krakow, Poznań, Gdansk, Łódz, and Katowice, there were nineteen happenings that took place. There are of course only the major street actions, not to mention leaflet distribution, wall painting, and small gatherings in public (e.g. the court building during Waldemar Fydrych's trial).

The actions of street happening organizing were initiated in Wrocław, but in time, they were also taken to other cities, mainly to Warsaw, Krakow, Poznań, and Gdansk. They often took place in strategic locations for various holidays and national anniversaries, which guaranteed the attention of all citizens. These actions were apparently only street theater, public fun. On the posters, billboards, banners, and leaflets, there were grotesque mockups of leading members of the government and the party, of public holidays, government decisions, or unpopular results of the economic crisis (e.g. lack of personal hygiene products). Most of the slogans displayed during the happenings were of an allusive character, though easily legible. However, we have also witnessed personal attacks, like when people shouted "Go away party" (*Precz z* PZPR)[13] in Łódz on Children's Day or "We don't want Wojtuś" ("*Nie chcemy Wojtusia*")[14] in Warsaw.

Parallel to the growth of happenings, the number of means of gaining social attention grew. Provocative, grotesque clothing, sound systems (musical instruments, megaphones, rattles, pipes, hood guns), characteristic paper, cardboard, and wood tools (tank mock-ups, flowers, and guns), as well as banners, leaflet distribution, posters, wall paintings, shouting slogans, or singing songs—these were all tools used during the happenings. They had to be loud, attractive, provocative, unusual.

Despite the stubbornly proclaimed opinion that street happenings are a "particular" form of art, a way of having fun, a student joke, that they reflect the "creative anxiety" of the people, devoid of political meaning—the truth is quite different. Alternative movement groups, mainly the Orange Alternative, the "Alternative Thinking Movement" ("Ruch Myślenia Alternatywnego, Wrocław"), White Alternative ("Biała Alternatywa," Warsaw), Mathias-Rust-Happening-Agency "Happyness" (Agencja Happeningowa "Fart" im Mathias Rust, Katowice), or the "Little Red Riding Hood Defense Committee named after Matthias Rust" (Komitet Obrony Czerwonych Kapturków, Poznań)—are they indeed strictly student tomfoolery, or are they political opposition groups?

The street actions organized by them are not a way of let off steam, but precisely planned and conducted political demonstrations. Organized without proper permits in places of heavy traffic and among pedestrians, they disturb this order, and also significantly disturb the public peace, that results in forcing officials to intervene, stop, and sentence the responsible organizers and the most devoted activists to prison.

It is difficult though to treat happenings as a specific form of entertainment. And certainly fit is not a game, distributing anti-state leaflets, painting the walls, or the action of three members of the Mathias-Rust-Happening-Agency "Happyness"[15] from Katowice, who on the first day of spring went onto the roof of a bus stop and chained themselves to the ladder. From this position, they gave a laudatory speech for the "Freedom and Peace" Movement and protested against the "conscious degradation" of the human natural environment and against obligatory military service. At the same time, they threw down leaflets with antistate content.

...

March 1: *Secret Agent's Day* (Dzień Tajniaka)[16]
The Happening was organized in Wrocław by Orange Alternative. Leaflets stating, "Secret Agent's Day" and "A great day, unforgettable impressions, do not miss this unique opportunity!"[17]
A group of twenty people marched the city streets, "completely dressed like secret agents"—hats, coats with collars up, dark glasses, with the signs: SB, KGB, CIA and SB signs on their coat sleeves—and demanded pedestrians to identify themselves.[18] They shouted: "Long live the police" and "Do not resist, let yourself be picked up—the militia officers invite us!"

Translated from Polish by Orange Alternative: http://www.orangealternativemuseum.pl/files/12_Archiwa_Tajnych_Sluzb/03_Raport_kapitana_Zielinskiego/UB-Zielinski%20PA_ENG.pdf
Młodzież na rozstajach komunizmu 1944–1989 (Warszaw: 2009)

Endnotes

1 Translator's note: The happenings are based on the holiday calendar. According to this calendar, the State Security has prepared an overview of the happenings to which Zieliński refers here. The following notes are taken from the Polish publication of the document but were slightly adapted and supplemented for the German publication.
2 Interview with Krzysztof Albin, a spokesperson of the Orange Alternative.
3 Interview with Waldemar Fydrych, Radio Free Europe, March 31, 1988.
4 Jerzy Grotowski (1933–1999): director, lecturer.
5 J. Klincz and A. Mól, "Panorama of Wrocław," *Mazowsze Weekly*, No. 247.
6 Ibid.
7 A common term used in the field of culture in Poland during the 1980s. Also in the study of cultural animation.
8 Interview with Krzysztof Albin, Radio Free Europe, March 30, 1988.
9 Radio Free Europe, March 11, 1988.
10 Artur Międzyrzecki (1922–1996) is a poet, translator, member of the Polish Writers' Association, and President of Polish Pen Club; Kazimierz Dziewanowski (1930–1998) is a writer, journalist, and diplomat. He's also the author of a speech given by Lech Wałęsa to the American Congress, Ambassador of Poland to the United States, 1990–1993; Halina Mikołajska (1925–1989) is an actress and opposition activist. She was imprisoned during the Martial Law, 1988–1989, and is a member of the Citizen Committee by the President of "Solidarity." She was also the wife of Marian Brandys; Jacek Kuroń (1934–2004) was a teacher, opposition activist, politician, and social activist. Also a member of Polish Youth Association and cofounder of Laborers' Defense Committee, as well as an advisor to Solidarity activists imprisoned during the Martial Law. During 1988–1989, he was a member of the Citizen Committee by the President of "Solidarity." 1989–2001, member of Parliament; Marian Brandys (1912–1998), writer, cooperated with Laborers' Defense Committee, member of Polish Pen Club; Andrzej Wajda (1926–2016), director, member of Polish Filmmakers Association during 1988–1989, member of the Citizen Committee by the President of "Solidarity." British Broadcasting Corporation and Radio Free Europe, March 22, 1988.
11 British Broadcasting Corporation, March 28, 1988.
12 This refers to the glasses of Wojciech Jaruzelski, who was the Prime Minister of the People's Republic of Poland from 1981 to 1985 and the head of state of Poland from 1985 to 1990.
13 In Polish literally: "Away with the PZPR" (*Polska Zjednoczona Partia Robotnicza*, Polish United Workers' Party).
14 Wojtuś is the diminutive form of Wojciech (Jaruzelski).
15 Mathias Rust (b. 1968) is a German pilot who flew from Helsinki to Moscow in 1987. He was detected early on by the Soviet air defense, but there was no immediate defensive action. He landed in Moscow and was arrested by the KGB. His flight was, according to him, a flight against all borders. The happening was widely commented on in the Western press. He was sentenced in the Soviet Union to four years of hard labor. All Soviet Air Force officers were fired by Mikhail Gorbachev. After being in Soviet prison for 432 days, he was allowed to come back to his home country. In 1994, he visited Moscow again.
16 Note from the translators: in Polish "tajniak," in contrast to "tajny agent" (secret agent), sounds disparaging.
17 "Agency News Review," Warsaw, No. 1, March 9, 1988.
18 British Broadcasting Corporation; Radio Free Europe Radio France Internationale, March 2, 1988.

The hostile artists from Karl-Marx-Stadt agreed with Dr.Klaus WERNER to carry out "action art" during the Pleinair, a project borrowed from the decadent western art scene. The goal of this was to set new standards for GDR art.
The essential content of "action art" is to produce decadent artistic images and then subsequently destroy them and to document these processes of movement.

The participants primarily received their information from Radio Germany (*Deutschlandfunk*) and disseminated in their circle the arguments broadcast there concerning political-ideological diversion.

Translated from German by Brian Alkire

MINISTERIUM FÜR STAATSSICHERHEIT

In der Zeit vom 17.09. bis 30.09.1977 fand in einem Ferienobjekt des Staatlichen Kunsthandels in Leussow, Bezirk Neubrandenburg, das sogenannte III. Pleinair des Staatlichen Kunsthandels der DDR statt.
Organisiert wurde dieses Treffen durch Mitarbeiter der Berliner Ausstellungsgalerie "Arkade" des Staatlichen Kunsthandels im Zusammenwirken mit der Genossenschaft bildender Künstler Karl-Marx-Stadt.
Als Hauptorganisatoren traten die Abteilungsleiter im Staatlichen Kunsthandel Berlin, Dr. Klaus WERNER und Peter GUSE, in Erscheinung.

Neben negativen Kunstschaffenden aus der Hauptstadt der DDR Berlin, den Bezirken Leipzig und Dresden, nahmen aus dem Bezirk Karl-Marx-Stadt die Maler und Grafiker

Thomas Ranft
Gregor-Torsten Schade
Michael Morgner und
[geschwärzt]

sowie weitere Kulturschaffende teil.

Die feindlichen Kunstschaffenden aus dem Bezirk Karl-Marx-Stadt hatten sich mit Dr. WERNER abgesprochen, während des Pleinairs ein aus der dekadenten westlichen Kunstszene entliehenes Projekt der "Aktionskunst" durchzuführen. Anliegen war, daß man damit neue Maßstäbe für die DDR-Kunst setzen wollte.
Wesentlicher Inhalt der "Aktionskunst" ist, daß dekadente künstlerische Gebilde hergestellt und anschließend wieder vernichtet und diese Bewegungsabläufe dokumentiert werden.

Von den Teilnehmern wurde sich vorwiegend im "Deutschlandfunk" informiert und die dort gesendeten Argumente der politisch-ideologischen Diversion unter ihrem Kreis weiterverbreitet.

Besonders der teilnehmende Personenkreis aus Karl-Marx-Stadt vertrat zu einer Reihe politisch-aktueller Probleme negative Auffassungen. So zum Beispiel:

- Schlechter als die gegenwärtige Lage sei, könne es nicht mehr werden, aber dieses sei eben typisch für die DDR.

- Sollten in einem Land die "Eurokommunisten" an die Macht kommen, dann werde die DDR nur noch einige Jahre existieren.

Erneut wurde die sozialistische Kulturentwicklung angegriffen. Die VIII. Kunstausstellung der DDR wurde als "Gruselkabinett" und "Scheißausstellung" bezeichnet und ausgeführt, als Karl-Marx-Städter Künstler werde man höchstens einen "Lästerdurchgang" machen.

In preparation of the Pleinair, Dr.Klaus Werner arranged with XXX to realize a so-called Land Art project ("Action Art"). This is intended, in his view, to set new standards for art in the GDR.
(The performance of so-called actions, with which this Land Art project is to be classed, is a component of the Western art scene. Representatives of this "idea of art" include among others the already operatively familiar connections of the suspect XXX, the West Germans BOYS and VOSTELL.)

Translated from German by Brian Alkire

weitere negative und feindliche Kunstschaffende aus den Bezirken Berlin, Leipzig, Dresden und Karl-Marx-Stadt teil. (Anlage) Die Auswahl dieser Personen wurde hauptsächlich durch Dr. Werner getroffen.

In Vorbereitung des Pleinairs hatte Dr. Klaus Werner mit ███ abgesprochen, daß sie anläßlich des Pleinairs ein sogenanntes Landart-Projekt ("Aktionskunst") verwirklichen. Damit sollten seiner Ansicht nach neue Maßstäbe in der Kunst der DDR gesetzt werden. (Die Durchführung von sogenannten Aktionen, unter denen auch dieses Landart-Projekt einzuordnen ist, ist ein Bestandteil der westlichen Kunstszene. Vertreter dieser "Kunstauffassung" sind u. a. die bereits operativ bekanntgewordenen Verbindungen des Verdächtigen ███, die Westdeutschen BOYS und VOSTELL7)

Im Verlaufe des Pleinairs entwickelten die Personen ███ ███ ███ und deren Verbindungen negativ-feindliche Aktivitäten. ███ informierte sich täglich in der Frühsendung des "Deutschlandfunk" (Kommentare des DLF zu ausländischen Pressestimmen) und verbreitete solche Argumente unter den Teilnehmern des Pleinairs zu den Mahlzeiten. Zum Thema Intershop bemerkte er, daß die DDR eine "klassenlose Klassengesellschaft" sei, die sich in drei Klassen gliedere:

1. Klasse der Devisenbesitzer, die im Intershop kaufen.
2. Klasse derer, die im Exquisit einkaufen können.
3. Klasse derjenigen, die beide Möglichkeiten nicht besitzen.

███ kommentierte vor den Teilnehmern aus dem ND vom 27. 9. 1977 einen Abschnitt aus der Rede des Generalsekretärs des ZK der SED, Gen. E. Honecker, anläßlich der Eröffnung des Parteilehrjahres. Als ███ die Passage: "Aber die Vergangenheit bleibt die Vergangenheit, die Zukunft bleibt die Zukunft", verlas, äußerte ███ dazu: "Schlimmer als jetzt kann es nicht kommen, so etwas ist eben typisch für die DDR." Diese Äußerungen, die vor einem breiten Teilnehmerkreis gemacht wurden, fanden den Beifall der anwesenden Künstler.

Als wesentlichster Beitrag des III. Pleinairs wurde der Vortrag von Lothar Lang, Berlin, über die Kunstausstellung "Dokumenta 77" in der BRD aufgenommen. Lang berichtete über seine Gespräche mit BRD-Künstlern und Kunstwissenschaftlern.

We were also able to determine that a certain gallery "Gerda Moschner" (or similar) is said to exist in Karl-Marx-Stadt, the existence of which is financed from the proceeds of paintings and photographs of "hoppenings" [*sic*] and "actions."

Translated from German by Brian Alkire

- Ablehnung der Grundtendenzen unserer Kulturpolitik und Notwendigkeit einer neuen künstlerischen Avantgarde;
  die Karl-Marx-Städter Teilnehmer zählen sich zu dieser Avantgarde und vertreten den Standpunkt, daß man versuchen muß, Kontakte mit dem "Westen" aufzunehmen, um sich international aufzuwerten;

- Sympathiebekundung mit einigen Künstlern, die die DDR verlassen haben, zum Beispiel RENFT.

Als Vertreter dieser Fragestellung und Probleme traten insbesondere nachfolgende Personen in Erscheinung:

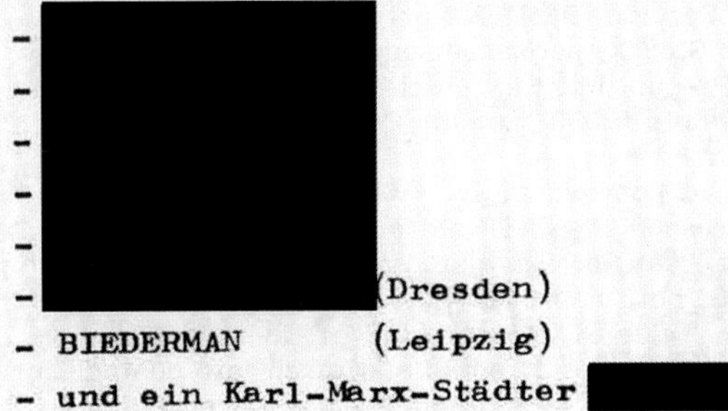

-
-
-
-
-
- (Dresden)
- BIEDERMAN (Leipzig)
- und ein Karl-Marx-Städter .

Weiterhin konnte erarbeitet werden, daß in Karl-Marx-Stadt eine Galerie "Gerda Moschner" o. ä. existieren soll, deren Existenz aus dem Erlös der Bilder und Fotos von "Hoppenings" und "Aktions" finanziert wird.

Auffällig war, daß zum Beispiel über erhebliche Geldmittel verfügen muß und daß er total in westlicher Konfektion gekleidet war. Er sprach von einer großen Investition in einer Sache, von der er noch nicht sprechen will.

Der gesamte Teilnehmerkreis will sich Anfang Oktober im Erzgebirge zu einem Künstlerfest treffen. Als Zeitpunkt wurde der 8. Oktober genannt, der Ort ist unbekannt.

Leiter der Abteilung	Leiter des Referates XX/7
Holtz	Freese
Oberstleutnant	Oberleutnant

Ref.:

Date: 10.31.66

Printed copy No.:

Matter: Action FLUXUS — report.

Comrade Col.
[1]K l í m a

P r a g u e

The StB (State Security)[2] Investigation Service of the VKR (Military Intelligence) initiated criminal proceedings and concurrent pursuit of Pvt.[3] (National Military Service) DEMJÉN Martin, born August 10, 1946, citizen: CSSR, nationality: Slovak, permanent address in Bratislava, Vysoká 32, from VÚ 3430[4] Prague (military unit)—for the criminal offense of defection abroad pursuant to § 283/1 of the Criminal Code (§ 283, odst. 1. tr. zákona).

On October 18, 1986 at approximately 14:00 hours, private DEMJÉN, in civilian clothes, crossed the CSSR state border at passport control point Folmava[5] into West Germany using the passport of a French citizen, Serge OLDENBOURG, born February 4, 1927 in Meudon with a permanent address in NICE 06, 2 Rue St.Geatan [*sic*], of liberal profession, divorced. OLDENBOURG was therefore arrested and taken into custody for a criminal offence pursuant §§ 10/1(c) and 283/1 of the Criminal Code (§§ 10, odst.1., písm. c, 283, odst.1 tr.zák.).

Inasmuch as they plausibly found out about the activities of private DEMJÉN and did not report them in a timely manner, criminal proceedings for the criminal offense of "not preventing a criminal offense" pursuant to §§ 167/1 and 283/1 of the Criminal Code (§§ 167, odst.1.; 283, odst.1. tr. zák.) have been initiated against the following persons: KNÍŽÁK Milan, born April 19, 1940 in Plzeň, artist with permanent residence in Prague 10, Sevastopolská 17; MACH Jan, born 31 May, 1943 in Prague, currently a manual laborer with permanent residence in Prague 8-Libeň, Na Rokytce 1106/18; ŽIŽKOVÁ Zdenka, born May 20, 1943 in Prague, photographer with the Office of the President of the Republic, permanent residence in Prague 2, Jenštejnská 3; Pvt. (National Military Service) SLACH Karel, born December 17, 1940 in Tábor, student cinematographer, currently with AUS-VN Praha[6] (military unit), permanent residence in Tábor, Zápotockého 830/8. Knížák and Mach were detained according to a warrant issued by a public prosecutor from the General Prosecution Office,[7] Pvt. SLACH Karel was detained according to a warrant issued by a prosecutor from the HVP[8] (Military Prosecution Office). Žižková was arrested according to § 67 of the Criminal Code (§67 tr.řádu) and released within the statutory period.

236

Čj.: Výtisk č.:

Dne 31.10.1966.

Věc: Akce FLUXUS - zpráva.

Náměstek ministra vnitra
s. plk. K l í m a

P r a h a

Vyšetřovací odbor Sto ve VKR zahájil tr. stihání a současně stihá voj.z.sl. DEMJÉN Martina, nar. 10.8.1946, čsl.st.přísl., národnosti slovenské, trvale bytem Bratislava, Vysoká č.32, příslušníka VÚ 3430 Praha - pro tr.čin zběhnutí do ciziny, podle ustanovení § 283,odst.1.tr.zákona.

Voj. DEMJÉN překročil státní hranice ČSSR přes OPK Folmava do NSR dne 18.10.1966 kolem 14,00hod., v civilním oděvu a na cestovní pas fr.st. příslušníka Serge OLDENBOURGA, nar. 4.2.1927 Meudon, bytem 2 Rue St Geatan, NICE 06, přísl. svobodného povolání, rozvedený. OLDENBOURG byl proto vzat do vazby pro tr.čin §§ 10, odst.1.,písm.c, 283,odst.1.tr,zák.

Vzhledem k tomu, že o činnosti voj. DEMJÉNA se hodnověrným způsobem dověděli KNÍŽÁK Milan, nar.19.4.1940 v Plzni, výtvarník, bytem Praha 10, Sevastopolská 17, MACH Jan, nar. 31.5.1943 v Praze,t.č. dělník, bytem Praha 8 Libeň, Na Rokytce 1106/18, ŽIŽKOVÁ Zdena, nar. 20.5.1943 v Praze, fotografka v Kanceláři presidenta republiky, bytem Praha 2., Jenštejnská č.3., voj.z.sl. SLACH Karel, nar.17.12.1940 v Táboře, student-kameraman, t.č. příslušník AUS-VN Praha, bytem Tábor, Zápotockého č. 830/8 a neučinili o něm včasné oznámení, bylo proti nim zahájeno tr. stihání pro tr.čin "Nepřekažení tr.činu" podle ustanovení §§ 167,odst.1.,283,odst.1. tr. zákona. Na Knížáka, Macha uvalil vazbu prokurátor GP, na voj. Slacha prokurátor HVP. Žižková byla zadrženapodle § 67 tr.řádu a v zákonné lhůtě propuštěna.

The investigation of the above-mentioned defendants has so far revealed:

A festival of the FLUXUS group took place in Prague on October 13, 14, and 17, 1966, the venues were Gallery Mánes, the Museum of Czech Literature (*Památník národního písemnictví*),[9] and Gallery Platýz. It is still unknown who granted the official permission for the festival to go ahead. The foreign participants in this festival included Alison KNOWLES with her husband Dick HIGGINS from New York, Ben VAUTIER and Serge OLDENBOURG from NICE in France, and Jeff BERNER from San Francisco. The self-appointed representative of FLUXUS[10] in CSSR is Milan Knížák, who corresponds with group members in the USA, and who is also in possession of some of the material published by the FLUXUS publisher in the USA. Knížák provided some of these materials to the exhibition AVANT-GARDNÍ EDICE (Avant-Garde Edition) that took place at the Museum of Czech Literature on October 14, 1966. The Fluxus events were attended by other young people, mostly students, approximately forty people.
As an illustration of the character of the FLUXUS group, I quote from the FLUXUS Manifesto:

> Art – anti-art – entertainment – Fluxus ignores the difference between art and anti-art, ignores the necessity of an artist, the exclusivity, uniqueness, ambition, ignores all claims of significance, rarity, inspiration, skill, complexity, depth, grandeur, novelty, shock, institutional and commercial values. It strives for monostructural, nontheatrical, nonbaroque impersonal values of common natural events, objects, games or gags. Fluxus – it is Spike Jones, gags, child's play, John Cage and Duchamp put together.[11]

Oldenbourg's written material also includes responses to Vladimír BURDA [*sic*], the contributing editor of the LITERÁRNÍ NOVINY newspaper, from where I quote a description of FLUXUS:

> The source of inspiration is mainly the present – politics, sexuality, civilization, technology, and so on. Some say that the activity of Fluxus is art, others maintain that it is anti-art. It depends on personal leanings. The starting point and the material are all areas of present life, be it artistic or non artistic. Each action, such as a hand movement, pushing the cigarette packet from one place to another, is already in its substance a happening. If these actions take place simultaneously, the relationship of those performing them determines whether an actual happening will come out of it. Present Fluxus can be likened to a kind of library or catalogue of happenings, and the FLUXUS magazine published by George MACIUNAS is a propaganda of these happenings.

The cited material takes as its theoretical basis

Z dosavadního vyšetřování výše uvedených obviněných vyplynulo:

Ve dnech 13., 14., 17.10.1966 se konal v Praze /Mánes, Památník nár.písemnictví, Platýz/ festival příslušníků skupiny FLUXUS. Kdo dával oficielní souhlas ke konání festivalu není dosud známo. Ze zahraničních účastníků byli na festivalu přítomni Alison KNOWLESOVÁ se svým manželem Dick HIGGINS z New Yorku, Ben VAUTIER a Serge OLDENBOURG z NICE Francie, Jeff BERNER ze San Franciska. Samozvaným představitelem FLUXUSU v ČSSR je Milan Knížák, který udržuje písemný styk se členy skupiny v USA a který také vlastní část materiálů vydávaných nakladatelstvím Fluxusu v USA. Knížák dodával část techto materiálů na výstavu AVANTGARDNÍ EDICE pořádanou v Památníku nár.písemnictví dne 14.10.1966. Akcí Fluxuse se zúčastnili další mladí lidé, většinou studenti, v počtu asi 40 lidí.

K charakteristice skupiny FLUXUS cituji z Manifestu FLUXU: " Umění - neumění - zábava - fluxus pomíjí rozdíl mezi uměním a neuměním, pomíjí umělcovu nezbytnost, výlučnost, jedinečnost, ctižádost, pomíjí všecky nároky na významnost, vzácnost, inspiraci, dovednost, složitost, hloubku, velikost, novost, škování, instituční a komerční hodnoty. Usiluje o monostrukturální, nedivadelní, nebarokní, neosobní hodnoty prostých přirozených událostí, předmětů, her nebo gagů. Je to Spikes Jones, gagy, dětské hry, John Cage a Duchamp dohromady."

V písemných materiálech Oldenbourga jsou také odpovědi na otázky redaktora LITERÁRNÍCH NOVIN Vladimíra BURDY, z nichž k charakteristice FLUXUSU cituji:

" Inspiračním zdrojem je především současnost - politika, sexualita, civilizace, technika atd. Někteří říkají, že aktivita Fluxusu je uměním, jiní tvrdí, že je to neumění. Záleží na osobním zaměření. Východiskem i materiálem jsou veškeré oblasti současného života, ať umělecké, či neumělecké. Každá akce jako pohyb rukou, přesunutí krabičky cigaret z místa na místo je už v podstatě happeningem. Podnikajíli se tyto akce společně, záleží na vztazích mezi jednajícími, zda vznikne vlastní happening. Dnešní Fluxus můžeme přirovnat k jakési knihovně nebo katalogu happeningů a časopis FLUXUS vydávaný Georgem MACIUNASem je propagandou happeningu."

Uvedené materiály z teoretického hlediska vycházejí

Dadaism – the literary and artistic movement which had at its heart the individualistic rebellion of artists who through their primitivism wanted to express their disgust with traditional art. Their sarcastic and destructive criticism of traditional art, not supported by any clear worldview, inevitably leads in its outcomes to reactionary decadence. At the same time, it is a certain variety of futurism which basically concerns anarchic protests leading to the rejection of cultural traditions and to the ideological support of fascism, racism, and imperialism.

The actual content of the FLUXUS festival in CSSR and its activities is documented by the attached photographs. These photos were taken by Zd. ŽIŽKOVÁ, who surrendered the negatives for the purpose of the investigation. Furthermore, Ben VAUTIER and Dick HIGGINS brought to CSSR several films which have not been screened at any official gathering. Their screening had been organized by Zd. ŽIŽKOVÁ in the "Dům dětí" [a youth center "Children's House" located in the Burgrave's Palace – translator's note] at the Prague Castle. The films were screened by ŽIŽKOVÁ's superior, comrade SUK in the presence of Knížák, Žižková, and Mach. Anna Vondrů and Private Slach were present at some of the screenings. The content of the films shown corresponded with the orientation of the FLUXUS group. According to Žižková's statement, the film should be in Knížak's flat, but it has not been recovered yet.

On October 15, 1966, KNOWLES and HIGGINS left the CSSR, Ben VAUTIER left on October 16, 1966. Serge OLDENBOURG remained in the CSSR and after the FLUXUS concert on October 17, 1966, together with Knížák, Mach, Slach, Žižková, Vondrů, MENS (Dutch citizen), and Private DEMJÉN, went to Knížák's flat at Na Novém Světě[12] 19, where the party continued. / His flat – art studio – can hardly be considered a flat, more of a "hovel"—it is sparsely furnished, dirty, not cozy, he uses a paraffin lamp for lighting. / The company ended their party at around 02:00 hours. Knížák went to bed, Mach accompanied Vondrů, Demjén accompanied Žižková, the rest went home. Demjén later returned to OLDENBOURG, who remained at Knížák's and they had a conversation, which OLDENBOURG in his statement describes as follows:

> As the other soldier /not Karel Slach/ constantly moaned that he did not like the military service, that he would like to go away, I took out my passport and I told him: "I am losing my passport and if you are a man, you have found it." He took it and told me that he would also need civilian clothes. So, I gave him my summer outfit.

z dadaismu - literárního a uměleckého směru jehož smyslem byla individualistická vzpoura intelektuálů, kteří chtěli svým primitivizmem vyjádřit svůj odpor k tradičnímu umění. Jejich sarkastická a destruktivní kritika tradičního umění, neopřená o janý světový názor vyústila nutně v dekadenci, ve svých důsledcích reakční. Stejně tak jde o určitý odstín futurismu, v němž jde v podstatě o anarchistické protesty odmítání kulturní tradice a k ideologické podpoře fašismu, rasismu a imperialismu.

Vlastním obsahem činnosti na festivalu FLUXUSU v ČSSR byla činnost dokumentovaná na přiložených snímcích. Snímky pořídila Zd. ŽIŽKOVÁ, která vydala negativy pro potřeby vyšetřování. Mimoto přivezli do ČSSR Ben VAUTIER a Dick HIGGINS několik filmů, které nebyly na žádném oficielním shromáždění promítány. Jejich promítání zařídila Zd. ŽIŽKOVÁ v "Domě dětí" na pražském Hradu. Filmy promítal nadřízený ŽIŽKOVÉ s. SUK za přítomnosti Knížáka, Žižkové, Macha a na části promítání byla přítomna Anna Vondrů a voj. Slach. Obsah promítaných filmů odpovídal zaměření skupiny FLUXUSU. Podle výpovědi Žižkové má mít film Knížák ve svém bytě. Dosud nebyl získán.

Dne 15.10.1966 odejeli z ČSSR KNOWLESOVÁ, HIGGINS, dne 16.10.1966 odejel Ben VAUTIER. Serge OLDENBOURG zůstal v ČSSR a po koncertě FLUXUSU dne 17.10.1966 odešel spolu s Knížákem, Machem, Slachem, Žižkovou, Vondrů, hol.st.přísl. MENSEM, voj. DEMJÉNEM do bytu Knížáka, Na Novém Světě č.19, kde se pokračovalo v zábavě. / Jeho byt - atelier - lze stěží charakterizovat jako byt, spíše "špeluněk" - je spoře zařízen, špinavý, neútulný, k osvětlení používá petrolejovou lampu./ Uvedená společnost ukončila zábavu kolem 02,00hod. Knížák odešel spat, Mach doprovodil Vondrů, Demjén doprovodil Žižkovou, ostatní odešli domů. Demjén se později vrátil k OLDENBOURGOVI, který zůstal u Knížáka a došlo mezi nimi k rozhovoru o němž OLDENBOURG vypovídá:

> " Protože ten druhý voják /nejedná se o Karla Slacha/ neustále naříkal, že se mu na vojně nelíbí, že by chtěl pryč, vyndal jsem svůj pas a řekl jsem mu: " Já ztrácím pas a jestli jsi muž, tak jsi ho našel." On si jej vzal a řekl mi, že by k tomu potřeboval civilní oděv. Proto jsem mu dal svůj letní oděv."

After this conversation, at around 04:30 hours, Private DEMJÉN, in civilian clothes, came to ŽIŽKOVÁ and told her that he would not return to his unit, that he had an opportunity to do anything, that he had a possibility even to cross the border, but that he needed 100 korunas from her. He said he even had the possibility to get to his father. ŽIŽKOVÁ did not give him the money, and according to her statement, tried to convince him to return to his unit. From that point on, there is no information about private DEMJÉN until his arrival at passport control point Folmava. According to the testimony of Marie KOBESOVÁ,[13] customs officer at OPK Folmava, on October 18, 1966 in the afternoon she had been processing a French national when she realized he spoke no French. She then remarked, in Czech, that he was a strange Frenchman. Further communication between them was in Russian. According to KOBESOVÉ, the Frenchman spoke Russian very badly too – for example, he said – in response to a question where he obtained Czechoslovak currency–"ya paluchil [Russian for "I borrowed"–translator's note] jich od [Czech: *it from*] frojnda [German: *from a friend*], razumeyete [Russian: *do you understand*], frojnd [German: *friend*]?" Following KOBESOVÁ's remark about this being a strange Frenchman, a German national present, who was returning to West Germany, said that it seemed strange to him too, that he did not speak much, and that he picked him up in his car in Domažlice, where he was hitchhiking. KOBESOVÁ, therefore, alerted Capt. VLASÁK, officer of control point Folmava. Officers of control point Folmava, Capt. VLASÁK, First Lt. Chum, and Warrant Officer MATHAUSER, confirmed that KOBESOVÁ did inform them of these facts, but they unanimously stated that it was Serge OLDENBOURG who had left the CSSR–even though it had to be obvious to them that the man claiming to be OLDENBOURG was much younger, that the photo in the document did not correspond to reality, etc. In spite of that, they allowed Private DEMJÉN to leave the CSSR.
On October 19, 1966, OLDENBOURG reported the "loss" of his passport to the French embassy, where he was told to report the loss to the Czechoslovak authorities. The French embassy then requested in its file to the KS of SNB14 (Prague police)15 that a replacement document be issued. When the SPV16 (Passport and Visa department) found out that someone had used these documents to travel out of the Republic, the SPV initiated an investigation of the loss of the passport and the investigation was taken over by the StB in the VKR17 (Military Counterintelligence).
Further characteristic and operative data obtained by the investigation into Milan KNÍŽÁK:

KNÍŽÁK considers himself a self-appointed leader of FLUXUS in CSSR. He is a member of the SVÚ (Union of Visual Artists)18, a member of the liberal professions, graduated from a secondary school (eleven-year secondary school with final "matura" exam), studied at the Academy of Fine Arts (AVU) for one year and left the Academy due to his disapproval of the official view

Po tomto rozhovoru asi ve 04,30hod. přišel voj. DEMJÉN v civilním oděvu za ŽIŽKOVOU a řekl jí, že se nebrátí ke svému útvaru, že má možnost nyní dělat všechno, že má možnost dostat se i za hranice, ale že od ní potřebuje 100Kčs. Uváděl, že má možnost dostat se i za otcem. ŽIŽKOVÁ mu peníze nedala a podle její výpovědi působila na něho, aby se vrátil k útvaru. Od té doby není o voj. DEMJÉNOVI žádných poznatků až do doby jeho příchodu na OPK Folmava. Podle svědkyně Marie KOBESOVÉ, celní úřednice na OPK Folmava tato odbavovala v odpoledních hodinách dne 18.10.1966 fr.st.přísl. a při rozhovoru s ním zjistila, že nehovoří francouzsky. Česky proto prohodila, že jde o divného Francouze. Další rozhovor vedli spolu v ruštině. Podle KOBESOVÉ hovořil Francouz i velmi špatně rusky - na př. uvedl - na otázku, kde získal čsl.peníze odpověděl - " já palučil jich od frojnda, rozuměješ frojnd?" Po vyjádření KOBESOVÉ, že jde o divného Francouze, řekl přítomný obč. něm. národnosti, který se vracel do NSR, že jemu je to také divné, že moc nemluvil a že ho vzal do vozu v Domažlicích, kde ho stopoval. KOBESOVÁ proto na něho upozornila kpt. VLASÁKA, přísl. OPK Folmava. Příslušníci OPK Folmava kpt. VLASÁK, npor. Chum, prap.MATHAUSER potvrdili, že KOBESOVÁ je na uvedené skutečnosti upozornila, ale shodně uvedli, že z ČSSR vycestoval Serge OLDENBOURG - ač jim muselo být zřejmé, že muž vydávající se za OLDENBOURGA je mnohem mladší, fotografie v dokladech nesouhlasí se skutečností a pod. Přesto voj. DEMJÉNA nechali z ČSSR vycestovat.

Dne 19.10.1966 ohlásil OLDENBOURG fr.zast.úřadu "ztrátu" svého pasu, kde mu bylo doporučeno, aby ztrátu ohlásil čsl. úřadům. Fr. ambasáda pak žádala svým spisem KS SNB Praha o vydání náhradních dokladů. Po zjištění na SPV, že na uvedené doklady již někdo vycestoval, zahájila SAV šetření ztráty pasu a další vyšetřování převzal odbor vyšetřování stb ve VKR.

Další charakteristické a operativní údaje získané vyšetřováním k osobě Milana KNÍŽAKA:

KNÍŽAK se pokládá za samozvaného vedoucího FLUXUSU v ČSSR. Je členem SVÚ, příslušník svobodného povolání, má 11-ti letou střední školu s maturitou, 1 rok akademie výtvarných umění, odkud odešel pro nesouhlas s oficielním názorem

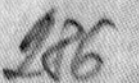

of the fine arts expressed during the lectures there. KNÍŽÁK comes from a broken home, his parents are divorced, both live in Mariánské Lázně. His father is a teacher, his mother is a housewife, she has remarried – now has the surname PŠAJDLOVÁ, his stepbrother Jan KNÍŽÁK is a major in the ČSLA (Czechoslovak People's Army).[19] KNÍŽÁK lives from a bursary he gets from the SVÚ and from what he earns by casual work. He is currently employed as a digger by the road and railway construction company *Staveb silnic a železnic* at the Bořislavka construction site. In 1966, he was offered a study bursary by the U.S. FLUXUS group for a stay in the USA. KNÍŽÁK submitted an application to travel out of the Republic. His application was rejected on the grounds that his appearance – his long hair (*mánička*, "mophead"[20])–would reflect badly on the CSSR. On October 14, 1966, after an intervention by the police (*Veřejná bezpečnost*, VB[21]), he was given a haircut. He protested vehemently and consequently, the same day, also gave a mandate to his solicitor, graduated lawyer Mil. MAŘÍK, to represent him in this matter. KNÍŽÁK believed that he had been given a haircut unlawfully.

KNÍŽÁK owns a car AERO-500. He has a so-called art studio in Prague 1, Nový Svět 19. In reality, these are two rooms, often left unlocked, used for parties of dubious character, for overnight stays of various Czechoslovak and foreign nationals. At the same time, he has another flat in Prague 10, Sevastopolská 10.

From an operational point of view, interesting information came from the written statement by the Dutch national Winands MENS, who states: "On October 21, 1966, when I was in KNÍŽÁK's flat, a married couple arrived in the flat. They came with their own car and were looking for KNÍŽÁK. I told them to wait and that's how I got to know them. They only came to pass on the greetings of a certain Ritter KLAUS from West Berlin, an acquaintance of KNÍŽÁK." As per the verbal statement by the officers of the II. SMV,[22] KLAUS Ritter is supposed to be engaged in taking people from the GDR to West Germany through our territory.

Encl.: 5/

Chief of the department of investigations of the StB in VKR
(Military Intelligence)
Podplukovník (Lieutenant Colonel) Karel P a u l

Translated from Czech by Dagmar Wallace-Tarry

240

na výtvarné umění, který se přednáší na škole. KNÍŽÁK pochází z rozvrácené rodiny, rodiče jsou rozvedeni, oba žijí v Mar. Lázních. Jeho otec je učitelem, matka v domácnosti, je znovu provdána - PŠAJDLOVÁ, nevlastní bratr Jan KNÍŽÁK je majorem ČSLA. KNÍŽÁK se živí ze stipendia, které dostává od SVÚ a z výdělků za brigádní práce. T.č. je zaměstnán jako kopáč u Staveb silnic a železnic s pracovištěm na Bořislavce. V r. 1966 mu bylo nabídnuto skupinou FLUXUSU z USA studijní stipendium pro pobyt v USA. KNÍŽÁK si podal žádost o vycestování. Výjezd mu však nebyl povolen proto, že by svým zjevem vlasatec-mánička špatně representoval ČSSR. Dne 14.10.1966 byl na zásah VB ostříhán. Ostře proti tomu protestoval a dal také toho dne plnou moc svému právnímu zástupci prom.práv. Mil. MAŘÍKovi, aby jej v této věci zastupoval. KNÍŽÁK se domníval, že byl ostříhán protiprávně.

KNÍŽÁK vlastní osobní automobil AERO-500. Má t.zv. umělecký atelier v Praze 1., Nový Svět č. 19. Jde prakticky o dvě místnosti, které jsou často neuzamčeny, jsou využívány k zábavám pochybného rázu, k přenocování různých čsl.občanů i cizinců. Přitom má další byt v Praze 10., Sevastopolská 10.

Z operativního hlediska je zajímavý poznatek, který vyplynul z protokolární výpovědi hol.st.přísl. Winands MENS, který uvádí: " Dne 21.10.1966 když jsem byl v bytě u KNÍŽÁKA přišli k němu do bytu manželé, kteří přijeli svým vlastním vozem VOLKSWAGEN a hledali KNÍŽÁKA. Řekl jsem jim, aby počkali a tak jsem se s nimi seznámil. Tito vyřizovali pouze pozdrav od jistého Ritter KLAUSE, ze Záp. Berlína, se kterým se KNÍŽÁK znal. S těmito lidmi, které jsem poznal pod jménem WOLFOVI - muž se jmenoval Ditter jsem se pak setkal v neděli, kdy tito hledali bezvýsledně KNÍŽÁKA." Podle ústního sdělení pracovníků II. SMV se má KLAUS Ritter zabývat převáděním občanů NDR přes naše území do NSR.

Přílohy: 5/

Náčelník vyš.odboru stb ve VKR
podplukovník

Karel Paul

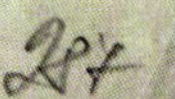

Endnotes

1 S. plk. – Soudruh plukovník (Comrade Col).
2 StB – Státní Bezpečnost (State Security).
3 Voj. z. sl. – Voják základní služby (Soldier in basic military service).
4 VÚ – Vojenský útvar (Military Formation).
5 OPK Folmava – Oddělení Pasové Kontroly Folmava (passport checkpoint Vollmau).
6 AUS VN – Armádní Umělecký Soubor Víta Nejedlého (Armee-Ensemble Vít Nejedlý), an elite corps.
7 GP – Generální Prokuratura (Attorney General's Office).
8 HVP – Hlavní Vojenská Prokuratura (chief public prosecutor's office of the military).
9 Památník Nár. [odního] Pisemnictví, also PNP (National Literary Archive).
10 The State Security declines the word FLUXUS, so that, among others, FLUXUSE, FLUXUSU, FLUXU can be read. These are almost impossible to translate into English.
11 In the common tradition of the *Manifesto of George Macunias* (1963), two words are missing that appear here in the Czech text. All in all, the lexicon is slightly shifted by the translation into and from Czech, the original states: "Fluxus FLUX ART: nonart – amusement forgoes distinction between art and nonart forgoes artist's indispensability, exclusiveness, individuality, ambition, forgoes all pretension towards a significance, variety, inspiration, skill, complexity, profundity, greatness, institutional and commodity value. It strives for nonstructural, nontheatrical, nonbaroque, impersonal qualities of a simple natural element, an object, a game, a puzzle or a gag." George Macunias quoted in Craig Saper, "Fluxus as a Laboratory" in *The Fluxus Reader*, ed. Ken Friedman (Wiley: New York 1998), 150.
12 The indication of the street by the StB is wrong. It should read: Nový Svet.
13 OPK (Oddělení Pohraniční Kontroly) – Border Control Division.
14 SNB – Sbor Národní Bezpečnosti (Corps of National Security Forces).
15 KS SNB – Krajská Správa Sboru Národní Bezpečnosti (District Authority of the National Security Forces Corps).
16 SPV – Správa Pasů a Viz (Passport and visa authority).
17 VKR – Vojenská Kontraro-Zvědka (Military counterintelligence).
18 SVU – Svaz Výtvarních Úmělců (Union of Visual Artists).
19 ČSLA - Československá Lidová Armáda (Czechoslovakian People's Army).
20 *Vlasatec-mánička* was a scornful expression used during that time for young men with long hair, whereby *mánička* goes back to the diminutive form *mánička* for Marie – long-haired men were to be ridiculed as unmanly, soft, and feminine.
21 VB – Veřejná Bezpečnost (public safety), the official term for the police.
22 II. SMV – II. Správa M(inisterva) V(nitra) (II. Authority of the Ministry of the Interior), code name for the KRS, Kontrarozvedná Správa VM (counterintelligence service of the MI).

Documentations

"It has unofficially come to our attention…": The Double Performance of Documents

Sylvia Sasse

Typically, the official records of secret services reveal far less about those being observed than they do about the various anxieties of those doing the observing. We encounter these anxieties throughout the files: in their inappropriately caustic language, recurring formulas, and exaggerated forensics. More than almost any other kind of text or image, they reveal that every attempt to define otherness or difference contains within itself, above all else, an act of self-constitution. This is particularly true of the observation of art and artists. State security and secret police services did not know what to do with the art trends emerging in the underground; they often pathologized and criminalized them, attempted to define and obstruct that which they did not understand. In the process, they sometimes—unknowingly—observed themselves, i.e. the "artistic" activities of the spies and informants who had been deployed for the surveillance and "decomposition" of artists. The following example illustrates this kind of self-observation.

Somewhere on a country road in the Ore Mountain countryside during the early 1980s, someone wrote down the slogan: "The Sience [*sic*] of Clara Mosch is Underrated," an allusion to Joseph Beuys's 1964 action *The Silence of Marcel Duchamp is Overrated.* While the slogan gradually dissolved in the russet dust of the road, it was preserved for posterity in the Stasi archives: "Unofficially, it has come to our attention," they wrote—using their usual formula for investigations—"that the above-named connecting road has for some time been bearing a scrawling … This scrawling has been documented by Section VIII."[1]

"This scrawling" was recorded by state security in a short information report and photo series. In the information report, we read: "On the basis of information provided by the Head of AKG/K, the following measures were undertaken on June 2, 1984, 14:30 hours: 200 m before the

Erdmannsdorf town exit, direction Gornau, turn right onto the Agricultural Cooperative Road and follow this road approx. 5 km in the direction of Dittmannsdorf. Shortly before entering the village of Dittmannsdorf, in a slight bulge in the street, will be found the slogan 'THE SIENCE OF CLARA MOSCH IS UNDERRATED.' This slogan is painted in white, presumably latex paint. It is approx. 3 m long and the individual letters are 30 cm to 20 cm tall. The present condition of the paint is old, and it is already partially peeling away. The slogan has been partially destroyed by skid marks from a truck. Head of Section, Schnabel Lieutenant Colonel." The report itself reveals more about the work of state security than the semantics of the slogan. Apparently, state security had received a tip, a "piece of information," and then tasked an employee with finding the location and describing it exactly, measuring the letters and describing the condition of the paint. The slogan itself is not interpreted in the file note. The connection to Beuys was not "ascertained." The captain seemed to assume that the action was carried out by a member of the artist group Clara Mosch, founded on May 30, 1977 by the artists Michael Morgner, Thomas Ranft, Carlfriedrich Claus, Gregor-Torsten Schade, and Dagmar Ranft-Schinke.[2] Accordingly, the documentation was placed in the file of member Thomas Ranft, in an "operative case file" with the pejorative name "Maggot."

The members of the group had been, as we now know, under surveillance by state security for some time. In November 1977, they compiled a fifteen-page "Plan for the Differentiation and Elimination of Staff Focus 'Avant-Garde Circle,'"[3] with the purpose of "decomposing" the group. The "operative measures" included the intention to destroy the Ranfts' marriage;[4] to "promote" Michael Morgner through increased responsibilities and participation in exhibitions in Western Europe; and to spread the rumor that Gregor-Torsten Schade was "unofficially" working for the Stasi. But the informant was someone else. A friend of the Mosch group, a man named Ralf-Rainer Wasse who carried out extensive photo documentation of Clara Mosch under the cover name "Frank Körner,"[5] provided meticulous reports to the Stasi. He recorded their artistic activity and even took part in actions as a photographer. The "unofficial collaborator" (*inoffizieller Mitarbeiter*, IM) assigned to the Clara Mosch group was thus simultaneously the group's artistic *and* secret police documenter, or put another way: documentation of their artistic activities was either, in the case of reports, directed towards the Stasi, or, in the case of photographs, made for both the Stasi and the artists. Wasse/"Körner" needed to prove himself both as an informant and as a friend and documenter. This double function of Ralf-Rainer Wasse/ Informant "Frank Körner" is neither exceptional nor coincidental: state security specifically planned these hybrid situations. They were reliant on unofficial collaborators with strong networks in the art world, as only such persons could infiltrate and understand this world. Their documentation is now the clearest evidence we have of the ambivalent orientation of both secret police and artist documents.

The case of the above-mentioned slogan action is even more complicated.

Unofficial Collaborator "Frank Körner" provided a report on the action, which was deposited in his informant file as well. On November 27, 1984, a bit later than Captain Schnabel, he wrote that Kurt Buchwald, also a photographer, was the one who wrote the lettering on the street: "In 1981, together with Wasse and other members of the special school, he organized a happening in Sternmühlental. In any case, he wrote the following on an industrial road of LPG Kleinolbersdorf/Altenhain in alkyd resin paint: "The Sience of Clara Mosch is Underrated"—in his understanding of as a spontaneous action in response to the closing of the gallery.[6]

In his report as an unofficial collaborator, Wasse, alias Körner, is writing "art history." He asserts that Buchwald was the author of the slogan and names himself—in his own report—as a participant in the action: a common Stasi procedure for "inner conspiracy."[7] When Kurt Buchwald, the photographer named by "Frank Körner," later read this report in the 1990s, he was surprised by the date and authorship: "I organized the happening on the occasion of my twenty-seventh birthday in June 1980. My friends and I met on a meadow near Kleinolbersdorf where we carried out a number of spontaneous actions like painting the street, adding my signature K. B. as a concluding gesture." Buchwald writes that it was Wasse himself, i.e. Unofficial Collaborator "Frank Körner," who painted the slogan on the street: "In contrast to his claim in the Stasi report, he himself painted 'The Sience of Clara Mosch is Underrated' on the street in latex-white, leaving out the letter 'l' in 'silence.' Afterwards he denounced the closing of the gallery."[8] Buchwald does not know why the letter is missing; could it be that the missing W—it reads *Scheigen* instead of *Schweigen* in German—points to Wasse himself, a signature *in absentia* to mark himself as an artist and not an informant?[9]

Buchwald was correct that it was an Unofficial Collaborator for state security who wrote the slogan on the country road. The Stasi had, in a sense, documented their own "creative" work—the "performance art" of an unofficial collaborator—without knowing that the slogan's author was their own informant.[10] That Wasse/“Körner” ascribed his “action” to another was probably related to his desire to discredit Buchwald. Buchwald's admission request to the Association of Visual Artists was well underway in 1984. Four years later, the informant shifted authorship to another, photographer Kurt Buchwald, whose work he was also ordered to spy on.

I have reconstructed this action and its documentation in detail to show what it means to work with state security files from the perspective of art historical research. In this case, we are dealing with an absurd case of self-surveillance and self-documentation. The Stasi is documenting a slogan painted on the street by its own informant. This example reveals not only how the Stasi worked in its attempts to forensically document supposedly critical art; the action also reveals that the Stasi was documenting itself and its own work.

These files are thus ambiguous in their forensic facticity; they lie about the authorship of the artistic action, while simultaneously stating the truth about the Stasi's actions. They also remain ambiguous with respect to the evaluation of the action as an artistic and/or secret police performance. Does our aesthetic evaluation or interpretation of the slogan change through knowledge of its authorship? Does this knowledge make it less artistic?[11] For the informant/photographer Wasse/“Frank Körner,” in turn, this action was an opportunity to act as an artist in the name of Clara Mosch and to be recognized by a potential art public through an act attributed to the photographer Buchwald. The material confronts us with this tricky question about the status of art independent of its authorship. Giving one answer to the question is impossible, but the question itself addresses important aspects of artistic production.

Documents For What? Facts About What?

Secret police files can only be used as art historical sources if we read them in light of their doubled performance. They are testaments to the secret police's “surveillance” and “handling” of art and artists and allow us to witness these acts in the document itself.

In the photographs of art actions, we thus always see at least two events: the actions of the artists *and* the work of the informant, whether as Stasi collaborator and/or as artist. The photos also show whether the documentation took place openly or in secret, whether the Stasi Unofficial Collaborator was an actor in the group, as well as whether he or she was a member of the audience or sat hidden behind a hedge. The documentation also shows the "inner conspiracy" of state security, i.e. the reciprocal surveillance of informants without their knowledge. Even the photographer who takes the forensic effort to measure the size of the slogan letters, "The Sience of Clara Mosch is Underrated," knows nothing about the informant who painted the letters in the first place.

We are thus dealing with documents which inextricably link both the act of documentation and the act which is to be documented. This double character is specific to each document; in secret police photographs of action art, it becomes particularly virulent. So, the question when we look at these photographs is less what actually happened, i.e. how the artistic action took place, than how the documents reveal the perspective and actions of the Stasi and their performance.

In this way, we are at least partially engaging with the reading of sources as Michel Foucault described it during the late 1960s in the *The Archaeology of Knowledge*. He distinguished between *document* and *monument* with a demand to read the document as a monument. He wanted an "archaeological description" of sources rather than a hermeneutic one. The point was not to "interpret." He did not want "to decide whether it is telling the truth or what is its expressive value, but to work on it from within and to develop it."[12] Foucault's intention was to dedicate himself to the document as material, to recognize its structures, its seriality, particularities, and relations, and not that which it supposedly referred to as a trace.

The files in the Stasi archives provide an excellent illustration of Foucault's distinction, of that which it "referred to as a trace." They are not documents about the "hostile activities"—as the Stasi would have formulated it—of the citizens under surveillance, but rather documents about how events were intended to be seen, documented, and interpreted as potentially hostile through the eyes of an informant. In this sense, these sources are monuments of the secret police's inner functioning—not only in their materiality, seriality, and correlativity, but above all, in their *performance.* They do not simply document the event; they reveal the performative production of their own documentary character, the documentation of the monument and the process of it becoming a document. They create what they supposedly reference as a trace. This documentary character of the monument applies to a broad variety of record-taking practices—for photography but also for textual records. In our case, action records where art actions are not only described but defined as potentially hostile from the start. Numerous opportunities for manipulation arise in the process of this production: the subject of surveillance is *made into* a hostile element in the first place, and surveillance itself can be a lie that is freely invented. The Russian writer Vladimir Voinovich, who attempted to gain access to his files in the early 1990s and ultimately had to settle for only a few pages, writes in his book *File No. 34840* (*Delo № 34840*) of "inner disinformation." With this term, he means a certain "eyewash" (*tufta*)[13] in the files, a kind of "lying upwards" and "lying downwards" that serves to soup up the files to make a "career" or simply fulfill a quota.[14]

At this juncture, it might be interesting to bring these secret police documents into conversation not only with Foucault's document-monument distinction, but also with the debate surrounding the documentation of performance art in art and theater history. For here too, a certain perspective has existed for a while now: that a photograph or report should not be read as a simple document recording the occurrence of an action, but as a monument, an independent artistic expression. Philip Auslander, in "The Performativity of Performance Documentation" (2006), drew attention to the fact—with reference to the artistic documentation of performances—that every form of documentation is itself performative; in extreme cases, the document *produces* the performance. Without making the distinction himself, he made reference simultaneously to performance (as the event of documentation) and to the ability of documents (as a type of speech act, as perlocutionary or illocutionary image acts) to produce that to which they refer: "If I may analogize the images that document performances with verbal statements, the traditional view sees performance documents as constatives that describe performances and state that they occurred. I am suggesting that performance documents are not analogous to constatives, but to performatives: in other words, the act of documenting an event as a performance is what constitutes it as such. Documentation does not simply generate image/statements that describe an autonomous performance and state that it occurred: it produces an event as a performance and, as Frazer Ward suggests, the performer as 'artist.'"[15]

Auslander first distinguished between a photograph from Chris Burden's *Shoot* (1971) and Yves Klein's *Leap into the Void* (1960).[16] The photo from Burden's *Shoot*, according to Auslander, documents an action which actually occurred. In contrast, Klein's *Leap into the Void* does not document at all: it produces rather than reproduces the action. Thinking with Foucault, it is produced as a monument from the start. Auslander thus differentiates between two categories of performance documentation: the theatrical and the documentary. Yves Klein's *Leap into the Void* is theatrical in this schema, a "performative photography," while Burden's photograph is documentary.

Auslander distances himself on the one hand from the theatrical documentation of analyses that regard documentation as supplemental (Amelia Jones)[17] or focus on the "contingency" of the document (Kristine Stiles).[18] On the other hand, his division remains closed to other documentary options.

We can identify other functions alongside the documentary and the theatrical, e.g. something like a conceptual function of documentation. In these cases, documentation is simultaneously part and subject of the performance; it is not only performative in the sense of producing the event *as* performance, it is at the same time performance itself,[19] i.e. part of the artistic process which, as documentation itself, is part of the performance. The Russian artist group Collective Actions, for example, carried out actions about the documentation of actions. The act of documentation was conceptualized as a field of action (a factographic field) that is only produced through the documentations, participant commentaries, author instructions, and photographs. In this field, the act of documenting and its effects during the action become instruments of artistic production and are inquiries into how the action is generated, altered, and continued through the documentation.[20]

The Documentary Act

If we now take these considerations together with the specific character of state security photography, we can see how the documentary act or image act must be thought of as bidirectional. I am less interested in distinguishing between theatrical, conceptual, and "documentary" documentation than in reading all forms of documentation, like Auslander, as performative, or even more: as at least doubly performative. Doubled in the sense of bidirectionality, as the document simultaneously constitutes the event and the person who documents in his or her role as documenter. This is what state security records reveal perhaps even more clearly than other "performance documents": a form of documentation which simultaneously *constitutes* the addressee (event as performance) and the sender (informant or informant/artist) performing the documentation.

This doubled performativity is not only part of the documentary act: it is a characteristic of every kind of speech and image act. However, because speech-act theories primarily focus on performance directed at the addressee, the examination of the bidirectionality of the document—as provoked by the secret police photographs—enables a revision of theories of performance, a revision which also incorporates the speaker in the event. What do I mean by this? J. L. Austin was the one who formulated the concept of performativity—that is, acting through speech as a model that only refers to the recipient or the addressed event. Judith Butler, in her influential study *Excitable Speech: A Politics of the Performative* (1997), linked Austin's theory with another addressee model, that of the French structuralist and Marxist Louis Althusser. Althusser's thesis is that in "western Christian culture," the individual is fundamentally constituted through "invocation."[21] That means that an individual becomes a subject through the way in which (and initially through the fact that) they are called by a name and shaped by speech acts. The subject in this understanding is a *subjectum* in the literal Latin sense: it is subject to something else which, in this case, is the violence of the language or the image with or by which it is addressed.

If we attempt to incorporate the speaker into the event, the question emerges as to why this speaker should not also be equally affected (in an illocutionary or perlocutionary sense) by his or her own speech act or image act—i.e. why do speech-act theories conceal the speaker as the one who might be constituted *as* someone by his or her own speech? A shift in our line of vision would require an interrogation not only of the "western" tradition of invocation (and its interpreters), but also the concept of the witness who observes something or the documenter who records something. Both generate not only that which is witnessed and documented, but, above all, themselves *as* witnesses, as someone who sees in a specific way and/or conditions the act of seeing.[22]

According to this thesis, every documentation of an event implies something like self-definition on the part of the speaker. Put another way: every documentation of an art action is simultaneously directed towards that which is documented as well as to the act of documentation (subject, medium). This "self-constitution" on the part of the documenter gives rise to witnesses and observers who are, by turn, unreliable or meticulously ambitious, artistic, or thoroughly loyal to the state. So, the act of documenting "is" not simply performative in the sense that it cocreates or simply creates the event; instead it shows that the document (as monument) is auto performative, i.e. constitutes the documenter and testifies to the act of documentation.

The Double Performance of the Document

Performance artists began to work with this doubled character of the document early, specifically with visual references to the documentary aesthetic of the secret services. Tomáš Pospiszyl and Amy Bryzgel,[23] for example, refer to the work of Czech artist Jiří Kovanda—e.g. *Contact* (*Kontakt*, 1974), *Theater* (*Divadlo*, 1976), or *Attempted Acquaintance* (*Pokus o seznámení*, 1977)—where he had himself photographed in the city as if under surveillance by state security. Or at least we could interpret it that way from today's perspective. The documentations of actions, according to Pospiszyl, resemble the photographs since found in the state security archives.[24]

In Kovanda's work, it is not just an action that is performed but the perspective of the observer as well. In other words, it is not entirely clear where the performance is taking place, in front of or behind the camera. In the photos, we see Kovanda walking around the city, bumping into people, and performing small gestures from a small, self-written script. The camera follows Kovanda, capturing his actions.[25] We thus see the photographer following Kovanda through the city with his camera, while other passersby remain unaware that a performance is even taking place. Kovanda writes: "Gestures and movements have been selected such that passers-by have no idea that they are watching a 'performance.'" Kovanda is only performing for the person who is pointing the camera at him.

In 1977, Kovanda again intensified the observational situation in *Attempted Acquaintances*. He not only had himself photographed as he attempted to make the acquaintance of a girl on the street, he also informed his friends that they would also be recorded as they observed this event. The photographer as documenter of the action thus captures an additional part of the performance, the act of observation, and refers back to his own action in the process.

In other cases, the artists act with the knowledge or suspicion that they are being watched by state security. This happens in *Secret Agent's Day* (*Dzień Tajniaka*), which the Orange Alternative organized in Poland on March 1, 1988 "in honor of" those watching them. During this happening, the artists demanded passersby, in the name of the Ministry for State Security, to act as agents: "Come appropriately dressed for the occasion: wear black sunglasses, a hat, a trench coat, or a leather cape. Bring along a recording device: a microphone, a funnel, or a trumpet. We particularly recommend microphones installed in umbrellas or canes."[26] The only record we have of this happening today was made by state security.

Something similar happened with the happening *Flour-Art*, which the artist collective Clara Mosch carried out in Glauchau in 1988. The artists gathered in a bakery to bake art and to transform mail art (*Mail-Art)* into flour art (*Mehl-Art*). They knew that they were under surveillance and the Stasi also knew, as we read in the files, that the artists knew.[27] It is hard not to interpret this action as an action *for* state security, i.e. as one addressed *to* surveillance. In the Stasi's detailed surveillance records and photographs, we see an almost exemplary case of the double performativity of the document. We not only learn about the observed action *Flour-Art*, we also learn about the act of spying: the permanent presence of numerous observers who, in addition to secretly taking photographs outside on the street, also used their "inspection patrols" to observe the artists during a visit to a restaurant or eavesdrop on their conversations in the hotel foyer. "And so we baked in the nude, clothed only in an apron,"[28] one of the informants heard an artist say. The observers also report when they are no longer able to follow their subjects and when they break off surveillance in the evening. They always address their report to their superior, to whom they needed to justify their act of surveillance. The report is one which is simultaneously directed towards the act of surveillance and the persons under surveillance. For Stasi agents, it was not easy to judge whether the observed actions were relevant, whether they constituted "negative-hostile" art actions, or when the action was finished and when it began. These are questions which action artists continually made a subject of in their own performances. In this case though, we see what it means when multiple inexpert observers minutely document an art action. It leads not just to the creation of a surveillance report, but also an observer report, the report of reception from the point of view of witnesses who could only write down what they were in a position to see.

Artists and activists have taken the surveillance of surveillance itself as a subject of their work, e.g. Ion Grigorescu in his 1975 *Electoral Meeting*. Grigorescu secretly photographed protests against the elections with a handheld camera, protests which were themselves being observed by secret police. The Moscow-based group Collective Actions conceived of potential surveillance as an event which unpredictably intervenes in the action and referred to it as an "expositional sign field" (*ekspozicionnoe znakovoe pole*). This includes unpredictable occurrences (weather, geographical conditions, chance observers, signs and symbols on trees, and other objects lying around that automatically become elements of the action), but also elements such as a black limousine that was parked at the forest's edge during an action, leading to speculation.[29]

While informants and spies could inevitably be seen at many performances (i.e. much of the photography of performance art in Eastern Europe is a gallery of spies), intentional photographs of state security at work are rare, as it was ultimately dangerous to document the observers. In 1982, Roland Jahn managed to take such photos while watching the Stasi remove a sculpture in the Johannisfriedhof cemetery in Jena. The sculpture commemorated civil rights activist Matthias Domaschk, who had died a year before in a Stasi interrogation center under mysterious circumstances. His death was dubiously ruled a suicide. To take the photographs, Jahn sought out a hiding spot in a neighboring Catholic retirement home, secretly photographing the equally clandestine removal of the sculpture.[30] The photos were then sent to the writer Lutz Rathenow, who then sent them to Jürgen Fuchs, who in turn gave them to *Der Spiegel*, making a public action of a doubly secret one. This inverted perspective, the surveillance of those doing the surveilling, reveals not only the work of the secret police—it also reveals an act of dissidence.

Translated from German by Brian Alkire

Endnotes

1 BStU, MfS BV Karl-Marx-Stadt, XIV, 996/78, Vol. 8, 018–023.

2 The name of the group is taken from the first letters of the artists' last names: CLA = Claus, RA = Ranft, MO = Morgner, SCH = Schade.

3 BStU, MfS, BV Chemnitz, XIV/73/75, Vol. 1, 018–032.

4 "Through political-operative measures, starting points for marital conflict are to be created, with the goal of divorce. This requires: use of reliable and verified informant on R [Ranft] and his wife, unsettling both persons through intimate notes, letters, etc. suited to deepening marital discord." BStU, MfS, Chemnitz Branch, "Massnahmeplan zur Bearbeitung des OV 'Made,'" §§ 106/107 StGB, Karl-Marx-Stadt, January 26, 1978, Vol. 1, 021.

5 "Körner" was an IMB ("Unofficial Collaborator for Homeland Defense with Enemy Connections and for the Immediate Handling of Persons Suspected of Hostile Actions"). IMBs were particularly important IMs. They enjoyed the confidence of the Stasi, and they also had direct contact with the people that the Stasi classified as hostile. See glossary: Unofficial Collaborator (IM).

6 http://www.wahrnehmung.de/Akte.htm (accessed June 2, 2019), as well as a conversation with Kurt Buchwald.

7 State security uses the term "inner conspiracy" to indicate the concealment of information among both informants and commanding officers and their respective "operative case files." This means that one is not aware of the other. This leads to informants constantly reporting about other informants as well as about themselves in the third person, i.e. appear under their real name as participants in events and art actions.

8 http://www.wahrnehmung.de/Akte.html (accessed June 2, 2019).

9 I thank Sandra Dugonjić for pointing this out.

10 The unofficial collaborator "Frank Körner," with reference to the "decomposition" of the Clara Mosch group, received an order to earn and build up trust, to inform and to ensure loyalty "without personally becoming hostile to the state," and if possible, to "conspire" with the group and report about the results of the "decomposition." "Konzeption zur Differenzierung und Zerschlagung des personellen Schwerpunktes 'Avantgardistischer Kreis,'" BStU, MfS BV Karl-Marx-Stadt, AKG–3485, Vol.1, 31.

11 This "error" has also been perpetuated in art history. In the index of Kurt Buchwald's work, the action is listed under his name and dated to 1979 (June 28, 1979, Chemnitz: "'Das Schweigen von Clara Mosch wird unterbewertet' ('The Sience of Clara Mosch is Underrated'). Cardboard boxes, paint, foil, wooden sticks. Documented with photographs in sequence and individual photos of various formats. Sandwich technique. Happening on a meadow by Kleinolbersdorf, assisted by Ralf Rainer Wasse [*sic*] and friends. The action's motto spreads the remark of Joseph Beuys: 'The silence of Marcel Duchamp is underrated' [Beuys falsely cited here]. The Chemnitz artist collective Clara Mosch (1976–83), then called 'Karl-Marx-Stadt,' was one of the first effective centers of avantgarde art in the former GDR."), in: Kurt Buchwald, *Fotografie in Aktion* (Berlin: Ex Pose Verlag, 1992), 70.

12 Michel Foucault, *Archaeology of Knowl*edge (New York: Pantheon Books, 1972), 6.

13 Vladimir Voinovich, "Delo № 34840," in *Maloe sobraniye sochineniye v 5 tomach, Zamysel* (Moscow, 1994), 344.

14 Ibid., 359: "Я всегда знал, что феномен советской системы в том и состоит, что низы лгут верхам, верхи низами и сами от низов требуют лжи." In the files of Stasi "unofficial collaborators," where they are themselves

evaluated as informants, there is always a division between the "estimation of truth-content and completeness" that had to be filled out during the respective meeting with the collaborator and the commanding officer. Now and then, we also find comments about "tendentious reports" and about requests or sworn statements on the truth of the reports. "Stephan," BStU, MfS BV Erfurt IXI 486/71, fol. 1/344, 01–02.

15 Philip Auslander, "The Performativity of Performance Documentation," *A Journal of Performance and Art* 28, no. 3 (September 2006): 5.

16 Ibid., 5.

17 Amelia Jones, "'Presence' in Absentia: Experiencing Performance as Document," *Art Journal* 56, no. 4 (Winter 1997): 16.

18 Kristin Stiles, "Performance and its Objects," *Arts Magazine* 65, no. 3 (1990): 35. See also: *Histories of Performance Documentation. Museum, Artistic, and Scholarly Practices*, ed. Giannachi/ Westerman—from the perspective of practice; Reason, *Documentation, Disappearance, and the Representation of Life Performance*. Boris Groys even critically stated that interest in performance art has shifted to an interest in the documentation of performances or art. See Groys, "Art in the Age of Biopolitics: From Artwork to Art Documentation," 53.

19 I distinguish here between performativity, the act of constituting reality through generating or producing that which it is doing, and the mode of executing this performance itself. This suggests that *performativea* (in Austin's sense) themselves have a performance which codetermines the mode of reality production.

20 Sasse, *Texte in Aktion. Sprech- und Sprachakte im Moskauer Konzeptualismus* (Munich: Fink, 1999).

21 Louis Althusser, "Idéologie et appareils idéologiques d'État (Notes pour une recherche)," in *Positions. 1964–1975* (Paris, 1976), 67–125.

22 Sasse/ Zanetti, "Hate Speech. Der Bumerangeffekt," *Geschichte der Gegenwart*, https://geschichte dergegenwart.ch/hate-speech-der-bumerangeffekt/ (accessed June 6, 2019).

23 Amy Bryzgel, "Performing for the Camera in Central and Eastern Europe," in *post.Notes on Modern and Contemporary Art Around the Globe*, https://post.at.moma.org/content_items/817-performing-for-the-camera-in-central-and-eastern-europe (accessed June 2, 2019).

24 Tomáš Pospiszyl, "Look Who's Watching: Photographic Documentation of Happenings and Performances in Czechoslovakia," in *1968–1989. Political Upheaval and Artistic Change*, ed. Claire

Bishop and Marta Dziewańska (Warsaw: Museum of Modern Art, 2009), 74–87.

25 Ibid.

26 Orange Alternative, "Day of the Secret Agents" ("*Dzień Tajniaka*"), Leaflet, http://www.orangealternativemuseum.pl/#dzien-tajniaka (accessed June 2, 2019).

27 "On Sunday afternoon, October 5, 1980, Dr. Werner came and informed us, specifically Ranft, Wasse, and Morgner, that we were being watched. ... Dr. Werner believed that their hotel registration had arrived with the police and the Stasi wanted to see who the many artists were in Glauchau before October 7, 1980," p. 26.

28 BStU, MfS BV Karl-Marx-Stadt XIV 73/75, Vol. 5, 16.

29 During the action *A Work of Visual Art—The Image* (1987), a military Jeep even drove into the middle of the demonstration field. Kabakov describes how he was initially afraid, even though the strike took place during perestroika. In his commentary report, we read that the jeep drove towards Andrey Fillipov, with the unknown driver asking Fillipov what was going on here. When he finally answered that it was a secret, the driver simply drove away. Ilya Kabakov, "Commentary," in *Kollektivnye deystviya, Poezdki za gorod* (Moscow: 1998), 696.

30 Both Blumhagen, who made the sculpture, and Jahn were later expatriated from the GDR. See Scheer, *Vision und Wirklichkeit: die Opposition in Jena in den siebziger und achtziger Jahren*, 212.

The Sience of Clara Mosch is Underrated

Kurt Buchwald

When the Berlin-based photographer Kurt Buchwald requested his file from the BStU in the 1990s, he was disappointed: he had no file, only references to him in the files of others, e.g. in Ralf-Rainer Wasse's. Wasse, alias Informant "Frank Körner," was not only a long-standing informant but also the "court"-photographer of the 1977-founded Chemnitz-based artist group "Clara Mosch," which was brutally disrupted by the Stasi and closed in 1982. Wasse, a.k.a. "Frank Körner," claimed in a report in November 27, 1984 that Buchwald, during a happening, painted the slogan "The Sience of Clara Mosch is Underrated" (*Das Scheigen von Clara Mosch wird unterbewertet)* on a country road. But in fact, it was informant "Frank Körner" himself who wrote the slogan—a reference to Joseph Beuys's 1964 action "The Silence of Marcel Duchamp is overrated"—on the road during Buchwald's birthday happening in July 1980. Why did "Frank Körner" falsely attribute the action to Kurt Buchwald? Why did the Stasi—a full four years later—document the action in pseudo-forensic detail? Probably because Buchwald attempted to be accepted to the Verein Bildender Künstler (Association of Artists in the GDR) in 1984. This happening by a Stasi informant was largely unknown to art history up until it was discovered in the files from 1984. So, the pseudo-forensic documentation of the Stasi is juxtaposed with the artistic documentation of the actions by Buchwald. In one of Buchwald's photos of this action you can see Ralf-Rainer Wasse himself standing with his motorcycle helmet next to a Trabant, as well as next to his written slogan as evidence of his action. (S/K)

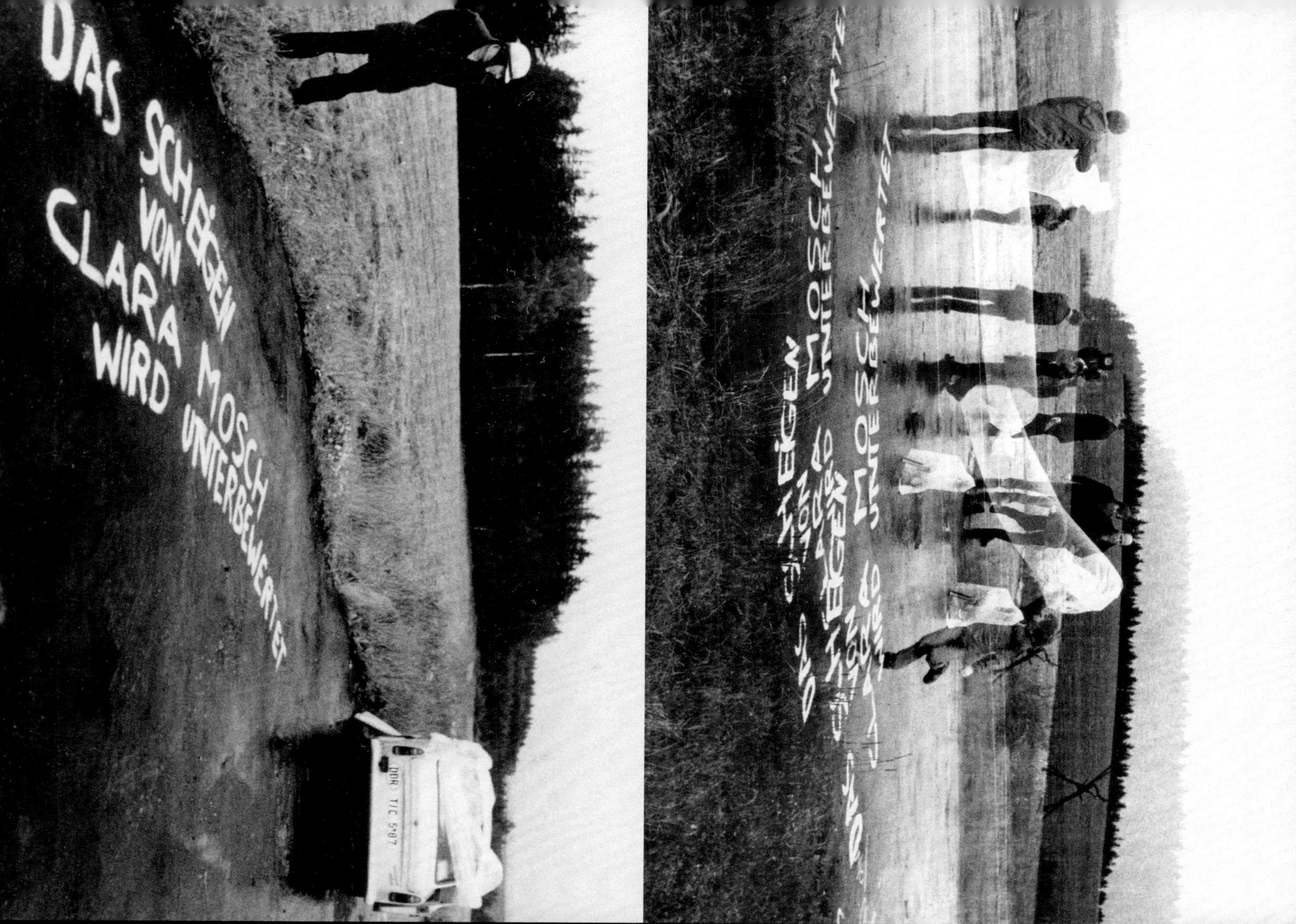

Two black-and-white photographs, 19.5 × 26.5 cm
Courtesy of Kurt Buchwald Archive, Berlin

Photo Documentation of *The Sience of Clara Mosch is Underrated*

MfS (GDR)

On June 6, 1984, the monitoring group of the District Administration for State Security of Karl-Marx-Stadt produced pseudo-forensic documentation of the slogan "The Sience of Clara Mosch is Underrated." "It has unofficially come to our attention"—the usual Stasi opening for investigations which they themselves ordered— "that the named connecting road has for some time been bearing a scrawling on the surface of the road." "This scrawling" was preserved for posterity in a short information report and photo series. In the "Photo Documentation of the Specified Slogan," we see, in a collection of nine photos, the still easily readable slogan—even measured with a folding rule: "the individual letters are of a height of 30 cm or 20 cm." Why the Stasi only became aware of the slogan after four years cannot be determined from the files. The informant was also not named. (S/K)

District Administration for
State Security, Karl-Marx-Stadt
AKG/Analysis & Control Group

Karl-Marx-Stadt, June 6, 1984
537/84

Stamp on the original:
Karl-Marx-Stadt
Received: 8.6.
Referencenr: 48701
Forward to: illegible

Head of Department XX
Comrade Lieutenant Colonel ENGELHARDT

Information concerning scrawling on the connecting road between Erdmannsdorf and Dittmannsdorf

It has unofficially come to our attention that the named connecting road has for some time been bearing a scrawling stating

"THE SIENCE OF CLARA MOSCH IS UNDERRATED"

on the surface of the road.

This scrawling has been documented by Department VIII (see attachment).
I request confirmation of receipt and further instructions.

Head of AKG/K
[Signature]
Seifert
Lieutenant Colonel

Attachment

Bezirksverwaltung für
Staatssicherheit Karl-Marx-Stadt
AKG/Kontrollgruppe

Karl-Marx-Stadt, 6. 6. 84

537/84

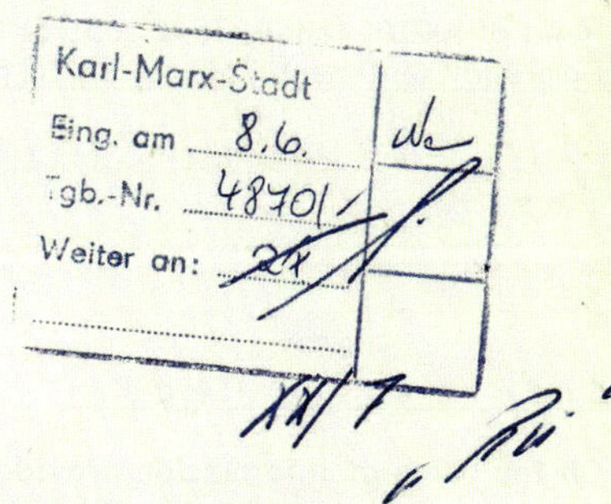

Leiter der Abteilung XX
Genossen Oberstleutnant ENGELHARDT

Information über eine Schmiererei auf der Verbindungsstraße zwischen Erdmannsdorf und Dittmannsdorf

Inoffiziell wurde bekannt, daß auf der genannten Verbindungsstraße eine bereits seit längere Zeit auf dem Straßenbelag vorhandene Schmiererei

"DAS SCHEIGEN VON CLARA MOSCH WIRD UNTERBEWERTET",

vorhanden ist.

Durch die Abteilung VIII wurde diese Schmiererei dokumentiert (siehe Anlage).
Ich bitte um Kenntnisnahme und weitere Veranlassung.

Leiter der AKG/K

Seifert
Oberstleutnant

Anlage

District Administration for State Security
Karl-Marx-Stadt
Department VIII

Karl-Marx-Stadt, June 3, 1984

Head of AKG/K (Analysis & Control Group/Control)
Comrade Lieutenant Colonel Seifert

Information Report

On the basis of information provided by the Head of AKG/K, the following measures were undertaken on June 2, 1984, 14:30 hours:

200 m before the Erdmannsdorf town exit, direction Gornau, turn right onto the Agricultural Cooperative Road and follow this road approx. 5km in the direction of Dittmannsdorf. Shortly before entering the village of Dittmannsdorf, in a slight bulge in the street, will be found the slogan

"THE SIENCE OF CLARA MOSCH IS UNDERRATED"

This slogan is painted in white, presumably latex paint. It is approx. 3m long and the individual letters are 30cm to 20cm tall. The present condition of the paint is old and it is already partially peeling away. The slogan has been partially destroyed by skid marks from a truck.

Head of Department
[Signature]
Schnabel
Lieutenant Colonel

Attachment
Photo documentation

BV für Staatssicherheit
Karl-Marx-Stadt
Abteilung VIII

Karl-Marx-Stadt, 3. Juni 1984

Leiter AKG/K
Genossen Oberstleutnant Seifert

Informationsbericht

Auf der Grundlage einer Information durch den Leiter der AKG/K wurde am 2. 6. 1984, 14.30 Uhr folgendes erarbeitet:

200 m vor dem Ortsausgang Erdmannsdorf in Richtung Gornau rechts einbiegen in die LPG-Straße, diese ca. 5 km weiter in Richtung Dittmannsdorf. Kurz vor der Ortschaft Dittmannsdorf an einer Ausbuchtung steht entlang des Straßenverlaufes die Losung

"DAS SCHEIGEN VON CLARA MOSCH WIRD UNTERBEWERTET".

Diese Losung ist mit weißer Farbe, vermutlich Latex, gemalt. Sie ist ca. 3 m lang und die einzelnen Buchstaben haben eine Größe von 30 cm bzw. 20 cm. Der gegenwärtige Zustand der Farbe ist alt und sie bröckelt zum Teil schon ab. Durch eine Bremsspur von einem Kfz ist die Losung zum Teil zerstört.

Leiter der Abteilung

Schnabel
Oberstleutnant

Anlage
Bilddokumentation

Six file pages, photo documentation
Source: BStU, MfS BV K-M-St XIV 996/75, Vol. 8, 18–23.
1984

PHOTO DOCUMENTATION

for the specified slogan of June 2, 1984, 14:30 hours
on the Agricultural Cooperative Road between Gornau and Dittmannsdorf

BILDDOKUMENTATION

zur festgestellten Losung vom 2. 6. 1984, 14.30 Uhr
auf der LPG-Straße zwischen Gornau und Dittmannsdorf

Six file pages, photo documentation
Source: BStU, MfS BV K-M-St XIV 996/75, Vol. 8, 18–23.

Image 1: Indicator arrows pointing towards the slogan, approx. 2 m front

Image 2: Overall view of the written slogan

Image 3: Same as image 2

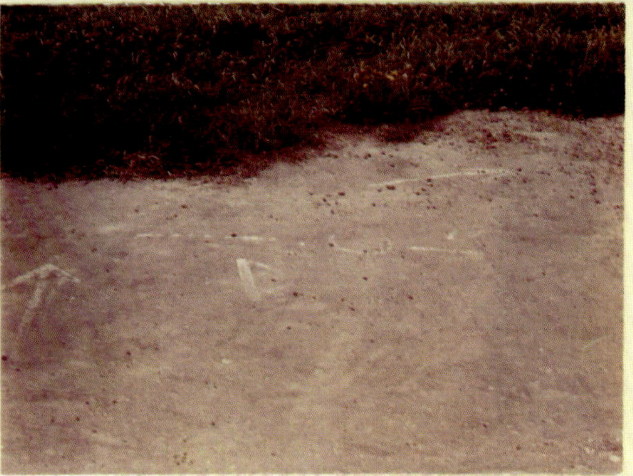

Bild 1: Hinweispfeile auf die Losung, ca. 2 m davor

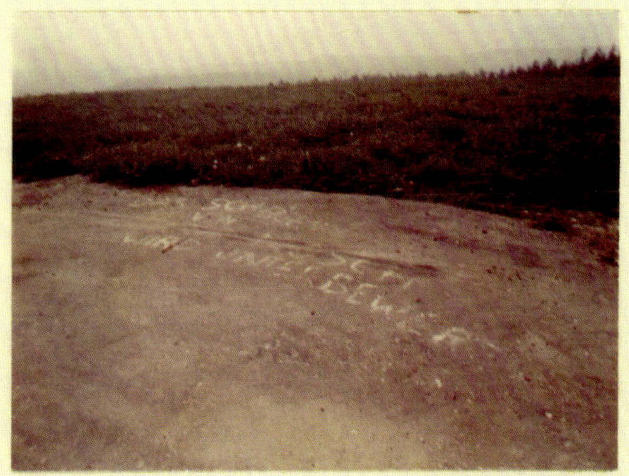

Bild 2: Gesamtansicht der niedergeschriebenen Losung

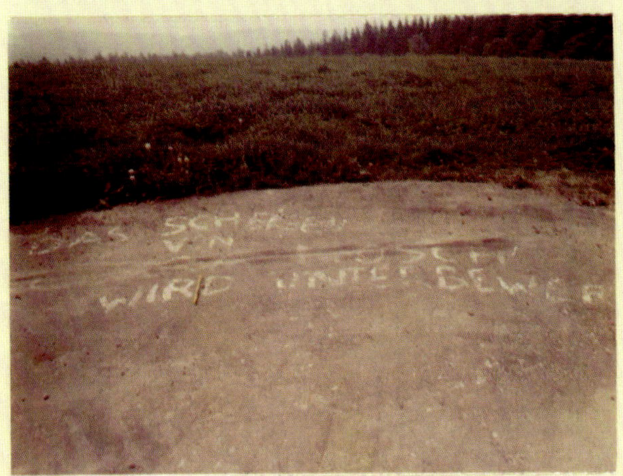

Bild 3: wie Bild 2

Six file pages, photo documentation
Source: BStU, MfS BV K-M-St XIV 996/75, Vol. 8, 18–23.
1984

Image 4: Partial words from the written slogan

Image 5: Same as image 4

Image 6: Same as image 4

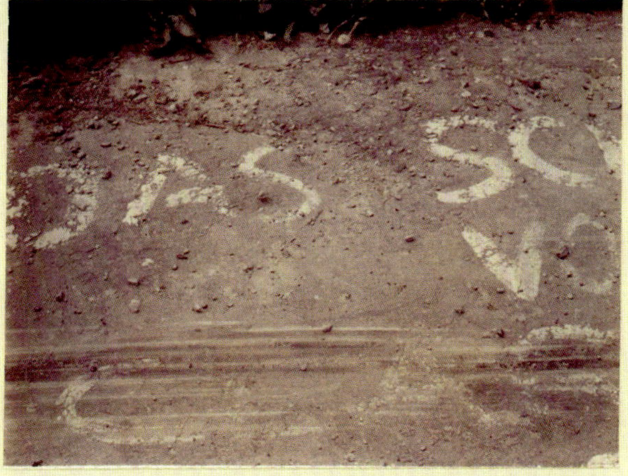

Bild 4: Teilwörter aus der niedergeschriebenen Losung

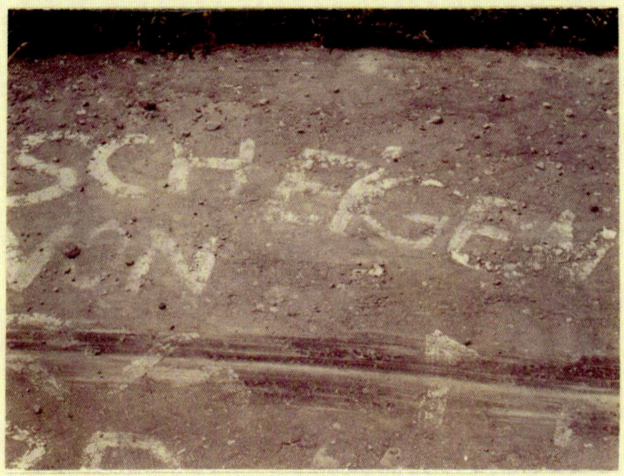

Bild 5: wie Bild 4

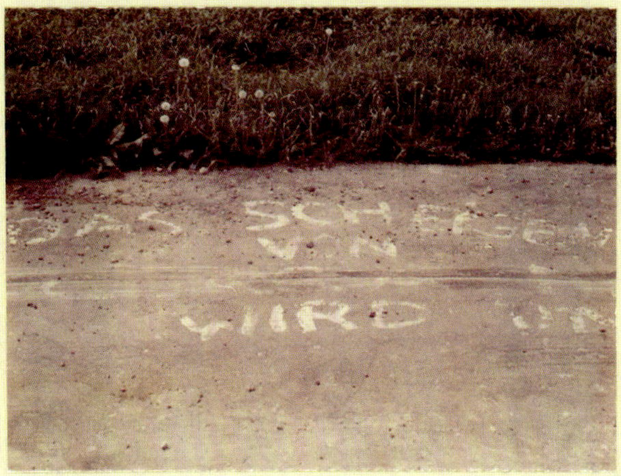

Bild 6: wie Bild 4

Image 7: Same as image 4

Image 8: Size of the letters of the written slogan

Image 9: Same as image 8

Translated from German by Brian Alkire

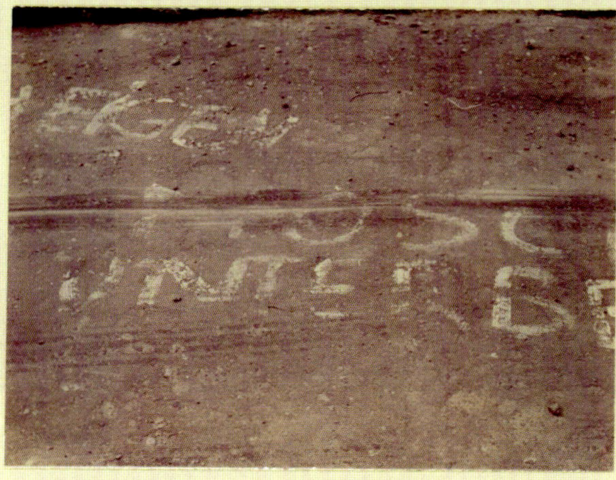

Bild 7: wie Bild 4

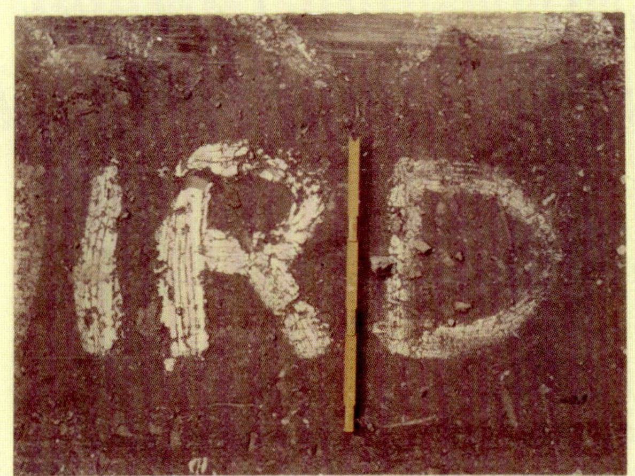

Bild 8: Größe der Buchstaben der niedergeschriebenen Losung

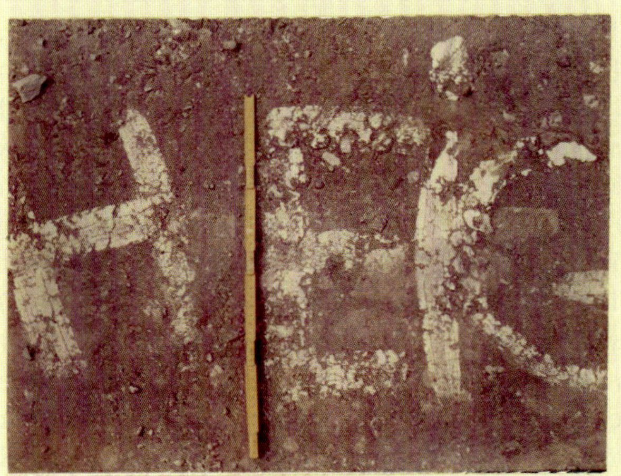

Bild 9: wie Bild 8

Six file pages, photo documentation
Source: BStU, MfS BV K-M-St XIV 996/75, Vol. 8, 18–23. 1984

Inke Arns, Kata Krasznahorkai, Sylvia Sasse

The Sience of Clara Mosch is Underrated

A Search for Traces

What happens if we take Stasi reports seriously? On September 2, 2019, we made an attempt to find remnants of the slogan "The sience of Clara Mosch is underrated." This slogan was written on a country road near Dittmansdorf in 1980 during a happening of Kurt Buchwald. We wanted to find out if the Stasi report written four years later, which also contains photo documentation, would actually lead us to the location of slogan. We found the place. Not, however, thanks to the Stasi's directions, which were only partially correct. We were helped by the taxi drivers Toni from Chemnitz and Enrico from the Local History Society (*Heimatverein*) of Dittmansdorf. The latter recognized the location from the horizon in a photograph and led us to the correct location on the former Agricultural Production Cooperative (*Landwirtschaftliche Produktionsgenossenschaft*—LPG) road. The writing was unfortunately gone, tarred over, and no one in town could remember that there was once—forty years ago—a mysterious slogan written on a rural road at the edge of town. As a reminder of the slogan action, we handed the Stasi report over to the Dittmansdorf Local History Society.

Four photographs, Dittmannsdorf near Chemnitz, Saxony 2019

Michael Morgner, b. 1942 in Chemnitz, GDR, lives and works bei Chemnitz, Germany.
Thomas Ranft, b. 1945 Königssee, GDR, lives and works bei Chemnitz, Germany.
Carlfriedrich Claus, b. 1930 in Annaberg GDR, died 1998 in Chemnitz, Germany.
Gregor-Torsten Schade, b. 1948 Hildburghausen, GDR, lives and works in Chemnitz, Germany.
Dagmar Ranft-Schinke, b. 1944 Chemnitz, GDR, lives and works in Chemnitz, Germany.

Flour-Art 80

Clara Mosch

In October of 1980, the happening *Flour-Art 80* (*Mehl-Art 80*) of the artist group Clara Mosch (1977–1982) took place in Glauchau, which the Berliner gallerist (Galerie Arkade) and art historian Klaus Werner traveled to take part in. The group was founded on May 30, 1977 by artists Michael Morgner, Thomas Ranft, Carlfriedrich Claus, Gregor-Torsten Schade, and Dagmar Ranft-Schinke. The idea for the name came from Thomas Ranft and was formed from the starting letters of their last names:
CLA = Claus
RA = Ranft
MO = Morgner
SCH = Schade
The artists met for a flour-art happening for an entire day. In two different bakeries, which they drove between in cars, they baked art, including *mail art* (a play on words; the German word for "flour" is "*mehl*," pronounced like the English *mail*). They knew that they were being watched by the Stasi, and the Stasi knew, as we read in the files, that the artists knew. (S)

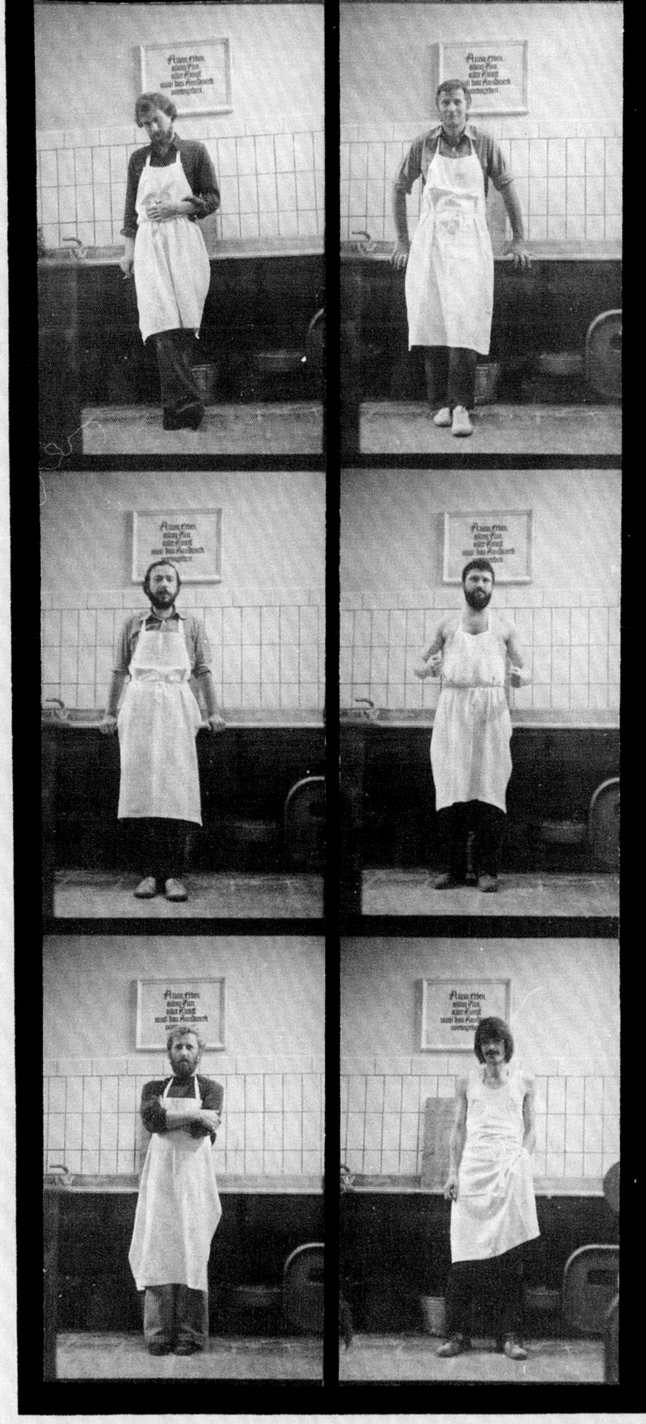

Der Spruch 3/7 1980

Ralf-Rainer Wasse (Photo)
Hans-Georg Gaul (Repro) Documentations

Slogan (Der Spruch), October 6, 1980, 3/7, black-and-white photograph on canvas, 66 × 50 cm, Courtesy: Gallery Barthel+Tetzner, Berlin

1980

Ralf-Rainer Wasse (Foto) Documentations
Hans-Georg Gaul (Repro)

Stone Breads (Die Steinbrote), October 6, 1980, 3/7, black-and-white photograph on canvas, 84.1 × 118.9 cm, Courtesy: Gallery Barthel+Tetzner, Berlin

1980

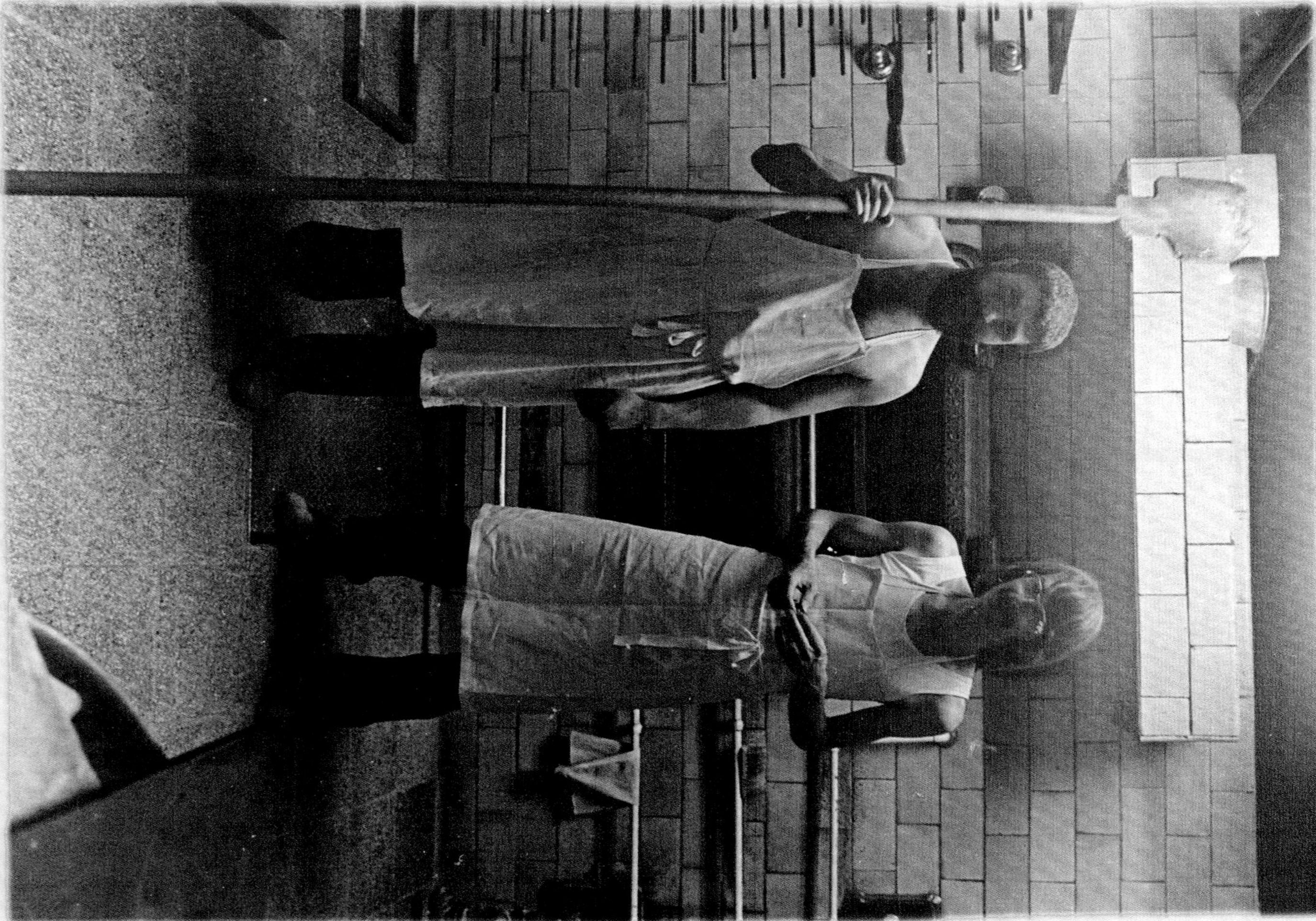

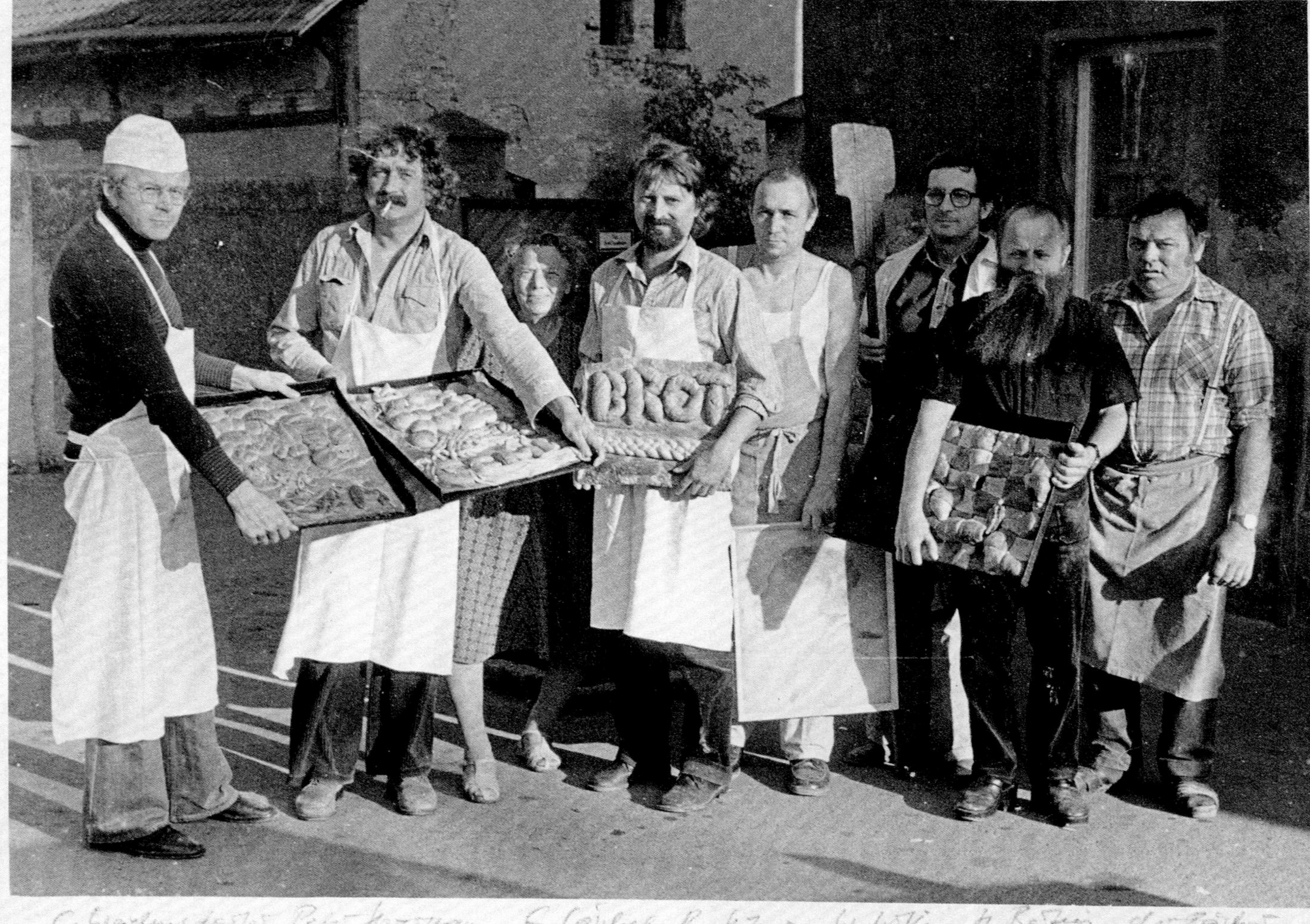

Ralf-Rainer Wasse (Photo)
Hans-Georg Gaul (Repro), Documentations

Group Image (Gruppenbild), October 6, 1980, black-and-white photograph on barium paper, 29.7 x 21 cm, Courtesy: Gallery Barthel+Tetzner, Berlin

Surveillance Report

MfS (GDR)

This surveillance report about the happening *Flour Art 80* (*Mehl-Art 80*) is found in the case file for Operation "Grub" which was compiled about Thomas Ranft. We learn from the almost forensically-detailed Stasi action records and the surveillance photos not just something about the action itself, but also something about the actual act of spying: the observers were present for two whole days and were continuously observing the artists not only outside on the street but also in the restaurant and at the hotel bar. They provided detailed reports with time signatures and took photos of the happening. During one of their "monitoring rounds," they also eavesdropped on the artists in the hotel foyer: "... and we were baking naked, wearing only an apron," one of the informants heard an artist say. In the final report, the Stasi had to admit that they were unable to discover any "operative indications" of "state-hostile con-nections" (StGB/1968 § 106 according to the criminal code of the GDR) or "state-hostile agitation." (S)

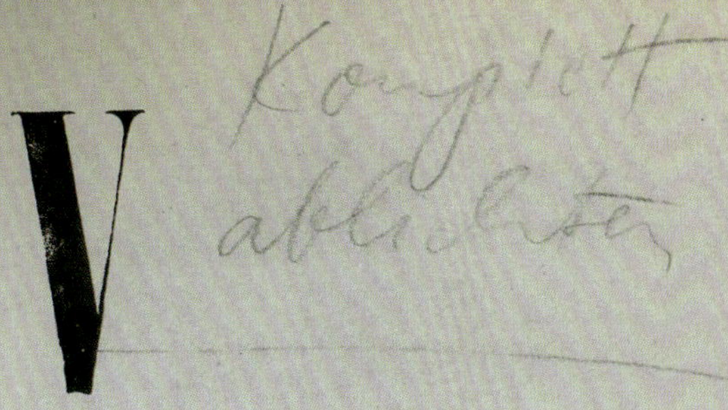

Reg.-Nr. XIV/73/75 / Karl-Marx-Stadt

„Made"

Beginn 31. Jan. 1984 H

Beendet

Archiv-Nr.

Band-Nr. 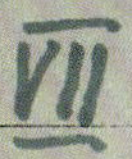

T-GLEIT-Hefter
Bestell-Nr. T 108/So
VEB Organisations-Technik Eisenberg
V 10 25 AG 515-97-79

BStU

Archiv der Außenstelle Chemnitz

MfS BV Karl-Marx-Stadt

XIV 73/75 7/14

Source: BStU, MfS BV K-M-St XIV 73/75, Vol. 7, file cover.

211

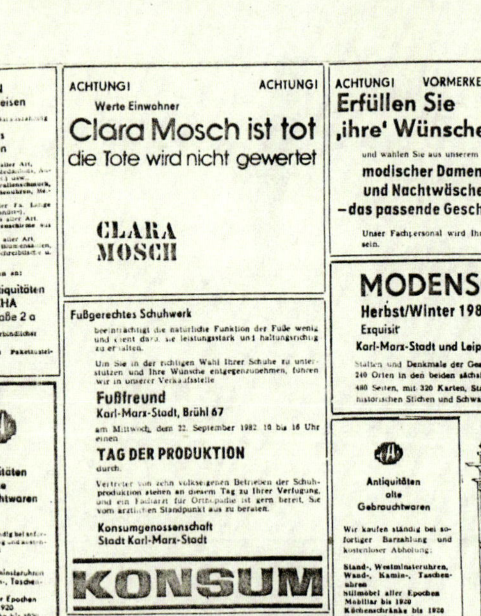

KAUFEN
Höchstpreisen
sofortiger Barauszahlung
...uck aus
...s Zeiten

Werk "...k"-Antiquitäten
TAUCHA
...hofstraße 2 a

ACHTUNG! ACHTUNG!
Werte Einwohner
Clara Mosch ist tot
die Tote wird nicht gewertet

CLARA
MOSCH

ACHTUNG! VORMERKEN! ACHTU...
Erfüllen Sie ‚ihre' Wünsche zum F...
und wählen Sie aus unserem reichhaltigen Angeb...
**modischer Damen-Tageswäs...
und Nachtwäsche
– das passende Geschenk –**
Unser Fachpersonal wird Ihnen dabei gern beh... sein.

Fußgerechtes Schuhwerk
beeinträchtigt die natürliche Funktion der Füße wenig und dient dazu, sie leistungsstark und haltungsrichtig zu erhalten.
Um Sie in der richtigen Wahl Ihrer Schuhe zu unterstützen und Ihre Wünsche entgegenzunehmen, führen wir in unserer Verkaufsstelle
Fußfreund
Karl-Marx-Stadt, Brühl 67
am Mittwoch, dem 22. September 1982 10 bis 16 Uhr einen
TAG DER PRODUKTION
durch.
Vertreter von zehn volkseigenen Betrieben der Schuhproduktion stehen an diesem Tag zu Ihrer Verfügung, und ein Facharzt für Orthopädie ist gern bereit, Sie vom ärztlichen Standpunkt aus zu beraten.
**Konsumgenossenschaft
Stadt Karl-Marx-Stadt**
KONSUM

**MODENSCHAU
Herbst/Winter 1982**
Exquisit
Karl-Marx-Stadt und Leipzig

Stätten und Denkmale der Geschichte und Kultur ... 240 Orten in den beiden sächsischen Bezirken.
480 Seiten, mit 320 Karten, Stadtgrundrissen, Wap... historischen Stichen und Schwarzweißfotos.

Antiquitäten
alte
Gebrauchtwaren

FDJ
**Großer
Solidaritäts-
Flohmarkt**
FDJ

- Den Besuch unserer international bekannten Nachtbar sollten Sie sich schon jetzt vormerken. Ab 1. Oktober 1982 bis 31. Dezember 1982 spielt für Sie die Formation Caja aus der ČSSR.
- **VORSCHAU:**
Wir laden Sie wieder ein zum 2. Chemnitzer-Hof-Ball am 19. November 1982 – extra mit Tanzpausenbüfett.
- Auf Grund einer Großveranstaltung am 22. Oktober 1982 ist unser Interhotel ab 14 Uhr geschlossen.
- Ab 1. November 1982 spielt für Sie jeweils dienstags bis sonnabends Rainer Kügler zur Unterhaltung in der Erzgebirgsstube.
- Für die Jugendweihefeiern 1983 haben Sie noch die Möglichkeit, Bestellungen aufzugeben.

Antiquitäten
alte
Gebrauchtwaren
Wir kaufen ständig bei sofortiger Barzahlung und kostenloser Abholung:
Stand-, Westminsteruhren, Wand-, Kamin-, Taschenuhren
Stilmöbel aller Epochen
Mobiliar bis 1920
Küchenschränke bis 1920
Bauernmöbel und -truhen
Porzellane, Ölgemälde
altes Kinderspielzeug
alte Puppen, Puppenmöbel
Spieldosen, Polyphone
Orchestrions, Klaviere
Zinn-, Kupfer- und Bronzegegenstände
Angebote bitte an:
VEB (K) Antikhandel Pirna
Einkaufsbereich Karl-Marx-Stadt
9006 Karl-Marx-Stadt
G.-Adolf-Straße 35 a
Ruf Karl-Marx-Stadt 33434
Für die Kreise Reichenbach, Auerbach, Plauen, Oelsnitz, Klingenthal:
9920 Oelsnitz (V.), PSF 34
Ruf Oelsnitz 2181
von 7 bis 8 Uhr

Wir kaufen:
Möbel (vor 1920)
Uhren (vor 1930)
Puppen Blechspielzeug
Musikinstrumente
speziell Klaviere
alten Hausrat
Nippes
VEB (B) DLK
Gebrauchtwaren

Gummischutz
NEU
H. KÄSTNER

Kaufen ab Oktober 1982
Posten
Blaufichten- und Koniferengrün
GPG Karl-Marx-...

Verkaufspreis
3,00 Mark

Clara Mosch ist tot

Clara Mosch ist tot

Verkaufspreis
1,00 Mark

Clara Mosch ist tot

126

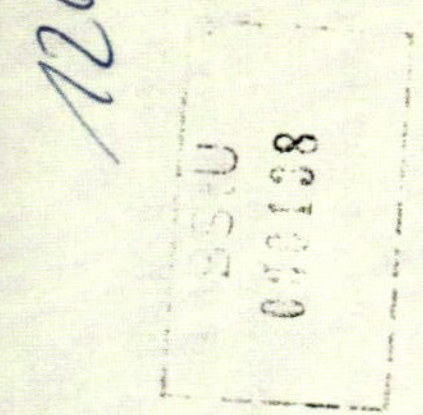

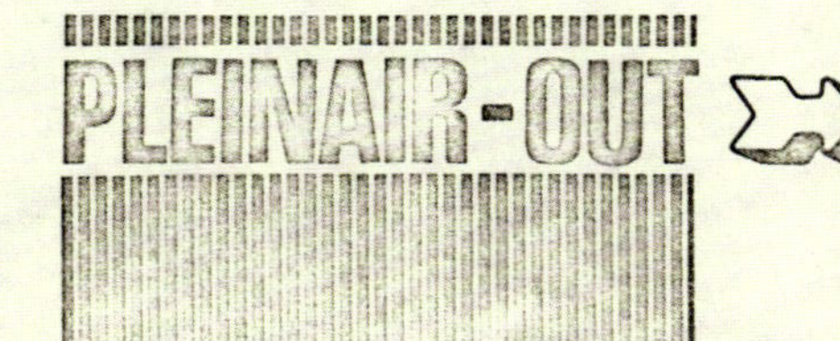

Einladung
zum private
EAT-ART-
NONFESTIVAL

MEHL-ART '80

Zwei Bäckereien stehen zur Verfügung. Kosten tragen die Teilnehmer. Anreise 4.10. mittags LINDENHOTEL
Erbitten Rückantwort.

Glauchau 4.10.-7.10.

Management Stübner & Werner

COUNCIL OF MINISTERS
OF THE GERMAN DEMOCRATIC REPUBLIC
Ministry for State Security

Department/Section/Subsection

District Administration/Administration

Responsible Person

Telephone

Department/Section XX/7 — Karl-Marx-Stadt, Oct. 9, 1980

District Administration/Administration Karl-Marx-Stadt

Ward/building office of the Ministry for State Security — Section Head-personal

Surveillance Report

Re: XXX — Date/Place of Birth XXX

Address: XXX

Cover name: "Maggot 80" — Mission Reg. No: VIII/B/

Oct. 4, 1980

12:00 Surveillance of XXX in Hotel Lindenhof, Glauchau begun.

12:12
Dr.Werner, Klaus
Address: 102 Berlin
Berolinastrasse 10

drove with his vehicle

Make/model: VW Golf
Color: blue
License No.: IBV 8 – 24

MINISTERRAT
DER DEUTSCHEN DEMOKRATISCHEN REPUBLIK
Ministerium für Staatssicherheit

Hauptabteilung/Abteilung/Referat ....

Bezirksverwaltung/Verwaltung ....

Sachbearbeiter ....

Telefon ....

Hauptabteilung/Abteilung XX/7

Karl-Marx-Stadt, 9.Okt.1980
schu-zö

Bezirksverwaltung/Verwaltung Karl-Marx-Stadt

Kreis-/Objektdienststelle des Ministeriums für Staatssicherheit ....

Leiter-persönlich

Beobachtungsbericht

Betr. [redacted] geb.am,in, [redacted]

Wohnhaft [redacted]

Decknamen "Made 80" Reg.-Nr. des Auftragsersuchens VIII/B/

Für die Zeit vom 4.10.80 12.00 Uhr bis 6.10.1980 10.00 Uhr

4.10.1980

12.00 Uhr wurde mit der Beobachtung des [redacted] in Glauchau am
Hotel "Lindenhof"
begonnen.

12.12 Uhr fuhr der

Dr. W e r n e r, Klaus
wohnhaft: 102 Berlin
Berolinastraße 10

mit seinem PKW

Typ: VW Golf
Farbe: blau
pol.Kennz.: IBV 8 - 24

0 098 177 75.0

to the parking lot of the aforementioned hotel and parked his vehicle. A short time later another vehicle,

Make/model: XXX
Color: XXX
License No.: XXX

parked next to the already parked vehicle, make: VW Golf.

The owner of the Wartburg vehicle is:

Name: XXX
Date/place of birth: XXX
Address: XXX
Employment: XXX

The following persons exited the vehicle:

XXX

Address: XXX
Employment: XXX

Address: XXX
Employment: XXX

as well as the driver:

Address: XXX
Employment: XXX

12:15 The above-named four persons greeted Dr.Werner, who was still standing next to his vehicle, with handshakes and shoulder slapping. They then unloaded their hand luggage from the vehicles,

auf den Parkplatz des vorgenannten Hotels und parkte seinen PKW ab.
Kurze Zeit später fuhr ein PKW

Typ:
Farbe:
pol.Kennz.:

neben den bereits abgeparkten PKW Typ:VW Golf.

Bei dem Halter des PKW Wartburg handelt es sich um die

geb.:
geb.am,in,
wohnhaft:
Tätigkeit:

Folgende Personen entstiegen dem PKW:

wohnhaft:

Tätigkeit:

wohnhaft:

Tätigkeit:

sowie der Fahrer

wohnhaft:

Tätigkeit:

12.15 Uhr begrüßten die vorgenannten vier Personen den noch an seinem PKW stehenden Dr. Werner mit Handschlag und Schulterklopfen. Im weiteren Verlauf entluden sie aus den PKW's ihr Handgepäck,

Photo 1

Photo 2

Photo 3

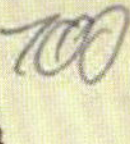

3

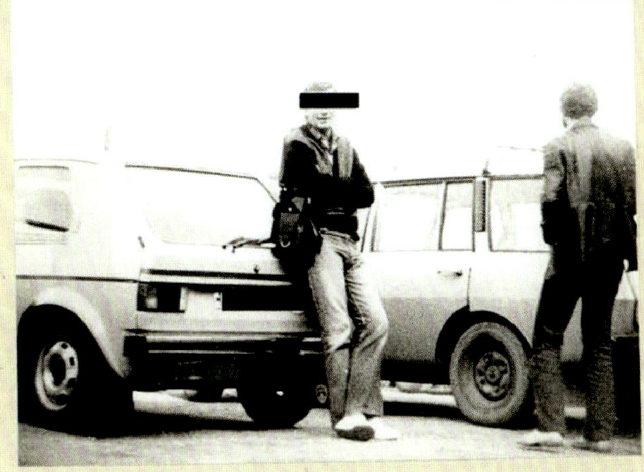

Bild 1

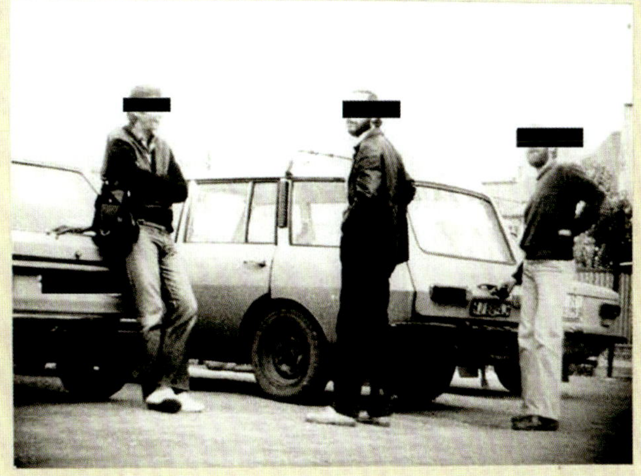

Bild 2

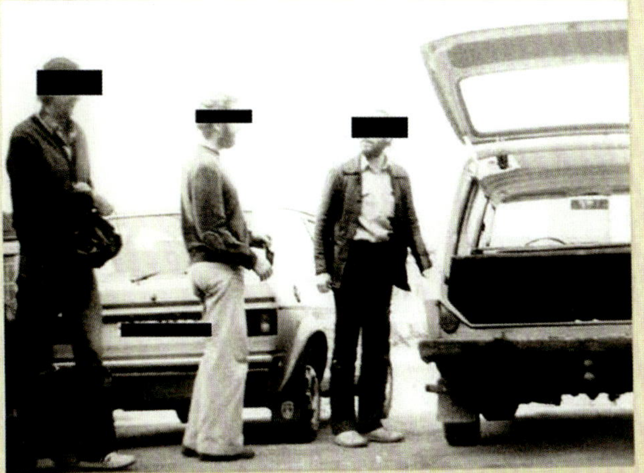

Bild 3

Photo 4

entered the hotel at

12:19 and went to the reception. After filling out the registration form, they received keys for rooms No. 307 and 104.
They then visited their rooms.

13:08 All of the known five persons returned from their hotel rooms and went to the hotel restaurant, where they sat at two tables in the section reserved for hotel guests.
A further six persons were already sitting at these tables, who greeted them and then carried on a conversation with them.
Upon inspection, it was able to be determined that all persons ate lunch and consumed alcoholic as well as nonalcoholic beverages.

14:51 XXX, Dr.Werner, XXX, XXX, XXX and three other male persons departed the hotel

Photo 5

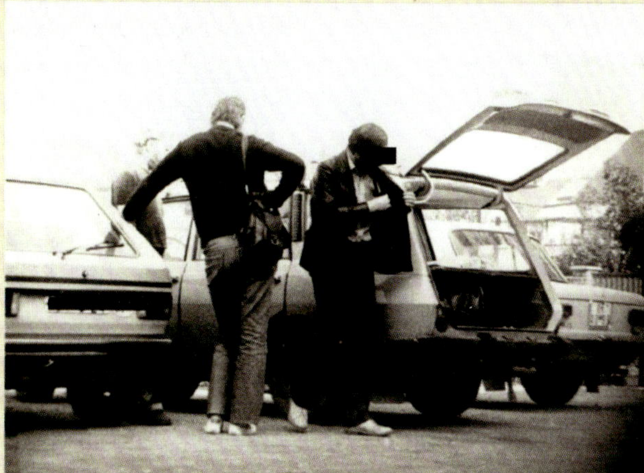

Bild 4

betraten um

12.19 Uhr das Hotel und begaben sich zur Rezeption. Nachdem sie die Anmeldeformulare ausgefüllt hatten, erhielten sie die Zimmerschlüssel Nr. 307 und 104. Im Anschluß daran suchten sie ihre Zimmer auf.

13.08 Uhr kamen alle bekannten fünf Personen von ihren Hotelzimmern zurück und begaben sich in das Hotelrestaurant, wo sie im reservierten Teil für Hotelgäste an zwei Tischen platz nahmen.
An diesen Tischen saßen bereits weitere sechs Personen, welche sie begrüßten und im weiteren Verlauf eine angeregte Unterhaltung führten.

Bei einer Kontrolle konnte festgestellt werden, daß alle Personen zu Mittag speisten und alkoholische und alkoholfreie Getränke zu sich nahmen.

14.51 Uhr verließen der , der Dr. Werner, der , der , der sowie weitere drei männliche Personen das Hotel

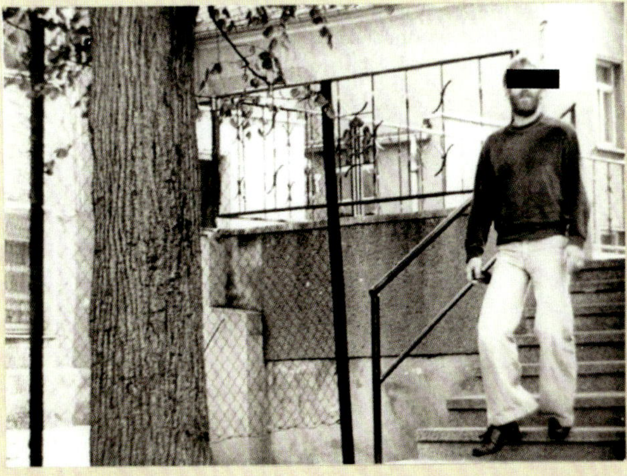

Bild 5

Photo 6

and proceeded to the hotel parking lot.
They entered the following vehicle:

Make/model: XXX
Color: XXX
License No.: XXX

The owner of the Trabant vehicle is:

XXX
Date/place of birth XXX
Address: XXX
Employment: XXX
XXX

All three vehicles drove together directly via Dr.-Friedrich-Strasse to Solidarity Square, where they parked the vehicles.

102

5

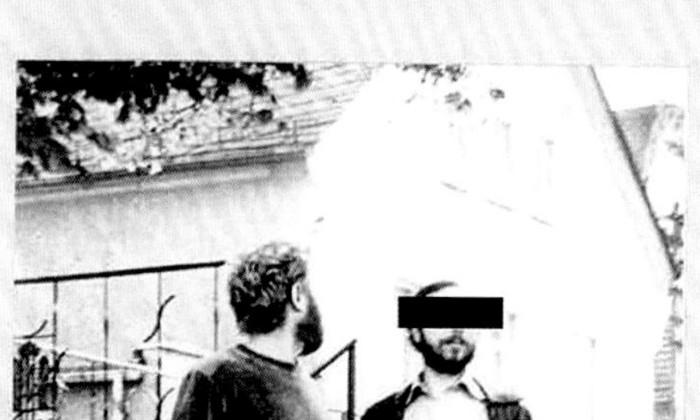

Bild 6

und begaben sich zum Hotelparkplatz.
Hier nahmen sie in den PKW's VW Golf, Wartburg sowie in einem PKW

Typ:
Farbe:
pol.Kennz.:

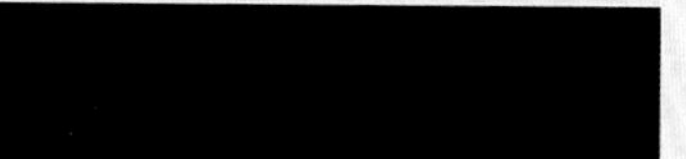

platz.

Beim Halter des PKW Trabant handelt es sich um den

geb.am,in,
wohnhaft:
Tätigkeit:

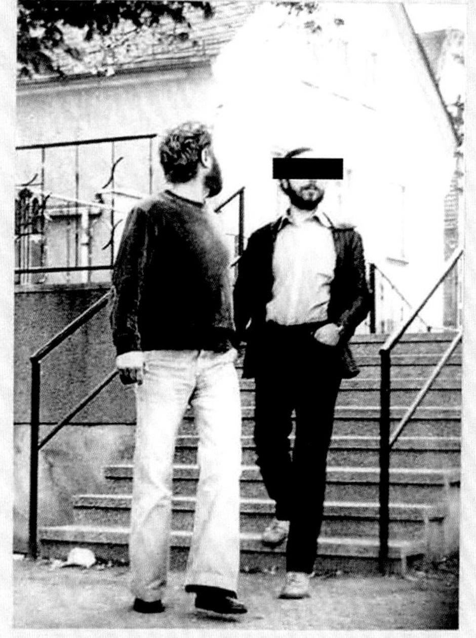

Gemeinsam fuhren alle drei PKW auf direktem Wege über die Dr.-Friedrich-Straße zum Platz der Solidarität, wo sie die PKW abparkten.

15:08 All eight persons entered the Glauchau Municipal Library at Otto-Schimmel-Strasse 30.

Due to conspiracy, further pursuit was not possible.

15:52 The persons returned from the library and entered the vehicles

Photo 7

Photo 8

15.08 Uhr betraten alle acht Personen die Stadtbibliothek Glauchau auf der Otto-Schimmel-Straße 30.

Aus Gründen der Konspiration wurde hier nicht gefolgt.

15.52 Uhr kehrten sie aus der Bibliothek zurück, nahmen in den PKW's platz

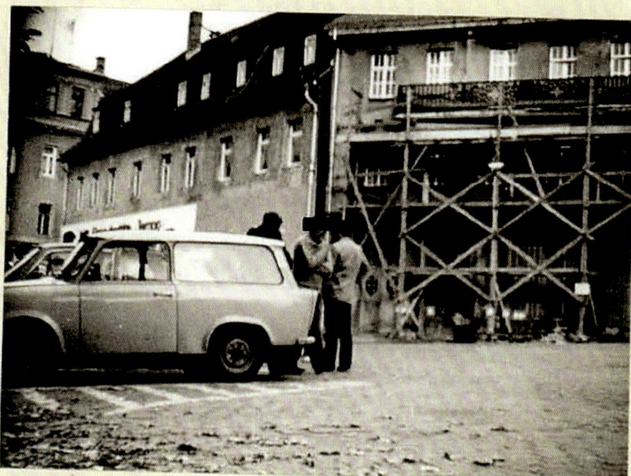

Bild 7

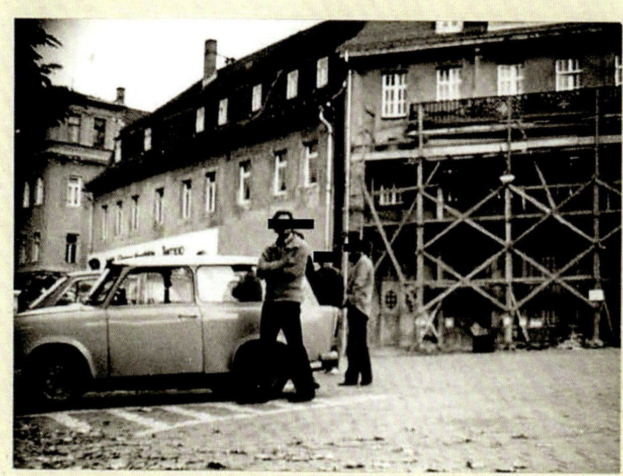

Bild 8

Photo 9

and drove back to Hotel "Lindenhof," which they reached at

16:02 They proceeded together to the hotel restaurant, where they subsequently drank coffee.

17:06 XXX, XXX, and XXX arrived at the hotel parking lot and entered the Wartburg/Tourist vehicle. They were followed by Dr.Werner and XXX, who entered the VW Golf vehicle. They then drove together via Zwickauer Strasse to Meeraner Strasse.

17:11 The following person stopped in front of the bakery:

XXX XXX
XXX XXX
XXX XXX

They parked their vehicle here

Photo 10

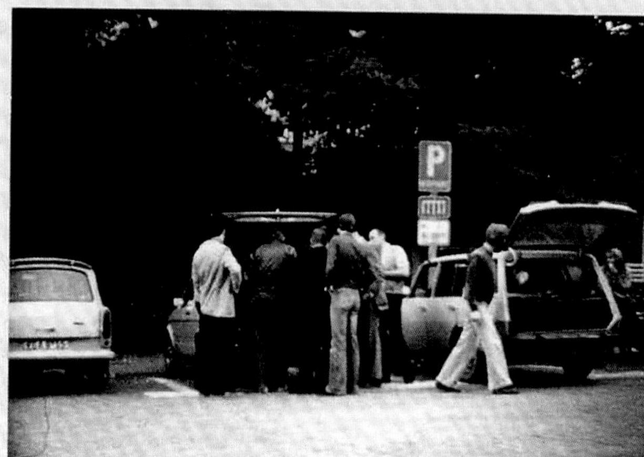

Bild 9

und fuhren zurück zum Hotel "Lindenhof", welches sie um

16.02 Uhr erreichten. Gemeinsam begaben sie sich in das Hotelrestaurant, wo sie im weiteren Verlauf Kaffee tranken.

17.06 Uhr kamen der ███, der ███ sowie der ███ zum Hotelparkplatz und nahmen im PKW Wartburg/Tourist platz. Ihnen folgten der Dr. Werner und der ███, welche im PKW VW Golf platz nahmen. Anschließend fuhren sie gemeinsam über die Zwickauer Straße zur Meeraner Straße.

17.11 Uhr hielten sie vor der Bäckerei

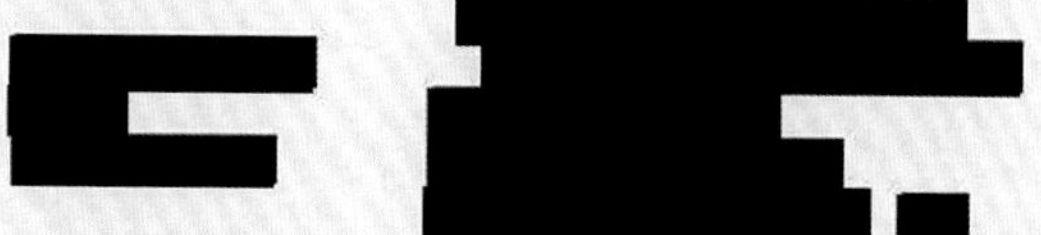

Hier parkten sie ihre PKW ab

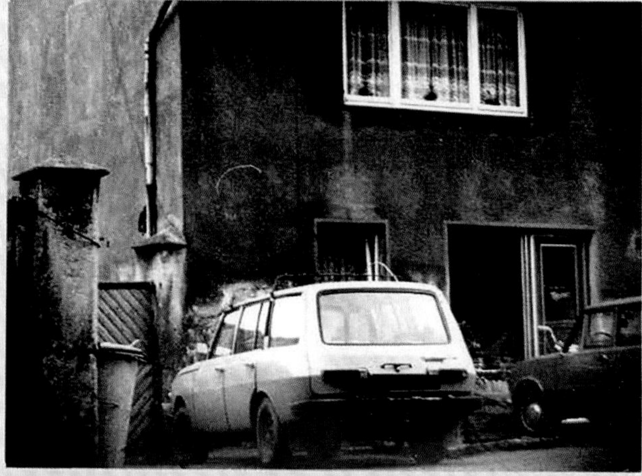

Bild 10

Photo 11

Photo 12

and entered the bakery via the rear entrance.

18:20 The five persons departed the above-named bakery, entered the vehicle, and drove through the Glauchau city center to Fischergasse, where they parked the vehicles and, via the rear entrance,

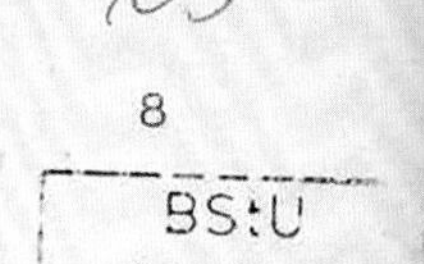

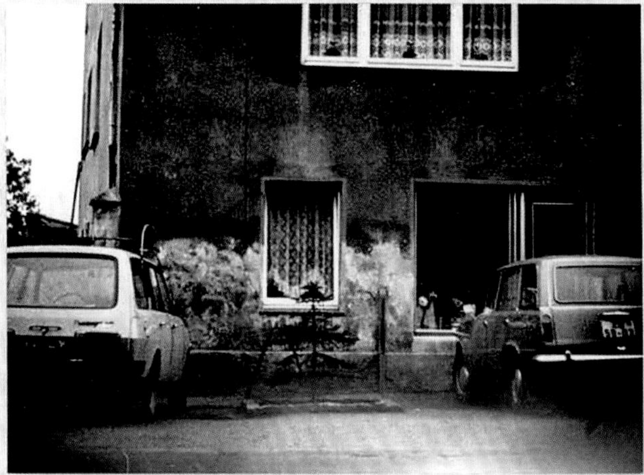

Bild 11

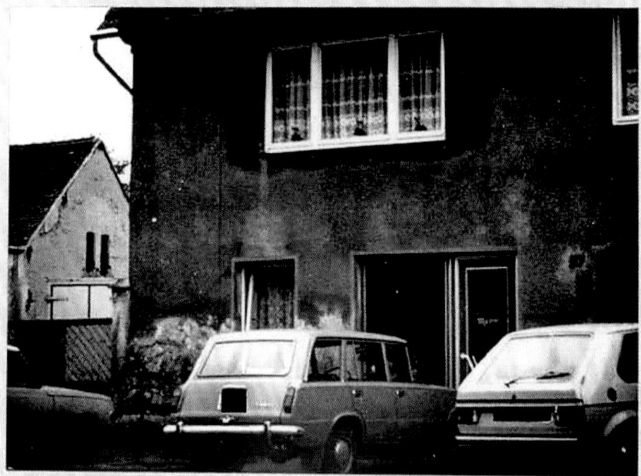

Bild 12

und betraten über den Hintereingang die Bäckerei.

18.20 Uhr verließen die fünf Personen die vorgenannte Bäckerei, nahmen in dem PKW platz und fuhren durch das Stadtzentrum von Glauchau zur Fischergasse, wo sie die Fahrzeuge abparkten und über den Hintereingang die entered the bakery.

Date/place of birth: XXX
Address: XXX

19:05 The named persons returned to Fischergasse, entered their vehicles, and drove to the hotel.

During an inspection of the hotel parking lot around

19:30 an invitation flyer was identified on the Wartburg/Tourist vehicle, approx. 25x35cm and attached to the rear window.
It read as follows:

Pleinair – Out

Invitation
to private EAT – ART
NON FESTIVAL

F L O U R A R T – 8 0

Two bakeries available
Costs borne by participants
Arrival Oct. 4 at noon

Linden Hotel

Please RSVP

Glauchau
Oct. 4 – Oct. 7

Management

Stuberarl & Werner

Edition Arkada [*sic*]

19:35 All known persons could be seen inside of the hotel.

Further surveillance in the hotel was not carried out.

Because none of these people departed the hotel until

22:00 surveillance was suspended.

 106

Bäckerei

geb.am,in,
wohnhaft:

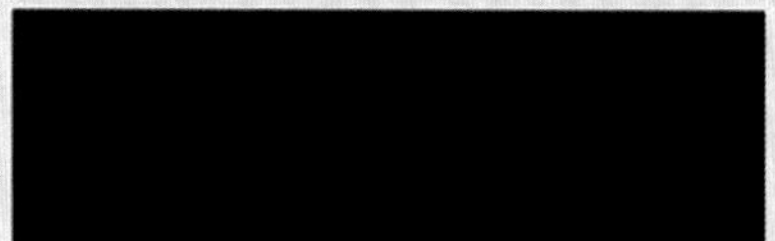

betraten.

19.05 Uhr kamen die genannten Personen zur Fischergasse zurück, bestiegen ihre PKW und fuhren zum Hotel.

Bei einer Kontrolle gegen

19.30 Uhr auf dem Parkplatz des Hotels, konnte am PKW Wartburg/Tourist ein Einladungsplakat ca. 25x35 cm, welches an der hinteren Fensterseite angebracht war, festgestellt werden.
Es hatte folgenden Wortlaut:

Pleinair - Out

Einladung
zum private EAT - ART
NON FESTIVAL

M E H L - A R T - 8 0

Zwei Bäckereien stehen
zur Verfügung Kosten
tragen die Teilnehmer
Anreise 4.10. mittags
Lindenhotel
Erbitten Rückanwort

Managment
Stuberarl & Werner
Edition Arkada

Glauchau
4.10. - 7.10.

19.35 Uhr konnten alle bekannten Personen im Hotelinneren gesehen werden.

Eine weitere Beobachtung im Hotel wurde nicht geführt.

Da bis

22.00 Uhr keiner dieser Personen das Hotel verließ, wurde die Beobachtung unterbrochen.

Source: BStU, MfS BV K-M-St XIV 73/75, Vol. 5, pp. 103–119.

Oct. 5, 1980

8:00 Surveillance was resumed at the Hotel Lindenhof in Glauchau. At this time, the vehicles which appeared at the lecture were still parked in the hotel parking lot.

9:43 Seven male persons left the hotel and walked via Zwickauer Strasse and Meerander Strasse to the bakery:

XXX
XXX
XXX

which they entered at

10:16 through the rear entrance.

9:50 Dr.Werner, XXX, XXX, XXX, XXX and one further male person left the hotel. All persons got into their two vehicles and drove directly to Fischergasse.

10:05 The above-named persons entered the bakery XXX through the main entrance on XXX.They carried along with them a large cutting board as well as a photographic presentation (A4) with the inscription

F L O U R – A R T – 8 0

11:35 Dr.Werner and XXX departed the bakery, entered the VW Golf and drove directly to Bakery XXX.

In the time period from

12:00 to

17:00 Dr.Werner and XXX were constantly shuttling between both bakeries in the VW Golf.

14:39 XXX, XXX, XXX, and XXX departed the Bakery XXX and proceeded to the Wartburg/Tourist vehicle.
All persons were clothed in white baker's aprons.
They subsequently drove directly via Zwickauer Strasse to Bakery XXX.

14:47 The above-named four persons entered this bakery.

5.10.1980

8.00 Uhr wurde die Beobachtung am Hotel "Lindenhof" Glauchau fortgeführt.
Zu diesem Zeitpunkt waren die am Vortag aufgetretenen PKW noch immer auf dem Hotelparkplatz abgeparkt.

9.43 Uhr verließen sieben männliche Personen das Hotel und liefen über die Zwickauer Straße, Meeraner Straße zur Bäckerei [redacted]
welche sie

10.16 Uhr durch den Hintereingang betraten.

9.50 Uhr verließen der Dr. Werner sowie der [redacted], der [redacted], der [redacted], der [redacted] und eine weitere männliche Person das Hotel.
Alle Personen nahmen in ihren zwei PKW's platz und fuhren auf direktem Wege zur Fischergasse.

10.05 Uhr betraten o.g. Personen die Bäckerei [redacted] durch den Haupteingang auf der [redacted].
Bei sich führten sie ein goßeres Kuchenbrett sowie eine fotografische Vorlage (A 4) mit der Aufschrift

M E H L - A R T - 8 0

11.35 Uhr verließen der Dr. Werner und der [redacted] die Bäckerei, bestiegen den PKW Golf und fuhren auf direktem Wege zur Bäckerei [redacted]

In der Zeit von

12.00 Uhr bis

17.00 Uhr pendelten der Dr. Werner sowie der [redacted] mit dem PKW Golf ständig zwischen den beiden Bäckereien.

14.39 Uhr verließen der [redacted], der [redacted], der [redacted] und der [redacted] die Bäckerei [redacted] und begaben sich zum PKW Wartburg/Tourist.
Alle Personen waren mit weißen Bäckerschürzen bekleidet.
Anschließend fuhren sie auf direktem Wege über die Zwickauer Straße zur Bäckerei [redacted]

14.47 Uhr betraten die o.g. vier Personen diese Bäckerei.

15:15 They again left the bakery, entered the vehicle, and drove to Hotel "Lindenhof," where they remained for approx. 2 minutes.

Photo 13

Photo 14

15.15 Uhr verließen sie die Bäckerei wieder, nahmen im PKW platz und fuhren zum Hotel "Lindenhof", welches sie für ca. 2 min aufsuchten.

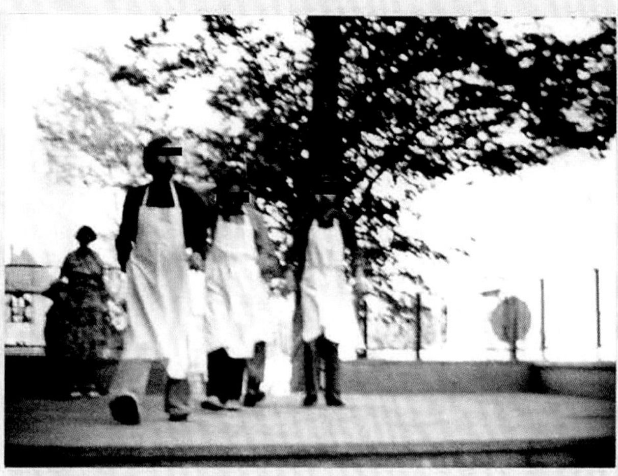

Bild 13

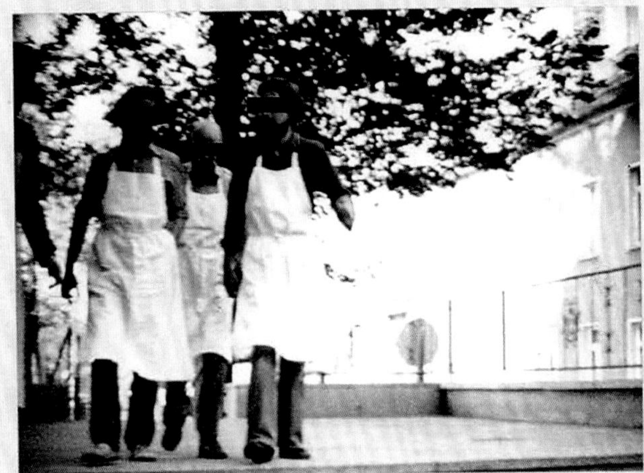

Bild 14

Photo 15

Photo 16

Photo 17

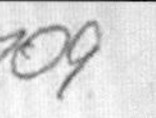

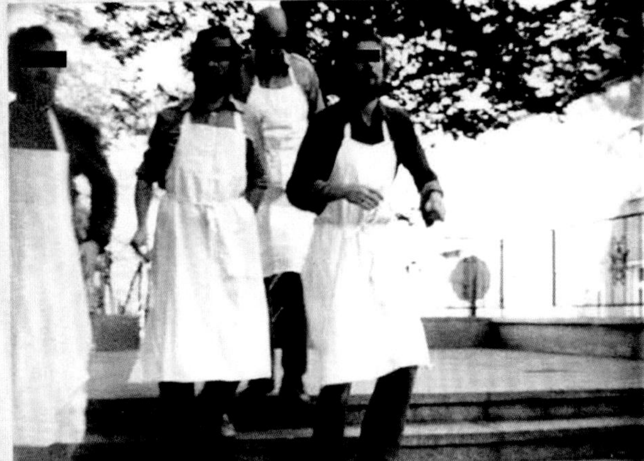

Bild 15

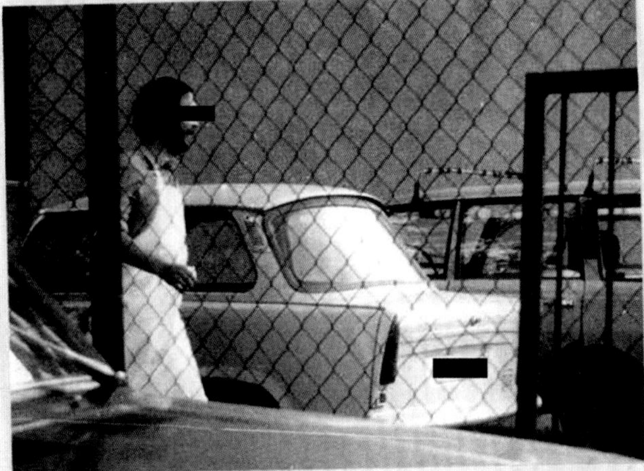

Bild 16

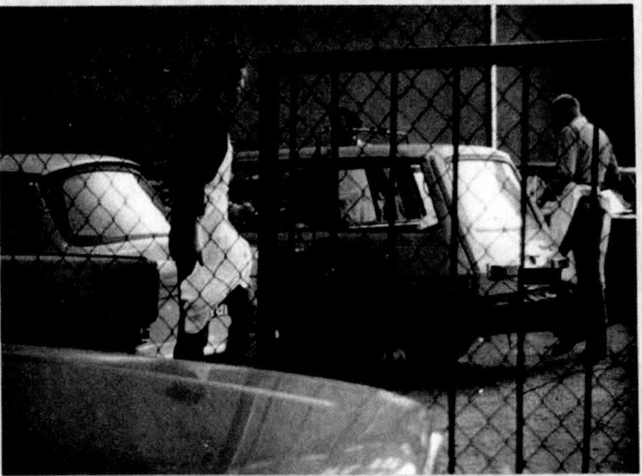

Bild 17

Source: BStU, MfS BV K-M-St XIV 73/75, Vol. 5, pp. 103–119.

Photo 18

Photo 19

They then continued their drive to Bakery XXXX and entered said bakery.

17:08 It was noticed that the Wartburg/Tourist vehicle with XXX, XXX, XXX and the male person drove again in the direction of the hotel.

Upon inspection of the hotel, the above-mentioned four persons were seen entering the hotel.

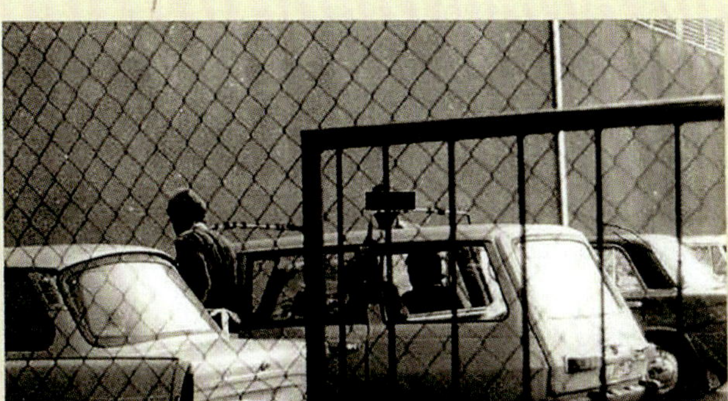

Bild 18

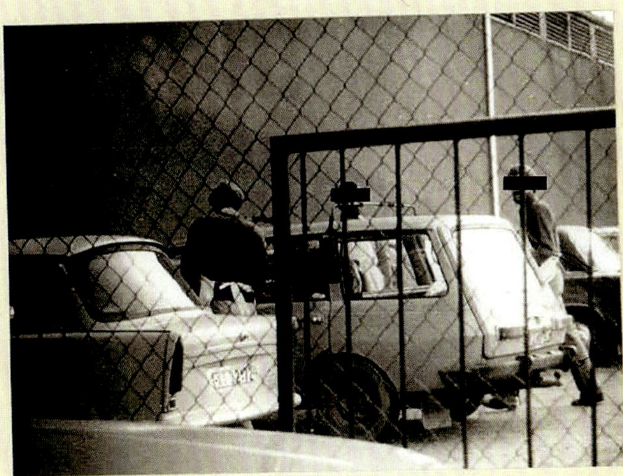

Bild 19

Danach setzten sie ihre Fahrt zur Bäckerei ■■■■■ fort und betraten diese.

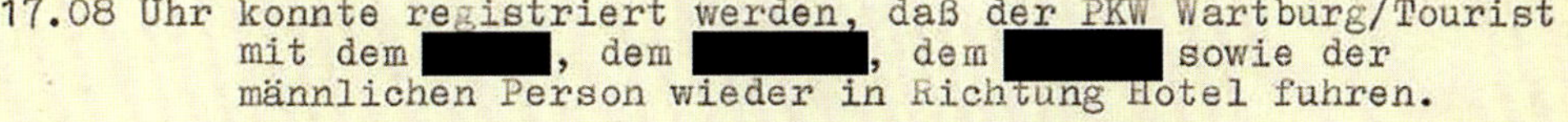

17.08 Uhr konnte registriert werden, daß der PKW Wartburg/Tourist mit dem ■■■■■, dem ■■■■■, dem ■■■■■ sowie der männlichen Person wieder in Richtung Hotel fuhren.

Bei einer Kontrolle am Hotel konnte gesehen werden, daß die o.g. vier Personen dieses betraten.

The Wartburg/Tourist vehicle was parked in the hotel parking lot. It was determined that some of the finished baked goods were located in the rear compartment of the vehicle.
Among these baked goods were muskets made of bread dough as well as several postcards made of roll dough bearing postage stamps and addresses.

In the hotel, they took seats in the foyer bar.

17:48 The seven male persons who were at the Bakery XXX also entered the hotel and took seats at the foyer bar.
There then developed a lively conversation which all persons participated in while consuming alcoholic beverages.
The following was able to be overheard:
"...it was invigorating work..."

"...and we were baking naked, wearing only an apron..."

"...an unbelievable amount of sweat due to the heavy physical effort as well as the dough..."

"...it was such an artistic connection..."

"...it was a real experience, and even though the result was satisfying, the dough took on a different shape than intended..."

"...the bakers totally followed their artistic ambitions and were really cooperative..."

"...we ate part of what we baked but some of it was determined to be inedible..."

"...we drank and ate a lot during the baking..."

In the time period from

18:15 to
18:30 all persons proceeded to their rooms with the elevator.

19:08 XXX, XXX, XXX, and XXX left the hotel with a Japanese cassette recorder and entered the Wartburg/Tourist vehicle.

Der PKW Wartburg/Tourist war auf dem Hotelparkplatz abgeparkt.
Es konnte festgestellt werden, daß im Fond des PKW einige der gefertigten Backwaren abgelegt waren. Hierbei handelte es sich unteranderen um eine aus Brotteig gebackene Muskete sowie um mehrere aus Semmelteig gebackene Postkarten auf denen die Briefmarken sowie Adressen angedeutet waren.

Im Hotel nahmen sie an der Foyer-Bar platz.

17.48 Uhr betraten die sieben männlichen Personen, welche beim Bäcker ██████ waren, ebenfalls das Hotel und platzierten sich an der Foyer-Bar.
Im weiteren Verlauf entwickelte sich eine angeregte Unterhaltung, an der sich alle Personen beteiligten und dabei alkoholische Getränke zu sich nahmen.

Hierbei konnten folgte Phasen mitgehört werden:
".... es war ein belebendes Arbeiten ....",

"... so haben wir nackt, nur mit einer Schürze bekleidet, gebacken ...",

"... eine unheimliche Schweißbildung durch die harte körperliche Beteiligung sowie des Brotteiges ..."

"... das war eine künstlerische Verbindung ..."

"... es war ein Erlebnis, trotz befriedigendem Ergebnis, aufgrund da sich der Brotteig anders verformt hat als gewünscht ..."

"... die Bäcker sind ihren künstlerischen Ambitionen voll gefolgt und sind richtig mitgegangen...",

"... ein Teil des Gebackenen haben wir gegessen, ein Teil wurde als ungenießbar erklärt ...",

"... beim Backen haben wir größere Mengen getrunken und viel gegessen ...".

In der Zeit von

18.15 Uhr bis

18.30 Uhr begaben sich alle Personen mit dem Fahrstuhl auf ihre Zimmer.

19.08 Uhr verließen der ██████ der ██████ der ██████ sowie der ██████ mit einem japanischen Stereokassettenrecorder das Hotel und nahmen im PKW Wartburg/Tourist platz.

They then drove to Fischergasse and entered the bowling alley

"Meisterhalle"

19:15 The wife of baker XXX

Name:	XXX
Date of birth:	XXX
Address:	XXX

drove with vehicle

Make/model:	XXX
Color:	XXX
License No.:	XXX

to the parking lot of the bowling alley, which she entered, carrying a number of objects.

19:25 She drove back in the direction of the city center.
She was not pursued.
Upon inspection, it was determined that the "Meisterhalle" was closed to the public on this day.
Through the window, however, the four known persons could be seen bowling and liberally partaking of alcohol (primarily beer).

Because the four persons had not departed the bowling alley by

22:30 and because no other persons could be identified here, surveillance was suspended both here and at the hotel.

<u>Oct. 6, 1980</u>

8:00 Surveillance of XXX was resumed at Hotel "Lindenhof" in Glauchau.
At this time, the only vehicles parked in the parking lot were the known VW Golf and the Trabant, license no. XXX.

Anschließend fuhren sie zur Fischergasse und betraten hier die Kegelbahn

"Meisterhalle".

19.15 Uhr fuhr die Ehefrau des Bäcker [redacted]

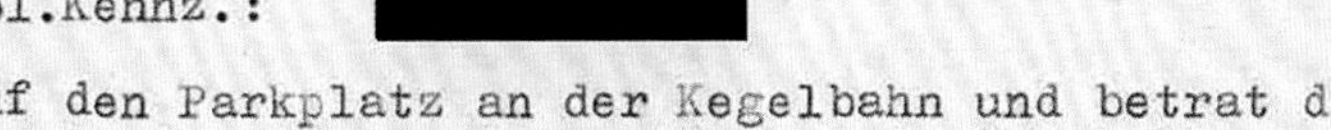

geb.:
geb.am,
wohnhaft:

mit dem PKW

Typ:
Farbe:
pol.Kennz.:

auf den Parkplatz an der Kegelbahn und betrat diese, wobei sie mehrere Gegenstände bei sich hatte.

19.25 Uhr fuhr sie in Richtung Stadtzentrum weiter.

Ihr wurde nicht gefolgt.

Bei einer Kontrolle konnte festgestellt werden, daß die "Meisterhalle" an diesen Tag für die Öffentlichkeit geschlossen hatte.
Durch die Fenster konnte jedoch gesehen werden, wie die vier bekannten Personen kegelten und dabei reichlich dem Alkohol (vorwiegend Bier) zusprachen.

Da bis

22.30 Uhr die vier Personen die Kegelbahn nicht verlassen hatten sowie keine weiteren Personen in dieser registriert werden konnten, wurde zu diesem Zeitpunkt hier sowie am Hotel die Beobachtung unterbrochen.

6.10.1980

8.00 Uhr wurde die Beobachtung des [redacted] am Hotel "Lindenhof" Glauchau weitergeführt.
Zu diesem Zeitpunkt parkten auf dem Hotelparkplatz nur der bereits bekannte PKW VW Golf sowie der Trabant, pol.Kennz. [redacted]

During an inspection of the bowling alley as well as the bakeries XXX and XXX as well as the in the city of Glauchau, the Wartburg/Tourist vehicle could no longer be located.

8:58 Dr.Werner, XXX, and three other male persons consumed breakfast in the hotel restaurant.

Upon inspection with the help of hotel records, the following persons were identified as having taken part in the group baking event. These persons are:

1.
Place/date of birth: XXX
Address: XXX
Employment: XXX

2.
Place/date of birth: XXX
Address: XXX
Employment: XXX

3.
Place/date of birth: XXX
Address: XXX
Employment: XXX

4.
Place/date of birth: XXX
Address: XXX
Employment: XXX

5.
Place/date of birth: XXX
Address: XXX
Employment: XXX

6.
Place/date of birth: XXX
Address: XXX
Employment: XXX

BStU
000118

113

16

Bei einer durchgeführten Kontrolle an der Kegelbahn sowie an den Bäckereien ████ und ████ sowie im Stadtgebiet von Glauchau konnte der PKW Wartburg/Tourist nicht mehr aufgenommen werden.

8.58 Uhr nahm der Dr. Werner, der ████ sowie drei weitere männliche Personen im Hotelrestaurant ein Frühstück zu sich.

Durch Überprüfungsmaßnahmen konnte an Hand der Hotelzimmerbelegungen nachfolgende Personen identifiziert werden, die sich am gemeinsamen Backen beteiligten. Bei diesen Personen handelt es sich um den:

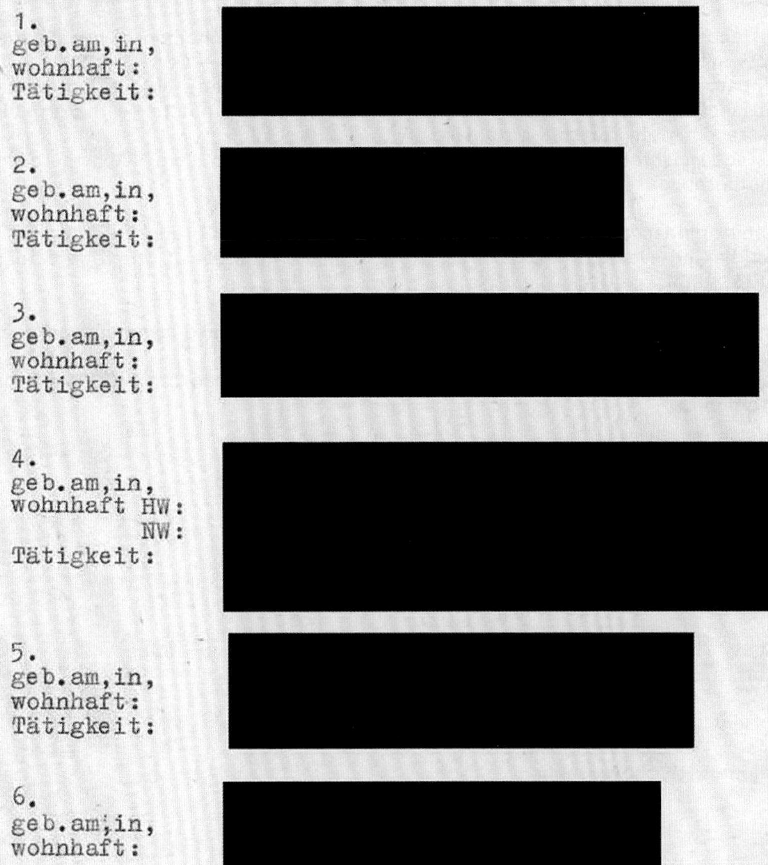

1.
geb.am,in,
wohnhaft:
Tätigkeit:

2.
geb.am,in,
wohnhaft:
Tätigkeit:

3.
geb.am,in,
wohnhaft:
Tätigkeit:

4.
geb.am,in,
wohnhaft HW:
NW:
Tätigkeit:

5.
geb.am,in,
wohnhaft:
Tätigkeit:

6.
geb.am,in,
wohnhaft:

9:15 All named persons departed the hotel with their luggage and proceeded to the hotel parking lot. They stored their luggage in the three vehicles. After all had said goodbye to one another and entered the vehicles, they drove away from the hotel parking lot in the direction of the freeway exit toward Glauchau.

As a result, surveillance was concluded.

A s s e s s m e n t

Surveillance measures were able to determine that the gathering of negative and hostile GDR artists took place in Glauchau from Oct. 4, 1980 – Oct. 6, 1980.
Taking part in this gathering were thirteen persons who were able to be identified.
Surveillance was able to determine that Dr.Werner turned out to be the organizer and person responsible for this gathering.
He was accompanied mainly by XXX, who was determined to have taken the corresponding photographs.

It was determined that the thirteen persons split into two groups and carried out the planned baking event at two bakeries in Glauchau, the staff of which were identified, on Oct. 5, 1980.

Outside the framework of the baking event, XXX did not make many appearances.

In the course of surveillance, no operative indications according to §§ 100, 106 could be determined.

Head of Section	Head of Department
[Signature]	[Signature]
Schnabel Captain	Schumann Major

Attachment

1 envelope with photographs

Translated from German by Brian Alkire

9.15 Uhr verließen alle genannten Personen mit ihrem Reisegepäck das Hotel und begaben sich auf den Hotelparkplatz. Hier verstauten sie in den drei PKW ihr Gepäck.
Nachdem sie sich alle von einander verabschiedet und in den Fahrzeugen platz genommen hatten, fuhren sie vom Hotelparkplatz in Richtung Autobahnauffahrt Glauchau.

Daraufhin wurde die Beobachtung beendet.

E i n s c h ä t z u n g

Durch die Beobachtungsmaßnahme konnte erarbeitet werden, daß das Treffen der negativ und feindlichen Kunstschaffenden der DDR in Glauchau in der Zeit vom 4.10.1980 - 6.10.1980 stattfand.
An diesem Treffen nahmen 13 Personen teil, die aufgeklärt werden konnten. Durch die beobachtungsführende Seite kann eingeschätzt werden, daß sich als Organisator und Verantwortlicher dieses Treffens sich der Dr. W e r n e r herauskristallisierte.
In seiner Begleitung befand sich vorwiegend der ██████████ wozu eingeschätzt wird, daß dieser die entsprechenden Fotos fertigte.

Es konnte erarbeitet werden, daß sich die 13 Personen in zwei Gruppen teilten und bei zwei Bäcker in Glauchau, die personell aufgeklärt werden konnten, am 5.10.1980 das geplante Backen durchführten.

Außerhalb des Backens trat der ██████████ nicht besonders in Erscheinung.
Im Verlaufe der Beobachtung konnten keine operativen Hinweise zu §§ 100,106 erarbeitet werden.

Leiter der Abteilung	Leiter des Referates
i.V. [signature]	[signature]
Schnabel	Schumann
Oberstleutnant	Major

Anlage

1 Kuvert mit Fotos

Gábor Altorjay, b. 1946 in Budapest, Hungary, lives and works in Berlin, Germany.
Tamás St. Turba (NETRAF-agent), b. 1944 in Fót, Hungary, lives and works in Budapest, Hungary.
Happening by Tamás Szentjóby (Tamás St. Turba [NETRAF-agent]) and Gábor Altorjay in cooperation with Miklós Jankovics and István Varannai supported by Enikő Balla, Miklós Erdély and Csaba Koncz

The Lunch (In Memoriam Batu Khan)

Tamás St. Turba (NETRAF-agent) / Gábor Altorjay

The first Hungarian happening took place on June 25, 1966 in the basement of a private house in Budapest—so, literally "underground." The audience had to walk through a garden where Szentjóby, who was buried up to his stomach in soil, typed on a typewriter. Behind this scene was a burning baby carriage. Once in the basement, an altered version of Krzysztof Penderecki's *Threnody for the Victims of Hiroshima* was droning, Szentjóby and Altorjay sat at a table, and a chicken was fastened in a pot. There followed a series of actions on multiple levels which Gábor Altorjay himself could no longer reconstruct: eating, vomiting, putting the chicken in a bag, throwing goose feathers, filling a condom with plaster ... In the video, the two people who smoke are informants of the State Security, as told to us by Szentjóby's voiceover. According to him, the consequences of this first happening are still "surprisingly present" today. Since 1966, the happening has had a cult character, especially in artist circles, although it is only in the last ten years that art historians have begun to reappraise it. (K)

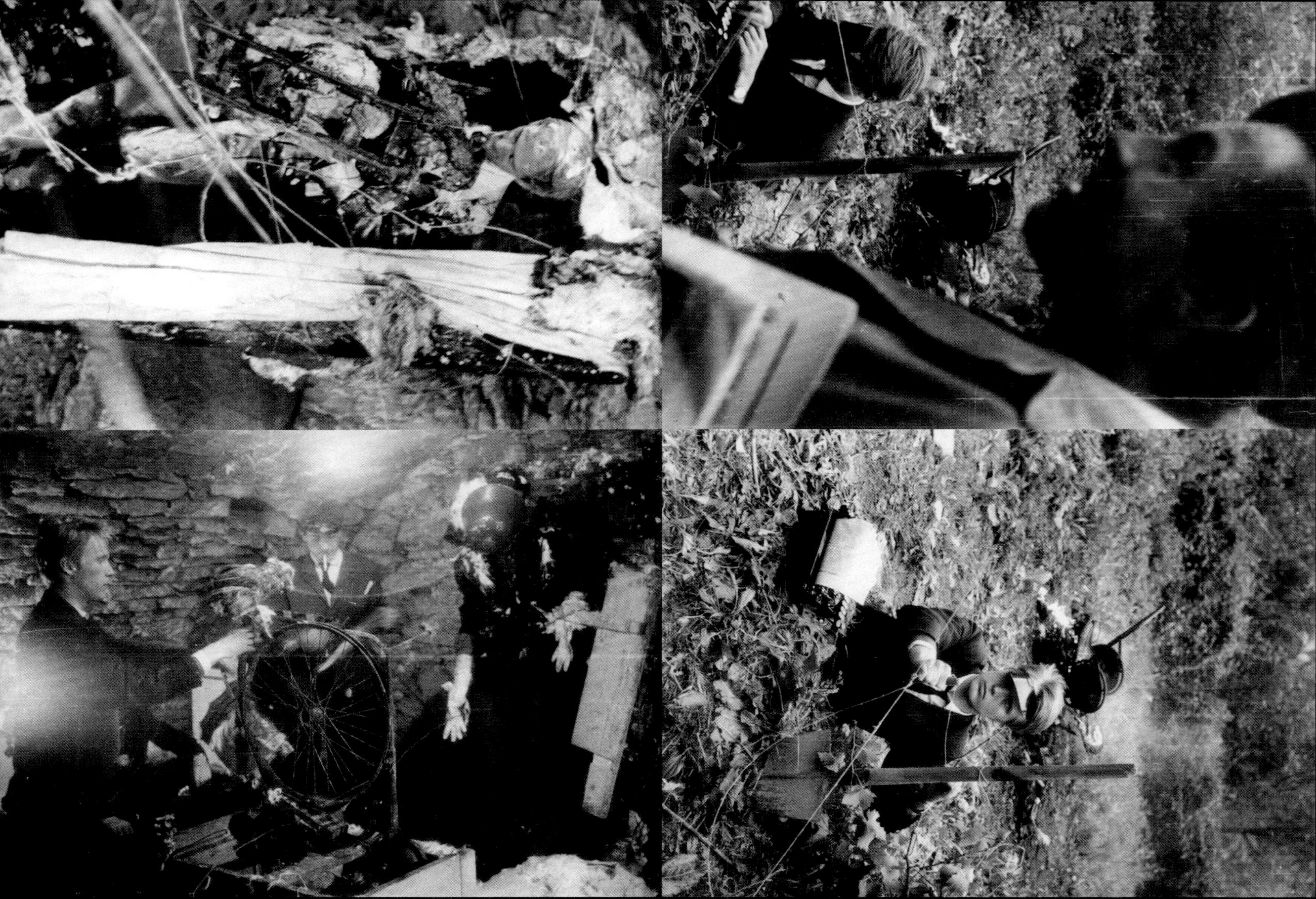

Tamás St. Turba, Gábor Altorjay

Documentations

Four b/w photographs, Photos by Gyula Zaránd, Courtesy: IPUT Archives, Budapest

1966

Video still, Super-8 film by László Gyémánt, with a voiceover by Tamás St. Turba (2013), Courtesy of IPUT Archives, Budapest

The "Mészáros," "László," and "Hajdu" Reports on *The Lunch (In Memoriam Batu Khan)*

BM (People's Republic of Hungary)

"Mészáros," "László," and "Hajdu" are the code names of three informants who all provided reports on the first happening in Hungary without being aware of each other's presence. From their reports we learn not just about a mysterious chicken but also about the audience. Who came? How did the audience react? We also learn which historical sources about happenings the Hungarian state security service at the BM used. Comparing the three reports, it becomes obvious how contradictory and fabricated the information is—one of the informants was not even present. We do not know anything about the actual happening from these reports—but what we do know is how the informants thought they should report on them so that the expectations of the state security are met, and the role and "importance" of the informants justified. Excerpts from these reports had indeed a long career within Hungarian state security: they were endlessly repeated in action plans and reports. Terms like "hostile," "nihilistic," "Western," and "anarchist" became markers through which state security classified happenings as a serious danger for socialist society—and then spent a decade surveilling, "disrupting," and "liquidating" them. (K)

BM. III. Departmental Directorate
III. Dept. Direct. 2/b. subdivision

Strictly confidential!

No. copies: 1
Submitted by: inf. n. "Mészáros T"
Received by: Pol. Lieut. János Krimmel
Date: July 1, 1966.

Subject: about the HAPPENING

Report

Budapest, July 1, 1966

The first happening in Hungary was advertised to start at 4:00 in the afternoon on June 25, 1966 at Hegyalja Road 20/b. Invitation cards were printed on a strict, named-invitee-only basis.

Before I get to an account of the facts, I should note that this concept is well known in certain circles, and thus the role of chance is more or less excluded. I must admit this at the outset because the entire background and spirit of this social phenomenon is such a fundamentally determined thing, that its aim to exclude all doubt and even its forms of appearance are not always explicit. The happening – although not under this name – has a rather long past, beginning with the gatherings of avant-gardist movements (e.g. Dadaism) in the thirties and ending with the activities of the school's direct founding father, Salvadore [*sic*] Dalí, which were an institutionalized variant of this pastime. Salvadore Dalí mostlyinvented this form of "entertainment" for business reasons, as ornamentation for his works, and of course, aimed at the propaganda around his person. It first became institutionalized in America. Happenings took place under this name and spread in Los Angeles, Greenwich Village, and other beatnik and hipster centers. Alan [*sic*] Ginsberg defined the aim of the happening as: "subjugation by the logic of a confused world, ... in other words when participants give up their illusory rights, which they believe can influence chance, and admit the fact of their absolute defenselessness right up until their own physical destruction."

I believe no further commentary is needed on how much this statement, whose platform is avowed nihilism and the "desire to shock," is required as a crisis phenomenon in order to stupefy the bourgeoisie and some sort of exaggerated decadence.

15. [handwritten]

BM. III. Főcsoportfőnökség
III. Csfség 2/b.alosztálya.

"Szigoruan titkos!"

1. sz. pld.

Adta: "Mészáros T" fn. inf.
Vette: Krimmel János r.fhdgy.
Idő: 1966. VII. 1.

Tárgy: HAPPENING-ről -

J e l e n t é s

Budapest, 1966. julius 1.

1966 junius 25-én délután négy órai kezdettel a Hegyalja ut 20/b. alatt meghirdették az első magyarországi happeninget. Meghivókat nyomtattak és szigoruan zártkörüre, névre szóló formában szervezték.

Mielőtt a tények ismertetésére rátérnék, meg kell jegyeznem, hogy bizonyos körökben ez a fogalom jól ismert és igy a véletlenség szerepe, majdnem kizárt. Ezt azért kellett előre bocsátanom, mert ennek a társadalmi jelenségnek egész háttere és szelleme annyira alapvetően determinált valami, hogy minden kétséget kizáró céljaival, mégha megjelenési formái olykor nem is egyértelmüek. A happening- jóllehet nem ezzel a névvel - elég nagy multra tekint vissza, kezdve a harmincas évek avantgardista mozgalmainak /pl. dadaizmus/ összejöveteleitől én befejezve az irányzat közvetlen szülőatyjának, Salvadore Dalinak megmozdulásain, amelynek intézményesitett változata ez az időtöltés. Salvadore Dali leginkább üzleti érdekből, alkotásai köritésére találta fel ezt a "szórakozást", no és persze személye körüli propaganda céljából. Elintézményesedni Amerikában intézményesedett el. Los Angeles, Greenwich Village és a beatnik és hipster központok más helyei a happening ezen a néven való megjelenésének és elterjedésének szinhelyei. Alan Ginsberg igy határozta meg a happening célját: "a zavaros világ logikájának való alávetettség... vagyis: a résztvevők lemondanak arról az illuzorikus jogukról, hogy a véletlen felett befolyást gyakoroljanak és beismerik tökéletes kiszolgáltatottságuk tényét egész a fizikai megsemmisülésig".

Azt hiszem nem kell bővebb kommentár, mennyire válságjelenségként a polgár elképesztésére és valamiféle tulhajtott dekadencia kiszolgálására kell ez a megnyilvánulás, amelynek programja a bevallott nihilizmus, a "megrendülés vágya".

- 2 -

The American variety, in its final phase, led to a deluge of violent acts, the mass enjoyment of narcotics, and open clashes with the police. This apart from the fact that they sometimes turned into pro-Cuba demonstrations, to the annoyance of the police and the authorities, because the aim and those who supported it could potentially be useful there [in Cuba]—although this is also doubtful. Their conviction is darkness and irrationalism, their religion is violence and hysteria.

István Szenes is the owner of Hegyalja Road 20/B.

/The next row is redacted/[1] Otherwise it started a little late, because nobody had been allowed near the event until the bulk of the guests had arrived. During this time, I saw, from among the old acquaintances, János Kenedi, János Streliczky, Ungvári, then Károly Doromby, Csaba [sic] Koncz, and the ten to twenty omnipresent snobs, whom I do not however personally know.

Finally the sign was given, and then we retreated to the back of the garden, where there was an entrance to a Tatar-era cellar. In front of the entrance, there was a figure typing, buried in a pit up to his armpits with a green shade on his head, and in the background, a baby carriage was set on fire with gasoline. Some of the steps leading down to the cellar had been removed, yet there was no lighting. Only once we reached the cellar, in semi darkness, was there any form of lighting. Presently however, every light went out and it was completely dark for approx. fifteen minutes. In the darkness, Stockhausen's electronic musical piece "Victory" (*Gyozelem*) suddenly came on. This is pretty much effect-music, meaning that its first movement is a recording of air raid noises mixed with snatches of incoherent (French) dialogue by people in a shelter, buried under the earth. Then there were echoes of electronic noises followed by some sort of music. Finally, a human voice spoke again. Here only the first two movements of the work were heard. Afterwards the light went on again. At the back of the venue there was some neglected part of the space where a kitchen table stood, with two people sitting next to it and a third person doing something in the background. In the right-hand corner, a grandfather clock mounted in a rusty wheel of a bicycle hang, its revolving arms moving around the axis. The backdrop ended with a door frame. When the lights came on, they poured potato stew out of a metal bowl and started eating, throwing the metal pots onto the ground. They occasionally belched loudly, which was amplified for the room by the microphone on echo. At the end of the lunch, they brought out a large nylon bag, into which one actor vomited the lunch back up. Meanwhile the third person was continuously occupied with a hen tied to a red pot.

After the vomiting, various articles appeared from an old, worn fridge standing in the background. The first was a black handbag which they gave to the audience; it contained white mice. Then came hammers with which they broke the plates, and then the table and the chairs. The broken pieces [of the plates]

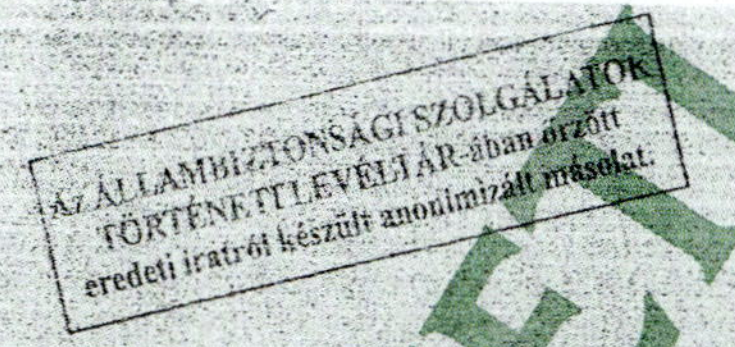

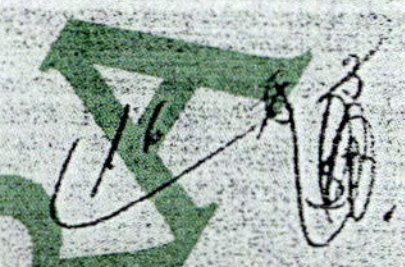

Amerikai válfaja végső stádiumában erőszakos cselekedtek özönéhez, tömeges kábitószerélvezethez, a rendőrséggel való nyilt megütközésekhez vezetett. Ezt nem befolyásolja az a tény, hogy időnként a rendőrség és a hatóságok bosszantására Kuba-párti tüntetést is létrehoztak belőle, mert a cél és a mögötte csoportosulók lehetnek esetleg hasznosak ott - bár ez is kétséges, - de meggyőződésük a sötétség az irracionalizmus, vallásuk az erőszak és a hisztéria.

A Hegyalja ut 20/B Szenes István tulajdona,

Egyébként kis késéssel kezdődött, mert mindaddig, nem engedtek az esemény közelébe, amig össze nem gyült a vendégek zöme. Ez alatt az idő alatt régebbi ismerősök közül Kenedi Jánost, Streliczky Jánost, Ungvárit, majd Dorømby Károlyt, Koncz Csabát és tizhusz mindenütt jelenlevő sznobot láttam, akik azonban személy szerint nem ismerőseim.

Végül jelt adtak és ekkor hátravonultunk a kert tulsó részébe. Itt volt egy tatárkori pince lejárata. A lejárat előtt egy gödörben hónaljig eltemetve, fején zöld ellenzővel gépelt egy figura, háttérben egy benzinnel leöntött gyermekkocsi lángolt. A pincébe vezető lépcsőkből néhányat kiszedtek, világitás pedig nem volt. Csak amikor leértünk, a félhomályban akkor világitott egy és más. Kisvártatva azonban minden fény kialudt és kb. tizenöt percig teljes sötétség volt. A sötétben váratlanul hangzott fel Stockhausen "Győzelem" cimü elektronikus zeneszáma. Ez egy meglehetősen effekt-zene, vagyis első tétele egy légitámadás zajainak hangfelvétele, amibe zavaros szöveg vegyül /franciául/ egy óvóhelyen lévő társaság szövegfoszlányai, akiket betemetett a föld. Utána elektromos zajokból szerelt visszhangok, majd valami zeneszerüség következnek. Végül ismét egy emberi hang szólal meg. Itt csak a mü első két tétele hangzott el. Utána felgyulladt a villany. A helyiség hátterében valami kihagyott rész volt. Itt egy konyhaasztal állt, mellette ketten ültek, a harmadik személy a háttérben tevékenykedett. A jobb sarokban egy kerékpár rozsdás kerekébe szerelt ütőóra lógott, amely egyre körbejáró mutatókkal a tengelye körül forgott. A hátteret egy ajtókeret zárta le. A villany felgyulladásakor csajkákból kitöltötték a paprikáskrumplit és enni kezdtek, a csajkákat ledobálták a földre. Időközönként nagyokat böffentettek, amit a visszhangositott mikrofon felerősitett a terem számára. Az ebéd végeztével egy nagy nejlonzacskót huztak elő, amelybe az egyik visszahányta az ebédjét. A harmadik személy ez alatt megállás nélkül egy piros fazékhoz kötözött tyukkal tevékenykedett.

A hányás után egy ócska jégszekrényből, amely a háttérben állt különféle tárgyak kerültek elő. Először egy fekete retikül, amit a közönségnek adtak és amelyben fehér egerek voltak. Utána kalapácsok, amellyel össztörték előbb a tányérokat, majd az asztalt és a székeket. A darabokat madzagon were distributed with twine all around the room. Meanwhile, the second actor tied the third one to the door frame, and then they mixed lime and water on a plate and poured it over his clothing before smearing him with a tube of toothpaste. Meanwhile the first finished with the hanging up stuff and then joined the third: he covered his face with a combat helmet and threw the feathers from a torn-up eiderdown over him. He threw the rest of the feathers at the audience. Then they took out a rubber prophylactic and filled it with some red goo, hung it up, and lit a candle beneath it. They switched on the cassette recorder again, which played a distorted Twentieth Symphony. Meanwhile they continued to rub more goo onto the one attached to the door. Then they got to work on the ruins and improvised some botched op-art, and put the chicken tied to a pot on the top, which naturally fell off head over heels. Then the second figure got to work again systematically tying the whole room up with twine, like a spider's web. Once it was hardly possible to move any more in the room, so that nobody could escape from the tensed cords, he returned to the center and smashed the light bulb.

I left for my part while it was dark. Dr.Végh arrived during the performance with two acquaintances and a girl called Gladys (I do not know her real name). She graduated from the Fine and Applied Arts Grammar School in 1965 (and a blonde bearded young man wearing a high-wind anorak). They attempted to join in by throwing stars and setting light to wastepaper, but because they didn't attract enough attention, they left. Végh said as he was leaving that he would organize an anti happening, because he doesn't like people bringing a system to anarchy. He, for example, would now like to take a shit in public.

I left with some others at the exit. At the villa, we tried to somehow remove the dirt stuck on our clothes, when István Ventilla popped up (late) and was very sorry he wasn't able to make it.

Otherwise, I forgot to mention at the start that they collected a ten-forint entry fee right at the beginning, before they let you down into the cellar. There must have been 50 - 70 people in the cellar, as far as one could see in the bad light. Otherwise, many people had brought cameras, even film cameras, but I don't think it was possible to record anything in that lighting, even with ultra-rapid film.

“Mészáros Tibor”

Evaluation: The report is valuable from an operative standpoint. It mirrors a new phenomenon which is starting to spread among youth circles in Hungary under Western influence.

In the future, they plan to hold more “happenings” described in the report and expand on them.

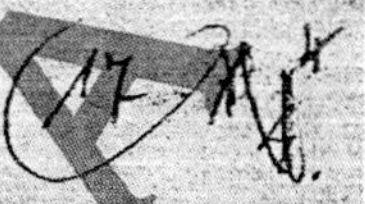

szétszaggatták a terem minden részébe. Közben a harmadikat a második odakötözte az ajtókerethez, utána egy tálban meszet és vizet kevert és leöntötte vele a ruháját, majd egy tubus fogkrémet is rákent. Az első közben elkészült az aggatással és bekapcsolódott a harmadik dolgába: ő egy rohamsisakkal elfedte az arcát, majd egy széttépett dunnából tollat zuditott rá. A többi tollat a közönséghez vágta. Utána elővettek egy gumi óvszert és valami vörös ragaccsal töltötték tele és felakasztották, alája egy gyertyát gyujtottak. A magnót is bekapcsolták ismét, az eltorzitva a XX. szinfoniát játszotta. Közben ujabb ragacsokkal tovább kenegették az ajtóhoz kötözöttet. Utána a romokon nekiálltak és összetákoltak egy op-art tákolmányt, a tetejére odatették a tyukot a lábára kötözött lábassal. Az persze leesett és fejjel lefelé kalimpált. Utána a második alak ismét nekiállt és madzaggal szisztematikusan át-meg átkötözte az egész termet, pókhálószerüen. Mikor már alig lehetett volna megmozdulni a teremben, hogy el ne bukjon valaki a kifeszitett kötelekben, visszament a középre és szétütötte a villanykörtét.

A sötétben részemről távoztam. Egyébként már az előadás folyamán megjelent dr. Végh is két ismerősével egy Gladys nevü lánnyal /nem tudom a valódi nevét/. Egyébként 1965-ben végzett a Képző- és Iparmüvészeti Gimnáziumban/ és egy orkán-anorákos szőke körszakállt viselő fiatalemberrel. Megkisérelték bekapcsolódni a cselekménybe, csillagszóróval és a papirszemét felgyujtásával, de mert nem keltettek elég feltünést, elmentek. Végh kijelentette távozóban, hogy ő anti-happeninget fog rendezni, mert nem szereti, ha valaki rendszert visz az anarchiába. Ő például most nyilvánosan szarni szeretne.

A kijáratnál többek társaságában mentem el. A villánál még igyekeztünk valahogy letisztitani a piszkot, ami a ruhánkra ragadt, amikor - késve - felbukkant Ventilla István is, és nagyon sajnálta, hogy nem lehetett jelen.

Egyébként az elején elfelejtettem mondani, hogy 10 Ft.- belépti dijat szedtek a kezdet kezdetén, mielőtt hátraengedtek a pincéhez. A pincében 50-70 személy lehetett jelen, amennyire a rossz világitásban látni lehetett. Egyébként többen hoztak fényképezőgépet, sőt kamerát is, de szerintem még ultrarapid filmmel sem lehetett volna semmit kihozni abból a világitásból.

"Mészáros Tibor"

Értékelés: A jelentés operativ szempontból értékes. Uj jelzést tükröz, ami az ifjuság körében Magyarországon is kezd elterjedni a nyugati behatás alapján.

A jövőben több esetben szándékoznak a jelentésben szereplő módon, illetve azt kibővitve "happening"-et tartani.

The persons mentioned in the report are usually university students, or college students, or graduates.

Measures: Via informants we will uncover the intellectual drivers behind the group and what kind of conceptual impulse the gatherings have.

Task: The inf. has been instructed to maintain further contact with the group's leaders.

Pol. Lieut. János Krimmel[2]

Prepared: KJ/M
No. copies: 2
To: CC: Copy no. 1 papka
Copy no. 2 táj.
Reg.Nr.: 2/7–36

Translated from Hungarian by Gwen Jones

Endnotes

1 Translator's note: Here and in other places: /redacted/ means that the relevant passage on the basis of §25/G of Act XXIII. of 1994 was anonymized.

2 Translator's note: The < entries on this page are illegible.

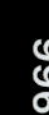

A jelentésben szereplő személyek általában egyetemisták, vagy főiskolát, vagy egyetemet végzett személyek.

Intézkedés: Az informátoron keresztül felderitjük a csoport szellemi mozgatóit és hogy az összejöveteleket milyen eszmei sugalatra rendezik.

Feladat: Az inf. feladatul kapta, hogy a csoport vezetőivel tartsa továbbra is a kapcsolatot.

/:Krimmel János r.fhdgy.:/

Készitette: KJ/M.
Készült: 2 pld.
Kapja: 1 sz. pld. papka
2 sz. pld. táj.
Nyt.sz.: 2/7-36.

Krimmel elvt.,

A jelentésben szereplő személyeket pontosítani kell.

[redacted] altgy.-val egyeztetten intézkedjék

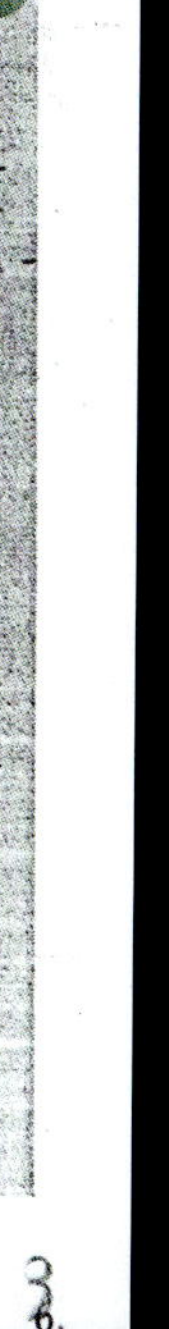

BM. III. Head Departmental Directorate
III. Dept. Direct. 2/b. subdivision

Strictly confidential!

No. copies: 1

Submitted by: a. n. "László"
Received by: Pol. Capt. Tipold
Date: July 22, 1966.

Subject: First Heppening [*sic*] party

Report

Budapest, July 22, 1966

An acquaintance of mine visited Balatonfüred in the first week of July. There he met László Benke and Tibor Sörös; both of whom are members of the Perlaky group of friends in Budapest. Even they were already talking a lot about the "Happening" gathering on July 2. This was held in the Buda Castle in a cellar, so they said, /a part of the sentence is redacted/[1] more than one hundred Pest intellectuals were invited, with a printed invitation to the "First Happening in Hungary." Among them were the film director János Herskó, Sándor Weöres, János Pilinszky, István Ventalin, the editor of "Vigilia" Károly Doromby, etc. At first, they wanted to hold it in Károly Doromby's apartment, but Doromby did not give permission. Most of the invitees attended: around sixty people.

/two rows redacted/

The show began in the complete darkness of the cellar. Among other things, they gave a chicken an enema, and the sound effects were transmitted through enormous electrical amplifiers into loudspeakers, so even the weakest sound had an impact like a thunderclap. The audience was fascinated by these never-before-seen phenomena. /one and a half rows redacted/ Meanwhile a piece of music called "Hiroshima" was heard from the loudspeakers. Over the course of the evening, a few other similar curiosities were presented.

/two rows redacted/

Essentially, viewers could witness new, shocking, never-before-seen spectacles. The whole phenomenon was analogous to going to church or the theater, in which the important thing is the shared experience.

/two rows redacted/

The "happening" is a regular form of entertainment in the West and has also been popular for years in Poland. /The first part of the sentence redacted/ why comrade Aczél did not like it. The news that the deputy minister was also concerned with the matter was brought by László Benke.

13 ~~16~~ 8.

BM. III. Főcsoportfőnökség
III.Csfség 2/b.alosztálya.

"Szigoruan titkos!"
1.. sz. pld.

Adta: "László" fn. u.
Vette: Tipold r.szds.
Idő: 1966. VII. 22.

Tárgy: I. Heppening partyról.

Jelentés

Budapest, 1966. julius 22.

Julius első hetében egyik ismerősöm Balatonfüreden járt. Itt találkozott Benke Lászlóval és Sörös Tiborral; mindketten a Perlaky-féle belvárosi társaság tagjai. Már ők is sokat meséltek a julius 2-án rendezett "Happening"-szerü összejövetelről. Ez a budai Várban, egy pincehelyiségben került megrendezésre, ugy mondták,

több mint száz pesti értelmiségit hivtak meg, nyomtatott meghivóval az "Első magyarországi Happening"-re. Közöttük Herskó János filmrendezőt, Weöres Sándort, Pilinszky Jánost, Ventalin Istvánt, Dorombi Károlyt, a "Vigilia" szerkesztőjét, stb. Először Doromby Károly lakásán akarták megrendezni, Doromby azonban nem engedte meg. A meghivottak nagyobbik része megjelent: kb. 60 személy.

A pincében teljes sötétségben kezdődött el a müsor. Többek között beöntést adtak egy csirkének, s a hang-effektusokat hatalmas elektromos erősitők közvetitették hangszórókba, igy a leggyengébb hang is égzengésként hatott. A közönség lenyügzően figyelte ezeket a soha nem látott jelenségeket.

Közben a hangszórókból egy "Hirosima" nevü zenemü hallatszott. Az est folyamán még néhány hasonló furcsaságot mutattak be.

A lényege az, hogy uj, megdöbbentő, soha még nem látott látványokban részesitik a nézőket. Az egész jelenség rokon a templommal és a szinházzal, fontossága a közös élmény.

A "happening" rendszeres szórakozásforma Nyugaton

ÁBTL -3.1.9. - V - 156455. /53

/redacted passage/

Many people from Pest and the inner city were present at Balatonfüred. Most of them stayed at Szabolcs Bognár and Tas Bognár's house. Also present were the photographer Csaba Konc [*sic*], and Péter Szalay, Elek Straub, Benke as well as Sörös, who were working as waiters and will be at Balatonfüred for the whole summer. All of them were talking about the international campsite meeting a lot. The two Bognár brothers play in the café guitar band "Kedves" (Dear). The familiar Pest types who come to Balaton come here first for a shorter or longer amount of time, and also go to Alsóörs, where the band "Omega" is playing.

"László"

Note: The first Happening party in Hungary was not among the agent's tasks.

Evaluation: The report is valuable. It describes a new direction of events in Hungary. Its essence is the audience witnessing unexpected, never-before-seen, thrilling experiences for the first time. Shortly after this we can report the attendance of intellectuals – writers, artists, etc., and young people.

Measures: Collecting material on participants. Observation.

Task: Agent received none because of his trip to Poland.

[signed]
Pol. Capt. Ferenc Tipold

Prepared: TF/M
No. copies: 3
To: Copy no. 1 papka
Copy no. 2 M. dossier
Copy no. 3 táj.
Registration Nr.: 2-7/140.

Translated from Hungarian Gwen Jones

Endnotes

1 Translator's note: Here and in other places: /redacted/ means that the relevant passage on the basis of §25/G of Act XXIII. of 1994 was anonymized.
2 Translator's note: This refers to the Hungarian art historian László Beke.

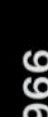

és évek óta már Lengyelországban is. Aczél elvtársnak miért nem tetszett. /Ezt a hirt, hogy a miniszterhelyettes is foglalkozik az üggyel, Benke László hozta/.

Balatonfüreden sok pesti és belvárosi személy is megfordul. Többnyire Bognár Szabolcs és Bognár Tas házában szállnak meg. Itt volt most még Konc Csaba fotós, Szalay Péter, Straub Elek, Benke és Sörös pincéri állást vállaltak és egész nyáron Balatonfüreden lesznek. Valamennyien sokat emlegetik a nemzetközi camping-találkozót. A két Bognár testvér a "Kedves" espressó gitár-zenekarában játszik. A Balatonra jövő ismerős pestiek elsőnek ide jönnek hosszabb-rövidebb időre és Alsóörsre is, ahol a "Omega" zenekar játszik.

"László"

Megjegyzés: Az ü. feladatán kivül jelent az I. magyarországi Happening partyról.

Értékelés: A jelentés értékes. Egy uj irányzat magyarországi megjelenéséről számol be. Lényege a közönségnek váratlan, soha nem látott, megragadó élményben, ujban való részesitése. Rövidesen ezt követően megjelenésével az értelmiségi - irók, müvészek, stb. fiatalok között számolhatunk be.

Intézkedés: Szereplő személyek anyagainak összegyüjtése. Ellenőrzés.

Feladat: Az ü. lengyelországi utja miatt nem kapott.

/:Tipold Ferenc r.szds.:/

Készitette: TF/M
Készült: 3 pld.
Kapja: 1 sz. pld. papka
2 sz. " M.dosszié
3 sz. " táj.
Nyt.sz.: 2/7-140.

Interior Ministry
III/III/2-a sub-division

Strictly confidential!

Submitted by: "Hajdu"
Received by: Pol. Maj. Jenő Frigyik
Date: July 30, 1966
Subject: [redacted]

No. copies: 1

R e p o r t

Budapest, August 4, 1966

"Hajdu" reports:

/blackened passage/

According to the first plan, the site of the happening would have been in the Buda villa of Károly D o r o m b y, the editor of *Vigilia*. Doromby was allegedly enthusiastic about the idea, but then said no. On the one hand, it worried him that his neighbour was Sándor Gáspár,

and that there was a permanent police guard there. On the other hand, his daughter had gone to inquire at the local police station, where she was told by the chief that they could do what they want. At the same time, he made it clear that they knew about the earlier events, and also mentioned a house party in February. Doromby and his family took fright. The next candidate was the painter László Gyémánt. At this point, there was also talk of filming the event. Gyémánt however "grew very ill."

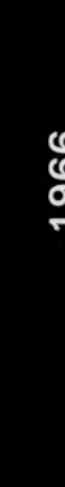
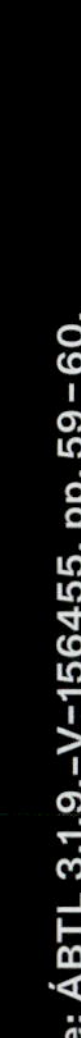

Belügyminisztérium
III/III/2-a. alosztály.

Szigorúan titkos!

Adta: "Hajdu"
Vette: Frigyik Jenő r. órgy.
1966. július 3o.

Tárgy:

.1. sz.pld.

ÁBTL -3.1.9. - V - 156455 /59

J e l e n t é s
Budapest, 1966. augusztus 4.

"Hajdu" jelenti:

Első elgondolás szerint a happening helyszine D o r o m b y Károly, a Vigilia szerkesztőjének budai villájában lett volna. Doromby állitólag lelkesedett az ötletért, de aztán mégis nemet mondott. Egyrészt aggasztotta őt, hogy szomszédja: Gáspár Sándor, és ott állandóan rendőr posztol. Másrészt lánya bement a ker. kapitányságra érdeklődni. Ott azt mondta neki a kapitányság vezetője, hogy azt csinálnak amit akarnak, ugyanakkor éreztette, hogy tudnak a korábbi rendezvényekről, igy egy februári házibulit meg is emlitett. Dorombyék megijedtek. A következő jelölt G y é m á n t László festő volt. Akkor még arról is szó volt, hogy filmezéssel kötik össze az eseményt. Gyémánt azonban "sulyosan megbetegedett".

A happening napján azonban olyan itéletidő volt, hogy nem hihettem a megtartásában. Igy nem mentem el az eseményre, ahol a kb. 15o meghivott közül csak kb. 5o jelent meg. Nem jöttek el a meghivott nagy irók: Weöres Sándor, Pilinszky János, Hamvas Béla, Szentkuthy Miklós, Passuth lánya, Passuth Krisztina művészettörténész megjelent.

./.

2-829 42-701

97.

/redacted passage/

On the day of the happening, the weather was so terrible I did not believe it would be held. This is why I did not go to the event, where [redacted phrase] only around fifty people attended out of around 150 invitees. The great writers invited did not attend: Sándor Weöres, János Pilinszky, Béla Hamvas, Miklós Szentkuthy. Passuth's daughter, the art historian Krisztina Passuth, attended.

/redacted passage/

The physician Dr.László V é g h was so "incited" by the happening taking place that he decided to hold a counterhappening.I do not know the invitees, but they were from the Petrigalla-Végh group of friends and artistic circles. From among my acquaintances, I know that Sándor Molnár the abstract painter had been invited.

/redacted passage/

I do not know much about how the happening took place. /redacted row/ A cat's tail was attached to the machine with a cord, which reached a painted pot. Honey was poured slowly out of a girl's shoe that they had spontaneously removed. The audience was sprinkled with water. I don't want to talk about the carved-up chicken, because even the thought of it makes me want to be sick.

In the background a baby carriage burned slowly.

"Hajdu"

Note: "Hajdu" was ordered to write the report.

Evaluation: The report is valuable. It concurs with a report by another agent on the subject.

Task: To be received after speaking to comrade Tipold, since they are dealing with the matter.

[signed]
Pol. Maj. Jenő Frigyik

Registration No.: 2 - 6/151
Prepared: 3 copies
2 pp.
To: C. Tipold
táj
"M." dossier
Zné

Translated from Hungarian by Gwen Jones

Endnotes
1 Translator's note: Sándor Gáspár (1917 - 2002) was a Hungarian communist politician.
2 Translator's note: Here and in other places: /redacted/ means that the relevant passage on the basis of §25/G of Act XXIII. of 1994 was anonymized.

dr. V é g h László orvost annyira "feltüzelte" a happening megtartása, hogy ellen-happening megtartását határozta el.

A meghivottakat nem ismerem, azonban ezek a Petrigalla-Végh társaságból, valamint müvészkörökből kerültek ki. Ismerőseim közül Molnár Sándor absztrakt festőről tudom azt, hogy meghivták.

Magáról a happening lefolyásáról nem sokat tudok. A géphez egy zsinórral egy macska farka volt hozzákötve, amelyik egy festékes edénybe ért. Egy lánynak a cipőjéből, amit spontánul huztak le, mézet csurgattak. Vizzel locsolták le a közönséget. A feltrancsirozott csirkéről nem akarok beszélni, mert már a gondolatára elhányom magam.

A háttérben egy babakocsi égett lassu tüzzel."

"Hajdu"

Megjegyzés: "Hajdu" utasitásra irta a jelentést.

Értékelés: A jelentés értékes. Megegyezik az e tárgyban kapott másik ügynök jelentésével.

Feladat: Tipold elvtárssal való megbeszélés után kap, mivel ők foglalkoznak az üggyel.

Frigyik Jenő r. őrgy.

Nyt.sz: 2-6/151.
Készült: 3 pld.
2 old.
Kapja: Tipold e.
táj.
"M" d.
Zné.

ÁBTL -3.1.9. - V - 156455 /60

Traces of Performance Art Events in the Archives of the Former Securitate:

Two Case Studies from Transylvanian Artistic Networks[1]

Mădălina Brașoveanu

Introduction: Premises and Dilemmas

I think that this study's first question, which is awaiting clarification, is how and why a historical research about recent art from the 1980s, created by certain artistic communities from Romania, comes to look for sources in the archives of the former Securitate.[2] The answer requires a more detailed treatment.

In Târgu Mureş, a self-titled "artistic society" called MAMŰ,[3] or the Atelier Circle, functioned as early as the end of the 1970s and until the mid-80s as an unofficial group of artists formed on the basis of a program with membership rules, stable participants, and invited members and supporters.[4] In the case of several artists, the composition of the group overlapped with that of the Youth Circle of the Union of Plastic Artists of Târgu Mureşi, but these structures were not interchangeable.

Moreover, MAMŰ was configured as an attempt to establish an alternative institutional structure to the existing ones, which were criticized for being limited to traditional forms of art and pushing official ideology. Within MAMŰ, the artists discussed, theorized, and encouraged forms of conceptual art, interventions in nature, art of collective or individual action, but also abstraction in painting or mail art.

The group's exhibitions were held in a space independent of the Union of Plastic Artists— namely in the lobby of Studio Theater in Târgu Mureş. They needed, like any other public cultural form of the period, the permission from the local Committee for Socialist Culture and Education. Indeed, they received these permissions until a certain moment, when the impossibility of exhibiting here, along with other personal factors, led to the massive emigration of the young artists. The group's meetings and the recurring place of their actions and interventions were the "wet hills" (*vizeshalmok*), located in nature near the city.

The activity of this artistic community, as well as those of Oradea, Cluj, and St. Gheorghe (George) with which MAMŰ maintained contact, can only be documented from the artists' private archives, at least the ones which still exist and are preserved adequately. The main argument for accessing the collection in the National Council of the Study of Security Archives (CNSAS) comes from an absence of any documentary resources: both in terms of what's been produced by the period's cultural institutions as well as the lack of records showing the existence of these artistic communities and their interactions with communist organizations.

My interest in this category of documents was mainly due to a desire to recover the official discourse, i.e. the arguments and techniques by which the bureaucracy of the socialist state appropriated some avant-garde cultural forms by instrumentalizing them ideologically, whereas these same forms were repressed by the same ideology in other contexts or in other artistic centers of the country. Assuming that such a category of documents—reports, situations, assessments, statements—had a high status of importance in their respective administration, but finding nothing of the kind in the public archives,[5] I sensed that in the archives of the former political police, I could identify some clues about the real connections that existed between the activity of the studied artists and the institutions of censorship.

If these were, broadly speaking, the arguments and the starting questions of the research in the CNSAS archive, some remained at least partially unanswered. However, as the number of accessed documents multiplied, they generated a whole branch of methodological queries and new puzzles. Firstly, they spurred questions starting from the premise that there is no such thing as an innocent archive that guarantees to harbor an objective and unaltered historical truth or an image of the past "as it happened," which creates complications when it comes to the archives of the former political police.

Like any other archive, it also has a reason for having been created, one that ultimately derives from its status as an instrument for exercising a power function.[6] This status, combined with the former totalitarian political regime, gives the documents a double function. On the one hand, it is directly utilitarian in terms of orchestrating the desired total control of the social spheres, and on the other, it arouses a mythologizing public perception, punctuated by exaggerations and prejudices at times. The documents produced by the secret service—in this case, the Securitate—are not only not designed to transmit historical information, but in many cases, they do not even speak for themselves. Instead, they can mislead or even lie.[7] For a political police force that was serving a power whose stability heavily depended on the management of its fictional constructions of reality, both to the outside world and to its direct witnesses, the problem of manipulating truth acquires an ontological dimension. The social perception of these sources, always marked by a tendency to mythologize, may result in an artificial, symbolic transfer on the documents: they may be given a disproportionate meaning only because they were created and kept under the status of "strictly secret."

This fact in itself has special implications for the archives' historiographic recovery and perhaps sometimes even more so in the eventuality of an exhibition. In the academic context, there is a discursive space for interrogating and analyzing the symbolic changes in the status of some documents based on the modifications in their preservation register. This includes the types of narratives that these documents create when correlated with each other (as archival presence) as well as with the outside (from the private collections of the artists to their oral histories). There is room, in other words, to comment on the historiographical relevance of these sources and the possible mnemonic functions they can support.

By displaying them in a documentary exhibition, perhaps the greatest risk the curator faces is that of monumentalization arising from this new change in their dissemination register—from "strictly secret" to public—and from the less transparent chain of circumstances which led these particular documents, and not others, to be created and preserved in this archive. Last but not least, an additional risk arises from the very selection of the exhibited documents and their organization, one that does not mirror the (dis)order of the archive, but a reconfiguration of it guided by the researcher's interests.[8]

MAMŰ Group –
Multimedia Birthday Action, 1982

The secret police file on the artist Károly Elekes was opened on August 12, 1982 in Mureş (county of which Târgu Mureş is the capital), due to suspicions regarding his links with what the Securitate code-named the "Poarta case/action." The "Poarta case" consisted of the appearance of some "unwritten" inscriptions in the public space of Târgu Mureş, referring to Károly Király,[9] more precisely a stamp with the text "Király Károly az üstökös" (Károly Király comet).[10] It had been applied to some posters of the local theater appearing in several areas of the city. Surveilled informationally since 1978, the time of the launch of the "Poarta case," Elekes's file dates to three years later, adding to the initial suspicions against him of "nationalist-chauvinist demonstrations, likely to protest."[11]

On July 17, 1982, the artists Károly Elekes and Árpád Nagy (Pika), both participating in the nucleus of the MAMŰ group, decided to organize a celebration of their common birthday at Nagy's house near Târgu Mureş. In preparation for the respective party, they sent out written invitations to their friends in Romania and Hungary. Some also confirmed their attendance in writing.

The event itself, as well as its preparations, provoked great interest among the officers involved in the Elekes case. It offered them the opportunity to set up a database containing the "network" of artists' close relations—the names gathered there being exclusively artists or art professionals—as well as the chance to closely observe and document photographically what seemed to be, of course, a meeting that had great potential for their security work.

The drawing up of the lists with the contacts of the "Ervin target"—the pseudonym under which Károly Elekes was pursued—was based on data obtained from the intercepted correspondence, all those to whom the artists had sent invitations. Thus: from Cluj, there is the artist Sándor Alexandu Antik; from Oradea, the artists Ioan Bunus and György Jovián; from St. Gheorghe/George, the artist Imre Baász; and from Bucharest, the artists Zoltán Szilágyi, András Butak, Wanda Mihuleac, Lili Mathe, and the art critic Mihai Drişcu. Among his friends in Hungary, are the artist Gábor Szörtsey and the art critic Bálint Chikán.[12] The text of the invitation, which is identical on three copies in the file, said: "We invite you to Nagy Árpád's and Elekes Károly's birthday. An alternative evening is being held on July 17th. We are waiting for you with fertilized thoughts, on Horizon Street, number 20." [trad. n.]

In a study note from July 15th, where the suspicions—nationalist-chauvinist protests which led to Elekes being pursued—are repeated summarily, the holographic inscription of an officer explicitly mentions the necessity of "controlling this meeting with all the means of security work."[13] The note also states that the people from Târgu Mureş who will attend the party are not known and that measures will be taken to identify all those who will be present, as well as any possible telephone communications before, during, and after the event. Thus, the monitoring of any correspondence will be intensified, telephone calls will be intercepted to identify possible messages, and a fixed stakeout post will be installed near the house where the party will be held, from where guests will be photographed and their means of transport recorded.[14] In the same conspiratorial impulse, the Mureş Securitate sent a series of communiqués to the County Security Inspectorates in Bucharest, Cluj, Covasna, and Bihor, requesting information about the invited artists from those respective centers. These communiqués mention the suspicions for which Károly Elekes is being pursued, the context in which the information about the guests to the celebration became relevant, as well as the urgency with which the requested response is expected.[15] The received replies from all four contacted counties are archived in the artist's file.

Subsequently, from Cluj, we find out that Alexandru Sándor Antik, a visual artist employed as a product designer at the "Iris" porcelain factory, does not appear in the Securitate records, but that the preserved data about him reveals he has some nationalist manifestations, and his disobedient position toward the organs of security is already known.[16] The Covasna County Securitate communicated that Emeric-Ladislau Baász[17] is monitored through an informative follow-up file for his "hostile nationalist-irredentist manifestations" and his preoccupations that are deemed "void for the politics of the party and the state."[18] The Bucharest Securitate responds with a presentation of Wanda Mihuleac, who is reported among the persons with whom Elekes keeps in contact. Also, it is mentioned that Zoltán Szilágyi is in the attention of the institution and was investigated in May 1981.[19] Finally, a note from Bihor informs that neither Ioan Bunus nor György Jovián are known to have problems relevant to security work.[20]

The stakeout at the "Horizon House," the code name given to Nagy Árpád's residence where the anniversary party was to take place, was held on the night of July 17th. In Károly Elekes's file there are photographs taken by security **agents** during this monitoring, together with the note-report describing the events observed during the stakeout—more precisely who came at what time and with what, who left and at what time—as well as a series of "monitoring and identification notes" of all the people who were observed and photographed as having entered the yard of the house. Some of the participants were not identified (or not listed as such), but among those named are Aladár Garda and his wife, Zoltán Szabó—the latter photographed but misidentified—Károly Elekes and his wife, and Ioan Bunuş, alongside the host of the event, Nagy Árpád.[21]

In addition to the artists, some people who were not directly connected with the anniversary were also photographed and identified, individuals probably visiting Nagy's in-laws who lived in the same house. During the anniversary party, a performative event that will appear later in the MAMŰ retrospective catalog, published under the title *Multimedia Birthday Action*,[22] was held inside the monitored house. Árpád Nagy had conceived an installation in one of the rooms of the house whose scenery was as follows: a white cloth curtain flowed from the ceiling to the floor, covered the TV but left its screen visible through a cut in the curtain; on a small, nearby table, stood an aquarium with only one fish in it, the aquarium being connected to the TV by a string; next to the aquarium was a glass vessel filled with water, in which several black-and-white photographs representing different everyday situations "swam"; the ambient sound was given by a tape on which the artist recorded the murmur produced by rubbing sandpaper, the murmur interrupted periodically by short laughter.

In addition, each of the guests wore a badge on their chest with the icon of a man, while the badge of Árpád Nagy displayed the icon of a fish. It was in this context that the *Multimedia Birthday Action* took place: the news, constantly extolling the extraordinary achievements of the party and the comrade, was broadcast on television; the TV screen was covered with a piece of cardboard with holes drilled in the raster on which the artist was trying to draw certain moments seen on the screen. When completing such a drawing, he would take a photograph out of the glass vessel and paste it on one of the walls of the aquarium so that, at the end of the approximately twenty-five minutes of the action, you could no longer see the fish in the aquarium because of the photos that completely covered the glass walls; the action ended with the laying of a wreath in front of the TV.[23]

The idea of this installation and the performance that activates it belongs to Árpád Nagy (Pika), although it was retrospectively claimed as a group action of MAMŰ, a situation valid for most of the actions performed by individual artists in public space (mainly from Târgu Mureş) or in nature outside the city during the first part of the 1980s. If I were to draw comparative lines from the local alternative art scene of the period, I would mention the house pARTy series, which took place in Bucharest and were organized by a group of artists at the house of the couple Nadina and Decebal Scriba,[24] where there was a similar isolation of some officially discouraged artistic practices in private space. The *Multimedia Birthday Action* within the MAMŰ group, however, remains an "indoor" artistic experiment that is complemented by its reflection in the former Securitate documents, which differentiates its historiographic profile.

Through indirect (and unmentioned) sources, the officers on the case found out what actually happened at the party, away from the intrusive gaze of those at the stakeout post, namely that Zoltán Szabó would have said that "there were interesting problems."[25] Along with the old suspicions of Hungarian nationalism, this statement appears enunciated in the August 11, 1982 decision to open the dossier for an informative follow-up of Elekes—a file where the anniversary party acquired the status of "suspicious clue." On the other hand, Károly Elekes testified that those who had been present at the party knew from the beginning that photographs were being taken from the house across the street, the owner of which was a military doctor who maintained good relationships with his neighbors.

However, at the same time, they were used to the monitoring, marked by the appearance of the "Black Dacia" that watched them from a distance on various occasions. They were convinced that they were doing nothing wrong and did not understand the reason for why they were being surveilled.[26]

The possibility of placing the two perspectives of the same event side-by-side—what the Securitate saw, photographed, and analyzed on one side, and what the artists actually did, intended, and archived on the other—gives an image of that event's reality seen from extreme poles (and can even function as an example of how a banal event sees its own historical reflection transposed in opposing forms).

By juxtaposing the photographs taken from the stakeout with those taken inside the house by the artists, a true memento of that context is created: the Securitate seeks something hidden that did not actually exist, failing to observe the immediate evidence that they were monitoring a trivial birthday party, while the artists continued, knowing that they were being watched without knowing why. The *Multimedia Birthday Action* was a performative moment that, if it had been known in its true intentions and details, could have attracted unwanted repercussions. But the action was far from being the main purpose of the party. What, of all these aspects, was the hidden part of reality, and what was its visible part? And that which was hidden was hidden from whom: the actions of the artists from the Securitate or the actions of the Securitate from the artists? Both situations seem equally true, and from the spectral interweaving of these two realities, an accurate image emerges. Reality was constituted precisely by the parallelism of the two perspectives, which are in a state of latent tension with each other. Due to the fact that it did not result in negative consequences, the "alternative" birthday party can be regarded in rather amused terms due to the somewhat ridiculous alarmism created by the officers **handling** the "Elekes case." But this ridiculousness could be transformed at any time, at the slightest concrete clue, into harassment, with the worst possible consequences.

Alexandru (Sándor) Antik – *The Dream Has Not Died*, 1986

Alexandru (Sándor) Antik is registered among the "contacts" maintained by Elekes, proof being the invitation to the "alternative party" of July 1982. In the informative communiqué requested by the officers from Mures, he is presented by the Cluj Securitate as an element with "nationalist manifestations" and a "refractory (disobedient) position" towards the political police, this at a time when the artist was not yet officially pursued.[27]

The information-tracking file on behalf of Alexandru Antik was opened in 1988, with the main suspicion revolving around him being provided to the Securitate by the **informant** "Ana Maria" in Sibiu. The latter, visiting Cluj together with Mircea Stănescu and Vladimir Munteanu, met with several visual artists from the city and, according to the training received from the officers of Sibiu, offered the collected information upon her return.

Among the artists from Cluj, the **informant** "Ana Maria" notes Antik as one of the most recognized in the art world. In the discussions they had together, she inquired into the issue of the Hungarians in Romania. To this Antik replied by mentioning some attempts to organize the young Hungarians through several student meetings at the Art House in Cluj, in which he also participated sporadically. From the **informant's** reports Antik considered these meetings "useless, insignificant, as long as the Romanians from Transylvania do not take their own attitudes against the politics of the state and the party, concluding that it would be natural for the Romanians to protest if they have a real reason to, and by no means the Hungarians." The **informant** also commented that, from her time in Cluj, as well as from other occasions when she met Antik, she could tell that "*he is an opinion leader that polarized the artists around him, especially young people, and has a great deal of influence over them.*" [Emphasis in orig.][28] Starting from this data received from Sibiu, the Cluj Securitate initiated the informative pursuit of Antik under the suspicion of Hungarian nationalism and his negative influence on young artists. This pursuit ended with the change of the Romanian political regime in 1990.

From this artist's file, the document that may have direct relevance to the history of recent art is an informative note, also coming from Sibiu and provided by the **informant** "Alexandra" on August 4, 1986. She states:

"Alexandru Antik, one of the best artists of his generation, rightly considered in most media, brilliant, has a great capacity to influence Hungarian artists in Romania, and is a kind of representative of good Romanian art abroad, especially [*sic*] in regards to Hungary, where he is fully accepted as a human and extraordinarily admired as an artist in the most exclusive artist circles of Budapest. (His brother is married in Hungary.) He makes experimental art, an art of great boldness, but of the best professional quality. His performance (a very modern artistic genre, a full spectacle in which the audience participates without intervening), presented in the Sibiu Camp, was one of the best done recently, it even seems in the entire world (this confirmation was made right away by Marcel Bunea [Cisnădie], Mircea Ignat [Sibiu], who came with a former colleague of theirs, currently in Karlsruhe, FRG [Federal Republic of Germany] who is also an artist and who spoke about the European level of the event). Since such experiments are shocking to the audience's antiquated visual perception, the organizers decided that at these experimental exhibitions (taking place at the Museum of Pharmacy History), the public would enter with the camp's badge; however, many came from outside the camp, and the risk of not letting them enter was too high. The embarrassment and the false ideas started from the fact that at one point in the performance, the artist undressed, which is more than natural for people in the arts, for whom the human body is as commonplace as any other artistic element. There was actually no justification for this, since the artist wished to represent in the performance the nakedness, purity, sincerity of the creator in front of his audience. Everything competed to present a more accurate explication of the risk of creation, of the torment that it demands. In fact, it was an experiment of the best artistic quality and nothing else."[29]

The **informant**'s account refers to the performance *The Dream Has Not Died* (*Visul n-a murit*), which Alexandru Antik presented in the Sibiu Camp exhibition of artistic creation and art criticism organized in the basement of the Museum of Pharmacy in 1986.[30] At that time, the artist's performance was interrupted by the intervention of the Securitate, thus the event entered oral circulation (oral history), and later the historiographic dimension as one of the most brutal episodes of political censorship in the visual arts sphere. Due to the legendary status that this event reached, both in the last years of the Romanian dictatorship and afterwards, the expectations of identifying consistent material on this subject in the artist's follow-up file were as great as they were illusory. The **informant** "Alexandra's" brief account is the only document of the intensely discussed "Sibiu moment '86" that was included in Antik's tracking file, a file only opened in 1988 and based on accusations independent of the artistic event that had taken place two years before.

The informative note signed by "Alexandra" is archived in the artist's file in the form of a typewritten copy and was most likely sent to the Cluj Securitate in Sibiu. This detail could acquire a certain importance in analyzing the document's testimony: on the one hand, it illustrates the image of the "good **informant**," obviously an art professional, knowledgeable, and with a perspective on the direction of alternative artistic production; on the other hand, small grammatical disagreements and stumbling phraseology can attest to either an (unspecified) translation from Hungarian, or the transcription of a handwritten text that was difficult to decipher, or the writing of the text after an oral account, or simple mistakes made during the typing process of the informative note's copy. Finally, I would point out the possibility that this art professional suspected of being the **informant** "Alexandra" could have been an artist rather than a theoretician—a case that can leave room for clumsy expression.

The **Network**

A recurring aspect analyzed by the Securitate in the artists' files of informative tracking refers to their **network** of interpersonal relationships. The lists of the "contacts" that the artists maintained with people inside and outside the country are reflected in the current composition of the files, which were completed and revised on various occasions. In the frame of this tracking, they played an essential role, ensuring the coverage of a possible spread of inappropriate attitudes or intentions, as well as guaranteeing sources of information about the tracked target. For the microhistorical analysis of the dynamics within these artistic communities, the notes of relations drawn up by the Securitate somehow acquire the status of a document attesting to the interaction between them and confirm the secret police's knowledge—partially and discontinuously—of their existence. The "network" of relationships and interactions among the artists in the studied centers is reduced in the Securitate's data and documents (and probably even, interest) to a few leads.

They represent more than what a complete absence would have, but for many reasons, are almost reducible to it: this is partially due to the complexity of the state of affairs—the artistic communities were much more numerous and active than those reflected in the document archive. It is also a result of the lack of justification for the particular attention with which even these aspects found in the archives were tracked and documented, because none of them concealed in themselves the guilt of which they were suspected. From here I think we can draw at least a statistical conclusion of what the documentary material indicates: all the artists from the studied centers that were monitored by the Securitate came to its attention because of the accusation of Hungarian nationalism. According to the arguments on which these accusations were based, which can also be deduced from among the few situations of repression exerted on some art works, they were less anchored in the artists' individual profiles but rather, pointed towards a collective profile of the Hungarian ethnicity and maybe, more specifically, of Hungarian intellectuals. Art, when questioned, was not questioned "in itself," i.e. in its stylistic and aesthetic intentionality, nor in its nature and cultural value, but in the content of its message in the strict sense of the ethnic and political references, and even more so, in terms of the reactions that the receptive public manifested in its message.

The "Art and Culture" (*artă-cultură*) Dilemma

In order to recover the general terms with which the Securitate formulated and organized its surveillance and intervention activities in the cultural sphere, numerous "problem" files are available, which are part of the archive's documentary fund and bring together plans of measures or guidelines regarding the collection of information in the art-culture field. As a chronological treatment of the evolution of the regime's vision in this arena would far exceed this study's theme, I will limit myself to summarizing ideas of such documents dating from the 1980s, looking for the coordinates that defined the vulnerability of this sector from an official ideology's point of view.

A "Program of measures regarding the improvement of the security activity in the arts and culture sectors" (*Program de măsuri privind* îmbunătăţirea *activităţii de securitate* în *sectoarele artei* şi *culturii*) was approved in the meeting of the Executive Board of the Governing Council of the Department of State Security on February 16, 1983.[31] The program structures its content, like all documents of this type, in two sections: the analysis of specific problems that this arena poses and specifically the measures that are required to make counteraction more effective. In its structure and content, the document functions as an indicative framework, according to which each county security inspectorate was to organize its activity,[32] with applicability to the concrete situations they oversaw. The main points of vulnerability cited in this program concern the anticommunist propaganda that is supported through a series of reactionary circles from abroad and its negative influence on a category of creators of literature and art in Romania, which aim to create a "dissident movement" within the country.

Of these, the only one nominated in the document is the radio station "self-titled Free Europe,"[33] to which there were transmissions of unofficial links that various cultural people maintain with individuals abroad, as well as information of a "socio-political nature that is used tendentiously in hostile propaganda carried out abroad against our country." Through the prism of this foreign influence, or independently of it, the document finds: the large number of illegal stays abroad among the creators; the taking of a position hostile to the party's politics by some, especially the writers; the creation and publication of "deficient" works of art in terms of ideological content; the segregation of the literary-artistic world in different groups with divergent interests, beliefs and ideas, which may degenerate into hostile manifestations; attempts to address inadequate aspects of the Romanian people's historical past along with a distorted and biased presentation of this history through cultural productions or in museum institutions; or, finally, the emergence of inappropriate moods among the creators who, if "not dealt with in a timely manner, can affect the atmosphere in the environment or lead to anarchist-protest actions."[34]

These broad directives of "hostile manifestations" are then treated exhaustively by listing all the categories of people or situations that they absorb, from finding the communication channels between the "circles of intellectuals from the reactionary emigration" and cultural people in the country, to identifying content in cultural productions that is hostile, interpretable or equivocal (!) from an ideological point of view—including mystical or Freemason ideas. This can include the seemingly aesthetic polemics, but with political subtext and with implications for the security of the state.[35]

The picture constructed by all the directions and categories in the culture field that are subject to the political police's scrutiny, exhausts the possible zones of ideological release: it closes a seemingly impenetrable circle of total control. The inherent nature of artistic production—in this context, the "material" to be controlled—remains, however, eminently connotative, therefore rather resistant to a univocal decoding. On the contrary, there is a cultivation of the potential of a plurality of interpretations. Besides this "abstract" character of the content of ideas in the cultural product, its form, given by the mode/language/medium of materialization of the respective content of ideas, also intervenes. In its reception, beyond the theoretical and ideological precepts of the viewer, the factor of "taste" also plays a role. The worker of the state security responsible for the art-culture sector in contact with the productions and activities specific to this field is, first of all, placed in the position of the receiving public—the only position from which the evaluative judgments about the presence of possible politically subversive intentions in any artistic work are possible.

In the chapter titled "Improving the specific means and methods of work, increasing the degree of professionalism in the work of information gathering" (*Perfecţionarea mijloacelor* şi *metodelor specifice de muncă, sporirea gradului de profesionalitate în lucrarea informaţiilor*) of the cited document, this problem is also addressed, after enumerating strategies for diversifying and strengthening the information network and the means of monitoring the cultural "sector." First, it specifies the need to directly involve the hierarchical heads in clarifying the cases with a higher degree of difficulty. Then, it is pointed out that "in the verification and appreciation of the information, special care will be taken to remove any manifestations of subjectivism, the exaggerations that may arise due to the aesthetic preferences of the sources, or their belonging or sympathies with one group or another of creators."[36] Here the justice of the sources' aesthetic appraisals, specifically informants or collaborators, which can be altered by the individual aesthetic preferences, is directly questioned, but, in the subtext, the warning about the "careful rejection of subjectivism" is offered.

This was precisely one of the zones that could break the closed circle of the intentional total control of the art-culture sector and, in some cases, even functioned in this role. I think that the reaction of the public towards a certain artistic production—be it a professional or a simple consumer of culture—finds its place and importance in relation to this zone: if something inappropriate escaped the "subjective" aesthetic appreciation of the censorship board members, that something could become the subject of increased vigilance after it came into contact with the receiving public.

In light of the criteria and themes of surveillance and censorship of culture very schematically listed here, the security work in the field was meant to have a preventive character first, as insisted in the mentioned 1983 document of the program of measures. The security work had to combat and reject attempts to undermine official policy, or negative influences from the outside. The fear of dissemination of inappropriate ideas meant the fear of dissent, in whatever form and direction it was undertaken, but the culture field was considered to be the most susceptible. The cited document—similar to the satellite documents that it generated at the county level—consists much on measures to prevent dissent, or to prevent its spread or popularization at least. Thus, the people in the sphere of art and culture who could initiate actions to constitute dissent in the cultural environment will be "positively influenced" and convinced not to resort to such acts. If they do, then "isolation, discouragement, neutralization, humiliation" and other measures will be taken against them.[37]

Regarding the dissidence of that period, seen through the prism of the general documents which I accessed in the archives on the art and culture sector, they do not attest to its existence as an orchestrated phenomenon in the strong sense of the term, but they do certify that there was an organized and official policy to deny or neutralize it. Another factor is its difficulty in delineating where exactly the political register began and ended within the perception of the communist state, and consequently, it is even more difficult to trace possible points of contention and manifestation of dissent.[38]

In the institutional hierarchy, the Securitate was, above all, the structures involved in the administration/production of culture, also controlling the "censorship institutions," represented by the County Councils of Culture and Socialist Education. The latter were in charge of the entire cultural activity carried out on the surface of the home counties. The monitoring activity of the cultural field fell within the tasks of the Securitate Directorate I for the republican institutions, while for the members and collaborators of the creative unions and associations, it fell within the responsibility of the county Securitate.

The Publication of the Material

I began my search in this archive to discover data that would help reconstitute the official discourse of the censorship institutions on the practice of the studied artists, and have come across its extreme form, produced by the ultimate institution of control: Securitate. Beyond the immediate utility that derives from here—i.e. the possibility of reconstructing the hierarchies of control, where the Councils of Culture and Socialist Education occupy a middle rank among the executives and decision-makers and are in turn subject to the political police's monitoring—this utility also brings a warning with it: that the documents we have analyzed come from one extreme of the respective reality. They represent this reality from a tendentious perspective and therefore, have access to a narrow and deformed angle of it. The possibility of compensating for this shortcoming lies in the oral history testimonies of the artists themselves—and these too carry risks arising from the identity constructions to which they belong, as well as to the inflections of memory in relation to the needs of the present—which may represent the very opposite angle of the initial realities. The reconciliation of these "extremes" should fall primarily on the public sphere.

The organization of the documentary material within the frame of an exhibition raises a number of corresponding problems, which emerge both from its very nature, as well as from the recovery strategies and curatorial intentions.

The private *Multimedia Birthday Action* event from the MAMŰ group's perimeter will be shown in the exhibition from its two perspectives: the "inside," recorded in the archives (and portfolio) of the artists, and the "outside," recorded in the Securitate files and reports. This display is motivated through negotiating the two perspectives—diametrically opposed—on the memory of that past: perspectives that, even if they come from the same place and time, were never meant to meet.

Alexandru Antik's *The Dream Has Not Died* can be exhibited through an approach similar in form, but noticeably different in content. Alongside the few photographs made during the performance that can be found in the artist's personal archive, one would add the informative note provided by the informant "Alexandra," the only document of a legendary episode for the local art scene from the 1980s that was kept in the Securitate. What neither the artist's photos nor the informative note can show are the precise causes that led to the Securitate's intervention in the artistic act, as well as the effects that the respective intervention had on the way in which *The Dream Has Not Died* entered oral and historiographic circulation.

A publication and an exhibition still have to manage a difficult aspect, which is that which refers to the silence and absence of this archive. One of the most unfortunate conclusions—and a frequent disappointment expressed by many of the artists—concerns the absence of follow-up files on all artists. This absence tends to be evaluated as proof of "insufficiency": insufficient detachment from the regime, insufficient creative freedom, insufficient importance. The risks of such an assertion are obvious and very inadequate in relation to this archive in particular. It may be that the actual display of these lacunae—in the archive and in the exhibition itself, and either through recourse to oral history or other categories of sources—is at least as necessary as the display of the existing documentary materials.

The exhibition of these documents intends to undertake, at least in part, a demystification of the relationship between the former Securitate and contemporary art. Each exhibition builds its discourse through the pieces it exhibits, which are at the same time the reference point and, to an extent, the discursive material itself. This exhibition aspires to sabotage its own exhibits, which it presents and questions simultaneously, because it works with material loaded with contradictory meanings. The greatest danger that the exhibition faces is that of involuntarily monumentalizing its material. The transfer of these documents from the status of "strictly secret" directly into history as major sources shares the same risk. An exhibition's main role should be to remove the documentary material from its mystifying isolation and reintroduce it into the public space in order to be seen, reclaimed, and digested, as well as to contribute to the consolidation of this space.

When I asked Károly Elekes about his general impressions after browsing his security file, the artist replied: "[...] it should not be taken very tragically, it is tragic for them, because they had to do it. But maybe it was also something positive for them, the fact that they had contact with an artistic thought that does not resemble their own thinking, and probably now [Alexandru] Agoşton [head of Mures Security, n.n.] is an art collector."

Translated from Romanian by Olga Stefan

Endnotes

1 Excerpts from: Mădălina Brașoveanu, "Thoughts for a documentary exhibition: traces of the artistic network Oradea—Târgu Mureș—Sfântu Gheorghe in the Archive of the former Securitate," *Caietele C. N. S. A. S.* 14, nor. 2 (2014): 85–166. Available online at: http://www.cnsas.ro/documente/caiete/Caiete_CNSAS_nr_14_2014.pdf (in Romanian). The present version of the study focuses on the few performance events that are traceable in the Securitate's archives, leaving aside an extensive part referring to the mail-art corre-spondence within these artistic communities, which has been monitored and archived by the secret police and was included in the original study.

2 The current study is part of a broader research project undertaken at The Doctoral School of the Faculty of the History and Theory of Art, National University of Bucharest, supervised by Professor Anca Oroveanu, titled "Community, artistic practice, discourse: Atelier 35 Oradea and Cluj, MAMÜ group, Târgu Mureș."

3 The initials come from *Ma*rosvásárhelyi *Mű*hel*y* (in Hungarian—the studio from Târgu Mureş or Târgu Mureş Studio).

4 The artists that took part in the MAMÜ group: Alexandru (Sándor) Antik (from Cluj), Csaba György Borgó, Ioan Bunus, Attila Diénes, Károly Elekes, Aladár Garda, Sándor Krizbai, Dénes Kuti, Árpád Nagy (Pika), Zoltán Szabó (Judoka), Pálma Szigeti-Baász, Zoltán Szilágyi, Gábor Szörtsey. Károly Elekes was the leader of the group and the initiator of the exhibition program.

5 In the inventory of the Mureş National Archives, there is no registered document from the Committee of Socialist Education and Culture, nor from the county's Union of Plastic Artists. The situation is similar regarding the Bihor National archives, where the quantity of documentation of the visual arts is very small among the files kept by the county's Committee of Socialist Education and Culture.

6 Jacques Derrida, "Archive Fever. A Freudian Impression," in *Diacritics* 25, no. 2 (Summer 1995): 9–63, see especially 9–12; Michel Foucault, *Arheologia cunoaşterii*, (en. *The Archeology of Knowledge*) (Bucureşti: Editura Univers, 1999), 156–163; Francis X. Blouin Jr. and William G. Rosenberg eds., *Archives, Documentation, and Institutions of Social Memory. Essays from the Sawyer Seminar*, (Ann Arbor: The University of Michigan Press, 2006).

7 R. Gerald Hughes, Peter Jackson, and Len Scott, eds., *Exploring Intelligence Archives. Enquiries into the secret state* (New York: Routledge, 2008), 2–3.

8 These observations make up the preliminary introduction of the exhibition I curated, *The Traces of the Art Network Oradea-Târgu Mures—St. George in the Archives of the Former Securitate*, which opened at Gallery B5 Studio in Targu Mureș, Oct. 2015, and itinerated to at MAGMA Contemporary Art Space, St. George, in the frame of netWorks, June 2017.

9 Gheorgheni District's, and later Covasna County's, First Secretary of the Romanian Communist Party between 1965 and 1972, a function from which he quits, as he claims, as a result of ideological conflicts, repeatedly criticizing antipopulist politics and the regime's discrimination towards the national minorities. He is the author of several protest letters regarding the situation of minorities in Romania, which reached Radio Free Europe and Voice of America, through his relations with a series of people from the nomenclature, and a personal relationship, until a certain point, with Nicolae Ceauşescu. Király became a figure of dissent surrounded by some controversy but with a certain notoriety, at least among the Hungarians in Romania. More details can be found at: http://kiralykaroly.blogspot.ro/p/biografie-1949-la-canalul-dunare-marea.html; Károly Király, *Nyílt Kártyákkal I.* Önéletírás és *naplójegyzetek* (Pécs: Sétatér Alapítvány Press, 2013).

10 Among the documents kept in Károly Elekes's file, the text of the stamp reads in this way. However, in the discussions with the artist, he recalled a more developed form: "*Király Károly az üstökös, a jel 896 'Király Károly cometa, sign 896.'*"

11 The National Council for the Study of the Securitate Archives (A.C.N.S.A.S.), Informative Fund, file nr. 085302, 15–36.

12 Among the invitations sent through the mail only those that were sent to Antik, Baász, Bunuş, and Jovián are archived in the file. A.C.N.S.A.S., Informative fund, file nr. 085302, 127–32. The other names were found on a list drawn up by the "S" Service with Elekes's "established contacts"from a recent period, communicated on July 14, 1982. Ibid., 114.

13 Ibid., 42: "It is necessary to control this meeting with all the means of security work at our disposal. Let's continue the information tracking measures placed on Elekes to clarify any suspicions we have about him. All operational moments will be reported to me and we will analyze the case on a weekly basis."

14 Ibid., 43.

15 Ibid., 80 (addressed to Bucharest); 77 (addressed to Cluj); 79 (addressed to Covasna); 78 (addressed to Bihor).

16 Ibid., 203.

17 The version translated the Hungarian name of the artist into Romanian. In most cases, Hungarian names that are translatable into Romanian appear in the Securitate's documents only in this form.

18 Ibid., 220.

19 Ibid., 45; 55.

20 Ibid., 71.

21 Ibid., 85–94.

22 Tihamér Novotny, ed., MAMŰ. *Marosvásárhely Műhely 1978–1984. Tegnap és Ma* (Szentendre: Szentendrei Képtár, 1990).

23 The action was described to me by Nagy Árpád in an email dialogue from May 2014. The idea of this installation and the performance that activates it belongs to Árpád Nagy (Pika), although it was retrospectively claimed as MAMŰ's action, a situation valid for most of the actions performed by individual artists in public space (from Târgu Mureş mainly) or in nature outside the city, in the first part of the 1980s.

24 The occasional meetings titled "house pARTy" were attended by the spouses Nadina Scriba, Wanda Mihuleac, Dan Mihălţianu, Călin Dan, Dan Stanciu, Andrei Oişteanu, and later Teodor Graur and Iosif Király. See Pintilie, *Actionism in Romania during Communism, Idea Design & Print*; Oişteanu, "Experimentul House pARTy (1987–1988)."

25 A.C.N.S.A.S., Informative Fund, file no. 085302, 36: "On July 17 a.c. celebrated his birthday together with, and at the residence of, Nagy Árpád, assistant painter-scenographer, at the National Theater in Tg-Mureş, an event at which were invited, and participated, the following: Ioan Bunuş, Imre Baász, Sándor Antik, Zoltán Szabó, Ladislau Garda from Tg-Mureş and others, a meeting about which Zoltán Szabó said that 'there were interesting problems.'"

26 "The project ContraFouché was done at Krizbai's house [Sándor], and the car [of the Securitate] stayed all night under the tree across the street; it was a willow, under which I could see the black Dacia, with the engine running until morning as I stood there making the newspaper sculptures. ... Or we had guests from here [from Budapest] from the Studio [Young Artists Studio], Bálint Chikán, and others. They came there every summer and we talked, but we didn't do anything political. When they were sleeping in my house, and then that car, the black Dacia, ... was staying there until morning. The next evening it was there again." From the discussions with Károly Elekes, February 2014, Budapest.

27 Alexandru Antik lived and worked in Cluj after finishing college, being more adaptable to the artistic environment of Cluj. The arguments for his inclusion in this study are the close links he had, even before his college years, with the cultural environment of Mureş; born in Reghin, a school colleague with Ioan Bunuş, he was among the members of the MAMŰ in the early 1980s.

28 A.C.N.S.A.S., Informative Fund, file nr. 234058, 11.

29 Ibid., 8.

30 For more details on this performance, see Antik, *Inventory*.

31 A.C.N.S.A.S., Documentary Fund, file nr. 3095, 83–90.

32 When comparing this program of measures with a "Work Plan on the issue of Art-Culture for 1988" ("*Plan de muncă* în *problema Artă-Cultură pentru anul 1988*"), elaborated by Covasna County Inspectorate, it becomes obvious that, despite the five-year difference between the two documents, the second incorporates a great deal of the first, but applies it to the specifics of the cases underway. See A.C.N.S.A.S., Documentary Background, file no. 3092, 17–20.

33 In a 1988 document titled "Documents on the circles and the reactionary elements from abroad that act on the line of negative influence and incitement of the people of art and culture in our country" ("*Documentar privind cercurile* şi *elementele reacţionare din exterior care acţionează pe linia influenţării negative* şi *incitării oamenilor de artă* şi *cultură din* ţara *noastră*"), these institutions are listed: Foundation for Intellectual Help in Paris; Sections in France and the USA of the Pen Club International, originally based in London; Union of Romanian Free Artists (Ars Libera) from FRG; Hyperion Association of Paris; Romanian Research Center, affiliated with the Paris Academy; Association for the Protection of Historical and Art Monuments in Romania in Paris; Romanian Research Institute in Munich; Constantin Noica's Friends Association in Paris; Society for the Preservation and Promotion of Romanian culture in West Germany; Inter Nationes Society, a West German institution from the Ministry of Foreign Affairs; the Humboldt Foundation of West Germany; and The American Romanian Academy of Arts and Sciences. In the chapter on publications issued by reactionary groups in emigration: *Cartea românească în Occident* (*The Romanian Book in the West*), and a semiannual bulletin published in France, *Limits* and *Ethos*, both published by the Romanian editorial staff in Paris of Radio Free Europe, *Săptămâna Müncheneză* (Munich Week)

in Munich, *Agora*, published in Philadelphia, *Universul* (*Universe*) and *Micromagazin*, published in New York. To this grouping are added the Romanian and Hungarian sections of the radio station Radio Free Europe, as well as a list of "Writers, plastic artists, lyricists, instrumentalists and circus workers who stayed abroad, who are used by various institutions or circles interested in collecting and determined to refuse to return to the country and to engage art and cultural people temporarily in the West in hostile activities." A.C.N.S.A.S., Documentary Fund, file no. 3095, 20–33.

34 A.C.N.S.A.S., Documentary Fund, file nr. 3095, 83–84.

35 In a document titled "Guide on collecting information on the issue of 'Art-culture'" ("*Tematică orientativă privind culegerea de informaţii în problema 'Artă-cultură'*"), also listed is: "The systematic refusal of some art and culture people to represent in their artistic work topics about the past struggle of the party and our people, the construction of socialism in Romania, to pay tribute to the political moments and political personalities." Or "inadequate states of mind and their causes, the concerns and preoccupations of persons from institutions in the field of culture and art, which may generate facts, phenomena or actions that may affect the politics of our party and state", or "decrease in cultural propaganda abroad, the reduced efficiency of the trips abroad of the delegations of the cultural-artistic institutions or of other actions abroad." A.C.N.S.A.S., Documentary Fund, file no. 5522, Vol. I, 30–31.

36 A.C.N.S.A.S., Documentary Fund, file nr. 3095, sheet 88 (verso).

37 Ibid., 89 (verso). Here the notion of "dissent" subsumes any form of protest, from "political meanings conferred on personal dissatisfaction" to "acts of protest or public disorder" or "turbulent acts of protest capable of gaining notoriety."

38 For an analysis of the legislation that defined and defended state secrecy, the obligations of citizens regarding the disclosure of information, etc., but also on the notoriety of writers / intellectuals who criticized the regime and how this notoriety protected them from serious sanctions on the part of the state, see: Iuliu Crăcană, "Legislative aspects of the repression of Romanian dissent. The Goma Case," in the Specifications C.N.S.A.S., no. 2/2008, 339–347. The Goma case had no brutal consequences, says the author, because the regime was not yet ready to face the new form of opposition-dissent; but the legislation was changed, and any anticommunist public manifestation could be blocked before it began to take place.

Károly Elekes, b. 1951 in Cristuru Secuiesc, Romania, lives and works in Budapest, Hungary.
Árpád Nagy, b. 1950 in Sângeru de Pădure, Romania, lives and works in Budapest, Hungary.

Multimedia Birthday Action

Károly Elekes / Árpád Nagy / MAMŰ Group

On July 17, 1982, two members of the artist collective MAMÜ, Árpád Nagy and Károly Elekes, celebrated their birthday at Nagy's house in Târgu Mureș. The celebration became a collective performance. Invitations were sent in advance to both Hungarian and Romanian artists, including Wanda Mihuleac, Mihai Drișcu, Zoltán Szilágyi, András Butak, and Alexandru Antik. During the performance, Nagy created live drawings about the social and economic achievements of the Party and its top leaders. After completing each drawing, a photograph with everyday scenes from an aquarium was taken and stuck to the side of an aquarium while a recording of the sounds of murmuring and sandpaper played, as well as laughter. The twenty-five-minute-long performance ended when the aquarium was completely covered with photos and the television, upon which lay a white curtain, received a wreath of flowers. The performance was intended to have a "therapeutic effect" in the midst of increasing cultural repression. (K)

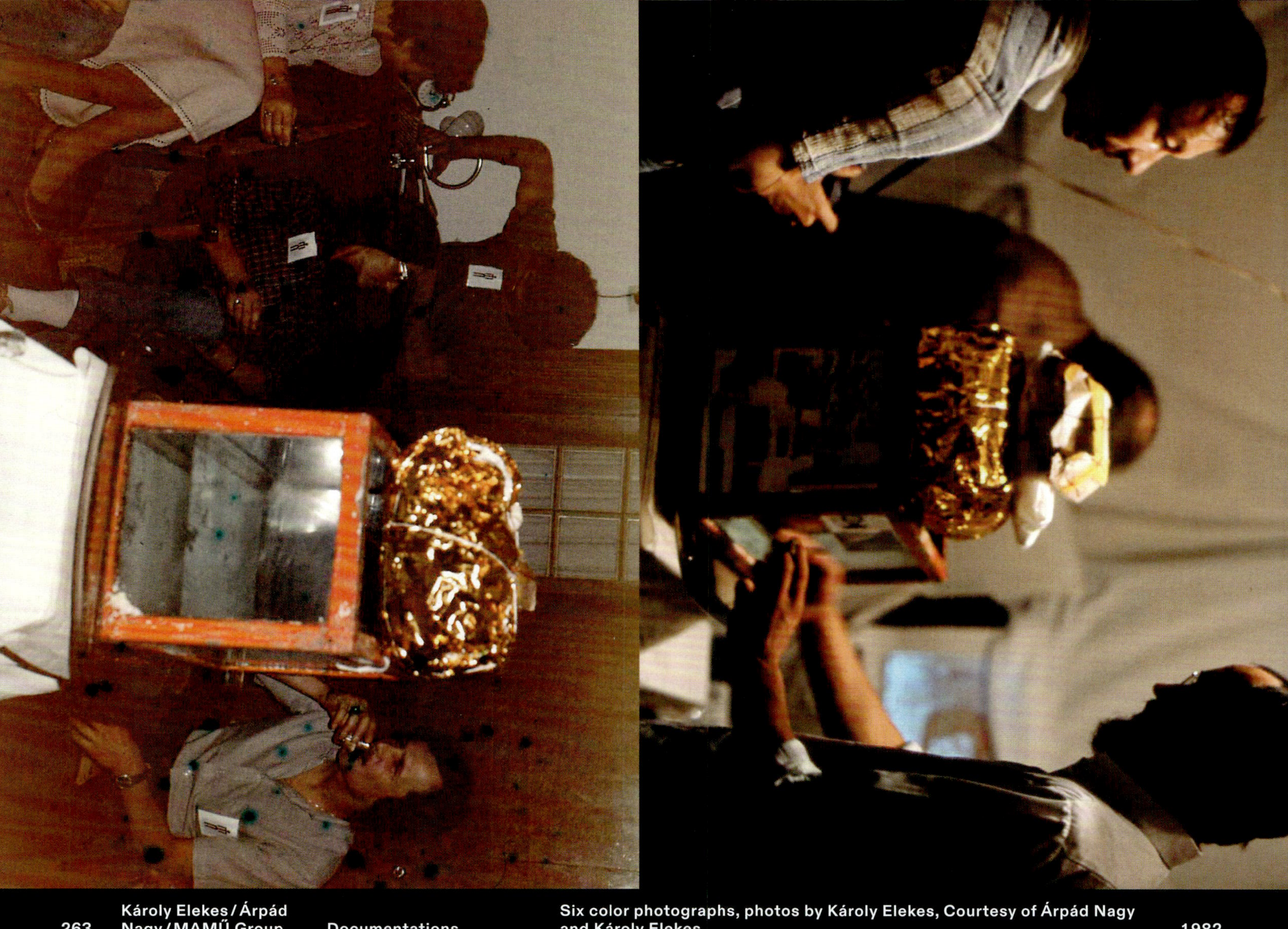

Six color photographs, photos by Károly Elekes, Courtesy of Árpád Nagy and Károly Elekes 1982

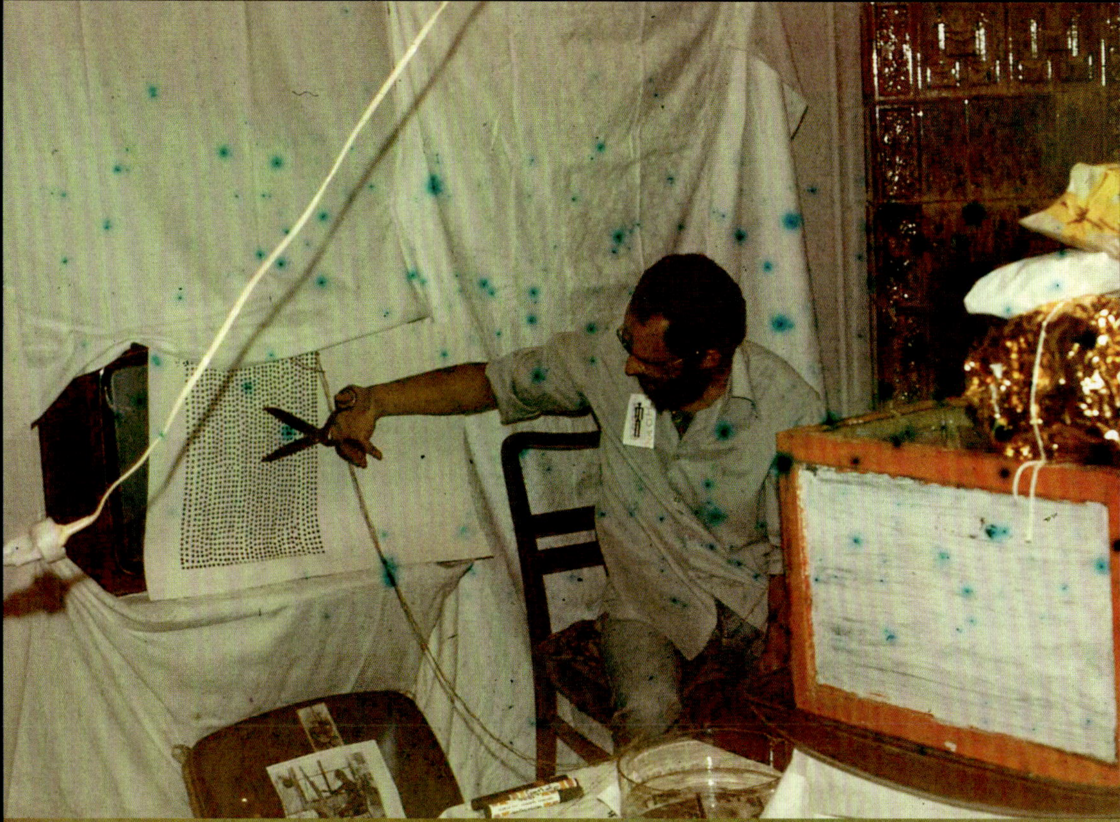

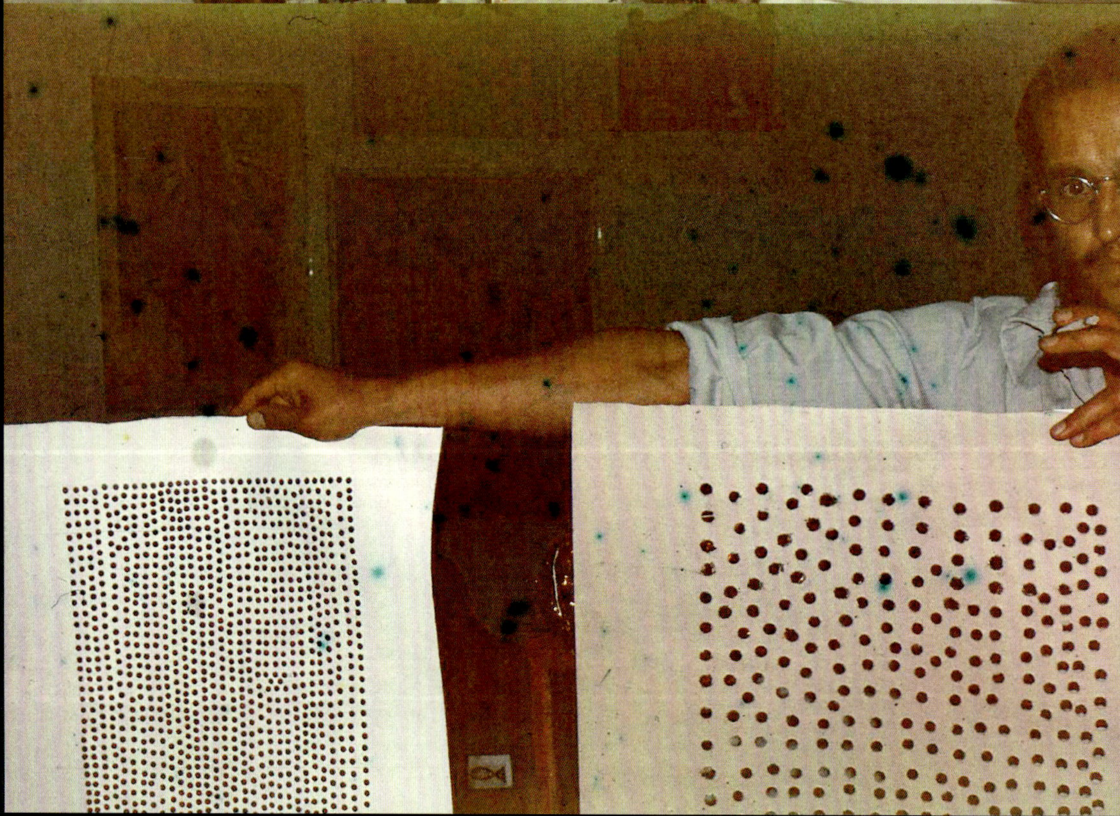

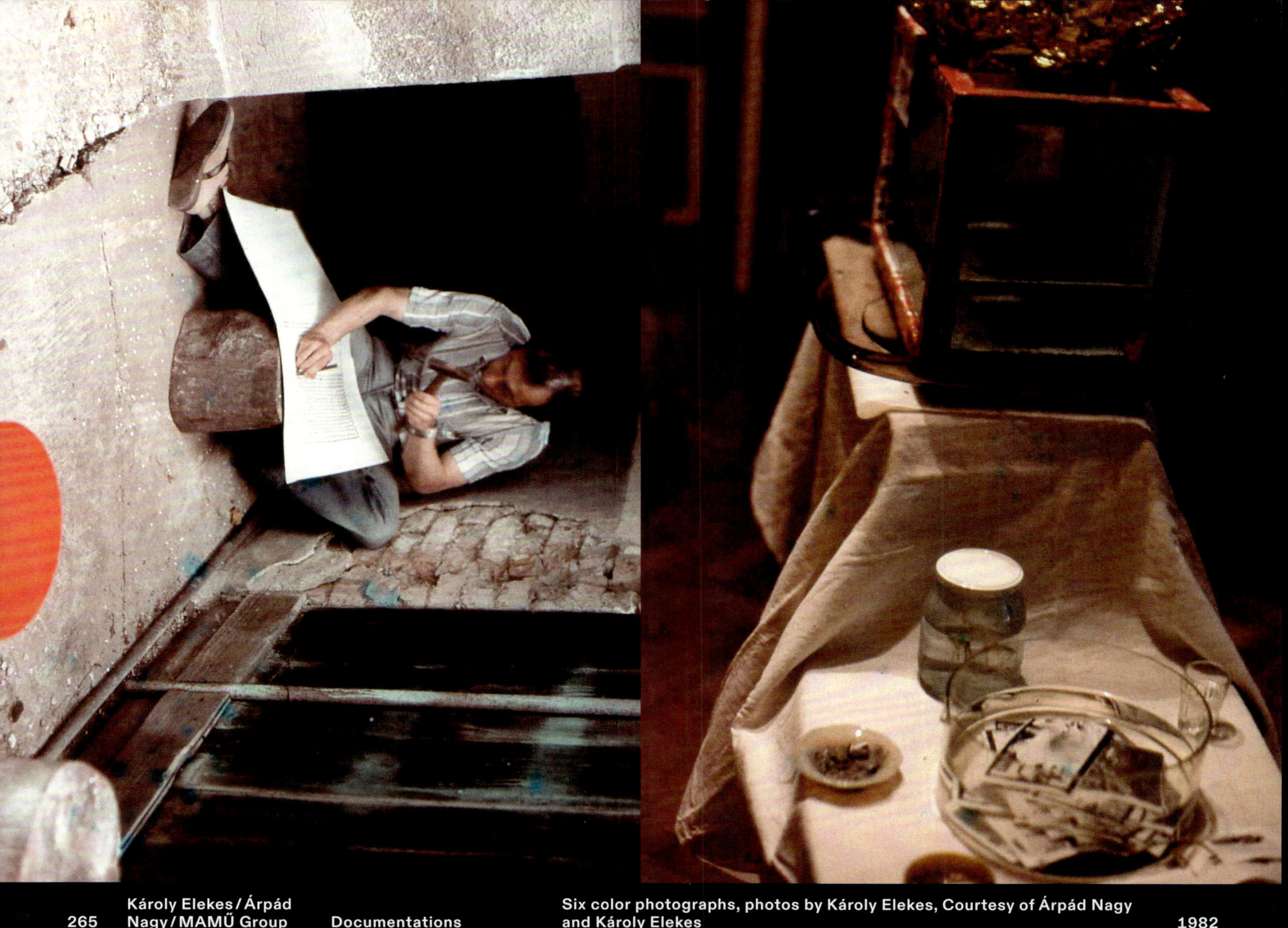

 Károly Elekes / Árpád Nagy / MAMŰ Group Documentations Six color photographs, photos by Károly Elekes, Courtesy of Árpád Nagy and Károly Elekes 1982

Surveillance Photos

Securitate (SR Romania)

The file of the Romanian artist Károly Elekes, who was placed under surveillance starting in 1978, contains a photographic surveillance report about persons entering and leaving the house of Árpád Nagy. (Even the house had a code name: "Orizont House.") All of these persons were artists and were coming to the *Multimedia Birthday Action*. This *Birthday Action* aroused significant interest in the Securitate: they would be able to both uncover the "network" of the artists through a Who's-Who report and attempt to compile relevant "evidence" against the participants. The photo documentation meticulously records who came and went and when, and "surveillance and identification notes" were made on every person. The Securitate desperately sought after some hidden element which did not exist and thus overlooked the facts of the matter, namely that the event was a harmless art action disguised as a birthday party, put on by artists who knew that they were being watched without knowing why. (K)

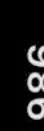

94

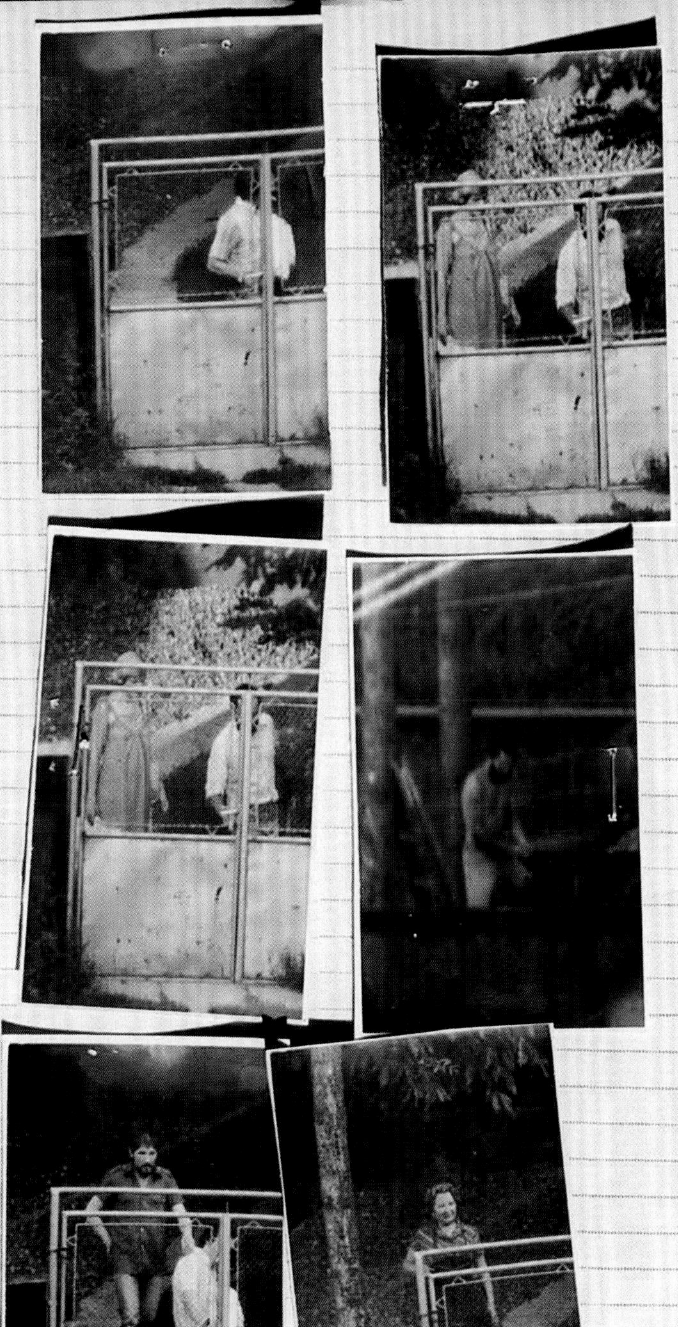

ORGAN D

Martor.

One page of surveillance photos from the file of Károly Elekes
Source: C. N. S. A. S I 085302, 94

Interactions and Counteractions

"Plainclothes Art Historians": On Performative Censorship

Sylvia Sasse

In December 2016, an unconventional censorship action took place in Moscow. The most well-known, independent theater in Russia—teatr.doc, founded in 2002—wanted to show the documentary *Stronger than Arms* (2014) by #BABYLON'13, a group of ten Ukrainian cinematographers, in its basement space in Moscow. The film concerns the resistance to Maidan and the war in eastern Ukraine. Though the screening was not banned in advance, shortly before the performance, about twenty police officers and officials from the Ministry of Culture burst into the basement and yelled that there was a bomb in the building. The audience was driven into the streets and, once there, were all registered. The residents of the building above the theater were not evacuated and were allowed—despite the bomb threat—to stay in their apartments. After this, the bomb squad barricaded themselves in the theater for approximately two hours. The "bomb search" quickly became a search for extremist materials that might violate the interests of the Russian state. Almost as an afterthought, the police disassembled the film projector, confiscated the film, laid waste to the space, and destroyed the props. The screening could no longer take place.[1]

This event was an act of censorship which I refer to as "performative censorship" or, in secret police jargon, "operative censorship." This practice was typical of the Soviet Union and other states in the former Eastern Bloc; since about 2000, it has started to be used again, even more intensely, in Russia.[2] I understand "performative censorship" to mean an action of the authorities or secret services which is intended to conceal but at the same time, also to demonstrate the actual activity of censorship. The action functions as a kind of Fake-Event, analogous to Fake News, which is to say that these events do actually occur but are only pretending "as if" they do. They occur but are not what they seem to be; they are "made," planned, cast, sometimes even rehearsed to supply a reason for why an exhibition isn't opened, a film not shown, a performance not carried out, or indeed an artistic work not continued. Thus, they engage with our idea of history's contingency.

Events like these make clear that any planned exhibition, film, or play can be prevented—within the bounds of the law—at any time. This is perhaps the decisive point: **performative censorship** is not only intended to make it seem like there is in fact no censorship, but also to demonstrate the existence of an intact legal system that takes bomb warnings seriously, is concerned about fire-prevention measures, or protects viewers and readers from pornographic or blasphemous art and literature.

The frequency of these events in recent years shows that the logic of secret service operations has again become part of censorship activities, at least in Russia. In the case of teatr.doc too, it was not a one-time occurrence: half a year before the alleged bomb threat, one day after the premiere of a piece on May 6, 2014, an unannounced fire safety inspection was carried out and the theater temporarily closed. The connection with the premiere of the presented piece is obvious. In her piece, the author and director, Polina Borodina, referred to a 2012 trial on charges of "resistance to state power" ("organization of public unrest" [*organizaciya massovykh bezporyadok*]). The accused were the organizers of the March of Millions to Bolotnaya Square. Half a year later, in October, it became known that the city of Moscow had terminated the lease without notice. The theater was accused of having improperly placed an entrance. This occurred, however, in May, at the order of the fire safety authorities that could have otherwise denied the operating permit.

Operativity

The Russian philosopher Mikhail Ryklin describes the current practice of politics in Russia, not only in relation to potential censorship measures but also in general, as "operative power," which is characteristically able to subordinate current politics to the logic of secret service methods: "Putinism is basically the politicization of secret service methods," Ryklin writes. The result of such politics is that its public, visible part is a "fiction" for or of "outsiders"; that is, "of those not party to the actual secret knowledge."[3] One might object that this had also been the case during Soviet times, and Ryklin certainly would not deny this. But while operative politics during this period still followed or aided an ideology in addition to covering over a reality that contradicted the ideology itself, current secret service practices merely serve the retention of power.

When Ryklin writes "operative," he does not mean the recently discussed media-philosophical question of the technical or performative aspects of operations; he is referring instead to the unpredictability and dissimulation involved in secret service operativity. A good idea of how this dissimulation functions can be obtained by looking at the Stasi guidelines for the Inoffizielle Mitarbeiter (IM, "unofficial collaborator"), as informants were known in the GDR. According to Stasi Directive 1/76, "decomposition," perhaps the most important activity of the Stasi, is the "systematic discrediting of public reputation, standing, and prestige on the basis of true and verifiable discrediting information in combination with false, believable, non-disprovable, and thus equally discrediting information."[4] One could say here that the Stasi oriented themselves towards Aristotle, who rightly noted that with regard to fiction, probable impossibilities are to be preferred to improbable possibilities. The Stasi also aimed to produce probable events intended to manipulate the lives of artists or dissidents. But these "falsely probable" events didn't remain fictive; they became biographical reality for those who were affected.

How do we want to theoretically conceive of the secret service's operative theater? Theater and politics have always been historically and conceptually closely connected. As early as the 1910s, the Russian theater historian Nikolay Evreinov spoke of a political "theatrocracy," suggesting that it is naïve to assume that theater is not also being performed in everyday life. Representation and surrogacy are in this sense necessary forms of democratic performance which do not conceive of political power as *providentia dei* (divine providence) or as natural law (an inherited right to power), but as contractual and elective. This does not mean that political theater is spoken of as fraudulent or fake—only as "made." But it was also Evreinov who published an article in 1921 directly addressing the theater of the secret police.[5] Evreinov recommends that the secret police work with more theatricality, which, in his view, would lead to more professionalism in the fight against crime. Evreinov had no idea that this theatricality would itself become a means of crime. Only with the writing of a piece about the theater of the Moscow show trials in the 1930s does he show the country's subjection to the methods of the secret police, how theater and playacting had themselves become means of political crime.

Whoever refers to the party dictatorships in Eastern Europe simply as societies of control or surveillance misses an essential political function of the domestic secret service: its performance mandate. It is thus entirely correct to call, as historian Malte Rolf did, the Eastern European party dictatorships "performance dictatorships."[6] Rolf meant, however, something else with this term: he was identifying the permanent performance of ideology in visual rituals and festivals. Fundamentally, he is interested in analyzing the "aestheticization of politics," which Walter Benjamin also investigated in the context of German fascism. Benjamin criticized art that puts itself in the service of such aestheticization.[7] In 1967, Guy Debord also referred to, in his book *Society of the Spectacle*, the staging of ideology and its function of pure spectacle. Later, in the 1980s, Debord extended his perspective of seeing society and ideology as fully spectacle, adding a focus on elements of the internal spectacle. The production of secret knowledge or training in "secret activities," Debord writes, produces "uncertainties" and "**diversions**" that add "countless specific frauds" to the "general fraud of the spectacle."[8]

The operative censorship or theatricality of the secret police targets this "internal spectacle," not just ideology in its existence as a stage. It not only translates a theory or metatext into a festival, ritual, protest march, or the setting of a party conference. Operative censorship functions not only on the level of representation; it also *alters* reality so that it can even be politically represented in the first place. These are criminal practices carried out by the state with the intention of obscuring its own actions as a censor, and of concealing the fact that the state is unlawfully acting as a censor and harassing artists.[9]

"Plainclothes Art Historians"

While the theatrical practices of the secret police can now be researched in most Eastern European countries where former secret police **archives** have been opened, in Russia we can only speculate about the files of "**performative censorship.**" As summarized by Arseny Roginsky and Nikita Okhotin in 1993 at a symposium on the topic of "State Security Services and Literature," a total destruction of the **Unofficial Collaborator** (IM) files was ordered in 1990. In 1991, many of the files of victims, "including the writers,"[10] were destroyed. The Russian commentator Vitaly Shentalinsky sought for years, in the middle of Perestroika, to acquire the files of murdered writers from the 1930s, which he managed to accomplish. He found, for example, Osip Mandelstam's poem against Stalin, the only copy of which Mandelstam was forced to surrender. This copy was later deposited in the KGB archives. He also found texts and diaries from other writers, their indictments, hearing records, etc. But Shentalinsky was not able to come near files from the 1950s to the 1990s.

Acts of "operative measures" can only be analyzed there from the affected artists' point of view, from their diaries and memoirs, or in other records from the civil rights movement, such as the *Chronicle of Ongoing Events* (*Khronika tekushchikh sobytiy*), which was typed on carbon paper in the Soviet Union from 1968 to 1983. They show the "normal case" of an interpretation of strange events whose authorship was attributed to so-called plainclothes art historians, as the agents in the Russian art scene were called. They should have actually been called "plainclothes performers."

In the *Chronicle*, artists report of obstructed or "impeded" exhibitions, of "fire safety measures," "burst pipes," and arson, as well as studio and private apartment burglaries aimed at destroying art. The *Chronicle* portrays these events in great detail, doing so with the full knowledge that they were initiated by the KGB. This knowledge gives rise to a complex interplay between artists and "plainclothes art historians." Reading the reports is interesting not only historically but also from a cultural studies perspective, as it is not the knowledge or facticity of secret service operations which is revealed, but rather, contemporary ideas about the secret service's actions in the sphere of art.

Reading the *Chronicle* reveals that the planning of public events, such as the hidden exhibitions, always took place in anticipation of potential KGB actions. In 1975, it was reported that during an exhibit in the Palace of Culture, located on the premises of the Exhibition of Achievements of National Economy (VDNKh)[11], the rooms were heated to over thirty-five degrees Celsius, despite the warm weather. The exhibit was thus made extremely unpleasant, almost unbearable. At night, undesirable works were taken down by "plainclothes art historians" and replaced with other randomly chosen ones. Other works were removed for alleged fire safety reasons or for technical reasons, because the stairs under which a work was hanging were in danger of collapsing.[12] The *Chronicle of Ongoing Events* also records that six works by Samuil Rubashkin were intended to be shown in the Moscow Artists' House in the Bolshaya Bronnaya Synagogue. After a quiet first day of the exhibition, members of the KGB appeared the next day to see the house's director in order to attempt prohibiting the exhibition on the basis of Jewish image captions or captions related to the Jewish religion (Jewish Holidays series). The pictures were removed, placed in the director's office, and banned. The curators turned to the Propaganda Department of the Central Committee (CC); the CC ordered a commission, and this commission permitted the pictures to be left in the exhibition for reasons of "national color."[13] But immediately after the approval, an act of performative censorship occurred: the fire brigade arrived and decided that the rooms were not secured against fire and then closed the exhibition.

While arrests served to decompose the art scene, to force artists to surrender their plan for the exhibition, and to announce the observation of their actions, the fires served to entirely prevent the upcoming exhibition. The visible, noticeable actions were replaced by covert and random ones. One example of this occurred in 1979 during an art festival which took place simultaneously in Moscow, Leningrad, and Paris. After the arrest of the painter Georgy Mikhailov and his sentencing for "private business activities and commercial exchange," the approach changed to repeatedly inviting other artists, destroying the door locks of studios, stealing frames, destroying works, turning off telephone lines, or starting fires. In the course of this, thirty artworks were completely destroyed and twenty partially destroyed.[14]

I name these actions in such detail because they clearly show the interplay of visibility and invisibility, conspicuousness and hiddenness. It is always about marking the presence of the "plainclothes art historians." This is followed by a second step, the decomposition of the artists, and ultimately, if this is unsuccessful, the destruction of art.

The Big Performance

Alongside these typical break-ins, there were also highly lavish productions. The most spectacular covert censorship action was undoubtedly the so-called Bulldozer Exhibition in Moscow in September 1974.

In the late 1960s, Oscar Rabin, a Moscow underground artist, had repeatedly attempted to organize an open-air exhibition, referencing the first open-air "protest exhibition" of 1962. In early September, several artists sent a letter to the Moscow City Council informing them of their intention to hold an open-air exhibition on Sunday, September 15, on an undeveloped piece of land. Because there was no law that planned for, denied, or forbade an "open-air picture exhibition," the exhibition was not officially forbidden, even if it was not explicitly approved. Because of this ambiguous gap in the law, the state planned on a highly elaborate performance.

On September 15, 1974, everything initially went according to plan. The artists travelled via metro to the city outskirts with the intention of presenting their pictures in the open field. The first intervention of the state had already happened, however, in the metro station. Oscar Rabin and Alexander Glezer, both organizers of the exhibition, were stopped by militia members and accused of theft. In Rabin's case, the theft of his own pictures. After a while, they were released again. From the outset, this first act of chicanery called attention to the presence[15] of these "plainclothes art historians."[16]

When the organizers reached the field, as the art collector Alexander Glezer reports, the set-up of the exhibition had just begun. Some of the artists present at the time were the now internationally known Komar and Melamid, Lidiya Masterkova, and Igor Sinyavin.

Parallel to this, workers were busying themselves on the open field with plants and seedlings, preparing to transform it into a culture park and public square. They were evidently recruited by the KGB to simultaneously carry out a *subbotnik*, a voluntary community service action. The militia were also securing the area with bulldozers and water guns. The workers were apparently instructed, according to Glezer, to perform their day's work on the square in a completely natural way. After a while, with calls to order like, "Out of the way! Do not prevent the workers from earning their daily bread! Everything for Lenin's *subbotnik*!", they tore the pictures out of the artists' hands and hurled them into the trucks. The drivers who were also recruited did not hesitate to drive their bulldozers towards the audience and artists, and to crush and then burn the pictures. Most of the painters were arrested. The bulldozers turned out to be involuntary exhibition objects, which is why the event is now called the Bulldozer Exhibition.

After the action, the participants in the *subbotnik* apparently wrote a letter to the editors of the *Sovetskaya Kul'tura* in which they complained that the artists had prevented their clean-up activities: "In the morning, we, the local residents and workers of the factory, voluntarily appeared for a *subbotnik* to set up autumn green spaces. How great was our incomprehension and then our outrage when, around noon, at the intersection ... one car after another suddenly stopped and out climbed these brazen, carelessly dressed people. They began dragging in the strangest pictures, without frames, to place them in the open air, and exactly there where we were working. Their arrival disturbed the work rhythm of the volunteer class."[17]

Why all this theater? They could have simply denied approval for the exhibition. What were the advantages of such a "performative censorship" as opposed to a simple ban? We can cite four points as an answer:

1) First of all, "performative censorship" conceals the fact that there is no cause for the censorship that's being enacted. That is why the approval was initially issued. The rights guaranteed in the constitution of the USSR included not only the right to free speech, a free press, and free association and assembly, but also the right to perform street marches and demonstrations. "Performative censorship" conceals the fact that the state is violating its own constitution. Thus, the state creates causes retrospectively to justify certain consequences (*metalepsis*).

2) The intricately staged counteraction intended to portray not the authorities, but the people as the action's opponent. The hired workers, by way of the *subbotnik*, turned the artists into occupiers of an already-occupied space, a space to which all Soviet citizens have a claim: the park.

3) Thirdly, this act of "performative censorship" was also a performance of the ideological metatext, in this case the voluntary Saturday work of the people. It did not just prevent something; it also demonstrated something—a typical socialist ritual. The performance of voluntary community service and the performance of constitutionality are among the continually repeated performances of the dictatorship.

4) Finally, there is an additional, highly pragmatic reason. This form of censorship enabled "getting to know" the artists who took part in the exhibition, i.e. getting an overview of the potentially subversive milieu. Participating in such an exhibition required great courage. Ilya Kabakov, for example, cancelled his participation due to his own panic, as he himself wrote in his memoirs.[18]

"Operative Measures"

Only the examination of available secret service files can reveal how partial this view from the outside is. They not only give information about acts of operative censorship in the art scene but also about the theatrical training of informants and Unofficial Collaborators. One can read about the criteria according to which agents are cast, trained in acting, and schooled in the methods of operative psychology. Their respective roles are recorded in the so-called legend. The "legend"—meaning the role and the scene of camouflage—consists, according to the dictionary, of "operational, staged facts and pretexts that trigger desired behaviors in certain persons and/or should put the Stasi in a position to arrive at certain information. The legend should be believable and based on real, verifiable facts. Depending on focus, there were travel legends, investigation legends, contact legends, evasive legends, and retreat legends."[19]

People needed to be found who would not attract attention in the artistic milieu, and who would be capable of simulating critical or subversive artistic activity. The "job requirements" of such Unofficial Informants, as in the case of artist Gabriele Stötzer, who I will consider in more detail below, looked like this, for example: "Lifestyle must conform to the above-named circles of persons or be easily adapted," "artistic talent," "strong general education."[20]

We are dealing here with subversive state practices intended to undermine the art scene. It becomes clear that subversive operations do not necessarily need to be aimed at a state power or ideology; the state can also use them effectively in order to infiltrate the underground.

The files of the artist and writer Gabriele Stötzer are a particularly vivid example of the Stasi's theatrical disruptive activity in artist circles. Decomposition with both true and untrue—though credible—means was directly aimed at her network of relationships, her psyche, and her artistic activity. It was intended to undermine her perception of reality and the self. The key to resisting power lies, as Foucault has written,[21] in the relationship to oneself. If this is decomposed, then no more resistance is possible. In the vocabulary of the Stasi, this involved the "systematic organization of professional and social failures for the undermining of self-confidence."[22] The Stasi called upon the methods of "operational psychology" as they were developed at the Law school of the MfS.[23]

In the case of Gabriele Stötzer, it was the IM David Menzer (Alexander "Sascha" Anderson), among many other informants, who devalued her artistic and literary activities through his work as a Stasi critic. Informants, but primarily their leading officers, usually put the words "artistic" and "literary"[24] in quotation marks, or wrote "so-called artistic work," "pamphlets," or "shoddy efforts."[25] They also disparaged the literary texts as "incomprehensible" or "unqualified," or pathologized them as "partially psychopathic."[26]

In the case of the writer Reiner Kunze, to name another example, it was said in the operational plan that "evidence shall be provided that Kunz's prose is bad prose and serves the sole purpose of agitation and the political-ideological diversion of the opponent."[27] From Stötzer's file, we also learn that attempts were made to convince her social circle that she was incapable of "successfully carrying out planned activities,"[28] although it was, of course, the Stasi itself that was secretly impeding these activities.

The decomposition of one's relationship to oneself occurred not only through causing uncertainty and through the minimizing of artistic work, or bad reviews, but also through performative censorship: exhibitions abroad, for example, were prevented from occurring by issuing rejections in the name of foreign curators; publishers were pressured not to publish texts, and so on. The Stasi also "liquidated" Stötzer's private gallery by terminating the lease on her apartment, which made the continuance of the gallery impossible. In Stötzer's files, this was referred to as the "formulation of a liquidation and decomposition plan," and as an "elaboration" or "exhaustion" of "every possible legal option for the restriction of the activities"[29] or as the elaboration of "preconditions ... against K.[30] carrying out administrative sanctions from the point of view of tax evasion."[31]

In a status report connected with "Operation Toxin" (AOP Toxin), we read the following: "To summarize, we can say that success was achieved in the framework of the operation in keeping the most essential activities of K. under control and in liquidating in a timely and sustainable fashion the operationally-relevant actions of K. which are to be classified as the organization of an underground political activity."[32]

In his book *Stasi Konkret* (*Stasi Concretely*), the historian Ilko-Sascha Kowalczuk lists over two pages of further examples of common decomposition practices, including consciously spreading the rumor that one was working with the Stasi![33] The most fantastic sounding are, however, the numerous "decomposition measures" that were imposed on Jürgen Fuchs. These include a bomb explosion in front of his house in 1986 and the sabotage of his vehicle's brake hoses. The Stasi Main Department VIII for Observation and Transit Traffic in 1988 also planned the installation of a radioactive source in Fuchs's home by an Unofficial Collaborator,[34] though this was never executed.

Especially perfidious are those "decomposition measures" which appear as their opposite, as something good, caring. To decompose the artist group Clara Mosch, for example, an artist of the group was actively "encouraged" to sow mistrust and resentment in the group.[35] In the files of the Berlin gallery Arkade (Operation Arkade), we read that Stasi invitation cards were sent with the wrong date in order to discredit the gallerist, Jürgen Schweinebraden. In addition, "contaminations" were carried out in the building (stairwell, landing) "with the goal of arousing disgust in older renters towards the behavior of the artists." The plan was to place "porn and other filth," and to send around "hooligans" to turn the building residents against the gallery. Schweinebraden was discredited with his West German colleagues through the purchase of expensive articles in his name in the West (via Intershop), which were then paid for by his Western contacts. In the operational plan of November 13, 1978 on the liquidation of the gallery, the decision was also made to send Stasi-hostile poems to artists.[36] In another instance, the Stasi forged a complete issue of an underground GDR magazine in order to target specific individual dissidents with false information.[37] All of these examples demonstrate "decomposing creativity," the subversion of the secret service apparatus. Some methods of secret service subversion can hardly be distinguished from those of the art scene. This shows that these methods and practices are not, in their form or performance, intrinsically artistic or critical—they become so only in correlation to their function. Decomposition can be both critical of power and power-stabilizing; affirmative, parodic practices do not automatically become criticism or demonstration: they can just as well be destructive and deceptive in promoting an ideology or state power. That is what the disruptive operational measures of the secret police listed above plainly show. They thus also throw into question the basic starting dialectic of research into subversion, which places subversion in opposition to the normativity which it seeks to undermine. Secret police subversion, however, is there to solidify normativity *through* subversion.[38]

The spy in the picture

In Gabriele Stötzer's case, the Stasi directed its "decomposition activities" not only towards the person but also towards the art. To do this, the Stasi planted Unofficial Collaborators as models in Stötzer's photo campaigns. The word that was spreading among her close acquaintances was that Stötzer was interested in photographing transvestites—and so the Stasi promptly provided a transvestite, who was brought to her by the unofficial collaborator "Konrad." Stötzer herself suspected that their intention was to radicalize her photographic works. They attempted to elicit pornographic photos from her in order to "be able to introduce criminal proceedings." Stötzer reports that—when she first semipublicly showed the photographs—she received a criminal charge for pornography, which is not itself contained in the Stasi files and is also not otherwise traceable. Another Unofficial Collaborator who was observing Stötzer made fun of the photos. He noted it in his record without realizing that the photo model was also an Unofficial Collaborator: "To express herself, she composed difficult-to-understand prose texts, but also photo series and substandard films which take for their content, people as a 'medium.' For example, she produced a photo series with a transvestite of about 150–200 photos, in which she believed that the transvestite had, at the end of the series, 'found herself and is able to know herself more self-confidently.'"[39]

Looking at the photographs with the Unofficial Collaborator"-Winfried" today, one sees the whole ambivalence of the Stasi's interference, but also their failure to degrade Stötzer's art. For "Winfried" was a gifted photo model, and the photographic works are art both because of and despite "Winfried." Even if we recognize "Winfried" as an agent and see him as an agent, we witness a pleasure in posing, which was justified even by the clandestine order: he is here, in front of Stötzer's camera, a transvestite, and could show himself as such. It is Stötzer who turns the agent into a photo model who loves the camera more than his duty.

Stötzer thus worked involuntarily with informants in her artistic photo and film works. "Winfried" was not the only one "supplied" to her, but also unofficial collaborator Breaky, who can now be seen as the leading actor in Super 8 films. In her film production *The Peak* (*Die Spitze*), he climbs "phallic objects" in Erfurt as an acrobatic punk. In a later status report, Breaky's own opinion of the action is cited: "When I pointed to the cathedral during filming, she misinterpreted that as a Hitler salute and immediately corrected me."[40] Breaky's report testifies to Stötzer's attentiveness, but also to the fact that he would never go so far as to smuggle a fascist gesture into her work with the purpose of criminalizing the artist.[41]

The informants were ultimately unable to impede Gabriele Stötzer's artistic work. In a certain sense, they also demonstrate a failure of secret police decomposition: some informants, not only those who were assigned to Stötzer, neglected their secret service missions for their own artistic interests or their desire to be a model or figure. Thus, Stötzer's works today are not only works of art—which interventions aimed to prevent—they are also a document of failed performative censorship in the GDR.

Translated from German by Brian Alkire

Endnotes

1 Ol'ga Slobodchikova, "'Teatr.Doc': politsiya prevrala pokaz fil'ma ob Ukraine", BBC *News, Russkaya Sluzhba*, https://www.bbc.com/russian/russia/2014/12/141231_moscow_teatr_doc_police (accessed October 19, 2020).

2 Davor Beganović made me aware that exhibitions in Belgrade and Sarajevo have recently been prevented with performative methods.

3 "Operative Macht. Sylvia Sasse im Gespräch mit Mikhail Ryklin," in *Geschichte der Gegenwart*, https: // geschichtedergegenwart.ch/operative-macht-ein-gespraech-mit-michail-ryklin/

4 "Zersetzung" in *Das MfS-Lexikon. Begriffe, Personen und Strukturen der Staatssicherheit der* DDR (Berlin: Ch. Links Verlag, 2016), 390ff.

5 Nikolay Evreinov, "Teatral'noe iskusstvo na sluzhbe u obshchestvennoy bezopasnosti," *Zhizn Iskusstva* 792–797 (August 1921): 4.

6 Malte Rolf, *Das sowjetische Massenfest* (Hamburg: Hamburger Edition, 2006).

7 Walter Benjamin, "Das Kunstwerk im Zeitalter seiner technischen Reproduzierbarkeit," in *Gesammelte Schriften I. Abhandlungen*, eds. Rolf Tiedemann and Hermann Schweppenhäuser (Frankfurt am Main: Suhrkamp Verlag, 1991).

8 Guy Debord, *Commentaires sur la société du spectacle* (Paris: Éditions Gerard Lebovici, 1988), 20.

9 Historically, we might refer to these theatrical censorship practices as *chicanery*. The term *chicane* or chicanery was originally used in sixteenth-century French to indicate that a fact was "distorted" or "falsified." It could also mean that someone was being harassed with exaggerated trivialities and was also being sued in court. While the focus here is still on the distortion, falsification, and harassment, all aesthetic and theatrical acts in the German term *schikane* relate more to its function (in *Meyers Lexikon* of 1908: a "difficulty caused with malicious intent, namely one by which another's intended performance of a something shall be delayed or prevented.") The main focus here, like in the Russian *pridrika*, is on delay and prevention tactics: meaning, approvals that are not issued, hurdles laid in the way, and conditions that are imposed for no apparent reason. "Difficulty," "delay," and "prevention" also fit the pattern of the first example. The fire safety inspectors arrive to delay or prevent something; the lease is terminated to present difficulties; work is hindered; and premieres are delayed

with the goal of making theater work generally impossible. Chicanery is part of a subversion strategy directed at individuals or at institutions. It can occur in secret or—as the French etymology suggests—with a great deal of theater, as, for example, in the bomb threat action. Vladimir Voinovich refers to them as "wet things" ("*mokrye dela*"). Vladimir Voynovich, "Maloye sobraniye sochinenii v 5 tomach, *tom 5*, Zamysel," *Delo № 34840* (Moscow, 1995), 372.

10 Cf. Roginski and Okhotin, "Archivquellen zum Thema KGB und Literatur"; Shentalinsky, *Arrested Voices. Resurrecting the Disappeared Writers of the Soviet Regime.* Unfortunately, Shentalinsky does not show the dossier, instead renarrating them to the point where they can hardly be used as a source anymore.

11 I.e. the Exhibition of Achievements of National Economy (VDNKh, Russian: ВДНХ) in Moscow.

12 Irina Alpatova and Leonid Talokhkin, eds., *"Drugoye Iskusstvo": Moskva 1956–1988*, (Moscow: Galart, 1999), 45.

13 "Kratkiye soobshcheniya,"*Khronika tekushchikh sobytii* 41 (1976), http://hts.memo.ru/.

14 See Gleser, *Kunst gegen Bulldozer: Memoiren eines russischen Sammlers.*

15 Sven Gundlach writes that "'plainclothes art historians' [*iskusstvovedy v shtatskom*] were present, costumed as drivers." Sven Gundlach, "Vystavka kak aktsiya," *Dekorativnoye iskusstvo* 5, 33.

16 There were also reports of the Bulldozer Exhibition in numerous Western newspapers. The *Spiegel* reported on the excesses during the action exhibition under the headline "On the field." *Spiegel* 39 (1974): 82–83.

17 Alexander Gleser, *Kunst gegen Bulldozer: Memoiren eines russischen Sammlers* (Berlin: Ullstein Verlag, 1982), 306; Andrey Erofeyev and Jean-Hubert Martin, eds., *Kunst im Verborgenen. Nonkonformisten Russland 1957–1995* (Munich/New York: Prestel, 1995), 36.

18 Ilya Kabakov, *60–70-e...: Zapiski o Neofitsial'noy Zhizni v Moskve* (*1960s–1970s...: Notes about Unofficial Artistic Life in Moscow*) (Moscow: Novoye literaturnoye obozreniye, 1997), 199.

19 "Legende," in *Das MfS-Lexikon* (Berlin: Ch. Links Verlag, 2016), 222f.

20 *Eingeschränkte Freiheit. Der Fall Gabriele Stötzer* (BStU, 2014), 51.

21 Michel Foucault, *L'herméneutique du sujet. Cours au Collège de France, 1981–1982* (Paris: Éditions du Seuil/Éditions Gallimard, 2001) 241.

22 *Das MfS-Lexikon*, 391.

23 Günter Förster, *Die Dissertationen an der "Juristischen Hochschule"*

des MfS. Eine annotierte Bibliographie, (Berlin: BStU, 1997).

24 OV "Toxin," BStU, MfS, 4, 127.

25 OV "Toxin," BStU, MfS, 4, 21.

26 OV "Toxin," BStU, MfS, 5.

27 Marko Martin, "'Geschaffene Machwerke.' Die Sprache der Stasi," in *Text+Kritik, Feinderklärung. Literatur und Staatssicherheitsdienst*, ed. Heinz Ludwig Arnold, Vol. 120 (October 1993), 51.

28 OV "Toxin," BStU, MfS, 4, 11.

29 OV "Toxin," BStU, MfS, OV Toxin, Vol. 4, 13.

30 "K" indicates Gabriele Kachold. Stötzer was married from 1973–79 and bore the name of her husband.

31 OV "Toxin," BStU, MfS, 4, 6.

32 *Eingeschränkte Freiheit. Der Fall Gabriele Stötzer*(BStU, 2014), 51.

33 Ilko-Sascha Kowalczuk, *Stasi Konkret.* Überwachung und Repression in der DDR (Munich: Beck C.H 2013), 174. See also Pingel-Schliemann's book *Zersetzen. Strategie einer Diktatur*, which names and analyses other decomposition measures.

34 "Bericht zum Projekt 'Einsatz von Röntgenstrahlen und radioaktiven Stoffen durch das MfS – Fiktion oder Realität?'", BStU, 215.

35 BStU, MfS BV KMSt XIV 73/75, Vol. 5, 18–30.

36 BStU, MfS BV Bln AOP 7030-82, Vol. 3.

37 The journal was a forgery of *Friedrichsfelder Feuermelder.*

38 Cf. recent contributions in: Gerber and Hausladen, eds., *Compared to What? Pop zwischen Normativität und Subversion.*

39 *Eingeschränkte Freiheit. Der Fall Gabriele Stötzer* (BStU, 2014), 235.

40 Ibid.

41 Conversation with the artist, September 14, 2018.

The Bulldozer Exhibition:

Reconstruction of a KGB (Russian Committee for State Security) Performance

The Bulldozer Exhibition (*Buldozernaya vystavka*) was one of the most influential events of the nonconformist art scene in the Soviet Union. It was an act of performative and violent censorship against a public exhibition planned by various artists in the Moscow outskirts on September 15, 1974. The authorities and "plainclothes art historians" (KGB agents) brought this exhibition to an end with an elaborate counterperformance. They sent workers to the exhibition location with the assignment of planting trees at exactly those locations where the artists wanted to exhibit their art. The "workers" had seedlings, spades, and rakes in their hands with which they knocked the artists' pictures from their hands and hurled them into trucks. The driver, also hired for the occasion, drove over the pictures with two bulldozers. The selected five photographs presented here from the Bar-Gera Collection were smuggled out of the Soviet Union, as well as thirteen facsimile booklet pages from the archive of Mikhail Abrosimov, a former KGB officer responsible for the Moscow artistic underground. In his booklet there are not only photos from the bulldozer exhibition, but also from the exhibition in Izmaylovo, which was approved a short time later. The letter originated with the alleged workers and appeared a couple of days later in the newspaper *Sovetskaya Kul'tura*. (S)

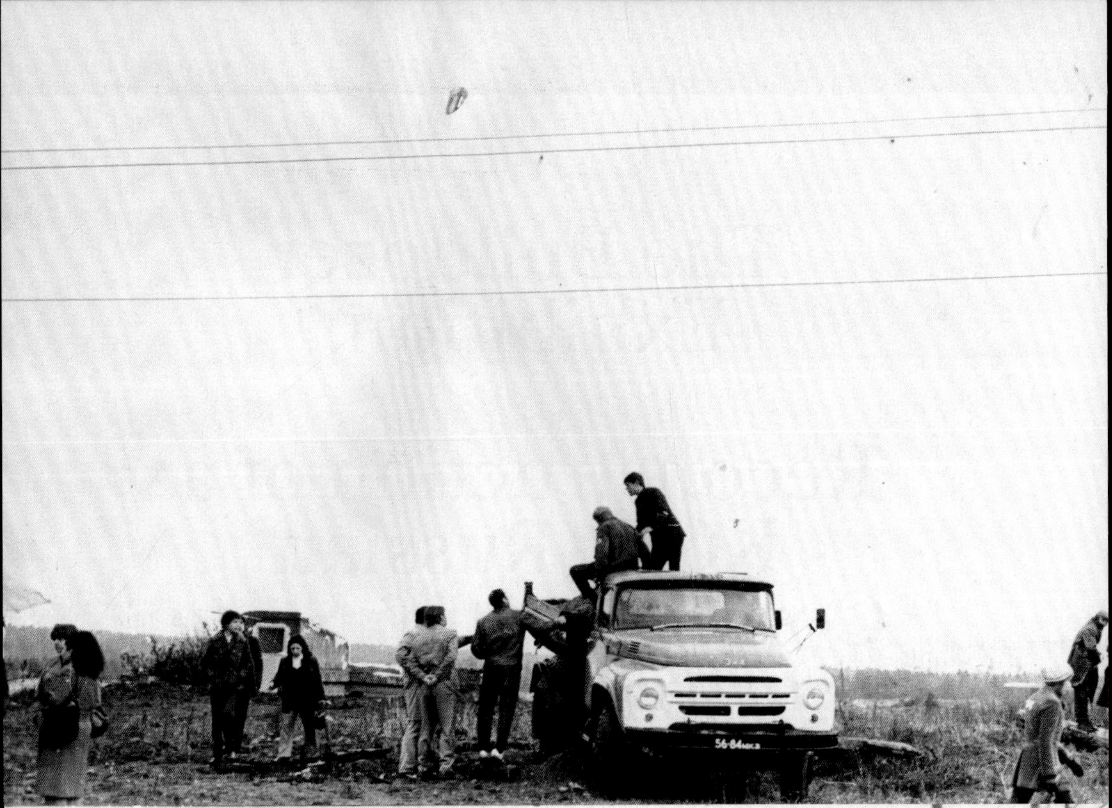

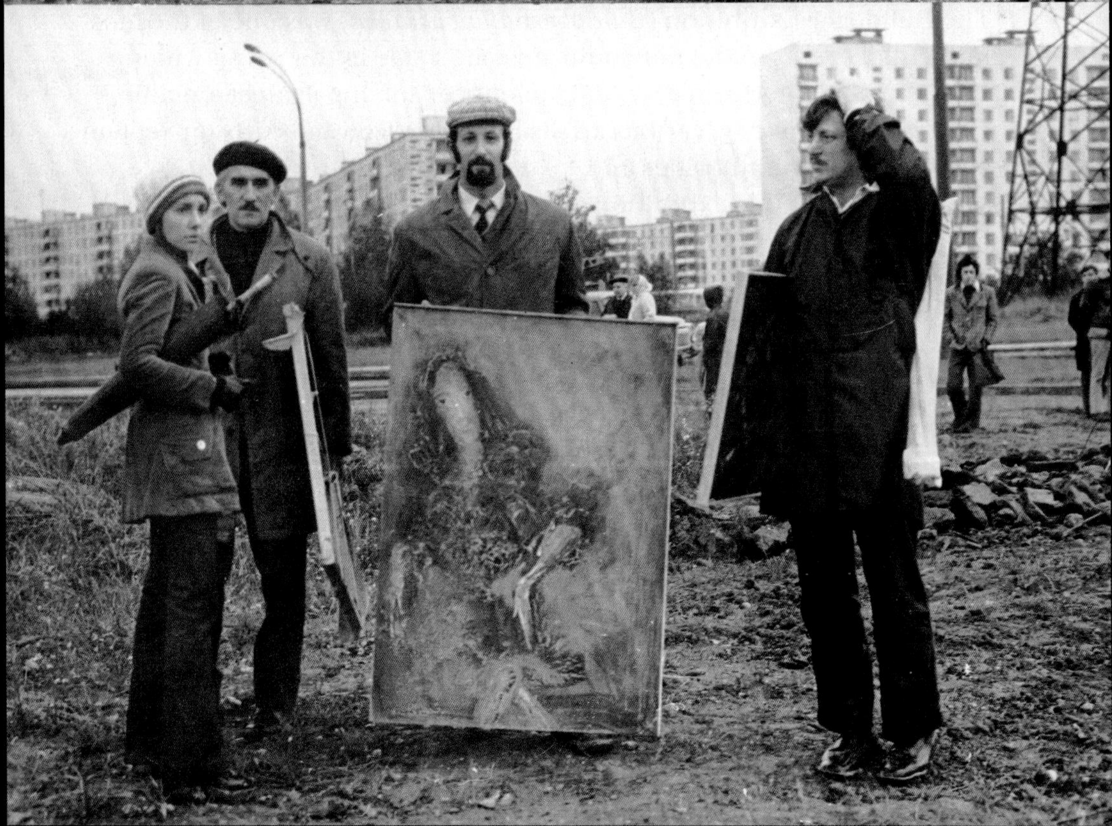

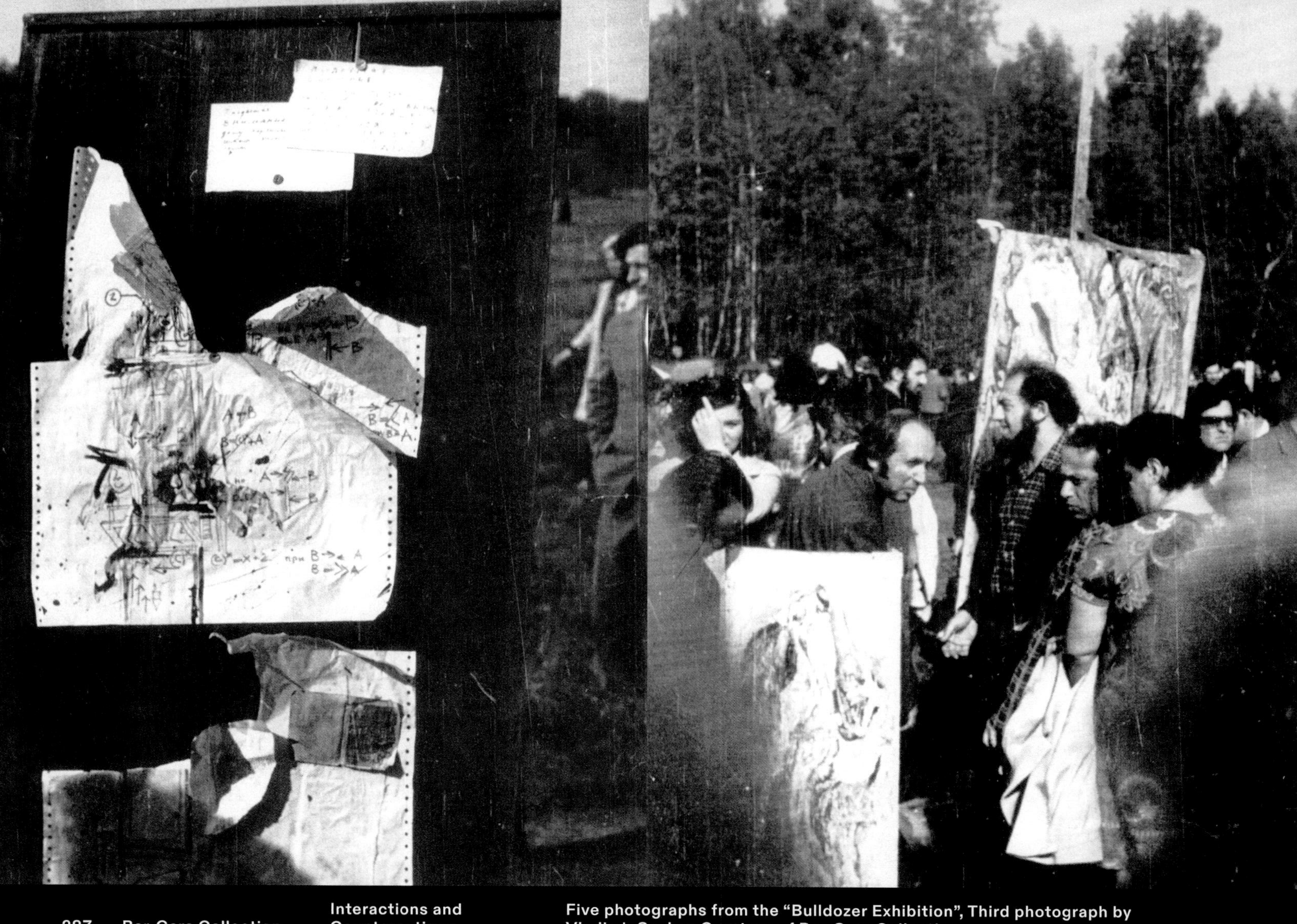

Five photographs from the “Bulldozer Exhibition”, Third photograph by Vladimir Sychev Courtesy of Bar-Gera Collection

1974

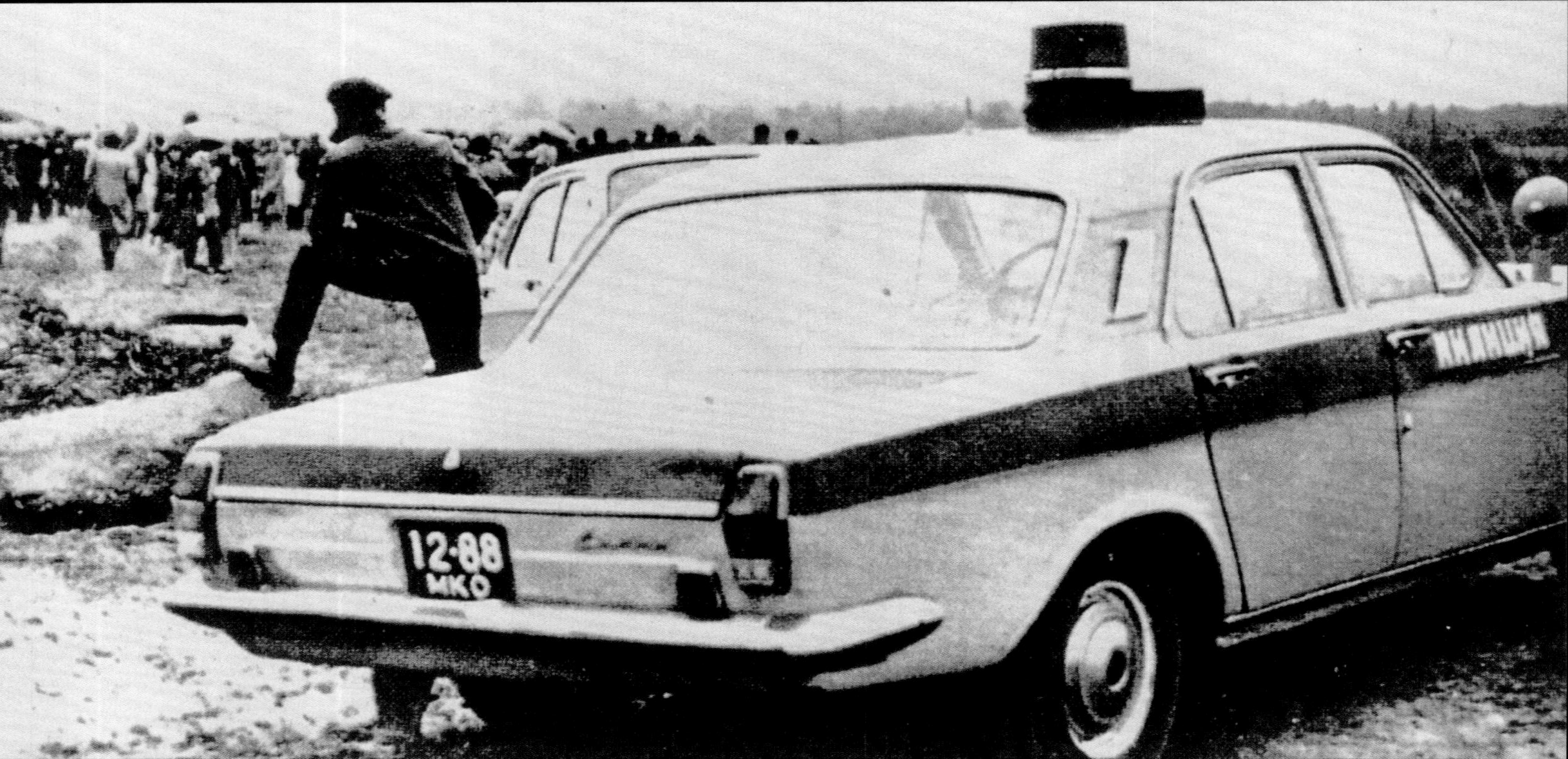
12-88
MKO

Cover and thirteen facsimile pages out of a booklet with forty-four photographs, Courtesy of Iskusstvo magazine 1974

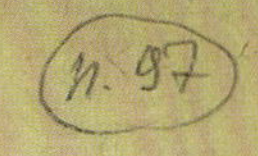

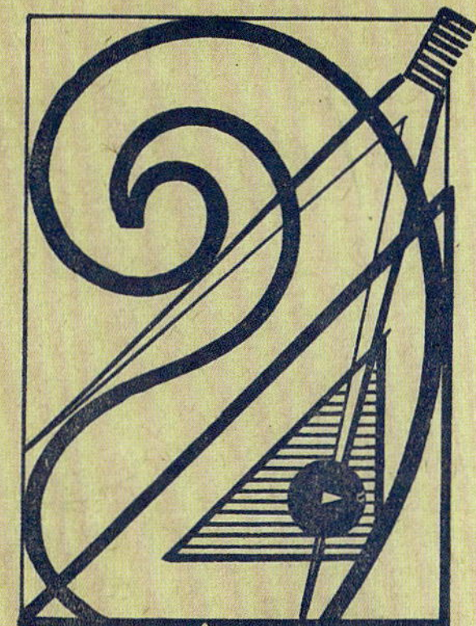

ДЛЯ ЧЕРЧЕНИЯ

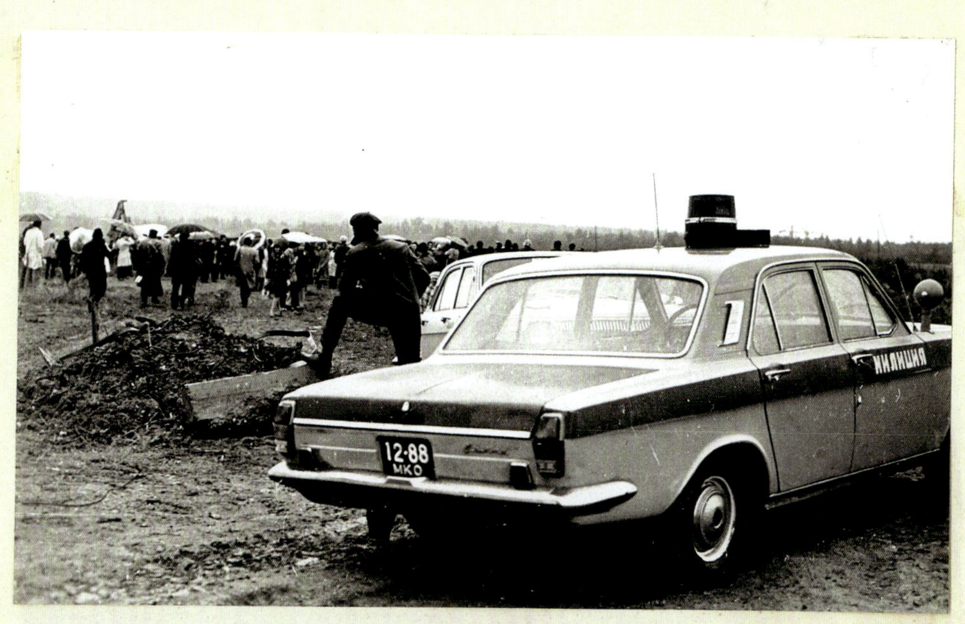

Thirteen facsimile pages out of a booklet with forty-four photographs from 1974 the archive of Mikhail Abrosimov, Courtesy of Iskusstvo magazine

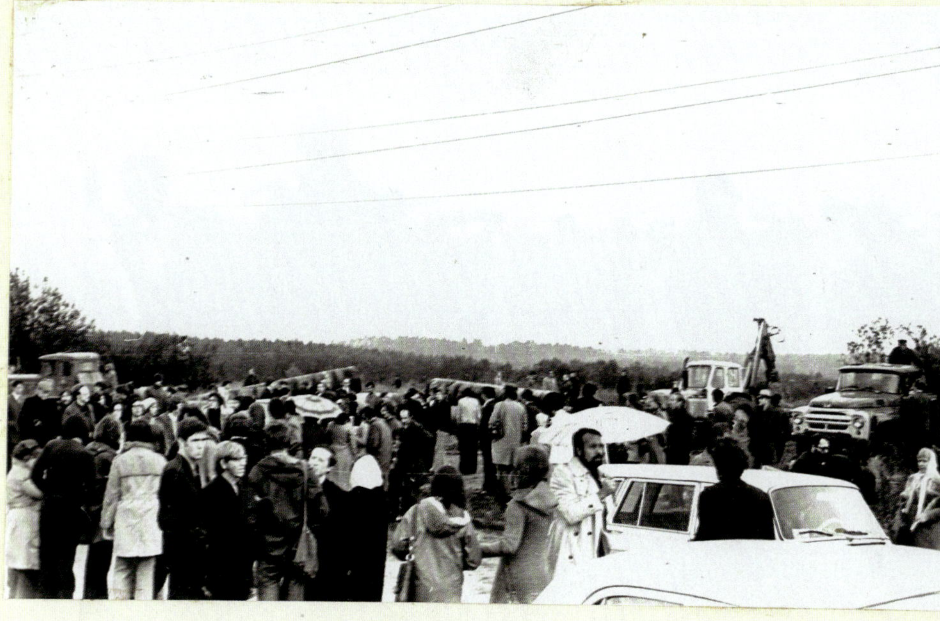

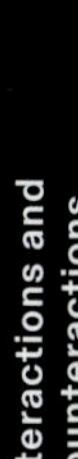

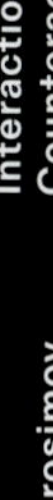

Thirteen facsimile pages out of a booklet with forty-four photographs from the archive of Mikhail Abrosimov, Courtesy of Iskusstvo magazine

1974

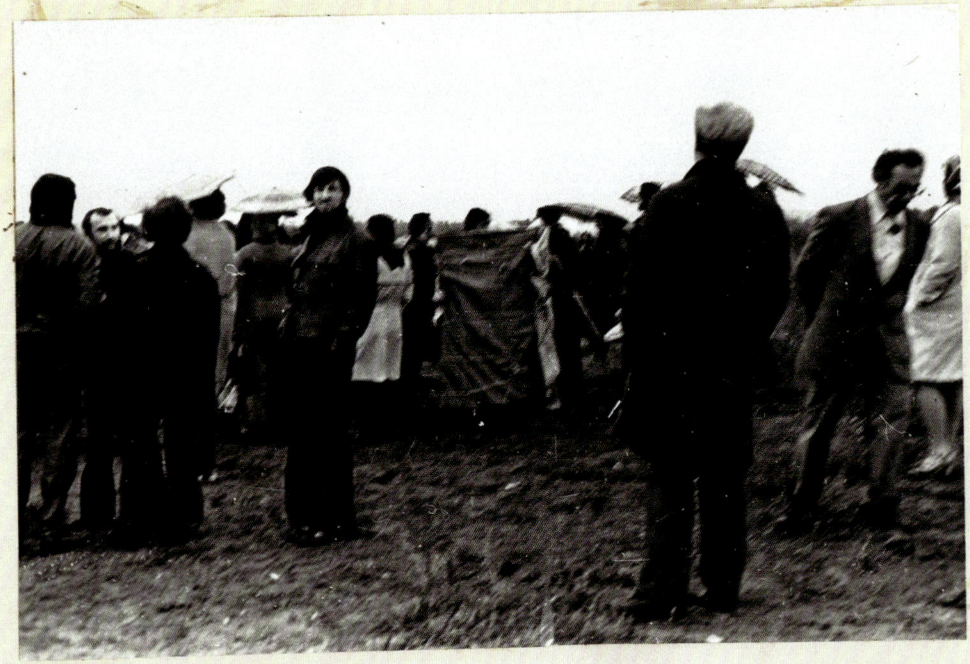

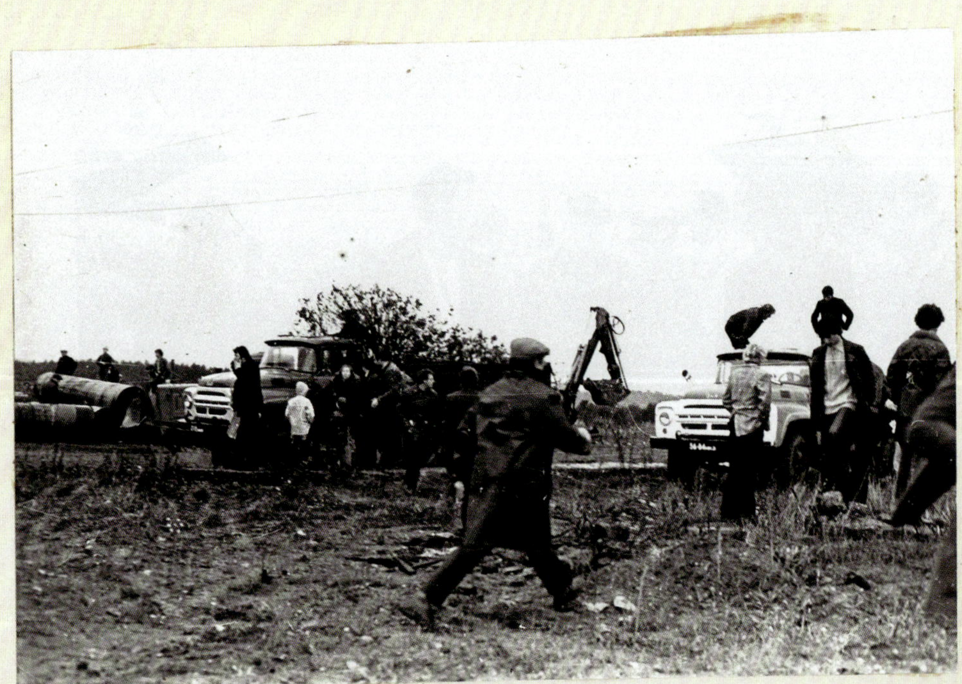

the archive of Mikhail Abrosimov, Courtesy of Iskusstvo magazine

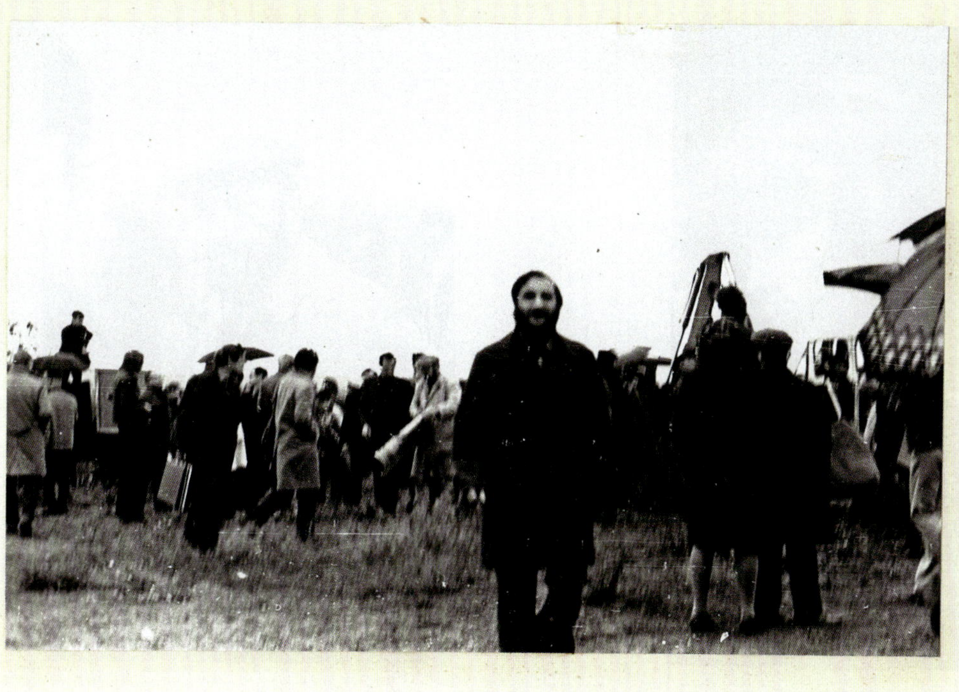

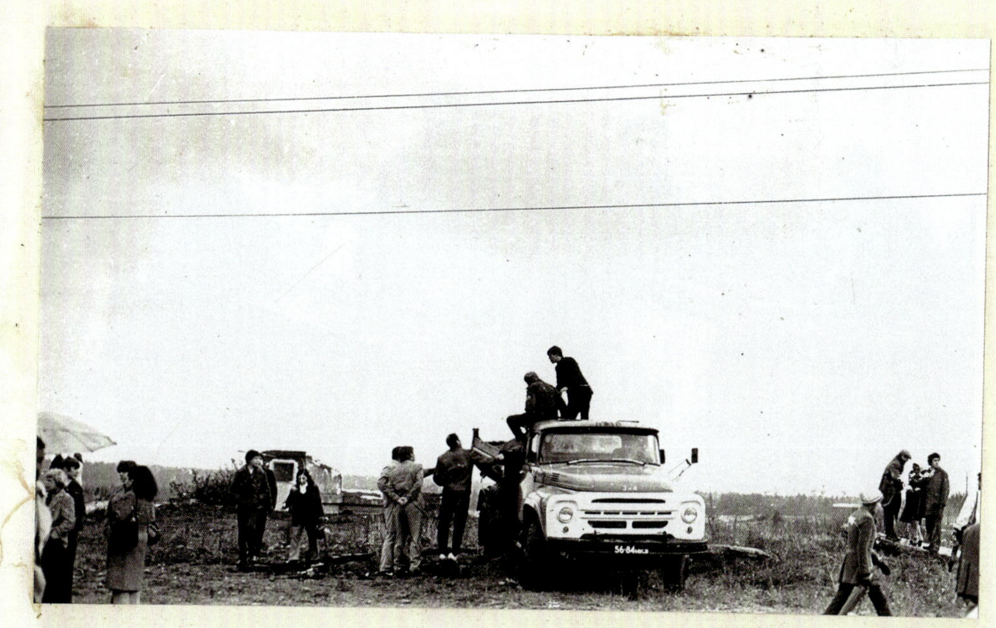

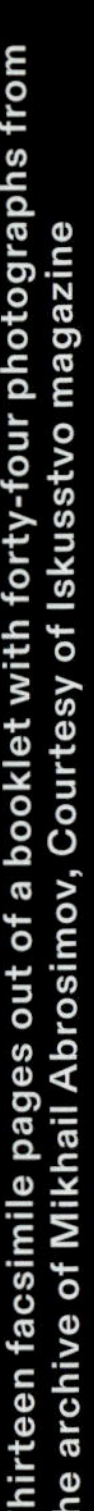

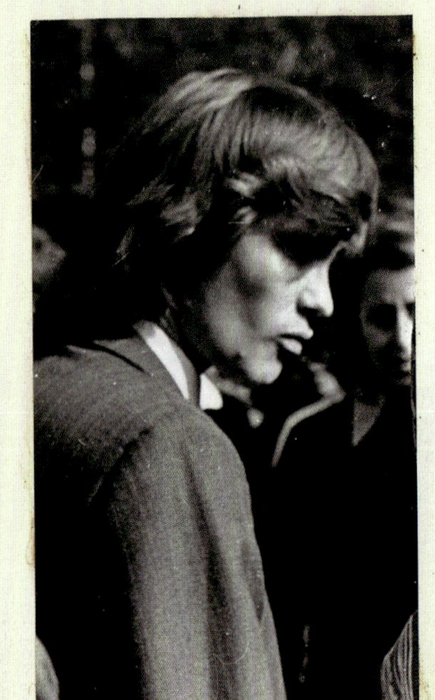

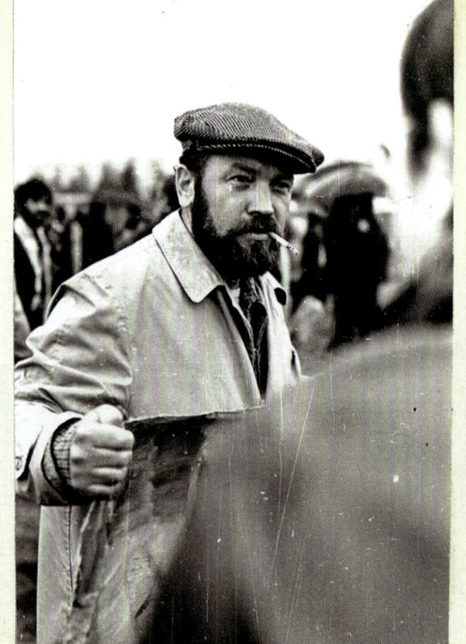

Thirteen facsimile pages out of a booklet with forty-four photographs from 1974 the archive of Mikhail Abrosimov, Courtesy of Iskusstvo magazine

Thirteen facsimile pages out of a booklet with forty-four photographs from the archive of Mikhail Abrosimov, Courtesy of Iskusstvo magazine

1974

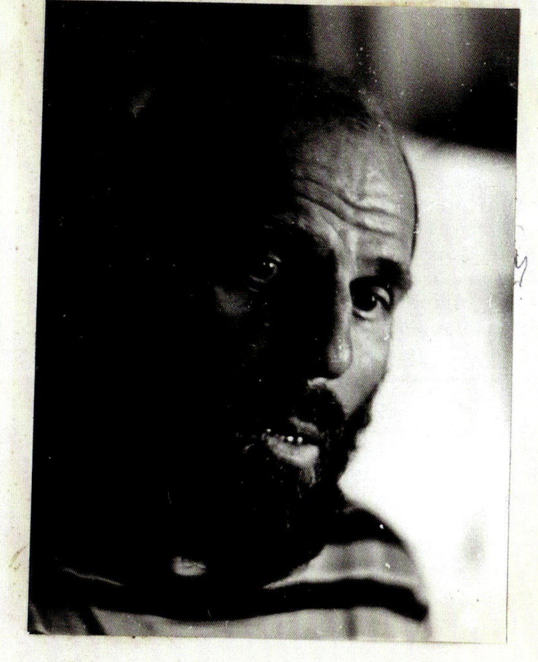

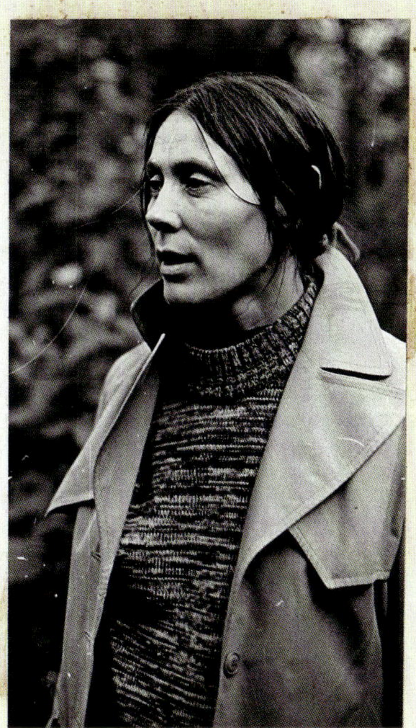

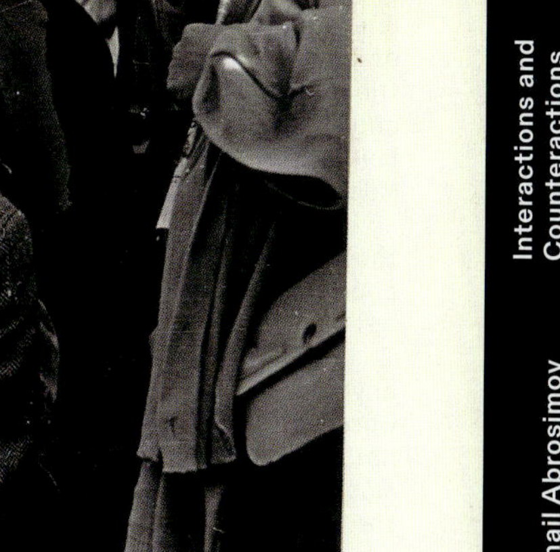

Dear Comrade Editor!

Are you informed about the occurrences in our neighborhood of Cheryomushki, yesterday, on September 15?

In the morning, we, a group of local citizens and workers from nearby enterprises, went out on that day full of enthusiasm to join this preplanned mass *voskresnik* (Sunday volunteer work) foran autumn cleanup and beautification. Imagine our confusion and then our dismay. It was noon on the intersection of Profsoyuznaya and Ostrovityanova when one car after another stopped and different, shoddily clothed people began to unload rather strangely painted canvases in frames and without them, with the intention of putting them on display here, in the open air, to arrange an exhibition of their painterly efforts in that same place where people were working. With their arrival, the rhythm of the Sunday volunteer work was disrupted. Pushing and shoving, noise, and disorder took over the quiet intersection: the uninvited guests behaved provocatively. They tore shovels and rakes from the workers, who they pushed off the lawns, and they tore up a poster calling for participation in the *voskresnik*, disrupted traffic, and used foul language and profanity.

What seems interesting, however, is that together with these so-called artists and even a little before, some foreigners also arrived. They came in cars with diplomatic license plates from the embassies of a number of capitalist countries. In fact, some of the pictures were brought in embassy cars. As it later turned out, there were quite a few correspondents of the international press among these foreigners. It was clear that they had not come here just to cover an "art exhibit." They demonstratively photographed all this mayhem and actively took part in it. Udgord Nils Morten [*sic*], a correspondent for the Norwegian newspaper *Aftenposten* even permitted himself to strike a volunteer guard in the face when the latter tried to restrain him. There were other similar cases.

In this way, the unseemly invasion of a group of formalist artists took on the character of a planned political provocation.

Volunteer guards intervened on the request of the Sunday work volunteers, who then called the militia. Several of the "exhibition's" organizers, who behaved themselves especially inappropriately, were taken in to local militia stations for identification. These turned out to be the self-proclaimed "free artists" and "nonconformists" O. Rabin, A. Krapivnitsiky [*sic*], V. Sychev, N. Elskaya, A. Tal, M. Slavutskaya, V. Tupitsyn and others, up to fifty in number. The pictures that they brought along clearly had an anti-artistic character and inspired nothing but disgust and derision.

Since all these people called themselves artists, we are writing to the Artists' Union today for an explanation. It turns out that none of these people are members of the Artists' Union of the USSR; it follows that they only acted after conspiring with one another. A week before, they had applied for permission at the Executive Committee of the Moscow City Council of the Communist Party, where they were informed about the regulations concerning the organization and carrying-out of art exhibits in our capital city. These they chose to ignore. On request of the Moscow City Council Executive Committee, corresponding information was also conveyed to them through the Moscow branch of the Artists' Union, but this also failed to impress them.

It also became apparent that some of these "artists," who decided to exhibit their work in such a strange manner, planned to sell their paintings to foreign countries. Some of them have even already exhibited there, maybe not earning money, but [instead], the prestige of "talent unrecognized in the motherland."

We know, however, that shameful speculation on nonrecognition has never earned anyone victory laurels. All the more because the events on Sunday in Cheryomushki were accompanied by breaches of the public order and hooliganism, and these should not be forgiven. As witnesses to this disorderly conduct, we, the citizens of Cheryomushki, categorically protest again such "artistic" actions. We demand respect for the laws of our country and its public order from both the so-called free artists who seemingly lack any idea of true art, and from their foreign friends and protectors.

Sunday-volunteering participants

V. Fedoseyev Welder, Shockworker of Communist Labor

J. Svistunov
Radio technician, Shockworker of Communist Labor

V. Polovinka
Administration Head for Roads and Parks in Cheryomushki, Area Worker's Soviet Deputy

B. Timashev
Electrician

Translated from Russian by David Riff.

Comment by Alexander Glezer (art collector), who participated in the exhibition: "None of the painters came to the exhibition grounds in a car, let alone a foreign one. No one snatched shovels and rakes from anyone, because there were no devices at all. Nils Morten, whom I know well, could never have beaten a helper – his upbringing speaks against it. But he himself was pushed around, his camera was taken away and microfilms that had nothing to do with the exhibition were stolen. And where in their vocabulary had the turners and fitters only found the refined term 'nonconformists' (*nekonformisty*) (the artists never called themselves that)?"
Translation from: Alexander Gleser, *Kunst gegen Bulldozer. Memoiren eines russischen Sammlers* (München: Ullstein, 1982), 305f.

Notice to the Politburo of the Central Committee of the CPSU (Committee Party of the Soviet Union)

On September 2 a group of artists addressed a letter to the Moscow City Council announcing its intention of organizing an open-air display of paintings far from the causeways of city traffic. The authors of the letter were invited to the Moscow City Council, where they spoke twice to the group of responsible council members headed by comrade K.A. Sukhinich.

The final meeting took place on September 13. Moscow City Council did not officially prohibit the open-air exhibit of paintings and issued no warning that the site would be occupied by a *voskresnik* [Sunday volunteer work]. This is why artists from Moscow, Leningrad, Vladimir, and Pskov (twenty-four persons total) took their paintings to the site of the exhibition near Belyayevo metro station on Sunday, September 15.

It was already at the exit of the metro station that the militia detained the artist Oscar Rabin and the poet and collector Alexander Glezer, accusing them of theft. They were released after twenty minutes, i.e. after the beginning of the planned exhibit. At the site of the planned exhibit, events unfolded as follows:

Around 12 p.m., the exhibition site was cordoned off by the militia and plainclothes operatives. Artists and audience had paintings torn from their hands, their arms twisted; they were beaten and run over by bulldozers and tractors. The only explanation offered was the need to vacate the location to make room for a tree-planting *voskresnik*. These insulting words and actions lasted for an hour. Paintings were trampled in the mud, thrown into the back of a truck, and taken off in an unknown direction.

The artists Evgeniy Rukhin, Oscar Rabin, Sascha Rabin, Nadezhda El'skaya, and Valentin Vorob'ev were detained by the militia.

We express our decisive protest against this lawless and arbitrary treatment, against the infraction against our rights and freedoms as guaranteed by the Constitution of the USSR and the Declaration of Human Rights.

We demand an investigation into this shameful matter, the return of the artworks, and that those responsible for this arbitrary action be punished.

Artists:

Vladimir Nemukhin
Lidiya Masterkova
Igor' Kholin
Yuri Zharkikh
Borukh Shteinberg
Alexander Melamid

Vitaliy Komar
Yekaterina Arnol'd
Rimma Zanevskaya
Oleg Tripol'sky
Valentin Vorob'ev

A number of visitors also protest against this lawlessness and the arrest of artists. They include:

Nikolay Bokov – Philosopher
Alexander Glezer – Poet
Mikhail Odnoralov – Artist
Vladimir Fuchs – Worker
Lyudmila Kaminskaya – Engineer
Margarita Masterkova – Student
Irina Bokova – Student

September 15, 1974

Translated from Russian by David Riff

Заявление в Политбюро ЦК КПСС

Второго сентября группа художников направила письмо в Моссовет, в котором сообщила о своем намерении организовать первый просмотр картин на открытом воздухе вдали от трасс уличного движения. Авторы письма были приглашены в Моссовет, где с ними дважды беседовали ответственные работники Моссовета во главе с т. Сухиничем К.А.

Последняя встреча состоялась в пятницу, 13 сентября. Моссовет официально не запретил просмотр картин на открытом воздухе и не предупредил, что территория будет занята под воскресник. Поэтому художники из Москвы, Ленинграда, Владимира и Пскова (всего 24 чел.) в воскресенье 15 сентября направились с картинами к месту просмотра, в районе станции метро "Беляево".

Уже на выходе из метро милиция задержала художника Оскара Рабина и поэта, коллекционера картин Александра Глезера, обвинив их в ограблении. Через 20 минут, т.е. после предполагаемого начала показа картин, их выпустили. На месте предполагаемого просмотра события разворачивались следующим образом:

Около двенадцати часов место показа было оцеплено милицией и гражданами в штатском. У художников и зрителей вырывали картины, выламывали руки, избивали, на них наезжали бульдозерами и тракторами. Объяснение было одно - требование освободить территорию в виду проводимого здесь воскресника по озеленению. Оскорбления словом и действием продолжались в течение часа. Картины затаптывали в грязь, бросали в кузова грузовых автомобилей и увозили в неизвестном направлении.

Художники Рухин Евгений, Рабин Оскар, Рабин Саша, Эльская Надежда, Воробьев Валентин были задержаны милицией.

Мы выражаем решительный протест против беззакония и произвола, против нарушения наших прав и свобод, гарантированных Конституцией СССР и Декларацией прав человека и гражданина.

Мы требуем разбирательства этого позорного дела, возвращения работ и наказания виновников произвола.

Художники: Владимир Немухин
Лидия Мастеркова
Игорь Холин
Юрий Жарких
Борух Штейнберг
Александр Меламид
Виталий Комар
Екатерина Арнольд
Римма Заневская
Олег Трипольский
Валентин Воробьев

Также возражают против беззакония и арестов художников и ряда зрителей:

Николай Боков - философ
Александр Глезер - поэт
Михаил Одноралов - художник
Владимир Фукс - рабочий
Людмила Каминская - инженер
Маргарита Мастеркова - студентка
Ирина Бокова - студентка

15 сентября 1974

Source: "Zayavlenie v Politbyuro CK KPSS," Memorial Moskva, Fond 102, Op.1., D.24., L.8.

Two Days in September

Nikolay Bokov

“The Hun knows no middle ground. He is either at your throat or at your feet,”[1] said Winston Churchill. But the middle ground is what guarantees stability. It is made of the compromises required wherever conflicts between society and the state arise. A stable social life is the goal of state institutions.

These are the generalities, if not banalities, that come to mind after visiting an autumn exhibit of pictures, which artists from Moscow, Leningrad, and Vladimir tried to organize. The exhibit was planned for September 15, 1974. This celebration of art turned into a riot, regrettably organized by the authorities. Its results are pitiful: around twenty paintings were damaged and five destroyed, some of them by fire, others crushed by bulldozers.

During the morning of September 15th, the most active connoisseurs of painting were already standing guard on the crossing next to the vacant lot in Belyaevo where the exhibit was to take place. There were about a hundred of them. Due to the rain and the fog, it was hard to discern any colors.

Just one artist managed to lift his painting onto a stretcher, but it was immediately thrown to the ground. All the other artists then gathered around. They were met by representatives of the authorities in uniform. *Nota bene*: the militia in uniform then disappeared, although the apprehended artists were accused of “resisting the authorities.” However, they did not decide to reveal themselves as such at that time: most of the damage was done by citizens “in plain clothes,” without presenting any documents.

Here, the visitor could see: a truck with saplings, a tractor, bulldozers, and three sanitation vehicles that they use in Europe to sprinkle the streets.

The artist Oscar Rabin and the collector Alexander Glezer were detained at the metro. They were accused of stealing paintings. The traditions of Russian culture came alive: if it was the officer’s widow (in Nikolay Gogol’s *The Government Inspector*) who flogged herself, it was Rabin who stole the paintings from himself, of course. But counter to tradition, Rabin and Glezer were released by the hands detaining them and could reach the artistic festivities.

What did lovers of painting see next? The militia disappeared, leaving only plainclothes officers, who were more active than the men in uniform. Who were these people? One thing is clear: these were real experts who had "appropriated all culture that humanity had accumulated before them." The bulldozers started up. Of course, the visitors scattered to avoid them. Of course, paintings were torn from their authors' hands and thrown onto lorries full of mud and soil. The artists cried, "Where can we find them?" "What do you mean, where?" answered the true lovers of art, regulars at the Louvre, the Tretyakov Gallery, and other mineralogical museums. "At the garbage dump!" The artist Rukhin was led off with his arms twisted behind his back. "Garbage," declared one connoisseur standing next to me, and kicked a canvas by Nadezhda El'skaya with his lacquered shoe. Other connoisseurs silently trampled one of Lidiya Masterkova's works.

But the art lover at the controls of the bulldozer, pardon me, already ran over Oscar Rabin's "garbage," and nearly crushed the artist too. One elegant maneuver and the paintings "crunch." Another maneuver and the artist fell over, knocked down by the bulldozer's blade together with his son, another artist named Alexander, though not to the ground! That cannot be permitted by the true lovers of art who have appropriated all of humanity's cultural legacy to become sincere connoisseurs. They twist the arms of the painters and lead them off to cars.

Of course, there were foreigners. It wouldn't be the same without them. "Everything is finite this time around," I said in French to the one who happened to be next to me. "Där Tysch,"[2] he answered. It was only later that I was to find an explanation for this strange event.

So where were the authorities? "Don't provoke us," yelled one of the plainclothesmen while attacking the artists. "You're educated people, but you don't understand that you're bound to fail," another plainclothesman next to me said. "If you don't leave, we'll burn your paintings," another one of them yelled, evoking scenes from Mikhail Romm's famous film.[3]

And suddenly, car finally pulled up. A heavyset woman pulled out some red bunting, which she began to unravel. "Why have you come here?" she yelled weakly, swaying back and forth. "Why won't you let the workers work? Go back to where you came from!" The slogan "Off to the *Subbotnik* [Saturday Volunteer Work]" appeared. (Maybe it should have been *Voskresnik* [Sunday Volunteer Work]).[4] But the *subbotnik* had already been carried out, and very successfully: around twenty paintings were confiscated and five artists were already under arrest. It is unclear why the slogan came so late.

It was then that some foreign correspondent got punched in the diaphragm, another foreigner had his forehead cracked open with his own photo camera. The *subbotnik* was going according to plan.

Then it became clear that a group of Soviet citizens had dressed up as "foreigners." I had the pleasure to talk to one them before the action, which was when my suspicions were aroused. It turned out that at the bus stop next to the scene, there were some more art lovers. When passersby asked them what was going on, they answered, "These are foreigners about to leave Russia, they are planting some trees to commemorate the moment. Some hooligans are getting in the way, they're breaking it up right now."

It's really true: water sprayed out from the street-cleaning vehicle and pushed away those spectators who crossed over to the hillock across from where the autumnal display of paintings was supposed to take place. The vehicle sprayed water till everyone ran away. An eager bulldozer driver demonstrated brilliant command of his vehicle in chasing down stragglers.

This is how the first open-air exhibition happened, which the artists had registered with the Moscow Council. The Council did not issue any prohibition, and effectively avoided making any decision on this request, until the problem was solved in its own peculiar way.

I decisively disagree with the accusations made against Oscar Rabin, Evgeny Rukhin, Alexander Rabin, Nadezhda El'skaya, and Vladimir Sychev, implicating them in resistance to the authorities. To prevent people from breaking the law, that law must be made public. To make sure that one does not resist the authorities, one has to know that one's attackers are representative of the law. On September 15, 1974, the authorities did not make themselves recognized as such. Authorities should always be authorities, under all circumstances ... That is a basic condition of the rule of law, especially, of course, a socialist one.

Let us try to reconstruct the plan followed by the municipal authorities on September 15, 1974. On September 2, a group of Moscow artists informed the Moscow City Council of the Communist Party of its intention to hold an exhibition of paintings. The question was discussed by the administration for two weeks. The MOSKh (Moscow Artists' Union)[5] did not supply a written expert opinion on the paintings supplied to them by the participating artists on the request of the Moscow City Council. The Moscow City Council issued no prohibition of the display.

On September 15, a group of persons clothed as foreigners came to the empty lot near the Belyaevo metro station that was indicated in the formal request. Corresponding persons also blocked the nearby asphalt parking lot to make sure the artists didn't "cheat" and put their paintings there. Before the exhibition started, a slogan was unfolded, reading "Everyone to the *Voskresnik*" (in fact, it said *subbotnik* because it was written in haste). The "foreigners" present (Där Tysch) began to plant two dozen saplings on an empty lot where you could plant a thousand trees. They met the arriving artists with angry shouts and corresponding exclamations on the appropriation of all culture accumulated before them by a grateful humanity, and, angry at the artists' interference in their intention of beautifying the capital, began to beautify the artists' faces with the help of shovels and other similar tools. The action concluded with the identification and punishment of the "rowdys."

Several qualities characterize the actions of the Moscow municipal administration on that day. One is inconsistency: Oscar Rabin and Alexander Glezer were detained at the metro station and released, only to allow them to reach the scene of the action and to be run over by bulldozers in front of a large number of Muscovites, foreign diplomats, and journalists. Rabin was only arrested after his run-in with the bulldozer. Indecision: by announcing their intention to hold an exhibition, the artists declared their loyalty. A permit or prohibition was to follow. Instead of a clear decision, an attempt was made to create an idiotic "Potemkin village," a truck with "special equipment," a prison van with the sign reading "Products" on the side. The representatives of the authorities committed an impermissible action (a punishable offence in developed countries): the loyalty of the citizens was not taken into account!

The following is the most important: in coming to a decision, the organs of the state should not just consider reality, but the reality principle. Let us clarify through a simple example: if you stop supplying the city with food, speculation and theft will follow, sometimes to the point of rioting.

In the present case, the reality principle was that the destruction of paintings and arrest of artists would become known to public opinion, and foremost, they would be publicized abroad. Although it was no doubt was informed of this fact, the municipal administration trampled the reality principle and soon encountered reality itself.

The disgusting incident of September 15 became a factor in foreign policy and world politics. And the problem was defined as such only on a level much higher than that of the Moscow Council and the City Party Committee. It follows that the municipal authorities avoid addressing local cultural-political problems, and that they are incapable of the most elementary political analysis. One sees a gulf in the capacity for political action between higher organs and organs with a mid-range authority. But it is precisely the latter that are dealing with the country's population on an everyday basis.

When it encountered this problem, the administration forgot about the appropriate legislation and reacted emotionally. "Don't provoke us," demanded one of those who broke up the exhibition. In that way, the administration tramples upon the reality principle and consigns itself to irresponsibility—unlike the citizens, in this case, the artists declared their loyalty. Such conditions turn the relationship between the state and its citizens on its head, and bear witness to the poverty and instability of social life.

In the end, an exhibition did take place on September 29, 1974 at Izmaylovo and became the object of attention for an international audience; that is, a factor in foreign policy, following lengthy negotiations between artists and the authorities. "Give us a situation report," they ordered the militia sergeant standing next to me. "Reporting on the situation: the situation is normal," the sergeant answered.

Indeed, the situation on September 29 was normal. Everyone kept to their own business: the militia made sure the situation remained orderly, artists displayed their paintings, the audience looked at them. There were sixty-four artists and around five thousand visitors from 12 pm to 4 pm! The specialized audience behaved with restraint this time and stayed in the frame of primitive criticism. The artists had received permission a day before, though only in spoken form, to show their canvases. Written permission would have probably prevented them from chasing away the audience and the artists, should the need arise. Written permission would have broken the traditional ban on initiatives by individual citizens. This tradition, vibrant and aggressive, has no juridical base and directly contradicts the letter of Soviet legislation—most importantly, the principle one, the Constitution.

The exhibition at Izmaylovo presented an extremely colorful picture: the tragic and expressive realism of Oscar Rabin, the near-figurative painting of Vorobyov, the youthful surrealism of Zhdan, as well as abstract burlesques. I daresay only new work was presented, even if some paintings were reminiscent of other schools, past and present.

After all, what matters is not just a style's novelty in principle, but the social context in which that style emerges, comes back to life or is appropriated. The cultural context, sanctioned by the socialist state, unconditionally prohibits artists to study Kandinsky, Malevich, and any other artist who doesn't correspond to the standard of pseudo-realism of the kind that gathers dust on the lower floor of the Tretyakov Gallery and floods the curricula of educational institutions. Under such conditions, the study of Kandinsky is an act of bravery and comes with a certain novelty; this study restores the "link to the past," the destroyed tradition of Russian painting and culture at large. Today, pseudo-realism needs a bulldozer to hold onto its position.

Belyaevo and Izmaylovo are important milestones in contemporary cultural life. The organs of the state encountered a nonstandard problem and proved incapable of solving it properly, i.e. according to the reality principle. This is an alarming symptom, as it is obvious that the sanctioned forms of cultural life are limited and incapable of accommodating new cultural phenomena and newly emerging culture. The problem was solved shoddily, also from the perspective of foreign policy. This bears witness to the unviability of the state's inner politics, and to the fact that domestic policy is a mirror of society and not an industrial branch of social control.

The exhibition at Izmaylovo is important not only because that it liberated painting from under the weight of oppression. This is a fact of social life that is new for both society and the organs of the state. It became clear that such manifestations of cultural maturity bear no threat to the organs of the state, that there can be no conflict, because it is the state that acts as an aggressor, not its citizens. This is a new experience that both sides will need to consider.

September 15 and September 29 have become symbols of two different cultural policies. Only the future will show which path the organs of the state will chose—that of destruction, of September 15, or the path of control corresponding to the reality principle as such, September 29.

Nikolay Bokov
Moscow, 1974

Translated from Russian by David Riff

Source: Nikolay Bokov, "*Dva dnya v sentyabre*," in *Iskusstvo pod bul'dozerom. Sinyaya kniga* (Paris, 1976), 135–143.

Endnotes

1 The original quote from Churchill's speech to Congress on May 19, 1943 was: "...the proud German Army has once again proved the truth of the saying, 'The Hun is always either at your throat or your feet.'" http://www.ibiblio.org/pha/policy/1943/1943-05-19a.html (last accessed December 3, 2019).

2 Parody of the pronunciation of the German phrase "the table," which means that the "foreigner" was not one at all. His answer is wrong, both phonetically and with regards to content.

3 What is meant here is *Ordinary Fascism* (*Obyknovenny fashizm*), or, *Triumph Over Violence*—a Soviet documentary by Mikhail Romm from 1965.

4 The *subbotnik* (from Russian *subbota*, meaning Saturday) is a name originating in Soviet Russia for an unpaid work assignment on Saturday. *Voskresnik* (from the Russian *voskreseniya*, meaning Sunday) would therefore be the name for a work assignment on Sunday.

5 MOSKh, 1969–1990 (Russian MOCX—*Moskovskaya Organizatsiya Soyuza Khudozhnikov*), a Moscow association of artists and art historians. After the dissolution of independent artist associations in the 1930s, it served the central direction of artistic creation and pursued ideological goals.

Gabriele Stötzer, b. 1953 in Emleben, GDR, lives and works in Erfurt, Germany.

Trans-Series

Gabriele Stötzer

When the Erfurt-based artist Gabriele Stötzer wanted, in 1984, to compose a photo series with a cross-dresser, she could have had no idea that it was the Stasi (the State Security of the GDR) that sent her "Winfried." "Winfried" was not just a cross-dresser—he was also an unofficial collaborator of the Stasi. He had been ordered to radicalize the photo performance in the direction of pornography and thus to create a potential criminal charge against Stötzer. But "Winfried" embodied the double role of artist and informant in a way the Stasi had not planned on. Even if we recognize the spy in "Winfried" and see him as a spy, we also see his pleasure in posing, which is not disturbed by his clandestine mission but is instead given justification. It is Stötzer who turns the spy into a photo model who seems to love the camera more than his mission. Stötzer produced a total of seven series with Winfried, none of which she ever publicly exhibited in the GDR. (S)

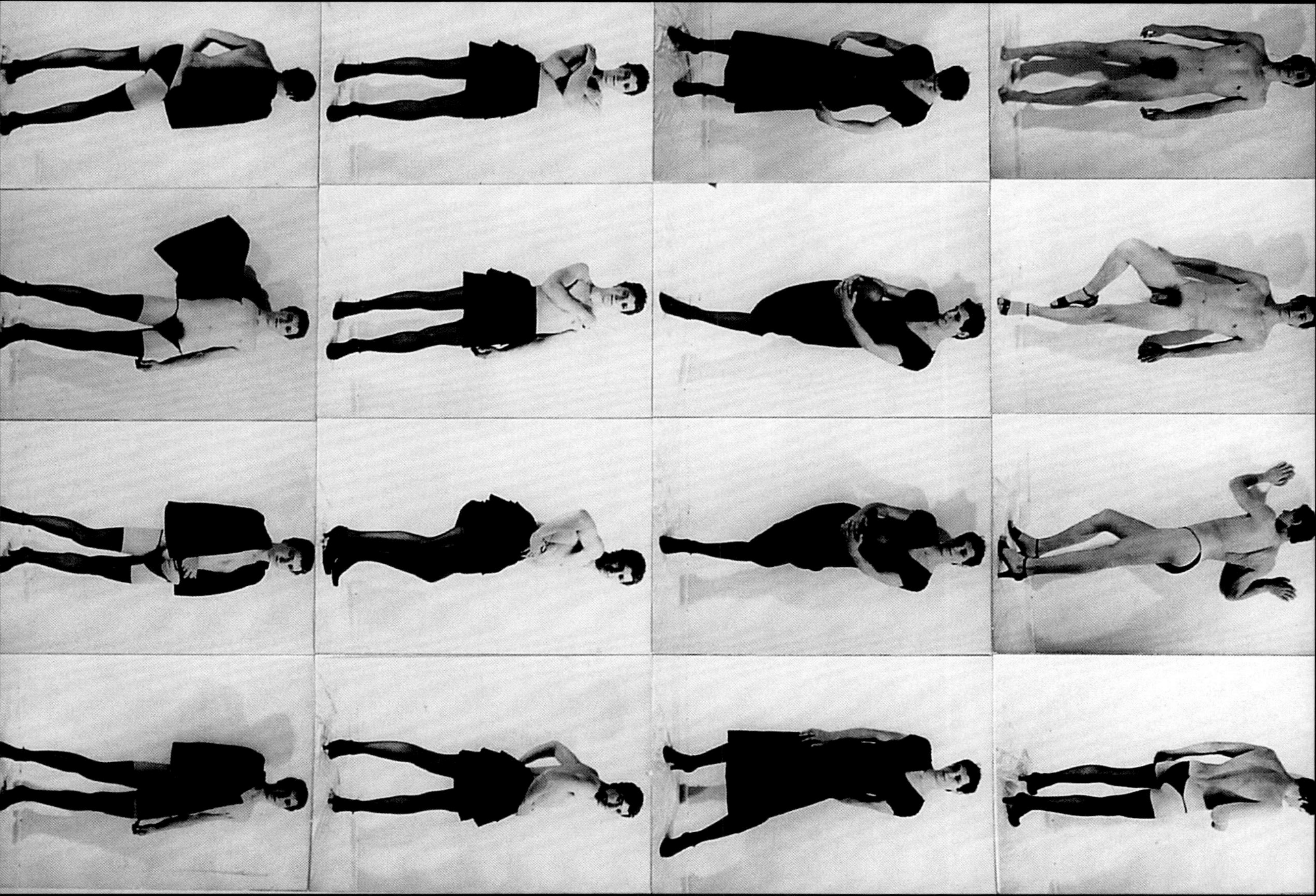

Trans in Black, silver-gelatin prints, mounted on cardboard, 80 × 60 cm, 1985
Courtesy of Gabriele Stötzer

Interactions and Counteractions

Trans as Mother-Child, silver-gelatin prints, mounted on cardboard, 180 × 60 cm Courtesy of Gabriele Stötzer

1985

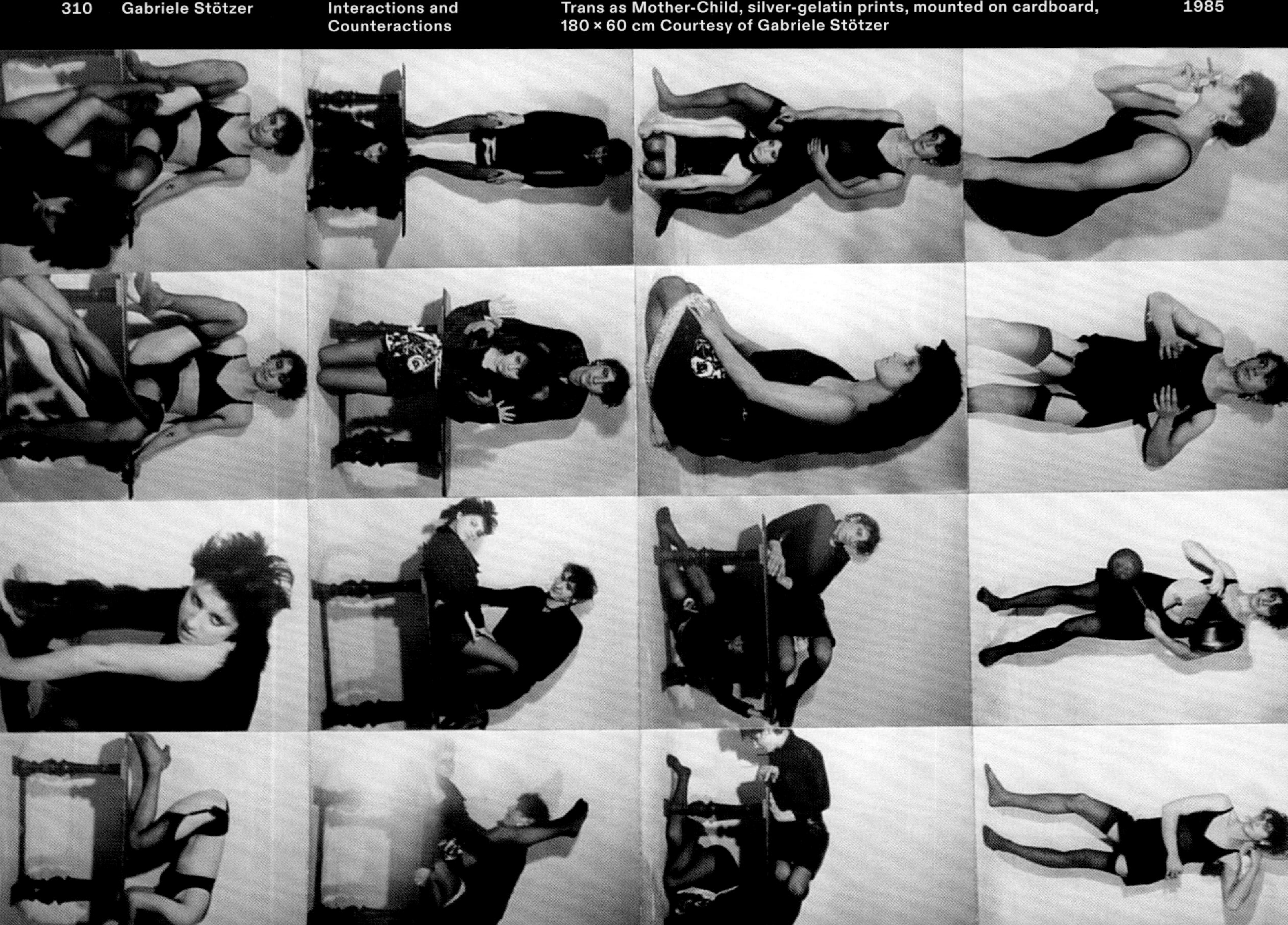

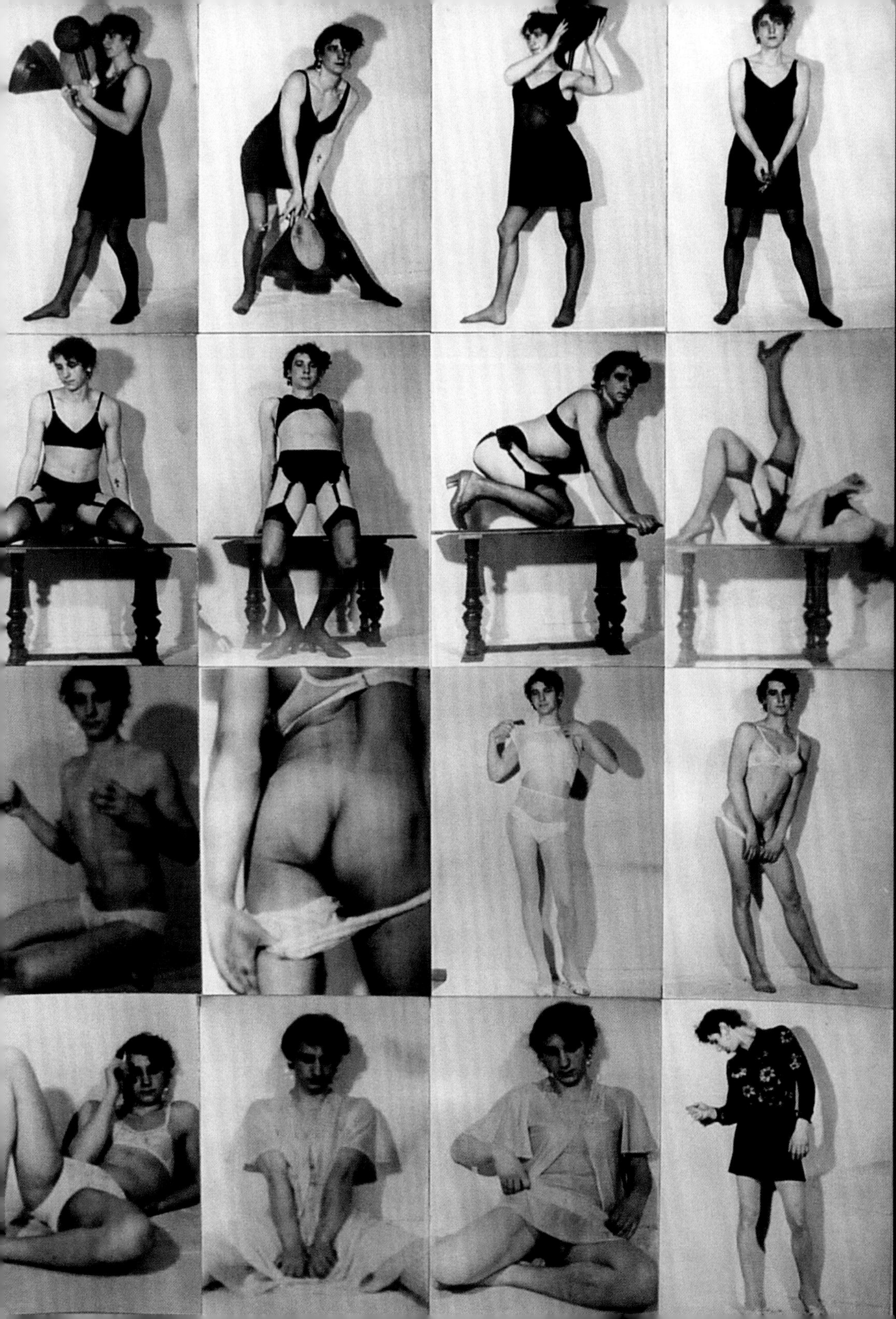

Trans with Kitchen Utensils, silver-gelatin prints, mounted on cardboard, 80 x 60 cm Courtesy of Gabriele Stötzer

1985

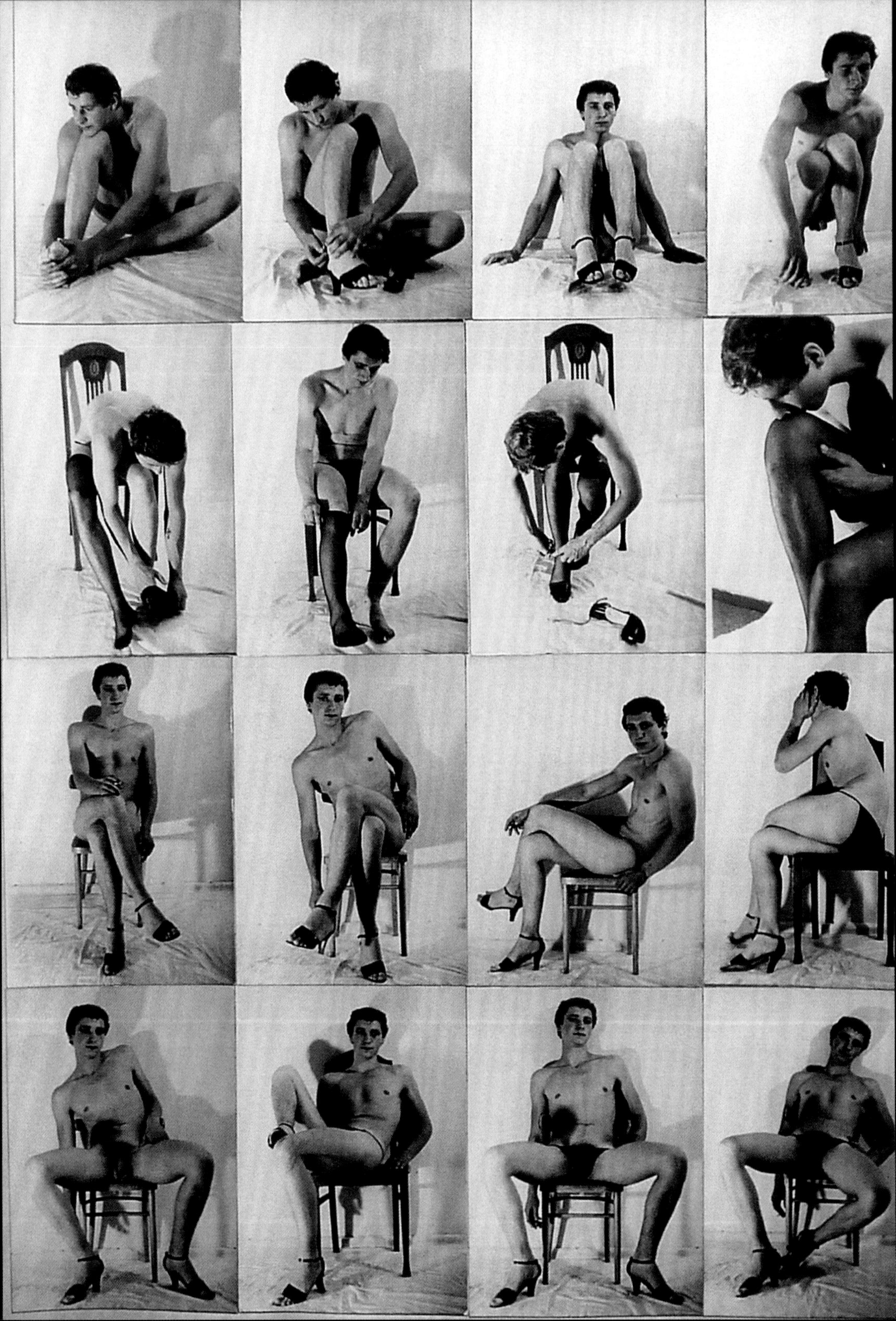

Trans as Man, silver-gelatin prints, mounted on cardboard, 80 × 60 cm, 1985
Courtesy: Gabriele Stötzer

Recruitment Photos

MfS (GDR): Unofficial Collaborator "Konrad"

Before GDR state security "supplied" the artist Gabriele Stötzer (then named Kachold) with "Winfried," they themselves took recruitment photos (Stötzer calls them "*Fangfotos*," or "catch photos"). These photos are not to be found in the BStU; they are not archived there. Gabriele Stötzer was given these photos by another unofficial collaborator, IMB "Konrad." IMB "Konrad" was assigned to Stötzer and was continually writing reports about her. He was the one who was supposed to supply her with "Winfried." In his informant report on Gabriele Stötzer, he writes that Stötzer knows that he himself was in prison for the "dissemination of pornographic images" and "political activities": "When I made passing reference to being acquainted with a transvestite, she looked forward excitedly to meeting them personally. On this basis, I attempted to secure contact with K. (Gabi Stötzer, at the time Kachold)." **(S)**

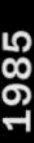

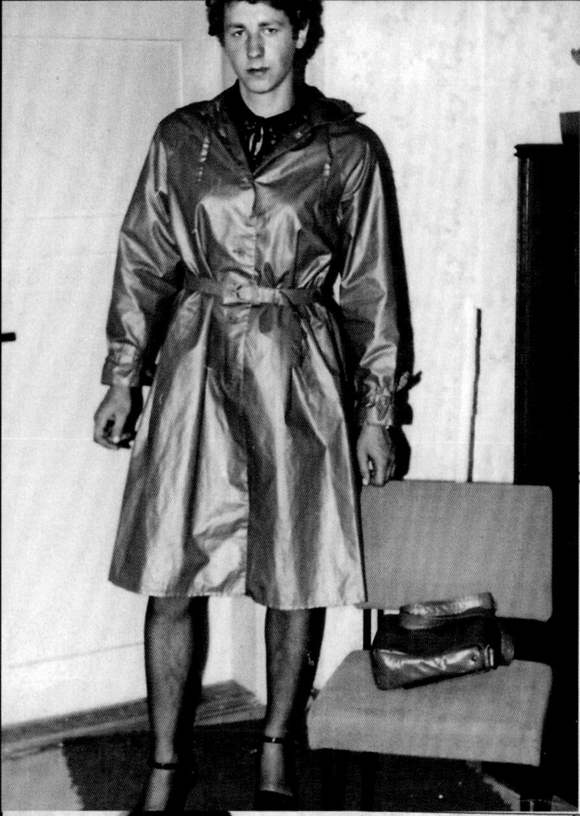

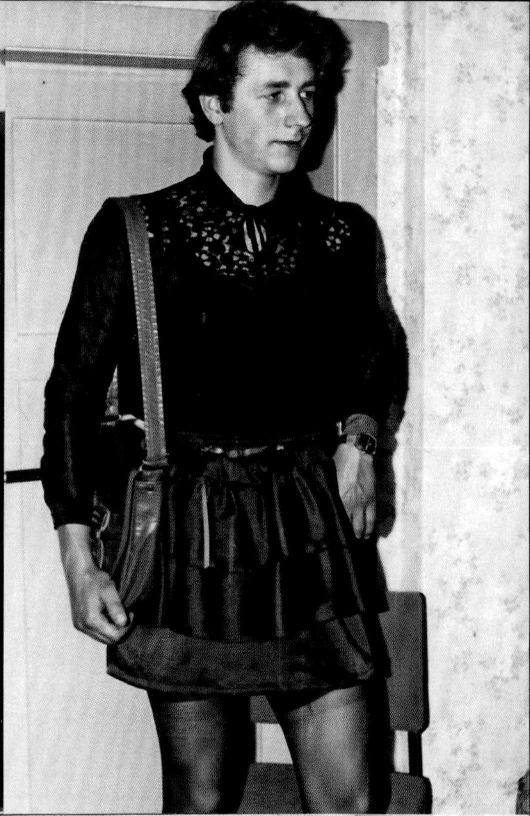

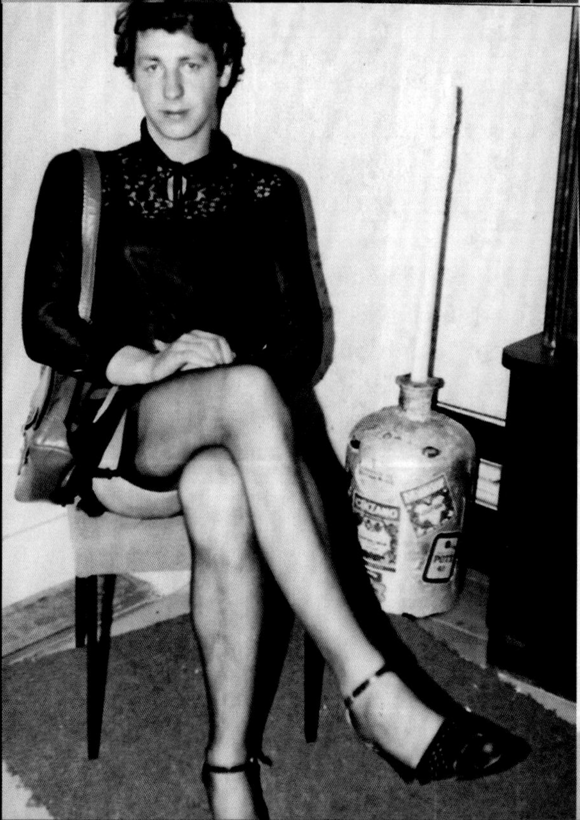

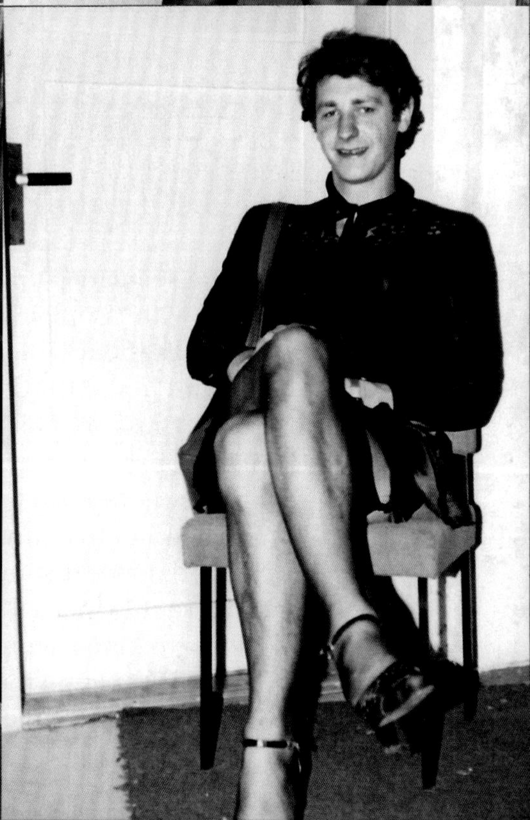

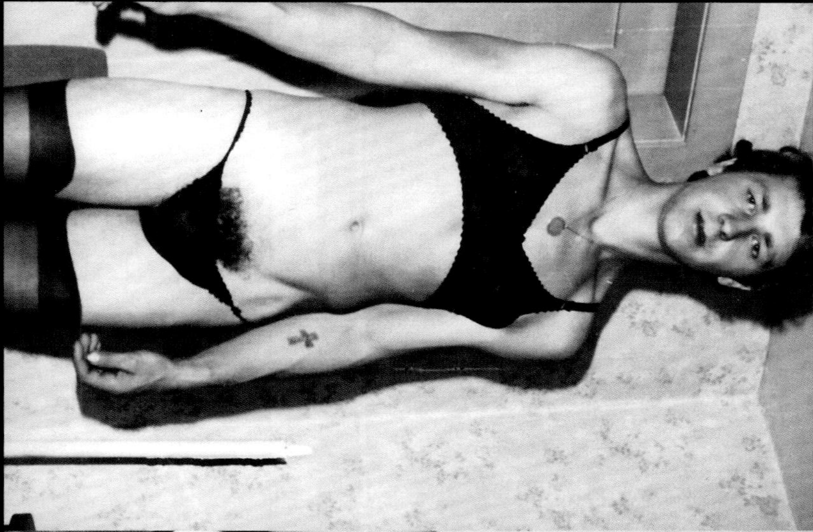

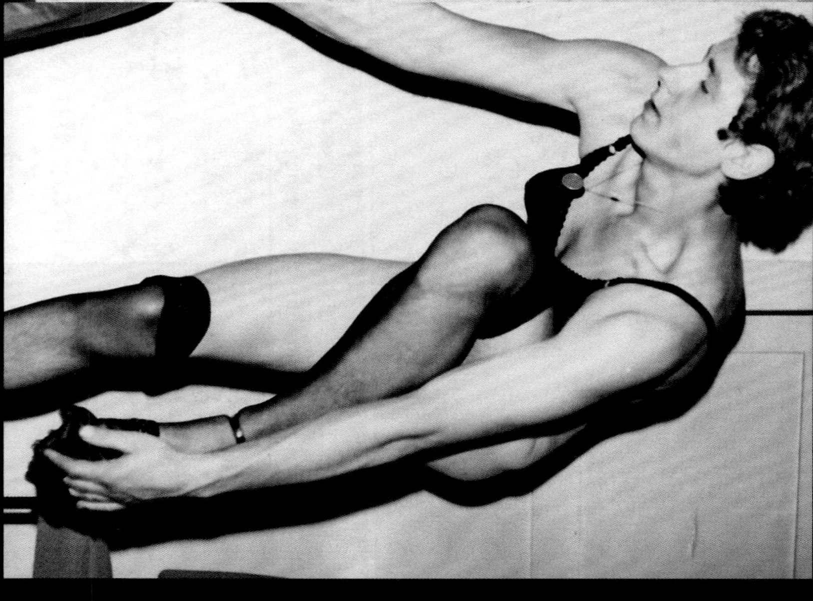

 IMB "Konrad" Interactions and Counteractions Six black-and-white photographs, 13.3 × 9.4 cm 1985

The Dream Has Not Died

Alexandru (Sándor) Antik

In the basement of the Pharmaceutical History Museum in Sibiu in 1986, Antik staged a thirty-five-minute performance that had an earth-shattering effect on subsequent performance artists in Romania. It took place in two rooms. Inside the first room was an exhibition of "pseudo-personal things." One could hear songs by Katalin Karády which were interrupted by passages of text announcing the happening and informing the audience that they were about to be witnesses to an unusual event. Antik read texts, a woman shaved his hair, and then he undressed and climbed into a cage-like room with the inscription: "Room of Unrealized Things." The audience could only follow this all through the barred windows. Music droned in the background. Antik shaped bloody cow intestines with his breath (which he then gave to the audience) to the rhythm of a waltz as he cited other texts and attempted to write the slogan "The Dream Has Not Died" on the cell wall with a gas lamp. Antik writes: "The action, however, could not be completed because a man in a suit suddenly showed up and ordered us to end the event and to remove all traces of it. We had to bring the bloody shapes to the city outskirts, for example." This brutal intervention by the Securitate hindered the performance from being finished, and it is also thus that it is "reenacted" to this day. (K)

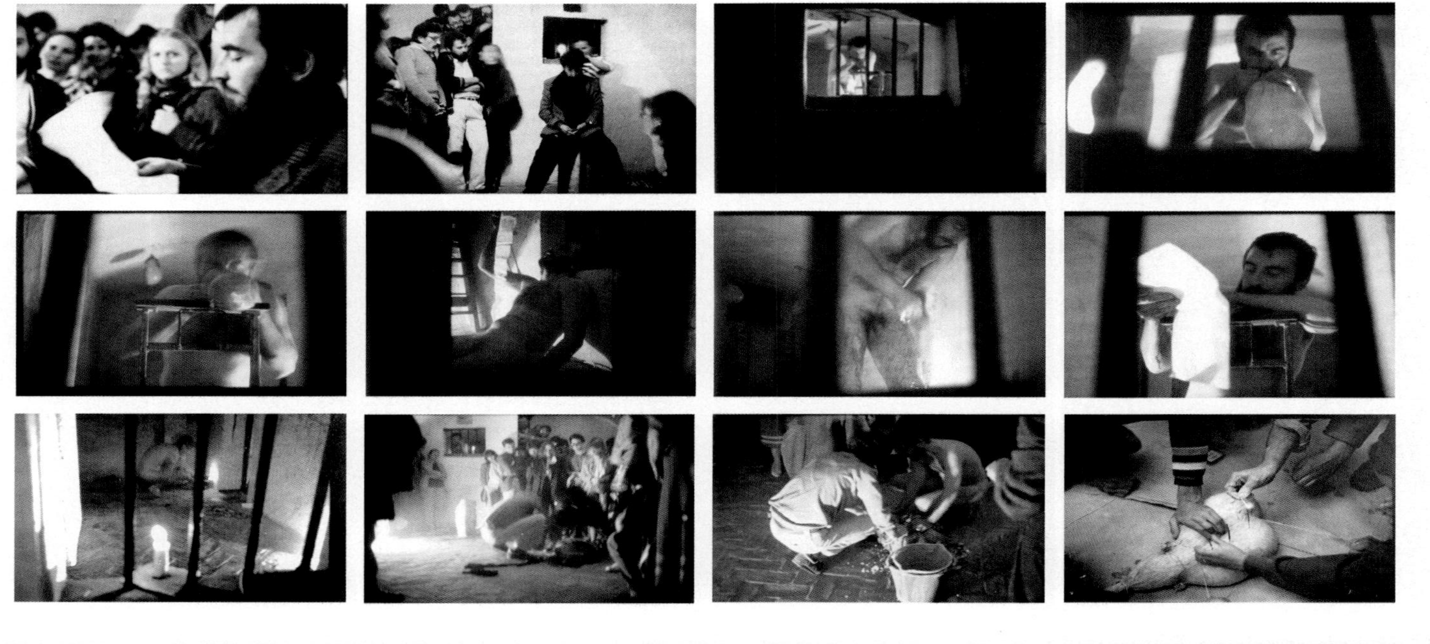

Alexandru (Sándor) Antik — Interactions and Counteractions — 1986, mounted as a photo collage 2013, 189.7 × 80.01 cm — Photos by Radu Igazsag, Courtesy of Alexandru (Sándor) Antik — 1986 / 2013

Report "Alexandra"

Securitate (SR Romania)

The Securitate officially began keeping tabs on Alexandru Antik in 1988 on suspicion of spreading Hungarian nationalism and because of his negative influence on young artists. But his 1986 performance, *The Dream Has Not Died*, had already triggered one of the Securitate's most brutal counteractions. "Alexandra"—clearly an art expert and theorist—wrote a report about the performance in 1986 where she explicitly addresses performance art and categorizes it as a "very modern artistic genre." In her explanation, "Alexandra" also attempts to temper the accusation of obscenity.

The Securitate's brutal and abrupt intervention has become the classic example of censorship in Romanian art history. But the files do not speak of an intervention at all; it was only transmitted orally. The Securitate itself did not document its own "counteraction"—only of "inner conspiracy" or the covering up of tracks. Antik writes that he "found nothing in his files" that would explain "why the happening got in the way of the system" and why the well-meaning report portrays the performance in such a distorted manner. (K)

Service I/B
Preserved: Captain Schiopoate Mircea
Submitted: Source "Alexandra"
No.00177/4.8.1986

Top secret
ex.unic

<u>M E M O</u>
-Copy-

The source reports the following:

Alexandru Antik, one of the best artists of his generation, rightly considered in most media, brilliant, has a great capacity to influence Hungarian artists in Romania, and is a kind of representative of good Romanian art abroad, especially [sic] in regards to Hungary, where he is fully accepted as a human and extraordinarily admired as an artist in the most exclusive artist circles of Budapest. (His brother is married in Hungary). He makes experimental art, an art of great boldness, but of the best professional quality. His performance (a very modern artistic genre, a full spectacle in which the audience participates without intervening), presented in the Sibiu Camp, was one of the best done recently, it even seems in the entire world (this confirmation was made right away by Marcel Bunea (Cisnădie), Mircea Ignat (Sibiu), who came with a former colleague of theirs, currently in Karlsruhe — RFG who is aso an artist, and who spoke about the European level of the event). Since such experiments are shocking to the audience's antiquated visual perception, the organizers decided that at these experimental exhibitions (taking place at the Museum of Pharmacy History) the public would enter with the camp's badge; however, many came from outside the camp, and the risk of not letting them enter was too high. The embarrassment and the false ideas started from the fact that at one point, in the performance, the artist undressed, which is more than natural for people in the arts, for whom the human body is as commonplace as any other artistic element. There was actually no justification for this, since the artist wished to represent in the performance the nakedness, purity, sincerity of the creator in front of his audience. Everything competed to present a more accurate explication of the risk of creation, of the torment that it demands. In fact it was an experiment of the best artistic quality and nothing else.

"Alexandra"

In Sibiu there was a camp for young visual artists from different corners of the country.

Antik Alexandru is under observation [by?] I.J. Cluj, where the material will be sent in copy, for investigation.]

Cpt. [= căpitan = Captain] Schiopoate Mircea

SM/SM
RD: 2849/

Translated from Romanian by Olga Stefan

Serviciul I/B
Primit:cpt. SCHIOPOAIE MIRCEA
Predat: sursa "ALEXANDRA"
Nr.00177/04.08.1986

STRICT SECRET
ex.unic

N O T A

- copie -

Sursa relatează următoarele:

ALEXANDRU ANTIK, unul dintre cei mai buni artişti ai generaţiei sale, considerat în majoritatea mediilor pe bună dreptate genial, are o mare capacitate de influenţă asupra artiştilor maghiari din România şi este un fel de reprezentant al artei bune din România în străinătate, precedentul crește în ceea ce priveşte Ungaria unde este acceptat deplin ca om şi admirat extraordinar ca artist în cele mai exclusive cercuri de artişti din Budapesta. (Fratele lui este căsătorit în Ungaria). Face o artă experimentală, o artă de ultimă îndrăzneală, însă de cea mai bună calitate profesională. Performanţă (gen artistic foarte modern,spectacol deplin la care publicul participă fără să intervină), prezentată în Tabăra de la Sibiu a fost una din cele mai bune făcute în ultimul timp, se pare în lume (confirmarea s-a făcut chiar pe loc, MARCEL BUNEA (Cisnădie), MIRCEA IGNAT (Sibiu) au venit cu un fost coleg de-al lor, actualmente la Karlsruhe - R.F.G. şi el artist, care a vorbit despre nivelul european al manifestării. Cum astfel de experimente sînt şocante pentru publicul rămas cu percepţia vizuală undeva mult în urmă, organizatorii au hotărît ca la expoziţiile experimentale (Muzeul de istoria farmaicie) să se intre pe bază de ecuson al Taberei; au venit totuşi mulţi din afara Taberei, iar riscul de a nu-i lăsa să intre era prea mare, neonoarea şi falsele idei au pornit de la faptul că la un moment dat, în cadrul performanţei, artistul s-a dezbrăcat, lucru mai mult decît firesc pentru oamenii de artă, pentru care trupul uman este la fel de obişnuit ca orice altă componentă artistică, nu a fost nici o justificare de fapt, artistul dorind să reprezinte în performanţă nuditatea, puritatea, sinceritatea creatorului în faţa publicului său. Totul a concurat la o explicare cît mai exactă a riscului creaţiei, a chinului pe care ea îl cere.

De fapt a fost un experiment de cea mai bună calitate artistică şi nimic altceva.

4 august, 1986, Sibiu

"ALEXANDRA"

N.O.: La Sibiu a avut loc o tabără a tinerilor artişti plastici din diferite localităţi ale ţării.

ANTIK ALEXANDRU se află în atenţia I.J.Cluj unde se va trimite materialul în copie, pentru exploatare.

Cpt. SCHIOPOAIE MIRCEA

ex.unic
SM/SM
RD:2849/

Source: C.N.S.A.S. Nr. 234058, p. 8. Courtesy of Mădălina Brașoveanu. 1986

Private Property

György Galántai

In 1970–73, during the time he was organizing the legendary chapel-studio exhibitions and art festivals in Balatonboglár, György Galántai put up signs on three different roads leading to the chapel saying "private property." These were intended to inform the police and other officials that Galántai was on a legally rented piece of property where the police has no right to control him or other persons. *Private Property* also appeared as a work of art by Galántai on the chapel door—an "ambiguous" road sign of a main road. In the middle of the yellow square stood the words "private property" (*Magánterület*). According to Galántai, the visual and verbal meanings functioned simultaneously, like a metaphor: "the main road is private property" (for them), or "the private property is a main road" (for us).

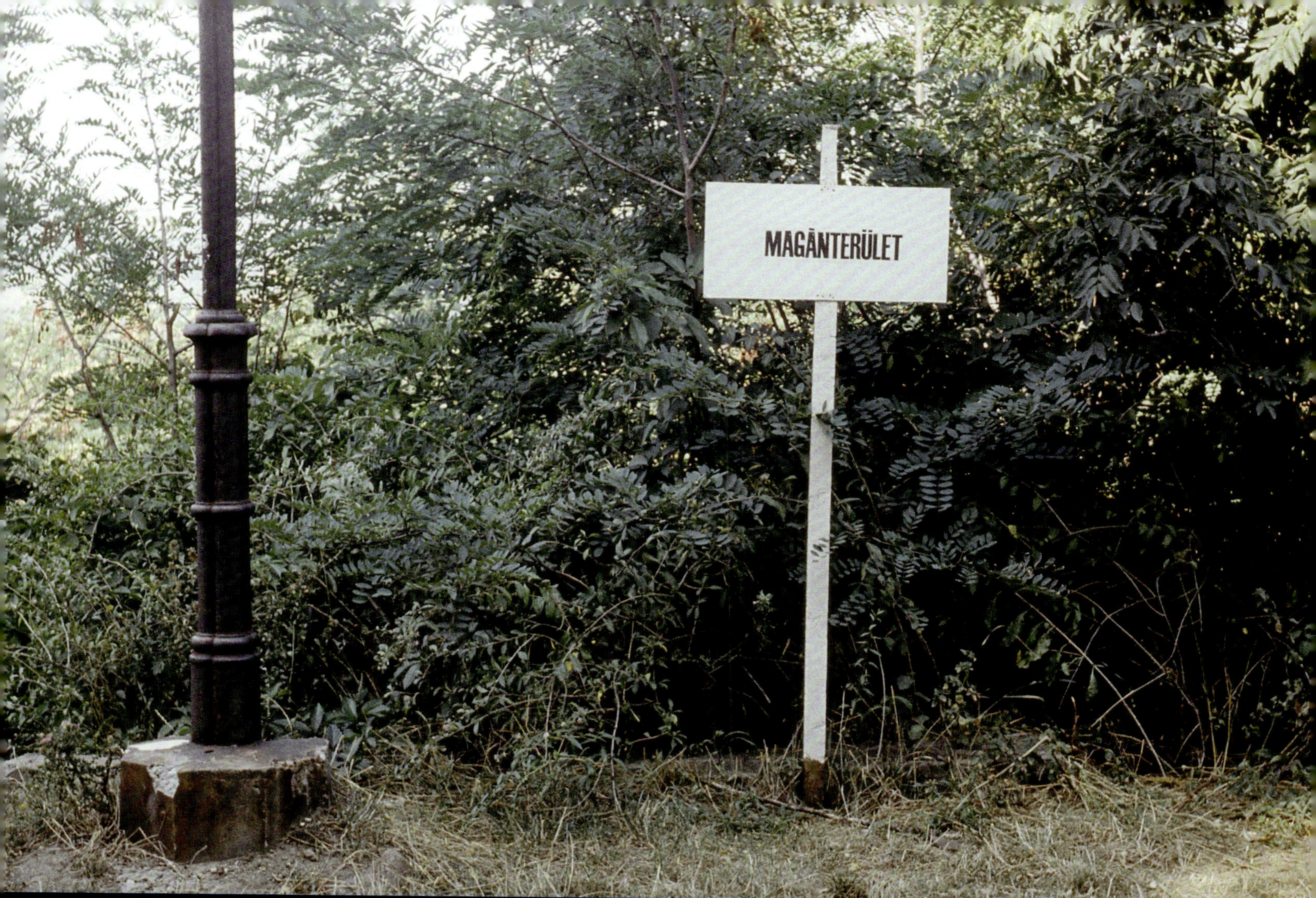

323 György Galántai (Foto)

Interactions and Counteractions

One color photograph, July 21, 1973
Courtesy: Artpool Art Research Center / Museum of Fine Arts, Budapest

1973

György Galántai, b. 1941 in Bikács, Hungary, lives and works in Budapest, Hungary.

Friendly Treatment

György Galántai

The panel *Friendly Treatment* (*Barátságos bánásmód*) comes from a performance by László Najmányi, which he made on July 21, 1973 in Balatonboglár. During the action, Najmányi sat on a chair behind an area delimited by ropes, with a plaque attached to his neck that read: "*Barátságos bánásmód.*" Galántai has re-used the panel and hung it on a tree as the police actions intensified that year against the Chapel. Galántai was under intense surveillance at this time and was referred to by the Hungarian State Security under the code name "Festő" (Painter). When the Balatonboglár Studio Chapel Atelier was forced to close after massive insults on August 23, 1973 Galántai had the sign "Friendly Treatment"hung on his shoulder as he was leaving the Chapel for the last time—a "farewell action."

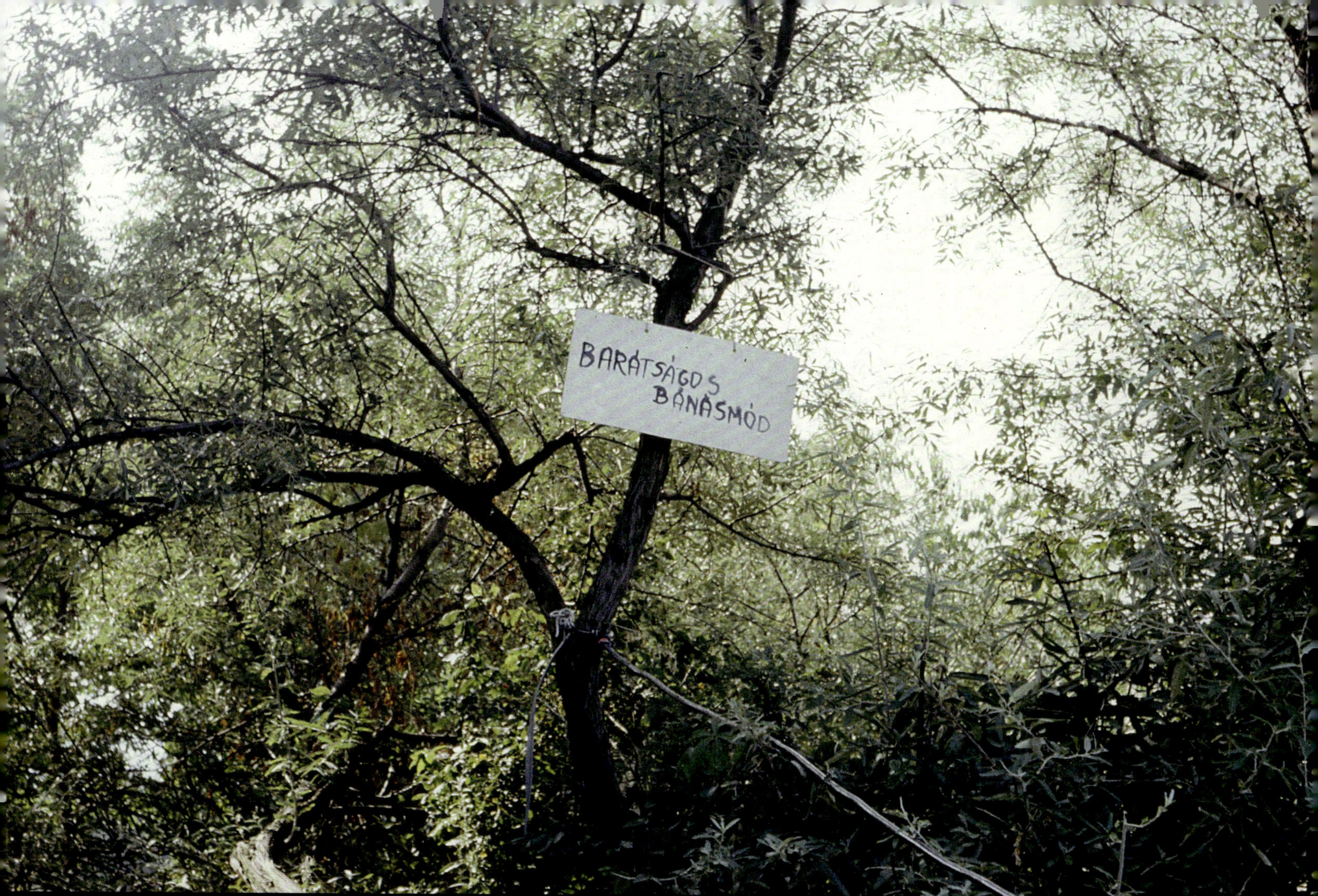

325 György Galántai (Foto) — Interactions and Counteractions — One color photograph, July 21, 1973. Courtesy: Artpool Art Research Center / Museum of Fine Arts, Budapest — 1973

Counteraction to Private Property/Friendly Treatment

Local Police (Balatonboglár)

In his diary, Galántai describes a spontaneous action performed by the local police on August 6, 1973 as follows: "At four in the morning, a strange incident took place at the locked gate of the chapel. From an artistic point of view, it was an 'action' performed by two policeman-artist-patrol-officers. They began their performance by repeatedly shouting 'sir,' and then used the wooden gate and their batons to 'give a concert'.... After this, and as a kind of intermission, the policeman-artists attempted to open the lock; but since they failed, they documented their passing presence—in the spirit of the concert and conceptual art—by leaving a mark on the freshly painted white gate: using their batons and the key, they wrote POLICEMAN on the gate. Finally, as the concrete poetical act of their departure, they turned upside down the signs saying, "FRIENDLY TREATMENT" and "PRIVATE PROPERTY," which both hung outside on an olive tree."
(https://www.artpool.hu/boglar/project/1973.html)
Galántai judges this to be an "artistic" action—the hammering with rubber clubs becoming a "concert" and a form of "experimental music"—as a conceptual gesture which he subsequently appropriated as a counteraction and integrated into the program of the chapel studio exhibitions. "What I saw from this non-artistic viewpoint was an atrocity happening below, on the ground level, in connection with me, even if merely symbolically"—as Galántai recalls. (K)

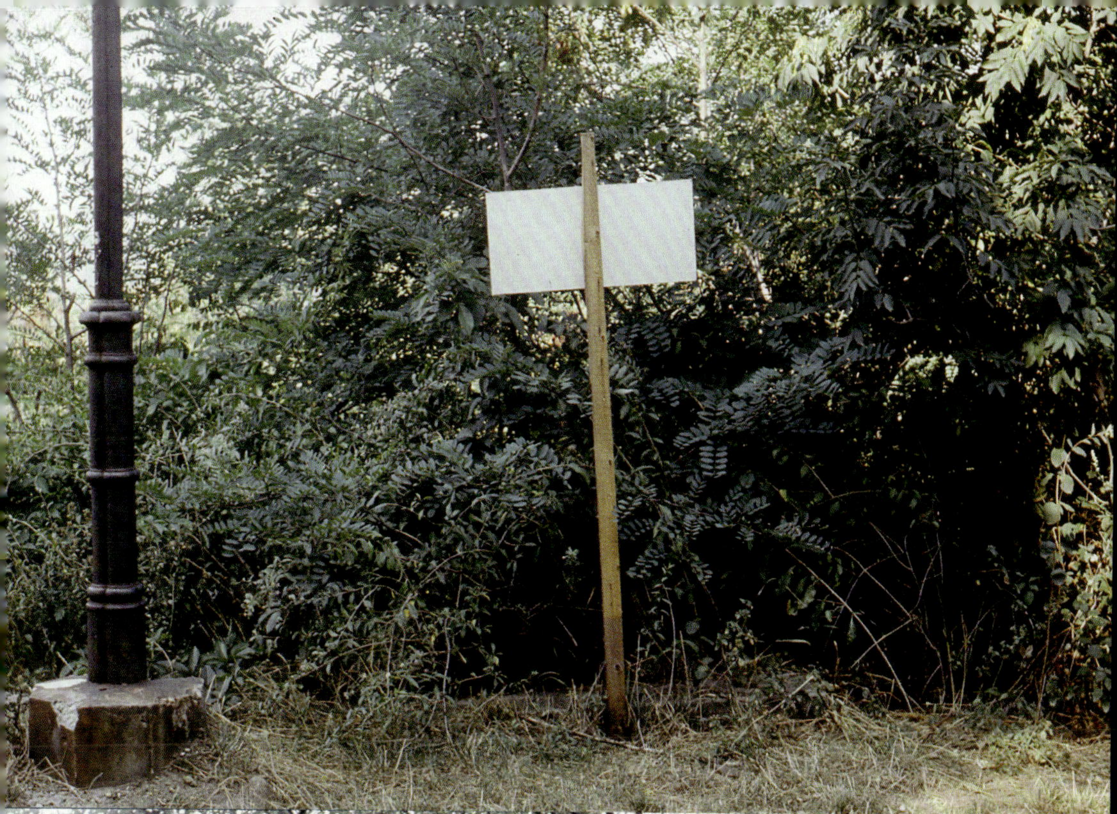

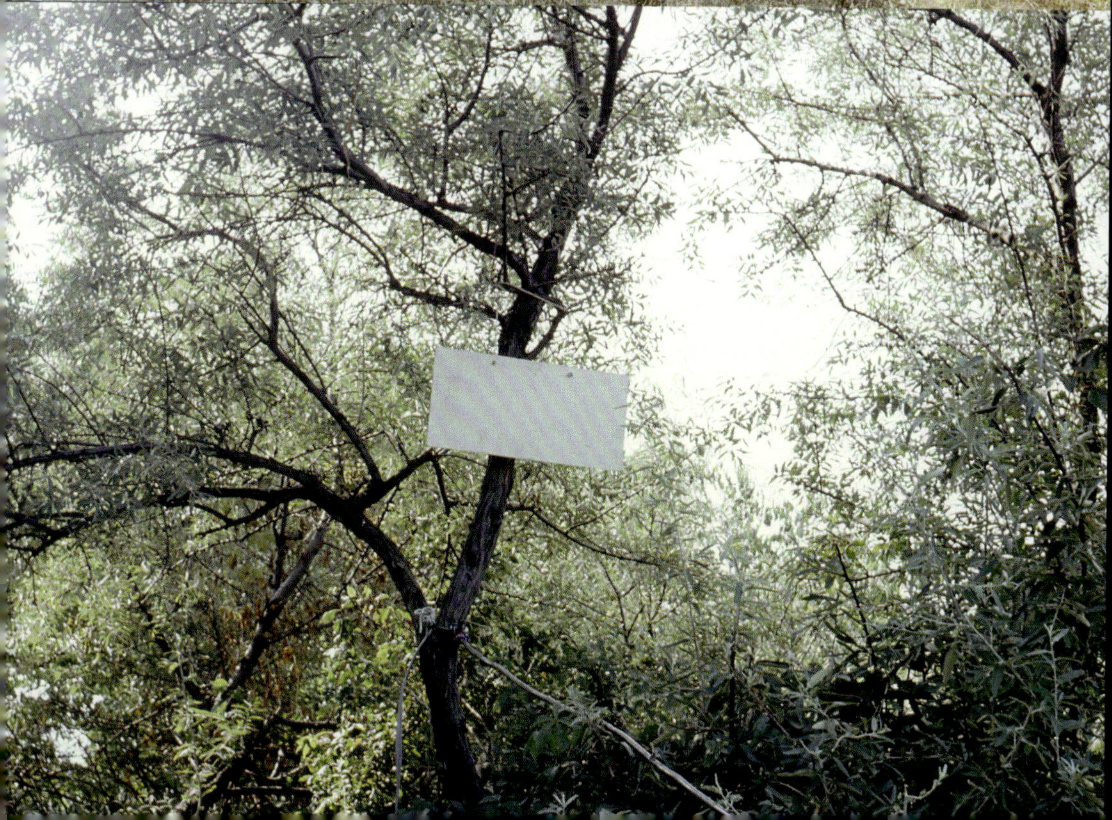

Local Police (Balatonboglár)

Three color photographs, Photos by György Galántai
Courtesy of Artpool Art Research Center / Museum of Fine Arts, Budapest

1972

3 Farbfotos, Foto: György Galántai,
Courtesy: Artpool Art Research Center / Museum of Fine Arts, Budapest

1973

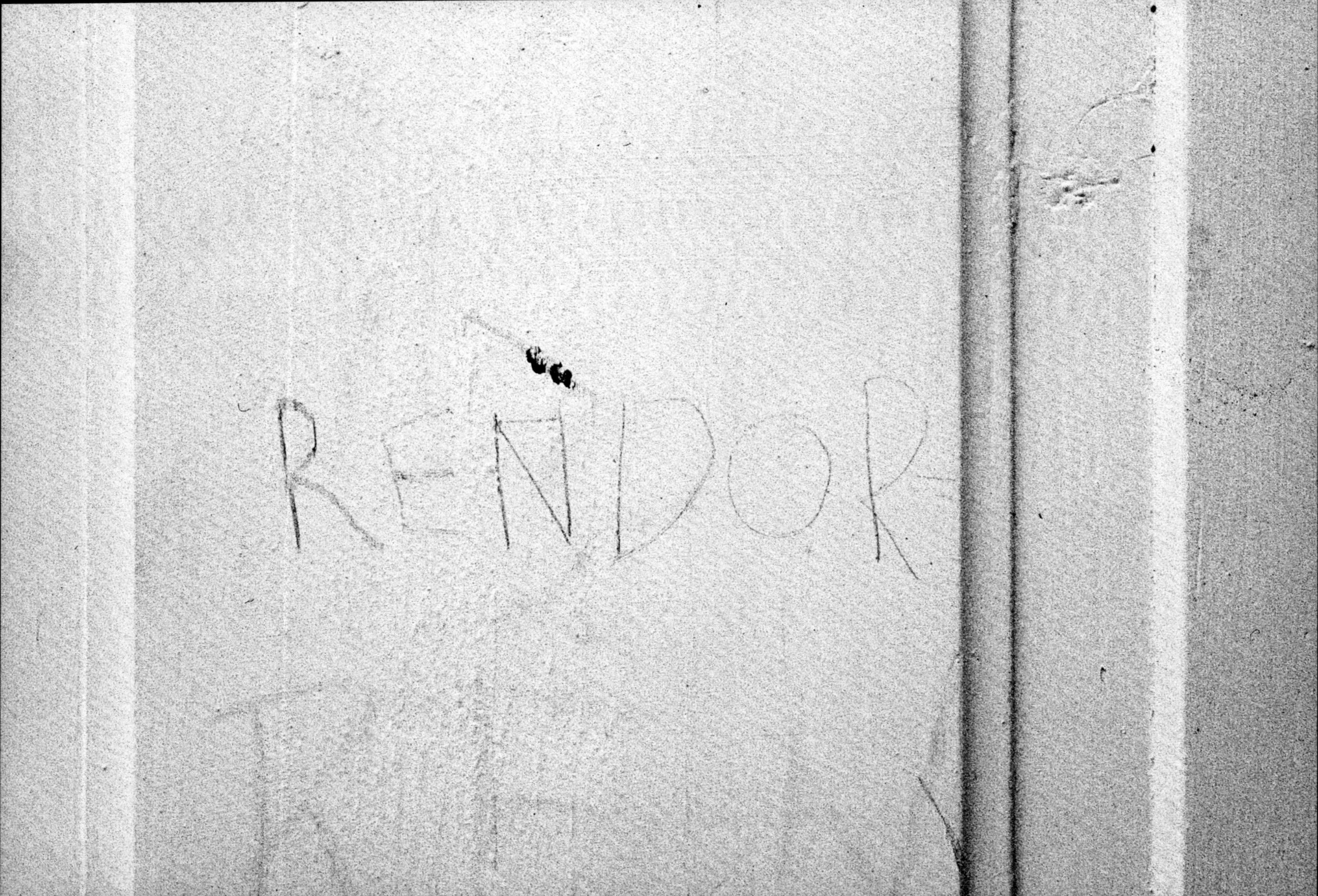

Countersurveillance

Did the Polish Secret Police Have a Sense of Humor?

Anna Krakus

"Sto lat, sto lat, niech żyje, żyje nam."

This celebratory song, sung in Poland for birthdays and victories, expresses a general good wish: "May you live for 100 years." One night in the early 1980s, a group of young men rushed out onto the street in Wrocław and surrounded police officers who were taking down political posters. The men ironically sang precisely this song to the police: *May you live for 100 years*. With this action, the Orange Alternative performance group was born, and their way of sarcastically communicating with the police through art was immediately established.[1]

Before becoming a performance group, "Orange Alternative" was the name of a journal founded in the early 1980s. During a 1981 student strike in Wrocław, the name was used and became the title of seven journal issues run by Ruch Nowej Kultury.[2] The journal's motto was "All proletarians, be beautiful!" and it mixed satirical content with more overt politics as well as artistic contributions. After singing to the police, the proper Orange Alternative practices began, and they took place in response to seemingly unimportant municipal police work, like the painting over of political posters, which the police were doing that night. The white patches that were left behind became the canvas for and the beginning of the Orange Alternative. Members of the group would create new pictures to cover the spots left from the police's censoring and tidying efforts. Typically, they would graffiti gnomes, a figure they became known for: "We'll paint dwarves on those patches." There are thousands or tens of thousands of paint patches in Wrocław, and probably a million in the entire country. "If a million dwarves get painted on a million patches, people will find strength and the government will fall," reasoned the group's founder and leader, Waldemar Fydrych.[3] Their art was constantly covered up again by police, and so a war of the street walls began, and the absence of text spoke as loudly as the text itself as well as the art that the paint concealed. The goal was to make people hang up *more* posters and graffiti *more* messages so that *more* blank patches would appear, and the graphic look of the city would change.

But Orange Alternative did not just take over the streets with graffiti and visual art, they also did so with their bodies. In the mid- and late 1980s, they organized street parties, "happenings" where they themselves became 3D versions of those painted gnomes: wearing smurf hats, they started a "gnome revolution."[4] They carried nonsensical posters and banners, and created a general sense of both fun and disruption in the city of Wrocław. Unlike the journal *Orange Alternative*, there was no real political program for the performance group, at least none declared in writing. According to young police officer Grzegorz Betka's thesis, written at the Polish police academy in 1990, "the intention of these actions was to liberate people of different psychological deviations from fear and strict rationalism of life. Happenings in surrealist socialist style were meant to show that art and life are one and the same."[5] The thesis goes on to suggest that perhaps the lack of program is the program.[6] Concerning political programs, Fydrych, or the Major as he calls himself, has said that: "... from an intellectual point of view the return to the concept of political programs is funny. ... It is museum-like historicism. A nineteenth century kind of traditional thinking, and nothing will change using conservative categories."[7] Even without a stated program, this was nevertheless a large alternative youth movement and their popular happenings, drawing hundreds of participants, were a mix of play, art, and politics. Except for one occasion,[8] there was never any violence at the Orange Alternative happenings or at those of the Warsaw faction, the White Alternative.

One of their favorite types of play involved the police, like the night they sung ironically in their honor. The police became their favorite interlocutors, and video footage taken by the former secret police (now available at the Nation's Memory Institute, *Instytut Pamięci Narodowej*, which houses former secret police files in Poland) shows that it was mostly mutual. "Okay, eagles, it's time to go home," shouts the police officer—or rather, a member of MO (*Milicja Obywatelska*, the citizens' militia)—at the end of a rally. Like stubborn children, the demonstrators ask for another nine minutes: "we have until two o'clock!" they insist. Eventually their chants turn into mocking the police: "you are being mischievous, go home!" ("*rozrabiacie, wracajcie do domu!*"). They sarcastically and repetitively cheer the kinds of things the police might tell them, but also the kinds of reprimands a parent might tell a petulant child. They are well aware of their role. Yet the police do not seem to mind. The police officer refers to a hat-wearing participant as Gargamel, a fictional character from the Smurfs, and everybody laughs. The Orange Alternative had a surprisingly positive relationship with the militia, in spite of their constant mocking of the institution.

Part of this mocking included one of their most famous events: Militia Day, in supposed celebration of the police. October 7th was celebrated as Militia Day in Poland, an opportunity for police to receive medals and honors. The *Militia Day* (*Dzień Milicjanta*) happening was organized simultaneously in two different places. One of the actions went by the name *A Flower for the Militia* (*Kwiatek dla Milicjanta*); the second one was entitled *We are Helping the Militia* (*Pomagamy Milicji*). The goal was to distribute flowers to all policemen. Police cars arrived and confiscated all the flowers, perhaps by different means than hoped for, but the police also politely thanked the attendants of the happenings before leaving. They were partaking in the game, acting in a sense as cocreators of the performance; their role was a positive one, as humorous as the tone set by the Orange Alternative itself, who could be seen as directors of this performance.

The language that Betka uses in 1990 reveals that he is aware of the performative nature of the happenings and, in a way, of the MO's part in them as well. He writes that by 1988, the Orange Alternative had essentially become boring and predictable: "The screenplay is always the same, the time and place, the slogans and props are the only things that change. You can actually predict the way things will go ahead of time. Their actions seem to reach an end that is inadequate in the new reality."[9] The police can plan ahead of time, having a form of script in hand, suggests Betka. The surprise element has been taken out of the performance and they are all just doing their jobs like actors on a stage. And yet, Betka's thesis asks whether the gatherings of alternative movements are truly "laughing at rituals and traditions of pompous academies in honor of surrealism, or are they perhaps a political battle?"[10] The author doesn't channel the feeling of a typical MO man, but rather of the secret police, *Służba bezpieczeństwa* (SB), who fear that there is something ominous lurking behind the supposed humor.[11]

The MO was certainly political and feared in Poland, especially the ZOMO (*Zmotoryzowane Odwody Milicji Obywatelskiej*, Motorized Reserves of the Citizens' Milita) units that controlled demonstrations by all possible means. But while their make-up was political, they certainly were no match for the SB, the secret security police who observed, filed, and controlled the behavior of citizens from a different kind of distance. And they, the SB, appear to have felt somewhat differently about the Orange Alternative than the MO did. And their role in the performances also differ as a result.

Reading Fydrych's book about the Orange Alternative's most important players, *Lives of Orange Men: A Biographical History of the*

Polish Orange Alternative Movement, you get a sense of how important the secret police were to Fydrych. They serve as an unavoidable interlocutor so vital to their happenings that he even thanks SB in his foreword, stating "I would also like to thank the personnel of the secret services. I will not give their names, owing to the delicacy of their position. One ought to remember that without their presence many interesting happenings wouldn't have occurred."[12] Yet for all the attention given to SB by Fydrych, there is a surprising lack of material at IPN about the Orange Alternative. Fydrych describes a kind of phobia, a "persecution mania,"[13] whereby people were afraid of the constant presence of undercover agents, whether or not they were actually there, and it seems he was a victim of it himself at times. Fydrych remembers an occasion when he is convinced that he is speaking to an undercover agent, but it turns out the man is just a regular person offering him a cigarette.[14]

The lack of attention from SB's side is surprising considering the fact that the SB are not known for their playfulness, and this comes through in the few Orange Alternative files left at IPN. In one case, an agent writes that the organizers of the group inspire others to join in "playing"; the idea of this playfulness is questionable to the agent.[15] After all, this is no laughing matter to the SB. This particular report, like most of the reports about the Orange and White Alternatives, is found in the context of dangerous groups that are prone to cause riots or spur political demonstrations. Of course, even the most joyous reasons for public unrest are dangerous for the people who need to keep the calm. What is worse for SB, they are forced to respond peacefully: Orange Alternative happenings restrict the kind of dangerous imposition the SB have become accustomed to using. The files that lay out the plans for the days of the events state clearly that they cannot use violence because there will be children present.[16]

According to Romanian visual artist, architect, and educator Iosif Király, in the course of observing a person, if the secret police did not understand something that that person was doing, they would simply order him to cease the action, whether it was intended to be subversive or not.[17] The Orange Alternative's main purpose was surrealistic confusion, so it certainly left many reasons for SB to want to intervene according to this principle. Yet, when there were children around, even this power to interrupt became somewhat limited. While the MO appear to have enjoyed their roles in the performances of happenings—playing the parent or acting as the grateful police officer who appreciates the flowers but does not grasp the sarcasm—SB are forced into a particular part as their hands are tied in ways that they typically are not. These agents, who like to consider themselves the directors of what happens in the public sphere, can only do what the performers allow them to.

Of course, there are also true negative aftereffects of the group's happenings: they leave behind devastation and destruction after their events, where attendants graffiti entire street blocks with paint, gnomes, and absurd slogans. Aside from this kind of destruction, and more dangerously, agents frequently suggest and fear that even the most innocent public events are opportunities for political pamphlets to be distributed. Worse—and this is precisely why SB can't have a sense of humor about the Alternatives, as Király explained—the misunderstood must be suspected as subversive, so it is not the political posters of the alternatives' happenings that are distressing to SB, but the funny and meaningless ones. "By working for your country, you are working for your country," states one big banner; "stop the peas!" and "shoe shine" read surprising posters at an Orange Alternative event.[18] This humor in itself seems to be an issue to SB, because humor may be political. Messages could be hidden underneath the fun, explains an agent.[19] Perhaps this is why the most upsetting banner to the SB is the one that reads: "The police in wonderland" (*Milicja w krainie czarów*).[20] This picture is captured in a file of photographs from one of the happenings, and out of the hundreds of posters and banners from the event, the reporting agent mentions this one in particular as an example of the event's goal: to mock state authorities such as themselves.[21] On this poster, there is a joke; it is about the police—perhaps even the SB are included in the designation—and yet what does it mean? There is all the reason in the world to assume the worst, and the SB agent takes it seriously when he states that there are actions like this all over the country, and that they "evoke unnecessary emotions and subgroups, the mood of dissatisfaction and the lack of trust in social consensus."[22] The kind of humorous rapport the group appears to have had with MO thus does not translate to SB.

Just like there were the successful Militia Day happenings, there was a happening organized in the name of the secret police, *Secret Agent's Day* (*Dzień Tajniaka*) in 1988. The SB were always there, reasoned the organizers, collecting information about the events and about their leaders. Their role was also to arrest and to interrogate, so certainly a happening should reflect their important role in the Orange Alternative's world. Participants were encouraged to disguise themselves as undercover spies in hats, coats, and dark glasses, as well as to act as such: check identities of passersby, take clandestine photographs, and stop and frisk suspects. It was a successful event in terms of its large participation, and some people even showed up with FBI and KGB badges that they carried around.[23] Yet the event did not make the kind of splash that was anticipated: SB files mention the event but only in lists of titles of Orange Alternative happenings, not in any greater detail.[24] According to Fydrych, there is perhaps more interaction between the SB and Orange Alternative participants outside of the files than in them. Sometimes, after arresting the participants, the **agents** would even share their opinions about the actions and complain about how they themselves had been portrayed. In a secret police file from Wrocław, an **agent** describes a conversation he had with Fydrych, who once came up to his car to chat. During the conversation, the SB **agent** slightly mocks Fydrych, saying that the demonstrations of some other groups have been more successful than those of the Orange Alternative. It seems as if the MO took an active part in the performance, while SB instead, however active in stopping it, appeared to consider themselves outside of the artistic situation—*critics*, not actors.

Archiving Performance

Of course, the SB plays one of the most predictable and important roles in the performance: that of the documenter. Amy Bryzgel writes that in Eastern Europe during socialism, and even after, performance has remained a preferred genre among many artists because of its open-endedness and the fact that "the work left no traces."[25] However, Bryzgel omits one particular type of physical trace: the video, photo, and written records of the secret police. Bryzgel notes that the Eastern European performance artists of the socialist period were actually quite good at self-documentation, but the efforts of SB in describing and recording were certainly more multisided, with multiple cameras on multiple people recording from every angle, as well as the critical responses described in the files and their attempts at capturing both the leaders as well as the talk from the sidelines. Both by the very process of documenting and in their choices of what to document, SB files raise the question of who the audience is in the case of the Orange Alternative happenings. Is it the collective itself? The SB camera? The SB **agent** who is being mocked by the event alone? What about the reader of the file, then or today? And it begs the question of what the performance is: is it the original event or is it (also) any documentation of the event after the fact?[26]

Amelia Jones has questioned the privileged status of live performance as opposed to documentation, claiming that performance is already mediated through one's own experience.[27] This is further explored by Erin Mizrahi, who writes that "documentation is just another form of an already existing mediated experience of the performance."[28] But what does it mean then, to have an Orange Alternative event be mediated by the secret police? What we have to go by today are the descriptions of events that Fydrych has collected in a virtual museum about the Orange Alternative,[29] as well as the SB's files. To what degree do reading and watching these materials make even myself a potential audience member? Documenting an event transforms the experience into public and collective memory, which allows for witnessing and accountability,[30] but what about *participation*, a key element of the Orange Alternative happenings? In a way, it is thanks to the archival efforts of the SB that I can most strongly relive the artistic happenings of the Orange Alternative, since the oppression by SB—an oppression so evocative and tangible to Fydrych, who thanks them in his book—is best captured precisely by the oppressors guiding the looming secret cameras. When viewing the materials at IPN, you find yourself in the middle of the performance. Nothing can make you feel more present than this shaky hidden camera moving around in the midst of other attendants. For instance, a video of a White Alternative event in Warsaw's old town shows close-ups of the happening organizers, zooming in especially close on Marcin Meller reading from Muammar Gaddafi's *Green Book*. The young man is reciting words about the undemocratic nature of referendums when the video pans and shows the heads and faces of other attendants at the margins. Through the mechanical eye of the SB agent, you see the main event as well as the spirit of the happening: the hundreds of participants, the rowdy mass of people, and towards the end of the video—as the secret police agent has moved to the edges of the square where it is all taking place—you also get a real sense of the police presence that has always haunted the Polish people. The agent positions himself in the midst of a large group of MO, with a dozen gray hats disrupting the view. The SB camera has captured the event, the audience, and the unintentional interlocutors: the police.[31] The participatory element of an Orange Alternative happening can today best be understood by reading about the events as written by the pen of an agent, and, thanks to clandestine recordings, the Orange and White Alternative events can be strikingly experienced through the record after the fact.

Endnotes

1 Bogdan Dobosz and Waldemar Fydrych, *Hokus Pokus czyli Pomarańczowa Alternatywa* (Wrocław: Inicjatywa Wydawnicza Aspekt, 1989), 8.

2 The cultural organization "New Cultural Movement." The inception of the Orange Alternative movement and the relationship with the New Cultural Movement is described in Grzegorz Betka's unpublished thesis: "WUSW we Wrocławiu," found in BU 1509/5445 at the Nation's Memory Institute.

3 Waldemar Fydrych, *Lives of Orange Men: A Biographical History of the Polish Orange Alternative Movement* (New York/Port Watson/Wivenhoe: Minor Compositions, 2014), 91.

4 J. Golec, "Rewolucja krasnoludków," *Nadodrze*, No. 1 (1989), https://www.inyourpocket.com/wroclaw/Alternative-orange-movement_70296f.(last accessed April 9, 2019).

5 Betka, "WUSW we Wrocławiu," trans. Anna Krakus, 10.

6 Ibid., 12.

7 E. Szemplińska, "Pomorańczowa Alterantywa," Ład, No. 43 (1988): 212.

8 IPN BU 2521/37, page 5 describes an incident in which two police officers were injured.

9 Betka, "WUSW we Wrocławiu," trans. Anna Krakus, 30.

10 Ibid., 19.

11 See also: Suleja, "The Orange Alternative from the perspective of the security forces (*Pomarańczowa Alternatywa z perspektywy Służby Bezpieczeństwa*)," in *Pomarańczowa Alternatywa—happeningiem w komunizm*, eds. Barbara Górska and Ben Koschalka (Kraków, 2011), 116–129.

12 Fydrych, *Lives of Orange Men*, 8.

13 Ibid., 26.

14 Ibid., 84.

15 IPN, BU 2837/522, 17.

16 IPN, BU 2836/36, 85.

17 Amy Bryzgel, *Performance Art in Eastern Europe since 1960* (Manchester: Manchester University Press, 2017), 74.

18 As seen in a White Alternative event in Warsaw on November 6, 1988. IPN, BU 1196/4.

19 IPN, BU 0258/384.

20 IPN, BU 3/16/32/26.

21 IPN, BU 0258/384.

22 Ibid.

23 Fydrych, *Lives of Orange Men*, 169.

24 IPN, BU 2836/36, 259. For instance, mentions of the White Alternative happening celebrating the SB; IPN, BU 1509/5445 specifically mentions the Secret Agent's Day. See also: Szymanski, *Theatraler Protest und der Weg Polens zu 1989. Zum Aushandeln von Öffentlichkeit im Jahrzehnt der Solidarność.*

25 Amy Bryzgel, *Performance Art in Eastern Europe since* 1960 (Manchester: Manchester University Press, 2017), 3.

26 Erin Mizrahi, "Witnessing Silence: Testimony, Performance, and the Poetics of the Unspeakable" (PhD Diss., University of Southern California, 2018), 15–16.

27 Amelia Jones,*Body Art/Performing the Subject* (Minneapolis: University of Minnesota Press, 1998), 15.

28 Mizrahi, "Witnessing Silence," 34.

29 http://www.orangealternativemuseum.pl/

30 Mizrahi, "Witnessing Silence," 19.

31 IPN, BU 1196/4.

Secret Agent's Day

Orange Alternative

On March 1, 1988, Orange Alternative organized the *Secret* Agent's *Day* (*Dzień Tajniaka*). The artist group thus not only captured a socialist holiday, they simultaneously acted as if state security itself had organized this happening. In view of the "happening prevention," which Polish state security was intensely engaged with at this time, this happening was also an ironic commentary on the effectiveness of secret-police work. The members of Orange Alternative wrote a flyer for the happening itself as well as a code of behavior for potential spies: "Wear black sunglasses, a hat, a trench coat, or a leather cape. Bring a listening device along: a microphone, a funnel, or a trumpet. Especially recommended are microphones installed in umbrellas or canes." Today we are also in possession of state security record as well as a report by Captain Zielinski for state security where he recalls: "They called out: 'Long live the secret police, don't resist, the secret police invite you.'" (S)

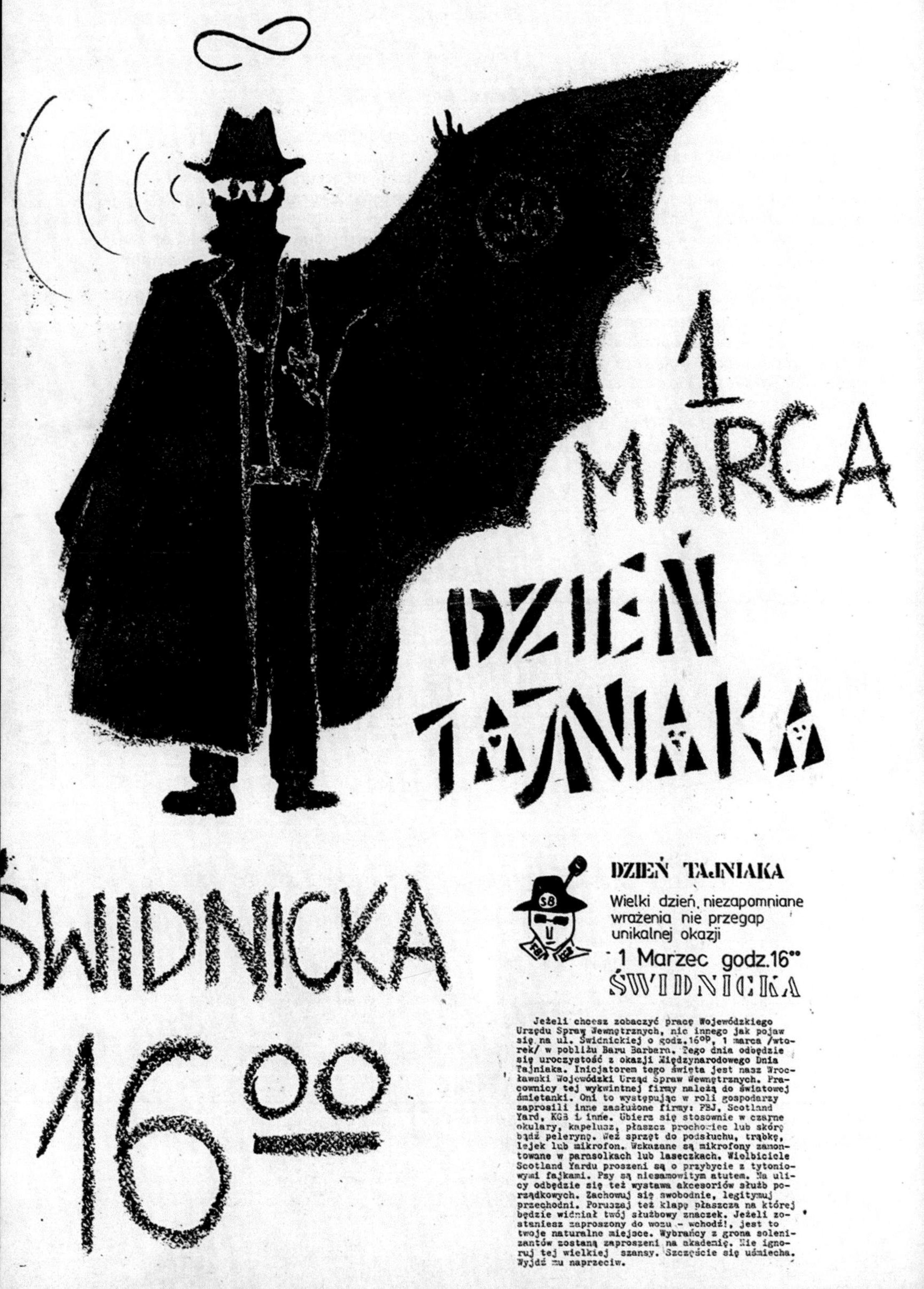

1 MARCA

DZIEŃ TAJNIAKA

ŚWIDNICKA

16^{00}

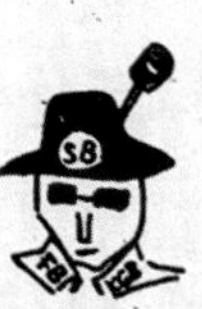

DZIEŃ TAJNIAKA

Wielki dzień, niezapomniane wrażenia nie przegap unikalnej okazji

1 Marzec godz.16^{00}

ŚWIDNICKA

Jeżeli chcesz zobaczyć pracę Wojewódzkiego Urzędu Spraw Wewnętrznych, nic innego jak pojaw się na ul. Świdnickiej o godz.16^{00}, 1 marca /wtorek/ w pobliżu Baru Barbara. Tego dnia odbędzie się uroczystość z okazji Międzynarodowego Dnia Tajniaka. Inicjatorem tego święta jest nasz Wrocławski Wojewódzki Urząd Spraw Wewnętrznych. Pracownicy tej wykwintnej firmy należą do światowej śmietanki. Oni to występując w roli gospodarzy zaprosili inne zasłużone firmy: FBJ, Scotland Yard, KGB i inne. Ubierz się stosownie w czarne okulary, kapelusz, płaszcz prochowiec lub skórę bądź pelerynę. Weź sprzęt do podsłuchu, trąbkę, lejek lub mikrofon. Wskazane są mikrofony zamontowane w parasolkach lub laseczkach. Wielbiciele Scotland Yardu proszeni są o przybycie z tytoniowymi fajkami. Psy są niesamowitym atutem. Na ulicy odbędzie się też wystawa akcesoriów służb porządkowych. Zachowuj się swobodnie, legitymuj przechodni. Poruszaj też klapę płaszcza na której będzie widniał twój służbowy znaczek. Jeżeli zostaniesz zaproszony do wozu - wchodź!, jest to twoje naturalne miejsce. Wybrańcy z grona solenizantów zostaną zaproszeni na akademię. Nie ignoruj tej wielkiej szansy. Szczęście się uśmiecha. Wyjdź mu naprzeciw.

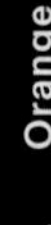

Orange Alternative Countersurveillance Invitation card Courtesy of Waldemar Fydrych, IPN Wr 142/10, 4z18 1988

Secret Agent's Day[1]

March 1, 4 p.m.

Świdnicka

A great day, unforgettable impressions, don't miss this unique opportunity. You want to see the ins and outs of the WUSW's [Provincial Office of Internal Affairs] operations? Then come on down to Świdnicka Street near Barbara's Bar on Tuesday, March 1 at 4 p.m. where the celebration of the international Secret Agent's Day will be held. The event sponsor is none other than our Wrocław Regional Office of Internal Affairs. The employees of this very select company belong to the world's cream of the crop. Being the hosts of this event, they have also invited other deserving companies: the FBI, Scotland Yard, the KGB, and others. Come dressed suitably to the occasion: wear black glasses, a hat, raincoat, leather coat, or a cape. Bring bugging equipment with you: a microphone, funnel, or a trumpet. Microphones installed in umbrellas or canes are in particular indicated. Fans of Scotland Yard are requested to arrive with their smoking pipes. Dogs are considered high value assets. There will be a street exposition of secret service accessories. Feel at ease, ask pedestrians for IDs. Expose your coat lapels where your service badge ought to be placed. Should you be asked into a car, go on! This is your natural environment. Only a few chosen ones will be invited to the ceremony to the academy. Do not ignore this great opportunity. Luck smiles at you. Go and meet it!

Translated from Polish by the Orange Alternative
http://www.orangealternativemuseum.pl/#secret-agents-day/posters

Endnotes

1 Translator's note: In Polish "tajniak," in contrast to "tajny agent" (secret agent), sounds disparaging.

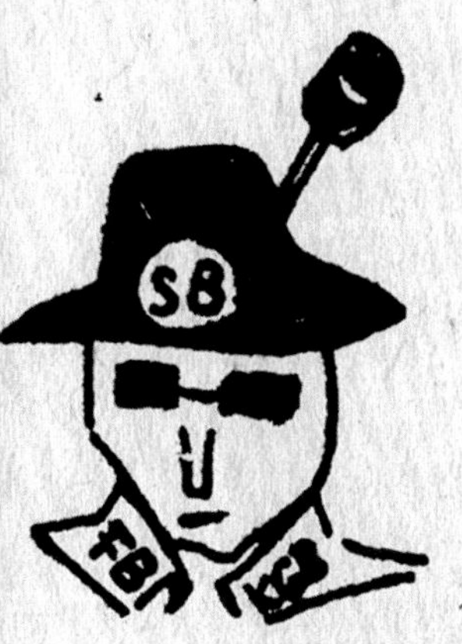

DZIEŃ TAJNIAKA

Wielki dzień, niezapomniane wrażenia nie przegap unikalnej okazji

1 Marzec godz.16°°

ŚWIDNICKA

Jeżeli chcesz zobaczyć pracę Wojewódzkiego Urzędu Spraw Wewnętrznych, nic innego jak pojaw się na ul. Świdnickiej o godz.16⁰⁰, 1 marca /wtórek/ w pobliżu Baru Barbara. Tego dnia odbędzie się uroczystość z okazji Międzynarodowego Dnia Tajniaka. Inicjatorem tego święta jest nasz Wrocławski Wojewódzki Urząd Spraw Wewnętrznych. Pracownicy tej wykwintnej firmy należą do światowej śmietanki. Oni to występując w roli gospodarzy zaprosili inne zasłużone firmy: FBJ, Scotland Yard, KGB i inne. Ubierz się stosownie w czarne okulary, kapelusz, płaszcz prochowiec lub skórę bądź pelerynę. Weź sprzęt do podsłuchu, trąbkę, lejek lub mikrofon. Wskazane są mikrofony zamontowane w parasolkach lub laseczkach. Wielbiciele Scotland Yardu proszeni są o przybycie z tytoniowymi fajkami. Psy są niesamowitym atutem. Na ulicy odbędzie się też wystawa akcesoriów służb porządkowych. Zachowuj się swobodnie, legitymuj przechodni. Poruszaj też klapę płaszcza na której będzie widniał twój służbowy znaczek. Jeżeli zostaniesz zaproszony do wozu - wchodź!, jest to twoje naturalne miejsce. Wybrańcy z grona solenizantów zostaną zaproszeni na akademię. Nie ignoruj tej wielkiej szansy. Szczęście się uśmiecha. Wyjdź mu naprzeciw.

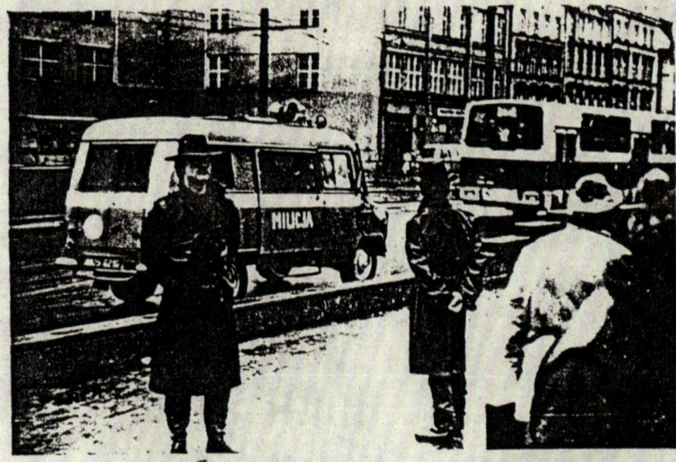

DZIEŃ TAJNIAKA ZIMNY

1.03.88

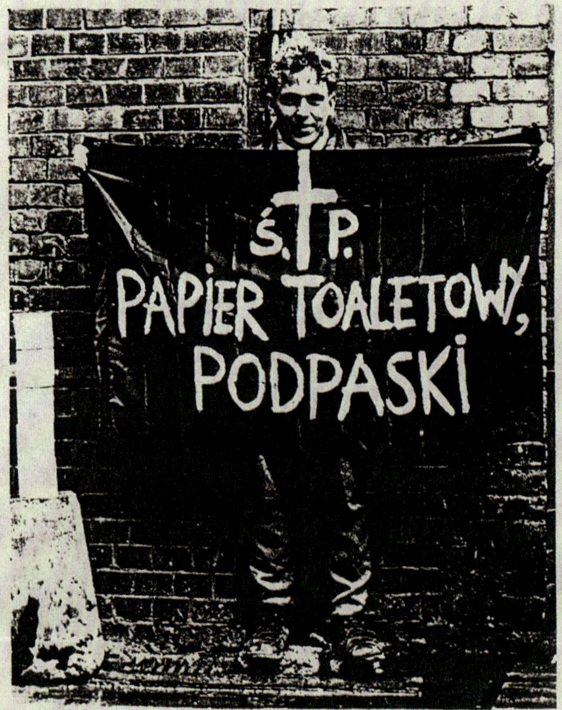

←

NAF DEMENTI

Look Who's Watching?

Photographic Documentation of Happenings and Performances in Czechoslovakia

Tomáš Pospiszyl

The argument of my paper is rather traditional: art is influenced by its historical context and we have to clarify this context again and again. In recent months, I became interested in photographic documentation of happenings and performances that took place in Czechoslovakia during the 1960s and 70s. These photographs include much more than just artists and their works, most notably audiences watching these actions. The onlookers are sometimes more interesting than the art itself. Quite often, we can even discern who is in the audience and what they think of what they're watching.

Let's begin with an action titled *Demonstration of One* (*Demonstrace jednoho*) by Milan Knížák from 1964. It is documented in a series of photographs and a text description:

"Stand still in a crowd, unfold a piece of paper, stand on it, take off your ordinary clothes and put on something unusual, a jacket half red, half green with a tiny saw hanging from the lapel, a piece of handkerchief pinned *to* the back. Display a poster on which is written: 'I beg the passer by, if possible, while passing this place *to* crow.' Lie down on a piece of paper, read a book, tear out the finished pages. Then stand up, crumple the paper, burn it, sweep up the ashes carefully, change your clothes, and leave."[1]

Photographs, taken by an unattributed photographer, document Knížák's accurate execution of this scenario.[2] What I found particularly interesting was that in every photograph we can see, not only Knížák, but also his audience. The photographer purposefully juxtaposes the performer and his audience in every shot. We can see that from the beginning of the event a small crowd had gathered around the artist. They were most likely people who were simply walking down the street and were struck by this unusual event happening on the sidewalk. We can see that they're curious, amazed; many are suspicious and some clearly find it funny. We can tell that it is a group of people brought together by chance, an audience unprepared for something like this, but interested in finding out what is going on. And it is clear that Knížák wanted to approach such an audience, to test their reactions, and at the same time, test the limits of public space. In 1964, the atmosphere in Czechoslovakia was relatively liberal, but there were still many limitations. The reason this action was not interrupted by the authorities was probably its short duration.

Roughly around the same time, Milan Knížák organized similar events that took place in different places around Prague. Another event, titled *A Walk in the New World. Demonstration for All Senses* (*Procházka po Novém Světě. Demonstrace na všechny smysly*, 1964), was prepared for an invited group of friends, but anyone who happened to be around could participate as well. The audience was to wander through a picturesque neighborhood where Knížák had a studio at the time. Various surprises, assemblages, and games were prepared for the participants. From photographic documentation, we can see that there was a clear distinction between performers dressed in costumes and guests in casual clothes. They were grouped into two separate crowds, the second following the lead of the first. Another Knížák project, *Demonstration for J. M.* (*Demonstrace pro J. M.*, 1965), took place in a similar environment. The audience was invited to perform simple tasks, like moving objects on the sidewalk or destroying paintings. The documentary photographs suggest a joyful atmosphere, but that sense is belied by the artist's own description of what took place. Here are his words: "Members of the State Security, who arrived in great force already at the beginning of the action, forbid all this, but after a lengthy and explosive discussion, I succeeded in persuading them it would take at least one hour to clean up all that mess and this was the guise under which the entire action took place. Therefore, the hectic clearing become a valid and inseparable part of the action."[3]

It would probably be unfair to call this event a game or a play; it was in fact the cleaning of the playground ordered by the police. Policemen are not captured in any of the existing photographs, but we should be aware of the fact that they were present. The police were an active third party—besides the artists and their audience—and had control over the whole action. Here we have an example of a secondary audience of a special kind: a state apparatus that can interpret every unusual activity as a threat to its security.[4]

Let's compare these photographs from the mid-1960s with documentation of artists active after 1968, during the time of the deepest political and cultural repression in Czechoslovakia. The work of Czech performers like Petr Štembera, Karel Miler, and Jan Mlčoch was much more private, known only to a small number of people. There was usually an audience at their performances, but it was comprised of people that already knew each other. Photographic documentation was thus crucial and developed a distinctive form: a single black-and-white photograph accompanied by a short text description. These performances did not take place in a public space or even in art galleries, but mostly in private apartments or other invite-only locations. Artists from this group often performed in a basement or the attic of their workplace, which was the building of the National Gallery in Prague, or in other nontraditional spaces.[5] Usually, five or ten people were present, but sometimes only the artist and a photographer took part. For example, Mlčoch's performance *Washing* (*Myti*), which took place in Prague on December 20, 1974, was described by the artist in these words: "In the presence of a few friends, I washed my whole body, including my hair."[6] What we can see in an unattributed photograph is an artist washing himself and two of his friends watching him: in other words, something very ordinary yet very private. One of the viewers, who can be identified as fellow artist Karel Miler, holds a burning candle as if he was participating in some semireligious ceremony. The audience here is put into a voyeuristic position that can be quite uncomfortable for both artist and viewers.

The relationship between performer and audience, which often became tense or even aggressive, is a subject of many performances by this group of artists. Both Petr Štembera and Jan Mlčoch put on performances in which they threatened their viewers. Let us read a description of a performance titled *Archer* (*Lukostrelec*) by Petr Štembera that took place in Hradec Králové on November 26, 1977:

> In a room full of people (dressed as a Black Shirt), I shot an arrow with a metal tip at a target on a wall, demonstrating the strength of a child's bow. I then dipped a second arrow (which also had a metal tip) into a bottle marked poison, I aimed it at the target but shot into the audience at the other end of the wall.[7]

In this work, Štembera, who was a performer known for putting himself into various dangerous situations, decided to do the opposite and endangered his audience. A more unpleasant situation was the basis for the 1977 performance *Night* (*Noc*) by Jan Mlčoch:

> A strange office in a strange building. A girl was brought to this office who did not know what was going to happen. I waited for her there with a tape recorder, camera, and a strong lamp. After an hour of questioning, I let her go. She left the building with the other people who were waiting outside.[8]

This is pretty much a police interrogation, and was probably very unpleasant even if the interrogated person knew it was only a simulation. The other audience members, waiting outside, probably also felt very uncomfortable, unsure if they should intervene, be concerned about their friend, and/or be bored from their passive position. We have to remember that this performance happened in 1977, the year of political unrest and Charter 77 in Czechoslovakia, when police interrogation become a regular part of life for many people trying to dissent from the totalitarian regime. The artist here also reversed his usual position: he was not to be a subject of watching and scrutinizing, but the opposite. He was the one in control, questioning his audience.

Mlčoch's performances often remind us of police investigations or situations more likely to be found in a detective novel. In the November 1977 performance *Classic Escape* (*Klasicky unik*), Mlčoch "threw out everyone present from a room of a borrowed flat into the corridor and nailed the door down from the inside. With help of a rope, I climbed down to the courtyard and left."[9] The photo documentation looks like the police reconstruction of a crime scene. This is a description of another Mlčoch work titled *There and Back* (*Tam a zpet*), performed on May 24, 1976:

> I wrote an anonymous letter in which I requested that an assault be carried out on the person described in the letter. I wrote down his name, address, and a basic description to which I added a photograph. I enclosed 100 crowns and promised more when the work was done. I was the person I described. I sent the letter to people who did not know me via an intermediary.[10]

The photograph that the artist decided to use as an illustration of this performance is slightly blurred. It shows a place that looks like an outdoor cafe, where we imagine the person that's about to be assaulted is sitting, unaware of being watched. The blurriness of the photograph reminds us of the era's photographs, taken by the secret police while surveying their suspects. Over one million photographs of this kind were recently discovered in the archives of the Ministry of Interior Affairs.[11] It is a fascinating mass of images. Their setup and even their aesthetic are sometimes very similar to the works under discussion by these Czech performers. People are being watched and photographed doing various cryptic activities in a strange environment. The meaning of their actions is clear only to informed people or to the ones reading a report explaining the situation. One of the photographs from the secret police archives depicts the writer Milan Kundera. He is with a woman on a street; she is giving him an envelope. As the series of images continues, he goes to a phone booth and then meets the same woman again. From the attached police report, we know that he had received his passport from a friendly clerk and was checking some details concerning his plans to leave the country. What at first looked like a casual meeting of two friends suddenly takes on a different meaning.

The audience in the photo documentation of Czech performers during the 1970s is not anonymous. This is not only because we often know them by name, and because they know very well that they are taking part in an art action. They also know that the photographs will be seen by a large secondary audience and maybe by the police, who can decode them as a disturbance of the peace. They take that risk. Their presence and willingness to be photographed means that they become part of the event. They are not people from the street, as in Knížák's happenings. Even if they remain passive throughout the whole event, they are participants, accomplices. In addition, performers themselves often put their audiences into situations in which the simple acts of being present and watching are emphasized by different symbolic or even aggressive scenarios.

Let us examine the work of Jiří Kovanda, who was very close to the aforementioned group of performers. His style was different—not as confrontational. He also executed some of his performances in public spaces. They took place at roughly the same place and time that the secret police were monitoring other people. The performances usually comprised something very close to ordinary activities. Sometimes nobody apart from the artist would guess that an artwork was being enacted. From 1976 to 1978, Kovanda used to set out for the busy city center to perform various activities. For example, a November 1976 piece called *Theater* (*Divadlo*) took place at Wenceslas Square, the busiest part of Prague: "I follow a previously written script to the letter. Gestures and movements have been selected so that passersby will not suspect that they are watching a performance."[12]

The artist touches his nose, moves his head, walks back and forth. His friend Pavel Tuč documented everything with a camera while remaining relatively free in the manner in which he captured his subject. Kovanda's most important requirement was that his friend not interrupt what he was doing while photographing him. The documentation was conducted in such a way that only the artist and the photographer would be aware of it. Many people whom the secret police photographed knew that they were under surveillance. They would adjust their behavior accordingly in order to avoid persecution, or they would use various methods to confuse the police. Kovanda knew that he was being photographed, since he himself had invited his friend to document his inconspicuous performances. Despite this, he acted as if he had no idea that this was the case.

Kovanda would later affix the photographic documentation of the work to a sheet of paper, write the name of the performance, the time and place of the event, and then add the script—as if he were making a report on his own activity. Two parallel activities were thus taking place in a public space, one by the secret police, the other executed by an artist. Both were originally not publicly available and were only accessible to a narrow circle of viewers. In addition, a proper understanding of both the police shots and Kovanda's performances requires that we know the motivation behind their origins and the foundations of their language. Kovanda makes no explicit reference to the secret police's work in his method of documentation. In all probability, he had no idea what their reports looked like.

Probably the most complex work from this period involving an audience is Kovanda's performance on October 19, 1977, entitled *Attempted Acquaintance* (*Pokus o seznámení*), described in the following words: "I invited some friends to watch me trying to make friends with a girl."[13] The group of friends watches an extraordinarily shy artist trying to talk to girls on the Old Town Square. The artist purposely put himself in the awkward situation of being **surveilled**. The fact of being watched was, at that time, a normal situation for thousands of other people in Prague. In this case the one being watched is trying to perform something very private, very intimate. He may be pushed to it because of the knowledge of external control over his actions.

The degree of state surveillance and its ubiquity in socialist countries has been underestimated not only by later generations who did not experience it, but also even by those who witnessed it. Jiři Kolář, for example, was under the constant surveillance of the secret police for a quarter of a century. Relentless official scrutiny of his everyday life did not cease until he emigrated in 1980.[14] It is very accurate to say that in Eastern Europe during the Communist era, all performance artists, and others whose work resembled performance art, attracted either the open or covert attention of the security services. This was true not only for openly provocative individuals such as Milan Knížák. The secret police were interested in Jan Mlčoch not as an artist, but because they hoped to make him inform on his artistic collaborators.[15] The name Petr Štembera can be found in various notes of Jiří Kolář's secret police dossier.

As a closing remark, I would like to emphasize the great change from the time of Milan Knížák's happenings to performances by artists in the 1970s. Milan Knížák was able—although with many limitations—to work in public spaces and to directly approach ordinary passersby on the streets. In the 1970s, artists could no longer work in a similar way, because there was no public space they could freely use. Therefore, they worked in small circles of friends and reached a secondary audience through photographic documentation. Their work reflects the control that the political regime had over people at that time. Audience participation has its own symbolic level of very close partnership. A relatively banal situation—since artists could not work openly due to political reasons—led to complex strategies for how to overcome this limitation.[16]

Endnotes

1 Milan Knížák, *Actions for which at least some documentation remains* (Prague: Gallery, 2000), 36.

2 Photographs were taken by Zdena Žižková, who was a close friend of Knížák's girlfriend at that time, Soňa Švecová. Žižková was interested in photography and documented most of the actions by Knížák and his friends during the second part of the 1960s.

3 Milan Knížák, *Some Documentary: 1961–1979* (Berlin: Edition Ars Viva, 1980), 80.

4 "Secondary audience" is a term for the recipients of art from outside of the artistic domain (those who are neither artists nor critics—i.e. the "primary audience"). In this particular case, the "secondary audience" was quite specific, as it was composed not only of "ordinary" spectators, but also of police officers and informants.

5 Karel Miler worked at the National Gallery as a curator; Petr Štembera and Jan Mlčoch worked in a depository.

6 Karel Miler, Petr Štembera, and Jan Mlčoch, *1970–1980* (Prague: Sorosovo centrum současného uměni, 1997), 51.

7 Ibid., 40.

8 Ibid., 58.

9 Ibid., 60.

10 Ibid., 57.

11 These secret police photos were published in *Praha objektivem tajne policie* (*Prague Through the Lens of the Secret Police*) (Prague: Institute for the Study of Totalitarian Regimes, 2009).

12 Hans Ulrich Obrist and Pawel Plit, *Jiří Kovanda: Actions & Installations 1975–2006* (Zurich: JRP Ringier/Tranzit series, 2006), 46.

13 Ibid., 36.

14 The Czechoslovakian secret police were convinced that Kolář had organized a subversive group. His files contain reports of monitoring, interrogations, a list of Kolář's friends and their characteristics, a floor plan of his apartment, and transcripts of telephone conversations, which police wiretapped for years. These files are held in the Security Services Archive at the Institute for the Study of Totalitarian Regimes in Prague.

15 Jan Mlčoch avoided collaborating with the secret police using a common strategy. In response to the offer of becoming an informer, he would tell a State Security officer that at his workplace, he had already announced his meeting with a Ministry of Interior employee, which immediately made him unsuitable as a reporter of information. A similar method worked particularly with people that the secret police considered less relevant or useful.

16 This text is a slightly updated version of Tomáš Pospiszyl's publication "Look Who's Watching. Photographic Documentation of Happenings and Performances in Czechoslovakia," in *1968–1989. Political Upheaval and Artistic Change*, eds. Claire Bishop and Marta Dziewańska (Warsaw: Museum of Modern Art, 2009), 74–87.

Contact
Theater
Attempted Acquaintance

Jiří Kovanda

In his art actions, the Czech artist Jiří Kovanda had himself photographed by his friend Pavel Tuč in works like *Contact* (*Kontakt*, 1977), *Theatre* (*Divadlo*, 1976), and *Attempted Acquaintance* (*Pokus o seznámení*, 1977). Kovanda's most important stipulation was that the friend doing the photographing not interrupt him. Only the artist and the photographer knew about the action. Later, Kovanda affixed the photographic documentation of the work to a sheet of paper, noted the name of the performance, its time and location, and attached the script—as if filing a report on his own activities. In one report, he even blacked text out. The camera pursues Kovanda, captures what he is doing. Kovanda puts the observed photographer into exactly that position which he intended for passers by on the street: "Gestures and movements have been selected so that passers-by have no idea that they are watching a 'performance.'" The photographs look like they were taken from the perspective of state security; or at least that is how we could interpret it today. (S)

Contact, Four b/w photographs, typescript on paper, 33 × 24 cm, 1977
Courtesy of Kontakt Collection, Vienna

"KONTAKT"

3.září 1977
Praha,Spálená a Vodičkova ulice

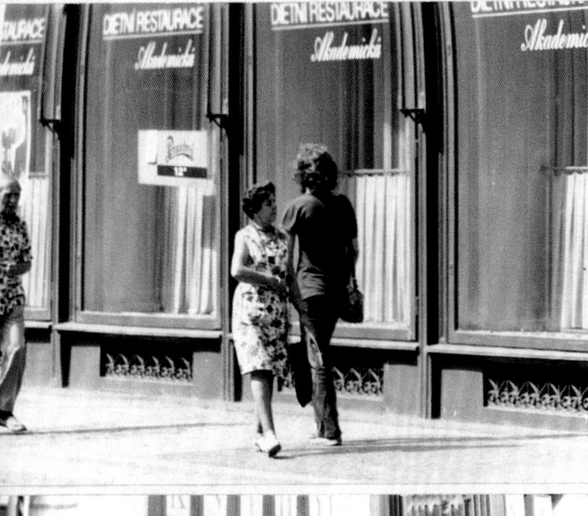

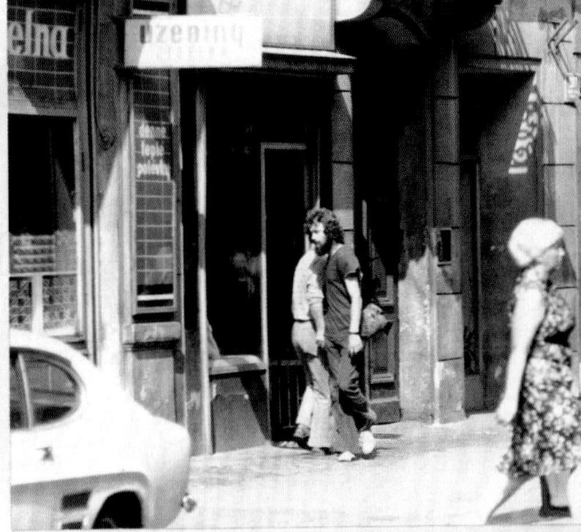

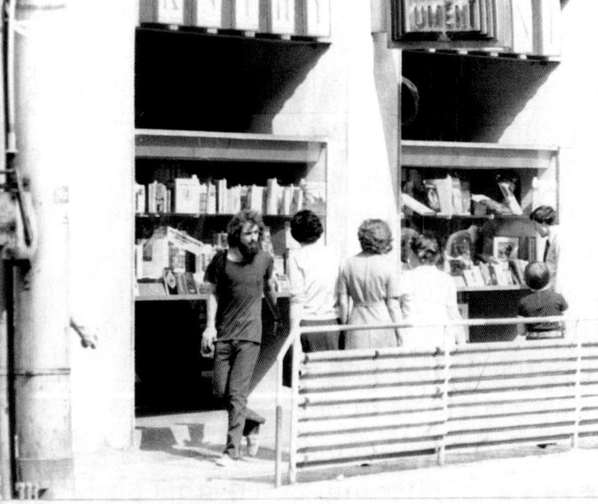

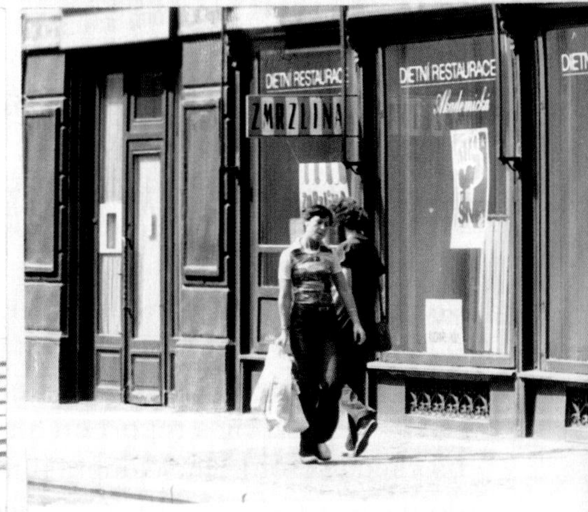

"DIVADLO"

listopad 1976
Praha, Václavské náměstí

Chovám se přesně podle předem napsaného scénáře. Gesta a pohyby jsou voleny tak, aby nikdo z kolemjdoucích netušil, že sleduje "představení".

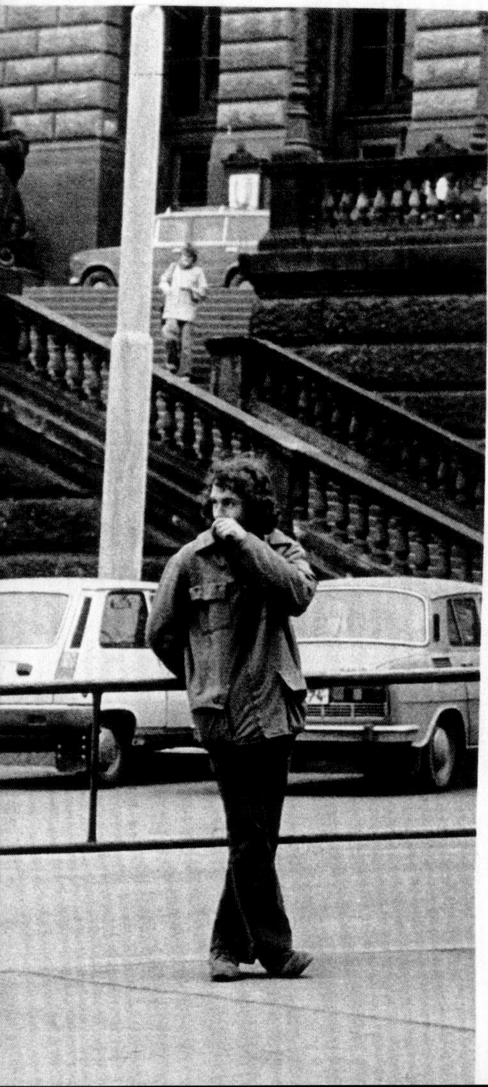

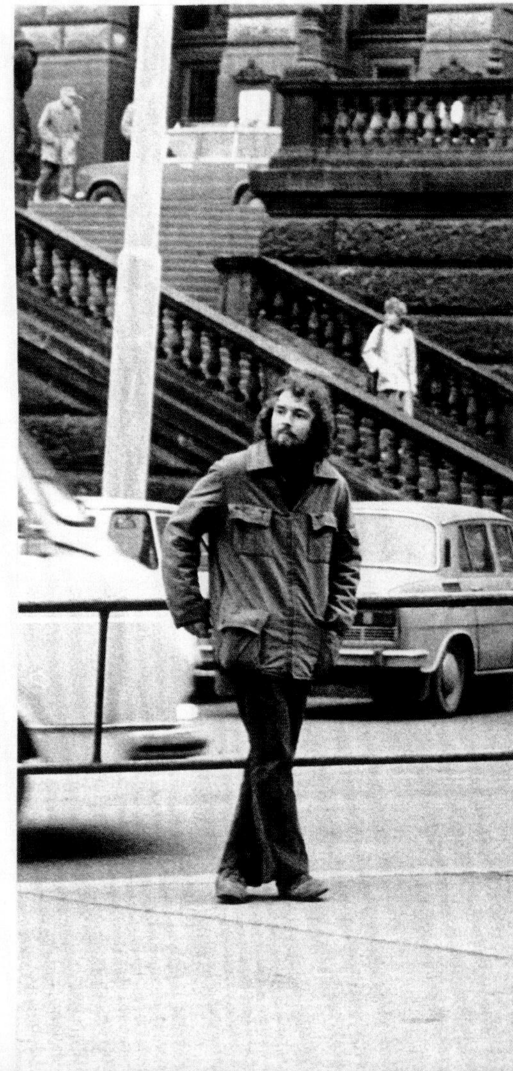

Theatre, Two black-and-white photographs, typescript on paper, 33 × 24 cm, Courtesy of Kontakt Collection, Vienna 1976

"POKUS O SEZNÁMENÍ"

19.října 1977
Praha,Staroměstské náměstí

Pozval jsem přátele,aby se podívali,jak se pokusím seznámit s holkou.

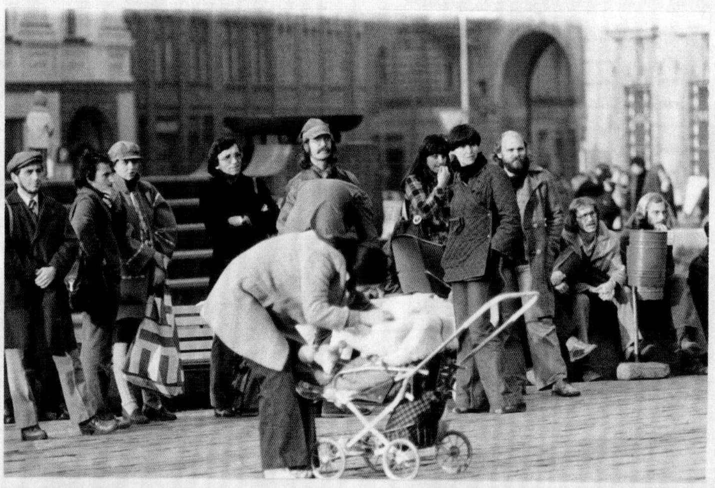

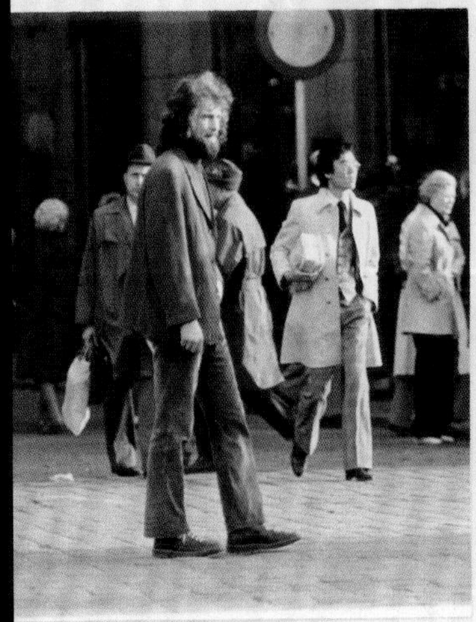

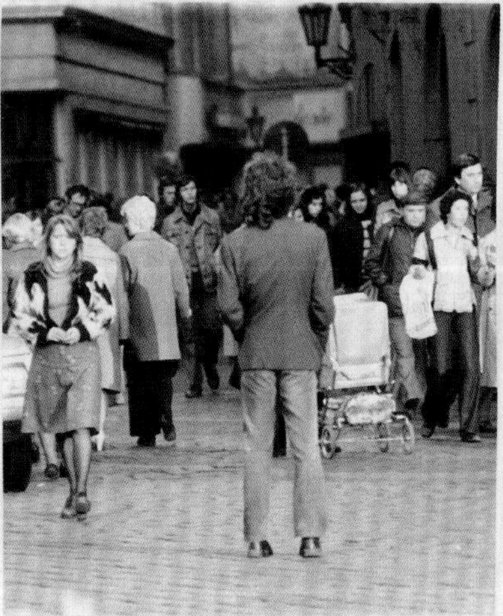

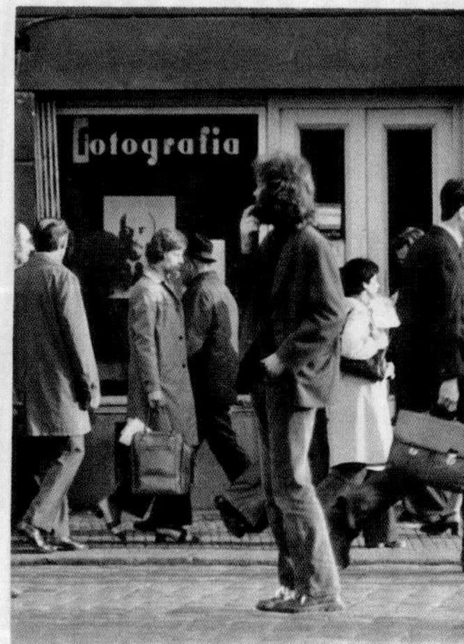

typescript on paper, 33 × 24 cm, Courtesy of Kontakt Collection, Vienna

Electoral Meeting

Ion Grigorescu

In communist Romania, state-managed electoral meetings were the order of the day. Under the oversight of the feared secret police, citizens had to testify to their adherence to the regime. Ion Grigorescu secretly photographed one of these meetings, organized on March 6, 1975. The results are especially revealing of the mechanism behind these demonstrations. The combination of the crowd, bewildered but docile, and the individual members of the secret police, created an absurd spectacle, lacking every form of spontaneity. These senseless and mechanical actions had no other purpose than to be a setting for role-playing, imposed by a system of discrete but ruthless oppression. Here, Grigorescu photographically assumes the perspective of state security: the scenes captured with a camera hidden at hip level are otherwise only found in the secret service files of persons under surveillance. (A)

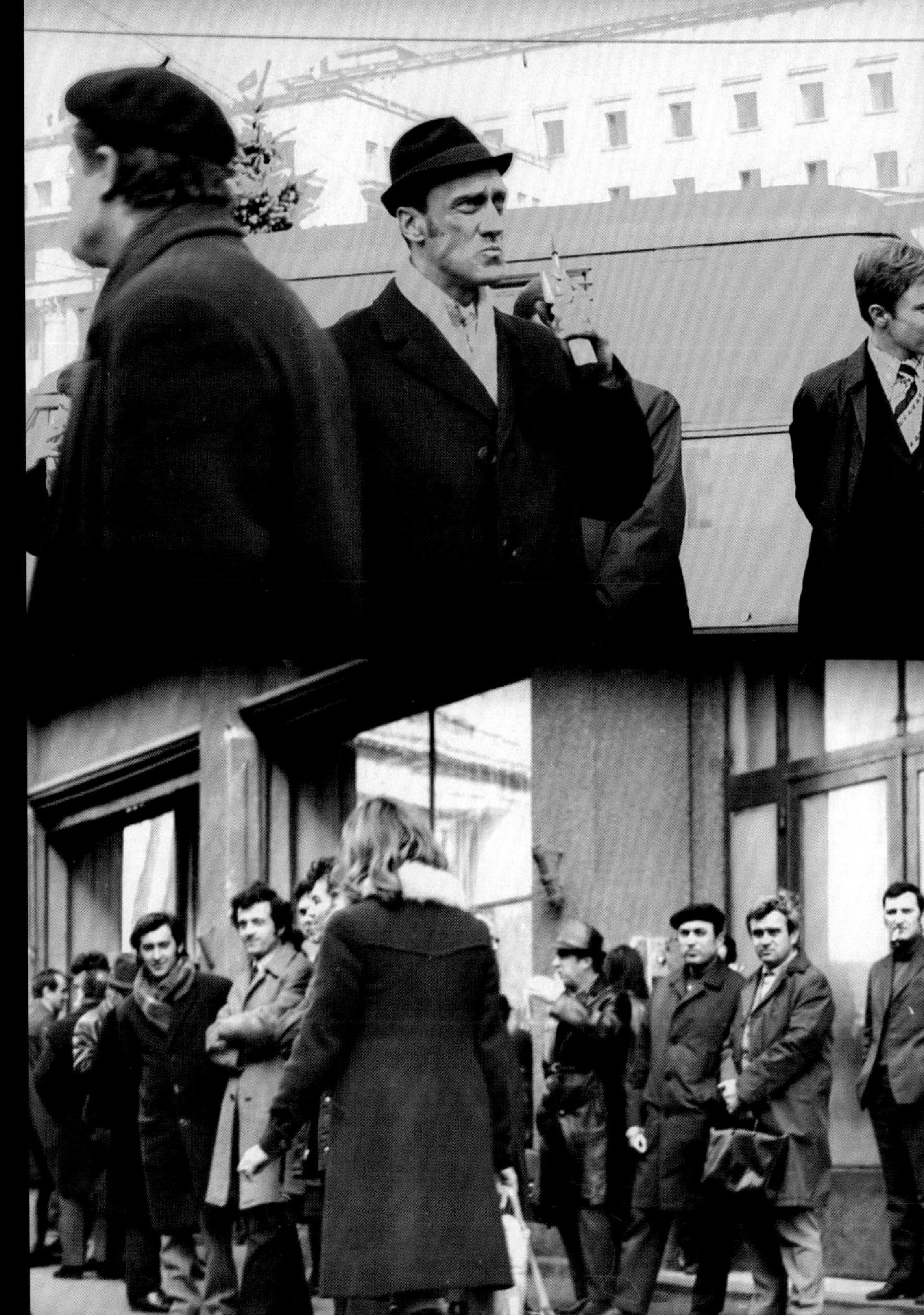

 Ion Grigorescu

Countersurveillance

Selection of seven black-and-white photographs, 28.20 × 14 cm
Courtesy of Ion Grigorescu

1975

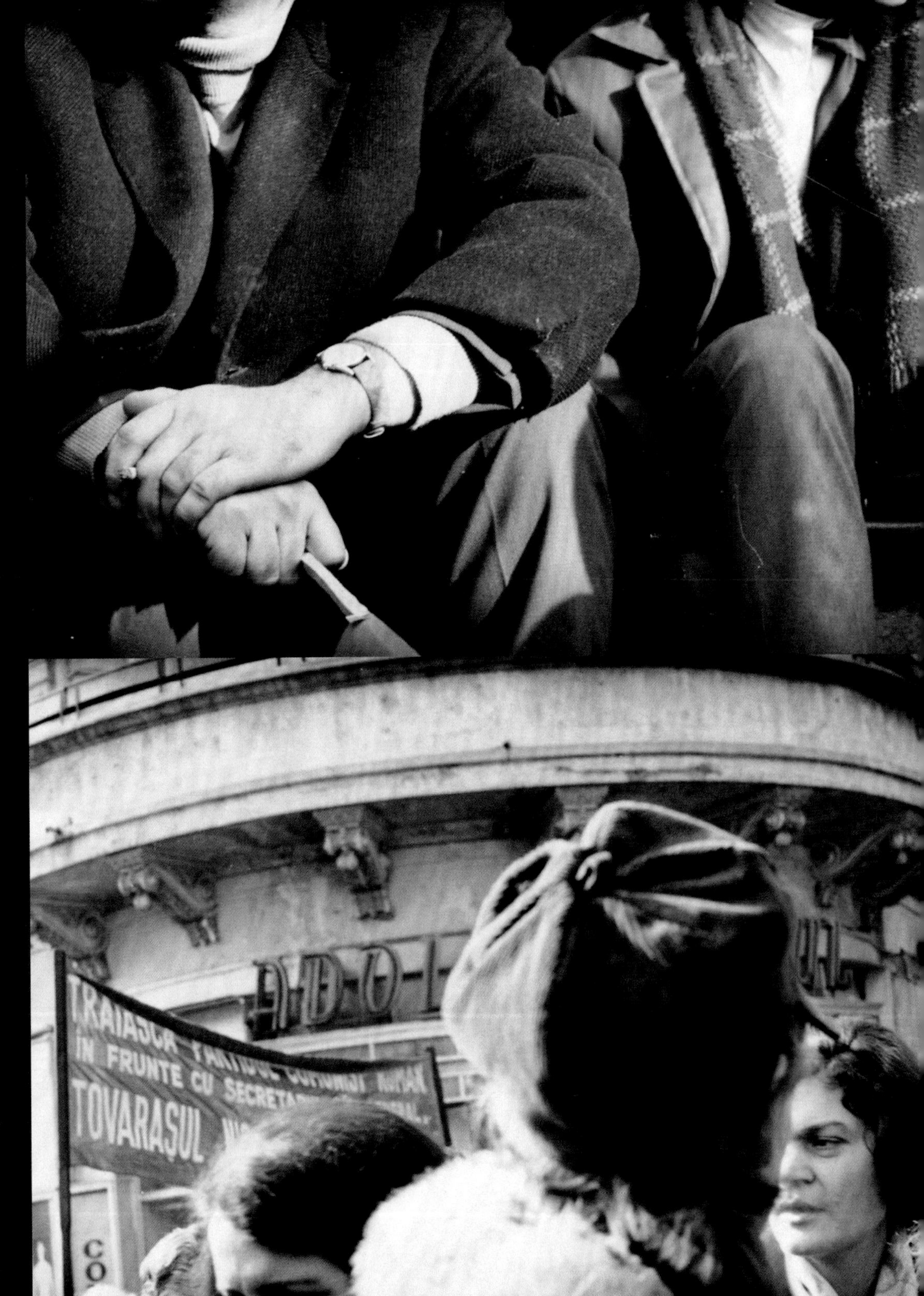
TRAIASCA
IN FRUNTE CU
TOVARAȘUL

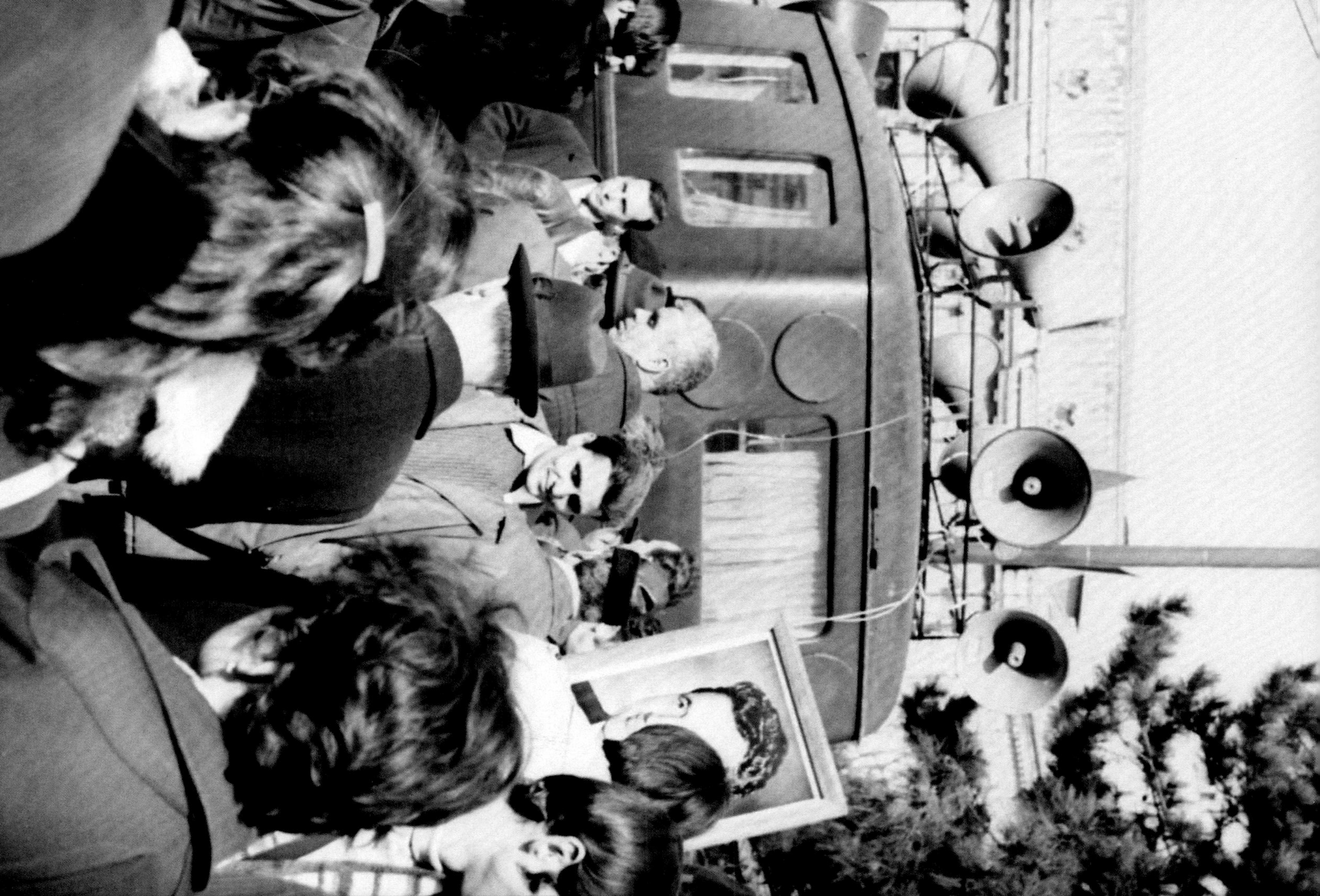

 Ion Grigorescu Countersurveillance

Selection of seven black-and-white photographs, 28.20 × 14 cm
Courtesy of Ion Grigorescu

1975

Sanja Iveković, b. 1949 in Zagreb, Yugoslavia, lives and works in Zagreb, Croatia.

Triangle

Sanja Iveković

The polyptych that consists of four photos and a text documents the eighteen-minute action *Triangle* (*Trokut*), which Sanja Iveković carried out on her balcony on May 10, 1979 in Zagreb. While the motorcade of the Yugoslavian President Josip Broz Tito passes on the street below, the artist sits on her balcony, reads a book, drinks whiskey, and acts as if she is masturbating. A sniper is on the roof across from her. Conceived of as a counteraction to the omnipresent surveillance, Iveković includes surveillance strategies in her performance, thus appropriating the methods of the secret services for her own artistic work. (A)

Trokut (Triangle)

Performance, photographs
Time: 18 min
1979

The action takes place on the day of the President's visit to the city, and it develops as intercommunication between three persons:

1. a person on the roof of a tall building across the street from my apartment;
2. myself, on the balcony;
3. a policeman in the street in front of the house.

Due to the cement construction of the balcony, only the person on the roof can actually see me and follow the action. My assumption is that this person has binoculars and a walkie-talkie apparatus. I notice that the policeman in the street also has a walkie-talkie.
The action begins when I walk out onto the balcony and sit on a chair, I sip whiskey, read a book, and make gestures as if I perform masturbation. After a period of time, the policeman rings my doorbell and orders that 'persons and objects are to be removed from the balcony.'

Savska 1, Zagreb
May 10, 1979

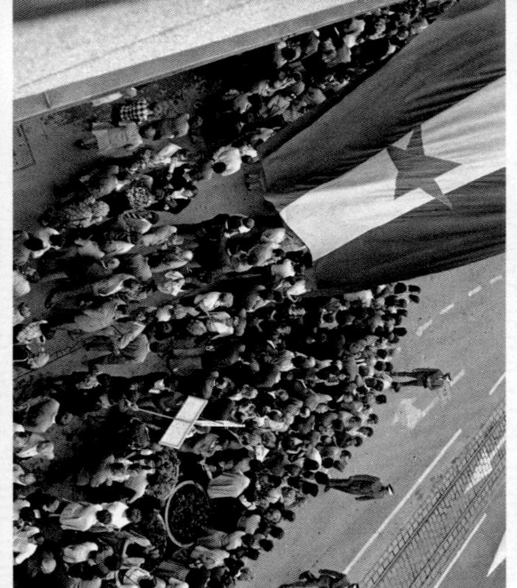

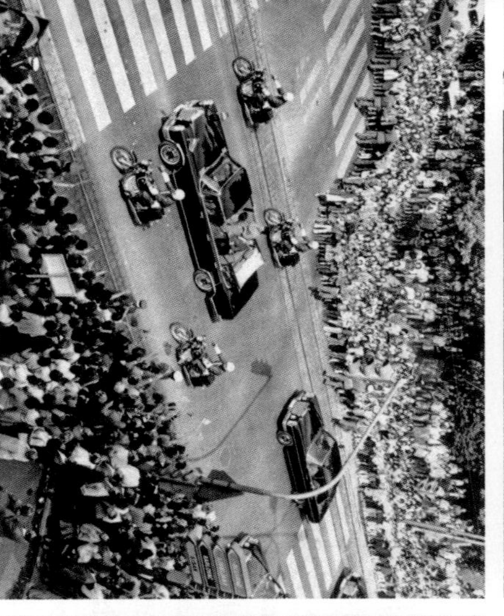

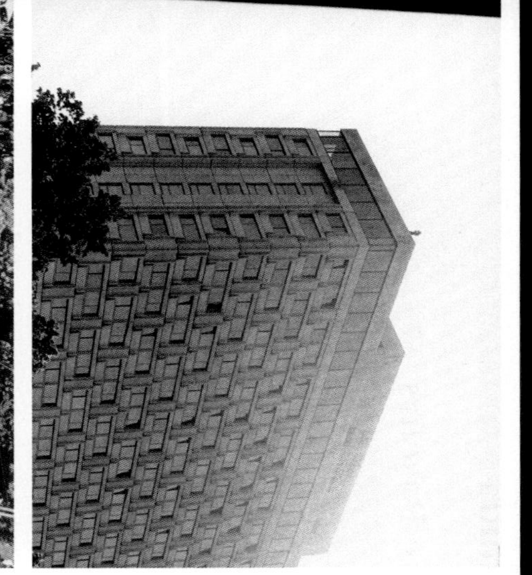

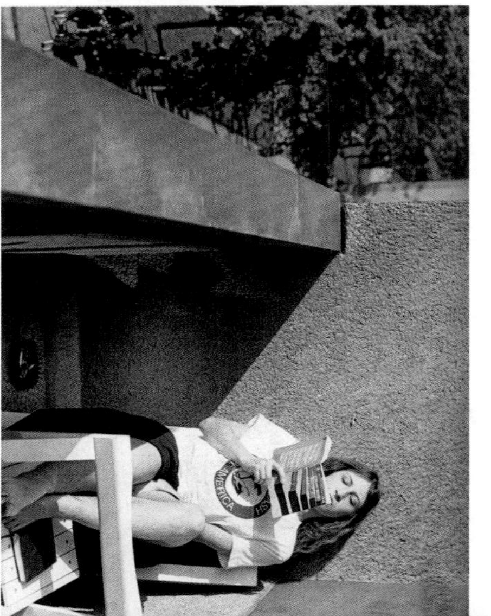

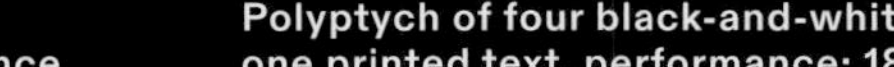

Sanja Iveković Countersurveillance

Polyptych of four black-and-white photographs, framed, 160 × 126 cm, one printed text, performance: 18 min, Courtesy of Sanja Iveković 19

Code Name "Letraset"[1]

Łukasz Ronduda

The Pawns and the Poseurs

On July 31, 1975, the Polish Security Service (*Służba Bezpieczeństwa*, SB) launched an "operational inquiry" code-named "Letraset."[2] The suspects under surveillance were artists Marek Konieczny and Przemysław Kwiek on account of the "threat" they were generating for the socialist state. In the opening of the "Letraset" file in the "Threat (Fact)" column, the following charge appears: "A dissident political initiative against the state/political authorities (petitions and collecting of signatures)."[3] The "Verbal Description of the Threat (Fact)" column contains the following report:

> In the course of operational activities for the case Letraset, information has been obtained about a protest being planned by a group of visual artists against the policies of the Visual Arts Workshops or PSP (*Pracownie Sztuk Plastycznych*) ... The protest's initiators are Marek Konieczny ... and Przemysław Kwiek. ...[4] The information we have suggests that the aforementioned intend to collect about forty signatures in their petition. ... The letter is to voice discontent with the policies and activities of the Visual Arts Workshops. ... The planned dissident initiative will be investigated in the course of an operational query by the local Department.[5]

At this point, it is worth remembering the role that the Visual Arts Workshops played in the context of the Polish People's Republic's (*Polska Rzeczpospolita Ludowa*, PRL) culture and economy. The state institution was the nationwide monopolist in charge of all public-sphere visual arts commissions, from shop window displays to large-scale, monumental environments. Visual arts commissions approved by the executive government or other branches of the communist state were then awarded by the Visual Arts Workshops leadership to the Association of Polish Artists and Designers (*Związek Polskich Artystów Plastyków*, ZPAP) artists.[6] Virtually all Polish artists of the communist period who, upon graduating from art school, decided to work "in the profession," lived off PSP commissions. Given the art market's vestigial nature[7] and the limited number of teaching jobs at art academies (and other schools), there existed virtually no other legal source of income for freelance visual artists.

In the early 1970s, Przemysław Kwiek and Marek Konieczny[8] represented neo-avant-garde trends in art and proreformist attitudes towards the political system (Kwiek was a candidate status holder and Konieczny, a full member of the Polish United Workers' Party, the communist party abbreviated as PZPR [*Polska Zjednoczona Partia Robotnicza*]). The protest they were organizing concerned the neglect of avant-garde propositions in the PSP's pricelists and commissions.[9] The commissions awarded by the PSP had to follow predetermined, traditional formats—painting, drawing, *sgraffito*, mosaic, monumental sculpture, bas-relief, medal—which were paid according to a square-meters-into-zlotys conversion rate defined in the PSP price list (the larger and taller the work, the better it paid).[10] Consequently, the PSP had a problem with accepting (and pricing)[11] new media works and artistic forms such as conceptual pieces, multimedia projections, intermedia shows and interactions, and so forth. It is worth remembering, in this context, the projects suggested to the authorities by the artists of the New Red Art movement,[12] such as Think Communism, Proagit 2, or Shapes of Red/A Path of Edward Gierek. The goal of the New Red artists was to reform politically involved art in the context of the socialist state so that it became more of an expression of grassroots communities and less of the authoritarian government. It was also meant to give people tools of self-organization and self-representation, as well as aid their creative and critical attitude towards reality. The New Red artists clearly differentiated between the socialist ideals in which they believed and their distortions, which they criticized in the context of institutions of the "real socialist" state. The question concerned not only a new concept of politically involved, avant-garde art, but also the general issue of whether there was room for neo-avant-garde art in the public space of communist Poland. KwieKulik (Zofia Kulik and Przemysław Kwiek) wrote:

> The point is that the forms of artistic expression are changing ... Through the "expert" committee he fully controls, Director Urbanowicz[13] is ordering artists to produce kitsch, unaware that the new, post-December policy[14] can't be expressed with old forms, or at least that we are unable, and unwilling, to do it using those old forms. And let us state it openly here—that if we are to produce an "in honor" plaque, then this is just a paid job for us that we want to do quickly, efficiently, well, and in the proper conditions. We don't treat it as part of our artistic output. ... On the other hand, we may be given the same "in honor" plaque to make, but with the assumption that it is to form part of our artistic output and that we can use all our

> skills to make it. We will be pleased to do it, but let no one be surprised if the final effect has a form never seen before. For instance, after his project of a monument in honor of the Nazi-executed hostages in Nowy Sącz[15] was rejected by the PSP, Władysław Hasior still made it, on his own responsibility, and the monument has now become the pride of "in honor" monumental works. We still remember today Hasior's article in *Odra* where he criticized, in formal, professional-artistic terms, the monuments and other works that the PSP had covered Poland with, to which Director Urbanowicz replied in *Polityka* by warning Hasior against sullying the places of national remembrance, soaked with the blood of freedom-fighting Poles, and so on.[16]

Besides fighting for a better place for new art, KwieKulik also had an existential aspect in mind—they wanted to be able to earn their living without having to do hackwork, to be able to carry out the PSP commissions using the new artistic language, which would further their own development as artists. Unlike those artists who had regular, full-time jobs (in cultural institutions or at art schools), KwieKulik's radical artistic attitude meant they were often in dire straits. At the same time, one of the aspects of that attitude was the attempt to consider the "material-spatial" conditions of reality, and therefore the functional, economic, and political context in which they happened to live and work.[17]

KwieKulik wrote in a letter to the Minister of Culture:

> At the same time, we are forced to carve out a living working for the PSP, the idiotic, swindling institution, doing "in honor" tablets, gravestones, calligraphing letters, priming surfaces, to then, if we are lucky, transfer someone else's designs onto them. No one, including the qualifying committee, believes in the sense and usefulness of these petty jobs. ... It is impossible not to do hack work when you work for the PSP. Our definition of hackwork: it is for-money work but only such where someone or something (the regulations) defines the field of your competence.[18]

This brings us to another charge against the PSP that was raised by Konieczny and Kwiek: one, in fact, that the majority of the artists working for the PSP (especially the more conservative members) agreed with. Namely, they accused the PSP authorities—and especially its director, Henryk Urbanowicz—of awarding commissions in a nontransparent manner, of corruption and cronyism.[19]

The fact that the SB decided to take Konieczny and Kwiek under surveillance on account of their planned protest against the PSP reflects not only the agency's obvious interest in all potentially subversive activity against the Polish People's Republic, but also shows the PSP's significance in the socialist regime's structures.

In charge of the regime's aesthetical and persuasive setting, the PSP was, alongside television, one of the strategic, strictly controlled elements of the state propaganda machine. That is why KwieKulik and Konieczny's attempts to wage criticism against the PSP triggered such a firm reaction from the state apparatus. In the course of the operation against Kwiek and, above all, Konieczny, who had turned out to be the action's initiator, the SB decided to tap artists' phones,[20] start reading their letters,[21] and set itself the task of finding out with whom they had recently been in touch.[22]

Particular emphasis was placed on determining the artists' (referred to as "pawns" in the SB documents) international contacts. For instance, Lieutenant Szymański, the officer in charge of the operation, ordered his subordinates to confirm a fact he had learned while intercepting Konieczny's telephone conversations:

> What does the "poser" from the Museum of New York represent as a person and why was he in Poland? Check him through Bureau C and Department I. ... Did the "pawn" meet the Canadians and what did they talk about?[23]

The SB probably wanted to find out whether Konieczny and Kwiek's initiative hadn't been inspired by an intelligence agency of some hostile capitalist state. Moreover, the SB file contains reports from "secret **agents**" and "operational contacts" (chiefly ZPAP members and Academy of Fine Arts employees),[24] concerning the "subjects" under **surveillance** and the situation at the PSP. Some of these are written by people relatively close to Konieczny. For instance, an operational contact code-named Zdzisław reported:

> Early on the 15th I called Marek Konieczny and got him interested in a commission to create decor for the space adapted for a café and restaurant on Senatorska street by Teatralny Square. He was interested and, to discuss the details, we met on the following day at the Mirowska café, because it's closest to where I live. Having discussed some professional matters and drunk a couple of cognacs, we proceeded to complain about the *Pracownie Sztuk Plastycznych* located on Foksal Street, and the institution's director, Mr. Urbanowicz. Among the visual artists, this is probably the most hotly discussed topic today, for I haven't met one who'd be satisfied with a PSP commission or their ways of pricing a job. This is a sore point for all the visual artists, one generating tensions and provoking harsh criticism.

The PSP officials get their "dole" from trusted artists, and everyone's happy. Unfortunately, this is how things are at the PSP, many people openly talk about it, but I'm sure that if a confrontation was held before the designated office or the party authorities willing to determine the truth, no one would say a word. It needs to be said that the current state of affairs is convenient for both sides, for you should know that the sums of money being exchanged range from tens of thousands to hundreds of thousands złotys. An artist who respects himself, but who also respects others, that is, the PSP officials, makes some 60,000 złotys a month. In this situation, a 5,000 złoty "gift" is nothing, little more than the cost of having a drink at a restaurant. This is a problem, but I don't think it can be solved as long as Urbanowicz keeps the job, and he's kept it for twenty-five years now, and [will keep] as long as he continues to have such mighty patrons in the top echelons of the party and government hierarchy. Such views were expressed in my conversation with Marek Konieczny. He then said he had entered into serious conflict with the PSP, a conflict for which, in a sense, not he was to blame, but rather the Ministry of Culture and Art's Visual Arts Department. He said he had been encouraged by the Ministry to lodge a fully documented complaint against the PSP. He did so, together with his colleague Bertrant, also a visual artist, believing their complaint would be reviewed by the Ministry and the appropriate measures would be taken against the PSP. Instead, the Visual Arts Department sent the complaint, with its own comment, to the PSP director Urbanowicz, asking him to take a position on it in writing. As the complaint contained rather harsh statements, Mr. Urbanowicz sued for slander of his institution. The case is pending, though it's in the appeals court now, because Konieczny lost in the first instance.

In another report, "op con" Zdzisław wrote about Konieczny:

I've been his guest many times. His wife is a math teacher. ... Konieczny is very intelligent and energetic. His wife helps him. Together, they possess inexhaustible energy and the ability to solve difficult, complex issues. He is a somewhat confrontational character, willing to stop at nothing in fighting for his personal interests. His official enemy is Director Urbanowicz and the *Pracownie Sztuk Plastycznych* as a whole. ... Politically, Konieczny isn't harmful, he plays the fool even though he's well educated and also professionally sound. I don't know much about Kwiek. I only know they've both joined the PZPR, though I wouldn't give them the recommendation.

Another "op con" (k.o.[25]), code name ZH, stated about Konieczny and Kwiek that they "belonged to the multitude of visual artists discontent with the way the PSP functions."

Other reports, drawn up on the basis of information obtained from "secret agents" and "operational contacts" from the artistic community, followed in a similar vein. Visual artists corrupted by the SB were using the opportunity to criticize the PSP. The SB drew the following conclusions from the body of material it had amassed:

> The evidence gathered so far doesn't suggest that Konieczny has been involved in subversive political activity. On the other hand, there are many indications to believe that irregularities, or even malfeasance, have been present at the PSP, of which the appropriate institutions should be notified at the right time.

And in another place:

> In the course of the operational activities undertaken, we've learned that the visual arts community is highly discontent with the functioning of the *Pracownie Sztuk Plastycznych*. It has been determined that the PSP is a nonsubsidized enterprise employing several hundred visual artists that provides services in the field of the visual arts—interior design, decor, displays—to commissioning companies and institutions. The PSP charges the artist a 15 percent middleman commission and an extra 4 percent for handling costs, plus the artists pays 8 percent income tax. Despite such overheads, an artist can make as much as 60,000 złotys a month, though the exact amount will depend on the number of commissions he gets and how big they are. It is at this point that misunderstandings and discord begin because the commissions are distributed by PSP officials who can give one artist a better job and with higher pay, and another a worse one. The older-generation artists know many of the PSP officials, often on a personal level, and in some cases present them with valuable objects as gifts, which means they get more, better paid commissions. This state of affairs is causing discontent among the younger-generation artists who sometimes perform more time- and effort-consuming but still less-paying jobs. ... it has been determined that Marek Konieczny and Przemysław Kwiek are not involved in any political activity and do not comment in any way on the country's present socio-political situation. Given the above, continuing the operation would be pointless and it has been sent to the archive of Department C, Warsaw Police Headquarters, for archivization.[26]

The SB discontinued the case against Konieczny and Kwiek, having decided that their protest was economically, rather than politically, motivated, and that it was a result of the two artists' discontent with the PSP's unfair practices. The file said nothing about Kwiek and Konieczny's postulates regarding the necessary reforms of the PSP's functioning, so that the institution moved away from primitive propaganda and instead opened itself to new trends in art (such as processualism, participation, interactivity, social activity). Moreover, contrary to the suggestions contained in the final report, the SB never notified the Supreme Chamber of Inspection of the alleged financial irregularities at the PSP. Nothing changed. Operation "Letraset" shows that the authorities were only interested in the propagandist effects of the PSP's work and not in the means the institution (and its director) used to achieve them. What mattered was its loyalty and subservience to the party's directives, as well as the lack of ideological controversy around its products.[27] In their letter of complaint to the Minister of Culture, KwieKulik wrote:

> Director Urbanowicz carries out an active artistic policy, which he makes no secret of. He says even more than that: he claims to be implementing in practice (via the specific works) the party's general directives. He proves that by saying that his company produces works such as eagles, commemorative tablets, national remembrance monuments, decorations for state holidays, medals and diplomas for good service ... You shouldn't tell the public, as Mr. Urbanowicz does, while claiming cynically to be expressing the views of the artists, on the one hand, and the authorities on the other, that all these works are an expression of the artists' utmost commitment to, and support for, the party's policy.

Marek Konieczny lost the slander lawsuit brought against him by Urbanowicz and had to pay a hefty fine. He no longer received commissions from the PSP.[28]

KwieKulik vs. the PSP

Przemysław Kwiek and Zofia Kulik perceived their critique of the PSP and other art institutions of the Polish People's Republic as part of their artistic practice. As early as 1971, Kwiek showed a file containing his letters to the Ministry of Culture and Art and as well as the official replies to them at the Galeria Współczesna, run by Maria and Janusz Bogucki in the Teatr Wielki building. The folder was marked "10 decagrams of Kwiek's papers" (a folder with petitions, opinions, and requests as the work *The Art of the Ministry of Culture and Art*).[29] It was a documentation of the official letters Kwiek had generated in 1971 and collected in the course of his wrestling with the bureaucratic apparatus of communist Poland's cultural officialdom. The work revealed the individual bureaucrats' positions (naming them personally), the hurdles raised by them, and their ignorance and opportunism. The writing of letters to institutions as a critical artistic activity was explicated in KwieKulik's 1975 letter to Deputy Culture Minister Tadeusz Kaczmarek, where they wrote:

> The work from the catalogue, the works on the photographs attached at the end of this file, our observations and views expressed in the form of public statements ... in the form of complaints and postulates concerning our problems—all this commentary that we practice, and because we practice it, we regard ourselves as being committed, so all this commentary writing distances us, with the distance creating a pathological anxiety, from our primary, planned, artistic activity, even though we believe this immediate commentary writing to be art too.[30]

In 1972, Przemysław Kwiek presented, at Galeria Sigma at Warsaw University, a work known as the *Vernissage of Meat and Osęka*, and, in 1975, a work from the Commentary Art series[31] (in collaboration with Zofia Kulik) entitled *A Portrait Study of Fourth-Rate Critic Skrodzki*. Both were satires on critics who had repeatedly condemned the neo-avant-garde and its representatives in press reviews. *The Vernissage of Meat and Osęka* was a big chunk of meat suspended in the middle of the exhibition space, to which was attached a photograph of the well-known critic Andrzej Osęka and a fragment of one of his reviews from the *Kultura Weekly*, which was derogatory of new art.

KwieKulik also complained to the Minister of Culture about the censoring of their works:

> We are presenting some of our materials at the Young Biennale in Paris, in the "documentation of artistic activities" section. The qualifying committees—there were about five of them—gave us extra work to do, because each wished to make changes in the selection and sequence of the slides. All were composed of officials and activists (?!) who, to make matters worse, were dealing for the first time in their lives with this kind of art! As a result, about three-fourths of the slide show presented by O. Truszczyński, the show's curator, and deemed by the authors to be final, were rejected. Among the rejected ones were all those that, projected simultaneously with the

> photographs of Edward Gierek visiting various places in Poland, formed part of the audiovisual show Proagit 2 [some of these slides were from the Activities with Dobromierz series—L. R.] ... the image of a naked infant juxtaposed with oranges and red cloth was interpreted as a "satire on China" and rejected. ... The visual exercises conducted on Michelangelo's *Moses* were condemned as "harming the religious feelings of Jews."[32]

KwieKulik spoke about their struggle with the state culture administrators, the PSP, and the censorship of their works during public presentations and lectures. The following is their own description of their meetings in Elbląg in 1974:

> We show them the slides, discuss them—reading out, for instance, our "complaint-petition" to the authorities about our work, our situation, about what we think about the course of qualifying the works for the Paris Biennale. We show those young people the works rejected by the committees. This is to fulfil our postulate of informing the audience not only about the form and content of our works and "activities," but also about the political circumstances of our artistic work.[33]

By attaching the above account to their scholarship application for the Ministry of Culture, right after receiving the same Ministry's reply to their letter about the censorship of their works, KwieKulik were presenting a disarming and arrogant attitude. They were, on the one hand, criticizing the authorities for their censorship, while, on the other, letting them know that they, KwieKulik, were notifying the public about how the government censored their works (and what the mechanisms of that censorship were).

KwieKulik's most radical institutional critique project was directed against the *Pracownie Sztuk Plastycznych*. As Academy of Fine Arts graduates, KwieKulik had no choice but to work for the monopolist. In 1975, concurrently with the attempts to organize a public protest against the PSP's practices, KwieKulik made the work *Plaster Bird for Bronze in the Visual Arts Barracks/Dick-Man* (*Ptak z gipsu do brązu w Barakach Sztuk Plastycznych/Człowiek-Kutas*). It consisted of two photographs accompanied by text and formed part of the Commentary Art series. The first photograph shows the interior of one of the PSP workshops where KwieKulik, while producing a potboiler (a commemorative tablet), are simultaneously performing documented material-spatial activities[34] that represent the essence of their practice. In the background, we can see a plaster eagle (the national emblem of communist Poland, made by their younger colleague Andrzej Pastwa), which is to be cast in bronze. The title—where, the word “workshops” has been replaced with “barracks” in the hated institution’s name, a word evoking oppressive associations—signals tension between the artists’ intentions and avant-garde ambitions on one side and on the other, the institution devaluing those ambitions, employing traditional methods to pursue propagandistic goals.

The other photo comes from the Bank of Aesthetical Time-Effects, the KwieKulik **archive** [from 1974, functioning as the Workshop of Activities, Documentation and Promulgation, or PDDiU—editor’s note].[35] Originally, it formed part of the documentation of the consecutive transformations of a clay nude that Przemysław Kwiek had made from a model in Jerzy Jarnuszkiewicz’s sculpture studio at the Warsaw Academy of Fine Arts in the academic year 1967/1968.[36] The juxtaposition of these two photographs, and the comments accompanying them, reflected the artists’ despair, disillusionment, and frustration. The *Dick-Man* became a metaphor of the existential humiliation and artistic degradation generated by the political system of communist Poland—a system demanding conformism, servility, and abandonment of one’s own ambitions and plans. The work was, as they described it, a “vengeance on reality,” an act of abreaction. It was a form of criticizing communist Poland’s art and culture policy, referring also to the dismal economic situation of neo-avant-garde artists sentenced to work for the PSP. In the years 1970–74, KwieKulik made efforts to find a place in the public sphere for the new artistic forms they had developed. That’s why they felt guilty making conventional artistic objects, an activity they perceived as cementing the paradigm of traditional art that they were fighting against. The work was also an expression of KwieKulik’s pessimism regarding the possibility of reforming the system, something that only a couple of years earlier, during the Soviet Pop Art period, they naively believed was possible. The clash between the official, propagandistic message endorsed by the PSP (the national emblem) and the clay figure—a symbol of the humiliation of artists trying to practice their own art in its shadow—is the core of this work. KwieKulik wrote:

> Highlighting the word “bird” in the commentary to the eagle photo was deliberate and purposeful. This purpose is explained, we believe, by the second part of the commentary: “the Visual Arts Barracks.” Had we highlighted some other object and written, for instance, “a wooden pedestal in the Visual Arts Barracks,” the work wouldn’t have made sense because it’d have failed to reveal the attitude of the director of the company, mockingly called “the barracks” here, a two-faced attitude: “outwardly” that of the perfect, devoted Citizen,

> Patriot, and Pole, and "inwardly" towards the artist-employees, that of, we're not afraid of the word, a "gangster."[37]

In September 1975 (at the time when the SB was investigating Kwiek), the work was presented (unbeknownst to Janusz Bogucki, the curator, and the Polish censors) in the catalogue of the exhibition of Polish art, *7 Young Poles*, at Malmö Konsthall. This provoked a violent reaction from the state authorities, which forbade KwieKulik from representing Polish art abroad and invoked a refusal to release their passports for the next couple of years. The Ministry of Culture may have been guided in this not only by concerns over communist Poland's image abroad, but also by its knowledge of the SB inquiry. The contents of the SB file clearly show that, during the course of Operation Letraset, the Ministry of Culture, the police, and the SB constantly exchanged information on the surveillance subjects with each other. The controversial anti-PSP work featured in the Malmö Konsthall catalogue was used by the authorities as a pretext for whipping the unruly artists into line. (It was at the same time that Konieczny lost the slander lawsuit brought against him by the PSP.) The official explanation was that the work defiled the national emblem by placing it next to vulgarities.[38] It was deliberate on KwieKulik's part to use such radical means of expression, a characteristic of contemporary critical art. By doing so, they wanted to provoke a debate on the PSP and its functioning:

> We know we've come close to the limit, because it takes little to metaphorically defile the eagle, but it turns out [that] only such a proximity causes a shock and attracts the authorities' attention, whereas even ten years of warnings that things are going in a bad direction wouldn't achieve this. What's important now, we believe, is to avoid squandering the opportunity, avoid turning attention away from the reasons such works are created and focusing instead on condemning the effects, avoid shushing, and instead to finally take up the burning issues and make the necessary decisions. The work is the final dramatic (and artistic) signal of our criticism and protest meant to bring attention to what the artists working for the PSP (because it's not only us) feel.[39]

KwieKulik's tactic had two aspects to it: to create the controversial work, while also sending complaints to the Ministry of Culture (which they perceived as an artistic activity)[40] and highlighting the issue in public statements. Upon returning from Sweden in 1976, in a protest action entitled *How Are You Ms Kulik? How Are You Mr Kwiek? You Are Polish Artists, Aren't You?* that takes place at Galeria Mospan, run by Tomasz Sikorski,

KwieKulik read out their letters to the Ministry of Culture concerning the "eagle case" as well as the official replies. They then unveil an exhibition of hardcore Swedish pornography, illegal in Poland at the time.

Because their passports had been withheld, Kwiek and Kulik were unable to take part in a number of important international events. In 1978, they were invited to participate in the Behavior Workshop in Arnhem, Netherlands. Being unable to appear physically, they suggested another form of participation: by mail. Before their "appearance," one of the organizers read out loud a letter in which KwieKulik explained why they couldn't take part in the event personally. Then, according to instructions mailed by KwieKulik, the Workshop's participants were to, within the time needed to bring a kettleful of water to boil, write heartening postcards to KwieKulik. The artists received a good dozen or so postcards (from, among others, Joseph Beuys). At the same time, frustrated by their inability to participate in foreign exhibitions and events to which they were invited, KwieKulik made a protest performance entitled *A Monument Without a Passport* in the Visual Arts Salons (Biennale of Young Art, Galeria BWA, Sopot 1978). The living monument—with Kulik standing (her legs immobilized in a lump of hardened plaster) and Kwiek sitting—was an ironic reference to the monuments produced to the PSP's commission, which the piece's title referred to. Kulik held a folder in her outstretched hand, marked "Ideas for Arnhem." The same year, KwieKulik staged a performance with trash bins on their heads, which can be interpreted as yet another metaphor of their degradation by the system (*Body, Performance*, Galeria Labirynt, 1978). They also created another critical piece aimed at the PSP, *Videodecoration*. Having no other choice, they were forced to keep taking commissions from the "gangster" institution. In this case, the subject matter was a conventional (as required by the employer) stage setting for the congress of the Polish Journalists Association (SDP). The artists filmed the setting's original design and a TV report from the official event, which was attended by the party leader, Edward Gierek, and the head of the PZPR Central Committee's Culture Department, Jerzy Lukaszewicz, the man through whose decision their passports were withheld. The TV report begins with the camera zooming in on their potboiler—the stage setting. The piece also settles the artists' accounts with their involvement in the Soviet Pop Art movement. One can see a change in their attitude towards power and politics, following the initial hopes stirred up by Edward Gierek's rise to power (*The Path of Edward Gierek*) for socialist state reforms, as well as for the neo-avantgarde playing a role in them; that is, the years of New Red Art (1970–1973), to a period of hopelessness and depression, when the artists have been reduced to the role of "decorators" of the communist state's propaganda ceremonials. Like the Bolsheviks in the 1920s, following initial signs of being interested in committed neo-avant-garde art, the Gierek government soon stopped pretending that it perceived artists as partners, rather than just as the artisans it needed to aestheticize the system.

Finally, it is worth noting the typically Polish (and original, even amongst the other Eastern Bloc countries) paradox in the relation between art and politics during the 1970s. Namely, that in the field of art, the only artists to conduct an open and bold critique of communist Poland's institutions, procedures, or ideologies were actually PZPR members (or candidates for members), who were also rooted in the subversive reformist position. As shown by the SB's inquiry into Konieczny and Kwiek, or the withholding of KwieKulik's passports, their critique was inconvenient for the regime (the authorities had earlier rejected Soviet Pop Art). The paradox was that in the reality of communist Poland, a more comfortable and privileged position was granted to the representatives of institutions as well as to artistic strategies propagating autonomy and the neutrality of art work aimed towards the political reality (e.g. Galeria Foksal PSP) than to reformist, political, left-leaning avant-garde artists. The authorities were mostly afraid of any open political critique, to which KwieKulik's Soviet Pop Art position and later activities clearly aspired. And those artists, in turn, found themselves at some point in the situation of double exclusion: by the regime from the field of politically involved socialist art, and by the contemporary art institutions, which preferred the safe utopia of the work's modernist disconnection from reality (guaranteeing the regime's noninterference with the art field).

Endnotes

1 First published in: Łukasz Ronduda, "*Neoawangarda w teczkach SB*/Neo-avant-garde Movement in the Security Service Files," *Piktogram* 9/10 (2007–2008): 53–69. The text is based on research at the Institute for National Memory (*Instytut Pamięci Narodowej*, IPN) where the files of the Security Service (*Służba Bezpieczeństwa*, SB) and Ministry of the Interior (Ministerstwo Spraw Wewnętrznych, MSW) 1945–1990 are stored. An analysis of the SB's operation against two members of the 1970s Polish neo-avant-garde and the effects that followed enables us to look at the relationships between art and politics in a different manner, as well as at the issue of institutional critique at the time. Working with the IPN archive is a rather tricky task these days. In recent years, the Polish public sphere has been dominated by ongoing, politically motivated manipulations of the archive, rather than by the effects of diligent scientific research that would show things in a broader context and take the complex nature of individual cases into account. The yearlong inquiry showed that the SB conducted the following operations against Polish artists. This included "Letraset" (1975), which affected Marek Konieczny and Przemysław Kwiek, who, in 1975, organized a protest against the *Pracownie Sztuk Plastycznych* (Visual Arts Workshops or PSP), the state institution in charge of public commissions in visual and applied arts The SB launched an inquiry into Kwiek, but it concerned his activities conducted together with Zofia Kulik as part of the KwieKulik duo. Additionally, there was "Strangers" (1972), carried out against the participants of a project by Jarosław Kozłowski and Andrzej Kostołowski titled NET, particularly targeting Jerzy Ludwiński, Zdzisław Jurkiewicz, Marianna Michałowska, Jerzy Rosołowicz, and Stanisław Dróżdż. Another operation was named "Visual Artist" (1975) against Janusz Haka (the most absurd of all the cases found as part of this query in the IPN flies). The operation "Gook" against Koji Kamoji (the code name clearly showing the SB officers' stupidity and racism) represents a separate issue because it did not concern Kamoji as an artist, but only his ethnic origin. The SB suspected Kamoji of contacting Japanese intelligence.

It needs to be remembered that, in many cases, the SB operational files have been lost or destroyed (sometimes deliberately), and many may not be credible. As objects of the SB's operational activities, all the abovementioned artists are entitled today to apply for the official status of "victims of the communist regime."

2 Operational Inquiry Case, archival no. II–3637 SUSW, State Protection Office (*Urząd Ochrony Państwa*, UOP) archive.

3 "Subject: culture and art. Object: Association of Polish Fine Artists (ZPAP). Ministry and department: Ministry of Culture and Art (*Ministerstwo Kultury i Sztuki*). Community: artistic. Date the threat (fact) occurred: July 28, 1975. Source: P.T. Source assessment: credible. Information assessment: credible."

4 The artists' names are followed by their personal details.

5 Signed: Head, 3rd Department, Warsaw Police Headquarters in Operational Inquiry Case (III *Komenda Stołeczna Milicji Obywatelskiej*, KSMO), archival no. II–3637 SUSW.

6 Signed: Head, 3rd Department, Warsaw Police Headquarters in Operational Inquiry Case (III *Komenda Stołeczna Milicji Obywatelskiej*, KSMO), archival no. II–3637 SUSW.

7 Besides highly limited purchases by museums, the only other official channels were the OESA galleries [a chain of state-owned commercial galleries selling traditional art and antiques—editor's note]. There was also the possibility of person-to-person sale. Even so, communist Poland's art market was rather minute.

8 See: *Piktogram*, No. 8 (2007).

9 The situation was somewhat better in PSP's architecture section, where far more avant-garde propositions were accepted than in the visual arts section.

10 To pursue the New Art's interests more effectively, KwieKulik had postulated from the early 1970s—to no avail—that what they termed the "Other Arts Section" (*Sekcja Sztuk Innych*) be set up within ZPAP.

11 The appraisals and valuations were conducted by a special committee composed of renowned traditional-media artists.

12 The term "New Red Art," forming part of the Soc-Art current, was coined by KwieKulik to describe their own activity and that of Anastazy Wiśniewski. See Ronduda, "Soc-Art: An Attempt to Revitalise the Strategy of Avantgarde in Socialist Poland." Excerpts published as: Ronduda, "New Red Art."

13 Henryk Urbanowicz was the Deputy Governor of the Kielce Province during the 1946 Kielce pogrom of Jews [in which over forty Jewish Poles were lynched—editor's note]. As a result of the political turbulence that followed, he was transferred to Warsaw and appointed head of the newly founded PSP. See: *Wokól pogromu kieleckiego* (*On the Kielce Pogrom*), ed. Kamiński and Żaryn. See also: Gross, *Strach* (*Fear*), 149–150.

14 This refers to the mass strikes in December 1970 and their suppression, resulting in over forty deaths—editor's note.

15 They were shot under the Nazi occupation—editor's note.

16 Zofia Kulik and Przemyslaw Kwiek, "Letter to Tadeusz Kaczmarek, Deputy Minister of Culture," Warsaw, February 3, 1976, unpublished, PDDiU archive.

17 See: *Piktogram* No. 5/6.

18 Zofia Kulik and Przemysław Kwiek, "Letter-complaint to the Ministry of Culture and Art," Warsaw, February 2, 1975, PDDiU archive.

19 The PSP had a substantial budget at that time. A major commission, e.g. for a monument, could buy a car. In the early 1970s, the average monthly pay in Poland was approximately 1,500 złotys, and some PSP commissions had budgets of about 100,000 złotys for design and execution.

20 In Konieczny's case, the phone tap resulted in orders of further operational activities: "Who is the woman, phone ...," "Who is Janek, phone ...," etc. Lieutenant Szymański, Classified, November 5, 1975, 12.

21 The file includes, for instance, photocopies of KwieKulik's artistic mailings, with the authors' names underlined.

22 The file contains a two-page list of persons that Konieczny had been in touch with, including their personal details. (Marek Konieczny's Personal Contacts, Operation "Letraset," 17).

23 Lieutenant Szymański, Classified, November 5, 1975, 12.

24 List of secret agents and operational contacts used in the case, p. 6.

25 "Op con" and k.o. means operative contact (*kontakt operacyjny*) —editor's note.

26 List of secret agents and operational contacts used in the case, p. 52.

27 It is worth noting that after discovering minute irregularities in the financial report of the Jarocin Music Festival (whose political tone in the 1980s was anti-establishment), the SB immediately notified the Supreme Chamber of Inspection (*Najwyższa lzba Kontroli*, NIK), which judged the organizers in a very harsh manner. See Lesiakowski, Perzyna, and Toborek, *Jarocin w obiektywie bezpieki* ("Jarocin as seen by the Secret Police").

28 A disturbing fact in the context of the lawsuit (mentioned by Konieczny and his wife, as well as Kwiek and Kulik, who were present during the trial) was that in order to discredit Konieczny,

the prosecutor (representing the PSP) quoted from the (in)famous article "The Pseudo-Avant-garde" by Wiesław Borowski, manager of Galeria Foksal PSP. In the article, published in the spring of 1975 [in the *Kultura Weekly*—editor's note], Borowski mentions Marek Konieczny and Przemysław Kwiek, alongside some other artists, as representatives of the "pseudo-avant-garde"—a current based on pseudo-artistic values. Still, Borowski probably did not know that his article would be used in this way.

29 Przemysław Kwiek, "*Awangarda bzy maluje*" ("The Avant-garde Painting Lilacs"), in *Wyszczególnienie działalności* (*Evidence of Activities*) (Warsaw: Galeria DAP, 1998), 3.

30 Zofia Kulik and Przemysław Kwiek, "Letter to Tadeusz Kaczmarek," Deputy Minister of Culture.

31 More on commentary art in: Ronduda, "*Działania na jednominutówkaeh innych KwieKulik* (KwieKulik's Activities on Others' One-minute Films)."

32 (Missing note)

33 KwieKulik, "Attachment to Scholarship Application," Part 2, 1974, unpublished, PDDiU archive.

34 The artists write "Activities" (*Działania*) with a capital as a proper noun.

35 From 1974, as a workshop for documentation and dissemination activities (*Pracownia Działań Dokumentacji i Upowszechniania*—editor's note). See Ronduda, "The KwieKulik Bank of Aesthetical Time-Effects."

36 See Ronduda, "*Doświadezenia medialne KwieKulik*" ("KwieKulik's Medial Experiences"). See Ronduda, "Przemysław Kwiek—Playing with Oneself."

37 "And we don't hesitate to speak like this because we know for sure that if other artists were given a voice, and if they weren't afraid to lose their jobs for being critical, they'd confirm our description of Director Urbanowicz." Kulik and Kwiek, "Letter to Tadeusz Kaczmarek."

38 Kulik and Kwiek, "Letter to Tadeusz Kaczmarek."

39 KwieKulik also wrote that the interpretation of their work could be manipulated by Urbanowicz. They wrote that he would "try to direct the interested parties'" attention to the following aspect: "look what the results are of being liberal towards artists, they go and defile the national emblem, you mustn't defile the national emblem without a purpose ... so these people are enemies of the PRL." Kulik and Kwiek, "Letter to Tadeusz Kaczmarek."

40 The proreform critique of the political and artistic establishment conducted by the Soc artists can, on a certain level, be likened to the activity of Jacek Kuroń and Karol Modzelewski who, as PZPR members, wrote an "open letter to the Party." See Bikont and Szczęsna, "*Jacek Kuroń—rewolucjonista z duszą negocjatora*" ("Jacek Kuron-A Revolutionary with the Soul of a Negotiator"). See also: Ronduda, "Soc-Art,"; Ronduda, "New Red Art."

From My Window 1978–1999

Józef Robakowski

From My Window 1978–1999 (*Z mojego okna*) documents daily life in a central square in Łodź, which Józef Robakowski observed from the window of his high-rise building for twenty years. In 1978, during a time when the Solidarność movement was still being severely repressed, Robakowski made the first 16mm film recordings of the so-called Manhattan of Łodź. He ended his video diary in 1999, shortly before a hotel for tourists was authorized by the city and built in front of his window, blocking his view. In characteristically laconic statements, Robakowski comments on events and changes from the socialist era into the postsocialist era. He grumbles about his neighbors' illegal meat sales on the seventh floor and about the career of the neighbor on the twelfth. New cars and new dogs are commented on, and now and then the camera lingers on a young woman, who turns out to be the wife of another neighbor. The view from the window, a common motif in art history since Romanticism, oscillates between subjective observation, illegal activity (recording tanks during martial law), and state surveillance. The observer makes connections between the observed persons across time and builds individual behavior profiles in the urban space. **(A)**

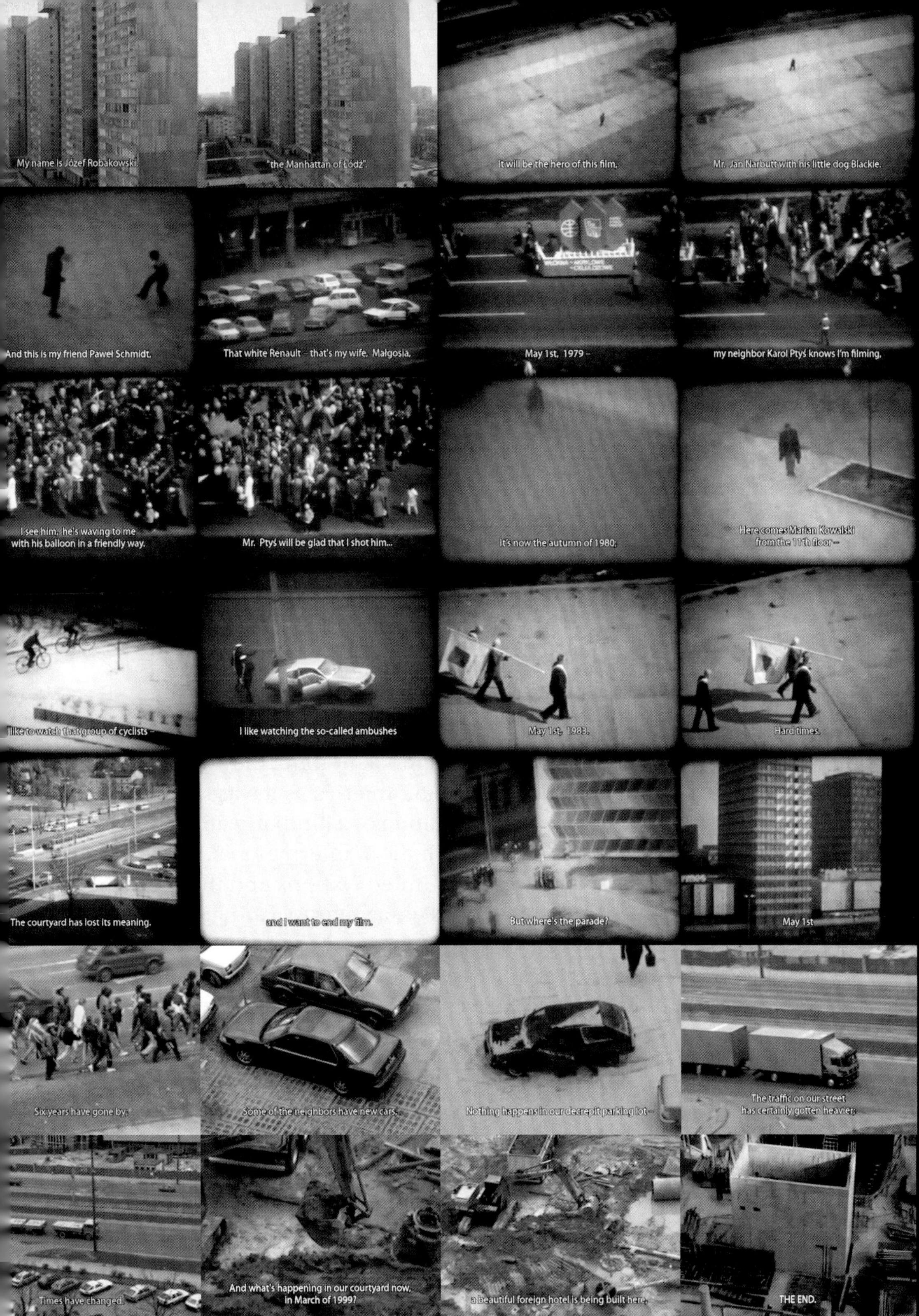

1978

Video stills, Black-and-white video, PAL, 19:09 min.

Andree Korpys, b. 1966 in Bremen, Germany.
Markus Löffler, b. 1963 in Bremen, Germany, live and work in Bremen, Germany.

America Films

Korpys/Löffler

On the tour of America that Korpys/Löffler took in 1996, they were interested above all in comparing their image of America as it was shaped by Hollywood movies with the actual locations—a kind of reality check. At the center of the short film trilogy are hubs of international, political, economic, and military power: the United Nations and the World Trade Center in New York as well as the Pentagon in Washington. The images remind one of those taken by amateur photographers, or the documentary recordings of investigative journalists or agents. Total intakes alternate with side scenes like emergency exits, tunnel entrances, empty corridors, and safes. Requisites, manhole covers, and ventilation shafts alike are filmed—potential weak points in security architecture. It is above all the daily coming and going of the staff that comes into view of the camera, the security guards, bodyguards, and chauffeurs in their cars. The camera repeatedly zooms in on individual people who are uninvolved passers by that give the impression of being potential state agents in a secret operation. The films thus remind one of surveillance scenes in which artists played with the gaze of the state security. (A)

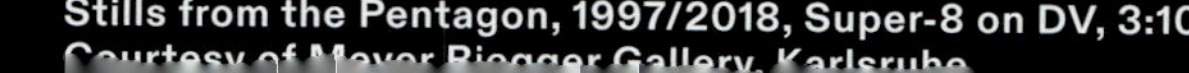

Stills from the Pentagon, 1997/2018, Super-8 on DV, 3:10 min.
Courtesy of Meyer Riegger Gallery, Karlsruhe

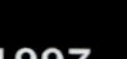

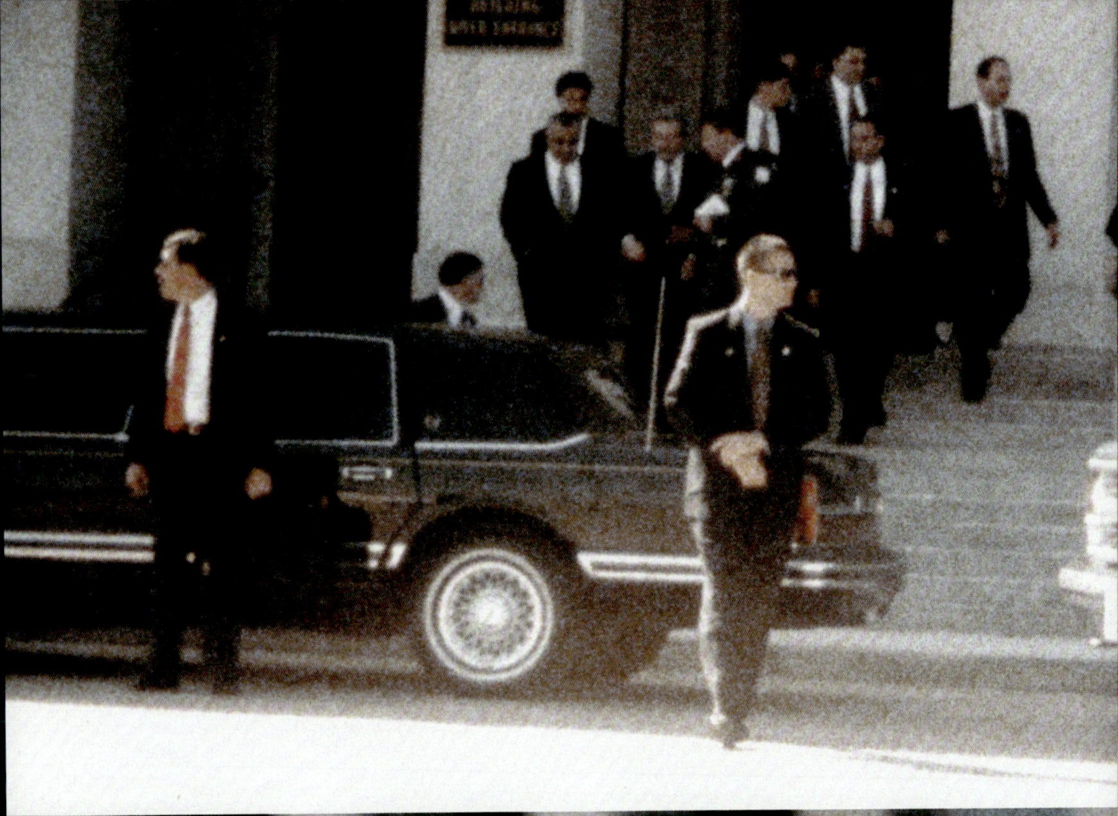

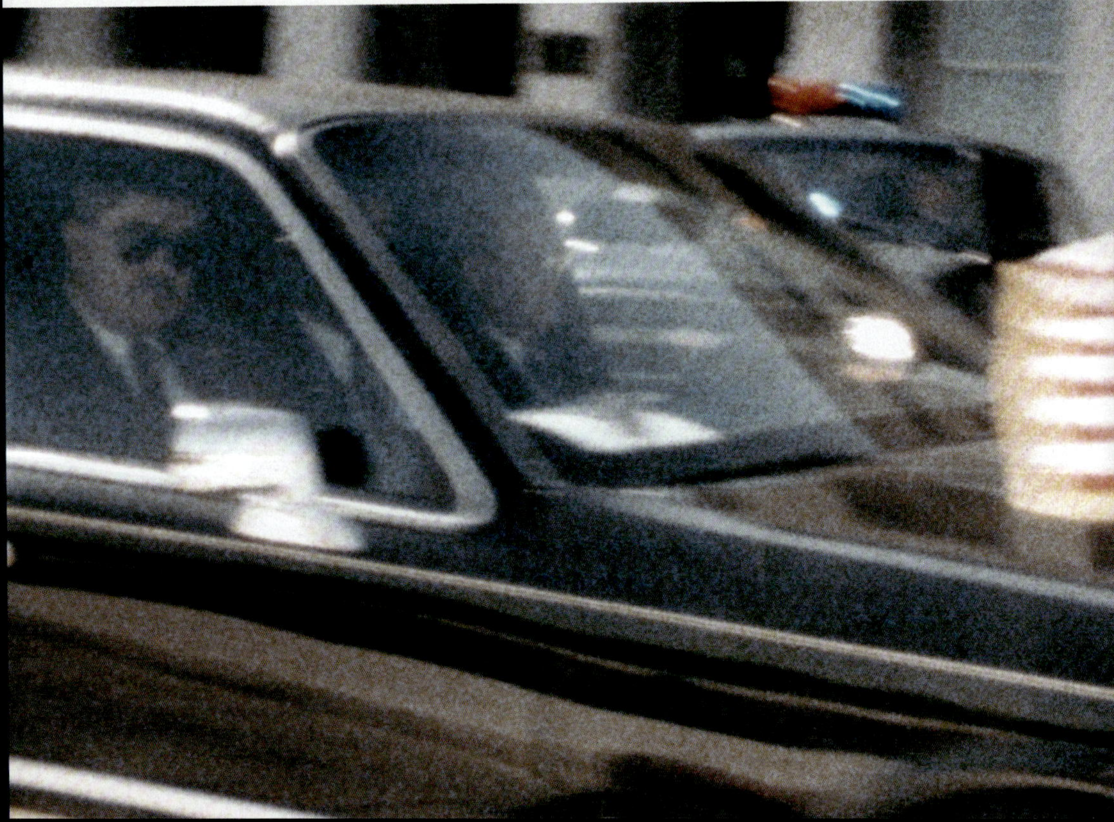

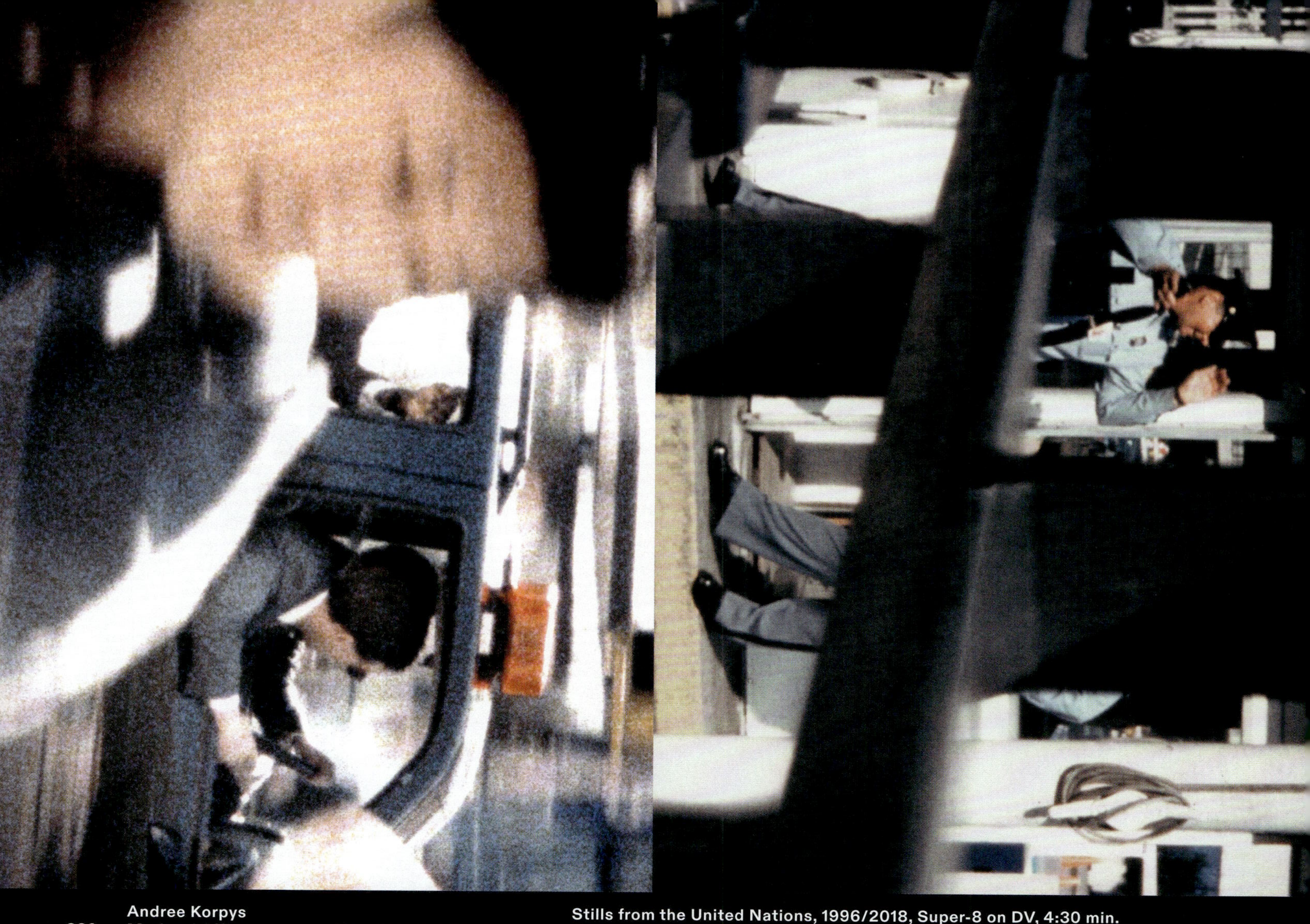

Stills from the United Nations, 1996/2018, Super-8 on DV, 4:30 min.
Courtesy of Meyer Riegger Gallery, Karlsruhe

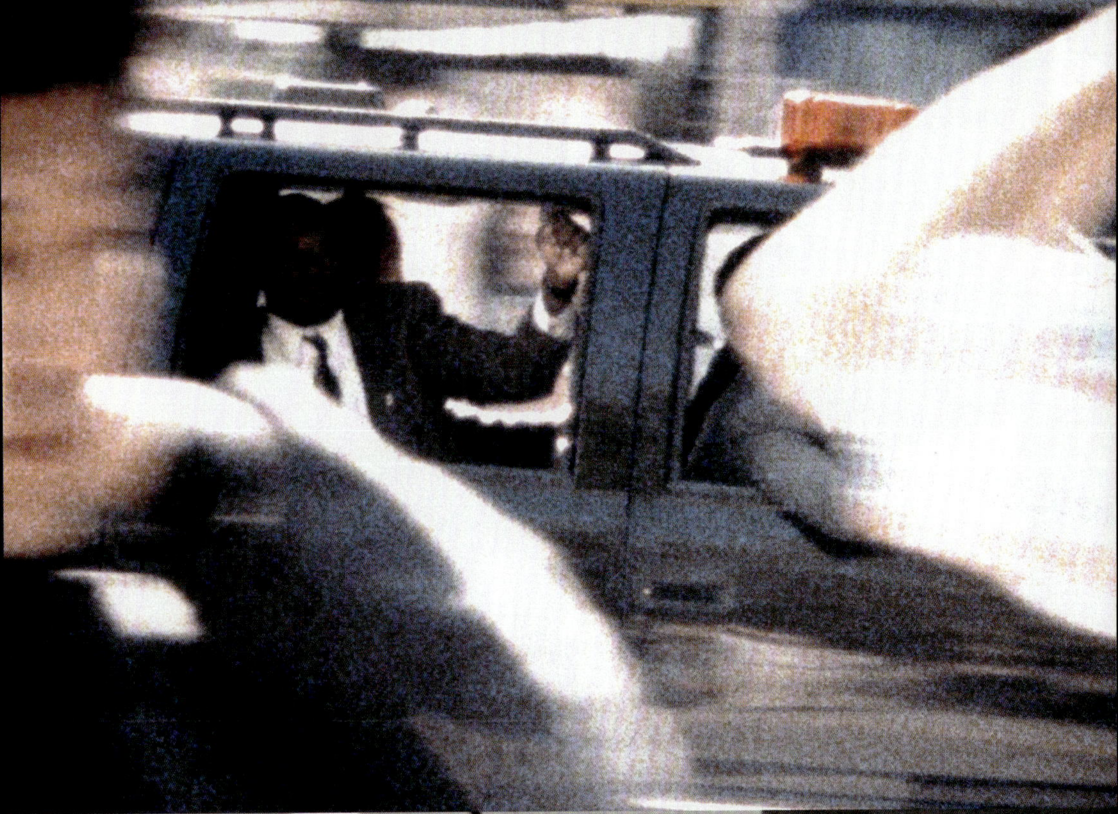

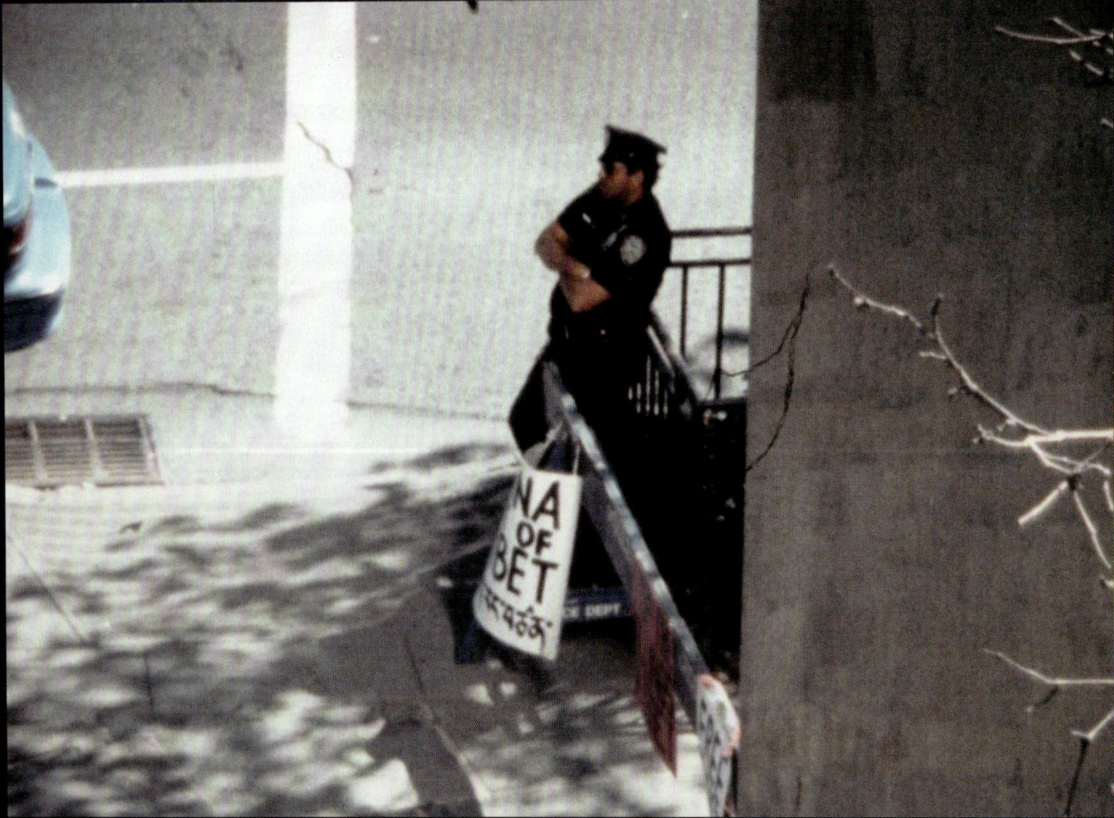

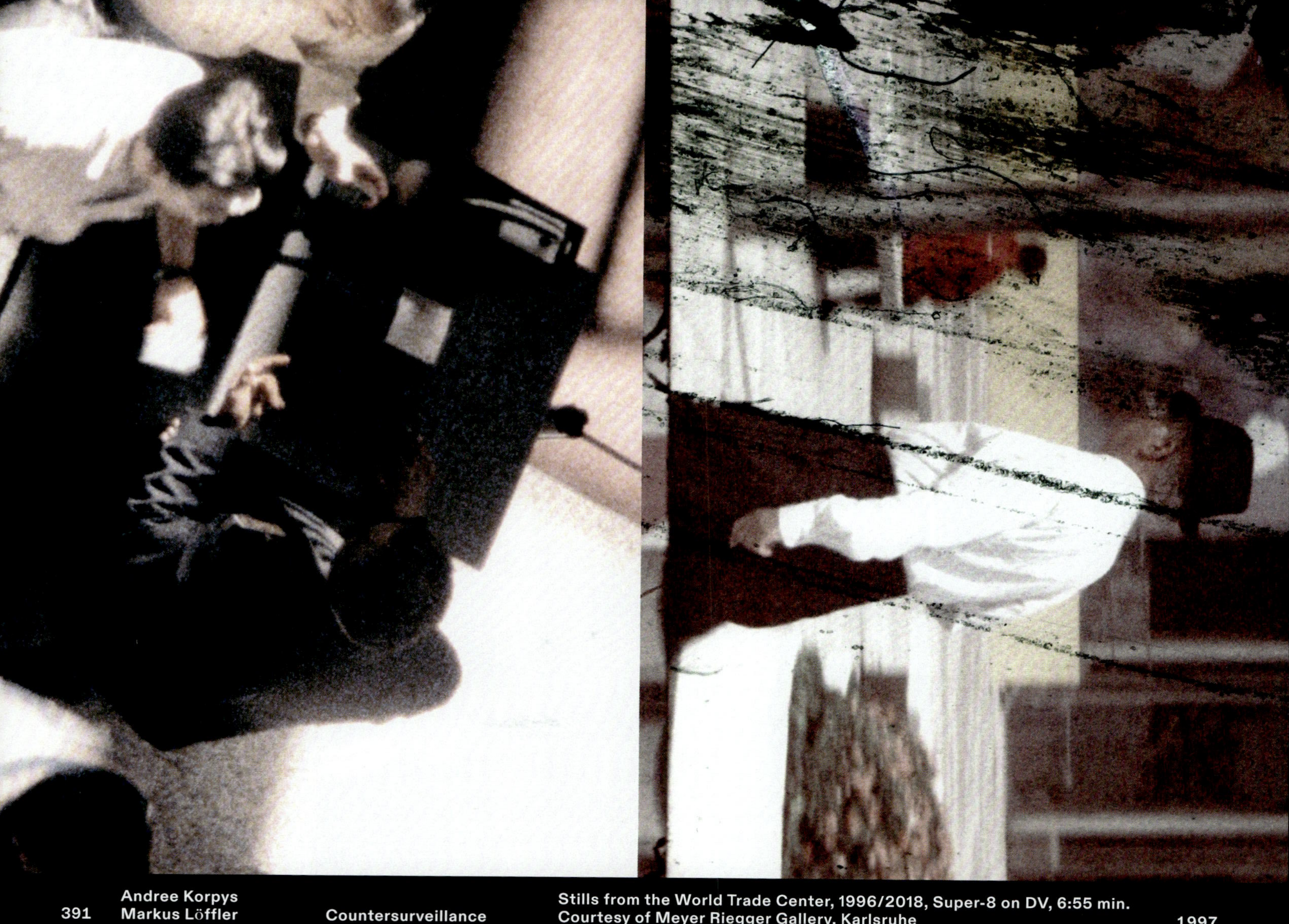

 Andree Korpys
Markus Löffler

Stills from the World Trade Center, 1996/2018, Super-8 on DV, 6:55 min.
Courtesy of Meyer Riegger Gallery, Karlsruhe

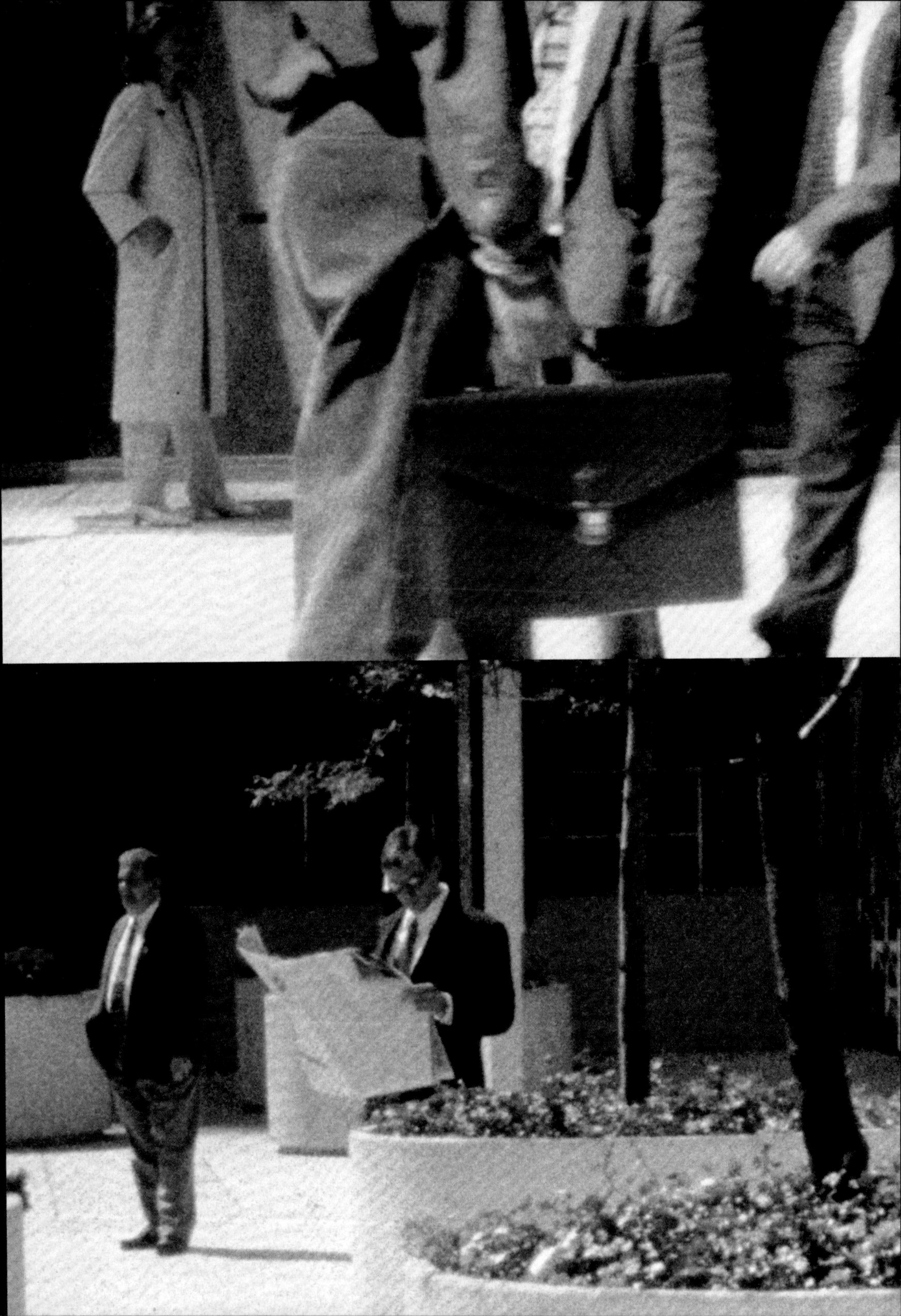

Measures and “Decompositions”

Survey of Bolshevik Activities of the Dadaist Group in Zurich

Political Police (Switzerland)

As this case demonstrates, it is not only in authoritarian regimes that artists were subject to surveillance, nor did it only begin with the Cold War. Surveillance of Dadaists by the Political Police of Switzerland was an immediate reaction to the October Revolution of 1917. One can sense the fear that the Political Police had concerning other revolutionary forces potentially residing in Switzerland and influencing Swiss politics. Lenin did, after all, go directly from Switzerland to Petrograd to spread the revolution. Accordingly, the Political Police classified the Dadaists Emmy Hennings, Hugo Ball, and Tristan Tzara (known in the files as Zara and whom they thought was a Russian), as a "Bolshevistic" threat or as Bolsheviks who wanted to spread Bolshevik propaganda. They even call the Dadaists a "revolutionary enterprise." Hennings and Ball were specifically suspected of "propagating revolutionary ideas." The goal of the surveillance was to submit a deportation request based not just on "revolutionary ideas," but on their "dissolute" lifestyle (Ball and Hennings lived together as an unmarried couple) and insufficient income sources, or rather, income sources that they "were not able to convincingly demonstrate." The file consists of a total of thirty pages from the years 1918 and 1919. **(S)**

Die Dadaisten in Zürich

E 21, 10535 - 10564 (=352)

1. Ball Hugo, alias Höxter John, born 1886, from Pirmasens (Bavaria),

writer, currently resident at Marzlilistrasse 30, Bern

Director of the "Free Press" (*Freien Verlags*) in Bern and employee of the "Free Newspaper" (*Freien Zeitung*). Suspected of being an associate of the radical leftist publication "Revolutionary" (*Revolutionär*) which is published in Mannheim, where his concubine Hennings (see above) also writes. Whether Ball also actively takes part in Swiss social movements has not yet been able to be determined.

Translated from German by Brian Alkire

1. <u>Ball Hugo</u>, alias Höxter John, geb.1886, von Pirmasens (Bayern), Schriftsteller, zur Zeit wohnhaft Marzilistrasse 30, Bern.

Direktor des Freien Verlags in Bern und Mitarbeiter der Freien Zeitung. Verdächtigt als Mitarbeiter des in Mannheim erscheinenden ganz links stehenden " Revolutionär ",in den auch seine Konkubine Hennings (siehe oben) schreibt.Dass Ball auch an den schweiz.sozialen Bewegungen aktiven Anteil nehme,konnte bis jetzt nicht festgestellt werden.

Cover and seven of nineteen file pages, 1918–19
Source: Swiss Federal Archive, Bern (21/10558)

Zurich
City Police

ZURICH, JULY 2, 1919

To: Commissioner's Office

Zurich

Several days ago, I was given the attached issue of "The Revolutionary" by proprietor Furrer at the Café Terrasse in Zurich, District 1, with a comment that the newspaper was offered to be put on display, but that he would not display it but instead handed it over to me.

I examined this newspaper and noted two familiar names among the listed authors, Hugo Ball and Editha von Münchhausen, a cohabitating couple who, in 1915, raised unwelcome attention in the city of Zurich. Hugo Ball was sentenced to one week in jail by the district court of Zurich due to the repeated, intentional use of identification papers bearing another name than his own. See Zurich Police Announcements 1915, no.6845.

Ball, Hugo, writer, from Pirmasens, Bavaria, b. February 23, 1886, identified himself to me as Höxter, John, painter, from Hanover, b. January 21, 1884, and had rented a typewriter under this false name. He had pasted his photograph in the passport of Höxter.
He was cohabitating at the time with HENNINGS, Emmy, née Cordsen, from Flenzburg, Hollstein, writer and nightclub singer, b. January 17, 1885 at Schoffelgasse 5.

According to the observations of proprietor Schneider, they lived on income from Hennings's immoral sexual acts, which provided assistance to Ball. Hennings had no identification papers at all and was at the time already writing for a magazine titled

"R e v o l t e r"

In an issue which was found on her person, she memorialized the execution of an anarchist. If I am not mistaken, she went at the time by the name of "Editha von Münchhausen."

Stadtpolizei
ZÜRICH

ZÜRICH, den 2. Juli 1919

mittags Uhr.

An das Criminalcommissariat

Zürich.

In Sachen
Stadtpolizei Zürich

gegen
Hugo Ball &
Hennigs, Emma, geb.
Cordsen,
vermutlich in Bern.

betreffend
gefährliche Ausländer.

Beilagen:
Der Revoltionär.

Vor einigen Tagen wurde mir von Wirt Furrer, zum Cafe „Terrasse" Zürich 1, die beiliegende Nummer "Der Revoltionär" übergeben mit dem Bemerken, die Zeitung sei hier zum Auflegen abgegeben worden, er lasse sie aber nicht auflegen und überlasse sie mir.

Jch sah mir diese an und bemerkte unter den Namen der Schriftsteller 2 mir bekannte, Hugo Ball, und Editha von Münchhausen, ein Concubinatspaar, das sich im Jahre 1915 in Zürich unliebsam bemerkbar gemacht hatte.

Hugo Ball ist vom Bezirksgericht Zürich, wegen wiederholtem wissentlichen Gebrauches eines auf einen andern Namen lautenden Ausweispapieres zu einer Woche Gefängnis verurteilt worden. Siehe Zürcher Polizei-Anzeiger 1915, Art. 6845.

Ball, Hugo, Schriftsteller, von Pirmasens, Bayern, geb. 23. Febr. 1886, hatte sich mir gegenüber als Höxter, John, Kunstmaler, von Hanover, geb. 21. 1. 1884, legitimiert und hatte unter dem falschen Namen eine Schreibmaschine gemietet. Er hatte seine Photographie in den Pass Höxter geklebt.

Er lebte damals mit Frau Hennings, Emmy, geb. Cordsen, von Flenzburg, Hollstein, Schriftstellerin und Tingel-Tangelsängerin, geb. 17. Januar 1885, an der Schoffelgasse 5 in Concubinat.

Nach den Beobachtungen des Hausmeisters, Wirt Schneider, lebten sie aus den Einkünften der Unzucht der Hennings, welche Ball begünstigte. Die Hennings hatte keinerlei Ausweispapiere und schrieb damals schon für eine Zeitschrift betitelt,

"Revoluzer"

in einer Nummer, welche bei ihr gefunden wurde, verherrlichte sie die Hinrichtung eines Anarchisten. Wenn ich nicht irre, zeichnete sie damals " Editha von Münchhausen".

No. 1. III. 19. 5000.

Cover and seven of nineteen file pages, 1918–19
Source: Swiss Federal Archive, Bern (21/10558)

The cohabitating couple lived in serious poverty because neither of them worked. They received support from Dr.Bruppacher in Zurich, a well-known anarchist. They also revered him. From a sense of pity, first Hennings and then later Ball were offered employment with the concert organizer "Marcelli."

Ball and Hennings often quarrel at night, during which fights Ball would strike Hennings.

During one such quarrel after midnight on or about September 20, 1915, Hennings attempted suicide by opening the veins on her arms with a pair of scissors. She quickly sought medical assistance, however, and was not permanently harmed.

The cause of these events could not be ascertained; both remained united and refused to betray each other. Other building residents concluded from this chaotic occurrence that the two were linked together by a crime.

Ball sought to defend himself by claiming that Hennings was a morphine addict.

Ball used the anarchist name Ha Hu Baley.

Hennings had told the concert organizer "Marcelli" that she and her husband had been imprisoned in Munich for espionage. Her husband had been shot while she was released on a bond provided by a wealthy gentleman. She then doctored her papers with respect to her age, which is how she crossed the border.

Marcelli lamented that Hennings did not come to her engagement and instead engaged in prostitution. She told him herself that Ball had forced her to do this, that he hit her when she delivered too little money. She claimed to be completely under the spell of Ball.

No further investigation into Hennings's forgery and Ball's pimping was carried out, presumably because they had again left Zurich. There are copies of the original reports in the Zurich Commissioner's Office.

Ball and Hennings might be residing in Bern and should be deported immediately

Translated from German by Brian Alkire

Das Concubinatspaar lebte, weil niemand arbeitete, in grosser Armut. Von Dr. Bruppacher, in Zürich, bekannter Anarchist, erhielten sie unterstützung. Sie gaben ihn auch als Reverenz an. Aus Erbarmen wurden zuerst die Hennings und nachher auch Ball bei Conzertunternehmer "Marcelli" angestellt.

Zwischen Ball und der Hennings spielten sich nächtliche Streit ab, bei welchen Ball die Hennings schlug.

Bei einem solchen Streit nach Mitternacht c. 20. Sept. 1915 machte die Hennings einen Selbstmordversuch, indem sie sich mit der Scheere die Schlagader am Arme öffnete. Sie begab sich aber bald in ärztliche Behandlung und nahm keinen Nachteil.

Den Grund dieser Vorkommnisse konnte man nicht erfahren, die beiden waren vorher wie nachher einig und verrieten sich nicht. Die Leute im Hause schlossen aus diesem Kesseltreiben, dass die Beiden durch ein Verbrechen miteinander verkettet seien.

Ball brach damals zu seiner Entschuldigung vor, die Hennings sei eine Morphinistin.

Ball führt den Anarchistennamen Ha Hu Baley.

Die Hennings hatte damals dem Conzertunternehmer "Marcelli" erzählt, sie und ihr Mann seien in München wegen Spionage verhaftet gewesen.. Jhr Mann sei erschossen worden, während sie gegen eine Kaution, die ein reicher Herr geleistet, entlassen worden sei, sie habe dann ihre Papiere in Bezug auf Alter gefälscht und sei so über die Grenze gekommen.

Marcelli klagte, dass die Hennings von ihrem Engagement weggeblieben und auf den Strich gegangen sei. Sie habe ihm selbst erzählt, dass sie Ball hiezu gezwungen habe, dass er sie geschlagen, wenn sie ihm zu wenig Geld abgeliefert habe. Sie sei ganz im Banne dieses Ball.

Wegen der Schriftenfälschung der Hennings und dem Zuhälterwesen des Ball wurde hier noch keine Untersuchung geführt, vermutlich weil sie wieder von Zürich fort waren. Es sind noch Copien der Originalrapporte auf dem Crimminalcommissariat Zürich. Wäll, Det.

3 VI 19

Ob C Unwey Com.

Ball u. der Hennigs dürften sich i. Bern aufhalten

Cover and seven of nineteen file pages, 1918–19
Source: Swiss Federal Archive, Bern (21/10558)

Post Office Room 142

July 7, 1919

Bern
Tel. No. 63[39]

To:

Detective Frey

B E R N

The Zurich Police have alerted us that the following persons are residing in Bern:

BALL Hugo (alias Höxter John and Ha Hu Baley), b. 1886, from Pirmasens (Bavaria), writer

and

HENNINGS Emmy (alias Editha von Münchhausen), b. 1886, from Flensburg (Holstein)

Both are apparently cohabitating outside of marriage. Both are suspected of propagating revolutionary ideas.

Do you want to organize questionings.

[Stamp: Swiss Investigatory Authority
for German and Italian Switzerland
Written by:]

Translated from German by Brian Alkire

Postgebäude Zimmer 142 7. Juli 1919.

Bern An

Tel.No.6339 Detektiv F r e y,

B E R N.

Es werden uns als in Bern sich aufhaltend von der Zürcher Polizei signalisiert:

B A L L Hugo (alias Höxter John und Ha Hu Baley), geb.1886, von Pirmasens (Bayern), Schriftsteller,

und

H E N N I N G S Emmy (alias Editha von Münchhausen), geb.1885, von Flensburg (Holstein).

Die beiden stehen angeblich im Konkubinat. Es besteht gegen beide der Verdacht, dass sie revolutionäre Ideen propagieren.

Wollen Sie in dieser Richtung Erhebungen veranstalten.

Eidg. Untersuchungsrichter
für die
deutsche und italienische Schweiz
Der Schriftführer:

Cover and seven of nineteen file pages, 1918–19
Source: Swiss Federal Archive, Bern (21/10558)

Bern, July 15, 1919

Report
to the Swiss Investigative Authority

Bern

The Hugo Ball named in the present commission is identical with BALL HUGO, son of Karl and Josefine (née Arnold) of Pirmasens, Bavaria, born February 22, 1886, writer, in Switzerland since 1915 in, among other places, Zurich, then in Ascona, and since the month of September 1917 in Bern, Marzilistrasse No. 30 with family Krähenbühl. Ball is still unmarried and holds the position of director at the "Free Press" (*Freier Verlag*) at Zieglerstrasse No. 8 in Bern, and is also employed at the "Free Newspaper" (*Freie Zeitung*) at Zieglerstrasse No. 8. He is in very intimate contact with the other person named in the commission, HENNINGS, née Cordsen Emma Marie, daughter of Ernst Cordsen and Anna, née Dorothe, divorced from Josef, born January 17, 1885 of Copenhagen, Denmark, writer and concert singer, living in Switzerland since 1915, Zurich, Ascona, and most recently Bern, resident with the Bichsel family, Marzilistrasse No. 23.

Both pretend to be engaged to be married. Ball, who has a good salary from his position, supports Hennings, as the latter's low income would not suffice for her and her twelve-year-old child. I was able to determine that Hennings is a writer for a publishing house named *Reissverlag* in Berlin. She is said to have been sentenced in Munich for anarchist propaganda. Hennings herself admits to having written for a newspaper "Revolter" (*Revoluzer*) during her stay in Zurich. Since then, she claims she has had nothing more to do with politics. In Bern to date, no indications have been found which would suggest that they are active in a political or revolutionary direction. The Municipal Police Directorship in Bern will nonetheless submit a deportation request, as Ball and Hennings were not able to convincingly demonstrate the source of their income.

[signature]
Furthermore:
re: the Dada Society

Bern , den 15. Juli 1919. L. A. 101d

Bericht

an das eidg. Untersuchungsrichteramt

Bern.

Der im vorstehenden Auftrag genannte Hugo Ball, ist identisch mit Ball Hugo, Sohn des Karl und der Josefine geb. Arnold von Pirmasens, Bayern, geb. den 22. Februar 1886, Schriftsteller, seit 1915 in der Schweiz, unter anderm in Zürich, dann in Ascona, und seit dem Monat September 1917 in Bern, Marzilistrasse No.30 bei Familie Krähenbühl. Ball ist noch ledig und versieht die Stelle eines Direktors im "Freien Verlag" Zieglerstrasse No. 8 in Bern, und ist aber zugleich noch Mitarbeiter der "Freien Zeitung" Zieglerstrasse No. 8 dahier. Er steht in ganz intimen Verkehr mit der im gleichen Auftrag genannten Hennings geb. Cordsen Emma Marie, Tochter des Ernst Cordsen, und der Anna geb. Dorothe, des Josefs abgeschiedene, geb. den 17. Januar 1885 von Kopenhagen, Dänemark, Schriftstellerin und Conzertsängerin, seit dem Jahr 1915 in der Schweiz, Zürich, Ascona und zuletzt in Bern, wohnhaft bei Familie Bichsel, Marzilistrasse No 23 dahier.

Beide geben sich als verlobt aus. Ball, welcher in seiner Stellung ein schöner Verdienst hat, erhält sozusagen die Hennings, da der geringe Verdienst der letzteren, für sie und für ihr 12 jähriges Kind nicht ausreichen würde. Wie ich vernehmen konnte, schreibt die Hennings als Schriftstellerin in einen Verlag , genannt "Reissverlag" in Berlin. Sie soll s.Z. in München wegen anarchistischer Propoganda verhaftet gewesen sein. Die Hennings gibt selber zu, wärend ihrem Aufenthalte in Zürich, in eine Zeitung "Revoluzer" geschrieben zu haben. Seither habe sie sich mit der Politik nicht mehr beschäftigt. Weder gegen ihren Verlobten Ball, noch gegen die Hennings konnten in Bern bis dato ~~keine~~ Anhaltspunkte festgestellt werden, dass sie sich politisch oder in revolutionärer Richtung sich betätigen. Die städt' Polizeidirektion in Bern, wird gleichwohl gegen Beide einen Ausweisungsantrag stellen, da sich Ball und die Hennings über ihre Erwerbsquellen zu wenig glaubwürdig ausweisen können.

Fug, Det.

Even if not all of them are Bolsheviks, most of them certainly are, and I suspect that Bolshevik propaganda is concealed behind this milieu. Häring, whom I named earlier, told me that the following members specifically were Bolsheviks:

Dr.Walter Serner
Tristan Zara

Häring believes that they are such more for reasons of money than conviction.

Dr.Walter Serner and Tristan Zara are intimately befriended with Schalk, Johann, from Baden, proprietor of the suspicious bookstore on Kirchgasse (previously Rosengasse).

With the earnings from his business it is unlikely that Schalk, who can be seen daily in cafés (Terrasse, Odeon), could maintain his lifestyle, leading one to suspect that he is a Bolshevik.

It would presumably be interesting to learn where Serner and Zara receive their means of subsistence from; presumably he can not live off of his activities as a writer. Serner is an Austrian deserter and claims to withdraw money from home under a false address, the Austrian Currency Center only allows 200 Kr. per month.

Häring described the Dada Society to me as a Bolshevik enterprise. I would like to note on this occasion that Häring describes himself as a major idealist, while I would claim that he is a major materialist.

The local Bolsheviks want to make direct contact with the Bolsheviks in Hungary by sending members to Hungary, especially since there are no sure messages coming from there.

unterstützt hat. Dabei ist zu sagen, dass Silberblatt sicher Bolschewiki ist, das kann jeder russ. Student bestätigen und er selbst macht ja nie ein Hehl daraus .

Arsenis Dionys lebt auf grossem Fuss, verkehrt in allen Cafés, ist sehr elegant gekleidet ; es dürfte ihm schwer fallen darzutun, woher er die Mittel hat für eine solche Lebenshaltung . Arsenis ist sehr vorsichtig, man sieht ihn nur in der Gesellschaft von Stramgas und Bambukis , mit Silberblatt zeigt er sich sehr wenig, fast nie.

Auf alle Fälle ist Arsenis nicht aus Ueberzeugung Bolschewiki, sondern nur des Geldes wegen . Was Bambukis anlangt, so kann ich nur so viel sagen, dass er auf alle Fälle der Mann ist, der sich für Geld zu etwas hergibt .

ferner :

betr. die Dada-Gesellschaft :

Wenn nicht alle, so sind sicher zum Teil Bolschewiki und ich vermute, dass sich hinter diesem Milieu eine Bolschewiki Propaganda verbirgt . Der früher von mir genannte Häring bezeichnete mir als Bolschewiki speziell die Mitglieder :

Dr. Walter Serner

Tristan Zara

wie Häring meint, seien es die zwar mehr des Geldes wegen als aus Ueberzeugung .

Dr. Walter Serner und Tristan Zara sind intim befreundet mit Schalk, Johann, ein Badenser , Jnhaber der fragl. Buchhandlung an der Kirchgasse (früher Rosengasse) .

Mit dem Verdienste aus seinem Geschäft, es geht sehr wenig , könnte Schalk, der täglich im Café zu sehen ist (Terrasse, Odeon) nicht bestehen, so dass man auf die Vermutung kommt, er sei Bolschewiki .

Jnteressant wäre vermutlich zu erfahren, woher Serner und Zara ihre Subsistenzmittel haben ; Zara ist Russe und bekommt kein Geld von zu Hause ; aus seiner schriftstellerischen Tätigkeit könnte er vermutlich nicht existiren . Serner ist Oesterr. Deserteur und behauptet deshalb unter falscher Adresse von zu Hause das Geld zu beziehen, allein die Oesterr. Devisencentrlae erlaubt nur 200 Kr. im Monat .

verte

Cover and seven of nineteen file pages, 1918–19
Source: Swiss Federal Archive, Bern (21/10558)

Häring bezeichnete mir gegenüber die Dada-Gesellschaft als Bolschewiki-Unternehmen . Bei dieser Gelegenheit mag bemerkt werden, dass Häring sich politisch als grosser Jdealist gerirt, während er meiner Ansicht nach ein grosser Materialist ist.

Die hiesigen Bolschewiki wollen mit den Bolschewiki in Ungarn direkt durch Sendlinge nach Ungarn in Verbindung treten, zumal man keine sichern Nachrichten aus Ungarn habe .

Momentan ist im Tun die Gründung einer französ. (Welsch - schweiz.) Socialisten Gruppe, vermutlich um die hiesigen Welsch - schweizer, die als solche weniger zum Bolschewismus neigen, in dieses Lager hinüberzuziehen, welchen Erfolg man sich verspricht, wenn man die Welschschweizer in ihrer Muttersprache bearbeiten könne, was nicht möglich ist in dem bestehenden gewerkschaftlichen und polizischen Organisationen .

Ob. Lieut. Müller. Comissär

The founding of a socialist group in French-speaking Switzerland is presently underway, presumably to recruit the local French-speaking Swiss, who are generally disinclined to Bolshevism, for their camp. This promises to be successful if they can speak to the French-speaking Swiss in their mother tongue, which is not currently possible in existing labor union and police organizations.

[signature]

Translated from German by Brian Alkire

The Dadaists in Zurich

Serner Walter, 1889*, Author
Tzara Tristan, ?, Author
Ball Hugo, 1886**, Author
Hennings Emma, b. Cordsen, 1885, Author

* Editor of "Sirius" in Zurich. With Otto Flake and Tristan Tzara, publisher of the journal "Der Zeltweg" (1919).

**Came to Zurich with Emmy Hennings in 1915, founded there the "Cabaret Voltaire" in February together with Hans Arp, Richard Heulsenbeck, Marcel Janco, Tristan Tzara and Walter Serner

Die Dadaisten in Zürich

Serner Walter, 1889*, Schriftsteller
Tzara Tristan, ?, Schriftsteller
Ball Hugo, 1886**, Schriftsteller
Hennings Emma, geb. Cordsen, 1885, Schriftstellerin

---

*Herausgeber des "Sirius" in Zürich. Mit Otto Flake und Tristan Tzara Herausgeber der Zeitschrift "Der Zeltweg" (1919)

**Kam mit Emmy Hennings 1915 in Zürich, gründete dort im Februar das "Cabaret Voltaire" zusammen mit Hans Arp, Richard Huelsenbeck, Marcel Janco, Tristan Tzara und Walter Serner

"But this kind of action art is a little foreign to me"

A Questioning

MfS (GDR)

Artists were often directly summoned to interviews by the Stasi. This was a typical "**decomposition measure**" with the purpose of "undermining self-confidence." In the Soviet Union, there were the so-called prophylactic warnings, which were also summonses to conversation. Between 1967 and 1975, more than 130,000 Soviet citizens were invited to these discussions and warned. But there were also cases where citizens were summoned to fake, "legendated discussions," i.e. to interviews where the purpose was to stoke suspicion that the summoned person was working with the state. These were "discussions" where both of the examining Stasi officers were interested not only in the artists, but also in action art as a genre. State security feared action art—as a genre from the West, as a praxis of the historical avant-garde, and as an unpredictable event. In the audio transcript, the examining officers ask the artists to talk about their own performances in detail. For reasons of privacy, we present here redacted versions of the whole discussion that avoids references to any specific actions. **(S)**

"But this kind of action art is a little foreign to me" —An Interrogation

Audio transcript

MfS: … We have made it a principle to talk directly to artists, to start a conversation. … What kind of problems do you have? Why do you think state security might have an interest in you?

Artist: I don't know. Maybe it's related to the fact that I, as you most likely know, create actions in the Association of Visual Artists. … Specifically, artistic actions. So, it's possible that someone is watching me now and then. But what does that mean? I did recently create a work with a definite political character. And I can imagine that you want to speak with me for that reason. Other than that, I don't actually know.

MfS: You know of no reason? Well, it's related, as you say, to the actions you've been putting on in your artistic orientation. It was a while ago, but what we're specifically thinking about …

Artist: Ah, now you're getting specific (laughs).

MfS: … is when you went to …

Artist: Ah …

MfS: I'll formulate it cautiously: with a truly spectacular action.

Artist: … if it's so specific, I can explain how it all relates. … But as you surely know – I don't know of course what you know and what you don't know …

MfS: No, we didn't know that …

Artist: But that's important, it's related.

MfS: Then you'll have to explain it to us.

Artist: (Laughs.) It's as follows, I don't know where to begin …

MfS: Huh?

MfS: What did you do?

Artist: … So I became very, very cautious because I was determined that someone spoke to me directly in …., well, how would you have liked it …

MfS: ?

Artist: … With what I am doing, you're amazed – and I can tell you this – that you live here, yeah you would actually have to, how do you manage … yeah, of course, I can, I have a scene here, I do what I want to, so far I have been very consistent about that.

MfS: ?

Artist: I was there with my wife and friends and what we did was we said we're making a decision; we're doing this action. You should look at that with quotation marks. Because anyone who goes there puts on a show of some sort, I just tried to feel like a free citizen of the GDR. To show those people who always just think we can't do it here anyways, and we have to invite … so that you know what's happening with us, and also to show GDR cultural workers that you can actually make pretty free decisions. And I hope that I can continue to do so.

I was continually approached and asked, are you from here or are you from the other side? I said I'm from here, and some people became pretty skeptical because they presume that a GDR artist … puts on such an apparently spectacular action. If you don't know what it's really supposed to mean, then I did nothing more tha n… Then I moved around totally normally in this exhibition. I just didn't drink any alcohol, and when someone approached me and talked to me, I answered their questions. And determined that I actually couldn't move freely …

MfS: (Laughs.)

Artist: So that's what I did and then it was done, then we went back outside, and no one tried to speak to us anymore.

MfS: Talked with no one, what?

Artist: Well that's probably because they did ID checks afterwards. But I think I can tell you something really interesting …

MfS: … This piece of paper is really clear …

Artist: This piece of paper is clear to the extent that people assumed that someone from the West was putting on an action for us GDR people, ...
Yeah, but no one asked me about it. So, I think it's pretty important how that's interpreted. So far, I have had hardly any reactions to the matter. What are your reactions? You can also express your opinion about it.

MfS: I can tell you. I, or we on this team, have a great deal of interest in art.

Artist: Yeah.

MfS: That's part of our work, but ... but this kind of action art is a little foreign to me.

Artist: Yeah, it's also foreign to certain artists in our association. I don't exclusively do actions, I also make pictures, and there I'm a bit of an outsider because in painting/graphics there's now a specific form all the way to space actions, you can paint pictures of things, but you can also just simply paint. And this is called "performance." It's a special form which doesn't have anything to do with happenings or actions in the broadest sense but still makes a division between the audience and the creator. You do something and the others watch, like in theater. It's actually a pretty simple ...

Artist: Yeah, yeah.

Artist: ... a pretty simple thing, merely through alienation. Because you're wearing something different from the others and go to receptions, a thing like that achieves an effect. It's just like when a naked woman is standing in the room among a bunch of clothed people ...

MfS: Exactly that was shown there, wasn't it?

Artist: Exactly that. Like I said, I'd have to show you photos. If I had known that we were going to be talking about this, I'd have brought photos for you.

MfS: You can still do that. ...

MfS: That's how it is. ... stressful. I wasn't there of course, but colleagues ... and they said ... people talked about ...
...
Yeah, yeah. You consider that obscene.

Artist: Obscene?

MfS: Yes, to the point that it seems offensive. Yes, something like that.

Artist: Well, I heard nothing about offensiveness. Afterwards they determined that nothing was actually happening there, many people also just ignored it.

MfS: How do you assess that there ... ? You were ... at the exhibition.

Artist: Yes, of course ...
...

MfS: Did you see there what ... You're saying there were punks, similar colleagues ...

Artist: Everything you can imagine is there because word got out that if you just, if you have the courage, you can go there and eat and drink really well and chat a bit ...

MfS: Art ...

Artist: Well, okay, I just want to allude to the fact that it's a bit more casual there now. You can also of course. ... You're very welcome to come. (Laughs loudly.) I mean, professionally ...

MfS: Yeah, yeah.

Artist: It is in fact in ... but I am a GDR artist. I live here. We can do that, too, we don't need any because most people are just afraid. Afraid of difficulties, of these kinds of pronouncements.

MfS: Is this fear real?

Artist: I can't really say. I can only speak for myself. I have so far been able to move very freely. And do what I wanted to do.
...

MfS: That's very good to know.

Artist: It's pretty accommodating in the Artists' Association, especially in Berlin ... With another type of work, I'd probably have been in there.

MfS: Do you want to … ?

Artist: No, not in the art exhibition. But that's also because of the insecurity of the painter. I myself have experienced how you don't really know what something is. Is that still art or is it theater or … I mean, it's not painted, so …

MfS Man 2: (from behind) … more interest in action art. … Whether there are more interested people through the action … ?

Artist: What do you mean? Whether this thing led to interest … ?

MfS Man 2: An increase in status … of this entire artistic direction?

Artist: No, no. Let's put it this way. Where some people say, oh, he's courageous, or I wouldn't do that, he's putting on airs, whatever, one person sees it that way while another person says: man, that's actually pretty interesting, or pretty good, and the other says the same thing again. But an increase in status …

MfS Man 2: Then not necessarily an increase in status, but an increase in interest in some circles – it's of course totally unknown. …

Artist: An Austrian approached me and said … there are indeed performance artists but many people don't know anything about them because it is a special artform. In this sense it's actually a really profane action. Dressing differently … it is actually really simple. But it still has a controversial effect … Oh, the Austrian approached me who said, how are you able to do this, are you allowed to do that?

MfS: Are you allowed to do that …

Artist: Someone approaches you and speaks to you and I repeatedly explained, to everyone who comes from the other side, yes, I say, I do that. They can't always think that you can only do that in the West, I say: of course, it might be under surveillance, but the fact that it's just a conversation, like now … it's totally logical.

MfS: Exactly.

Artist: Beuys has also not allowed himself to be taken in. … What I get asked is how it works, what I'm doing here. And I say, you don't need to have any fear of state security, because everyone just always assumes that.

MfS: Mhm, mhm.

Artist: That you're always thinking, look at what that guy's able to do, and then nothing happens. And I say, what do I do now? I'm doing nothing. That was another form, a different, special artform, but that doesn't mean you're hostile to the state or whatever. But like I said, you … have a bit of anxiety about me, that I could be corrupted. I can imagine. (Laughs.)

MfS: I can tell you in principle that you bypassed our legal system.

Artist: … bypassed? What does bypassed mean?

MfS: Well, because you violated the law. You say that you're not aware of that. But …

Artist: No, I'm not aware of that. That's why I'm asking.

MfS: Normally it's the case that citizens are expected to adhere to the system of laws. And that includes you …

MfS: It's about … The people creating all this fuss, they know their place, what's permissible in this state. … When they get taken in.

Artist: Then that's also my duty, … talking, talking, talking, because I'm in favor of mutual understanding, and then that's also a fantastic thing for example, on the other side … no one would care about that, but here it's crucial that it's happening here and now. … I also made this action to show GDR artists that it's possible. If you're familiar with other works you will figure out that it wasn't a gag, that it all relates somehow. … … I don't see it as my duty to be destructive. If crazy people do that, that's their problem … fabricating this kind of apocalyptic mood.

MfS: Then that becomes difficult politically …

Artists: I also don't let myself get caught up … in panic … and theater and actions. My thing is having a constructive effect. If I had known, if we had had this conversation two or three weeks ago, then I'd have invited you to a project that we did. …

MfS: You thought that was the impetus for our conversation?

Artist: Well, I had hoped. ...

MfS: As action art, too?

Artist: As action in the room. With an acquaintance of mine. I'd have invited you right away, to see that you shouldn't always see the negative aspects. Even though that's an issue too. ...

MfS: Was it also photographed?

Artist: Yes, it was also photographed. ...

MfS: (unintelligible)

Artist: It doesn't have that. You're in the here and now and you're active. I see that as a very constructive thing. But naturally you can start to speculate and say, well, he made an effort, but it's a completely different kind of effort. Or you could also be opposed, in the Stasi too, someone would certainly have been there ...

MfS: Yes, yes. Of course.

Artist: It's not that bad. I also see now, what I'm saying is that one should be able to know what's happening ...

MfS: While you say that you would invite us, I just wanted to say that it's part of our job, at a kind of presentation like that ... you're obviously not responsible for that.
(Artist laughs.)

MfS: No, just so you don't think that.

Artist: Yes, that's obvious. But why? I just say to myself, please, take a look at us and then you can make a judgment, rather than just hearing about something. You need to tackle these kinds of borderline cases, even if you already have a firm viewpoint. As I said, I came back, don't forget that, I will also stay here. But please, in that case I'd like to move freely within the GDR. That is what defines artistic activity, simply leaping over certain boundaries, yeah. ... And what we did, the actions, I see as very constructive, although you were probably very skeptical due to your lack of familiarity.

MfS: Yes, I would say that.

Artist: ... Yes, one should be able to calmly make that observation.

MfS: You can assume that. You could also convince me of the opposite. What you're doing, what an artist creates and what action art is. ... Who is the audience?

Artist: Yes, I of course have my own audience.

MfS: I don't want to, but do you know, ... there is a broad spectrum from far left to far right – how is that perceived by people?

Artist: Yeah, you also have to be able to hear it when you think back on it ...

MfS: I can imagine, and if, let's say, such artists ...

Artist: So, you think that there is a threat from those who don't know what it's all about, or who are already preparing to go over to the other side ...

MfS: I would at least not reject the danger outright. ... It depends on how the audience feels there.

Artist: Yeah, so far we have kept it that way, a certain confusion, that's of course conscious. Art of course does not surpass logic. Instead there are numerous irrational aspects. So you of course can't approach it with your head.

MfS: Yeah.

Artist: That's also the case with the actions ... That is naturally a kind of confusion ...

MfS Man 2: Or looks in the other direction ... (?)

Artist: (Laughs.) ... and, well, there's then a kind of confusion and uncertainty ...

MfS: Yes, I can imagine that when we're talking about clarifying these things ... of course there are also so many metaphors and ambiguities ... but ...

Artist: (loudly interrupting): ... You of course can't judge, as far as reflection ... because of course there are people who exploit it in one way or another, right?

MfS: How do you assess the interest in all of these problems ... actions against, a deep political effect …

Artist: What do you mean? I don't understand.

…

MfS: We have very specific rules and procedures we have to follow. …

Artist: Not there, which is why there are different kinds of people there, where you know they're from state security … But when you come out – no doubt everyone who goes in and out is registered. That's the fear of course. Most people say, I can't go in there, I'll get into trouble … somehow you just know it.

MfS: Did you know …

Artist: Whenever you come out, around to the right …, then police officers come or someone behind you and then please, very friendly, personal details.

MfSMan 2: Are you interested in a sequel … ?

Artist: Well, so you're doing something again, no, it was a one-time thing. (Laughs.)

MfS: Do it, you were so wonderfully noticeable, then do something. (Laughs.)

Artist: I only do things that I actually believe in. … And my advantage is that I see this connection … between these two poles. … That's why they had to have experienced an action like this from me, in order to be able to assess what's happening there, how their emotions are, how you handle the thing …

MfS: Yes.

Artist: Then give me your phone number, I'll write it down.

MfS: There is naturally a problem here that needs to be taken into account … that is also the basic principle of our work …We talked about problems which aren't very acceptable in public. That is in your interest and ours too …

…

Artist: Why shouldn't you either? Everyone knows the Stasi is there. I experience that every day, like when you feel like Dimitrov Street is Records Street. People are standing around there, are simply very present, and everyone notices it too. One doesn't need to pretend like it's not true, or agree to keep quiet about it, when everyone knows about it. I mean …

MfS: ?

Artist: I also wasn't surprised. I thought, well, two people are sitting in here, what's going on here, but …

MfS: The difference is that those who are present are intended to be present, you should be able to see them.

Artist: Yeah, of course …

MfS: Our duty with regard to protection is an entirely different one, also an entirely different demand …

Artist: Then one of your people will probably be in … ? Then we'll see each other again there.

MfS: We have no relationship there.

Artist: But you've got to do it sometime, you've got to experience it. … simply to be able to judge it. Exactly, and not just always hear about it from someone else.

…

MfS: … My recommendation is that we'll contact you if we have any problems.

Artist: Mhm.

MfS: We know where you live … we won't do it immediately, in another form, … with other names…

Artist: … So are we going to be examined individually or not? Is that the case with me? We can presume that, can't we? That you know in detail the individual steps one is taking …

MfS: You think we're responsible for that. … How many people do you think we have?

Artist: (Laughs.)

MfS: Our primary duty is to deal with actual enemies … there's already enough work to do there, no.

Artist:	Of course, of course. ...
MfS:	You're aware of our interests, above all to limit that ...
Artist:	Well, I feel like ... I just came from West Berlin, and every one of us was surprised at first, coming into a world like that. ... If you don't just simply flip out emotionally, then you don't have any emotions ... it's logical, it's also something which causes many to go over to the other side, because they say they're unable to do everything here ...
MfS:	You will manage ... it's also in your own interest ...
Artist:	Thank you, too, yes. Well, have a nice day and until we meet again. (Laughs.)

Translated from German by Brian Alkire

Private Reports

KGB (USSR)

The former KGB officer Mikhail Abrosimov, a KGB agent from 1967–79 in the Fifth Department of Moscow, which was responsible for handling artists, was involved in surveilling the Moscow underground art scene. When he died, he passed on his private archive to the art journal *Iskusstvo*. Among the contents of this archive were two notebooks with Abrimosov's observations of the art scene. We could call these notebooks a private "Who's-Who Report." The Who's-Who Report was a secret police method for recording and presenting persons and groups as well as the relevant relationships with each other.Abrosimov noted people like Yuri Albert, Sergey Anufriyev, Valery Gerlovin, Alexander Melamid, Genrich Sapgir, Nadya Stolpovskaya, and Vadim Zakharov. Abrosimov apparently attempted to arrange all of the members of the Moscow underground in alphabetical order and to assign photos to them. (S)

Alexander Mikhaylov's essay was published in 2013 in the Russian art journal *Iskusstvo*. Reading this essay, one has the sense of still being in the Cold War era. A KGB commanding officer is speaking with an alarming self-awareness. He continues to tell two constructed narratives —originating in the secret service itself—about, first, how most artists in the underground were good-for-nothings and their art worthless, and second, how surveillance of the art scene served to protect against Western influence. The first narrative is about discrediting artists whose art does not align with prevailing political interests, a devaluation of artists that we can witness in contemporary Russia, but also in contemporary Hungary. The second narrative advances the idea that criticism of the political system could only come from outside, that they are always financed by the West and that critical artists are vassals of the West. We found almost no other texts where these two narratives appear in such a concentrated form. (S)

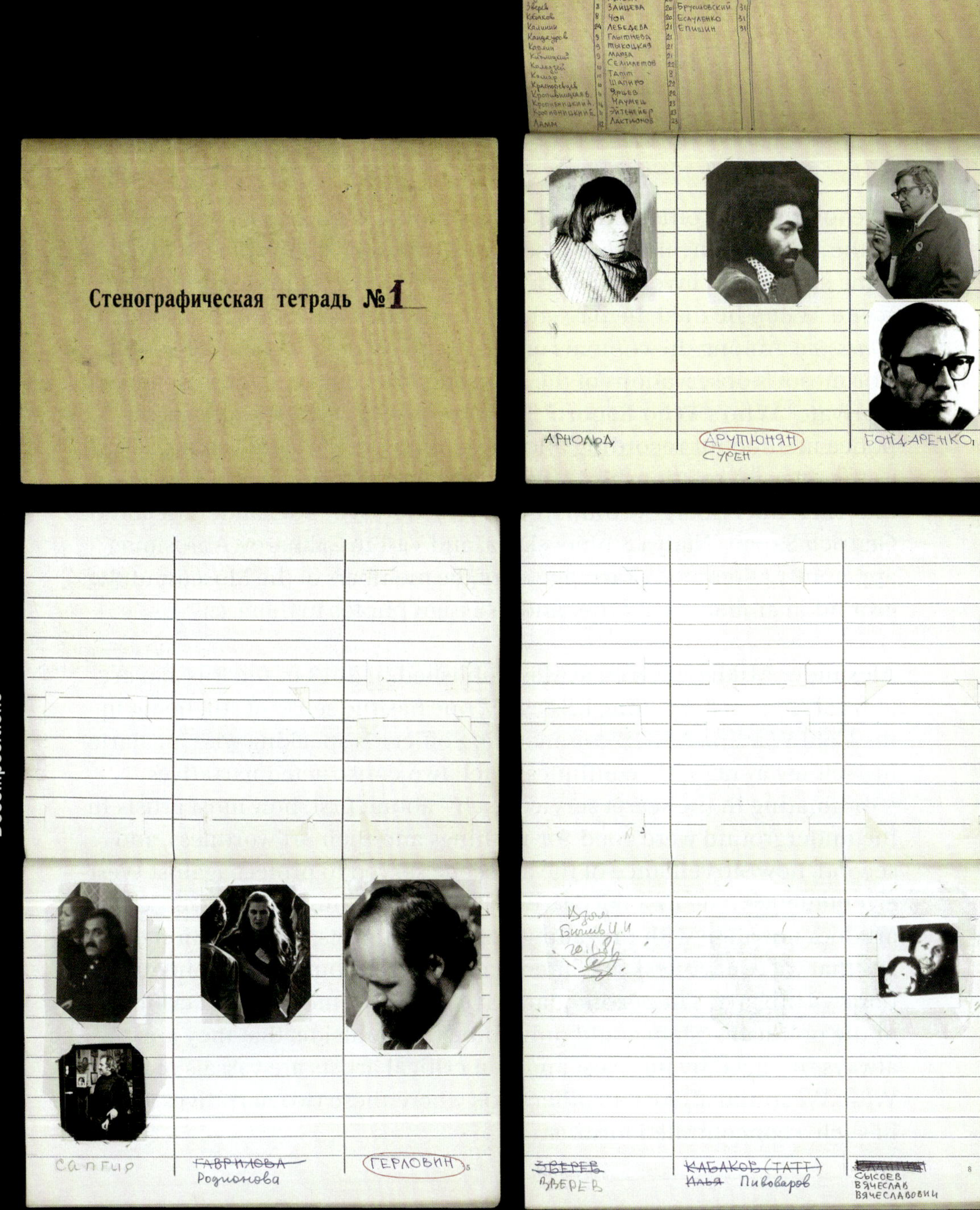
Стенографическая тетрадь №1
АРНОЛЬД
АРУТЮНЯН
СУРЕН
БОНДАРЕНКО
САПГИР
ГАВРИЛОВА
Родионова
ГЕРЛОВИН
ЗВЕРЕВ
ЗВЕРЕВ
КАБАКОВ (ТАТТ)
Илья Пивоваров
СЫСОЕВ
ВЯЧЕСЛАВ
ВЯЧЕСЛАВОВИЧ

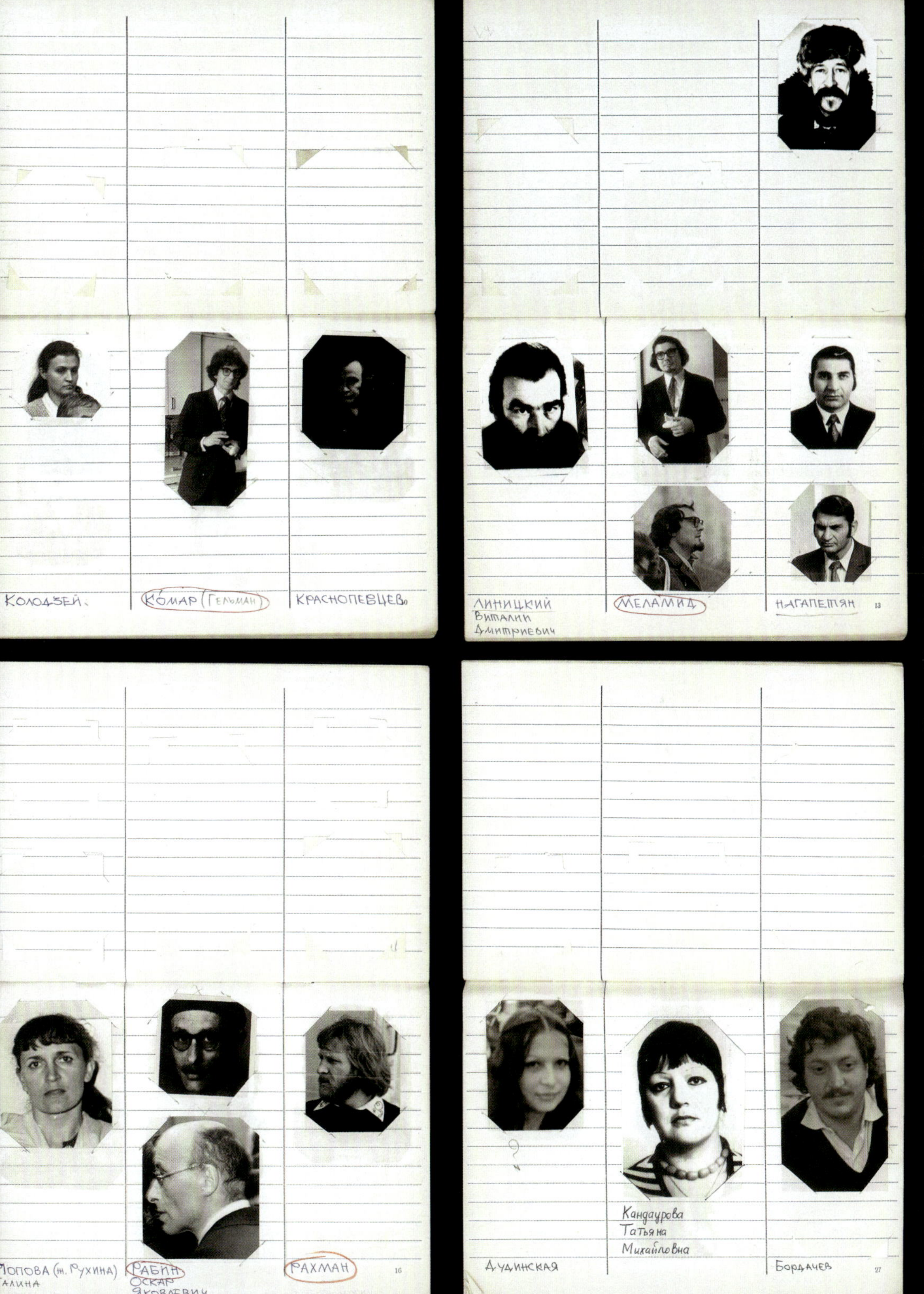

Two notebooks from the archive of Mikhail Abromisov, 1976–79
Courtesy of *Iskusstvo* archive

АБРАМЕНКОВ	1	ЛЕВИКОВА	11		20
АНУФРИЕВ	1	ЛИЛЬБОХ	11	КУЗНЕЦОВА Л.	21
АБРАМОВ	1	ЛУТЦ	11	ПРУДОВСКИЙ ЛЬ	21
АЛЕНА	2	ЛЮБУШКИН	12	ПАВЛОВ ЮВ	21
АРМЕН	2	МАРТЕМЬЯНОВА	12		
АВЕТИСЯН	2	МИЛЛЕР	12		
АФОНИЧЕВ	2	МЫШКОВ	13		
АЛЬБЕРТ	3	НОВИКОВ	13		
БАСИН	3	ПЕДЕШ	13		
БЕЛЕНОК	3	Провоторов	14		
БЕЛКИН	4	ПОПОВА В	14		
Борисов	4	Романов-Михайлов	14		
БОЧКАРЕВ	4	САВЕЛЬЕВ	15		
ВИК	5	СИДЕЛЬНИКОВ	15		
ГИДУЛЯНОВ А	5	СКЛЯРОВ	15		
ГИДУЛЯНОВ В	5	СЛЕПОВ	16		
ГИНДИН	6	СОКОВ	16		
ГРОМОВА	6	Ситников-Покровский	16		
Горишнев	6	Стокповская	17		
ДЛУГИЙ	7	ТИЛЬ	17		
ДРЮЧИН	7	МАРИЯ	17		
ДУБАХ	7	ТУМАНОВ	17		
ЖЕРДЕВ	8	ТИЛЬМАН	18		
ЗАХАРОВ	8				
ИСАЧЕВ	8	ТИТОВ	18		
КАМЕНЕВ	9	ТРОФИМОВ Вл-р	18		
КИРЦОВА	9	ТРЯМКИН	19		
КОВАЛЬСКИЙ	9	ХЭГАЙ	19		
КУБАСОВ	10	ЩНУРОВ	19		
КУЗНЕЦОВА Н.	10	ЩЕРБАКОВ	20		
ТОЛСТЫЙ	10	ВЕЛИКЖАНОВ	20		
КОТЛЯРОВ	10		20		

Стенографическая тетрадь № 2

Абраменков Анатолий Москва

Ануфриев Ал-др Одесса

Абрамов Андрей Москва

1

Сергеева Валентина Юрьевна, 1954 г.р. Ленинград

Армен (Аветисян) Ленинград

Афоничев Владимир Ленинград

2

Альберт Юрий Москва

Басин Анатолий Ленинград

Беленок Петр Москва

3

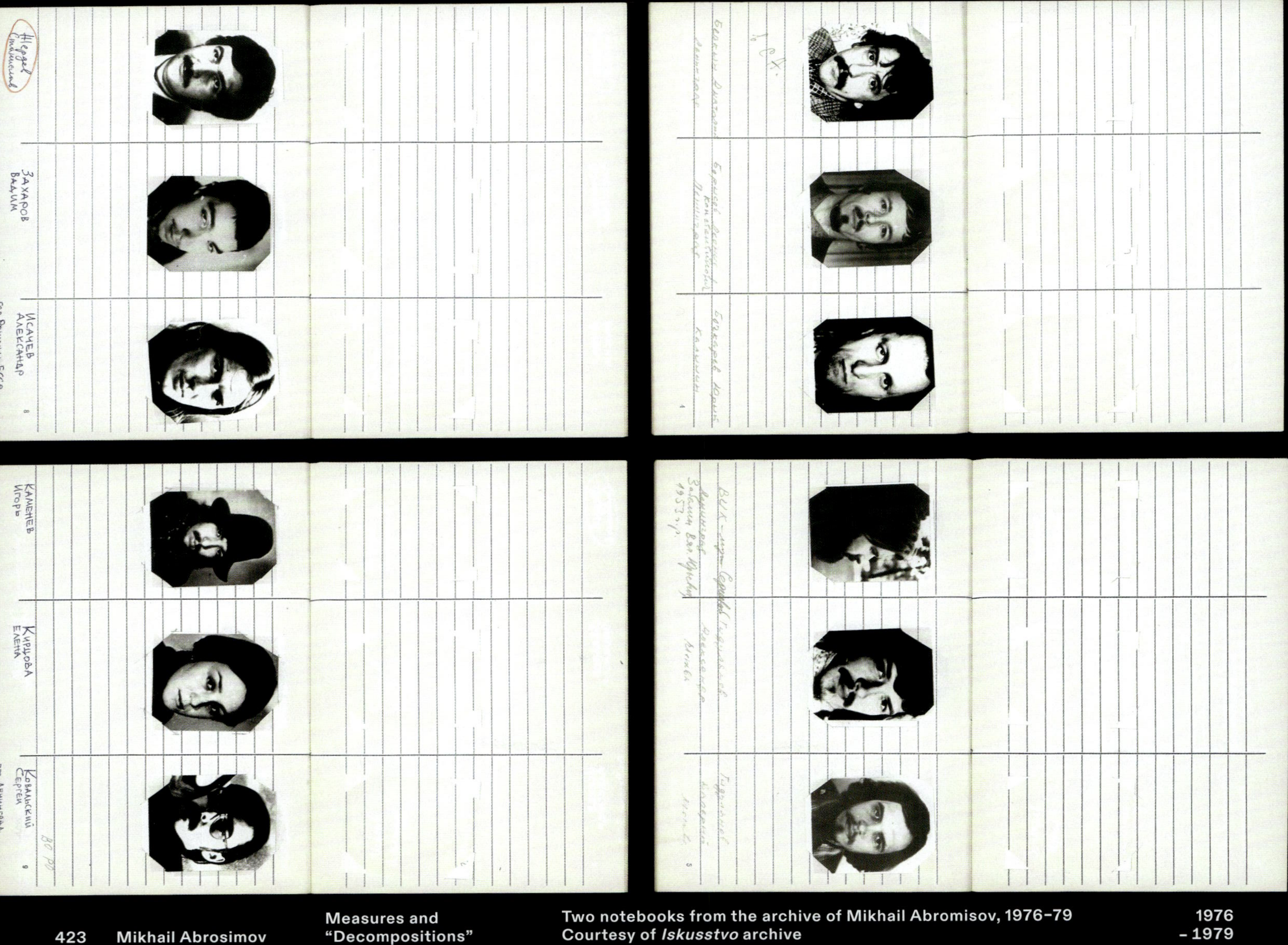

Two notebooks from the archive of Mikhail Abromisov, 1976–79
Courtesy of *Iskusstvo* archive

1976
–1979

"I have not made any decisions on censorship by the KGB"

Alexander Mikhaylov

The 5th Service of the Moscow Directorate of the KGB (USSR) was founded in 1976, and the people who worked with us there were unique. I myself was a graduate of the Faculty of Journalism of Moscow State University, the head of my department came from the Academy of the Arts in Leningrad, other employees were graduates of Moscow State University of Foreign Affairs, Moscow State University, the Literary Institute, the State Institute of Theater Arts (GITIS), even the All-Union Institute of Cinematography (VGIK), and the Shchukin Theater Institute. In those years, they didn't take [simply] anyone who wanted to join, but those who were actually needed. One of my colleagues had two educations, as an actor and as a director. He was also a professional opera singer. My partner was a graduate of the Moscow Institute of Architecture (MARKHI) who dreamed of building something all of his life but wound up serving in counterintelligence. Almost the entire division tasked with watching the creative intelligentsia consisted of representatives of the creative intelligentsia. Seryozha Truchin was a real Epicurean: fat, lazy, and cheerful. He graduated from the Moscow Conservatory and even took part in the P.I. Tchaikovsky Competition once. In 2003, he became Deputy Head of Counterterrorism in the Moscow Directorate of the FSB. I can tell you that this job didn't fit with his character in the least. For lack of better cadres, they put ill-suited people in the wrong positions. Then there was the "North-East"[1] hostage drama and Seryozha's head was on the line. First, he had a heart attack, then a stroke, and then he passed away.

Back then in Soviet times, the division's goal was shielding the creative (technical, scientific) intelligentsia from actions of "ideological diversion by the opponent," so our tasks included countermeasures to prevent Western influence onto this milieu. We all remember that the sixth article of the Constitution of the USSR defined the priority of only one ideology—that of communism—and there was a massive censorship apparatus in the USSR to maintain this primacy. The apparatus' goals were set by party organs. In its evaluation of artists, the Communist Party did not just lean upon Marxist-Leninist doctrine, but on principles declared by the Artists' Union. Joint decisions were made on what was good and what was bad, what to allow, and what might be harmful to the morale and morality of citizens or to the prestige of the Soviet Union. Any divergence from this dogma was unwelcome, and the KGB acted as a regulator of sorts, helping to control attitudes, intellectual trends, tendencies, hidden threats and dangers. Such are the tasks of any secret service in the world. They all are tasked with the early detection of potential threats, regardless of origin. At the same time, the KGB was never tasked with the criminal persecution of anyone if their actions didn't directly break the existing laws. The question of whether these people were good or bad is not under discussion. The law is the law. That was the work, all to the task of "defending." The services of the KGB were never self-sufficient; their function was only to inform the party organs of problems. The information we supplied provided the basis for political decisions. For example, the KGB would inform the party of the catastrophic conditions among the creative youth. Then the Central Committee of the Communist Party would study our material and issue a declaration "On Work with the Creative Youth," whose measures would include those of a financial character. I should say it again: the KGB did not make any decisions on censorship or other questions. We only informed our superiors and followed the decisions made above.

At the same time, there were never any direct orders from the Central Committee. It wasn't a coincidence that I quoted the function of the service as "shielding the creative (technical, scientific) intelligentsia from actions of ideological diversion by the opponent." The two key words here are "diversion" and "opponent." The KGB's opponents were not artists or writers, but the intelligence services of the West. They were to us what we were to them. Moreover, the KGB did not operate within the country, but "against the opponent" (against foreign intelligence services), uncovering the opponent's interest in concrete people. Our task was to determine how this interest arose, which goals foreign services were pursuing in working with this person or that. It was only in such cases that citizens of the Soviet Union could become the objects of our care. The main goal was to prevent the opponent from using Soviet artists in their subversive interests, to form a "fifth column." This is why "diversion" is the second key word. It was important to stop the opponent from using the intelligentsia to subvert the state order of the USSR or to sow discord in the relations between nationalities. The creative milieu is one that directly influences society. It can raise people up to great feats of courage, but it can also tear a country apart. The underestimation of this fact, and maybe even a natural regularity, led to the dissolution of the USSR and revolutions in the countries of Eastern Europe. The intelligentsia was the locomotive of all these "destructive" processes. A good example can be found in the poets and writers of the Soviet and Russian republics: Havel in Czechoslovakia [*sic*], Elchibey in Azerbaijan [*sic*], Gamsakhurdia in Georgia, or Yanderbiev [*sic*] in Chechnya. The intelligentsia can be used to sow discord between the peoples, to spread nationalist ideas that will later become the foundation for extremism and terrorism. This is why we scanned the situation in the creative milieu with such vigilance: to preempt the development of negative process. We were defending our government, much in the way that all intelligence services continue to do nowadays.

Of course, things went over the top sometimes: every municipal party committee had a cultural section tasked with visual art, among other things. Its employees were supposed to demonstrate ideological vigilance. They were supposed to permit some things and prohibit others. They also had to write reports, in which there was no need to write about individual harmful representatives of the intelligentsia, but about dangers, dubious tendencies that might have a negative impact upon the morals and artistic tastes of the citizens. As for exhibitions, this topic itself was absurd, simply because the total number of people involved in dubious exhibitions and apartment galleries in Moscow never exceeded three hundred, and many of them were not really fully involved at all. Most of the time, they exhibited totally realistic work, but hoped to gain some recognition in those circles, simply because they had no other place to turn, as the Artists' Union of the USSR only accepted a chosen few. So, they didn't really pose any threat to the government.

Of course, there were other folks too, those who didn't make pictures of the Komsomol or the Baikal–Amur Railway, but something of their own, something nonstandard. Traditionally, they were surrounded by a large number of provocateurs who bore little relation to art. This is a special category of people. And in 1974, that famous Bulldozer Exhibition was held in Belyaevo. It looked harmless at first glance: all the artists did was to go to an empty lot without bothering anybody, just to show their paintings. But this was planned as a demonstration for diplomats and Western mass media. In my opinion, the municipal authorities made a very "wise" decision: to interrupt the action by holding a *subbotnik* on a vacant lot where nothing ever happened before, and where there was nothing to clean up. This resulted in a grand scandal, because many foreigners, diplomats, [and] special correspondents had been invited, and they all planned to cover and discuss the event, which obviously, the government did not like. The government was appalled. The West exploded, and the event went down in history as a paradigm of thickheadedness and limitedness of party organs who fell for a provocation. To somehow smooth over the situation, the Moscow directorate of the KGB wrote to the Central Committee with the offer of organizing yet another exhibition, but this time, under supervision. The artists were given the Beekeeping Pavilion at the All-Union Exhibition of Economic Achievements, where they could show anything they wanted. The exhibition included works that are famous today, and stuff that was openly crap, like for example, a man sitting on eggs. The whole thing created such a commotion that the line had to be broken up into groups of five to ten people who went from one barrier to another to avoid creating a crowd. The main thing was that it became clear that some artists were capable, while others were posers, incapable of anything; they were only interested in vodka, girls, and drunken philosophizing on the meaning of life. It was then that it was decided to somehow organize these new forms by creating a section for painting at the City Committee of Graphic Artists, de facto equating them, if not to Artists' Union members, then to members of a creative workers' union. They were given a space on the ground floor of Malaya Gruzinskaya 28 and formed a core group of twenty-eight people. Of course, at that point, there were many more of them: there were different circles and even schools, like the students and admirers of Oscar Rabin, for example.

Then came the exhibitions at Izmaylovo Park, which we simply hated, because they were held on weekends, and we would have to go to work on Saturday morning after a Friday night. These exhibitions also turned into some kind of action. Once they brought a huge ball of string. Everybody had to help to unravel it and got a certificate that he or she was present when the string was unraveled. They would then drink on the occasion, so life was "fun." The artists were constantly harassed by individuals from so-called dissident circles. These included true romantics and open provocateurs. The latter often inspired the ire of law enforcement and party organs, they were often persecuted by criminal courts. One now usually thinks that they were persecuted for political reasons, but for the most part, these were simply pathological hooligans and hoodlums, like one priest who stole utensils, was defrocked, and went to prison, who considered himself a freethinker for the rest of his life.

The only people who were really interested in any of this, however, were not the authorities as such, but the members of the Artists' Union. They protested because their monopoly as a mirror of reality had been broken. There were many critical articles from their side, but the real social scandal dissipated into nothing. The forbidden fruit is tempting to everyone, but once you'd been to the All-Union Exhibition of Economic Achievements and seen everything legally, there would be no consequences. So, interest immediately waned. The next step were legal organizations. It was then that even Western journalists lost interest, not to mention a broader public, because what was interesting in this situation was not art, but interference from the KGB. It's one thing to go somewhere to see people getting their faces smashed in, and another to look at some incomprehensible nonsense in a cramped exhibition space. There were very few people with professional expertise in art, and they had seen everything in the studios anyway. But what does the crowd see? Just a painting? But where is the militia? Where are the men in black?

If it seems today that anybody stood up for the artists in the USSR or in the West, it's mostly an illusion of time. Almost nothing happened in our country (with the exception of isolated facts). There were several reasons for this: the creative methods of the avant-gardists sparked the interest of only a limited circle of people, mostly artists themselves, while the Western reaction was so-so. Mostly, because the quantity of available information was miniscule. There was no internet, both television and newspapers were under strict control, Western radio stations were scrambled. Most importantly, people were interested in something else entirely. Society was weaned on the films and literature of Socialist Realism. So, the goings-on in the circles that interest you didn't actually concern anyone. The overwhelming majority simply wasn't interested. Moreover, whenever it encountered a nonstandard product, society itself would demand that they "cease and desist."

Of course, Western interest actively created a commotion around the artists. They were surrounded by a great many people from the intelligence services, spies working under diplomatic cover, and journalists. The latter were out for a scoop, while the former considered these circles as a hotbed of protest, easily ignitable tinder. But there was too little tinder. Moreover, many people from this scene consciously stimulated interest in themselves in order to accumulate enough scandalous capital to "run off" to the West. Once they were there, they would quickly lose their "commodity value," simply because they were uninteresting, ungifted, and unwanted. That is, if we aren't talking about big figures like Mikhail Shemyakin [who emigrated to Paris and continued to enjoy artistic success well into the 1980s].

Naturally, the government did not like any of this. Four years after emigrating, Shemyakin decided to present some of his paintings to the Tretyakov Gallery as a gift. He sent them in 1977, but the Ministry of Culture declared: "We will not accept any gifts from Shemyakin." It was then in May 1977 that an exhibition was held in the apartment of Aida Chmelyova on the first floor of a building on Rozhdestvensky Boulevard. She and her husband Volodya Sychev invited diplomats and other guests, deciding that since the apartment belonged to them, they could do as they pleased. That's how it is now: "my home is my castle." But back then, the First Secretary of the Moscow City Committee of the Communist Party, Viktor Grishin said that there would be no exhibitions of Shemyakin in Moscow. This was enforced in the simplest way: we put a militiaman on guard in front of the apartment door. On the other side of the boulevard, in a space formerly belonging to communal services, our guys sat watching hockey and talking to the militiaman on a walkie-talkie. His task was to not let anyone into the house from six am till midnight. Today, this would be outrageous, but then, it was nothing out of the ordinary. The militia guard stood there for quite a while, the inhabitants could enter and leave, but guests weren't allowed in. There were constant scandals because crafty guests would try to gain entry or to distract the militiaman. It was a strange and crazy time. The situation in the country was reminiscent of a wound-up spring that had exploded in 1985—which is when Shemyakin's monument to Peter the Great popped up in Petersburg, or the square on Bolotnaya Square, and so on. Essentially, as negatively as we now look upon that time, it marked and crystallized artistic potential that could be realized later on. There were awkward stories like, for example, the famous work *Moscow-Petushki* by Venedikt Yerofeyev, found to be slanderous by nineteen Soviet courts. But here's what's interesting: nobody went out to look for the author! This means that a person who spread "slanderous" literature could be charged, but nobody went out to arrest an actual author. Because they didn't assume he or she would work under his or her actual name. Venechka himself was half-homeless, they didn't know where he lived, and didn't look for him, the book's author was considered a phantom. Readers could get in trouble, but not writers. As Venechka Yerofeyev, he became a public figure only after 1985.

As for today, well, in theory, we would have come down hard on Marat Gel'man[2] for many things: dubious exhibitions bordering on public provocations, cynicism, and artistic hooliganism. Of course, we would have prevented it. His exhibitions with the icons would not have opened by definition. I don't know whether they got rid of those wooden men in Perm, but our society doesn't accept things like that. They say that it would be better to give the money spent on art to war veterans. Of course, that's totally stupid. We've already given everybody something, and nobody has created anything. But the fact is when we talk about the tolerance exhibited by the current order, you have to understand that it barely conceals utter indifference. There used to be writers read only by the KGB. If you publish them today, nobody will read them, because they aren't very interesting in themselves. Still, all these people whined about how they couldn't get published, how the KGB pressured them. In fact, if the KGB put them under pressure, it was for the conscious provocations of the West and because they themselves wanted to gain scandalous attention without possessing any talent at all. People would draw general conclusions from particular cases and that was most irritating of all. Today, we have tolerance, and many figures have disappeared, people don't know their names. All the works kept in drawers in the 1960s and 70s have been published now, but they haven't found any popular resonance. It's the same with artists, only more complicated.

Recorded by Alya Tesis

Translated from Russian by David Riff
Alexander Mikhaylov, "Nikakikh resheniye pro tsenzure KGB ne prinimal", *Iskusstvo* 2 (585), 2013.

Endnotes

1 Translator's note: *North-East* was the title of the musical, which was performed in Moscow's Dubrovka Theatre and occupied by terrorists on October 23, 2002. Forty to fifty armed people entered the theater, took eight hundred and fifty people, while demanding the withdrawal of Russian troops from Chechnya. After the two-and-a-half-day hostage-taking, special units of the Russian domestic secret service FSB pumped an unknown chemical into the theater's ventilation system and stormed the building minutes later. The stunned terrorists were killed on the spot by the special units by shots to the head. 130 hostages died, 5 by the hostage-takers, 125 due to inadequate medical treatment as a result of the use of gas.

2 Translator's note: This refers to the well-known gallery owner and curator Marat Gel'man, whose Moscow gallery exhibited many important contemporary artists, especially in the 1990s. From 2008 to June 2013, Gel'man was the director of the Museum of Contemporary Art in the city of Perm (МУЗЕЙ СОВРЕМЕННОГО ИСКУССТВА ПЕРМЬ). After some politically controversial exhibitions, Gel'man was dismissed as the director of the museum in June of 2013.

Summary Report and Measure Plan in the Operative Case File "Schwitters"

BM (PR Hungary)

After three different informants submitted separate reports on the first happening in June 1966, Operation "Schwitters" was opened. The code name itself is already revealing: the Dadaist Kurt Schwitters was falsely specified by Stasi informants as the inventor of the happening—and so Szentjóby was also called by this name in the files. On the basis of this "Summary Report" from 1968, we can follow the "paths" of the individual reports within the state security apparatus. The first three informant reports are already cited in this report; they are one of the causes of the dramatic expansion of persecution of the happening scene and specifically of Tamás Szentjóby. Almost no other measure plan so clearly formulates the consequences: if Szentjóby continues to create happenings, then he will be admitted to a psychiatric hospital. (K)

BM. III. Departmental Directorate
III. Dept. Dir. 2/b sub-department

Strictly confidential!

Subject: "Schwitters"

Summary Report and Measure Plan

June 25, 1966 in Budapest, the first happening in Hungary was held. The word happening means an event, something that happens. The movement developed in the 20s and 30s of the twentieth century, and can be traced back to futurist and Dadaist endeavors in fine arts and literature. Its leading figures were: the Italian Marinetti, the French [*sic*] Salvador Dali, and the German Schwitters. For the latter, every object, from the tram ticket via cut-outs and discarded postcards to bent nails and rotting pieces of wood, every type of refuse from big-city life could be used, and indeed had documentary value as constituent parts of his art. Schwitters even saw useable, expressive tools and symbols in rubbish.

The happening was brought from Europe to America by László Moholy [*sic*] (the architect of Hungarian origin). One of its best-known representatives there is Robert Rauschenberg the founder of New York's Garbage Heap Junk Theatre. Today in America there are many kinds of happenings: purely artistic, musical, and theatrical–in Hungary, the last type has ended up being performed. The happening therefore is a theatre play which has no prewritten script. The performer does whatever comes to their mind during the performance; that is to say, they improvise. The aim is to compel the audience to similar active deeds.

The American Alan [*sic*] Ginsbert [*sic*] defined the aim of the happening as: "... subjugation by the logic of a confused world, in other words when participants give up their illusory rights, which they believe can influence chance, and admit the fact of their absolute defenselessness right up until their own physical destruction." Regarding the philosophical side of the happening, it promotes nihilism, darkness and irrationalism, the denial of the healthy person's activity. Their religion is violence and hysteria. Its practical realization serves to confuse the citizen and to enforce an exaggerated decadence.

The American variety, in its final phase, led to a deluge of violent acts, mass enjoyment of narcotics and open clashes with the police.

55.

BM. III. Főcsoportfőnökség.
III. Csfség.2/b alosztálya.

Szigorúan titkos!

Tárgy: "Schwitters" fn. jelzésben

ÖSSZEFOGLALÓ JELENTÉS ÉS INTÉZKEDÉSI TERV.

1966. junius 25-én Budapesten megtartották az első magyarországi happeninget. A happening szó eseményt, történést jelent. A mozgalom a XX. szd. 20-as 30-as éveiben fejlődött ki, s a képzőművészetből és irodalomból ismert futurista és dadaista kezdeményezésekre vezethető vissza. Vezéralakjai voltak: az olasz Marinetti, a francia Salvador Dali és a német Schwitters. A utóbbi számára minden tárgy, a villamosjegytől kezdve az eldobott kéeslap kivágásokon át a görbe szegekig, a korhadt fadarabokig, a nagyvárosi élet mindenféle hulladéka, hasznavehető, sőt dokumentális értékkel biró alkotórésze volt művészetének. Schwitters még a szemétben is felhasználható, kifejezhető eszközt, szimbolumot látott.

A happeninget Európából Moholy László /magyar származású építész/ vitte át Amerikába. Ott egyik legismertebb képviselője Robert Rauschenberg, a New York-i Szemétdombi Limlomok Szinházának megalapítója. Amerikában ma többféle happening van: tisztán képzőművészeti, zenei, s elszinházisodott - Magyarországon az utóbbi került bemutatásra. A happening tehát olyan szinjáték, amelynek nincs előre megirt szövegkönyve. Az előadó azt csinálja, ami éppen eszébe jut az előadás közben, vagyis rögtönöz. Célja, hogy a közönséget hasonló aktiv cselekvésre késztesse.

Az amerikai Alan Ginsbert igy határozza meg a happening célját: ". . . . a zavaros világ logikájának való alávetettség, vagyis a résztvevők lemondanak arról az illuzórikus jogukról, hogy a véletlen felett befolyást gyakoroljanak és beismerik tökéletes kiszolgáltatottságuk tényét egész a fizikai megsemmisülésig".

A happening filozófiai oldalát tekintve a nihilizmus, a sötétség, az irracionalizmus hirdetése, az egészséges emberi tevékenység tagadása. Vallásuk az erőszak és a hisztéria. Gyakorlati megvalósulása a polgár elképesztésére, a tulhajtott dekadencia érvényesi-

ÁBTL -3.1.9. - V - 156455 /127

Among the socialist countries, the happening spread most widely in Poland, where it also received wide press coverage.

The happening in the West is a gesture of "shocking the bourgeois" and may be called an antiboredom pastime. In Hungary, it is a rejection of active constructive activity, as such it can be assessed as an activity suitable for the politics of loosening, e.g. the *Press Review* edited in Hamburg – which published original articles by German journalists and is regularly sent from the BRD with imperialist aims to our universities, [and] published an article on the first page of its February 1968 edition entitled the "Forerunner of the Happening."

According to the information that has come into our possession, happening performances have so far been organized in Budapest at the following places:

The first was held on June 25, 1966, with a 4pm start in Budapest, I. district, Hegyalja Street 20/b, in the basement of István Szenes. Previously, they had wanted to hold it in the apartment of /blackened/ (the editor of /blackened/), who supported the initiative, however after certain inquiries, out of caution, he did not give permission.

The organizers of the first performance were: Gábor Altorjay /blackened/ college student and Tamás Szentjóby /blackened/ apartments.

The literature originated from Béla Arany, who works at the Culture Foreign Trade Company. This is where he found a foreign book in which the happening is described and illustrated with photographs.

Almost 150 invites were sent out for the performance, yet only 50 – 60 people attended. Printing of the invites was organized by the aforementioned Károly Doromby. The list of invitees was compiled by Szentjóby and Altorjay. The bulk of the invitees were graduate intellectuals, including poets, writers, journalists, painters, engineers, etc. Most of them came from Pál Petrigalla and Dr.László Végh's circle of friends from various artist circles and clubs, and from Gábor Altorjay and Tamás Szentjóby downtown acquaintances.

A 10-forint entrance fee was collected from each participant. When a sign was given, the viewers retreated into the garden where, in front of the entrance to a Tatar-era basement, Szentjóby was buried up to his waist, half naked, with a green lampshade on his head, typing onto newspaper. The typewriter was tied with string to a cattail, which reached a paint-stained pot. Behind was a child's pushchair covered with petrol and set on fire. Some of the wooden steps leading down to the basement had been removed, there was no lighting, this is how the viewers entered. Downstairs in the dark, Stockhausen's electronic musical piece Victory suddenly came on.

The first two movements were played, the first of which is an audio recording of the sounds of an air raid, mixed with snatches of incoherent French-language dialogue of the people assembled in the air-raid shelter, and who are buried underneath the earth.

After the lights come on, a kitchen table could be seen in the background, next to which two people were sitting, and the third person behind them was busy with a hen attached to a red pot. The two people seated at the table started eating. While eating, they occasionally belched loudly, which was amplified for the room with the help of a microphone and loudspeaker. At the end of lunch, they brought out a large nylon bag, into which one actor vomited the lunch back up.

After this, they took out a black handbag from a tatty icebox and gave it to the audience. It contained white mice. Then they brought out a hammer and broke the plates, the table, and the chairs. The third actor was tied to the door frame, then they mixed lime and water on a plate and poured it over his fastened clothing, before smearing him with a tube of toothpaste, and threw the feathers from a torn-up eiderdown over him, then distributed the other half of the feathers among the audience. After this, they filled a rubber prophylactic with some red sticky material, hung it up, and lit a candle beneath it. They switched on the cassette recorder and played distorted music. Then one of the actors tied up the whole room with string like a spider's web, returned to the middle, and attacked the lightbulb with a thermos. Meanwhile, someone blocked off the basement entrance, making it difficult to leave.

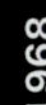

- 2 -

tésére szolgál. Amerikai válfaja végső stádiumában erőszakos cselekedetek özönéhez, tömeges kábítószer élvezethez, a rendőrséggel való nyilt megütközésekhez vezetett.

A happening a szocialista országok közül Lengyelországban terjedt el szélesebb méretekben és ott nagy sajtónyilvánosságot is kapott.

A happening nyugaton "polgárbotránkoztató" gesztus, unalomüző kedvtelésnek nevezhető. Magyarországon az aktiv konstruktiv tevékenységtől való elfordulás, mint ilyen a fellazitás politikájában beillő tevékenységként értékelhető. Pl. a Hamburgban szerkesztett "Sajtószemle" - amely német ujságokból eredeti cikkeket jelentetett meg és az NSZK-ból imperialista célzattal rendszeresen küldik egyetemeink cimeire, 1968. februári számában az első oldalon cikket közölt a "Happening előfutára" cimmel.

A birtokunkba jutott adatok szerint eddig Budapesten az alábbi helyeken rendeztek happening bemutatókat:

In response to the events, Dr.Végh stated he would organize an antihappening, because he didn't like it when someone systematized anarchy. Many of the audience liked it, while others reacted very cautiously. In general, audience members said that they liked the performance, they were scared of offering an opposing opinion in case they were regarded as conservative.

László Kamondy wrote an article with the title "Lunch in memoriam Batu Khan. Meditation on the first happening in Hungary" in the September 13, 1966 issue of Tükör weekly, which was published with photos of the performance taken by Gyula Zaránd. As well as this, the Esti Hírlap and the Népszabadság also published short articles on the performance.

2. The second happening event was initiated and directed by Gábor Altorjai [sic] under the title "Golden Sunday" on December 27, 1967. Rubin Szilárd offered the use of his apartment /blackened/ for the performance, however, when he learned that around 100 people would be invited, he withdrew. The event was held in Miklós Erdélyi's [sic] coal cellar. Altorjai [sic] sent invitations to 50 people, but only 15 people attended.

3. At the University Stage, there were 2 happening events as part of the "Horizon" program. This program is conceived and organized by the journalist György Horváth, and Péter Vágó also took part in the process.

The first happening performance at the University Stage was held by Tamás Szentjóby and György Lendvai on January 18, 1968. Before the performance, a talk was given, entitled "The impact of Zen Buddhism on American literature," then György Horváth gave an introduction, in which he explained the concept of the happening and read out relevant selected passages from Polish journalists.

4. On February 20, 1968 at the Travelers' Rest (Utasellátó) club on Arany János Street in Budapest, V. district, a pop-art evening was organized by István Poór under the title "Hidden parameters." During the show, Miklós Erdélyi [sic] (one of the ideological founders and enthusiastic organizers of happening performances in Hungary) gave a talk about happenings. This was followed by an improvised happening performance by Tamás Szentjóby.

According to the network report, on the evening of March 27, 1968, István Poór, Miklós Erdélyi [sic] and Tamás Szentjóby held a discussion at the Carpathia, where they considered the idea of organizing a larger happening performance.

They agreed that the performance organizer and host of the show would be István Poór. Miklós Erdélyi [sic] will give the ideological basis, if required, and provide the show's organizers with the latest foreign literature. Tamás Szentjóby will take care of the show's harmonic and artistic realization. They plan their next discussion for April 6, 1968, where they will try to agree further details of the show. Poór mentioned that the greatest problem was securing a location, at present.

/The next one and a half rows are black/

During the conversation, István Poór also mentioned that the police had recently been paying lots of attention to the word happening, and performances. The police are allergic to happenings, immediately flying into a rage upon hearing the word, and they will do everything they can to prevent performances. This is why the use of the word happening should be avoided when promoting performances in the future, instead they should use op-part, or pop-art, or similar words.

Measure Plan:

In light of the above, it can be established that the spread of happenings is harmful to young people's intellectual and political development, it is antiprogress, and a phenomenon that promotes imperialist circles' politics of loosening.

- In the interests of reducing the harmful impact on youth, the further spread of happenings must be prevented.
- The most important organizers of happenings in Hungary, and any of their potential foreign contacts, must be placed under control.
- Via open administrative and operative measures decomposition measures must be taken among the main organizers.
- Public appearances by the happening organizers must be prevented, it must be made impossible for them to use public forums to promote and popularize happenings.

In order to carry out the tasks listed above, the following concrete measure

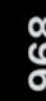

60

I n t é z k e d é s i   t e r v :

A fentiek alapján megállapitható, hogy a happening elterjedése az ifjuság eszmei, politikai fejlődésére káros, haladásellenes, az imperialista körök fellazitási politikáját elősegitő jelenség.

- Annak érdekében, hogy az ifjuságra kiterjedt káros hatását csökkentsük, meg kell akadályozni a happening továbbterjedését.

- Ellenőrzés alá kell vonni a happening legfontosabb hazai szervezőit és az esetlegesen felmerülő külföldi kapcsolataikat.

- Nyilt adminisztrativ, valamint operativ intézkedések utján bomlasztást kell végrehajtani a főbb szervezők körében.

- Meg kell akadályozni a happening szervezők nyilvános szereplését, lehetetlenné kell tenni, hogy nyilvános fórumokat felhasználhassanak a happening terjesztésére és népszerüsitésére.

A felsorolt általános feladatok megvalósitásához az alábbi konkrét intézkedések me tételét

1k

a r e r e c o m m e n d e d:

1./ According to an earlier conversation with the leader of the University Stage (the director Zoltán Rózsa), he too condemns the happenings, and in his opinion, there is no place for them at the University Stage. The director Zoltán Rózsa must be contacted again and influenced to also put his theoretical standpoint into practice.

Deadline: [*June 1, 1968*]
Responsible: /whitened/

- Informing the departmental KISZ and Party leadership of ELTE BTK with a view to prevention.

Deadline: [*June 1, 1968*]
Responsible: /whitened/

- Informing the ELTE KISZ VB and the leadership of the Eötvös Club so that they deny permission to happening performances.

Deadline: May 30, 1968
Responsible: First Lt. Mihály Balogh

2. / Signal to the Culture Ministry and the Metropolitan Council Cultural Affairs departments with the agreement of the III/III/4 department that they should not issue permits for "happening" performances.

Responsible: [illegible] /whitened/
Deadline: May 30, 1968

3./ Signal to the II. Dept. Directorate that, in the event they receive a request for a "happening performance," they deny its endorsement.

Deadline: May 30, 1968
Responsible: /whitened/

4./ A measure plan to be taken must be worked out to decompose the happening movement from within. According to our knowledge to date, the conflict of ideological principles on the question of happenings between Tibor Frankl and *Tamás Szentjóby* could easily be exploited to this end. Together with the III/III/4-a. sub-department we will organize the direction and coordination of those networked individuals who are in contact with the happening organizers.

Deadline:
Responsible: [illegible date]

5./ The known individuals must be monitored at the passport department. They must be placed under "K" surveillance.

Deadline: *Ltn.*
Responsible: *May 30, 1968*

61.

- 7 -

j a v a s o l j u k :

1./ Az Egyetemi Szinpad vezetőjével /Rózsa Zoltán igazgatóval/ történt korábbi beszélgetés szerint, ő is elitéli a happeninget, véleménye alapján ennek nincs helye az Egyetemi Szinpadon.
Ujból fel kell keresni Rózsa Zoltán igazgatót és oda kell hatni, hogy elvi álláspontját a gyakorlatbanis érvényesitse.

Határidő :
Felelős :

- Az ELTE BTK. kari KISZ és pártvezetőség hasonló tájékoztatása preventiv céllal.

Határidő :
Felelős :

- Az ELTE KISz VB és az Eötvös Klub vezetőség tájékoztatása annak érdekében, hogy a klubban ne engedélyezzék happening bemutató megtartását.

Határidő : 1968. május 30.
Felelős : Balogh Mihály fhdgy.

2./ Szignalizálni a Müvelődésügyi Minisztérium és a Fővárosi Tanács Müvelődésügyi osztályához a III/III/4. osztállyal egyetértésben, hogy a "happening" bemutatókra ne adjanak ki engedélyt.

Felelős :
Határidő : 1968. V. 30.

3./ Szignalizálni a II. Főcsfség. felé, amennyiben "happening bemutatóra kérelem érkezik hozzájuk, tagadják meg a láttamozást.

Határidő : 1968. V. 30.
Felelős :

4./ Intézkedési tervet kell kidolgozni a happening mozgalmon belüli bomlasztásra. Eddigi ismereteink szerint ilyen célra jól felhasználható a Frankl Tibor és [anonymized] meglévő elvi ellentét a happening kérdésében. A happening szervezőkkel kapcsolatban lévő hálózati személyek foglalkoztatásának központi irányitását, illetve összehangolását szervezzük meg a III/III/4-a. alosztállyal közösen.

Határidő :
Felelős :

5./ Az ismert személyeket figyelőztetni kell az utlevél osztályon. "K" ellenőrzés alá kell vonni őket.

Határidő :
Felelős :

ÁBTL -3.1.9. - V - 156455 /133

12.

6./ The main leaders of the happenings must be warned to desist from their planned performances in the future. *Special attention must be paid to Tamás Szentjóby, who is the most active in this field. Szentjóby's attention must be drawn to the fact that if he is not willing to desist from organizing happening performances in the future, then we will recommend that he be treated in a closed psychiatric institution.*

Deadline: June 30, 1968
Responsible: BRFK. Pol. Div. III. sub.

7./ The possibility of legally transferring Szentjóby to a psychiatric institution must be examined, and if justified, measures must be taken to remove him from circulation in this way

Deadline: ongoing
Responsible: BRFK. *Pol. Div.* III. *sub.*

8./ Agent named "László" to travel to Czechoslovakia and Poland to liquidate the illegal channels of happenings.

Deadline: May 15, 1968
Responsible: Cpt. Ferenc Tipold.

9./ We are aware that so far, the networked individuals named below have provided reports related to happenings, and have contacts to the happening organizers, via whom the network surveillance can be solved.

a./ Inf. named "Mészáros" provided a detailed report on the first performance and can potentially gather intelligence on the happenings' main organizers. He may be put to use for further surveillance.

Deadline: ongoing
Responsible: First Lt. János Krimmel

b./ Agent named "László" has provided a number of reports on happenings. He has the best potential to gather intelligence on the main organizers.

Deadline: ongoing
Responsible: Cpt. Ferenc Tipold

c./ Agent named "Hajdu" was among those invited to the first performance, and has certain potential to gather intelligence gathering on the happening organizers.

Deadline: ongoing
Responsible: Pol. Lt.-Col. Jenő Frigyik III/III/1-b.

d./ Inf. named "Tibor Kurucz" has the potential to acquire information via István Poór on the latest happening organizational plans.

Deadline: ongoing
Responsible: Pol. First Lt. Ferenc Bándi

62

6./ A happening főbb szervezőit figyelmeztetni kell annak érdekében, hogy a jövőben tervezett bemutatóktól álljanak el.

Határidő : 1968. VI. 30.
Felelős : BRFK. Pol. Oszt. III. alo.

7./

8./ "László" fn. ügynök Csehszlovákiába és Lengyelországba utaztatása a happening illegális csatornáinak felszámolására.

Határidő : 1968. V. 15.
Felelős : Tipold Ferenc szds.

9./ Tudomásunk szerint eddig a happeninggel kapcsolatosan az alábbi hálózati személyek hoztak jelentéseket, akik a happening szervezői felé kapcsolatokkal rendelkeznek, s akiken keresztül a hálózati ellenőrzés megoldható.

a./ "Mészáros" fn. inf. részletes jelentést hozott az első bemutatóval kapcsolatosan, s hírszerzési lehetőséggel rendelkezik a happening főbb szervezői felé. Ellenőrzésre továbbra is felhasználható.

Határidő : folyamatos
Felelős : Krimmel János fhdgy.

b./ "László" fn. ügynök több jelentést hozott a happening bemutatókkal kapcsolatban. A legjobb hírszerzési lehetősége van a főbb szervezők felé.

Határidő : folyamatos
Felelős : Tipold Ferenc szds.

c./ "Hajdu" fn. ü. aki az első bemutató meghívottai között volt, bizonyos hírszerzési lehetőségekkel rendelkezik a happening szervezői felé.

Határidő : folyamatos
Felelős : Frigyik Jenő r. alez. III/III/1-b.

d./ "Kurucz Tibor" fn. inf.-nak Poór Istvánon keresztül lehetősége van tudomást szerezni a legujabb happening szervezési tervekről.

Határidő : folyamatos
Felelős : Bándi Ferenc r. fhdgy.

ÁBTL -3.1.9. - V - 156455 /134

e./ Inf. named "György Fung" has provided a report on the recent organization of happening performances and can potentially report on happenings via István Poór.

Deadline: ongoing
Responsible: First Lt. Mihály Balogh

f./ Agent named "Bárány" provided a report on Sándor Sztaskó Török (Czechoslovak citizen) and his contacts to the happening organizers and has intelligence-gathering potential in this area.

Deadline: ongoing
Responsible: Cpt. Imre Seres
BRFK Pol. D. III/1-b. s.

10./ The development of a new measure plan based on existing operative measures, incoming network reports, and analysis of information acquired through other means.

Deadline: September 30, 1968
Responsible: BRFK. Pol. D. III. s.

Note:

The BM. Central Divisions contacts must be advised that if we learn of a report concerning happenings, the relevant subdivision must be informed promptly.

B u d a p e s t, May 11, 1968

Magdolna Földváry
(Magdolna Földváry Pol. Lt.)

Mihály Balogh
(Mihály Balogh Pol. Lt.)

No. Copies: 3
To: [illegible]
No.: 2-7-978

63

- 9 -

e./ "Fung György" fn. inf. jelentést adott a legujabb happening bemutató szervezésékről, kinek Poór Istvánon keresztül lehetősége van a happeningről jelenteni.

Határidő : folyamatos
Felelős : Balogh Mihály fhdgy.

f./ "Bárány" fn. ü. Sztaskó Török Sándorról /csehszlovák állampolgár/ és annak a happenin szervezőkkel való kapcsolatáról hozott jelentést, ezek irányában rendelkezik hirszerzési lehetőségekkel.

Határidő : folyamatos
Felelős : Seres Imre szds.
BRFK. Pol.O. III/b. alo.

10./ A megtett operativ intézkedések a beérkező hálózati jelentések és az egyéb uton szerzett adatok elemzése alapján ujabb intézkedési terv kidolgozása.

Határidő : 196.. szeptember 30.
Felelős : BRFK. Pol.O. III. alo.

Megjegyzés:

Fel kell hivni a BM. Közp-onti Osztályok tájékoztatóinak figyelmét, ha a happeninggel kapcsolatos jelentés jut a tudomásunkra, rövid uton tájékoztassák az üggyel foglalkozó illetékes alosztályt.

B u d a p e s t , 1968. május hó 11.

Földváry Magdolna

/: Földváry Magdolna r. fhdgy. :/

Balogh Mihály

/: Balogh Mihály r. fhdgy. :/

Készült: 3 péld.
Kapja : elo.sz.
Nyt.sz.: 2-7-978.
FM/B.

ÁBTL -3.1.9. - V - 156455 /135

Appendix

To the summary report code-named "Schwitters"

According to information received to date, the individuals named below were among those invited to the first happening in Hungary on June 25, 1966, at István Szenes's basement at Hegyalja S. 20/b, Budapest.

1./	Dr.László Végh	Doctor, Composer
2./	Miklós Erdélyi [sic]	Architect
3./	Szilárd Rubin	Writer, Journalist
4./	István Szenes	Interior Designer
5./	Károly Doromby	Journalist
6./	Sándor Molnár	Abstract Painter
7./	János Herskó	Film Director
8./	Sándor Weöres	Poet
9./	János Pilinszky	Poet
10./	Krisztina Pasuth [sic]	Art Historian
11./	Gyula Zaránd	Photo Reporter (magazine c. Tükör)
12./	László Kamondy	Journalist
13./	Csaba Koncz	Photographer
14./	János Kenedy [sic]	
15./	János Streliczky	
16./	Pál Petrigalla	
17./	J. István Ventalin	
18./	László Benke	
19./	Tibor Sörös	
20./	Elemér Zalotai	
21./	Béla Hamvas	
22./	Miklós Szentkuti [sic]	
23./	boy named Ungvári and	
24./	girl named Gladys	

Translated from Hungarian by Gwen Jones

The name of an artist and certain text parts are whitened (redacted) in the ÁBTL-version according to regulations on privacy of the archive. We have included these missing texts from the online version in the translation here in italics. The names of BM employees and certain personal data is blackened in the online version, but can be read partly unredacted in the ÁBTL version of the Report.

Cryptonym "Medium"

SB (Polish People's Republic)

When Orange Alternative began to put on happenings in Wrocław in 1987 and brightening up the city with dwarf graffiti, the Polish state security was alarmed. They began to design an operative case file with the name "Cryptonym 'Medium'" and to observe the individual happenings. They wrote reports, while also taking videos and photos of the happenings. In the measure plan, they determined that the "so-called street happenings" were a "danger for public order and security." The measure plan accordingly planned a "disintegration of the members," the "neutralization of the group's assets," the "prevention and ultimately the elimination of hostile activities," as well as the "documentation of illegal activities." The latter led to the storage of thirty-six photos of the happenings, as well as four videos and numerous reports on the actions. More than anything, they document state security's view of the Orange Alternative, in addition to showing the high participation numbers in the happenings, during which the Orange Alternative always incorporated the militia, police, and state security as additional actors. On the occasion of the happenings, state security also wrote an extensive report on the genre of the happening. (S)

MINISTERSTWO SPRAW WEWNĘTRZNYCH

JAWNE 5
Podstawa prawna — art. 86 ust. 3 ustawy z dnia 22 stycznia 1999 roku o ochronie informacji niejawnych (Dz. U. nr 11 poz. 95 z późn. zm.)
(1)
Wickaj

~~TAJNE~~
spec. znaczenia

SPRAWA
OPERACYJNEGO ROZPRACOWANIA

Tom I

ARCHIWUM
WUSW we Wrocławiu
Nr II-103542

Kryptonim „MEDIUM"

Nr ewidencyjny

ZAREJESTROWANO w WYDZIALE ... WUSW Wrocław
pod Nr 56700
11.05.88 r. podpis

Nr archiwalny	
Kategoria akt	

Zaczęto dnia .... 19.... r.

Zakończono dnia .... 19.... r.

IPN Wr 024/8883

EO-73/78

File cover Cryptonym "Medium"
Source: IPN WR 0 24 8883

1988

-Stamp-
WUSW[1]
State Security Wrocław
Col. Stanisław Biernacki

Wrocław, 06. 13. 1988
SECRET
spec. importance
Nr. of evidence: 56700

R E Q U E S T

For the initiation of an operation
against Cryptonym "Medium":

1. ....
(Name and surname)

....
Born (birth date and location)

....
(place of residence)

....
(occupation, post, company)

2. ....
(Name and surname)

....
Born (birth date and location)

....
(place of residence)

....
(occupation, post, company)

3. ....
(Name and surname)

....
Born (birth date and location)

....
(place of residence)

....
(occupation, post, company)

4. ....
(Name and surname)

....
Born (birth date and location)

....
(place of residence)

....
(occupation, post, company)

- A -

„ZATWIERDZAM"

ZASTĘPCA SZEFA
WOJEWÓDZKIEGO URZĘDU
SPRAW WEWNĘTRZNYCH
ds. Służby Bezpieczeństwa
we Wrocławiu

(podpis i pieczątka)

płk mgr Stanisław Biernacki

Dnia .... 19...... r.

Wrocław, dnia 13.06. 1988 r.

TAJNE
spec. znaczenia

Nr ewidencyjny 56100

WNIOSEK

o wszczęcie sprawy operacyjnego rozpracowania

kryptonim „M E D I U M" przeciwko:

1. .... s.(c.) ....
(nazwisko i imię)

ur. ....
(data i miejsce urodzenia)

....
(miejsce zamieszkania)

....
(zawód, stanowisko, miejsce pracy)

2. .... s.(c.) ....
(nazwisko i imię)

ur. ....
(data i miejsce urodzenia)

....
(miejsce zamieszkania)

....
(zawód, stanowisko, miejsce pracy)

3. .... s.(c.) ....
(nazwisko i imię)

ur. ....
(data i miejsce urodzenia)

....
(miejsce zamieszkania)

....
(zawód, stanowisko, miejsce pracy)

4. .... s.(c.) ....
(nazwisko i imię)

ur. ....
(data i miejsce urodzenia)

....
(miejsce zamieszkania)

....
(zawód, stanowisko, miejsce pracy)

5. .... s.(c.) ....
(nazwisko i imię)

ur. ....
(data i miejsce urodzenia)

....
(miejsce zamieszkania)

....
(zawód, stanowisko, miejsce pracy)

6. .... s.(c.) ....
(nazwisko i imię)

ur. ....
(data i miejsce urodzenia)

....
(miejsce zamieszkania)

....
(zawód, stanowisko, miejsce pracy)

7. .... s.(c.) ....
(nazwisko i imię)

ur. ....
(data i miejsce urodzenia)

....
(miejsce zamieszkania)

....
(zawód, stanowisko, miejsce pracy)

PODSTAWA WSZCZĘCIA SPRAWY w m-cu czerwcu 1987r powstała we Wrocławiu n
formalna grupa występująca pod nazwą "Pomarańczowa Alternatywa", której ak
i sympatyków stanowi głównie młodzież studencka Uniwersytetu Wrocławskieg
i uczniowie szkół średnich Wrocławia. Grupa ta manipulowana przez działac
opozycji politycznej /m.in. J.Pinior, W.Frasyniuk/organizuje tzw. happeni
uliczne stwarzając zagrożenie bezpieczeństwa i porządku publicznego. Pod
rem apolityczności propagowane są treści wrogie naszemu ustrojowi, wyszyd
jące instytucje i struktury państwowe oraz usankcjonowane formy aktywnośc
społecznej. Podczas happeningów młodzież szkolna przechodzi swoiste przes
lenie w ulicznej konfrontacji z organami MO i stanowi potencjalną bazę ka
wą przyszłej opozycji. Z operacyjnego rozpoznania wynika, że nastąpi eska
ja działalności grupy, jak również mogą zostać podjęte próby jej rozszerz
nia na inne środowiska.

CEL ROZPRACOWANIA: -rozpoznanie powiązań aktywu grupy z opozycją polityc
(określić jaki cel zamierza się osiągnąć w tym rozpracowaniu)
i inymi nielegalnymi organizacjami / "WiP", "PPS", "SW",RKW"S" /;

- dezintegracja członków nieformalnego ugrupowania;
- neutralizacja aktywu grupy;
- ograniczenie, a finalnie - przecięcie wrogiej działalności;
- procesowe dokumentowanie działalności niezgodnej z prawem.

kpt. Andrzej Beksa
(stopień, imię i nazwisko funkcjonariusza wnioskującego)

....
(podpis)

ZASTĘPCA NACZELNIKA WYDZIAŁU III WUSW we Wrocławiu
... Niemiec
(podpis i pieczątka przełożonego)

5. ....
(Name and surname)

....
Born (birth date and location)

....
(place of residence)

....
(occupation, post, company)

6. ....
(Name and surname)

....
Born (birth date and location)

....
(place of residence)

....
(occupation, post, company)

7.
(Name and surname)

....
Born (birth date and location)

....
(place of residence)

....
(occupation, post, company)

REASONS FOR INITIATING THE OPERATION: In the month of June 1987, an informal group under the name of "Orange Alternative" was created in Wrocław, whose human assets and sympathizers were mainly constituted by the students of the University of Wrocław and students of High Schools of the city of Wrocław. This group manipulated by political opposition activists (amongst others J. Pinior, W. Frasyniuk) organizes the so-called street happenings, thus creating the danger to the public order and safety. On the pretenses of not being politically connected, hostile messages to our political system are being propagated, the institutions and the structures of the state are ridiculed along with the established forms of social well-being. During happenings, school youth undergoes a sort of training in the street confrontation with MO (Citizens' Militia) units and constitutes the potential human resources of the future opposition. From our operative measures we have learned that the activity of the group has the potential to escalation; attempts at the broadening of its activity upon other social groups may also be undertaken.

THE AIM OF THE MEASURES:
- The determination of the relationship of the group's activism with the political opposition as well as other illegal organizations /"WiP", "PPS", "SW", RKW "S"/;
- Disintegration of members of the nonformal group
- Neutralization of group assets
- Limitation, and finally – putting an end to hostile activity
- Procedural documentation of the illegal activities

cpt. Andrzej Beksa

Translated by Orange Alternative: http://www.orangealternativemuseum.pl/#operation-medium-wroclaw/add_2

Secret
Number 308 (308)
Dated July 1, 1988, time 15:00 hrs
bg – 00290/88

<u>Commandant of the WUSW in Wrocław</u>
The head of the Inspectorate 2 SWUSW in Wrocław
The head of the III division–1 WUSW in Wrocław

In connection to the cryptogram sent by the inspectorate 2 WUSW in Wrocław, in connection to the organization, on the day of the seventh this month, the happening of the "Orange Alternative" amongst the students of the High School in Oleśnica I would like to inform that in the conversation with the Head Director SB (Security Service) initiated the concept which has been aimed at prevention for the organization of a happening. It has been agreed that the person who was responsible for the initiation of the action was the student of the first class Kaduczak Marek. In the morning hours during Classes the director of the High School conveyed a conversation with the aforementioned student within which he proposed that along with the delegation consisting of three students they will go to the headquarters of the RUSW in Oleśnica. About 8:30 the delegation visited the head of the RUSW who was presented with the bouquet of orange flowers.
At the long recess the director of the School organized appeal for the whole school, during which he thanked for the initiative of students aimed at the handing of flowers to the management of the RUSW, which statement caused consternation amongst the gathered youth. In the afternoon no incidents have been noted in connection to the aforementioned alternative. Currently operative measures aimed at the full recognition of the construction of the structures of the "Orange Alternative" are currently being recognized on the premises of the High School in Oleśnica, the results of the will be communicated on the ongoing bases.

The vice-head of the RUSW with regard to the Security Service Affairs in the city of Oleśnica captain T. Indycki.

Coded by Bednarz on the day of July 1, 1988 time, 15:30 hrs
Decoded by _______ Wysota 15:25 hrs

Translated by Orange Alternative:
http://www.orangealternativemuseum.pl/#operation-medium-wroclaw/add_2

-18-

Tow Płk Biernacki

88-10-10

SZYFROGRAM OTRZYMANY z OLEŚNICY 3721

ROZSZYFROWANO 1988 PAŹDZ 07

WOJ. URZĄD SPRAW WEWN. Wpłynęło 1988-10-12 Nr L-0 2617/88

tajne
nr 308 (308)
dnia 1988.01.07 godz 15.00
by -00290/88

szef wusw we wrocławiu
kierownik inspektoratu 2 swusw we wrocławiu
naczelnik wydziału iii- 1 wusw we wrocławiu

nawiązując do szyfrogramu przesłanego przez inspektorat 2 wusw we wrocławiu, dot. zorganizowania w dniu 7(7) bm. akcji ''pomarańczo alternatywy '' sposrod uczniow lo w olesnicy informuję,ze w rozmowie z dyr. lo tut. sb zainicjowała koncepcję mającą na celu nie dopuszczenia do zorganizowania imprezy. ustalono ze inicjatorem akcji był uczen kalasy pierwszej kaduczak marek . w godzinach rannych w trakcie lekcji dyr.lo przeprowadził zw/w rozmowe w ktorej zaproponował iz razem z delegajcją w składzie trzech osob pojdzei do rusw w olesniccy . okolo godz 8.30 delegacja przybyła do szefa ruw ktoremu wręczyła bukiet pomaranczowych kwiatow .
podczas duzej przerwy dyr.lo zorganizował apel całej szkoły ,podczas ktorego podziękował za inicjatywę uczniow wręczenia kwiatow kierownictwu rusw oswiadczenie to wywołało konsternację wsrod zebranej młodziezy . w godzinach popołudniowych nie zanotowano w zwięzku z sytuecją innych incydentow. prowadzone są czynnosci operacyjne zmierzające do pełnego rozpoznania zawięzywania sie na terenie lo w olesnicy struktur ''pomaranczowej alternatywy'' o wynaikach będziemy informowac na biezęco.

z-ca szefa rusw d/s sb w olesnicy kpt t.indycki

zaszyfrował bednarz dnia 1988.01 m.07 godz 15.30
rozsz frował?++vvv wysota godz.15.25

Ko-01138/88

In the location of

Within our operative investigation we come across operatives of the illegal organizations such as PPS, WiP and "Orange Alternative", who often organize protest actions on the premises of the city. The organized happenings are secured and observed in order to be documented with the application of photograph and video equipment. We cooperate with ZOMO as well as with Intelligence Company, who to a limited extent execute prophylactic activities and constitute the proof for the occasion of the necessary intervention of the Militia forces.

It has been stated that during such happenings what takes place are not only political occurrences but also what is committed are offences against general order, amongst others streets are littered with leaflets, banner, and other instruments applied during the aforementioned happenings.

In connection to the above I kindly request for your opinion and decision with regard to the described issue as well as for the provision of guidelines in what cases and what formal and legal means are to be applied and how should be such cases documented.

2 copies were executed
Copy number one - addressee
Copy number two - a/a.
Opr. St.Druk MCh
Nr ks.masz.0242/88

Translated by Orange Alternative:
http://www.orangealternativemuseum.pl/#operation-medium-wroclaw/add_2

17

WOJEWÓDZKI URZĄD
SPRAW WEWNĘTRZNYCH
we Wrocławiu

23 L. dz. I-02650/88

Wrocław 1988-10-14

T A J N E

Egz. nr 2..

NACZELNIK WYDZIAŁU ŚLEDCZEGO
WOJ. URZĘDU SPRAW WEWNĘTRZNYCH

w miejscu

W naszym operacyjnym zainteresowaniu przechodzą działacze nielegalnych organizacji PPS, WiP i "Pomarańczowej Alternatywy", którzy często organizują akcje protestacyjne na terenie miasta. Imprezy są zabezpieczane operacyjnie w celu identyfikowania osób, ich działań oraz są dokumentowane fotograficznie i na taśmie video. Współpracujemy z funkcjonariuszami ZOMO i Kompanii Wywiadowczej, którzy w ograniczonym zakresie prowadzą działania profilaktyczne i stanowią odwód na wypadek koniecznej interwencji sił MO.

Stwierdzono, że podczas takich imprez mają miejsce nie tylko wydarzenia polityczne, a często popełniane są wykroczenia natury porządkowej. Między innymi ulice miasta zaśmiecane są ulotkami oraz transparentami i innymi rekwizytami wykorzystywanymi w czasie trwających imprez.

W związku z powyższym uprzejmie proszę o zajęcie stanowiska w przedmiotowej sprawie i podanie w jakich przypadkach można stosować działania formalno - prawne i jak te przypadki winny być dokumentowane.

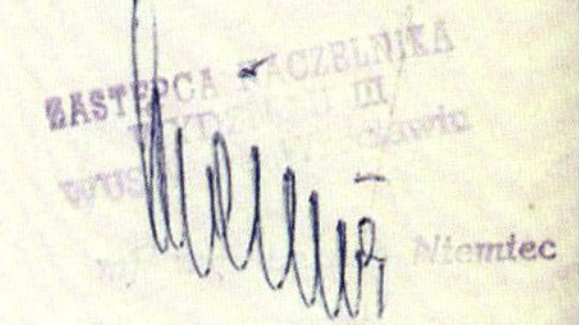

Wyk. 2 egz.
Egz. nr 1 - adresat
Egz. nr 2 - a/a
Opr. St.G druk MCh
nr ks.masz.0242/88

Junior Inspector Piotr Kończak
Intelligence Company
WUSW Wrocław

Wrocław, October 21, 1988

OFFICIAL NOTE

On October 21, 1988 upon the order received from WUSW Wrocław supervisors we went to Świdnicka Street in order to observe the progress of the happening organized by the so-called "Orange Alternative." The happening begun at 4 p.m. in front of "Barbara" bar, were gathered the group of dressed individuals with various accessories i.e. the old washing machine, "round table" toilet seat, deckchairs, "Wrozamet" gas cooker packing boxes with orange bricks painted upon them, which have been used to construct a wall. The mob of about 600 – 700 individuals gathered around, the majority of which were constituted by youth. The organizers played various musical instruments and were painting an orange "clock" next to the "Barbara" bar. About 4:40 p.m. the whole happening marched in the direction of the Old Market Square, where they marched around the square stopping next to the monument of A. Fredro and painting the monument orange. The citizen of Heller, Marcin was arrested in the square, the second year Historical Department student of the University of Warsaw, who with the application of spray paint was painting a phone booth and inside the booth he wrote "997."

mł. insp. Piotr Koniczek
Komp. Wywiad.
WUSW Wrocław

Wrocław 1988-10-21.

NOTATKA SŁUŻBOWA

W dniu 1988-10-21 na polecenie kierownictwa służbowego WUSW Wrocław udaliśmy się na ul. Świdnicką celem prowadzenia obserwacji przebiegu happeningu zorganizowanego przez t.zw. „Pomarańczową Alternatywę". Impreza rozpoczęła się ok. godz. 16⁰⁰, przed barem „Barbara" zebrała się grupa przebierańców z akcesoriami t.j. stara pralka, sedes „okrągły stół", leżaki, kartony po pakowaniu kuchenek gazowych z „Wrozamet" z pomalowaną na nich „bazią", z których uskuteczniali mór. Dookoła zebrali się gapie w sumie ok. 600-700 osób w przeważającej części młodzież. Organizatorzy grali na różnych instrumentach, oraz malowali wszystko przy barze „Barbara" na kolor pomarańczowy. Ok. godz. 16³⁰ całość przemaszerowała w stronę Rynku, obeszli cały Rynek zatrzymując się przy pomniku A. Fredry malując go na pomarańczowo. W Rynku zatrzymano ob. Heller Marcin s. Stefana student II roku Uniwersytetu Warszawskiego Wydział Historyczny który malował farbą w okresie budkę telefoniczną umieścił na niej napis „997".

z Rynku część grupy, ta najaktywniejsza wróciła pod „zegar" na ul. Świdnickiej. Pozostali rozeszli się po bokach. Grupa ta liczyła ok. 70 osób przebywała w tym miejscu do godz. 18^00^, w tym czasie jeden z nich malował ponownie zegar. Gdy grupa ta zmniejszyła się do ok 40 osób i ruszyła w kierunku Pl. Solnego zatrzymano w tej grupie mężczyznę który malował zegar, okazał się nim. Robert Jezierski s. Witold student II roku Uniwersytetu Wrocławskiego Wydział Filologii.

Obydwóch malarzy przekazano wraz z materiałami of. dyż. DUSW Wrocław, które Miasto celem dalszego postępowania.

Notatkę przekazuję kierownictwu służbowemu Komp. Wywiad. WUSW we Wrocławiu

[signature]

The part of the group returned to the area of the "clock" located at Świdnicka Street. The remaining part of the group dispersed. The group which returned was about 70 individuals and remained there until 6 p.m., in the meantime one of the participants continued to paint the clock. When the group decreased to about 40 individuals and started moving in the direction of Solny Square a man from the group was stopped, in the person of Robert Jezierski, the son of Witold, second year Philology Department student of the University of Wrocław. Both arrested individuals, along with their painting accessories were transferred to the on-duty officer of DUSW Wrocław Stare Miasto in order for the further processing,

This note is passed onto the hands of the supervisors of the Intelligence Company WUSW in Wrocław.

/illegible signature/

Translated by Orange Alternative:
http://www.orangealternativemuseum.pl/#operation-medium-wroclaw/add_2

Junior Inspector Piotr Kończak
Junior Inspector Ryszard Grum
Junior Inspector Paweł Rudło
Intelligence Company
WUSW Wrocław

Wrocław, October 21, 1988

OFFICIAL NOTE

On October 21, 1988 about 4:50 p.m. performing professional responsibilities within the region of Świdnicka Street and Market Square in Wrocław during the happening of the so-called "Orange Alternative" we saw a young man who, with the application of the spray paint colour orange was painting on the side window of the telephone booth located in the Square in front of Sukiennice the sign "997".

He was arrested, his ID was checked:

1) HELLER MARCIN, the son of Stefan, and Iwona maiden surname Galicka, October 23, 1968 Warsaw, Warsaw Waryńskiego Street 9/40, the second year Historical Department student of the Warsaw University. Personal ID number DB 2529800, Director WSA UDz. Warsaw Śródmeście.

The aforementioned individual contained spray paint of orange color manufactured in the West.
This note is passed onto the hands of the on-duty officer of DUSW Wrocław Stare Miasto.

/illegible signature/

Translated by Orange Alternative:
http://www.orangealternativemuseum.pl/#operation-medium-wroclaw/add_2

mł. insp. Piotr Konczak
-„- Ryszard Gawin
-„- Paweł Radło
komp. wywiad.
WUSW Wrocław

10

Wrocław 1988-10-21.

DUSW-03
WROCŁAW-ST[ARE] MIASTO

NOTATKA SŁUŻBOWA

W dniu 1988-10-21 od godz. 16[00] pełniąc obowiązki służbowe w rejonie ul. Świdnickiej i Rynek we Wrocławiu podczas trwania happeningu t.zw. „pomarańczowej alternatywy" zauważyliśmy w/n młodego mężczyznę który farbą koloru pomarańczowego w aerozolu malował na bocznej szybie budki telefonicznej usytuowanej w Rynku naprzeciw Sukiennic napis „997".

Zatrzymano go i wylegitymowano. Okazało się że jest to:

1/ HELLER MARCIN
s. Stefan, Ilona z d. Galicka
23. 10. 1968 r. Warszawa
Warszawa ul. Waryńskiego 9/46
student II roku Uniwersytetu ~~Wrocławski~~ Warszawskiego
Wydział Historyczny
DO DB 2529800 wyd. WSA
UDS Warszawa Śródmieście

W/w posiadał przy sobie pojemnik z farbą w aerozolu koloru pomarańczowego produkcji zachodniej.
Notatkę z zatrzymanym przekazuję d. dyż. DUSW Wrocław Stare Miasto.

Junior Inspector Pająkowski Tadeusz
Junior Inspector Drozdowicz Ryszard
Junior Inspector Szubestowicz Ryszard
Intelligence Company
WUSW Wrocław

Wrocław, October 21, 1988

OFFICIAL NOTE

October 21, 1988 while performing professional duties in the Świdnicka Street upon the order issued by the Supervisors we were observing an illegal happening organised by the illegal youth organization the so-called "Orange Alternative." About 5 p.m. an unknown man started to paint the foundations of the clock located in the Street of Świdnicka in Wrocław in front of the "Barbara" bar. This fact was communicated to the Supervisors. The decision with regard to the arrest and identification of the instigator was undertaken. Due to the large group of people present it has been unable to stop and identify the man and then arrest him, in the meantime the man painted the aforementioned foundations with the application of colorful spray paints. After the man got off the ladder an attempt to identify the man was undertaken, but due to the aggressiveness of the mob the attempt was withheld and the observation continued. The aforementioned man was stopped about 6:15 p.m. in the main square in the area of Fredro monument with the application of Militia trained martial arts, next gas thrower was used towards the individuals who attempted to reclaim him. After the transportation of the man to the headquarters of WUSW in Wrocław the aforementioned man was identified as:

Jezierski Robert **ARRESTED**
The son of Wiktor and Jadwiga, maiden surname Kaleczyk,
born on August 12, 1966 in Grudziądz
Wrocław, Racławicka Street 50
Polish Philology student of the University of Wrocław, Student ID 61424

In connection to the above the man's case was directed to the Collegiate Court, with the application of accelerated mode.

ml. szer. Szyszkowski Tadeusz
-II- Drzazdowicz Ryszard
-I- Szubertowicz Ryszard
Kmpt. wydział
WUSW Wrocław

W-W 88-10-21.

11

21.10.88
D.U. WROCŁAW-STARE MIASTO

Notatka urzędowa

W dniu 21-10-1988, pełniąc obowiązki służbowe przy ul. Świdnickiej zgodnie z poleceniem kierownictwa służbowego obserwowaliśmy nielegalną imprezę zorganizowaną przez nielegalne ugrupowanie młodzieżowe tzw. „Pomarańczowa alternatywa". Około godz. 17[20] n/n mężczyzna rozpoczął malowanie postumentu zegara przy ul. Świdnickiej we Wrocławiu przed Barem „Barbara". O fakcie tym powiadomiono kierownictwo służbowe. Została podjęta decyzja o wylegitymowaniu i zatrzymaniu tego osobnika. Ze względu na dużą gromadę ludzi nie można było go wylegitymować a następnie zatrzymać, w tym czasie mężczyzna ten wymalował postument kolorowymi farbami aerozolowymi. Po zejściu z drabiny mężczyznę tego próbowano wylegitymować lecz ze względu na agresywność tłumu odstąpiono i podjęto obserwację. Zatrzymania tego mężczyzny dokonano o godz. 18[15] w Rynku na wysokości pomnika Fredry używając chwytów obezwładniających [illegible] w stosunku do osób próbujących go odbić. Po doprowadzeniu do pomieszczeń służbowych WUSW we Wrocławiu okazał się to:

JEZIERSKI ROBERT
s. Wiktor Jadwiga z d. Kaleczyk
12.08.1966 Grudziądz
Wrocław ul. Radiówka 50
Student Filologii Polskiej
Uniwersytet Wrocławski
Leg. Stud. 61424.

ARESZT „F"

W związku z powyższym na n/n mężczyznę sporządzono wniosek do kolegium ds. wykroczeń w trybie przyspieszonym.

„VERTE"

Którego mam z notatką. informacją i raportem o zatrzymaniu
przekazuję dyr. DUSW Stare Miasto [illegible]

The man, along with this note was passed onto the hands of the on-duty officer of DUSW Wrocław Stare Miasto.

/illegible signature/

Translated by Orange Alternative:
http://www.orangealternativemuseum.pl/#operation-medium-wroclaw/add_2

Wrocław, November 21, 1988
SECRET
Single copy

OFFICIAL NOTE

In connection with the preparation of the members of "Orange Alternative" for the conveyance of the demonstration as of today

October 21, 1988 at about 12:50 p.m. comrade pseudonym "Helper" (Pomocnik) informed at the entrance to "Feniks" Department Store from the direction of Szewska Street in Wrocław 5 young people have gathered the considerable amount of packaging cartons. The portion of the gathered cartons have been laid at the sidewalk next to the entrance to the Department Store; they are guarded by two men. The remaining three men still continue to walk around the Store and gather cartons which later they carry out and lay on the sidewalk.

From the relation of the comrade it turns out that they are the members of "Orange Alternative."

MEASURES:

The information about the undertakings of the members of "Orange Alternative" is to be immediately communicated to comrade Stanisław GAJ the Head of the II Department.

Captain D.Taryma
/illegible signature/

I confirm the fact of receiving the aforementioned report
Captain Stanisław Gaj
10/21/88

Translated by the Orange Alternative

TAJNE:
Egz. pojed.

NOTATKA SŁUŻBOWA

dot. przygotowań członków „Pomarańczowej Alternatywy" do przeprowadzenia demonstracji w dniu dzisiejszym.

Dnia 21.10. br. o godz. 12^{50} t.w. ps. „POMOCNIK" poinformował, że przy wejściu do ŚDH „Feniks" od strony ul. Szewskiej we W-wie 5-ciu młodych mężczyzn zgromadziło znaczną ilość kartonów po opakowaniach.

Część zebranych kartonów zostało ułożonych na chodniku przy wejściu do ŚDH i pilnuje je dwóch mężczyzn. Pozostali trzej chodzą po sklepie i w dalszym ciągu zbierają ze stoisk handlowych kartony, które następnie wynoszą i układają na chodniku.

Z relacji t.w. wynika, że są to uczestnicy tzw. „Pomarańczowej Alternatywy".

PRZEDSIĘWZIĘCIA:

Informację o poczynaniach

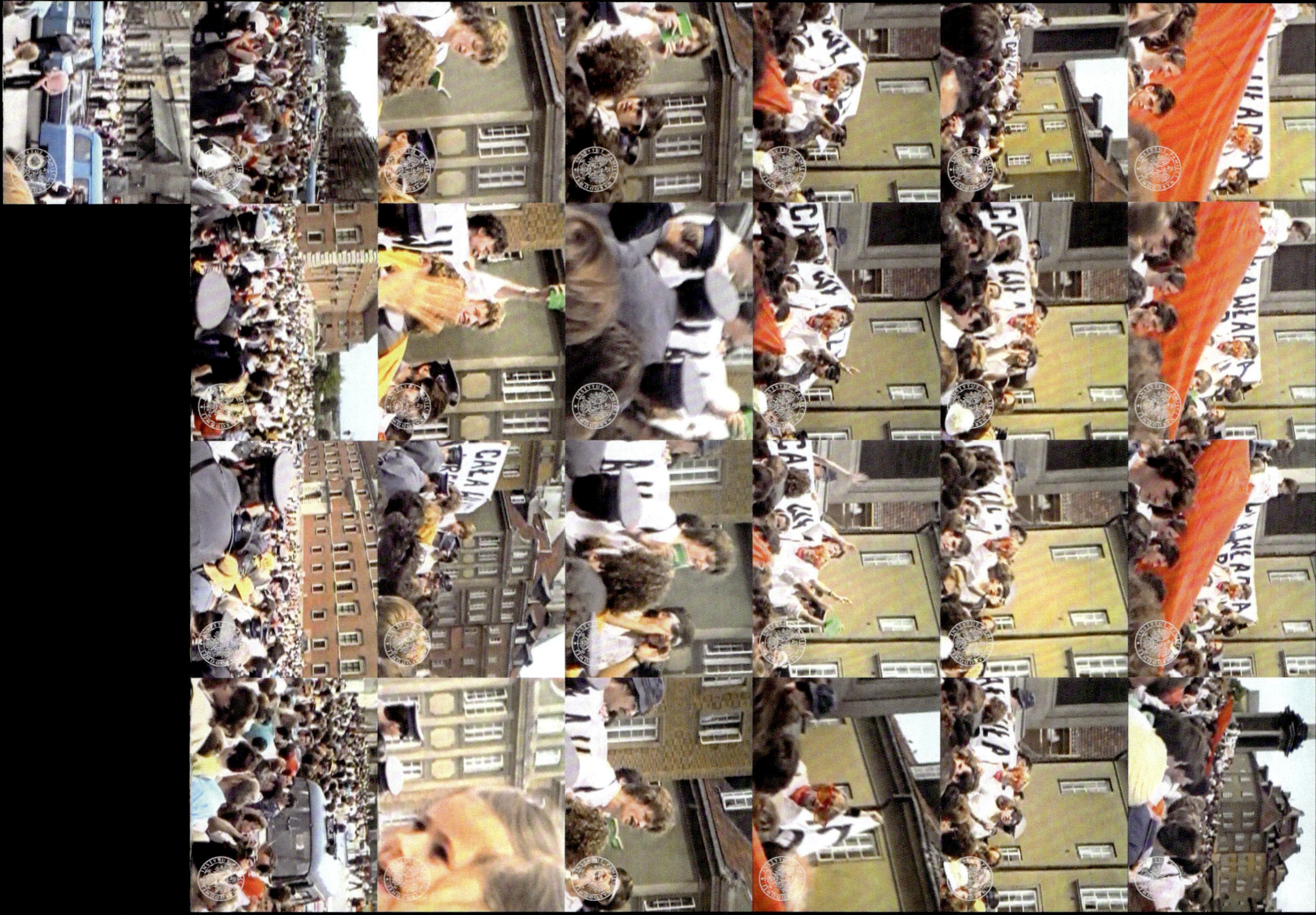

471 SB (Polish People's Republic) Measures and "Decompositions"

Video stills from surveillance video on an Orange Alternative happening by the SB, Source: IPN BU 1196 4 u cz1 C

1988

Happeningi
„Pomarańczowej Alternatywy"
1987 - 1988

UPACY 25.07.87

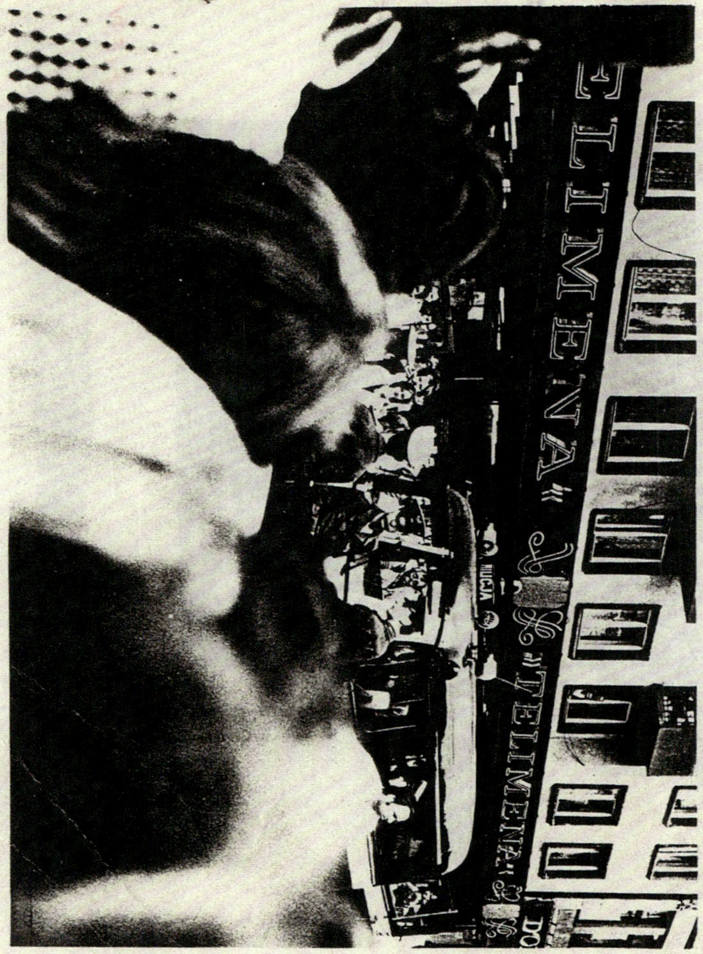

UPACY

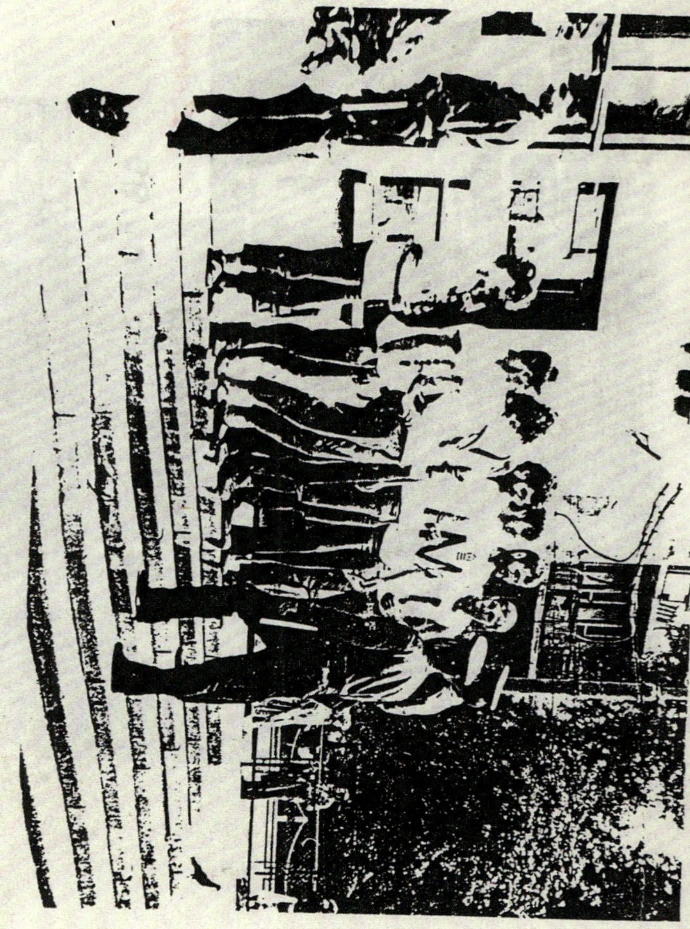

NAF DEMENT

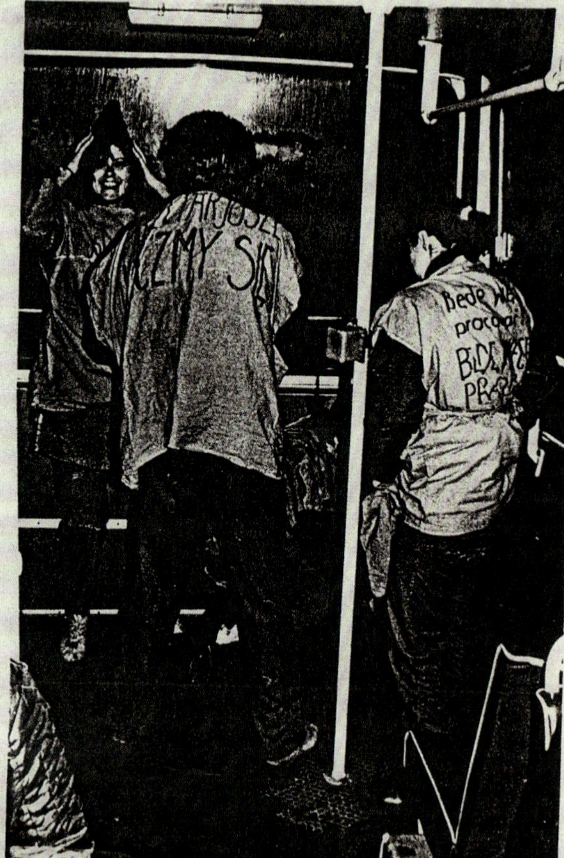

REWOLUCJA 7.11.87

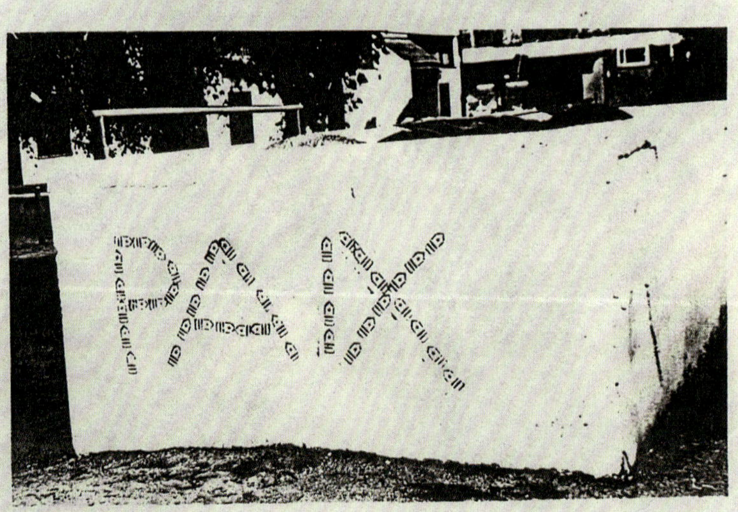

~~Jer~~ Graffiti październik 87

KALAKIOR

NAF DEMENTI

KALAFIOR

~~NAF DEMENTI~~

NAF DEMENTI

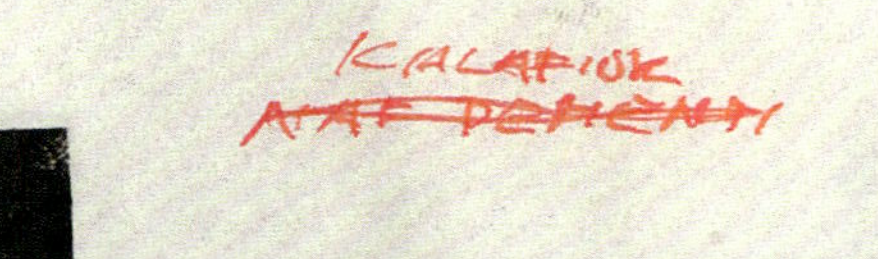

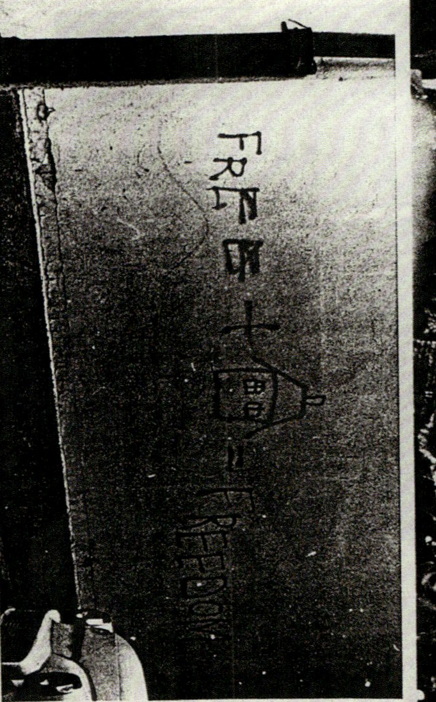

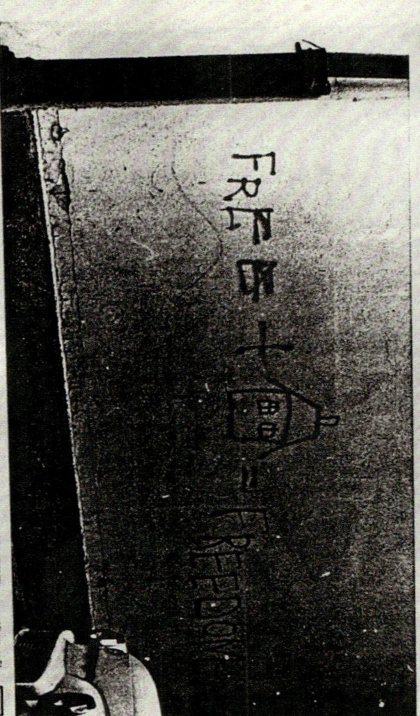

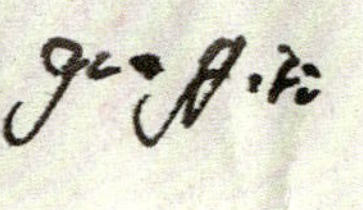

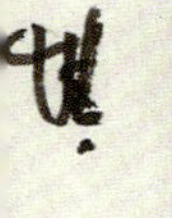

Dzień LWP
12. 10. 87

graffiti

KRASNOLUDKI
1. 06. 87

SB (Polish People's Measures and Fourteen photocopied photographs from a dossier "Happeningi Pomeranczowy

DZIEŃ MILICJANTA

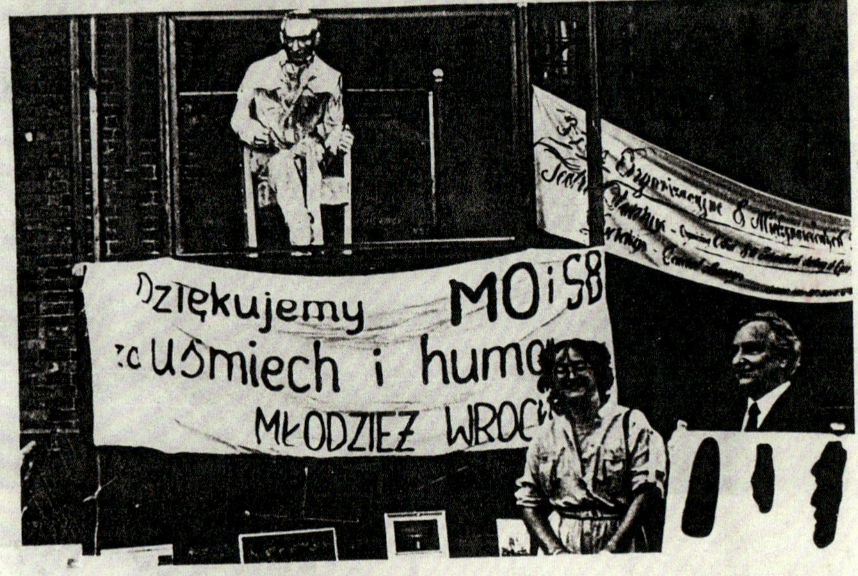

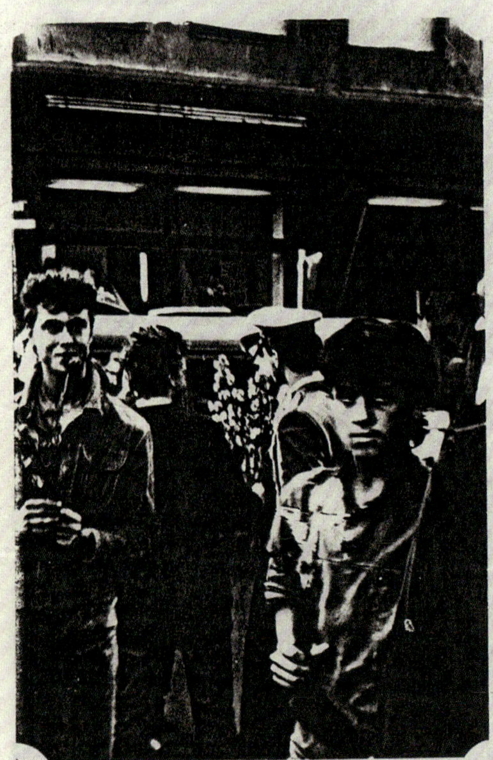

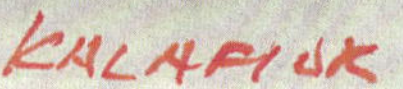

KALAFIOR

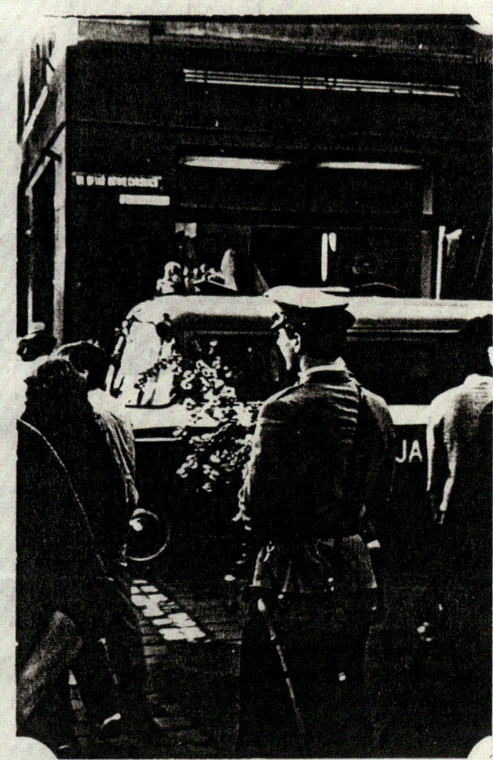

KALAFIOR

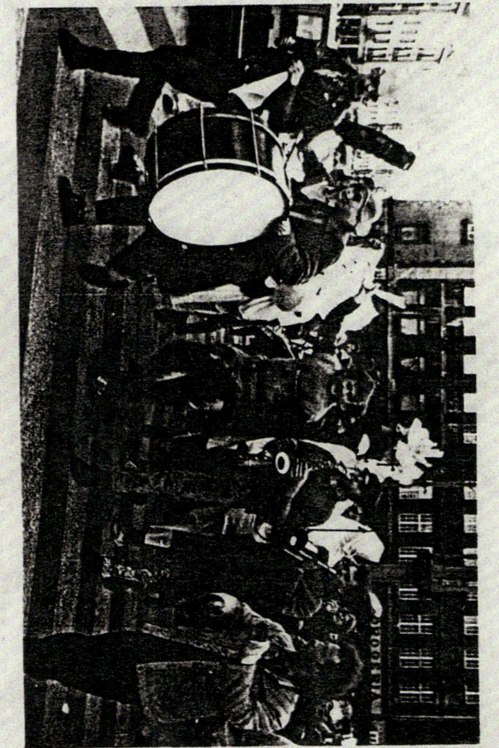

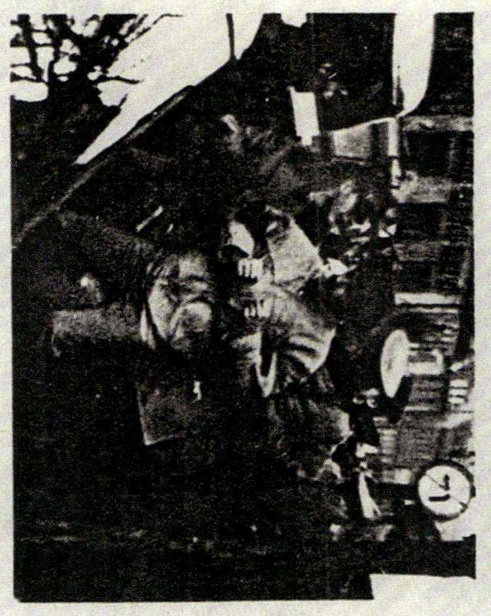

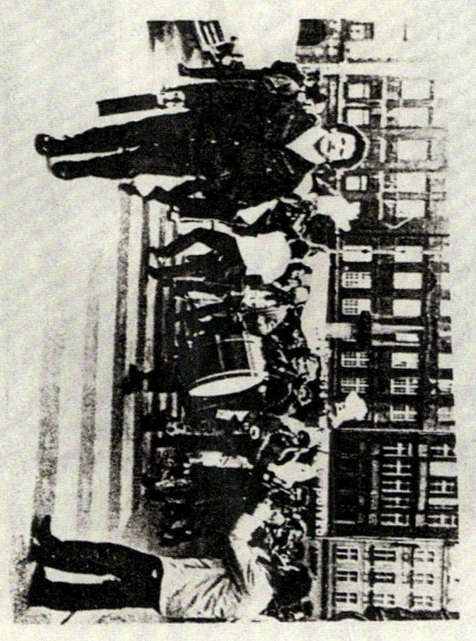

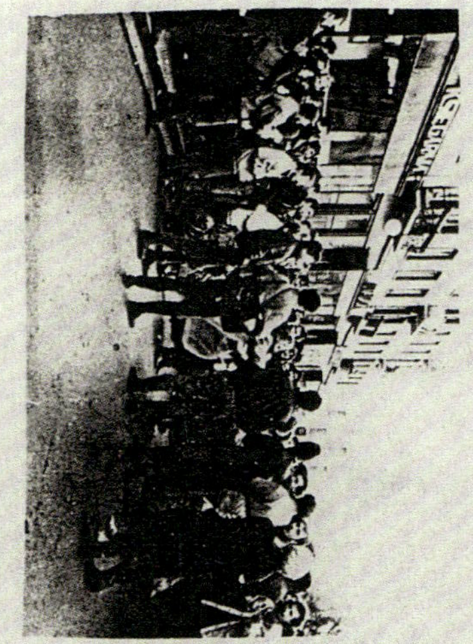

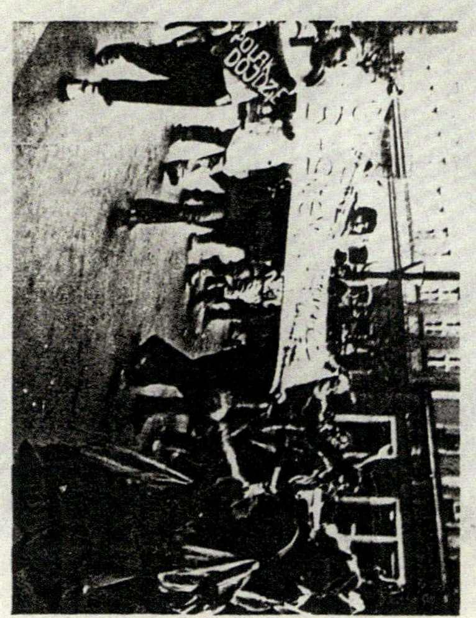

j.w.

Fourteen photocopied photographs from a dossier "Happeningi Pomeranczowy Alternatywy 1987–1988". Source: IPN WR 142/10, 2z18. Courtesy of W. Fydrych 1988

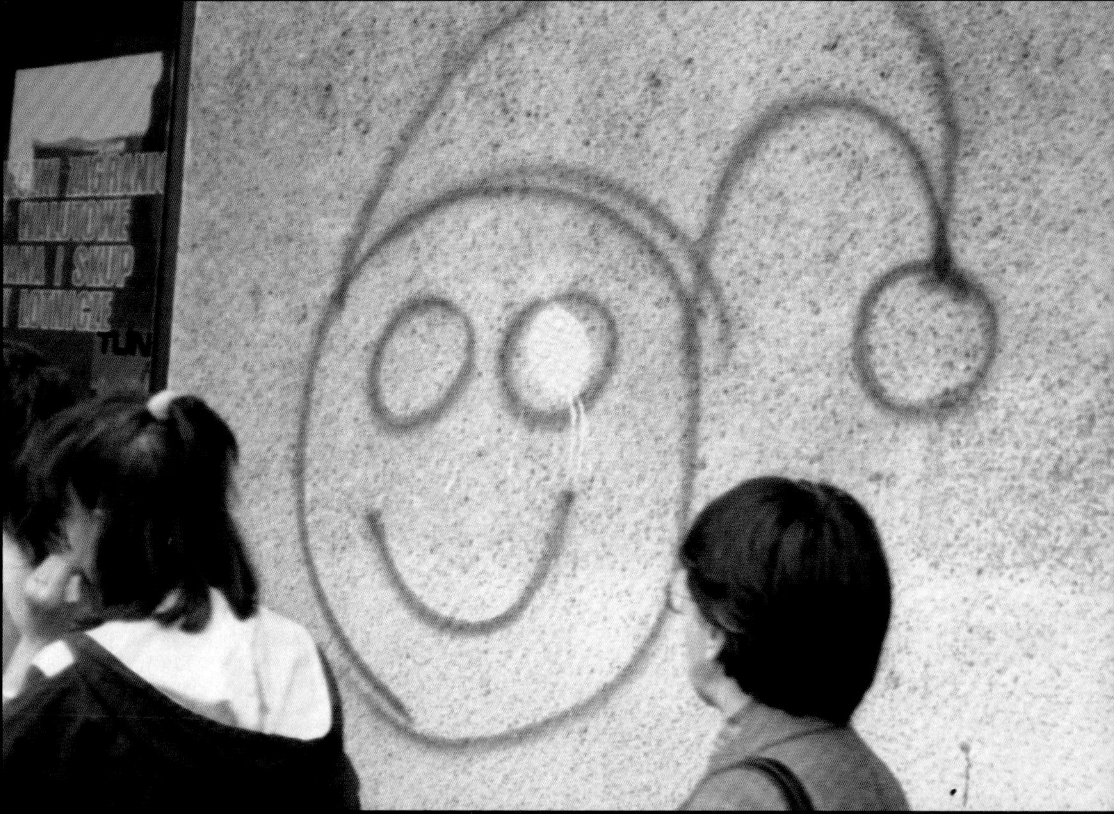

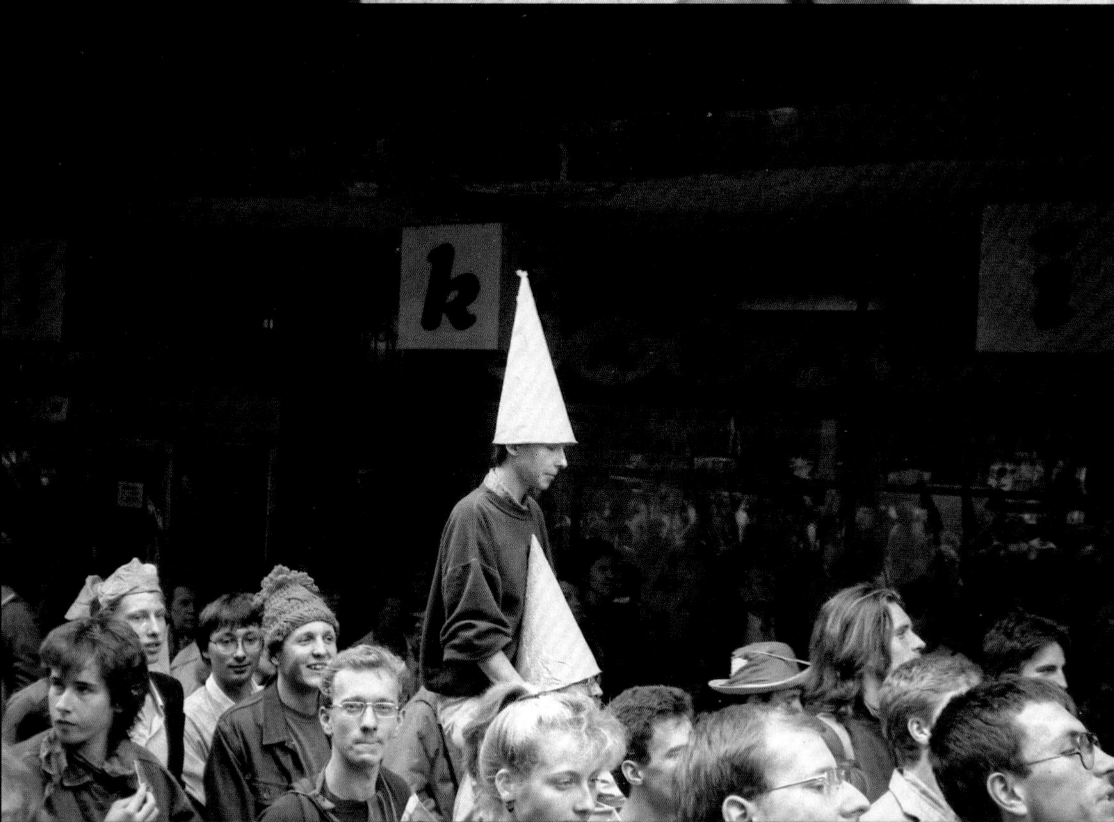

Four surveillance photos of the Orange Alternative
Source: IPN BU 3 16 32

1988

Operative Plan "Operation Arkade"

MfS (GDR)

In 1975, the Stasi began Operation "Arkade" with the purpose of observing and "disrupting" the gallery activities of Jürgen Schweinebraden on Dunckerstrasse St. in Berlin. In this gallery, Schweinebraden exhibited the work of artists from East Germany, Poland, Czechoslovakia, Hungary, and West Germany, particularly action artists. In the operative plan of April 5, 1976 on the "liquidation" of the gallery, we can read about how state security sent invitation cards to the vernissage with the wrong date and undertook a "dirtying up" of the building (in particular, the staircase and landings) "with the goal of arousing disgust about the artists' behavior among the older residents." We also learn how they planned to lay "porno photos and other smut" on the stairs and to dispatch "hooligans" who would set the building residents against the gallery. It was also decided to send Stasi-hostile poems to artists. These were poems the Stasi itself had written against the Stasi. (S)

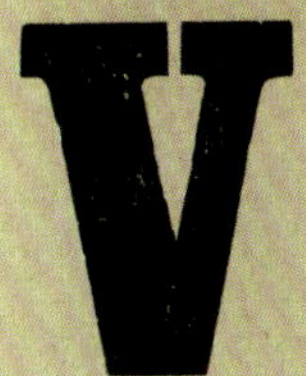

Reg.-Nr. 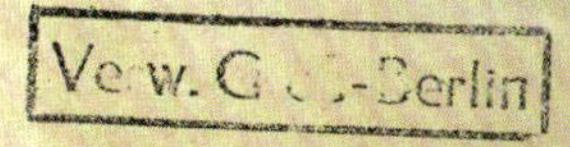 / XV/2870/75

„Arkade"

MfS

Beginn 29.09.75

Beendet

Archiv-Nr. 7030/82

Band-Nr. 1

Nicht gesperrt
Sammelakte

7030/82

T-GLEIT Hefter (DAPat.)
Bestell-Nr. T 108/So
VEB Organisations-Technik 652 Eisenberg/Thür.
V 10 25 Ma-G 3/11/72

Measures and "Decompositions"

Cover "Arkade" file
Source: BStU, MfS BV Bln AOP 7030/82, Vol.1

1975 –1976

Source: BStU, MfS BV Bln AOP 7030/82 Vol. 1, 153.

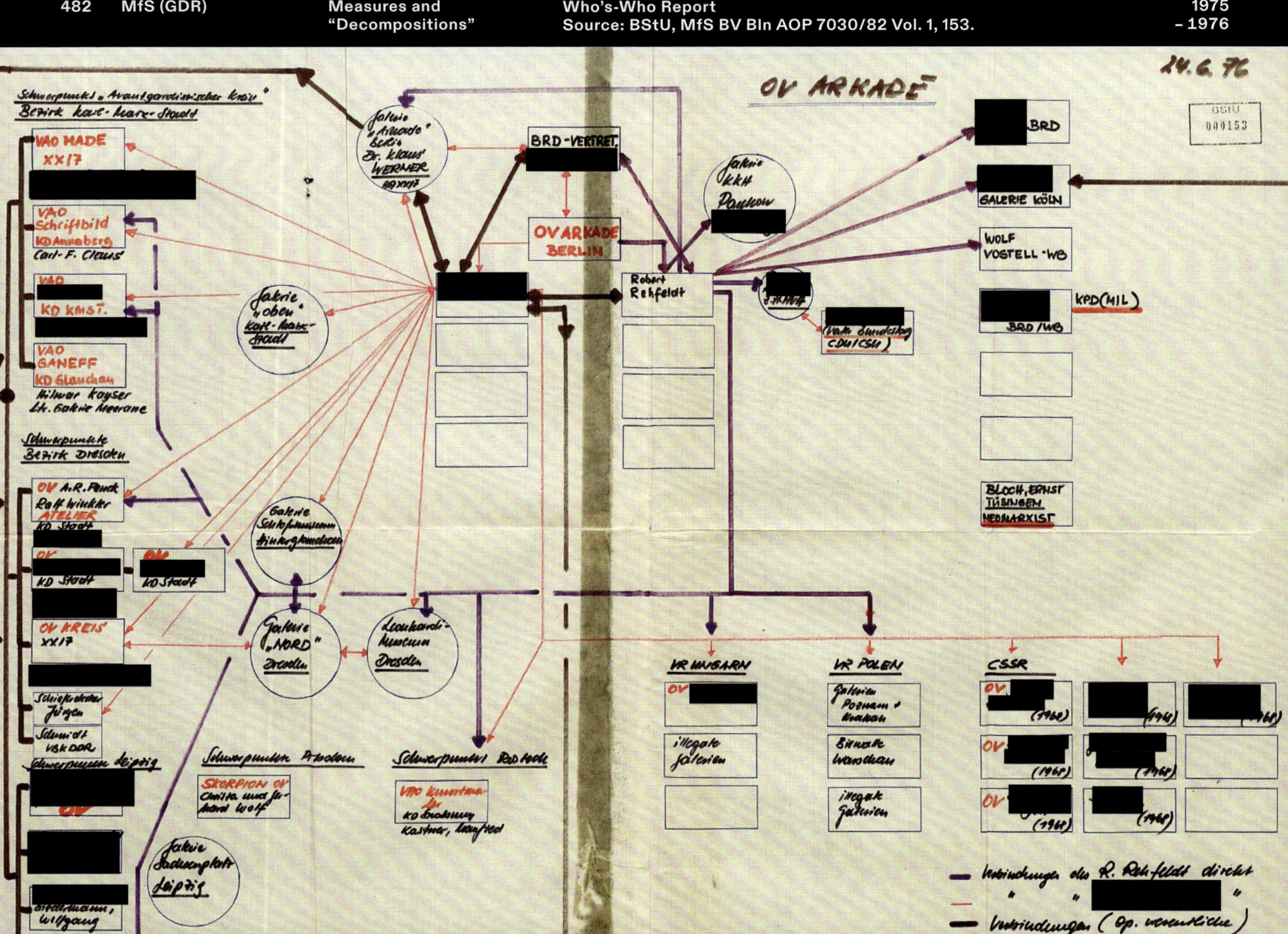

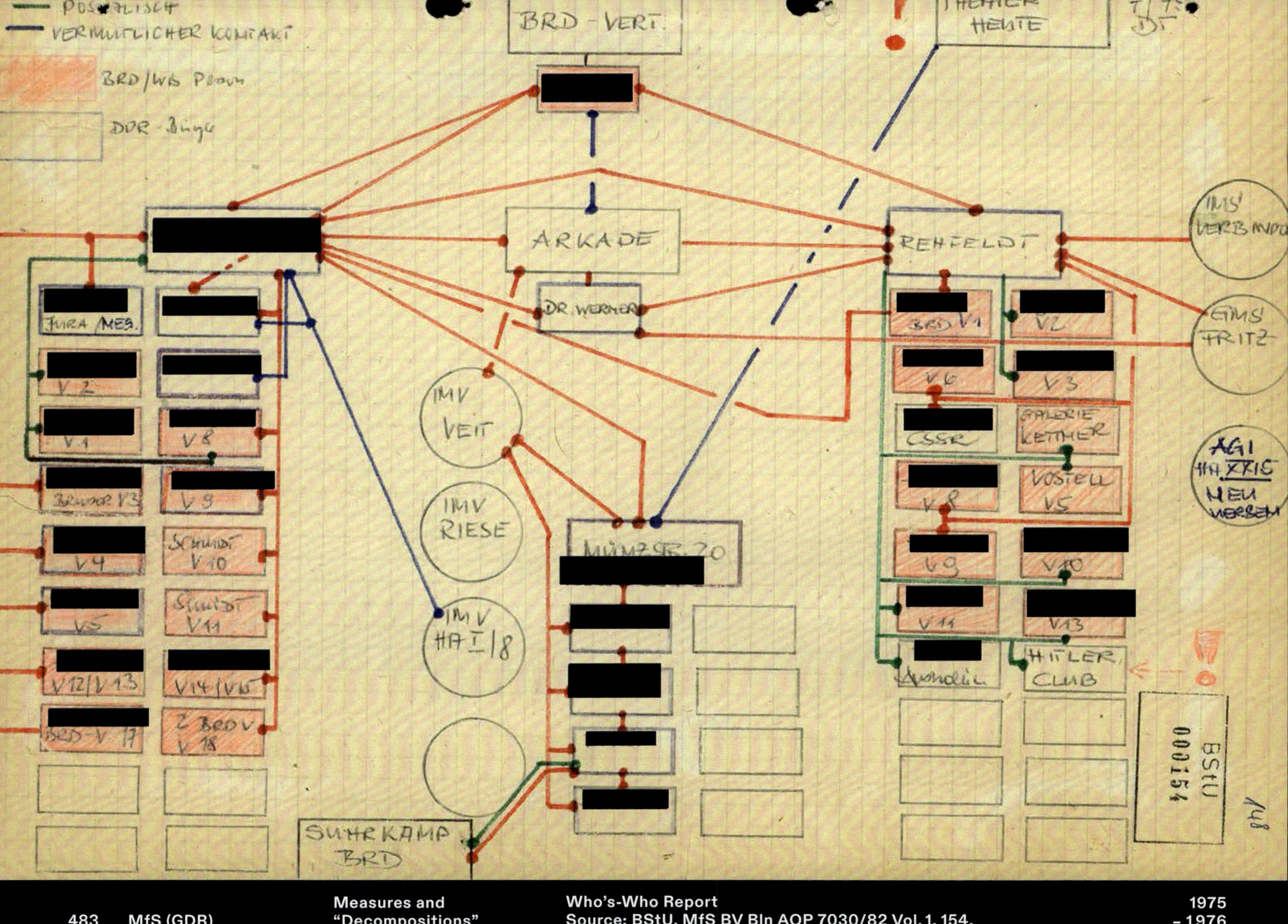

483 MfS (GDR)

Measures and "Decompositions"

Who's-Who Report
Source: BStU, MfS BV Bln AOP 7030/82 Vol. 1, 154.

1975 – 1976

Dept. XX/7

Berlin, February 9, 1976

Attachment to Operative Information No. 132/76

Sketch of Jürgen Schweinebraten's invitation to the opening of a private exhibition on February 7, 1976 in his apartment in Prenzlauer Berg Berlin, Dunckerstrasse 17

Front:
preprinted

Reverse side:
filled in with a typewriter

Nothing to note in the handwritten invitation card.

121

Abt. XX/7

Berlin, den 9.2.76

Anhang zur op. Information Nr. 132/76

Skizze der Einladung des Jürgen Schweinebraten zur Eröffnung einer Privatausstellung am 7.2.76 in seiner Wohnung, Berlin, Prenzlauer Berg, Dunckerstr. 17

Vorderseite:
vorgedruckt

Rückseite:
mit Schreibmaschine ausgefüllt

Telefon:
4492858

Plastik ●
Malerei ●
Grafik ●
Foto o

Dokumentation:
Tendenzen
moderne kunst o
Neue Musik ●
Jazz o
klassische Musik o
Chanson o

am 7.2. Zeit: 20⁰⁰ Uhr

vom 7.2. bis 12.3.76

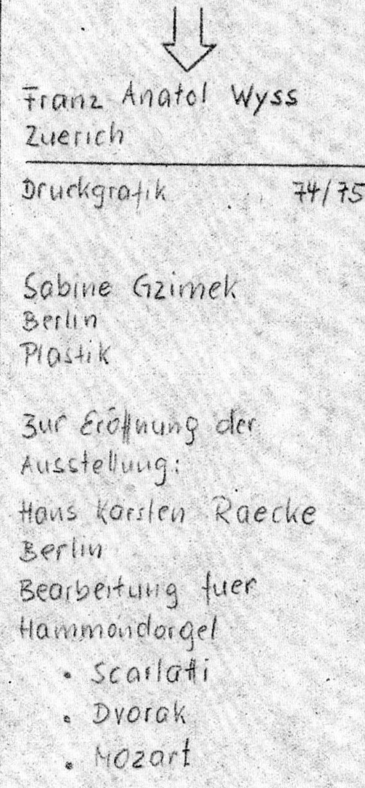

Franz Anatol Wyss
Zuerich

Druckgrafik 74/75

Sabine Gzimek
Berlin
Plastik

Zur Eröffnung der Ausstellung:
Hans Karsten Raecke
Berlin
Bearbeitung fuer Hammondorgel
• Scarlatti
• Dvorak
• Mozart

Von Originalvorlage abgezeichnet.

[signature]

Copied invitation card of an exhibition in the Schweinebraden Gallery
Source: BStU, MfS BV Bln AOP 7030/82, Vol. 3, 155.

THOMAS WIDERA

Warning to my friends

I am not who you think I am
I am not a nice, pacifist boy
with a good heart, I am not
someone who likes to help you
I care for you not at all
and your problems are bullshit to me
I just sit with you
to get to know you
I want to know who you are
hide your thoughts from me
like children from gypsies
I can be dangerous in my cowardice
and I am cowardly underhanded
I'll rat you out
close your doors and your hearts
there's someone with fall in his hair
and spring in his mouth

Translated from German by Brian Alkire

THOMAS WIDERA

Warnung an meine Freunde

ich bin nicht der für den ihr mich haltet
ich bin kein netter pazifistischer Junge
mit einem guten herzen, ich bin nicht
der euch gerne etwas zu gefallen tut
ich nehme auf euch keine rücksicht
und eure probleme interessieren mich einen dreck
ich sitze bei euch nur
um euch kennen zu lernen
ich will wissen wer ihr seid
versteckt eure gedanken vor mir
wie die kinder vor zigeunern
ich kann gefährlich sein in meiner feigheit
und ich bin feige hinterhältig
ich verpfeife euch
verschließt eure türen und eure herzen
da geht einer der hat den herbst in den haaren
und den frühling im mund

487 MfS (GDR) Measures and "Decompositions"
Poem, "Warning to my Friends" by Thomas Widera
Source: BStU, MfS BV Bln AOP 7030/82, Vol. 7, 120.
1975 - 1976

Some thoughts on Jürgen S.

At Dunckerstrasse 17,
in the 2nd wing, you'll find
a pleasant place which you'll be keen
to finally leave behind.

Now that we're taking a hard line
on a cultural level
someone's star has begun to shine –
one can only admire the devil.

If an artist says a single word
the result is quite unsavory
and in such a pleasant world –
where does Herr S. find the bravery?

His employers gladly close
their eyes, and swift
and Herr S., he'll never oppose
stooping to grab his Judas' gift.

The black ink on his card
could only have been be done
by a powerful patron with hard
markers had by almost no one.

Everything is tolerated in silence
there and pushed out of view –
a matter for all of simple compliance
but the victim – it is you!

Even when he's tossed from the job
Herr S. still makes a tidy sum
because his camouflage was – STOP
and we often needed something new to come.

And so the cashbox clinks out its song
and everyone knows who comes and talks
but you won't be able to rest very long
and no one needs the jail door's locks.

Trust is good – control is better, said Lenin
and then you'll be delivered
cold as ice to the hangman
and Herr S. receives his thirty silver.

Sketched from original model
Translated from German by Brian Alkire

1800 110

Nachdenken über Jürgen S.

In der Dunckerstraße 17
2. Seitenflügel steht
ein schöner Ort, wo man am liebsten
nicht mehr gerne hinein geht.

Seit auf kultureller Ebne
gefahren wird ein harter Kurs
setzt sich jemand groß in Szene
daß man sich nur wundern muß.

Sagt ein Künstler mal ein Wörtchen
bekommt er gleich eins auf den Hut
und an diesem schönen Örtchen -
woher nimmt Herr S. den Mut ?

Seine Auftraggeber drücken
gern die Augen zu und promt
und Herr S., er wird sich bücken
wenn ~~er~~ der Judaslohn dann ~~be~~kommt.

Schwarz zu drucken seine Karten
kann nur hierzulande einer
der mächtge Gönner hat mit harten
Märkern wie sonst keiner.

Alles wird dort still geduldet
man drückt beide Augen zu
keiner hat das dann verschuldet
doch das Opfer - das bist Du !

Selbst beim Rausschmiß aus dem Job
macht Herr S. noch Plus
denn zur Tarnung hieß es - STOP
weil öfter mal was neues kommen muß.

Und so klingt das Geld im Kasten
man weiß ja, wer dort kommt und spricht
doch man wird nicht lange rasten
und den Knast den braucht man nicht.

Vertrauen ist gut - Kontrolle ist besser
das sagte doch der Lenin schon
man liefert Dich eiskalt ans Messer
und Herr S. bekommt den Judaslohn.

Administration for State Security
Greater Berlin
Department XX

Berlin, April 4, 1976
Mü/lüc

3. Operative Plan

Operation (OV) XXX – Record No.XXX

1. Deployment of Unofficial Informants

Because we have so far been unable to carry out the targeted deployment of an Unofficial Informants in our work, the following urgent measure needs to be undertaken as quickly as possible as a basis for the disruption measures to be executed. The following procedures are in place for this purpose, implementable on the basis of current knowledge of the working methods of XXX.

1.1 Production of obviously fake invitation cards from XXX to an exhibition opening in May 1976. This measure shall be implemented by Section E in accordance with the existing model.

1.2 Mailing these invitation cards in accordance with the attached distribution list. The sending of these cards, including to our own Unofficial Informants, will result in:

a) opportunities for controlling the Unofficial Informants;

b) possibility of contact by the Unofficial Informant with XXX, as they will go to the exhibition opening with her invitation. At such time, it can and will occur that XXX notices that some persons are in possession of fake invitation cards. This accomplishes the goal of unsettling XXX and his circle and causing them to search for the "forger." XXX will not be able to notify the police as his exhibition has not been registered and approved by them. In this way we bring him into a position of contradiction from which he will be hard pressed to extricate himself, thus introducing anxiety and unease into their ranks. The Unofficial Informants will report that they received fake invitation cards. With the help of the Unofficial Informants, a search will be undertaken for the "forger" of the materials and they will attempt to explain the reasons for this action.

c) Furthermore, this form of invitation offers us the possibility of incorporating persons who we can assume will bring these invitations to the party secretary and/or their student advisers at the Berlin Academy of Arts. Because these parties will follow up with the signer, new paths will open for contacting these people and integrating them into operational handling and/or to recruit them.

Verwaltung für Staatssicherheit
Groß-Berlin
Abteilung XX

Berlin, o5. o4. 1976
Mü/lüc

27.4.76

3. Operativplan

OV █████ - Reg.-Nr. █████

1. Einsatz von IM

Da es bei der bisherigen Arbeit nicht gelang, einen gezielten IM-Einsatz durchzuführen, ist diese vordringliche Maßnahme, als Grundlage für die durchzuführenden Zersetzungsmaßnahmen schnellstens zu realisieren. Dazu gibt es folgenden Verfahrensweg, der aus der bisherigen Kenntnis der Arbeitsweise des █████ realisierbar ist.

1.1. Herstellung von offensichtlich gefälschten Einladungskarten des █████ zu einer Ausstellungseröffnung im Mai 1976. Diese Maßnahme wird entsprechend der vorgegebenen Muster durch das Referat E realisiert.

1.2. Versendung dieser Einladungskarten auf dem Postwege, entsprechend des beigefügten Verteilerschlüssels. Durch das Versenden der Einladungskarten, u.a. auch an eigene IM, ergeben sich

a) Überprüfungsmöglichkeiten der IM;
b) Möglichkeiten der Kontaktaufnahme der IM zu dem █████., weil sie mit ihrer Einladung zur Ausstellungseröffnung gehen werden. Dabei kann und wird es passieren, daß █████ feststellt, daß einige Personen im Besitz von gefälschten Einladungskarten sind. Dadurch wird erreicht, daß █████. und sein Kreis in Unruhe geraten und nach dem "Fälscher" suchen. Anzeige kann █████. bei der VP nicht erstatten, weil seine Veranstaltungen nicht polizeilich gemeldet und genehmigt sind. Dadurch bringen wir ihn in Widersprüche, aus denen er schwerlich einen Ausweg finden wird und somit in diesen Reihen Unruhe erzeugt. Die IM werden berichten, daß sie gefälschte Einladungskarten erhalten haben. Mit Hilfe der IM wird nach dem "Fälscher" der Materialien gesucht und versucht, diese Handlungsweise aufzuklären.
c) Weiterhin bietet diese Form der Einladungsversendung die Möglichkeit, Personen einzubeziehen, wo anzunehmen ist, daß sich diese mit den Einladungen an den Parteisekretär bzw. ihren Studienbetreuer der Kunsthochschule Berlin wenden. Da von dieser Stelle eine Rückmeldung an den Unterzeichner erfolgt, eröffnen sich Wege, die Personen zu kontaktieren und in die Bearbeitung einzubeziehen bzw. gegebenenfalls zu werben.

31

- 2 -

1.3
On the day of the exhibition opening, April 24, 1976, XXX
a comrade (Gen. Hasse) will be deployed with the following assignments:
- making a mess of the building, stairwell, landings (rubber protection, dirt, etc.) with the goal of arousing disgust in the building's older residents towards the behavior of the artists
- possible adhesion of pornographic photos and other smut, with the same objective.

The overall goal of this measure is the immediate creation of an informant in the staircase who, under the legend of fighting against the slobs, will be used as a police informant (fake backstory) for the observation of the artists. The goal is to recruit this person for long-term use.

1.4
Further use of Gen. Wild's informant IMP "Andre" with the specific assignment of further strengthening relations of trust with XXX and XXX. Informant IMP "Andre" will consistently take part in the exhibition openings and in doing so identify as many people as possible, particularly West German and West Berlin persons. This also includes employees of the West German-Representation. Presentation of the photo catalogue to the IMP for further identification of persons in the circle surrounding XXX.

1.5
Deployment of informants IMS "Clemens" and IMS"Gerda" on the basis of the status of contact peripheral to XXX. IMS "Clemens" will, in accordance with his assignment, continue to seek contact with the gallerist XXX via Robert Rehfeld. The goal is for "Clemens" to access and become part of Rehfeld's circle of trust. This measure and objective will be supported through visits by the IMS to
exhibition openings where R. will also make an appearance, thus demonstrating to R. that this "art" interests him and that he supports it.
Informant IMS "Gerda" is assigned the task of gaining access to Gallery XXX via her husband and then to identify persons she knows from the time of her studies at the Academy of Art in Berlin.

1.6
The Unofficial Informants of Main Dept. (HA) VII and Main Admin. Dept. (HVA) IV, who have also been compiling information on this operation, will continue to receive concrete assignments. This includes the signer carrying out consultations with relevant collaborators.
The goal of this deployment is to further specify the plans and intentions of XXX, in particular with regard to the exhibition activities and printing of graphics and the persons involved in these activities.

Date: April 23, 1976

1.3.
Am Tage der Ausstellungseröffnung am 24. 4. 1976 wird ███ ein Genosse (Gen. Hasse) zum Einsatz gebracht, der folgende Aufgabenstellungen hat:
- Verunreinigen des Hauses, Treppenaufgang, Treppenpodeste (Gummischutz, Dreck usw.) mit dem Ziel, bei den älteren Mietern Abscheu über das Verhalten der Künstler zu erregen.
- Evtl. Ankleben von Pornofotos und anderen Schmutz mit gleicher Zielstellung.

Gesamtziel dieser Maßnahme ist die Schaffung einer Auskunftsperson unmittelbar im Aufgang, die unter der Legende, daß man diese Schmutzfinken bekämpfen muß, durch einen Genossen unseres Referates als Auskunftsperson der VP (Legende) zum Beobachten der Künstler genutzt wird. Ziel ist es dabei, diese Auskunftsperson für einen langfristigen Einsatz zu gewinnen.

1.4.
Weiterer Einsatz des IMF "Andre" des Gen. Wild mit spezifischer Aufgabenstellung zur weiteren Festigung des Vertrauenskontaktes zu ███ und ███. IMF "Andre" wird stets an den Ausstellungseröffnungen teilnehmen und dabei so viel wie möglich Personen identifizieren und insbesondere BRD- und WB-Personen kontaktieren. Dazu gehören auch die Mitarbeiter der BRD-Vertretung. Vorlage des Bildkatalogs für den IMF zur weiteren Personenidentifizierung des Personenkreises, der bei ███ verkehrt.

1.5.
Einsatz des IMS "Clemens" und IMS "Gerda" ausgehend vom Stand des Kontaktes peripher. zu ███
Der IMS "Clemens" wird entsprechend seiner Aufgabenstellung weiterhin über den Robert Rehfeld den Kontakt zum Galeristen ███ suchen. Dabei geht es darum, daß "Clemens" den Vertrauenskreis von dem Rehfeld erreicht und in diesen eindringt. Diese Maßnahme und Zielstellung wird unterstützt dadurch, daß der IMS Ausstellungseröffnungen besucht, bei denen R. ebenfalls in Erscheinung tritt und dabei diesem gegenüber glaubhaft nachweist, daß ihn diese "Kunst" interessiert und er sich dafür einsetzt.
IMS "Gerda" ist beauftragt, über ihren Ehemann Zutritt zur Galerie ███ zu erlangen und dabei Personen zu identifizieren, die sie vom Studium an der Kunsthochschule Berlin kennt.

1.6.
Die IM der HA VII und der HVA IV, die bisher ebenfalls Informationen zum OV erarbeiteten, werden weiter konkretisierte Aufgabenstellungen erhalten. Dazu werden durch den Unterzeichner Absprachen mit den jeweiligen Mitarbeitern durchgeführt.
Ziel dieses Einsatzes ist es, die Pläne und Absichten von ███ weiter zu konkretisieren, insbesondere, was die Ausstellungstätigkeit und die Druckauflage von Grafiken und den daran beteiligten Personen betrifft.

Termin: 23. o4. 1976

Verantw.: Oltn. Müller

Responsible: Capt. Müller

– 3 –

1.7
Formulate a recommendation for the establishment of contact with XXX. She has been an associate of XXX and XXX since the gallery's beginning. Using the legend that she can support our work as a model at the Berlin Academy of Arts, with respect to contact development with students and the criminal activities of models, we should test whether XXX has the necessary prerequisites for supporting our work on Operation "Arkade."

Date: April 23, 1976
Responsible: Capt. Müller

1.8
Processing materials relating to instructor XXX, in order to be able to immediately contact him in the context of the measures under 1.2.

Date: April 21, 1976
Responsible: Capt. Müller

2. Further Measures

2.1
Creation of a neutral status report on the actions of XXX, in order to be able to provide this information to an Unofficial Informant from the area of law for review. This person should, in the context of criminal law, determine which opportunities for criminal acts exist at Gallery XXX.

Date: May 10, 1976
Responsible: Capt. Müller
Coordination: with Major Gen. Hansen

2.2
Continued cooperation with the Gen. of Dept. II regarding persons appearing in the area of the West German delegation. Also possible deployment of one of Gen. Seidler's Unofficial Informants in this area.

Date: April 30, 1976

1.7.
Vorschlag zur Kontaktaufnahme mit ████ formulieren. Diese verkehrt als Besucherin seit Existenz der Galerie bei ██ und ████ um den ██. Unter der Legende, daß sie als Modell an der Kunsthochschule Berlin unsere Arbeit unterstützten kann, was Fragen der Kontaktpflege von Studenten und kriminelle Handlungen von Modellen betrifft, soll getestet werden, ob die ██ die Voraussetzungen hat, unsere Arbeit hinsichtlich des VAO "Arkade" zu unterstützen.

Termin: 23. o4. 1976

Verantw.: Oltn. Müller

1.8.
Aufarbeiten des Materials über den Dozenten ████, um diesen im Rahmen der Maßnahmen unter 1.2. sofort kontaktieren zu können.

Termin: 21. o4. 1976

Verantw.: Oltn. Müller

2. Weitere Maßnahmen

2.1.
Herstellung eines neutralen Sachstandsberichtes über die Handlungen des ██, um dieses Material einem IM aus dem Bereich der Juristen zur Begutachtung übergeben zu können. Dieser soll strafrechtlich fixieren, welche Möglichkeiten eines strafrechtlichen Einwirkens bei der Galerie ██ existieren.

Termin: 10. 5. 1976

Verantw.: Oltn. Müller

Koord.: mit Gen. Major Hansen

2.2.
Weiteres Zusammenwirken mit den Gen. der Abt. II hinsichtlich der in Erscheinung getretenen Personen des Bereiches der BRD-Vertretung. Dazu evtl. Einsatz eines IM des Gen. Seidler in diesem Bereich.
Termin: 30. 4. 1976

– 4 –

2.3
Coordination with Section E of the Greater Berlin Administration, deployment of an infrared camera in the hallway XXX, in order to continue to comprehensively identify the stream of visitors to the exhibition opening.

Date: April 24, 1976
Resp.: Capt. Müller
Deployment: Gen. Girod

2.4
In accordance with Section E's offer, an industrial television system will be installed for the exhibition opening on April 24, 1976 at XXX. The necessary measures for this will be coordinated with Section E (test try).

Date: April 24, 1976
Resp.: Capt. Müller

2.5
Continue to expand cooperation with the responsible District Administration with respect to informant HFIM "Rene" in line with agreements made.

Date: ongoing

2.6
Investigative action pertaining to XXX Dunckerstrasse 17, XXX in order to check which questions the person can be asked about and used for.

Date: May 5, 1976
Resp.: Capt. Müller

Duration of operative plan: through May 15, 1976
New operative plan: May 16, 1976
Monitoring: Major Gen. Klemer

[signature]
Müller
Captain

Translated form German by Brian Alkire

2.3.
Abstimmungen mit dem Ref. E der Verw. Gr.-Bln., Einsatz eines Infrarot-Fotoapparates im Hausflur ████████, um den Besucherstrom und die Personen, die an der Ausstellungseröffnung teilnehmen, weiter und umfassend zu identifizieren.

Termin: 24. o4. 1976
Verantw.: Oltn. Müller
Einsatz: Gen. Girod

2.4.
Entsprechend der gebotenen Möglichkeit des Ref. E erfolgt der Einsatz einer Industriefernsehanlage am 24. o4. 1976 zur Ausstellungseröffnung bei ███. Dazu festzulegende Maßnahmen werden mit dem Ref. E abgestimmt (Testversuch).

Termin: 24. o4. 1976
Verantw.: Oltn. Müller

2.5.
Weitere Zusammenarbeit mit dem zuständigen ABV über den HFIM "Rene" entsprechend der getrofenenen Vereinbarungen weiter entwickeln.

Termin: laufend

2.6.
Aufklärungshandlungen zur ████████ Dunckerstr. 17, ████████ um zu prüfen, in welchen Fragen die Person ansprechbar und nutzbar erscheint.

Termin: o5. o5. 1976
Verantw.: Oltn. Müller

Laufzeit des Operativplanes bis 15. o5. 1976,
Neuer Operativplan: 16. o5. 1976
Kontrolle: Gen. Hptm. Klemer

Müller
Müller
Oberleutnant

Operative Plan "Avant-Garde Circle"

MfS (GDR)

In November 1977, the Stasi wrote a fifteen-page "Plan for the Differentiation and Elimination of Staff Focus Area 'Avant-Garde Circle'" with the purpose of "decomposing" the artist group Clara Mosch. The goals of the "operative measures" included destroying the Ranfts' marriage, "promoting" Michael Morgner through awarding more contracts, and participating in exhibitions abroad in Western Europe, in addition to planting the rumor that Gregor-Torsten Schade was "unofficially" collaborating with the Stasi. The informant, however, was someone else: it turned out to be the Mosch friend Ralf-Rainer Wasse who, as Unofficial Collaborator "Frank Körner," composed numerous photo documentations of Clara Mosch actions and meticulously reported on their artistic activity, as well as himself taking part in actions. The elimination plan shows in a particularly explicit way that artists were not only placed under surveillance but, especially in the GDR, that the plan was to eliminate artists and artist groups with disruptive creativity. (S)

District Administration for
State Security, Karl-Marx-Stadt
Department XX

Head of District Administration
Comrade Major General Gehlert

[stamp]

Internal

Operative Plan "Avant-Garde Circle"

Attached you will find a draft plan, approved by Deputy of Operations Comrade Captain Pierschel, for the differentiation and elimination of the focus area "Avant-Garde Circle" in the area of visual arts in the district of Karl-Marx-Stadt.

Because the implementation of this plan requires a series of far-reaching measures, I request your personal approval of the execution of the proposed measures.

Head of Department XX

Engelhart
Major

Attachment

Bezirksverwaltung für
Staatssicherheit Karl-Marx-Stadt
Abteilung XX

Karl-Marx-Stadt, 12. 04. 1977
Fr/oe
Tgb.-Nr.: XX/7/ 1531 /77

Leiter der Bezirksverwaltung
Genossen Generalmajor Gehlert

im Hause

Konzeption "Avantgardistischer Kreis"

Als Anlage übersende ich Ihnen eine, vom Stellvertreter Operativ, Genossen Oberstleutnant Pierschel, bestätigte, Konzeption zur Differenzierung und Zerschlagung des Schwerpunktes "Avantgardistischer Kreis" im Bereich der bildenden Kunst des Bezirkes Karl-Marx-Stadt.

Da sich zur Realisierung dieser Konzeption eine Reihe weitreichender Maßnahmen erforderlich machen, bitte ich Sie um Ihre persönliche Sanktionierung zur Durchführung der vorgeschlagenen Maßnahmen.

Leiter der Abteilung XX

Engelhardt
Major

Anlage

DA Karl-Marx-Stadt.
Department XX/7

Karl-Marx-Stadt, March 11, 1977
Hau/Ir

O P E R A T I V E P L A N

for the differentiation and elimination of personnel focus area "Avant-Garde Circle"

The suspects of Operation "Maggot" (Dept. XX) and Operation "Worm" (Karl-Marx-Stadt/City) are engaged in subversive efforts in close cooperation with known hostile forces in Berlin and other districts of the GDR. These efforts are directed in particular against the realization of our party's cultural politics in the area of visual arts in Karl-Marx-Stadt.

The present class struggle situation requires offensive measures to prevent the consolidation of emerging hostile footholds and the systematic differentiation and elimination of this concentration.

For this purpose, the following focus area tasks are to be resolved:

1. The especially close relationships between the visual artists
   XXX
   XXX
   XXX
   Operation "Maggot" of Dept. XX

   XXX
   XXX
   XXX
   Operation "Maggot" of Dept. XX

   XXX
   XXX
   XXX
   Operation "Worm" of KMStadt/City

BV Karl-Marx-Stadt
Abteilung XX/7

Karl-Marx-Stadt, 11. 03. 1977
Hau/Ir

K o n z e p t i o n

zur Differenzierung und Zerschlagung des personellen Schwerpunktes "Avantgardistischer Kreis"

Die Verdächtigen des OV "Made" (Abt. XX) und des OV "Wurm" (KD Karl-Marx-Stadt/Stadt) unternehmen in engen Wechselbeziehungen mit erkannten feindlichen Kräften in Berlin und anderen Bezirken der DDR subversive Bestrebungen, die sich insbesondere gegen die Verwirklichung der Kulturpolitik unserer Partei im Bereich der bildenden Kunst des Bezirkes Karl-Marx-Stadt richten.

Die gegenwärtige Klassenkampfsituation erfordert offensive Maßnahmen, um eine weitere Festigung des entstehenden feindlichen Stützpunktes zu verhindern und die planmäßige Differenzierung und Zerschlagung der Konzentration durchzuführen.

Dazu sind folgende Schwerpunktaufgaben zu lösen:

1. Die besonders engen Beziehungen zwischen den bild. Künstlern

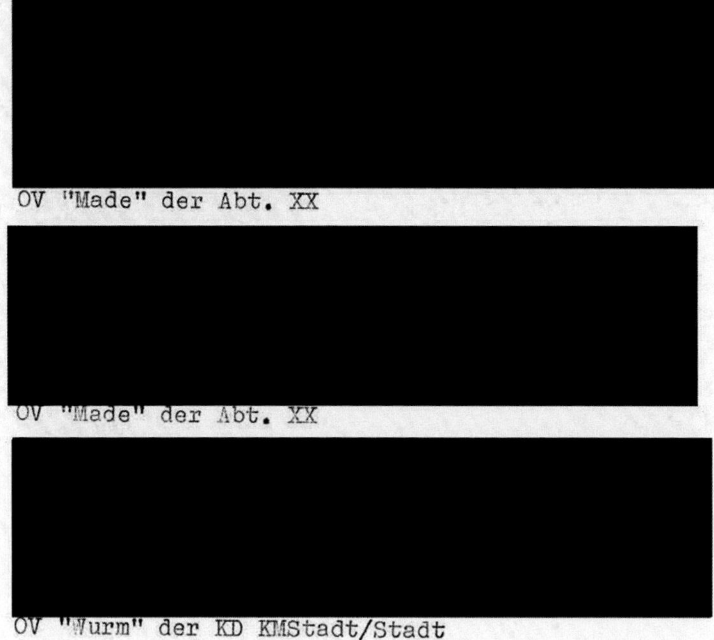

OV "Made" der Abt. XX

OV "Made" der Abt. XX

OV "Wurm" der KD KMStadt/Stadt

among each other and to their contacts in Berlin, Leipzig, Halle, and Dresden are to be disrupted through appropriate political-operative measures with the goal of differentiation and/or ultimate termination.

2. <u>Sympathizers with the suspects, in particular the following persons:</u>

XXX
XXX
XXX
XXX
XXX
XXX
XXX
XXX
XXX

Lutz V O I G T M A N N
January 29, 1941 in Krostitz
Freelance painter/graphic artist/KMStadt
Member of the Association of Visual Artists/KMStadt
Not a party member

Wolfgang E I N M A H L
April 5, 1944 in Euba
Freelance painter/graphic artist/KMStadt
Member of the Association of Visual Artists/KMStadt
Not a party member

XXX
XXX
XXX

shall be removed from the influence of the suspects.

untereinander sowie zu ihren Verbindungen in Berlin, Leipzig, Halle und Dresden sind durch geeignete pol.-operative Maßnahmen mit dem Ziel der Differenzierung bzw. des entgültigen Abbruchs zu stören.

2. Die Sympatisanten der Verdächtigen, insbesondere die Personen:

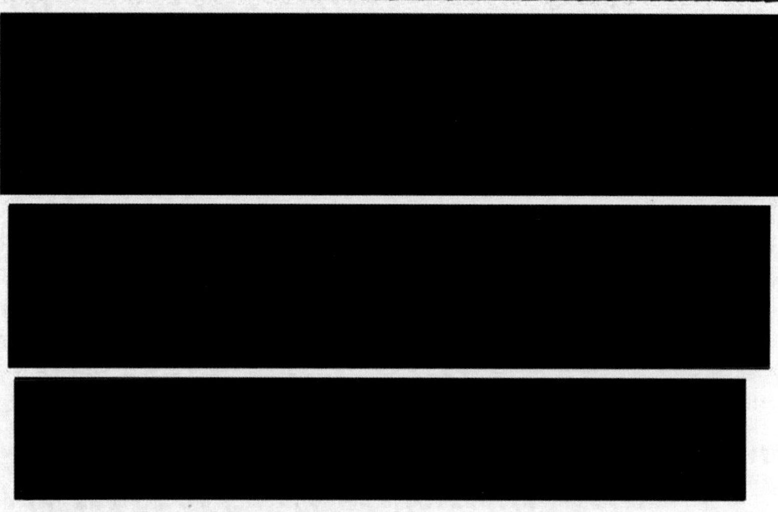

Lutz V o i g t m a n n
29. 01. 1941 in Krostitz
freischaffender Maler/Graphiker/KMStadt
Mitglied des Verbandes bild. Künstler/KMStadt
parteilos

Wolfgang E i n m a h l
05. 04. 1944 in Euba
freischaffender Maler/Graphiker/KMStadt
Mitglied des Verbandes bild. Künstler/KMStadt
parteilos

sind dem Einfluß der Verdächtigen zu entziehen.

3. The concentration points of the "Avant-Garde Circle" in the Karl-Marx-Stadt district:

   - "Galerie oben" KMStadt, Innere Klosterstrasse

   - "Intelligentsia Club Pablo Neruda" KMStadt

   are also to be removed from the influence of the suspects. Through preventative political-operative measures, the ability of new concentration points of these personal circles to emerge shall be prevented.

4. By means of a continual, significant, and fact-supported flow in information about the effectiveness and direction of attack of hostile forces in the area of visual art towards party leadership, it shall be ensured that the operative situation in this area be precisely judged and that ideological work with the artists can be effectively supported.

<u>Measures for differentiation and decomposition</u>

1. The goal of the political-operative measures with regard to the person
   XXX
   consists of isolation in public and withdrawing other artists from his influence.

1.1 The intensive political-ideological work of the responsible bodies and institutions shall ensure the restriction and systematic suppression of the negative political influence of XXX and his associates on the painting/graphic arts section of the Association of Visual Artists in KMStadt, as well as on the organization and execution of art exhibitions in Intelligentsia Club "Pablo Neruda" and "Galerie oben."

   This requires coordinated measures with the following bodies, institutions, and DE of the Ministry for State Security (MfS):

   - SED District Leadership KMStadt
   - HA (Main Department) XX (political-operative influence on the Association of Visual Artists of the GDR and the State Art Industry of the GDR)
   - District Secretary of the Cultural Association of the GDR/KMStadt ("Pablo Neruda" -Club)

3. Die Konzentrationspunkte des "Avantgardistischen Kreises" im Bezirk KMStadt:

- "Galerie oben" KMStadt, Innere Klosterstraße
- "Club der Intelligenz Pablo Neruda" KMStadt

sind ebenfalls dem Einfluß der Verdächtigen zu entziehen. Durch vorbeugende pol.-operative Maßnahmen ist zu verhindern, daß neue Konzentrationspunkte dieses Personenkreises entstehen können.

4. Durch einen ständigen, aussagekräftigen und tatsachengesicherten Informationsfluß über Wirksamkeit und Angriffsrichtung der feindlichen Kräfte auf dem Gebiet der bild. Kunst an die Parteiführung des Bezirkes ist zu sichern, daß die operative Lage in diesem Bereich exakt eingeschätzt und die ideologische Arbeit mit den Künstlern wirksam unterstützt werden kann.

Maßnahmen zur Differenzierung und Zersetzung

1. Das Ziel der politisch-operativen Maßnahmen zur Person

[redacted]

besteht in seiner Isolierung in der Öffentlichkeit und darin, andere Künstler seinem Einfluß zu entziehen.

1.1. Durch eine intensive politisch-ideologische Arbeit der zuständigen Organe und Institutionen ist zu gewährleisten, daß der negative politische Einfluß des [redacted] und seiner Vertrauten auf die Sektion Malerei/Graphik des Verbandes bild. Künstler/KMStadt sowie auf die Organisation und Durchführung von Kunstveranstaltungen im Club der Intelligenz "Pablo Neruda" und in der "Galerie oben" wesentlich eingeschränkt und systematisch zurückgedrängt wird.

Dazu sind koordinierte Maßnahmen mit folgenden Organen, Institutionen und DE des MfS notwendig:

- SED - Bezirksleitung KMStadt
- HA XX (pol.-op. Einflußnahme über den Verband bild. Künstler der DDR und den Staatlichen Kunsthandel der DDR)
- Bezirkssekretariat des Kulturbundes der DDR/KMStadt ("Pablo Neruda" - Club)

1.2 In the course of further op. handling, checks shall be continually performed whether evidence and indications of criminal activities or violations of state order by Ranft can be compiled.

For this purpose, all indicators shall be checked, such as:

- lack of a state-mandated business license for the sales gallery planned by XXX, indications of potential tax evasion,

- unauthorized export of his own works into foreign, capitalist countries, non-approved participation in exhibitions in foreign, capitalist countries, as well as the sale of his works in foreign, capitalist countries.

1.3 XXX
XXX
XXX

This requires:

- Deployment of a vetted and reliable Unofficial Informant on XXX
XXX

- Creating uncertainty for both persons through letters, calls, etc., which are suited to deepening marital conflict.

2. The goal of the political-operative measures for person
XXX
consists of compromising and isolating XXX vis-à-vis his friends and acquaintances.

2.1 The suspicion should be spread among his friends and acquaintances that he is continually informing the district party and state organs about confidential matters from his circles of acquaintance.

<u>For this purpose, the following measures shall be undertaken:</u>

- Contact shall be made with XXX by a functionary of the state, or of a social organization or institution. This functionary shall engage with XXX on a confidential basis while publicly avoiding XXX.

1\. 2. Im Zuge der weiteren op. Bearbeitung ist laufend zu prüfen, ob Hinweise und Beweise für kriminelle Handlungen oder Verstöße gegen die staatliche Ordnung des Ranft erarbeitet werden können.

Dazu sind alle Anhaltspunkte zu prüfen, wie:

- Nichtvorliegen einer staatlichen Gewerbegenehmigung für die durch █████ geplante private Verkaufsgalerie, Hinweise auf eventuelle Steuerhinterziehung,

- Unerlaubte Ausfuhr von eigenen Werken in das kapitalistische Ausland, nichtgenehmigte Beteiligung an Ausstellungen im kapitalistischen Ausland sowie der Verkauf seiner Werke im kapitalistischen Ausland.

1\. 3. █████

Dazu ist erforderlich:

- Einsatz von überprüften und zuverlässigen IM an █████ █████

- Verunsicherung beider Personen durch Zuschriften, Anrufe u. ä., die geeignet sind, eheliche Zerwürfnisse zu vertiefen.

2\. Das Ziel der pol.-operativen Maßnahmen zur Person

█████

besteht darin, █████ gegenüber seinem Freundes- und Bekanntenkreis zu kompromittieren und zu isolieren.

2\. 1. In den Freundes- und Bekanntkreis ist der Verdacht hineinzutragen, daß █████ ständig die Partei- und Staatsorgane des Bezirkes über vertrauliche Sachverhalte aus seinem Bekanntenkreis informiert.

Dazu sind folgende Maßnahmen durchzuführen:

- Durch einen Funktionär eines Staatsorgans, einer gesellschaftlichen Organisation oder Einrichtung ist Verbindung zu █████ aufzunehmen. Dieser Funktionär hat sich auf einer vertraulichen Basis mit █████ zu beschäftigen und gleichzeitig █████ offen zu meiden.

Moral and material connections shall be built through small jobs like the graphic design of posters or similar.

This procedure serves the purpose of damaging trust in XXX and to inspire in XXX a feeling of mistrust.

- It is recommended that this connection be taken up by Comrade XXX, leader of the Free German Youth of Karl-Marx-Stadt.
  Fake, legend-based interviews as Dept. K shall be held with XXX without meaningful content with the purpose, first, of simulating a relationship of trust with Dept. K and, second, of undermining the relationship between XXX and XXX and others.
  By means of these interviews, the suspicion shall be strengthened that XXX is forwarding confidential information to Dept. K.

  It is recommended that these measures be implemented by Gen. Major Franik of Department XX.

2.2 In the operative handling of XXX, it should always be checked whether evidence and indications of criminal activity and violations of state order can be compiled. All indications of this kind shall be comprehensively reviewed to find further criteria for the continuation of decomposition measures.

2.3 The public reputation of XXX shall be compromised through the exploitation of existing moral failings and the targeted use of reliable Unofficial Informants.

Forms of behavior to be used to damage the target include:

- excessive enjoyment of alcohol

- fluctuating intimate relationships with in some cases morally degenerate persons, sexual compulsivity, and interest in pornography

sporadic financial difficulties, loans of financial means.

Durch kleine Aufträge, wie graphische Gestaltung von Plakaten o. ä. sind moralische und materielle Bindungen herzustellen.

Dieses Vorgehen dient dem Zweck, daß Vertrauensverhältnis zu ████ zu stören und bei ████ ein Gefühl des Mißtrauens zu wecken.

Es wird vorgeschlagen, daß diese Verbindung durch Genossen ████████, FDJ Bezirksleitung Karl-Marx-Stadt, aufgenommen wird.

- Mit ████ sind legendierte Aussprachen als Abt. K ohne bedeutsamen Inhalt zu führen, um einerseits ein Vertrauensverhältnis der Abt. K zu ████ vorzutäuschen und andererseits die Verbindung des ████ zu ████ und anderen zu verunsichern.

  Durch diese Aussprachen ist der Verdacht zu bestärken, daß ████ vertrauliche Informationen an die Abt. K weitergibt.

  Es wird vorgeschlagen, daß diese Maßnahme durch Gen. Major Franik der Abteilung XX realisiert wird.

2. 2. In der operativen Bearbeitung des ████ ist ständig zu prüfen, ob Hinweise und Beweise für kriminelle Handlungen und Verstöße gegen die staatliche Ordnung erarbeitet werden können. Alle derartigen Hinweise sind umfassend zu prüfen, um weitere Anhaltspunkte für die Fortsetzung der Zersetzungsmaßnahmen zu finden.

2. 3. Das öffentliche Ansehen des ████ ist durch Ausnutzen vorhandener moralischer Schwächen und den zielgerichteten Einsatz zuverlässiger IM zu kompromittieren.

Dabei sind solche Verhaltensweisen des Schade auszunutzen, wie:

- übermäßiger Alkoholgenuß
- wechselnde intime Beziehungen zu teilweise moralisch verkommenen Personen, sexuelle Triebhaftigkeit und Interesse für Pornographie
- zweitweilige finanzielle Schwierigkeiten, Ausleihe finanzieller Mittel.

3. The goal of coordinated political-operative measures with respect to person

XXX

is to cause him, through intense political-ideological cultivation, support, and appropriate political-operational measures, to:

- publicly declare a growing commitment to the cultural politics of our party,
- document this commitment through the creation of party-oriented, realistic artworks close to the people,
- distance himself from the activities of persons XXX and XXX as well as their connections.

His public commitment to socialist cultural politics should achieve a loss of credibility for the antisocialist objectives of the persons surrounding the suspects XXX and XXX and thereby bring about a public break.

<u>The following measures should be carried out for this purpose:</u>

3.1 The Head of the Culture Department at the District Council of Karl-Marx-Stadt, Gen. Joachim Schlund, shall continue the already-issued order from the district leadership of the Karl-Marx-Stadt SED to undertake individual political-ideological work with XXX, increasing personal contact and ensuring the return flow of information about the results of the cultivation process.

3.2 Contracts for wall paintings, building-linked artworks, and graphics shall be contracted by clients in the community who shall support consistently party-oriented and people-friendly creation and enable intensive exertion of influence via the client. Suitable mentors shall be selected for this purpose.

<u>Such clients could include:</u>

- District Council of KMStadt, Dept. Culture – Gen. Schlund
- Free German Trade Union Federation (FDGB) District Chief KMStadt, Dept. Culture – Gen. Uschpilkat, Secretary of the FDGB District Committee (This measure will be implemented in cooperation with Dept. XVIII)

3. Das Ziel koordinierter politisch-operativer Maßnahmen zur Person

[redacted]

besteht darin, ihn durch intensive politisch-ideologische Erziehungsarbeit, Förderung und geeignete politisch-op. Maßnahmen zu veranlassen,

- ein wachsendes Bekenntnis zur Kulturpolitik unserer Partei öffentlich abzugeben,

- durch das Schaffen parteilicher, realistischer und volksverbundener Kunstwerke dieses Bekenntnis zu dokumentieren,

- sich gegenüber den Aktivitäten der Personen [redacted] und [redacted] sowie deren Verbindungen zu distanzieren.

Durch sein offenes Bekenntnis zur sozialistischen Kulturpolitik soll erreicht werden, daß [redacted] an Glaubwürdigkeit für die antisozialistischen Zielstellungen der Personen um die Verdächtigen [redacted] und [redacted] verliert und dadurch ein offener Bruch herbeigeführt wird.

Dazu sind folgende Maßnahmen durchzuführen:

3.1. Der Leiter der Abteilung Kultur beim Rat des Bezirkes Karl-Marx-Stadt, Gen. Joachim Schlund hat den bereits erteilten Auftrag der Bezirksleitung der SED/KMStadt zur individuellen politisch-ideologischen Arbeit mit [redacted] weiterzuführen, den persönlichen Kontakt zu intensivieren und den Rückfluß über die Ergebnisse des Erziehungsprozesses zu gewährleisten.

3.2. Durch gesellschaftliche Auftraggeber sind an [redacted] Aufträge für Wandbilder, baugebundene Kunstwerke und Graphiken zu vergeben, die von ihm ein konsequentes parteiliches und volksverbundenes Schaffen fordern und eine intensive ideologische Einflußnahme durch die Auftraggeber ermöglichen. Dazu sind jeweils geeignete Mentoren auszuwählen.

Solche Auftraggeber können sein:

- Rat des Bezirkes KMStadt, Abt. Kultur - Gen. Schlund

- FDGB-Bezirksvorstand KMStadt, Abt. Kultur- Gen. Uschpilkat, Sekretär des FDGB-Bezirksvorstandes (Diese Maßnahme wird in Abstimmung mit der Abt. XVIII realisiert)

- District Secretary of the GDR Cultural Association/KMStadt
  - Gen. Weber

- Free German Youth district leadership KMStadt – Gen. Kirchner

In addition, the following can be reviewed:

- Contract-awarding through the district committees of the Society for German-Soviet Friendship, the Sport and Technology Association, as well as through combines and industries of the KMStadt district.

3.3 Suitable political-operative measures shall be used to cause XXX to become effective in his function as XXX in the KMStadt regional district. Electoral orders shall recruit XXX in the solution of social problems.

Reliable unofficial collaborators/Unofficial Informant shall be deployed for the execution of these measures who present these electoral orders to XXX. Strict monitoring and instructions for execution of these contracts for XXX shall be organized by the responsible People's Representative.

3.4 Depending on the respective state of XXX's political-ideological development and his connection to the district party and state organs, more comprehensive support measures may be introduced such as:

- Sending representatives to exhibitions abroad, in both socialist and capitalist countries,
  (This requires coordinating measures with Main Dept. XX via the Central Committee of the GDR Association of Visual Artists/Berlin)

- Approval of travel, heretofore repeatedly denied, to capitalist countries to visit exhibitions, priority offering of study trips, etc.
  (This requires the coordination of measures with Main Dept. XX and district party leadership)

- Awards, prizes, and artistic recognition in the form of funded prizes from state and social organizations and institutions
  (These measures can be implemented through the District Council, Dept. Culture, through the FDGB district committee, Dept. Culture, and through the District Secretary of the GDR Cultural Association/KMStadt)

- Bezirkssekretariat des Kulturbundes der DDR/KMStadt - Gen. Weber

- FDJ Bezirksleitung KMStadt - Gen. Kirchner

Weiterhin kann geprüft werden:

- Auftragsvergabe durch die Bezirksvorstände der DSF, der GST, des DTSB sowie durch Kombinate und Betriebe des Bezirkes KMStadt.

3. 3. Durch geeignete politisch-operative Maßnahmen ist zu veranlassen, daß ██████ in seiner Funktion als ██████ im Landkreis KMStadt wirksam wird. Durch Wähleraufträge ist ██████ zu aktiver Mitwirkung bei der Lösung gesellschaftlicher Probleme heranzuziehen.

Zur Durchführung dieser Maßnahmen sind zuverlässige IM/GMS einzusetzen, die ██████ entsprechende Wähleranliegen vortragen. Über die zuständige Volksvertretung ist die straffe Kontrolle und Anleitung zur Durchführung der an ██████ ergangenen Aufträge zu organisieren.

3. 4. Abhängig vom jeweiligen Stand der politisch-ideologischen Entwicklung des ██████ und seiner Bindung an die Partei - und Staatsorgane des Bezirkes werden weitergehende Fördermaßnahmen eingeleitet, wie:

- Beschicken von Ausstellungen im sozialistischen und kapitalistischen Ausland, (hierzu sind koordinierte Maßnahmen mit der HA XX über den Zentralvorstand des Verbandes bildender Künstler der DDR/Berlin erforderlich)
- Genehmigung der bisher mehrfach abgelehnten Reisen in das kapitalistische Ausland zum Besuch von Ausstellungen, vorrangiges Angebot von Studienreisen u. a. (hierzu sind Maßnahmen mit der HA XX und der SED-Bezirksleitung abzustimmen)

- Auszeichnungen, Prämierungen und künstlerische Anerkennung in Form von Förderpreisen staatlicher und gesellschaftlicher Organisationen und Einrichtungen, (diese Maßnahmen können durch den Rat des Bezirkes, Abt. Kultur, durch den Bezirksvorstand des FDGB, Abt. Kultur und durch das Bezirkssekretariat des Kulturbundes der DDR/KMStadt realisiert werden)

3.5 Measures such as the following shall be reviewed for the creation of further ties between XXX and party and state organs:

- Temporary revocation of XXX's driver's license due to hazardous driving while drunk and short-term reinstatement by the apparatus of state.
  (This operative measure will be carried out in coordination with Departments VII and VIII)

- In the framework of his travel, customs controls shall be carried out upon reentry into the GDR. The return of temporarily confiscated items shall be organized.
  (Corresponding operative measures will be initiated via Dept. VI)

- Local organs of state shall develop a good relationship with the father of XXX XXX. As necessary, support shall be provided via XXX concerning technical improvements XXX to recruit laborers etc. in order to build trust and recognition of district party and state organs.
  (Material and moral support can be carried out by XXX and the local council. This requires coordination with the relevant MfS DE).

<u>Operative measures in suspect's circle of acquaintances</u>

1. The objective of the political-operative and political-ideological measures with respect to person

   XXX
   XXX
   XXX

   is to solidify XXX's trust in district party leadership. This is intended to achieve a gradual distancing and turning away from the circle of persons surrounding XXX.

3\. 5. Zur Schaffung weiterer Bindungen des an die Partei- und Staatsorgane des Bezirkes sind solche Maßnahmen zu prüfen, wie:

- Zeitweiliger Entzug der Fahrerlaubnis des wegen Verkehrsgefährdung durch Trunkenheit und kurzfristiger Rückgabe durch den Staatsapparat.
(diese operative Maßnahme wird in Koordination mit den Abteilungen VII und VIII durchgeführt)

- Im Rahmen seiner Reisetätigkeit sind Zollkontrollen bei Wiedereinreise in die DDR durchzuführen. Die Rückgabe von zeitweilig eingezogenen Sachen ist zu organisieren.
(entsprechende operative Maßnahmen werden über die Abt. VI veranlaßt)

- Zum Vater des ist durch die örtlichen Staatsorgane ein gutes Verhältnis herzustellen. Gegebenfalls erfolgt Unterstützung über zur möglichen technischen Verbesserung Zur Beschaffung von Handwerkern u. ä. um auf dieser Grundlage Vertrauen und Anerkennung der Partei- und Staatsorgane des Bezirkes zum Ausdruck zu bringen.
(die materielle und moralische Unterstützung kann über und den örtlichen Rat erfolgen. Dazu ist die Abstimmung mit den betreffenden DE des MfS notwendig).

Operative Maßnahmen im Verbindungskreis der Verdächtigen

1\. Die Zielstellung der politisch-operativen und politisch-ideologischen Maßnahmen zur Person

besteht darin, die Vertrauensbeziehungen des zur Parteiführung des Bezirkes zu festigen. Dadurch soll eine schrittweise Distanzierung und Abkehr vom Personenkreis um erreicht werden.

To achieve this objective, it is necessary for a select comrade of district party leadership to undertake intense political-ideological work with XXX.
We recommend that a responsible comrade from the area of economics be assigned to this task. XXX
The concrete details of these measures shall be determined in coordination with Dept. XVIII.

2. The objective of the political-operative measures with respect to person

XXX
XXX
XXX

is undermining and isolation vis-à-vis the XXX circle as well as the reduction of his influence in the "Neruda Club."

Through the deployment of suitable unofficial collaborators, existing personal differences between XXX and XXX shall be exacerbated and intensified, with the goal especially of causing XXX and XXX to distance themselves from XXX.

In XXXX's place of work, XXX shall be given more intensive political-ideological support through key positions in the KMStadt Technological Institute. He shall receive party contracts which will require his personal engagement, even in his free time.

Corresponding measures shall be carried out by Division XX/3.

3. Through continual political-ideological influence measures by party and state organs in the KMStadt district on the persons:

XXX
XXX
XXX
and

Lutz VOIGTMANN
January 29, 1941 in Krostitz
Freelance painter/graphic artist - KMStadt

Zum Erreichen dieser Zielstellung ist es erforderlich, daß ein ausgewählter Genosse der Bezirksleitung der Partei mit eine intensive politisch-ideologische Arbeit leistet.

Es wird vorgeschlagen, daß mit dieser Aufgabe ein verantwortlicher Genosse aus dem Bereich Wirtschaft beauftragt wird.

Zur Konkretisierung dieser Maßnahmen erfolgt die Abtimmung mit der Abt. XVIII.

2. Die Zielstellung der pol.-operativen Maßnahmen zur Person

besteht in der Verunsicherung und Isolierung gegenüber dem Kreis sowie im Abbau seines Einflusses im "Neruda-Club" KMStadt.

Durch den Einsatz geeigneter IM werden die zwischen und bestehenden persönlichen Differenzen verstärkt und zugespitzt, so daß vor allem von Seiten der Personen und eine Distanzierung gegenüber herbeigeführt wird.
Im Arbeitsbereich des wird durch Schlüsselpositionen an der TH KMStadt politisch-ideologisch stärker gefordert. Er erhält Parteiaufträge, die seinen persönlichen Einsatz auch bis in das Freizeitbereich verlangen.

Entsprechende Maßnahmen werden durch das Ref. XX/3 durchgeführt.

3. Durch eine kontinuierliche politisch-ideologische Einflußnahme der Partei und Staatsorgane des Bezirkes KMStadt auf die Personen

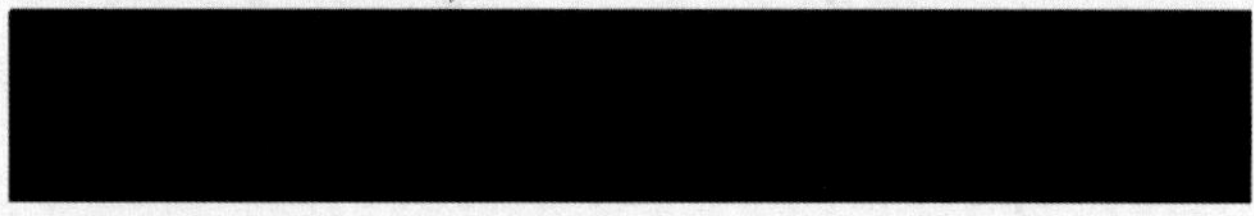

und

Lutz V o i g t m a n n
29. 01. 1941 in Krostitz
freischaffender Maler/Graphiker – KMStadt

it shall be ensured that the negative artistic and ideological influence of XXX and others shall not increase.

Targeted political-ideological influence measures shall be used to bring about the distancing of both artists from persons surrounding XXX.

Support measures are necessary for the achievement of this objective. These measures shall be carried out by the appropriate organs of state, e.g. the District Council of KMStadt, Dept. Culture, the FDGB District Committee, Dept. Culture, the District Secretary's Office of the GDR Cultural Association/KM-Stadt, etc.:

- Such support measures can take place in the context of the targeted granting of contracts for paintings and graphics. The content of the contracts shall be designed to demand consistent party- and people-friendly work and to ensure the political-ideological influence of the contract-giver.
- Both persons shall be given preferential treatment in selection for study trips to allied socialist countries. The delegating institutions shall exercise influence to ensure that the impressions gained on these study trips are realized artistically.
- Targeted ideological influence operations on these persons by progressive unofficial/social collaborators (IMs/GMSs) shall promote and support the process of their development into a socialist artistic personality.
  The deployed IMs/GMSs shall give these persons moral and material support, e.g. in the procurement and provision of better studios, etc.

4. The objective of the political-operative measures with respect to person

XXX
XXX
XXX

is to compile evidence and indications in the sense of §106 StGB through intensive operative handling. All evidence and indications gathered during this handling are to be checked for criminal actions.

ist zu sichern, daß sich der negative künstlerisch-ideologische Einfluß von [redacted] u. a. auf diese Personen nicht verstärkt.

Durch die zielgerichtete politisch-ideologische Einflußnahme ist zu erreichen, daß sich beide Künstler von den Personen um [redacted] distanzieren.

Zum Erreichen dieser Zielstellung ist es erforderlich, daß durch die entsprechenden Staatsorgane, wie den Rat des Bezirkes KMStadt, Abteilung Kultur, dem FDGB-Bezirksvorstand, Abt. Kultur, dem Bezirkssekretariat des Kulturbundes der DDR/KMStadt, u. ä. Fördermaßnahmen realisiert werden:

- Solche Fördermaßnahmen können im Rahmen einer gezielten Auftragserteilung zur Schaffung von Gemälden und Graphiken erfolgen. Die Aufträge sind inhaltlich so zu bestimmen, daß sie ein konsequentes parteiliches und volksverbundenes Schaffen erfordern und der pol.-ideologische Einfluß der Auftraggeber gewährleistet wird.
- Beide Personen sind bevorzugt für Studienreisen in die befreundeten sozialistischen Länder auszuwählen. Durch die delegierenden Einrichtungen ist darauf Einfluß zu nehmen, daß die während dieser Studienreisen gewonnenen Eindrücke künstlerisch umgesetzt werden.
- Durch die gezielte ideologische Einflußnahme progressiver IM/GMS auf diese Persoen ist ihr Entwicklungsprozeß im Sinne einer sozialistischen Künstlerpersönlichkeit zu fördern und zu unterstützen.
  Die eingesetzten IM/GMS geben diesen Personen moralische und materielle Unterstützung. Z. B. bei der Beschaffung und Bereitstellung besserer Ateliers u. ä.

4. Die Zielstellung der politisch-operativen Maßnahmen zur Person

[redacted]

besteht darin, durch eine intensive operative Bearbeitung in einer OPK Hinweise und Beweise gem. § 106 StGB zu erarbeiten. Im Rahmen der operativen Bearbeitung sind alle Hinweise und Beweise auf kriminelle Handlungen mit zu prüfen.

Seventeen file pages from the "Plan 'Avant-Garde Circle'" 1977
Source: BStU, MfS BV KMSt, AKG 3485, Vol. 1, 18–34.

A special action plan shall be developed for the operative handling of person XXX.
The results of operative handling shall be comprehensively used for continued decomposition and differentiation of the circle surrounding XXX.
Responsible: Head of Division XX/7

5. All of the suspect's known or emerging connections are to be quickly and meaningfully reported on. Decisions concerning the operative measures for achieving the objective of differentiation and decomposition shall depend on concrete circumstances and conditions.

The results of the Who's-Who Report shall be ready for delivery on demand, including a photograph.

Responsible: Head of Division XX/7

Securing Focus Subjects

6. "Galerie oben"
Karl-Marx-Stadt, Innere Klosterstrasse
(Agricola House)

Sales Cooperative of Visual Artists of the Karl-Marx-Stadt Association of Visual Artists

The objective of the political-operative work is that the "Galerie oben" guarantees clear political-ideological and party-oriented work with the artists and that the gallery is removed from the anti-socialist forces surrounding XXX.
The XXX "Galerie oben" XXX shall be pressured out through targeted operative measures, as he offers no guarantee of the consistent realization of party cultural politics in cooperation with the artists. This pressuring shall, however, occur in such a way that the relationship of trust between the artists and XXX is fortified.

Responsible: Head of Division XX/4

Zur op. Bearbeitung der Person █████ ist ein gesonderter Maßnahmeplan zu erarbeiten.
Das Ergebnis der operativen Bearbeitung ist umfassend für die weitere Zersetzung und Differenzierung des Kreises um █████ zu nutzen.

verantwortlich: Ref.-Ltr. XX/7

5. Alle bekannten und bekanntwerdenden Verbindungen der Verdächtigen sind kurzfristig und aussagekräftig aufzuklären. Nach den konkreten Umständen und Bedingungen ist zu entscheiden, welche op. Maßnahmen zur Durchsetzung der Zielstellung der Differenzierung und Zersetzung durchzuführen sind.

Die Ergebnisse der "Wer ist Wer?" - Aufklärung sind mit Foto abrufbereit zu halten.

verantwortlich: Ref.-Ltr. XX/7

Sicherung von Schwerpunktobjekten:

6. "Galerie oben"

Karl-Marx-Stadt, Innere Klosterstraße
(Agricolahaus)

Verkaufsgenossenschaft bild. Künstler des VBK
KMStadt

Die Zielstellung der pol.-operativen Arbeit besteht darin, daß in der "Galerie oben" eine klare politisch-ideologische und parteiliche Arbeit mit den Künstlern gewährleistet und die Galerie dem Einfluß der antisozialistischen Kräfte um █████ entzogen wird.
Der █████ "Galerie oben", █████ ist durch gezielte operative Maßnahmen herauszulösen, da er keine Gewähr für die konsequente Verwirklichung der Kulturpolitik der Partei in der Arbeit mit den Künstlern bietet. Die Herauslösung soll jedoch gleichzeitig so erfolgen, daß das Vertrauensverhältnis der Künstler zu █████ gefestigt wird.

verantwortlich: Referatsleiter XX/4

The new manager of the "Galerie oben" shall be a person selected and installed to ensure the enforcement of our party's cultural politics. The reliable and repeatedly vetted unofficial collaborator "Harald Hauser" should be reviewed for this position.

Responsible: Head of Division XX/7

7. "Intelligentsia Club, Pablo Neruda"
Karl-Marx-Stadt, GDR Cultural Association/KMStadt

and

Intelligentsia Club and the Small Gallery of the GDR Cultural Association in local communities.

The political-operative measures are to be carried out similarly to the objectives for "Galerie oben."

The following measures are necessary for the comprehensive securing of these areas:

- Among the organizers and regular visitors of the Pablo Neruda Club, unofficial collaborators/informants shall be deployed who can have an active influence on the content of visual artist exhibitions with regard to the Party's cultural politics.
  In this context, representatives of party-oriented realistic art among the artists are to be supported.

  Responsible: Head of Division XX/7

- With XXX "Neruda Club" XXX, fabricated unofficial interviews shall be carried out with the goal of strengthening their engagement with the representatives of realistic, party-oriented art. Absolutely no operative knowledge should be disclosed in these interviews.

  Responsible: Head of Division XX/7

- We recommend that the District Secretary's Office of the GDR Cultural Association/KMStadt be assigned the mission by district party leadership to report on accomplished political-ideological work with the intelligentsia, particularly with visual artists, for the implementation of party decisions in the sphere of socialist cultural politics. This reporting should also cover work in the

Als neuer Leiter der "Galerie oben" ist eine Persönlichkeit auszuwählen und einzusetzen, die die Durchsetzung der Kulturpolitik unserer Partei in der Galerie gewährleistet. Dazu ist der Einsatz des mehrfach überprüften und zuverlässigen IMV "Harald Hauser" zu prüfen.

verantwortlich: Referatsleiter XX/7

7. "Club der Intelligenz Pablo-Neruda"
Karl-Marx-Stadt, Kulturbund der DDR/KMStadt

sowie

Club der Intelligenz und Kleine Galerie des Kulturbundes der DDR in den Kreisen.

Die politisch-operativen Maßnahmen sind analog der Zielstellung für die "Galerie oben" durchzuführen.

Zur umfassenden Sicherung dieser Bereiche sind folgende Maßnahmen erforderlich:

- Im Kreis der Organisatoren und Stammbesucher des Pablo-Neruda-Clubs sind IM/GMS einzusetzen, die auf den Inhalt der Veranstaltungen bild. Künstler aktiven Einfluß im Sinne der Kulturpolitik der Partei nehmen.

  In diesem Zusammenhang sind Vertreter parteilicher und realistischer Kunst unter den bild. Künstlern zu fördern.

  verantwortlich: Referatsleiter XX/7

- Mit ████████ "Neruda-Clubs", ████████ sind legendierte inoffizielle Aussprachen zu führen mit dem Ziel, ihr Engagement für die Vertreter der realistischen, parteilichen und volksverbundenen Kunst zu verstärken. In diesen Gesprächen ist keinerlei operatives Wissen preiszugeben.

  verantwortlich: Referatsleiter XX/7

- Es wird vorgeschlagen, daß das Bezirkssekretariat des Kulturbundes der DDR/KMStadt durch die Bezirksleitung der SED/KMStadt den Auftrag erhält, periodisch über die geleistete politisch-ideologische Arbeit mit der Intelligenz, insbesondere mit den bild. Künstlern zur Durchsetzung der Parteibeschlüsse auf dem Gebiet der sozialistischen Kulturpolitik, Bericht erstatten. Diese Berichterstattung soll auch die Arbeit im

"Pablo Neruda Club" of Karl-Marx-Stadt as well as among the intelligentsia and galleries in local communities.

8. Use of Unofficial Informants (IMs)

8.1 IMV "Frank Körner," Dept. XX

The informant shall be assigned the task of continually developing existing relationships of trust with the suspects and on this basis to constantly inform the MfS about the ideological effectiveness of the suspects as well as the means and methods they use and their social connections. In the course of the decomposition process, he shall ensure the suspects of his loyalty without himself becoming actively hostile to the state.
If the suspects retreat into conspiracy, he shall be tasked with joining them in this conspiracy.
The informant shall perform continual, comprehensive monitoring of the reactions of the suspects in the course of decomposition and differentiation.

Responsible: Captain Haubold, Division XX/7

8.2 IMV "Peter," Dept. XX

This informant shall be released from his current function with a suitable fabricated backstory. This backstory should be designed to deepen the relationship of trust with the suspects.

Responsible: Major Decker, Head of Division XX/4

8.3 IMV "Voko Müller", District Office KMStadt/City

This informant shall maintain friendly relations with the suspects of Operation "Maggot" on the basis of technical assistance.
Via targeted contract awarding, the informant shall be deployed for comprehensive personal monitoring of the suspects in their homes as well as for the securing of operative-technical measures.

Responsible: Captain Lermer, District Office KMStadt/City

"Pablo-Neruda-Club" Karl-Marx-Stadt sowie in den Club der Intelligenz und Galerien des Kulturbundes in den Kreisen erfassen.

8. IM-Einsatz

8.1. IMV "Frank Körner" , Abt. XX

Der IMV erhält den Auftrag, kontinuierlich die bestehenden vertraulichen Beziehungen zu den Verdächtigen auszubauen und auf dieser Basis das MfS ständig über die ideologische Wirksamkeit, die angewandten Mittel und Methoden sowie über den Verbindungskreis der Verdächtigen zu informieren. Im Verlauf des Zersetzungsprozeßes hat er den Verdächtigen seine Loyalität zu versichern ohne selbst staatsfeindlich aktiv zu werden.
Bei Zurückziehen der Verdächtigen in die Konspiration erhält er den Auftrag, mit ihnen in die Konspiration zu gehen.
Über die Reaktionen der Verdächtigen im Verlauf der Zersetzung und Differenzierung ist durch den IMV eine ständige und umfassende Kontrolle auszuüben.

verantwortlich: Oberleutnant Haubold, Ref. XX/7

8.2. IMV "Peter", Abt. XX

Der IMV wird mit einer geeigneten Legende aus seiner bisherigen Funktion herausgelöst. Die Legende ist so zu gestalten, daß sich dadurch das Vertrauensverhältnis zu den Verdächtigen vertieft.

verantwortlich: Major Decker, Referatsleiter XX/4

8.3. IMV "Voko Müller", KD KMStadt/Stadt

Der IMV unterhält gegenwärtig ein freundschaftliches Verhältnis zu den Verdächtigen des OV "Made" auf der Basis handwerklicher Unterstützung.
Durch gezielte Auftragserteilung ist der IMV zur umfassenden Personenkontrolle der Verdächtigen im Wohnbereich sowie zur Sicherstellung op.-techn. Maßnahmen einzusetzen.

verantwortlich: Hauptmann Lermer, KD KMStadt/Stadt

8.4 IMV "Harald Hauser", Dept. XX

On the basis of his journalistic activity in the area of visual arts, he is in a position to provide evaluations of the public political-ideological effectiveness of the suspects. His deployment shall occur in accordance with the plan for taking over the key position of the "Galerie oben" in Karl-Marx-Stadt.
On the basis of his publishing activity and his personality, he is in a position to aid in the implementation of the Party's cultural politics in this sphere.

Responsible: Captain Freitag, Head of Division XX/7

8.5 IME "Paul Schmidt," Dept. XX

The existing friendly relationship to person XXX in the social circle surrounding XXX shall be further developed in order to gain entry into the circle around XXX.
Informant "Paul Schmidt" shall actively support the process of differentiation and decomposition through targeted missions.

Responsible: Captain Freitag, Head of Division XX/7

8.6 IMV "Horst Sommer", Dept. XVIII

This informant is acquainted with the suspects through repeated visits to "Neruda Club" events. The informant and the suspects have already engaged in ideological disputes about visual art.
The use of this informant will aim at carrying out an open, partisan debate with the suspects and their social circle.

Responsible: Head of Division XX/7 in conjunction with Dept. XVIII

8.4. IMV "Harald Hauser", Abt. XX

Auf der Grundlage seiner journalistischen Tätigkeit im Bereich der bild. Kunst ist er in der Lage, Einschätzungen über die politisch-ideologische Wirksamkeit der Verdächtigen in der Öffentlichkeit zu geben. Sein Einsatz erfolgt entsprechend der Konzeption zur geplanten Übernahme der Schlüsselposition in der "Galerie oben" Karl-Marx-Stadt.
Auf der Grundlage seiner publizistischen Tätigkeit und seiner Persönlichkeit ist er in der Lage, die Kulturpolitik der Partei in diesem Bereich durchsetzen zu helfen.

verantwortlich: Hauptmann Freitag, Referatsleiter XX/7

8.5. IME "Paul Schmidt", Abt. XX

Das bestehende freundschaftliche Verhältnis zur Person [redacted] aus dem Freundeskreis um [redacted] ist weiter auszubauen, um durch [redacted] in den Kreis um [redacted] eingeführt zu werden.
Durch gezielte Aufträge hat der IME "Paul Schmidt" aktiv den Differenzierungs- und Zersetzungsprozeß zu unterstützen.

verantwortlich: Hauptmann Freitag, Referatsleiter XX/7

8.6. IMV "Horst Sommer", Abt. XVIII

Durch kontinuierliche Besuche von Veranstaltungen des "Neruda-Clubs" ist der IMV mit den Verdächtigen bekannt. Im Rahmen der Gespräche über bild. Kunst kam es bereits zu ideologischen Auseinandersetzungen zwischen dem IMV und den Verdächtigen.

Mit dem Einsatz des IMV wird das Ziel verfolgt, in den Veranstaltungen der bild. Künstler eine parteiliche und offene Auseinandersetzung mit den Verdächtigen und deren Freundeskreis zu führen.

verantwortlich: Referatsleiter XX/7 in Verb. mit Abt. XVIII

8.7 IMV "Matthias Bosch", Dept. XX

This informant shall develop relations of trust to persons XXX and Lutz Voigtmann. On the basis of these relations of trust, the state of the artists' political-ideological attitude shall be continually analyzed in order to develop further operative conclusions.

Responsible: Captain Haubold, Division XX/7

8.8 IMS "Peter Schulz", Dept. XX

This informant's position within the Association of Visual Artists KMStadt, where he represents party interests, shall be used to promote the ideological clarification process. The informant shall be assigned the task of further developing friendly and collegial relations with painter XXX.
The goal is to exercise a positive influence if desired and to strengthen his relations of trust with district party leadership.

Responsible: Lieutenant Meyer, Division XX/7

9. Operative Control Measures:

9.1 Appropriate operative control measures of departments

VI, VII, M, PZF shall be introduced.

The objective is to:

continually determine the suspects' reactions to the introduced measures

- and to learn about their further plans and intentions, means and methods, as well as the character of their connections,
- in order to be able to determine appropriate conclusions and further actions on this basis.

Responsible: Head of Division XX/7

8.7. IMV "Matthias Bosch", Abt. XX

Durch den IMV sind die Vertrauensbeziehungen zu den Personen ███ und Lutz Voigtmann auszubauen. Auf Grundlage dieses Vertrauensverhältnisses ist der Stand der politisch-ideologischen Haltung der Künstler ständig zu analysieren, um daraus weitere operative Schlußfolgerungen ziehen zu können.

verantwortlich: Oberleutnant Haubold, Ref. XX/7

8.8. IMS "Peter Schulz", Abt. XX

Die parteiliche Position des IMS innerhalb des Verbandes bild. Künstler KMStadt wird genutzt, um den ideologischen Klärungsprozeß im Verband mit voranzutreiben. Der IMS erhält den Auftrag, das freundschaftlich-kollegiale Verhältnis zum Maler ███ weiter auszubauen.
Das Ziel besteht darin, eine positive Einflußnahme auf Wunsch auszuüben und dessen Vertrauensbeziehungen zur Parteiführung des Bezirkes zu festigen.

verantwortlich: Leutnant Meyer, Ref. XX/7

9. Operative Kontrollmaßnahmen:

9.1. Gegen die im Differenzierungsprozeß erfaßten Personen sind op. Kontrollmaßnahmen der Abteilungen

VI, VII, M, PZF u. a. geeignete Maßnahmen

einzuleiten.

Die Zielstellung besteht darin:

- alle Reaktionen der Verdächtigen auf die eingeleiteten Maßnahmen ständig in Erfahrung zu bringen,
- ihre weiteren Pläne und Absichten, Mittel und Methoden kennenzulernen sowie den Charakter ihrer Verbindungen weiter aufzuklären,

um auf dieser Grundlage geeignete Schlußfolgerungen ziehen zu können.

verantwortlich: Referatsleiter XX/7

9.2 In the case of suspects

XXX
XXX
XXX

secret searches are to be carried out in support of the above-named objectives.

Responsible: Head of Division XX/7

Confirmed:
Head of District Administration

[signature]

Gehlert
Major General

Head of Department XX

[signature]

Engelhardt
Major

9.2. Bei den Verdächtigen

sind zur Unterstützung der vorgenannten Zielstellung konspirative Durchsuchungen durchzuführen.

<u>verantwortlich:</u> Referatsleiter XX/7

bestätigt:
Leiter der Bezirksverwaltung

Gehlert
Generalmajor

Leiter der Abteilung XX

Engelhardt
Major

Subject "Větrník," Subject "Aktual"

StB (ČSSR)

In 1968, state security in Czechoslovakia opened an operative case file on Subject "Větrník" and in 1974, on Subject "Aktual." Both operations concerned the surveillance of Milan Knížák, considered the "Director of Fluxus East" since 1965, and Marie Saudková. The "Větrník" is also directed towards Knížák and his studio. The Czechoslovakian Stasi, however, does not document any art actions: only Knížák's and Saudková's banal, insignificant daily activities. Their most detailed documentation is reserved for themselves: their names, their clothing from their shoes to their hats, the cars they drive during observation, e.g. Volga and Simka (conspicuous brands at the time which only the nomenklatura owned), as well as the technology they used to carry out the surveillance. They also made drawings, not of the activities of Knížák and "Aktual" but instead of the locations where their spies and vehicles were standing. (S)

PŘÍSNĚ TAJNÉ!

MAPKA SLEDOVAČKY č. SI-00714/02S-68

1015/74

Objekt VĚTRNÍK-1

Atelier Milana Knížáka

Prováděno 9.10–16.10.1968 a.č. SL-90+

-64

 StB (ČSSR) Measures and "Decompositions" Cover, Větrník file Source: 81-001015/02-S-74-460, 0001 1968

S StB Praha (State Security Service)4th Division, 1st Dept. 1
SI 00714/02-S-68 TOP SECRET!
MINISTRY OF HOME AFFAIRS
KS SNB PRAGUE1

Section II/A, 7th Department
Ref. number: OS -002397/7-70-08

Approved by: Ivorsky[2]
Date: 10.8.1968

Request to establish and perform surveillance and gather intelligence

Operation code name: VĚTRNÍK 1

Name and surname: artistic studio of Milan KNÍŽÁK, Nový Svět 19, Prague 1

[The rest of the form including personal data is not filled in, transl. note]

Date and place of birth ______ Nationality ______ National citizenship ______

Political Membership ______ Civil Status ______ School Education ______

Permanent Residence ______ Phone ______

Temporary Residence ______ Phone ______

Profession (address – place, building, gate) ______ Working hours and break possibilities ______
(Professional position, special features)

Attached for the purpose of observation (photograph of the subject, exact description with all conspicuous and distinctive features, e.g. glasses, shape of face, any special characteristics, if the subject has already been recorded, etc.) ______

Special information about the subject (indicate the means of transport used – car, streetcar, bicycle, motorcycle, cab, whether subject visits restaurants, wine bars, sports facilities, whether the subject likes women, etc.) ______

(Family members:

Wife (name and surname) unmarried ______ Date of birth, address ______

(Do they live together or separately?) ______

Photography attached: yes - no; description of children ______

(number, age, include photo and profession for older kids) ______

MINISTERSTVO VNITRA
KS SNB Praha
II/A odbor, 7.oddělení
čj. OI - 002397/4-70.68

-8 X. 1968 81 00714/02-S-68 -8 X. 1968

PŘÍSNĚ TAJNÉ!

Schvaluji: ...
Dne 8.10.1968

Žádost o zavedení sledování, střežení a zjištění

krycí jméno akce: VĚTRNÍK 1

Jméno a příjmení atelier Milana KNÍŽÁKA, Nový Svět č. 19, Praha 1

datum a místo nar. ... národnost ... stát. přísl. ...

polit. přísl. ... stav ... škol. vzdělání ...

bydliště trvalé ... telefon ...

bydliště přechodné ... telefon ...

zaměstnání (adresa - místo, budova, vrátnice) ... prac. doba a možnosti odchodu ...
(postavení v zaměstnání, zvláštnosti)

Pro účely sledování přikládáme (fotografii objekta, jeho podrobný popis se všemi nápadnými a výraznými vlastnostmi, např. brýle, jakého tvaru, příp. zvláštní znamení, objekt bude vystaven, atd.) ...

Zvláštní údaje o objektu (uvést jakých používá doprav. prostředků - auto, tramvaj, kolo, motocykl, taxi, zda navštěvuje restaurace, vinárny, sport. podniky, divadla, má rád ženy apod.) ...

Rodinní příslušníci:

manželka (jméno a příjmení) ... za svobodna ...

datum nar. ... její adresa ...
(zda bydlí společně, odloučeně)

fotografie přiložena: ano - ne, popis ...

děti (počet, stáří, u starších toto a zaměst.) - ...

Relatives (name, surname, relationship, residence, photo)

Roommate (name, surname, profession, photo)

The known names of persons who are in contact with the subject or with whom it is possible to meet (name, surname, residence, profession, photo), note whether they should be observed after a meeting with the subject

The subject is being handled on the basis of suspicion (if he/she is a member of an il legal organization, function within this organization, is it an agent, resident, contact person, is it about the control of an agent etc.): that a group of young people meets there to handle chemicals.

The observation should identify (contacts, company, addresses visited, destinations, sending of mail) of individuals who come to the studio and subsequently, create their profile

Sent correspondence (intercepted or not)

Photographs of the subject (confiscate camera or not)

The observation shall be made over a period of days, starting with ..., without interruption

Possible interruption of the observation

The subject has already been checked (yes – no)

A profile[4] has already been created at the residence (yes - no).

Further findings relevant for the observation

Attached to the application
(number of photos, other attachments)

Classify reports under AZ: Name of the Referees: Maj. Dvořák Jiří

Approved: the head of the department Ivorský On 10.8.1968

92-59

Příbuzní (jméno a příjmení, rod. vztah, bydliště, foto)...

...

Spolubydlící (jméno a příjmení, zaměst., foto)...

...

Známá jména osob, s nimiž je objekt ve spojení nebo má možnost se s nimi sejít (jméno a příjmení, nar., bydliště, zaměstnání, foto), poznamenat, zda po setkání s objektem se mají sledovat...

...

Objekt je rozpracován na podkladě podezření (je-li členem illegální organizace, jaké je jeho postavení v org., je-li agentem, residentem, spojkou, jde-li o kontrolu agenta apod.) že se tam schází skupina mladých lidí, kteří mají manipulovat s chemikáliemi.

Sledováním se má zjistit (styky, společnost, navštívené adresy, kam cestuje, odesílání pošt. zásilek apod.) osoby docházející do atelieru a provést jejich ustanovení

...

Odesílanou korespondenci (zadržet nebo ne)...

Jestliže objekt fotografuje (odebrat nebo ne) fotograf. aparát...

Jestliže objekt opustí obec (zadržet, sledovat dále nebo ne)...

Sledování provádějte po dobu ... dnů, počínaje dnem ... od hod. ... do hod. ..., nepřetržitě ...

možno přerušit sledování ...

Objekt byl lustrován (ano - ne)...

V bydlišti byla už prováděna ustanovka (ano - ne)...

Další poznatky, které mohou býti důležité při sledování...

...

K žádosti přikládám ...
(počet ks foto, jiné přílohy)

Zprávy podávejte k čj.: ... jméno referenta mjr. Dvořák Jiří

na telef. čís./kl. 2132 v noci 2114

Souhlasím náčelník odboru ... Dne 8.10.1968 19...

92-59

Number 4/ red
Number 6/. red

Approved by:

TOP SECRET
[crossed out by hand]
number

Chief of III. Division of IV. Directorate HS-StB[5]
[hand signature]
/pplk. Josef Stuchlý/[6]

SURVEILLANCE PLAN

KNÍŽÁK Milan, proprietor of a studio at Nový Svět No.19, Prague 1. A group of around 15 to 20 people reportedly meets in this studio, this group allegedly manufactures explosives.

The operation will run under the code name VĚTRNÍK 1.

CHARACTERISTICS OF THE RESIDENCE

The said studio is located in the Nový Svět, street number 9, Prague 1, on the ground floor of a two-story house with exit onto the said street. This house is part of a complex of the same or smaller houses and on the opposite side of the street the houses reach only halfway along the street. The windows of this house are low above the street level and it is possible to climb out of them without much effort. The street itself is very narrow, therefore it is not possible neither to park a mobile support unit there, nor is it possible to perform a OB[7] via undercover operatives in the street. There is a small grocer's shop near the studio. There is a telephone booth opposite the entrance to the house. There is very little traffic in this lane, both pedestrian and vehicular.

SURVEILLANCE ORGANIZATION

Given that the operation involves watching out for people entering and exiting the studio, the observation will be performed by undercover operatives in disguise. These operatives will be stationed on a nearby slope, disguised as a pair of lovers. There are benches on this slope, and it provides direct line of sight to the exit from the ...

Schvaluji :

PŘÍSNĚ TAJNÉ

Počet listů: 4 6

náčelník III. odboru IV. správy HS-Stb.

/ pplk. Josef S t u ch l ý /

PLÁN SLEDOVÁNÍ

KNÍŽÁK Milan majitel ateliéru, Nový Svět č.19, Praha 1. Zde v tomto ateliéru se má údajně scházet asi 15 až 2o ti člená skupina osob, která se ma zabývat výrobou výbušnin.

Akce bude probíhat pod krycím jménem VĚTRNÍK 1.

CHARAKTERISTIKA MÍSTA BYDLIŠTĚ

Uvedený ateliér se nachází v ulici Nový Svět č.19, Praha 1., ve dvoupcschodovém domku v přízemí s východem do uvedené ulice. Tento domek stojí v komplexu stejných i menších domků a druhá strana ulice je zastavěna jen do poloviny. Okna z uvedeného domku jsou nízko nad ulicí je z nich možno bez většího usílí vylézt. Ulice sama je velmi úzká, takže zde nelze zaparkovat ani OB, ani zde nelze provádět záchyt z otevřené stojky. Nedaleko ateliéru je malý krámek Potraviny. Naproti v chodu se nachází tel.automat. Ulička je velmi málo frekventovaná jak chodci, tak i vozidly.

ORGANISACE SLEDOVÁNÍ

Vzhledem k tomu, že se jedná o záchyt osob přicházejících a odcházejících z ateliéru bude záchyt prováděn maskovací stojkou. Milenecký pár, který bude tuto stojku znázorňovat bude umístěn v nedaleké stráni, kde se nachází lavičky a odkud je vidět přímo na východ z uvede-

... studio. They will be equipped with binoculars and a connection to the mobile operatives. This connection will be with service vehicles stationed as follows:

1 Service vehicle will be stationed near the Hotel Savoy in a position to close off the stairs in Na Náspu street.
2 Service vehicles will be in the Loreta square (Loretánské náměstí), positioned to close off Černínská and Kapucínská streets.
2 Further service vehicles will be in the area of Hradčanské square. These will follow the subject/s in case they proceed in the direction of U Brusnice street.
1 Service vehicle will be in the Pohořelec parking lot, in case a taxi is used.

Should the pair performing the surveillance of the house communicate the direction of travel of a subject, all service vehicles are to proceed individually and in turn to pick up the surveillance.

In case of an observation point being set up in the House No. 2, opposite the studio's entrance, the vehicles will be stationed in the same way and the surveillance will be performed from there.

TECHNICAL EQUIPMENT

Two complete units will be assigned to the operation consisting of:
6 Service vehicles
4 Kits for covert photography /open/
1 Set of binoculars
1 Camera with telescopic lens for the observation point

LIST OF OPERATIVES

Unit A / lead [6 handwritten signatures]
Bětík ....
Novotná ....
Šrédl ....
Štádler ....
Karas.Jiří? ....
Krupka ....

ného ateliéru. K dispozici bude míti dalekohled a dále spojení pro chodce. Toto spojení bude mít se služebními vozy, které budou umístěny následovně:

1 služební vůz bude umístěn poblíž hotelu Savoy, tak aby uzavíral schody v ulici NA Náspu.
2 služební vozy budou na Loretánském nám, tak aby uzavíraly ulice Černínskou a Kapucínskou.
2 další služební vozy budou v prostoru Hračanského nám a případě, že objekt/i/ půjdou směrem do ul. U Brusnice na tyto se napojí.
1 služební vůz bude na parkovišti Pohořelec, vpřípadě použití taxi.

Všechny služební vozy mají za úkol v případě vyrozumění dvojice, která bude provádět záchyt, o směru odchodu objekta na tohoto se jednotlivě napojovat.

V případě, že bude vybudován OB v domě č.2 naproti východu z ateliéru rozmístění vozu bude stejné a záchyt bude prováděn odtud.

TECHNICKÉ PROSTŘEDKY

Na akci budou nasazeny dvě kompletní skupiny se :
6 ti služebními vozy
4 soupravy tajného fota /otevřeného/
1 dalekohledu
1 foto s teleskopem do OB

SEZNAM PRACOVNÍKŮ

Skupina A /vedoucí ....
....
....
....
....
....

Akce VĚTRNÍK (Action VĚTRNÍK)
GRAFICKÝ PLÁN MÍSTNOSTI - AKTUEL - CLUBU (Graphical room plan - Aktuel - Club)

Pohořelec
el. dr. č. 22 (elektrická dráha (Tram)
Keplerova
Hotel Savoy
Na náspu
MZV -- Ministerstvo zahraničních věcí (Foreign Office)
Černínská
Loretánské nám. (náměstí)
Loretánská
Loreta
Kapucínská
Nový svět
Dětské hřiště (Playground)
Zahradnictví (nursery)
U kasáren
Brusnice
Pasovka (Passport office)
Kanovnická
Hradčanské nám.

Legenda (Legende)

místnost AC (Actual Club Room)
Opěrný bod (mobile base)
Služ. vozy -- služební vozy (company cars)
orgánové (Jargon for Unofficial collaborator)
stanice el. dr. (elektrické dráhy) (tram stop)
Telefon

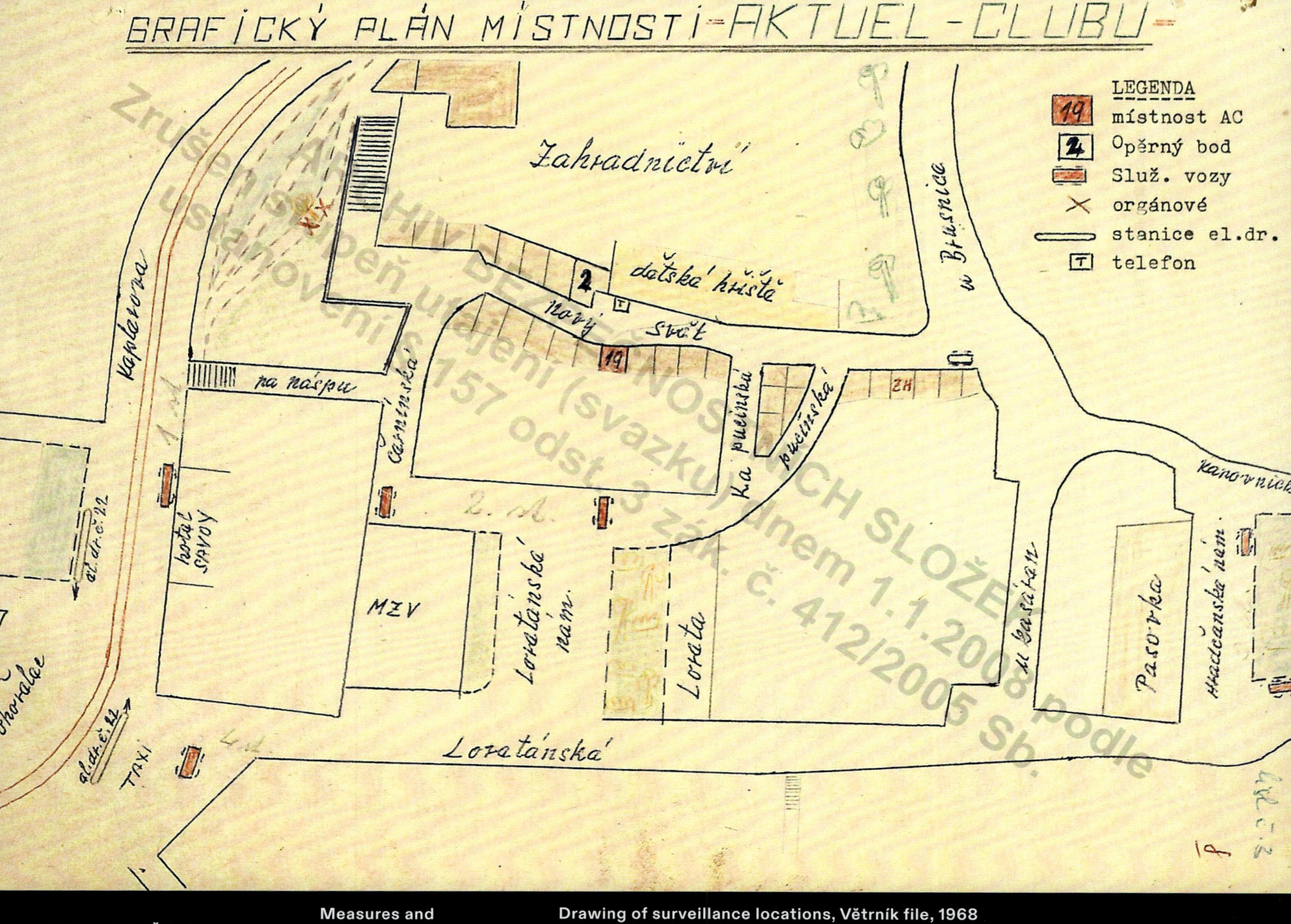

 StB (ČSSR) Measures and "Decompositions"

Drawing of surveillance locations, Větrník file, 1968
Source: 81-001015/02-S-74-460, 0001

1968

Operation – VĚTRNÍK I - surveillance: Prague 10.9.1968

Surveillance of the studio of Milan Kn i ž á k, permanent domicile in Prague 1, Nový Svět 19.

In further memos and summaries, the operation will be referred to under the code name

VĚ T R N Í K I.

09:00 hours commenced the surveillance of unknown persons who will enter or exit house number 19.

12:00 the surveillance operation VĚTRNÍK I was terminated here, no information obtained.

Operatives' attire: 10.10.1968

Pospišil: bareheaded, dark suit, blue windproof overcoat,[8] black shoes, H 5.
Říha: bareheaded, dark jacket, grey trousers, black shoes, H 5.
Lipták: bareheaded, dark suit, grey overcoat, black shoes.
Musil: bareheaded, dark suit, black shoes, grey jacket, H 5.
Fuksová: bareheaded, blue suit, black shoes, black ladies' handbag.
Macháček: bareheaded, blue jacket, blue trousers, brown shoes. H 5.
Brendl: bareheaded, black suit jacket, grey trousers, black shoes, H 5
Stedína: bareheaded, blue suit, black shoes.
Nezbeda: bareheaded, blue windproof coat, grey trousers, brown shoes, H 5.
Novotná: bareheaded, grey coat, black shoes, black handbag
Krupka: bareheaded, blue trench coat, grey trousers, black shoes, H 5 K60
Fuksa: bareheaded, blue windproof coat, grey trousers, black shoes, H 5

Vehicles:

black Tatra 603	AE 58-09	driven	5 km Com. Lipták
grey Volha	AB-13-42	"-"	7 km Com. Sedina [sic]
blue SIMCA	AJ-09-14	"-"	6 km Com. Krupka
blue SIMCA	AK-50-73	"-"	9 km Com. Musil

Control: Com. Svěrkoš 09:33 hrs

[handwritten signatures, illegible]

Translated form Czech by Dagmar Wallace-Tarry

Endnotes

1 KS SNB Praha (Krajská správa Sboru národní bezpečnosti, Regional directorate of SNB, National Security Service in Prague).
2 Handwritten signature.
3 English – windmill, weather vane.
4 The original speaks of *ustanovka*. The term is taken from Russian and refers to the report that a special unit of the State Security prepares on a person under their observation.
5 HS Stb. –Hlavní Správa Státní ezpečnosti (Main Office of State Security).
6 Pplk. –Podplůkovník (Lieutenant colonel OSL).
7 OB–Odbor Bezpečnosti (Security Department).
8 Translator's note: In the original, the colloquial expression is "šusťák." They were waterproof coats made of the synthetic fiber silon, produced only in Czechoslovakia.

Akce-VĚTRNÍK I-sledování: Praha 9.10.1968.

9

Střežení ataleiru Milana K n i ž á k a, bytem Praha I. ul. Nový Svět č.19.
V dalších svodkách bude akce uváděná pod krycím jmenem

V Ě T R N Í K I.

V 09.00 hodin bylo započato se sledováním neznámých osob, kteří zajdou, nebo opustí dům č.19.

V 12.00 hodin bylo zde sledování VĚTRNÍK I skončeno, bez poznatku.

Oblečení orgánů:

Pospišil:prostovlasý,tmavé šaty,modrý šusťák,černé boty H 5.
Říha:prostovlasý,tmavá bunda,šedá kalhoty,černe boty, H 5.
Lipták:prostovlasý,tmavé šady,šedý plášt,černé boty.
Musil:prostovlasý,tmavé šaty,černé boty,šedý kabát H 5.
Fuksová:prostovlasá,modrý kostým,černé boty,černá dámská kabelka.
Macháček:prostovlasý,modrá buda modré kalhoty,hnedé boty. H 5
Brendl:prostovlasý,čené sako,šedé kalhoty,černé boty, H 5
Stedína:prostovlasý,modré šaty,černé boty .
Nezbeda:prostovlasý,modrý šusťák,šedé kalhoty,hnědé boty, H 5.
Novotná:prostovlasá,šedý kabát,černé boty,černá kabelka
Krupka:prostovlasý, zelený plášt,tmavé kalhoty,hnědé boty H 5 K 60.
Fuksa:prostovlasý,modrý šusťák,šedé kalhoty,černé boty H 5.

AUTO:

černá T 603	AE 58-09	ujeto	5 km.	s. Lipták
šedá Volha	AB-13-42	-"-	7 km.	s. Sedina
modrá SIMCA	AJ-09-14	-"-	6 km.	s. Krupka
modrá SIMCA	AK-50-73	-"-	9 km.	s. Musil

~~Kontrola~~: s. Svěrkoš 09.33 hod.

III.

Bez poznatků.

1

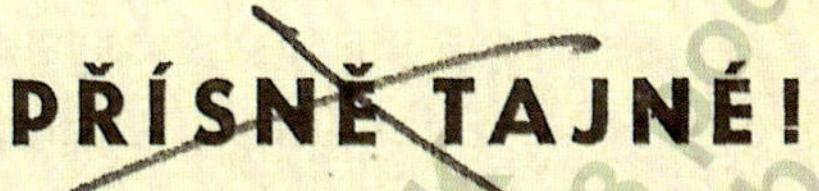

PŘÍSNĚ TAJNÉ!

Spisový svazek č. 81-001015/02-S-74-460

Objekt: AKTUÁL

Prováděno: 22-23. 10. 74, a.č. SL-90

State Security (StB) Operational Uni
Ref.: OS-007044/4-1-74
Encl.: 2 photos

Approved by: Chief of S-StB, Prague
pplk. Karel Kupec
(post, rank and surname to be typed as well)

Date 18. 10. 1974
[stamp: Registered on 29 Oct 1974]
TOP SECRET!
[stamp: illegible, 28 Oct 1974,
Handwritten: SI-001015/02-S-74-460]

SURVEILLANCE REQUEST

Surveillance is requested as part of (operation code name) A K T U Á L

Number and type of file

Grounds for surveillance:

suspicion of criminal activity pursuant Sect. 8/1, 112 of the Criminal Code (§§ 8/1, 112 tr. zák.)

Duration: 2 days, beginning on 22.10.1974 at 07.00 hours

Name: Milan Surname: K N I Ž Á K DOB: 19.4.1940

Nationality: Czech Citizenship: Czechoslovakia Marital status: single

Employment: liberal profession
Vehicle ownership: licence plate TC 74 38 type: Škoda-110 L parked: on the street in front of domicile

Resident: Prague 10, Tulipánova Street 2802
Operation to be supervised and personally handled by comrade: por. Svoboda (2nd lieutenant)

Contact details: tel.ext. 2165; 2710

Deputised by comrade: mjr. Hiřman (major) Tel.ext.: 2710

M o t i v e a n d o b j e c t i v e o f s u r v e i l l a n c e: Important information for preparation of surveillance, prevention, detection and documentation of criminal activity with regards to achieving the objective of the surveillance, namely the person's anticipated activity, known or assumed contacts, family members and similar.

The purpose of the surveillance is primarily to ascertain the daily routine. The subject lives with his partner Marie SAUDKOVÁ, who has 2 sons from her previous marriage /SAM, 9 years, DAVID, 8 years/. KNIŽÁK often uses his car, white Škoda-110L. It can be assumed that he rents a studio in Prague 6, Nový svět number 9

Signature of the operative [handwritten signature por. Svoboda]3
Approved by date
Chief of 4th Division of S StB date
[handwritten signature]
Pplk. Ladislav Irovský (Lt.Col.) date
[state: post, rank, name and surname]

S StB Praha

4. odbor, 1.odd.

operativní útvar StB

Čj. OC-007044/4-1-74

Přílohy: ~~2 foto~~

Schvaluji:

Náčelník S-StB Praha

pplk. Karel Kupec

(Fukce, hodnost a příjmení se vypisuje též strojem)

Dne 18.10.1974

PŘÍSNĚ TAJNÉ!

Návrh na sledování

S1-001015/02-S-74-460

Žádám o sledování v akci (krycí název) AKTUÁL

číslo a druh svazku

důvod rozpracování podezření z trestné činnosti podle §§ 8/1,112 tr. zák.

po dobu 2 dnů, počínaje dnem 22.10.1974 od 07.00 hodin.

Jméno Milan příjmení KNIŽÁK narozen 19.4.1940

národnost česká st. příslušnost čsl. stav svobodný

zaměstnán svobodné povolání

majitel vozidla SPZ TC 74 38 typ Š- 110 L garážuje v ulici před bydlištěm

bytem Praha 10 Tulipánova 2802

Za akci zodpovídá a osobně projedná s. por. Svoboda

bude k dosažení na telefonní lince 2165 ; 2710

Zastupuje s. mjr. Hiřman č. telefonu 2710

Důvod a cíl sledování: Důležité údaje pro přípravu sledování, předcházení, zabránění, odhalování a dokumentaci trestné činnosti vzhledem na dosažení cíle sledování, zejména předpokládaná činnost osoby, známé nebo předpokládané styky, rod. příslušníci ap.

Sledování provádět zejména za účelem zjištění režimu dne. Objekt žije ve společné domácnosti s družkou Marií SAUDKOVOU, která má z prvního manželství dva syny /9let SAM, 8let DAVID/. KNIŽÁK používá často své osobní vozidlo, bílá Š-110L. Lze předpokládat, že má pronajatý ateliér v Praze 6 Nový svět 9

Podpis operativního pracovníka por. Svoboda

Doporučuji: dne

Náčelník 4.odboru S StB dne

pplk. Ladislav Irovský dne

(Uvádí se funkce, hodnost, jméno a příjmení)

MV č. skl. 880

Plán bydliště objekta "AKTUÁL" (Plan of the object's residence)

Legenda (legend):
bydliště objekta (place of residence)

telefonní automat (telephone automat)

pojízdný opěrný bod (mobile base)
služební vozy (company cars)
autobusová zastávka (bus stop)

The streets:
V korytech
Narcisová
(parkov - parkoviště) - Parkplatz
Tulipánová
TRAFO ST. Trafo stanice
U Zahradního města
Slunečnicová
Karafiátová
Pomněnková

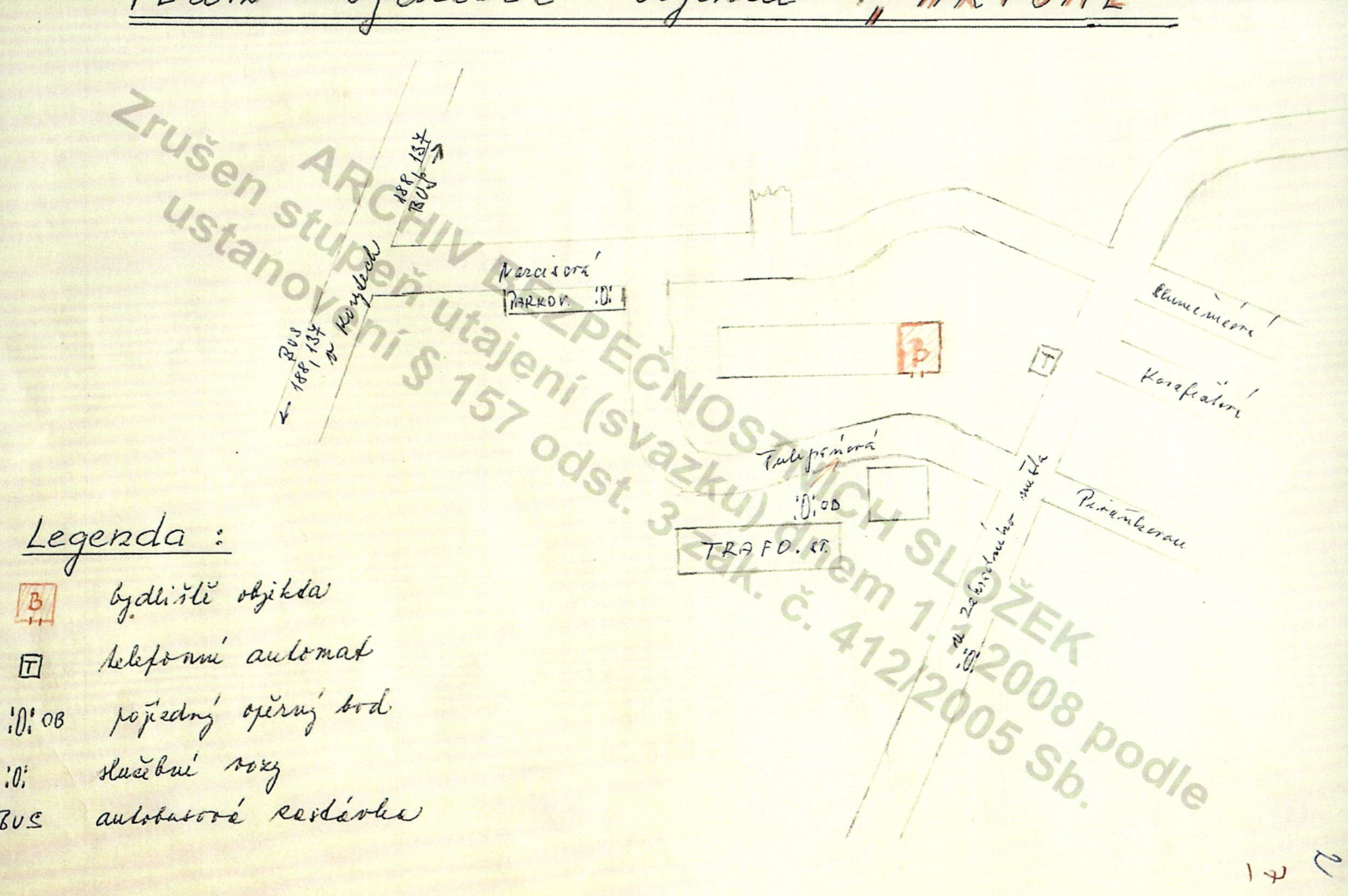

553 StB (ČSSR) Measures and "Decompositions" Drawing of surveillance locations, Aktual file Source: 81-001015/02-S-74-460, 0001 1974

A KT U Á L

<u>Date: October 22, 1974.</u>

06.30 hours The surveillance of AKTUÁL initiated at his domicile.

07.00 hours AKTUÁL left his domicile. He was wearing a large black hat – painter's hat. He was

wearing a green jacket, brown trousers, brown shoes. AKTUÁL has a moustache under his nose and long hair half-way down his back. He walked down the Tulipánová street towards his car, a light grey MB,[4] TC 74 - 38, which he unlocked and got in. He drove in front of his domicile, where a boy, about 13 years of age, got in the car with him. AKTUÁL then drove off taking the Tulipánová, Želivecká, Průběžná, and Na hroudě streets to Kubánské náměstí,[5] where he stopped. The boy got off the car and AKTUÁL continued driving along the street tř. SNB,[6] through the Náměstí Bratří Synků,[7] along the streets Boleslavova, Slavojova, Nezamyslova, Vyšehradská, Plavecká to Pod Slovany street, where he stopped in the car park. He got out of the car, locked it and set off to Na Moráni street, where at ...

07.35 hours Entered the building number 352/8. The parents of his partner live here.

08.00 hours AKTUÁL left this building. He was no longer carrying anything. He walked back the same way to his car, which he unlocked, got in and drove off along the street ...

[cont. on next page, transl. note]

Translated from Czech by Dagmar Wallace-Tarry

A K T U Á L

Dne 22. října 1974.

V 06.30 hodin bylo započato se záchytem AKTUÁLA u jeho bydliště.

V 07.00 hodin opustil AKTUÁL své bydliště. Na hlavě měl velký černý klobouk- malířský. Oblečen byl v zelenou bundu, hnědé kalhoty, hnědé boty. AKTUÁL má pod nosem knír a dlouhé vlasy do půli zad. Odebral se ul. Tulipánovou, ke svému vozu MB svělešedé TC 74-38, do kterého po odemknutí nasedl. Předjel před své bydliště a k němu si přisedl asi 13ti letý chlapec. Poté AKTUÁL odejel ul. Tulipánovou, Želiveckou, Průběžnou, Na hroudě, na Kubánské nám., kde zastavil. Chlapec z vozu vystoupil a AKTUÁL pokračoval dále v jízdě po tř. SNB, nám. bří Synků, Boleslavovou, Slavojovou, Nezamyslovou, Vyšehradskou, Plaveckou, do ul. Pod Slovany, kde na parkovišti zastavil. Z vozu vystoupil, uzamkl jej a odebral se do ul. Na Moráni, kde v ....

V 07.35 hodin zašel do domu č.352/8. Zde bydlí rodiče družky.

V 08.00 hodin opustil AKTUÁL uvedený dům. V ruce nic nenesl. Odešeb stejnou cestou zpět ke svému vozu, do kterého po odemčení nasedl a odejel ul.

[cont. from previous page, transl. note] ... Pod Slovany, Podskalskou, Vyšehradská, Nezamyslova to Slavojova street, where he stopped in front of the greengrocer's (Ovoce-zelenina). He got out of the car and entered the shop. He was carrying a red shopping bag. After 5 minutes, AKTUÁL left the said shop. It was evident that his shopping bag was full. He walked to his car, got in and carried on driving along the Slavojovà, P. Rezka, Táborská, Svatoslavova, Nuselská, U plynárny, Záběhlická, and Vkorytách streets to Tulipánovà street, where he stopped in the car park. He got out of his car carrying the said shopping bag in his hand, he locked the car and went off to his domicile, where he rang the doorbell. Then he looked up to the higher floors and at ...

08.20 hours He entered his domicile.

12.30 hours The surveillance was handed over to Comrade Němeček + 4 photographs.

II.

The subject was under control during the surveillance. His behavior is normal, his driving speed is a little fast. The address of No. 8, Na Moráni is the residence of the subject's partner's parents. Due to a very short duration of subject's movement, there are no further findings. The subject was recognized by: Maxa, Liptáková, Wolf, Zika, Veselý.

Operatives'attire:

Maxa: bareheaded, blue coat, dark suit, black shoes, blue nylon shopping carrier, white raincoat.

Veselý: bareheaded, beige coat, light-colored trousers, brown shoes. Brown briefcase.

Zika: bareheaded, black jacket, grey trousers, black shoes, dark-grey hat, black briefcase.

Pod Slovany, Podskalskou,Vyšehradskou, Nezamyslovou do ul. Slavojové,kde před prodejnou Ovoce-zelenina zastavil. Z vozu vystoupil a zašel do uvedené prodejny. V ruce nesl červenou nákupní tašku. Po 5 min. opustil AKTUÁL uvedenou prodejnu. Bylo vidět,že má plnou tašku.Odešel ke svému vozu, do kterého nasedl a pokračoval dále v jízdě ul.Slavojovou, P.Rezka,Táborskou,Svatoslavovou,Nuselskou, U plynárny, Záběhlickou, V korytách, do ul. Tulipánové,kde na parkovišti zastavil. Z vozu vystoupil, v ruce nesl uvedenou tašku ,vůz uzamkl a odešel ke svému bydlišti,kde u dveří zvonil na zvonek. Potom se díval do vyšších pater a v ...

V 08.20 hodin zašel do svého bydliště.

V 12.30 hodin bylo sledování AKTUÁLA předáno s.Němečkovi + 4 ks foto.

II.

Objekt byl po dobu sledování pod kontrolou. Jeho chování je normální, jeho jízda vozem je rychlejší.
V ul.Na Moráni v č.8 bydlí rodiče družky objekta.
Pro krátkost pohybu jiných poznatků není.
Objekta poznali: Maxa,Liptáková,Wolf,Zika,Veselý.

<u>Oblečení pracovníků :</u>

Maxa prostovlasý,modrý kabát,tmavý oblek,černé boty, modrá silon.taška, bílá pláštěnka.

Veselý prostovlasý,béž.kabát,světlé kalhoty,hnědé boty. Hnědá aktovka.

Zika prostovlasý,černá bunda,šedé kalhoty,černé boty, tmavošedý klobouk,černá aktovka.

Wolf: bareheaded, grey coat, grey suit, black shoes, black briefcase,

Liptáková: bareheaded, light-colored trench coat, blue trousers, brown shoes, black handbag, red coat, red and black umbrella, red bag.

Dusil: bareheaded, grey suit, black jacket, black shoes,

Vehicles:
Renault 16, grey, ABA 72 96, Wolf
Simca, red, ABA 72 49, Zika
Škoda 120, blue, ABK 95 43, Veselý
Renault 16, dark blue, ABR 62 51, Dusil

III.

Upon review, operation without defects.

Chytka
[hand signature]

Translated form Czech by Dagmar Wallace-Tarry

Endnotes
1 S StB–Správa Státní tajné Bezpečnosti (Authority of the State Secret Security Service).
2 Crossed out by hand.
3 Por.–poručík (Ltn = Lieutenant)
4 MB stands for the production plant in Mladá Boleslav, WW Škoda MB.
5 Kubanské Náměstí–Kuba Square.
6 Tř[ída] S[boru] N[árodní] B[ezpečnosti]–Boulevard of the Corps of National Security Forces.
7 Náměstí Bratří Synků–Square of the Synek brothers.

3

11

Wolf prostovlasý.šedý kabát,šedý oblek,černé boty, černá aktovka,

Liptáková prostovlasá,světlý balon.plášť,modré kalhoty, hnědé boty,černá kabelka,červený kabát,červenočerný deštník,červená taška.

Dusil prostovlasý,šedý oblek,černá bunda,černé boty,

Auta :

R 16 šedý ABA 72 96 Wolf
Simca červená ABA 72 49 Zika
Š 120 modrá ABK 95 43 Veselý
R 16 tm.modrý ABR 62 51 Dusil

III.

Při rozboru akce bez závad.

Chytka

Re-reading, Re-enactment, Re-construction

"Looking Forward to Further Collaboration": The Artistic "Handling" of the Files

Kata Krasznahorkai,
Sylvia Sasse

In the early 1990s, the Russian writer Vladimir Voinovich attempted to gain access to his KGB files. He wanted to know whether the symptoms he had experienced after being interrogated by KGB officers in April 1974 in the Hotel Metropol were caused by poisoning. Towards the end of the interrogation, Voinovich began to feel dizzy, becoming mentally absent and disoriented. This condition lasted for days and was later accompanied by heart palpitations and skin discoloration. Almost no one wanted to believe that his condition had something to do with the interview in the Hotel Metropol; many, including doctors, waved him away and called him paranoid or confused.[1]

Voinovich's story resembles another suspected poisoning, the truth of which will presumably remain forever unknown: the poisoning of Russian action artist Pyotr Verzilov. After a court hearing on September 11, 2018, Verzilov briefly lost his ability to speak, was unable to move, and was finally flown to the Charité hospital in Berlin at the urging of his friends. On the basis of his symptoms, the physicians in Berlin thought poisoning was likely.

Both stories sound like something out of a Cold War spy thriller: disagreeable writers are poisoned with the tip of an umbrella or a cigarette or are kidnapped by secret service agents and taken out of the country. But in this case, we are dealing not with fiction but with events that actually took place. The exiled Bulgarian writer Georgi Markov, for example, was an actual victim of the "Bulgarian umbrella" on the Waterloo Bridge in London on September 7, 1978. The Bulgarian Secret Service placed a small pellet in the tip of an umbrella and an agent then pricked Markov in the calf. There were about two hundred micrograms of ricin in the pellet. Markov died four days later, also on September 11, of fever and hypotonia from heart failure.

The Bulgarian journalist Hristo Hristov wrote a book about the case of Georgi Markov, while Vladimir Voinovich wrote a book about his own case. Hristov had to struggle with the problem that in the early 1990s, state security had destroyed two operative case files on Markov, containing about ten volumes of material, as well as with the fact that he was receiving death threats due to his research. Voinovich's search, however, remained even more fruitless. He was told, even after reaching out to Boris Yeltsin, that the files were destroyed in 1991, two weeks before his request. They did provide him with individual excerpts, but only with the purpose of *not* clarifying the case almost twenty years after the events, leaving Voinovich in a state of uncertainty. This uncertainty is the substance of Voinovich's book, a reconstruction of autobiographical fantasy.

Improbable Veracity

It is a kind of fantasy which has often been described in the language of psychology, literature, and literary studies.[2] Heinrich von Kleist called this phenomenon "improbable veracity," which is to say a phenomenon which takes place in reality but sounds so improbable that one can only believe that it is made up. The Bulgarian-French literary critic Tzvetan Todorov defines the fantastic as requiring—with reference to a literary text—a moment of indecision and hesitation: do the strange events of a story contain natural or supernatural origins?[3] And is what happened true? Readers (and meanwhile the protagonists too) do not, as a rule, know until the end and are left in this state of uncertainty. In psychology, this manufactured uncertainty, where private reality seems invented, imagined, and fantastic, has been referred to as gaslighting.

The term gaslighting itself originates in literature, its first use occurring in the 1938 play *Gaslight* by British dramatist Patrick Hamilton. In the play, Hamilton describes an act of psychological abuse that a husband inflicts on his wife. He consistently dismisses and manipulates her line of thinking until she begins to doubt her perception of reality. Voinovich's perception of being poisoned was also dismissed from numerous different angles.

While gaslighters, i.e. the perpetrators, are generally individual actors, secret service practice makes them part of a state-guided system of actors. It is the state which subjects its undesirable citizens to the situation of gaslighting. This manipulation occurs above all in the denial and constructed unbelievability of the practices which the state security itself carries out.

Reading secret service files, one discovers that the generation of this uncertainty was one of the strategies for disrupting self-awareness; the secret police used this in Eastern Europe to repress dissidents, particularly dissident artists. The strategy involves an inversion in the sphere of fictionality and reality. In the archives of the Stasi Records Agency (BStU, *Stasi-Unterlagen-Behörde*), there are files about the case of pediatrician Karin Ritter, who was also involved in dissident circles. Along with continuously spreading rumors about her, the secret police broke into her apartment numerous times, moved her pictures around, relocated her flowers, and switched around the types of tea in her cans. Actions like this evoked an inversion of the spheres of fictionality and reality. The secret police invented or faked an event in the life of another, which they contested the reality of in the same breath. Through its denial, the event shifts from reality and into the victim's imagination, their perception pathologized.

Years ago, literary critic Eva Horn wrote a much-discussed book titled *The Secret War: Treason, Espionage, and Modern Fiction*, where she argues that fictions are the "most lucid option" for "speaking in the modern period about political secrets." Literature is the location for "more precisely grasping the legends and fictions spread in politics," where they are not just represented but also made comprehensible. "Fiction," according to Horn, "gives up on the claim of historians and journalists of being able to present a *single* historical truth about an event." Fiction is, she claims, better suited than any other form of discourse "to speak about secrets and to explain their form—without being able or willing to conclusively reveal these secrets. It explored possible versions of an event without falling into the illusion of a conclusive solution."[4] To understand the logic of espionage, Horn exclusively examines fictional works, literature, films, and plays.

After years of studying the documents of secret services, it seems to us much more important to intensively foreground the fictional performances of nonliterary actors, i.e. the secret service. For if we are able to take anything from secret service files, it is certainly not the reality of the events—that would be a complete misunderstanding of the material—but instead quite the opposite: their fictional achievements. Exploring possible versions of an event is not reserved for literature but is, on the contrary, a typical practice of the secret services. The same is true of the generation of ambivalence and the impossibility of revealing secrets.

If we oppose fiction in literature to the "truth of documents," we confuse—in secret police files—method and subject. Because even if the "fictive historian" were to search for truth in the files, she would find exactly those fictions which make it clear that the material found is often hardly distinguishable from a novel, whether good or bad. Cristina Vatulescu has thus recommended reading secret police files as a "collective literary work,"[5] a kind of perverse novel based on the fantasies of bureaucrats and autocrats. To not ultimately reveal secrets might be a distinguishing feature of literature, but it is also precisely literature itself which knows that keeping secrets, even in real life, can be a means of "decomposition."

Re-reading

We would now like to draw attention to the artificiality of the secret service documents and actions, not only in terms of their fictionality and fantasy, but also with regards to their staged documentary character and their apparent forensics; not to mention, their banality, absurdity, and unintentional comedy. Artists long ago discovered this potential of the secret service files, indeed long before literary and art critics knew what to do with the material. For the point is surely not to examine these files for a *single* art-historical or literary-historical truth, but to understand how bureaucratically and, at the same time, fantastically "secret police knowledge" is produced and proliferated.

Writers were the first to transform their files (and lack of files) into new autobiographical texts and who were forced to reconceive of the simultaneously real and fictional dimensions of their lives in the files. Klaus Schlesinger describes the reading of his records as the sensation of becoming a protagonist in a book he was not the author of. It seemed to him that the "structure of this novel borrows from European Modernism, where the characters emerge from the glances other characters cast at them."[6] Conceiving of oneself as a character in a novel led to an incompatible "experience of contrast between the imagined reality of the files and events as I remembered them."[7] Péter Esterházy, in a different case, describes his shock upon reading his father's files as the feeling of having landed in a fantasy novel. Esterházy writes that the reality of the files was more fantastic than he imagined: "I can imagine many things, but what happens now, what I am in now, I could not."[8]

But it is not only authorship of one's own life that is lost in a single blow: one's own memory proves to be a false perception, that which was previously thought to be autobiography is now only one of multiple possible versions. Suddenly one's life is subject to the same rules that are otherwise only relevant for artistic activity. One is no longer an author but a character, not a subject, but an object of **observation**, description, stylization, polemics, even alienation.

Péter Esterházy, for example, turned the reading of his father's files into a book in which he makes us, as readers, participants in the writing exercises of his father as an **informant**. He reads and writes of how his father, as an **agent**, became an author. Jürgen Fuchs, too, one of the most spied-on and "handled" writer in the GDR, who alone had more than thirty file binders to read about himself, reacted immediately to how the reading of the documents concerned him. In 1991, he wrote a seven-part essay series for *Der Spiegel* entitled "Landscapes of Lies: On Writers in the Stasi Web"[9]:

> Not bad: the "thought process" comes into action. Pressure is applied to my family, done by Section 5 of HA XX ("Handling of Inspirers and Organizers of Underground Political Activity"), where I have been listed as an "opponent" since 1974 with the Operation "Pegasus," later "Central Operation." My wife has been closely accompanied by at least two men everywhere she goes, at a distance of one to two meters. In Jena with her parents they sit in the foyer of the apartment; a "viewing" every weekend; they even check the children's room to see whether any "unauthorized" persons have hidden themselves. This for nine months.[10]

Fuchs weaves file material into his autobiographical memories, notes individual words like "viewing," "unauthorized persons," and file numbers and abbreviations. These serve not simply to verify the spying: he simply can no longer, as he writes, remember his own past without this vocabulary. The language of the Stasi imposes itself, smuggles itself into autobiographical memory.

In contrast to Fuchs, Voinovich analyzes not his acts, but rather, their withholding. This only allows Voinovich to write a novel about uncertainty and its production, which the KGB used as a means of **decomposition**. In 1993, while attending a symposium in Moscow on the topic of "KGB, Stasi, and Literature" and also reaching the end of his search, Voinovich received, after everything, confirmation of his poisoning—from former KGB **agent** Yuri Korotky. This revelation changed everything for him. His allegedly morbid fantasy suddenly transformed into a reliable perception of reality.[11]

Reenactment

While Fuchs shows how Stasi language became part of his own autobiography, Gabriele Stötzer began to work with text fragments from her Stasi files, Dadaizing them, i.e. revealing their intrinsically Dadaistic, nonsensical core. Stötzer, an Erfurt-based artist and writer who also had several thousand pages of "situation reports," "observation minutes," and "action plans" to read about herself, now puts on performances of her file texts, sometimes alone, sometimes with an opera singer who warbles the alleged offences construed for her by the Stasi:

> ... the hostile-negative basic attitude of this person, her aim of spreading hostile ideas and joining together with other hostile-negative persons of the same mind is well-suited to assist in the realization of the goals of hostile groups in the organization of a political underground in the GDR.[12]

The mantra-like, even incantatory repetition of the vocabulary of hostility—hostile-negative person, hostile-negative basic attitude, enemy groups, hostile ideas—is recognizable not only to a commanding officer with a mastery of Stasi vocabulary.[13] Instead, the sentences hammer vocabulary into the files which, through their endless repetition and self-citation, produce the "enemy" in the first place. The files themselves become the site of action.

The sources, as Stötzer emphasizes, are what create the enemy: they do not document him or her but rather interpret everything observed as hostile. The sources, as documents, thus violate all rules of representation. But if we take them seriously as representations of reality, such as the artist Cornelia Schleime does in her work *Looking Forward to Further Collaboration* (*Bis auf weitere gute Zusammenarbeit*), absurd relations between image and text emerge. Schleime, who left the GDR in 1984 and was subject to intense surveillance both before and after, began her Stasi series *Looking Forward to Further Collaboration, No. 7284/85*[14] in 1992, offering thanks at the beginning for the "help of the Ministry for State Security of the GDR and its numerous aides" for the material. Schleime selected particularly banal sentences from her files, which she then turned into photographs. She truly staged the texts, specifically those that accuse her of an "antisocial lifestyle," a typical accusation for artists in the Eastern Bloc. She also affixed frivolous, decadent self-portraits to fifteen different original file pages: we see her lounging on her bed reading *Bravo*, dancing naked in a poppy field, posing in front of an American limousine. We could describe this series as an inverted *ekphrasis*, not as the description of an image but as the imagification of a text, not as a literary visualization strategy but as a *post hoc* photographic "documentation" of the events portrayed in the text.

In Schleime's Stasi file, we read: "The apartment is scantly [*sic*] furnished with old pieces of furniture, which is intended to seem modern. Her outer appearance is brought into harmony with the decor [misspelled in the file: *Aussattung*] of the apartment and also 'aims to' appear very modern."[15] In response, Schleime "verified" the observation with a self-portrait where she is wearing a high-necked black dress with a lace collar. She is sitting on an old chair at a table covered with a tablecloth with a brown-orange pattern. Next to her sits a German shepherd and, on the table, a fat cat; on her head is a hat reminiscent of traditional German dress.

We read in the file: "The ABV has become aware of no information or indications beyond the investigative report of 10/24/83 (Sheet 74–75) that Sch. is behaving highly inconspicuously."[16] Schleime again "verifies" her highly inconspicuous behavior with a self-portrait in which she is wearing a red wig and a two-meter-long plait on her head, pulling a children's wagon behind her.

Schleime ridicules the alleged reality of the verbal sources by allowing another reversal to take place alongside her reversal of text and photograph, a carnivalesque inversion directly confronting the documentary status of the sources.

Making the absurdity of "secret police knowledge production" visible was also the intention of Max Frisch's fastidious file reading *Ignorance as State Defense* (*Ignoranz als Staatsschutz*). After studying the files which Swiss state security kept on him for forty-two years, from 1948 to 1990, Frisch undertook a painstaking work of reappropriation. The existence of the Swiss files was "discovered" or disclosed at almost the exact same time as the files in Eastern Europe. Between 1900 and 1990, nine hundred thousand state defense files were assembled, covering more than seven hundred thousand persons.[17] Frisch meticulously corrected the mostly ludicrous entries about his meetings with intellectuals from the East, providing them with ironic commentary and above all, supplementing them with much more relevant events than those that state security had noted once or twice per year.[18] But it would be a mistake to conclude from Frisch's reading that Swiss state security's work was all sloppy. The meticulousness and inventiveness of the surveillance and bullying of the 1980s leftist photographer Miklós Klaus Rózsa has recently been demonstrated by the publication of his files, compiled between 1971 and 1990 by Swiss state security. Rózsa published the files and pasted photographs of himself from the period of surveillance over parts of the book, causing his own perspective to continually clash with that of state security. Christoph Nüssli and Christoph Oeschger, who put together the book along with Rózsa, speak here of an "involuntary humor," the "insufficiency of the analyses," the "mentioning of irrelevant details," and "wild speculations" like the idea that a sticker with a hand-drawn bomb was a sign of "suspicion of terrorism."[19]

The files demonstrate another kind of enemy production where youthful critics of contemporary Swiss society needed to be labeled as "anarchists," "socialists," "terror suspects," or "militants" to justify the heavy-handed approach of the police towards "the troubled," as the 1980s youth movement in Switzerland was called. In the Zurich movement of the 80s, Rózsa was a photographer of the youth scene and the police actions against demonstrators, where he took photos of, among other things, police performing their work. The photographs with their gaze directed towards the police ultimately made him a subject of surveillance by state security. Swiss state security files show that the production of enemies is not simply a phenomenon of dictatorships or autocracies; rather, secret police, in various different ways, portray social critics as enemies of the state or extremists—Rózsa, for example, ended up in the Swiss "extremist index." This history of Western democracies has always remained hidden—though reminding us exactly of the opened former secret police archives in Eastern Europe.

Re-archiving

The Hungarian artist György Galántai has an entirely different approach to the reading of his files. Around 1999, he gained access to his files and he was the first (and last till date) artist in Hungary to make his secret service files transparent. He made his dossier "Painter" publicly accessible on his personal website and on the website of Artpool Art Research Center/Museum of Fine Arts, Budapest,[20] an archive he cofounded with Júlia Klaniczay in 1979 in Budapest. Artpool Art Research Center/Museum of Fine Arts, Budapest has become one of the major archives on Eastern European Art, specializing in conceptual art, performance art, media art, mail art, fluxus, and *samizdat* publications.[21] Artpool emerged, according to Galántai and Júlia Klaniczay, from the activities in Balatonboglár, where members of the Hungarian art scene regularly met between 1970 and 1973.

The history of Balatonboglár would have also been unthinkable without the constant, active interaction with the police and the secret service. As Tamás Szentjóby described it in 1998: "There was a continual conflict between us and the apparatus of state—twenty-four hours a day. What they breathed out, we breathed in; what we breathed out, they breathed in.[22] And so we were in permanent general contact with this construction. You could actually say that if György Aczél[23] and the personnel in his service did not pursue the cultural politics they pursued, then that side of artistic activity would not have become so intense through bringing out the social element. So, we are very thankful to said state order."[24] Galántai himself referred to the chicanery of the police in his diary as performances: "From an artistic point of view it was an 'action' performed by two policeman-artist-patrol-officers. They began their performance by repeatedly shouting 'sir', and then used the wooden gate and their batons to 'give a concert.'"[25] (For example, when the police knocked rubber batons against the chapel door at night and then left their "signature" behind with the batons, or when they turned around Galántai's panels for an art action, see *Private Property/Friendly Treatment* in this volume.) Galántai appropriates this threatening action by the police as an integral part of the Chapel Studio Atelier exhibitions and as their own autonomous work: "The baton concert— as an experimental musical production—might have been an event worthy of being mentioned in the history of music."[26]

These "interactions" between Galántai and the state security before 1990 led to another "parallel action" after 1990. One which relates to the archive and the act of archiving as an "experimental" practice: both Galántai and state security collected "thousands of names and addresses"[27] and "tens of thousands of letters, drawings, journals, and artist's stamps, books, catalogues, posters, magazines, and audio materials."[28] Both thought in networks and took material from this network. Both sorted their respective (in the case of state security, fictionalized) facts into their respective archives in order to write other, additional, parallel art histories —but certainly this act of archiving material that partly they themselves produced could not be more different. But there are decisive parallels in their archival practices: Galántai describes in his manifesto, *Active Archive 1979–2003*,[29] the difference from "traditional archival practices" as follows: "The idea behind the Artpool project is to create an ACTIVE ARCHIVE built on specific artistic activities. This differs from traditional archival practices in that the ACTIVE ARCHIVE does not only collect material already existing 'out there,' but the way it operates also generates the very material to be archived."[30] Galántai here is describing a practice which not only collects and organizes existing material but rather generates this very material itself through its mode of functioning. Galántai himself refers to a form of artistic-curatorial production and collection of documentation. This practice correlates with the modes of functioning of secret service archives in one aspect—but certainly with diametral different aims and outcomes. Also, the state security was not only collecting material from "the outside," but themselves created material for the archive.

After the historical break of 1990, the state security archive was deactivated—and yet Galántai's Active Archive lived on. Even after 1990, the Active Archive stood for radical transparency: it is a historical act of a value that's hard to overestimate and Galántai making his files fully accessible is unique not only in the Hungarian art scene, but beyond as well. Thus he demands with an artistic act that which defines our interaction with secret service archives today, as also happened with the establishment of the state security archives: the disclosure and accessibility of materials. With this act, Galántai strongly argues for the management of former secret service documents in the form of an open, transparent archive within the archive. In an artist statement for readers and researchers, written as a note on the website where the files are published, he comments on this act of disclosure as follows:

To the attention of the readers/researchers: The information contained in the reports can only be treated as source material in regard to the activities of the secret services. The data they contain about the artistic scene of the era are to a great extent wrong or incorrect, therefore they should not under any circumstances be used as reference in any scientific research unless confirmed by data found in reliable sources. ...

GG: I decided to publish the material contained in the dossier codenamed "Painter" because my entire life's work can only be understood if the environment in which it was built is known. It was a world where through the practice of cultural security the secret police sought to control the general atmosphere, thinking and personal norms as well as the circumstances of acceptable social activity.

I can assertively say that the greatest loss suffered by Hungarian art was not the confiscation of large amounts of mail but the destrution of normal human relationships, which was achieved by the network through consistently (for decades) applying the method of decomposition, disinformation and signalization.[31]

In the ÁBTL (Historical Archive of the Secret Service, *Állambiztonsági Szolgátok Történeti Levéltára*, founded 2003), complete, transparent access has only partially been achieved—a portion of the documents is still being used to this day by the successor organization to the former secret services.[32] The complete disclosure of the files in Hungary—as happened in Germany with the Stasi archives—still has not been carried out. From this perspective, Galántai's artistic act of placing his files online is also a form of pre-enacting a (still) not accomplished phase of engagement with the secret service material in Hungary. His act is thus a sign of resistance to the ongoing playing down, covering up, and accompanying fictionalization of history through secret police documents. At the same time, his work in the archive is a call to reappraise these files according to the criteria of archival work, art history, and the protection of personal data—all along the lines of his very own case. In this way, the history of the Chapel Studio Atelier exhibitions in Balatonboglár became one of the best-documented events in Hungarian art history—also and partly with the "help" of secret service documents. But in this case, the counterarchiving of Galántai neutralizes and overwrites the long-lasting effects and consequences of operative archiving.

The opposite concept—an act of "de-archiving" by prohibiting any access—was carried out by Tamás Szentjóby in connection with his files. He was reacting to the publication of files by art historians in 1998, who had published file material without even the most basic observation of personal rights or concern for data privacy. Szentjóby caused access to all files relating to his person to be blocked; one of the purposes of this was to draw attention to the fact that work on and in the archive (then the *Történeti Hivatal*, founded in 1996 and the predecessor institution of the current ÁBTL) needed to be legally regulated. Szentjóby was rightfully horrified that highly sensitive material, including about his private life, was made available to the public. It is more than understandable that he blocked access to his files in an act of protest. While from his perspective the concealment of his files is completely understandable and legitimate, for researchers it is an immense loss. The file "Underground," for example, where all of the activities of the avant-garde scene were collected, are considered lost. Szentjóby's files with the cover name "Schwitters" are—alongside Péter Halász's and György Galántai's—one of the most extensive dossiers in the Hungarian art scene. There were presumably numerous overlaps with the "Underground" file; moreover, Szentjóby was at the center of the happening events in Hungary. The blocking of his file means that a large portion of documents on this topic are unable to be reviewed and also highlights the immense gaps and losses within these archives as well.

Relocation, Displacement

Gaps in the archive are also a space of projection for artists who use access to the files not for reappraising and/or supplementing their own biographies, nor for research into secret police practices, but who belong to a second generation which is primarily interested in the visual material of the archive. Jens Klein, who has been engaging with the photographic material of the former Stasi, has formed a number of artistic series from available visual and serial material—including *Mailboxes* (2012), *Walkers* (2012), *Balloons* (2013), and *Sunset* (2018). They are observational series based on Klein's research in the Stasi archives. In his presentation of the material, Klein cuts the connection to the original context, removes the photographs from their surroundings, draws attention away from the act of spying to what is actually being photographed. Klein writes: "In the pictures I chose, the people do not know they are being watched—or at least I presume not. It seems totally banal, nothing is happening where you could think, *Now that's suspicious.*"[33]

Artistic research in the archives has led to the discovery of series, or of the way secret police thought in series. That is not only the case with Klein, but also with Arwed Messmer (*Reenactment MfS*) or Simon Menner (*Top Secret*). All three artists saw the same series and logic of the series in the archive and used them in very different ways. Informant photographs follow the logic of long-term surveillance, of repetition, or in Stasi German, a "Who's-Who-Determination": who are the visitors to the gallery, who is going down this street, who is putting letters into these mailboxes? While series in art are aimed more at the difference of repetition, and produce this difference, the point here is to recognize visual patterns in order to understand the deviations in what is observed.

While Klein is less interested in scurrility and absurdity than in "everyday life," Simon Menner is interested in a completely different photo series for the disguise of Unofficial Collaborators, for secret signs, for *selfies* by these collaborators, for surveillance training, and for the reconstruction of a bomb from the stock of the Czech secret police. Messmer also takes material from the archives, photographs, and exhibits, and puts them in new orders and sizes. Subsequently, by choosing and re-ordering material, he concentrates less on series than on networks.[34] While Klein directs his gaze to what is observed, Menner and Messmer are focused on the self-documentation of the Stasi and, in the case of Menner, the *Státní bezpečnost*, the secret police of Czechoslovakia. Despite these differences, it just so happens that the exact same photo of a woman placing a letter in a mailbox shows up in the catalogue for Simon Menner's *Top Secret*, in Jens Klein's series *Mailboxes*, and in the permanent exhibition of the Stasi Museum at the site of the former Ministry for State Security Headquarters in Berlin-Lichtenberg. While Klein cuts the photo's relationship to its context, Menner borrows the brief description from the collection of the Stasi Records Agency (BStU). There we learn that numerous central mailboxes in the GDR were secretly surveilled by the Stasi in order to reconstruct who had posted the suspicious letters. The Stasi could also open the boxes on their own and simulate a regular emptying.[35]

When we see exactly the same exhibit or series—the people and the mailbox—in Klein, Menner, and in the Stasi Records Agency, we are confronted with the question of whether we look differently at Jens Klein's mailbox than we do at Simon Menner's, or at Simon Menner's differently than the Stasi Records Agency's. Klein is interested in the fact that nothing spectacular is happening in the images, or that we are unable to recognize anything spectacular. In contrast to Klein, the Stasi itself was not interested in everyday life when creating their surveillance series, but rather in the detection of hostile, dissident behavior. Their fear was that what looked like everyday life, or what was "disguised" as everyday life could be a kind of hazardous subversion—thus the surveillance. The photo itself cannot, however, represent this—it cannot show the act of subversion itself. It is the gaze alone which takes into account the possibility of the noneveryday.

Not least of all, the mailbox is among the most common image *topoi* of the secret police. The permanent exhibition of the Stasi Museum in Berlin has a special section dedicated to information about mail monitoring; in guided tours, they even reenact letter-opening techniques. With the adoption of this technique from Jens Klein and Simon Menner, the focus is not so much on the "everyday," but rather the self-mythologization of the Stasi: the apparent control they have over their surveillance.

Klein's and Menner's work with the photo series, who turned them into a ready-made, raises yet another question. Do the images which the artists find in the archive become *different* images when they are in an artistic context, in the gallery space, or on the art market? Is this displacement an art-critical strategy? Or a critical one with regard to secret police and the aesthetics of surveillance, presenting these photos ripped from their context? Further: does this concern an aestheticization of material, the original purpose of which was to harm others, to "decompose" them? For Klein, too, the question emerges: "*May* we do this?"[36]

An indirect answer to this question might be found in another work of art: “In the summer of 2007, I found a catalogue on the desk of my colleague Alba D’Urbano whose title photo jarred me in an unexpectedly strong way. The image on the cover showed a naked, seated young woman with a black bar over her eyes, and the subtitle was a stamp of the BStU. I was that woman 25 years ago. In the catalogue, there are other photos of naked women sitting on a lakeshore.”[37] These sentences were written by the artist and photographer Tina Bara. She discovered a photograph of herself which the Stasi confiscated and archived in 1983. The Stasi had opened the case file “Wasp” with the purpose of conducting surveillance of “Women for Peace,” a group of women who advocated for the demilitarization and disarmament of the GDR and for peace-oriented child education. The Spanish artist Dora García found these photos in the BStU archive and integrated them into her exhibition at the Gallery for Contemporary Art (gfzk) in Leipzig and the accompanying catalogue *Rooms, Conversations*. Later, they were circulated in the Art Forum in Berlin in two galleries as artworks of the Spanish artist—we can see the same fundamental process here as we did with Klein and Menner. Alba D’Urbano and Tina Bara decided, however, to reappropriate the photographs by revealing the circulation process of photographic material between the Stasi archives and the art market. Bara and D’Urbano—in a complex photo installation, a video, and a publication—show the original photos from the collection of the Stasi archives and then produce new photographs of the women portrayed in the original photos. The series thus becomes a web of references in space and time, a *chronotopos* of the reappropriation of photos from the archive and the art market. The installation thus connects the 1980s with the present, and a lake somewhere in East Germany, where the photos were taken, with the archive and with the gallery of Dora Garcia, and finally with their own exhibition. The production of these relationships is simultaneously a work about image rights, personal rights, authorship, and one’s own photos as ready-mades in the artwork of another. To Klein’s question of whether we *may* do that, the artists would most likely reply with a “yes,” as the Stasi archives obviously allow the redeployment of the photo material. But even if we *may* do this, the installation of Tina Bara and Alba D’Urbano shows that we must always reckon with finding our “own” ready-mades in the artwork of another, possibly even in the artwork of those depicted in the photograph.

Translated from German by Brian Alkire

Endnotes

1 Vladimir Voinovich, *Delo №34840* (*File No. 34840*) (Moscow, 1993).

2 Holger Richter, *Die operative Psychologie des Ministeriums für Staatssicherheit der DDR* (Frankfurt am Main, 2001); Klaus Behnke and Jürgen Fuch, eds., *Zersetzung der Seele. Psychologie und Psychiatrie im Dienste der Stasi* (Hamburg, et al., 2010).

3 Tzvetan Todorov, *The Fantastic. A Structural Approach to a Literary Genre* (Cornell University Press, 1975).

4 Eva Horn, *Der geheime Krieg. Verrat, Spionage und moderne Fiktion* (Frankfurt am Main, 2007), 10–11.

5 Cristina Vatulescu, *Police Aesthetics. Literature, Film, and the Secret Police in Soviet Times* (Stanford: Stanford University Press, 2010).

6 Klaus Schlesinger, "Macht, Literatur, Staatssicherheit," in *Text+Kritik, Feinderklärung. Literatur und Staatssicherheitsdienst*, ed. Heinz Ludwig Arnold, Vol. 120 (October 1993): 30.

7 Ibid., 31.

8 Péter Esterházy, *Javított kiadás – melléklet a Harmonia caelestishez, 2002* (Budapest: Magvető, 2002), 18.

9 Cf. Huberth, *Aufklärung zwischen den Zeilen. Stasi als Thema in der Literatur.*

10 Jürgen Fuchs, "Landschaften der Lüge. Über Schriftsteller im Stasinetz," in *Der Spiegel*, vol. 47 (1991): 282.

11 Voinovich, *Delo*, 225.

12 Gabriele Stötzer, *Dada*, manuscript.

13 Cf. Sasse, "Stasi-Dada. Was KünstlerInnen mit ihren Stasiakten machen."

14 Cornelia Schleime, *Bis auf weitere gute Zusammenarbeit, Nr. 7284/85*, http://www.artsite.de/cornelia.schleime-kap/stasi-uebersicht.html, (accessed June 8, 2019).

15 Ibid.

16 Ibid.

17 Jürg Frischknecht and Liliane Studer, eds., *Schnüffelstaat Schweiz. Hundert Jahre sind genug* (Zurich: Limmat, 1990).

18 Frisch's Stasi files contain no observations made by the Stasi themselves, only newspaper cuttings and a transcription of a radio broadcast with Frisch.

19 Christoph Nüssli and Christoph Oeschger, "Beobachtung und Überwachung," in *Miklós Klaus Rózsa* (Leipzig/New York: Spector Books, 2014), 593. The publishers draw attention to the fact that the publication

of the documents has been censored to this day, which affects both the image and film archives, referred to in the files themselves.

20 https://www.galantai.hu/festo/; https://www.artpool.hu/Research/Galantai.html.

21 Júlia Klaniczay and György Galántai, eds., *Artpool. The Experimental Art Archive of East-Central Europe*, eds. (Budapest: Artpool Research Center, 2013).

22 This is a reference to the *A-B* happening in Balatonboglár in 1971.

23 György Aczél was the chief cultural-political ideologue and close associate of President János Kádár, acting with unlimited authority in cultural affairs.

24 As cited in Edit Sasvári and Júlia Klaniczay, eds., *Törvénytelen Avantgárd. Galántai György Kápolnaműterme 1970–1973*, trans. Brian Alkire and Kata Krasznahorkai (Budapest: Artpool—Balassi Kiadó, 2003), 207.

25 György Galántai, "How Art Could Begin as Life: Supplement to the Boglár Story. The Last Kick-Off Year," trans. Artpool, https://www.artpool.hu/boglar/project/1973.html.

26 Ibid.

27 Galántai cited in Kristine Stiles, "Foreword," in *Artpool: The Experimental Art Archive of East-Central Europe*, eds. Júlia Klaniczay and György Galántai (Budapest: Artpool Research Center, 2013), 9.

28 Ibid.

29 György Galántai, "Active Archive 1979–2003," in *Artpool: Experimental Art Archive*, eds. Klaniczay, Galántai, 15.

30 Ibid.

31 György Galántai, "Note to the Readers/Researchers," http://www.galantai.hu/festo/jegyzet_e.html (accessed May 5, 2019).

32 After 1990, four thousand meters of state security documents were transferred into the ÁBTL archive, of which three hundred twenty meters, i.e. thirty-two thousand archive entries, are still managed by the secret services. The justification is that the publication of these documents would endanger national security. Historian Krisztián Ungváry, a member of the so-called Kenedi-Committee, asserts that the historical data banks would be available. There is a register both on magnetic stripes and on paper. According to Ungváry, it is still the responsibility of the Hungarian government to resolve the uncertainty connected with the state security documents, and then the data would be available. The issue mainly concerns the so-called B-Dossiers, the "obligation" or

"recruitment" dossiers, of which there are five thousand that remain of the original ten thousand. Many are presumed to be in Moscow. More information can be found at: https://index.hu/belfold/2014/07/20/nem_szamit_vane_moszkvaban_masolat_a_magyar_allambiztonsagi_iratokrol/ (accessed May 5, 2019) and https://hvg.hu/itthon/201711__allambiztonsag__ugynokok__60s_karton__a_megismerhetoseg_hatara (accessed May 5, 2019). The documents, partially under lock and key, remain an instrument of power and contribute substantially to the weakening of the democratic process in Hungary. See more in: Ungváry, *A szembenézés hiánya. Felelősségre vonás, iratnyilvánosság és átvilágítás Magyarországon 1990–2017.*

33 See Pichler, "The Survival and Revival of Images. Interview with Jens Klein," in this volume.

34 Arwed Messmer, *Reenactment MfS* (Ostfildern, 2014).

35 BStU, MfS, HAXX, Fo No. 177, image 17.

36 See Pichler, "The Survival and Revival of Images. Interview with Jens Klein," in this volume.

37 Tina Bara and Alba D'Urbano, "Covergirl: Wespenakte (2009)" in the exhibition *"Agents & Provocateurs,"* curated by Beáta Hock, Franciska Zólyom and Inke Arns, HMKV Dortmund 2010, https://www.hmkv.de/programm/programmpunkte/2010/Ausstellungen/2010_Agents_Provocateurs.php (accessed June 3, 2019).

Looking Forward to Further Collaboration, No. 7284/85

Cornelia Schleime

"This work was only made possible with [the] help of the Ministry for State Security of the GDR and its numerous aides, who contributed to the texts with their meticulous and painstaking work," wrote Cornelia Schleime in 1993. Schleime, who left the GDR in 1984 and who was intensively spied on both before and after, selected particularly banal sentences from files pertaining to her own person: the accusation of an "asocial lifestyle," a description of her apartment as "sparsely" furnished, that she only wore "western clothing," and that she "totally refuses to adapt to socialist society"—all typical accusatory narratives for artists in the GDR and the other party dictatorships of Eastern Europe. Schleime answered with frivolously decadent self-portraits which they affixed to fourteen different file pages. Here we see her lounging in bed reading *Bravo*; there we see here dancing in a poppy field or posing in front of an American limousine. Schleime laughs not only about the alleged reality of the verbal sources, but also about the documentary status of the files. (S)

Der Bundesbeauftragte für die
Unterlagen des Staatssicherheitsdienstes
der ehemaligen
Deutschen Demokratischen Republik
Postfach 1199, O-1086 Berlin

Kreisdienststelle Mitte

Der Bundesbeauftragte für die
Unterlagen des Staatssicherheitsdienstes
der ehemaligen
Deutschen Demokratischen Republik
Postfach 1199, O-1086 Berlin

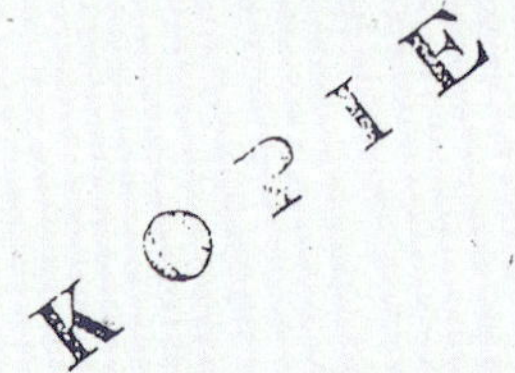

Dem ABV ███████████, sind keinerlei über den Ermittlungsbericht vom 24.10.83 (Blatt 74-75 des Mat.) hinausgehenden Informationen oder Hinweise bekannt geworden, da sich die Sch. äußerst unauffällig bewegt.

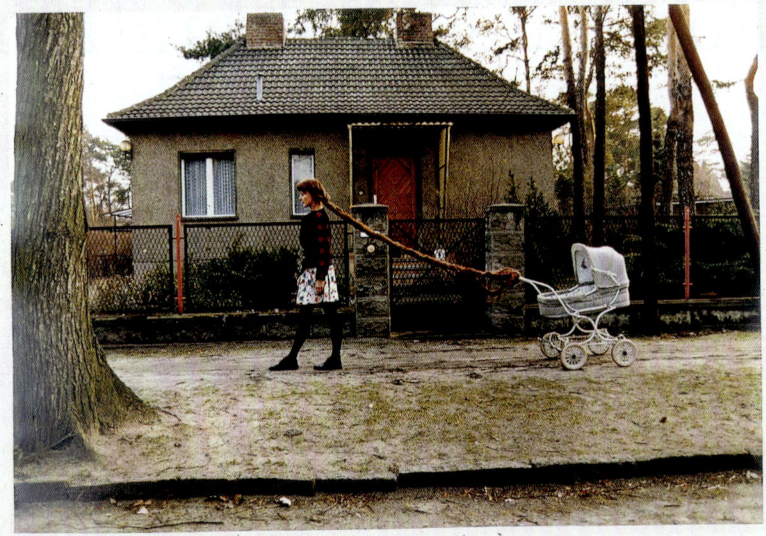

E

128

-3-

Der Bundesbeauftragte für die
Unterlagen des Staatssicherheitsdienstes
der ehemaligen
Deutschen Demokratischen Republik
Postfach 1199, O-1086 Berlin

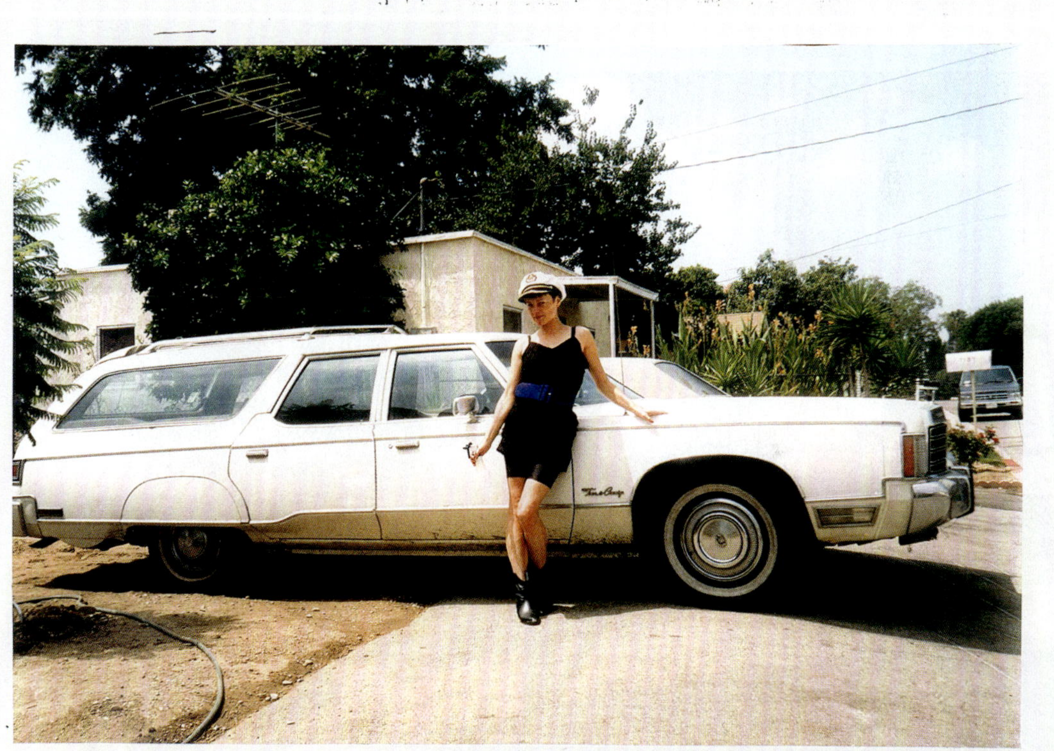

KOPIE

Die Ermittelte besitzt kein Kraftfahrzeug und auch kein Grundstück.

gez. IM "Martha Heine"

 Cornelia Schleime

Re-reading, Re-enactment, Re-construction

Six photographs on silk-screen from a series of fifteen, each 100 × 70 cm, 1993 collage. Courtesy of Cornelia Schleime

Der Bundesbeauftragte für die Unterlagen des Staatssicherheitsdienstes der ehemaligen Deutschen Demokratischen Republik Postfach 1199, O-1086 Berlin

15

Blatt II des E.-Berichtes S c h l e i m

Bisher wurden im jetzigen Wohngebiet keinerlei gesellschaftliche Aktivitäten festgestellt, was man auf Grund der bisher gewonnen Erkenntnisse über die Sch. auch kaum erwarten kann.

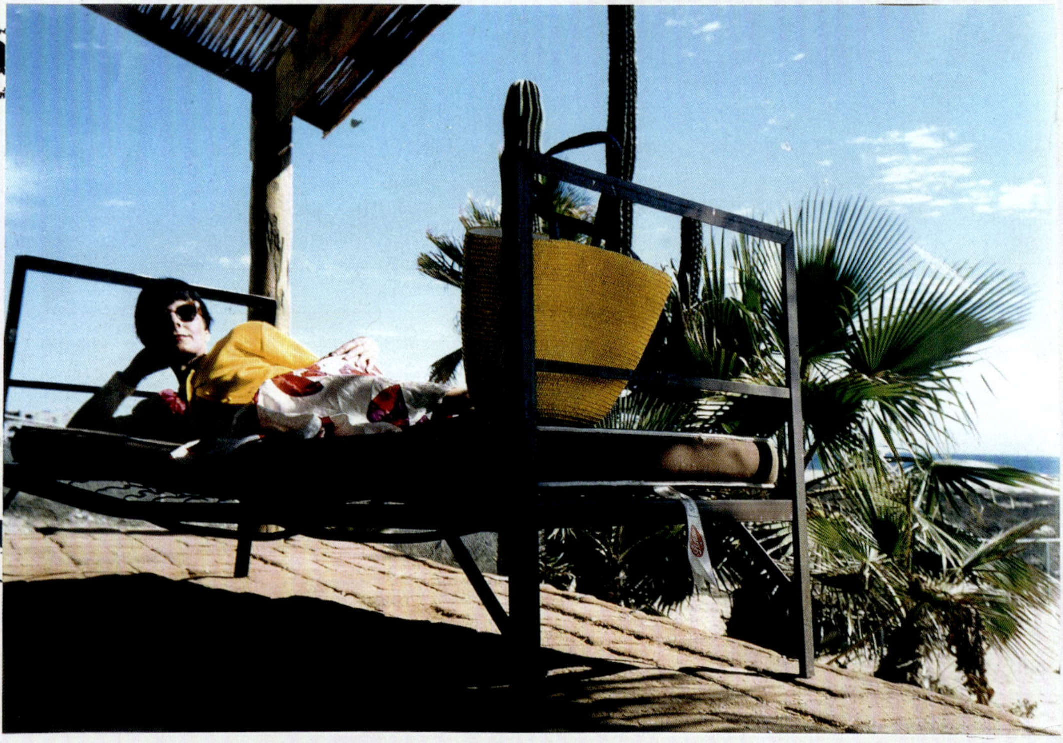

Die Ermittelte hat bisher noch nicht in ihrer Wohnung übernachtet

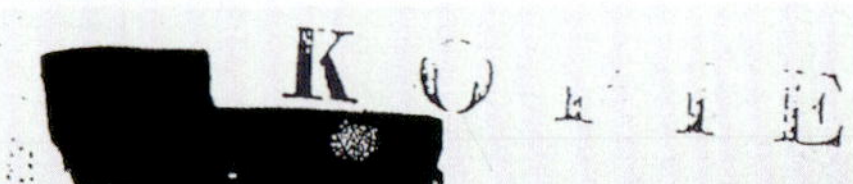

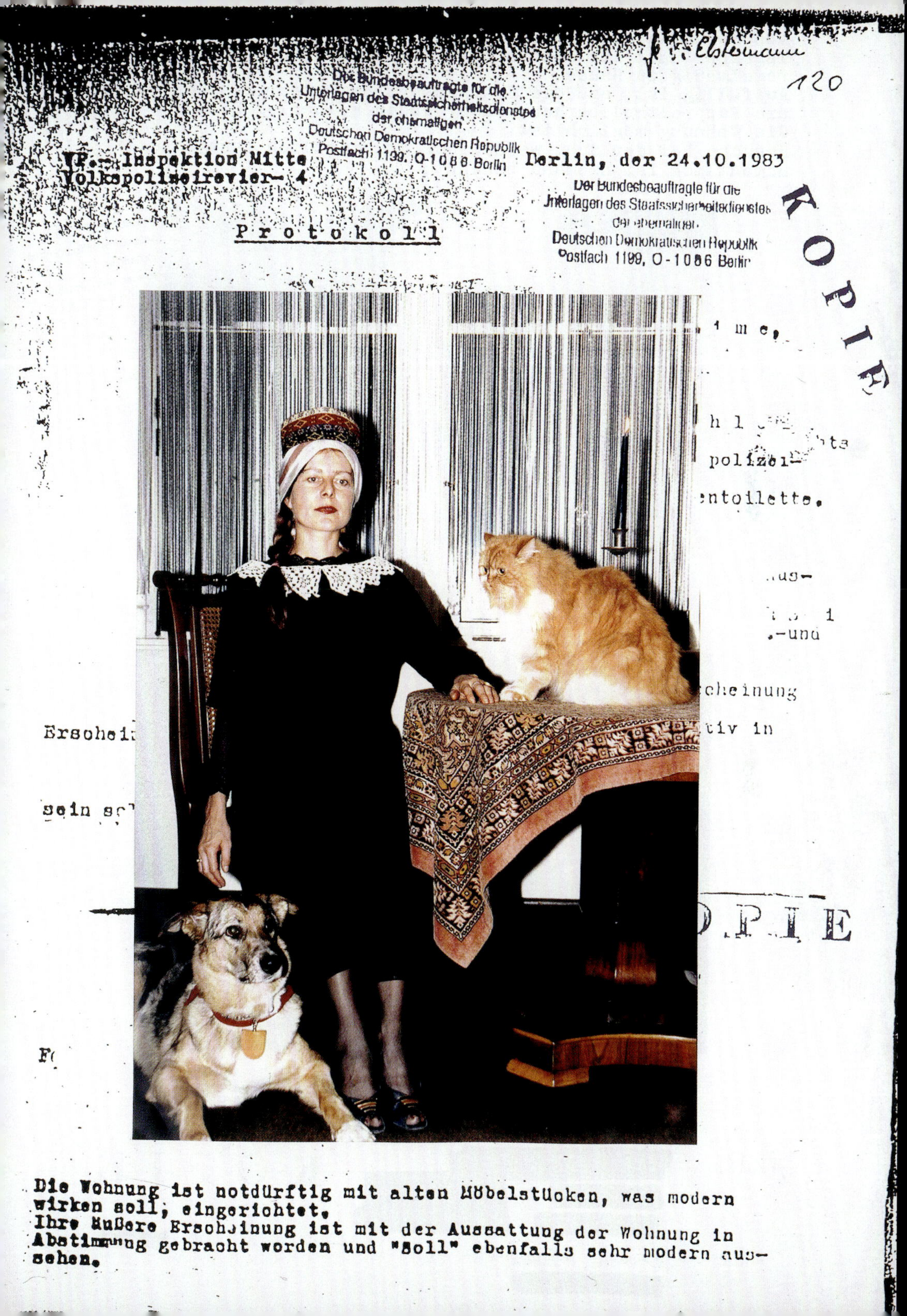

Elstermann

120

VP.-Inspektion Mitte
Volkspolizeirevier- 4

Berlin, der 24.10.1983

Der Bundesbeauftragte für die
Unterlagen des Staatssicherheitsdienstes
der ehemaligen
Deutschen Demokratischen Republik
Postfach 1199, O-1086 Berlin

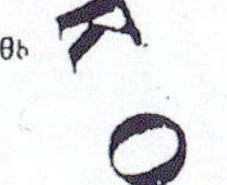

Protokoll

...ime,

h l ... hts

polizei-

...entoilette.

...aus-

...l
.-und

...scheinung

Erschei... ...tiv in

sein sc...

KOPIE

F(

Die Wohnung ist notdürftig mit alten Möbelstücken, was modern wirken soll, eingerichtet.
Ihre äußere Erscheinung ist mit der Aussattung der Wohnung in Abstimmung gebracht worden und "Soll" ebenfalls sehr modern aussehen.

Six photographs on silk-screen from a series of fifteen, each 100 × 70 cm, 1992, collage. Courtesy of Cornelia Schleime

Im Haus selbst ist von der Sch. lediglich bekannt, daß sie von Beruf Malerin ist.
Tagsüber hält sie sich nicht im Wohnhaus auf, ist abends aber regelmäßig zu Hause.
Auffällig ist, daß die Sch. sofort nach Betreten der Wohnung die Pappfaltrollos herabläßt, sodaß keinerlei Einblick in die Wohnung möglich ist.
Besuche bei der Sch. werden nur gelegentlich festgestellt, namentlich ist niemand bekannt.

beauftragte für die
atssicherheitsdienstes
hemaligen
kratischen Republik
O-1086 Berlin

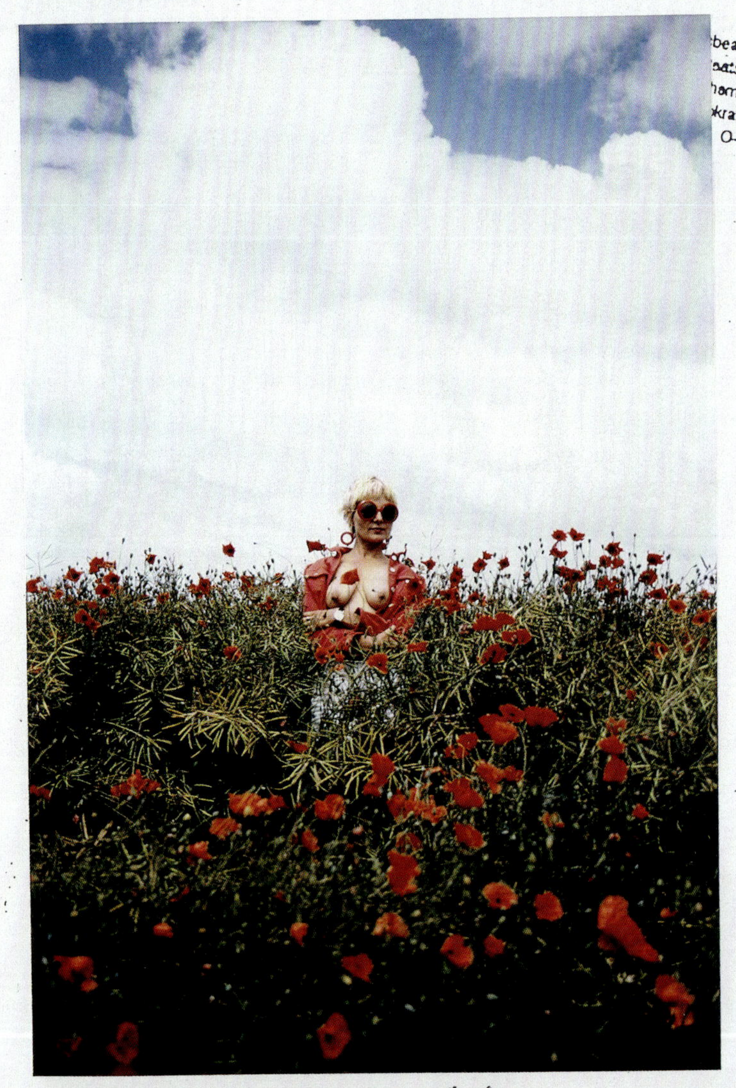

Elstermann
Ltn.

AKP: ████ im ████, ████ chem. IMB, als AKP bedingt geeignet, ████

KOPIE

Gs.

Volkspolizeikreisamt Dresden
Volkspolizeirevier Nord-ABV-

Dresden, den 24.03.82

KOPIE

BStU
000016

Volkspolizei-Inspektion
Kriminalpolizei Komm.VIII
Berlin-Köpenick
1170 Berlin

Wendenschloßstraße 130

Ihr Ermittlungsersuchen unter Az.:958 vom 09.03.82 über die Bürgerin
S c h l e i m e, Cornelia 04.07.53 ,1160 Berlin-Oberschöneweide,
Zeppelinstraße 79

Im Wohngrundstück wurde sie von den Mietern als asoziale Person eingeschätzt. Ihre Besucher nutzten die Fenster als Eingang. Die Wohnung ist verdeckt und es befindet sich außer einem Tisch, 2 Stühle und einer Pritsche nur Lumpen und Unrat in der Wohnung. Die Wände der Wohnung sind mit nackten Frauenfiguren bemalt. Die gesamte Wohnungstür ist zum Hausflur zu, mit Mitteilungen ihrer Bekannten mittels ölkreide beschmiert. Mit den Hausbewohnern hatte sie keinen Kontakt. Sie kam nur Nachbarn gegenüber aus der Reserve wenn sie wegen ihrer Lärmbelästigung durch Spielen ihrer mitgebrachten Freunde auf Musikinstrumenten-Gitarren, Baßgeigenusw.-zur Nachtzeit zur Ordnung gerufen wurde. Dabei trat sie fläzig und arrogant auf.

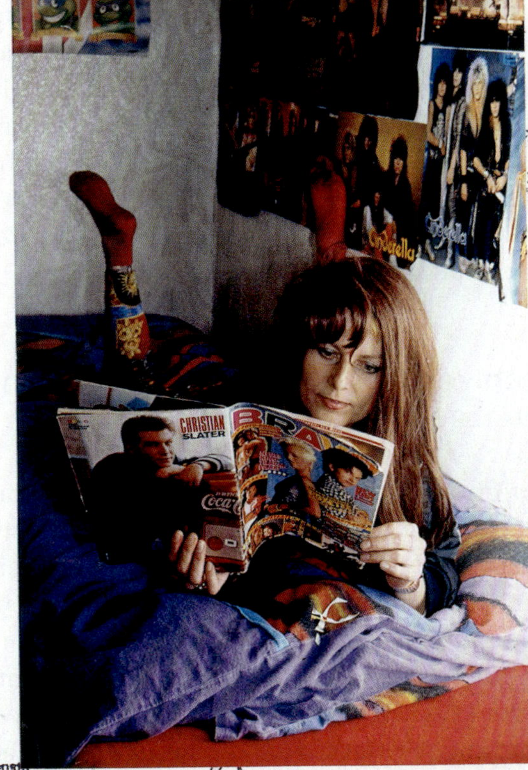

Oltn.d.VP

Re-reading, Re-enact- Six photographs on silk-screen from a series of fifteen, each 100 × 70 cm,

The Archives of Operation Condor: Dissonant Narratives in the Artworks of Paz Encina and Voluspa Jarpa

Liliana Gómez

VJ: "I consider historical narrative itself as a cultural symptom, that is, as an apparition of the repressed in the social body, and thus as a traumatic trace. We understand it as itself subject to editorial operations that are regulated by the repression, conversion and inversion of its signifiers in institutional contexts and for institutional ends, and those same operations are present in the construction of the subjective individual narrative"[1] (Voluspa Jarpa, *Historia, archivo e imagen*, pp.15–16, my translation)

The Archives of Operation Condor and Emergent Latin American Art

The invisibilization of conflict is a part of political violence. It fosters historical amnesia, creating voids in memories and archives. Against this amnesia, artists articulate countersemantics and challenge oblivion, silence, and forgetfulness in situations of post conflict and transition. In the following, I discuss the shifting ontology and politics of the archive of the secret services, examining the files related to Operation Condor, the name given to the initiative led by the United States' secret services during the Cold War to back right-wing dictatorships in Latin America. These have been aesthetically reassembled and rearranged by Paraguayan filmmaker Paz Encina and Chilean artist Voluspa Jarpa. Both artists delve into the logics of the archive while deconstructing it as a set-up of a legal-administrative assemblage to explore the aesthetic-political potentialities as dissonant narratives. They inquire into the way the documents are constituted—suppressing other narratives, while interrogating the mechanisms of the writing of history, as well as the repressions and omissions that are the lacunae of historiography, as a sort of Freudian unconscious archive.[2] Jarpa, for her part, thus tackles the notion of the archive as Jacques Derrida proposed it in *Mal d'*Archive*: Une Impression Freudienne*, conceiving of the archive as a trace or remainder of events that are questioned subjectively and collectively.[3] Following Derrida's "analogical association of the archived document and the psychoanalytical trauma" as archivable psychic material, Jarpa explores the materiality of the elaboration of historical narratives that reflect the same operations of psycholinguistic and discursive inscriptions.[4] Both artists, Paz Encina and Voluspa Jarpa, utilize visual and sonic means to reveal the affects that are trafficked in the archive, and the ways we ethically partake in the narration and comprehension of history. Furthermore, they ask: "When artists employ historical archives as media is history affected?"[5]

The archival turn or "archival impulse"[6] that has been taking place for the past two decades has also influenced the production of contemporary Latin American art and visual culture. The figure of the archive has its foundation in the gestures of recollection and montage, the storage of an image being a metaphor for contemporary art.[7] Both artists have made original use of the archive and its related files and documents in Latin American contemporary art. They problematize representation with regard to the potency of historical distance in order to "take a position on the imaginary of an epoch."[8] This implies engaging with different written sources, oral and photographic documents, and all sorts of archival materials that are part of a professional historical production to contest more fundamental notions like authenticity or evidence as a register of the documentary, but also the narrative and political discourse of an historical event. Jarpa's work delves into the functioning of the archive's historical force, and has become a major reference point for the relationship between minimalism, the art world, and the Cold War.[9] This has first been tested in the exhibition *En nuestra pequeña región de por acá* (*In our small region around here*), presented in the Archivo de Bogotá in 2014 in Colombia, and later as solo exhibition in the MALBA (Museo de Arte Latinoamericano de Buenos Aires) in 2016 in Argentina. It comprised a study of declassified secret service files, particularly from the Central Intelligence Agency, in the period from 1948 to 1994, known as Operation Condor.

The declassification of the files related to Operation Condor was acknowledged by the United Nations Educational, Scientific, and Cultural Organization (UNESCO) in 2009 to include parts of the so-called *Archivos del Terror* (Archives of Terror) in Paraguay, in the program of the Memory of the World initiated in 1992 to protect and increase awareness about the world's documentary heritage, particularly in regions that experience war, social upheaval, or lack of resources for the preservation of material and immaterial collections, archives, and other documents. This initiative certainly reflects increased awareness about the significance of preserving documentary heritage, and also relates to the globalization of other concepts, such as transitional justice, that give space to the collective dimension of truth and with it the conservation of archives "to guarantee the right to memory."[10] The state thus plays a leading role in the creation and preservation of historical memory and has an obligation to investigate. The conceptual framework of transitional justice, moreover, aims to facilitate "the right of victims to access judicial records so as to participate in processes of truth telling."[11] This is certainly reflected in the declassification of thousands of documents in 1975, related to the secret missions and the involvement of secret services in the dictatorships of Latin America, starting with the Pinochet regime. In 1993, the Center for Documentation and Archive for the Defense of Human Rights was established in the Palace of Justice in Asunción, Paraguay to house the Archives of Terror. The existence and conservation of these documents correspond to a number of complex factors: first of all, the pragmatics of the repression that required an efficient system of control; secondly, the legal façade adopted by the dictatorship of Alfredo Stroessner; and thirdly, the myth of the eternity of the system. Against this background of preserving archival records of conflict and dictatorship, the notions of evidence and testimony and thus, the construction of documents have been contested. This is at stake in the interventions by both artists: Encina's short films *Arribo* and *Familiar* (2014) and Jarpa's multimedia installation *En nuestra pequeña región de por acá* (2014–present) outline the omissions, suppressions, and repressions in the social body, and thus the traumatic trace, by creating dissonant narratives and alternative writings of the present past.

Dissonant Narratives: Paz Encina's Audio-Visual Artworks

In her audio-visual works, Paz Encina uses and assembles visual and sonic material from the **Archives** of Terror, reappropriating the **archives** in order to experiment with alternative ways of showing the repressive regime that the dictator Alfredo Stroessner installed from 1954 to 1989 in Paraguay. For instance, in the short film *Familiar* (2014), she renarrates a scene of betrayal by juxtaposing and reassembling archival material of images, text, and sound. Encina reorders the visual and sonic material creating a dissonant narrative of the stories untold. She is interested in a new configuration and modulation of the **archive** and in how affects are articulated by the displacement and juxtaposition that she undertakes in her audio-visual art. In this sense, she uses the image as an original police register to rework it as an aesthetic materiality. The art historian Natalia Taccetta suggests that Paz Encina "create[s] a dispositive to let the affects flow that enable the past. The terror of the **archives** combines itself with a certain cynicism to survive the absence of memory."[12] Moreover, Encina articulates a critique of the linearity of historiography while putting in evidence of the exceeding affects that produce the immateriality of the mental relations that emerge from and between the images.

In *Familiar*, she reassembles the archival material from an alleged crime and sabotage against the authorities in the zone of Caaguazú, Paraguay, in which a twelve-year-old girl named Apolonia Flores was said to have been involved (Fig.1). In a slow camera movement, we read the detention or police document about the crime, citing her family relations, age, physiognomic characteristics, and name. A witness's voice narrates the betrayal in a mixture of Spanish and Guaraní; the voice is part of the sonic **archive** of those years of terror and the witness forms part of the administrative-bureaucratic **archive**. Yet, it is the montage of the images and the narrative rhythm that turn the filmic construction into a dissonant narrative as it attempts to restore the documents' place in the historical process detached from the images' life. So it is that the image in Encina's work does not simply constitute the index of an event, but rather is to be understood as a theoretical investigation and configuration of an imaginary dimension of temporal spatiality. The film returns to the **archive** from the conflictive image and particularly from the sonic dimension to analyze imaginary survivals.[13] Encina proposes that this terror is the affect that configures the relation to the past and thus is not only the trace which would allow us to rethink the political, diplomatic, and police structures in Paraguay during the dictatorship, but also to understand memory today. So it is that with this short film, as montage, Encina establishes a relationship to memory and the past not as something that is already concluded when the dictatorship ends, but rather as sequences that are always narrated in the present and through the interpretation of images.[14] Accordingly, her audio-visual art reflects the construction of an archeology of the past understood as the practice of the archival document that implies the "deconstruction of usual categories to think of history as period, social agents, political actors, historical documents."[15] Her work, as it delves into the dissonance of narratives of the past, reflects a different order of history writing—retelling the stories untold, unlistened to, and unknown. Further, through this approach, she delves into a historical unconsciousness or cultural symptom—a dimension of collective trauma in which Voluspa Jarpa also takes an interest. Encina's work thus unfolds a phantasmal model, while she configures a heterodox or dissonant archive, in opposition to an archive understood as a repository of documents or facts; she focuses—in a similar way to Jarpa—on the voids, as these "unveil the affective plots (always inconclusive) of history."[16] The spectator is thus confronted with the conflicting image and sonic narration, both always in problematic and discontinuous movement from the police image and official documents.

In her audio-visual works, Encina questions the historical construction of the past that Paraguayan society has been confronted with. Ultimately, her montage technique problematizes the use of documents in historical narratives, and the ways in which stories about the past are told in political and ideological terms. By using the documents from the Archives of Terror, she delves into the social construction of that period, but also questions the temporality of the spectator and the historian.[17] As a dissonant archive, Encina's use of visual and sonic archival material fosters an ideological and imaginary inversion of the archive of terror, that is, "[a]n exhibition of terror," Taccetta suggests, "that empowers a reflexion about history and the activation of empathy from the present confronting fear that is never only past."[18]

Performing the Archive: Voluspa Jarpa's *En nuestra pequeña región de por acá*

Jarpa's work takes up recent tendencies of Latin American art that produce the archive as artwork. Accordingly, the archive as artwork "challenges the notion of history as a discourse based primarily upon chronology and documentation," so that there is no longer " a stable and retroactive archive, but often a generative one."[19] Jarpa questions this notion of history in her recent art installation *En nuestra pequeña región de por acá*. She assembles declassified files from various real archives relating to Operation Condor and delves with this performative installation into the events of the Pinochet years in Chile (1973–90), while questioning the archival logics within the files of the secret services. She explains: "The archive material, from the perspective of my work, should be capable of making visible the operations of 'edition and suppression' that are constitutive of the archive. Given that the archive material is the first trace of the 'truth of the events,' my intention is while revising it to establish a new meaning in the already narrated official history that excludes and omits certain elements of that story, which will be inevitably questioned by the documents of the archive."[20] With *En nuestra pequeña región de por acá*, Jarpa asks: "is it possible to change the course of history? And in this case: when and how does it happen? Also, the lack of judicial inquiry, the mantle of suspicion ... have had social and ethical consequences for our people and in their future development."[21] In her work, she develops the archive not as something that sorts out available things nor determines something as a reliable source, but rather she unfolds the performative nature of the archive as something that produces that which is archived, as is the case with the secret services. Accordingly, she reveals the unstable limits of the archive, which is situated between the fictional and factual. This is also reflected in Encina's audio-visual works, delving into the performative character of these collections as it constitutes ongoing social realities, the present and the past.

The declassification of secret service files has been explored by Jarpa since 1998[22] as a deconstruction of the archival logics of a legal-administrative assemblage to explore the aesthetic-political potentialities of dissonant narratives. In her work, one of the central themes is the visibilization and construction of artistic dispositives emerging from the declassified files of the Central Intelligence Agency and other secret services in Latin America. In the multimedia installation *En nuestra pequeña región de por acá* in particular, she delves into the linguistic regime of the text and the image, configuring a problematic space where the audience cannot access the files by reading, but rather by traversing and crossing them, as reading the files becomes impossible: the documents are shown with their erasures, stamps, illegible annotations, superimposed dates and textures, and finally many other traces that provoke the documents' unintelligibility. Jarpa suggests that these erasures speak of the secret and always-controlled access to the archives. So she understands that a series of signs, stamps, and traces reveal the forms in which the deletions and omissions alter the course of history. "The blemishes are the contemporary consciousness of our history," she writes.[23] These are the superimposed layers that the artist interprets in the register of trauma in psychoanalysis, the anxiety, confusion, the nonreconciliation that should be confronted with the articulation of some language.[24] Jarpa writes: "I resort to the idea of trauma as an archived and negated story, and to the symptom, as an encrypted archive ... impression, repression and suppression, reproduction, all valid concepts to propose a body of work addressed to question the construction that society makes of its past and, thus, its future."[25]

With *En nuestra pequeña región de por acá*, she "performs" the archive of secret service documents that shaped the course of history of Latin America, renarrating the archive through the painted portrait gallery, the main element of the installation (Fig. 2), which she juxtaposes with archival photographic images. She performs the archive against utopian narratives of the politics of the Cold War. Questioning these archival documents, she thus reveals the hidden dystopian reality "engendered by unresolved deaths" of political leaders in the Latin America she portrays.[26] The multimedia installation *En nuestra pequeña región de por acá* has evolved over time and has come to include more elements. For instance, in the video work *Translation Lessons*, she delves into the depth of language as a particular code for reflecting upon the hierarchical relationship between Washington's Cold War politics and the representation of Latin American history. Here she problematizes her own English lessons that she had to take over the years in order to be able to read and decipher the declassified CIA documents. During these lessons she is confronted with the fact that most of the documents' texts are blacked out, making their language and meaning unintelligible.

Further, she questions the fabrication of archives of the secret services that are situated at the border between fiction and nonfiction by reassembling copies of the archive files she inserts into Plexiglas boxes and juxtaposing them with sound recordings (Fig. 4). Using these boxes in reminiscence of Donald Judd's minimalist vocabulary, she articulates an implicit critique of the political decontextualization of minimalist art during Cold War. These copies of the redacted archive files also form part of the recent installation and her first solo exhibition in the MALBA in 2016 (Fig. 5) and, more recently, the Centro Cultural Matucana 100 in Santiago de Chile in 2017. By performing the archive, the artist thus questions the visitors' neutral position and invites them to participate in the critical reflection on the archive. Echoing other Latin American critical and participatory artworks, such as those by Eduardo Kac, Paulo Bruscky, and Hélio Oiticica, Jarpa reflects, overall, on "representation, vision and the invisible [that] often alter the conventional boundaries of fiction and non-fiction," making explicit the disruptions of representation.[27]

So she plots a space with multiple signifying layers, a Latin American map that cannot be reduced to historiographic pretensions. She rather exposes a geopolitical potency in the image and the occupation of space through the word.[28] Interestingly, in Jarpa's work the point is not to represent past events, nor to interpret history, but rather to conjoin image and text to problematize access to and comprehension of the past, and to illuminate the present. In her installation, she uses different archives and archival material, articulating multiple reference points. As part of a multiple-piece installation, her exhibition includes paintings, objects, installations, multichannel videos, and copied documents from the declassified CIA files that do not focus on the horrors of the Latin American dictatorships (like torture or enforced disappearance) or illuminate the operations of Plan Cóndor. Rather, because her work is an aesthetic and epistemological undertaking, she delves into the archive as a starting point for a writing of history and storytelling, questioning the biopolitical ordination of the present-past and the very act of the declassification of the documents as an "aesthetics of a legal-administrative organization."[29] Accordingly, from the very notion of the archive, both material and conceptual, Jarpa practices a "politics of interstices" through the technique of a montage of the pieces and their archival uses, questioning their relationship with the domiciliation, access to, organization, and figuration of the past.[30] The aesthetics of the archive is, Jarpa suggests, the interstice, the lacuna, the caesura, or that which "articulates the ontology of this Latin American archive."[31] She relates this dimension to the Freudian unconscious archive and thus, the dialectic of trauma and historical narrative as a cultural symptom and "an apparition of the repressed in the social body." Jarpa writes: "From this perspective, the archive would be a beginning from which one could anchor a narrative, a probative document, in which a narrative of any nature could rest from the delirium and lean on this probe to elaborate itself. ... For me, the archive inhabits a poetic space, as pure possibility between the real and the unreal. It is also a fuzzy interstice between the notions of the public and the private, the secret and the no-secret, the individual and the collective, the conscious and the unconscious. The archive, as a concept, confronts us with a problem of limits, and thus ethics."[32]

Jarpa's performance "in, with and of the archive," in resonance with other Latin American critical and participatory art since the 1970s, produces "an ontological change—from the archive as a repository of documents to the archive as a dynamic and generative tool. ... This change in the archive's ontology," the critic Simone Osthoff suggests, "produced in part by the contamination between artwork and documentation, positions history and theory neither completely outside the realm of art nor entirely inside of it, but in continuous relays."[33] Moreover, "the question of the institutional location of the archive—physical, ontological, and historical" has become pivotal in the writing of contemporary art history.[34] Transcending its double nature, the archive thus constitutes a reconsideration of history: on the one hand, it is a real repository in a material sense, a collection of objects that survive classification and selection; on the other, it constitutes the image of an event, the figuration of a series of incidences or a period. It further controls the apprehension of a time through a sovereign operation that is, again, the montage. So it is that Jarpa realizes a deconstructive relationship with the images in order to produce and give emphasis to the discrepancy and split.[35] Further, Jarpa's proposal is a form of the politics of the interstice, the cut and discontinuity that make the truth appear to be only provisional. Accordingly, her montage operations constitute modes of challenging aesthetic-political conventional views of history. Finally, she problematizes the ethical limits of the use of the archive and thus of the declassified files. These ethical limits are diffuse, she suggests, as there are documents of the institution that correspond with an administrative event. "In other words," she writes, "the scope of the potential of the archive and the ethical 'use' that we could make of it transgress the mere act of declassification."[36] So she further suggests that the one who preserves the archive does not possess it, nor can possess the consciousness of history or the consciousness of law.

Concluding Perspectives

Both Paz Encina's and Voluspa Jarpa's work make explicit that: "No longer able to maintain the neutral and safe spectator's position outside the space of representation, beholders, critics and historians alike are increasingly positioned as participants inside the artwork, who must author in real time and with all our senses the meaning of what we see and feel in multimedia installations."[37] They thus critically reflect the archival turn or the **archive** as a third paradigm that has shaped global contemporary art production.[38] Their performative work enables a collective space of knowledge and memory, as they contour "the most negligible as well as ... the most prominent of objects constitutive of an event."[39] Furthermore, they share "[a] psychological dimension [that] is contained in [a] mode of allegorical doubling, in saying something else in reference to something non-sayable, non-representable, one that transfers the purported authenticity and factuality of the [image and text], which after all are never presented in their original materiality but always as 'treated' pieces of archival evidence ..., completely from the domain of their various realities into the sphere of fictions."[40] Overall, these art interventions in the **archives** of the secret services make clear that "non-present spaces and times cannot be grasped simply as a closed past, for these documents are not perforce concerned with the past, non-passing and defying closure, ever continues to have an effect in the present."[41] They perform the **archive** in order to reveal that to perceive and interpret the past is a cultural process that enables us to comprehend "the incommensurability between factual events and individual-subjective experience."[42] So both artists engage, in a critical and poetic way, with the complex processes of writing history, creating their own dissonant narratives that invite us as spectators to ethically participate in.

Endnotes

1 "Considero al relato histórico en sí mismo como síntoma cultural, es decir, como la aparición de lo reprimido en el cuerpo social, y por ende como huella traumática. Lo entenderemos de por sí sometido a operaciones de edición que son reguladas por la represión, conversión e inversión de sus significantes en contextos y con fines institucionales, siendo estas mismas operaciones las que están presentes en la construcción del relato subjetivo individual." Voluspa Jarpa, "Historia, archivo

e imagen: sobre la necesidad de simbolizar la historia," in *A contracorriente. Una revista de historia social y literatura de América Latina* 12, Vol1. (2014): 14–29.

2 Voluspa Jarpa, "Historia, archivo e imagen: sobre la necesidad de simbolizar la historia," *A contracorriente. Una revista de historia social y literatura de América Latina* 12, Vol 1. (2014): 20.

3 Ibid., 15.

4 Ibid.

5 Simone Osthoff, *Performing the Archive: The Transformation of the Archive in Contemporary Art from Repository of Documents to Art Medium* (New York: Atropos Press, 2009), 12.

6 Hal Foster, "An Archival Impulse," *October* 110 (2004): 3–22.

7 Natalia Tacetta, "En nuestra pequeña región de por acá: de la declasificación del documento al contraarchivo en la obra de Voluspa Jarpa," *Meridional. Revista Chilena de Estudios Latinoamericanos* 9 (2017): 237.

8 Ibid., 239.

9 Ibid., 240.

10 Maria Victoria Uribe and Pilar Riaño Alcalá, "Constructing Memory amidst War: The Historical Memory Group of Colombia," *International Journal of Transitional Justice* 10, Vol.1 (2016): 3.

11 Ibid., 16.

12 Natalia Taccetta, "En nuestra pequeña región de por acá: de la declasificación del documento al contraarchivo en la obra de Voluspa Jarpa," *Meridional. Revista Chilena de Estudios Latinoamericanos* 9 (2017): 396.

13 Ibid., 400.

14 Ibid., 401.

15 Ibid., 402.

16 Ibid., 404.

17 Ibid., 405.

18 Ibid., 407

19 Simone Osthoff, *Performing the Archive: The Transformation of the Archive in Contemporary Art from Repository of Documents to Art Medium* (New York: Atropos Press, 2009), 12.

20 "El material de archivo, desde mi perspectiva de trabajo, debe ser capaz de hacer visible las operaciones de 'edición y supresión' que son constitutivas del archivo. Dado que el material de archivo es la huella primera de la 'verdad de los hechos', mi intención al revisarlo es establecer un nuevo sentido, entendiendo, por ello, que aquello que

ha sido narrado como historia oficial puede excluir u omitir ciertos elementos en dicho relato, lo que será inevitablemente cuestionado por los documentos de archivo." Voluspa Jarpa, "Historia, archivo e imagen: sobre la necesidad de simbolizar la historia," in *A contracorriente. Una revista de historia social y literatura de América Latina* 12, Vol 1. (2014): 16.

21 *Archivos para la paz: Voluspa Jarpa. Artista chilena. (Diálogos de la memoria)* (Bogotá: Centro Nacional de Memoria Histórica, 2014), 2–3.

22 Alexia Talia, "Entrevista a Voluspa Jarpa," *Artishock. Revista de arte contemporánea*, 2011.

23 "Por lo mismo, las tachas hablan del secreto y del acceso siempre vigilado a los archivos, ... en este sentido, una serie de signos, de designaciones, de sellos, revelan las formas en que la tachadura altera el curso de la historia. ... Las tachas son la conciencia contemporánea de nuestra historia." Voluspa Jarpa, "Historia, archivo e imagen: sobre la necesidad de simbolizar la historia," in *A contracorriente. Una revista de historia social y literatura de América Latina* 12, Vol 1. (2014): 26–27.

24 Natalia Tacetta, "En nuestra pequeña región de por acá: de la declasificación del documento al contraarchivo en la obra de Voluspa Jarpa," *Meridional. Revista Chilena de Estudios Latinoamericanos* 9 (2017): 238

25 "Recurro a la idea del trauma como relato archivado y negado, y al síntoma, como archivo cifrado ... impresión, represión y supresión, reproducción, todos ellos conceptos válidos para proponer un cuerpo de obra dirigido a construir e interpelar la construcción que la sociedad hace de su pasado y, por tanto, de su futuro." Voluspa Jarpa, "Historia, archivo e imagen: sobre la necesidad de simbolizar la historia," in *A contracorriente. Una revista de historia social y literatura de América Latina* 12, Vol 1. (2014): 17.

26 Voluspa Jarpa and Mor Charpentier, *En Nuestra Pequeña Región de Por Acá: October 20-November 6, 2014* (Bogotá: Archivo de Bogotá/ Centro de Memoria Histórica, 2014), exhibition catalogue.

27 Simone Osthoff, *Performing the Archive: The Transformation of the Archive in Contemporary Art from Repository of Documents to Art Medium* (New York: Atropos Press, 2009), 11.

28 Natalia Taccetta, "Afectos en el Archivo del Terror," *Imagofagia. Revista de la Asociación Argentina de Estudios de Cine y Audiovisual* 16 (2017): 241.

29 Benjamin Buchloh, "Atlas Archive," in *The Optic of Walter Benjamin, Vol. 3 De-, Dis-, Ex-* (London: Black Dog Publishing, 1999), 32.

30 Natalia Taccetta, "Afectos en el Archivo del Terror," *Imagofagia. Revista de la Asociación Argentina de Estudios de Cine y Audiovisual* 16 (2017): 241.

31 Ibid., 242.

32 Voluspa Jarpa, "Historia, archivo e imagen: sobre la necesidad de simbolizar la historia," *A contracorriente. Una revista de historia social y literatura de América Latina* 12, Vol 1. (2014): 22.

33 Simone Osthoff, *Performing the Archive: The Transformation of the Archive in Contemporary Art from Repository of Documents to Art Medium* (New York: Atropos Press, 2009), 11–12.

34 Ibid., 27.

35 Natalia Taccetta, "Afectos en el Archivo del Terror," *Imagofagia. Revista de la Asociación Argentina de Estudios de Cine y Audiovisual* 16 (2017): 244.

36 Voluspa Jarpa, "Historia, archivo e imagen: sobre la necesidad de simbolizar la historia," *A contracorriente. Una revista de historia social y literatura de América Latina* 12, Vol 1. (2014): 21.

37 Simone Osthoff, *Performing the Archive: The Transformation of the Archive in Contemporary Art from Repository of Documents to Art Medium* (New York: Atropos Press, 2009), 12.

38 Anna María Guasch, *Arte y archivo, 1920–2010. Genealogías, tipologías y discontinuidade* (Madrid: Ediciones Akal, S.A., 2011).

39 André Lepicki, "In the Mist of the Event: Performance and the Activation of Memory in The Atlas Group Archive," in *The Atlas Group (1989–2004): A Project by Walid Raad* , eds. Kassandra Nakas and Britta Schmitz (Cologne: Walther Konig, 2006), 64.

40 Kassandra Nakas, "Double Miss. On the Use of Photography in the Atlas Group Archive," in *The Atlas Group (1989–2004): A Project by Walid Raadb*, eds. Kassandra Nakas and Britta Schmitz (Cologne: Walther Konig, 2006), 51.

41 Ibid., 51.

42 Ibid., 52.

Translation Lessons

Voluspa Jarpa

In her work *Translation Lessons*, Voluspa Jarpa asks whether the artistic use of archival material has an effect on history. Her work is the result of Jarpa's years-long engagement with declassified U.S. Central Intelligence Agency files from Operation Condor in Chile between 1948 and 1994. Under this code name, the secret services of six Latin American countries worked together with the United States with the goal of pursuing and killing left-wing and dissident forces throughout the world. The files were declassified in 2009 in the context of the UNESCO program "Memory of the World." The CIA material is largely unreadable due to the massive amount of redaction. Jarpa's work presents the archive itself as an artwork, while grappling with gaps, illegibility, and the unstable borders between fact and fiction. In the video, Jarpa attempts to learn English on the basis of the CIA documents. The hopelessness of this endeavor rapidly becomes clear, however, for despite the feat of learning the hegemonic language, the documents remain unreadable. As Liliana Gómez writes, "making conflicts invisible is an element of political violence. It supports historical amnesia and creates gaps in memories and archives." **(S/K)**

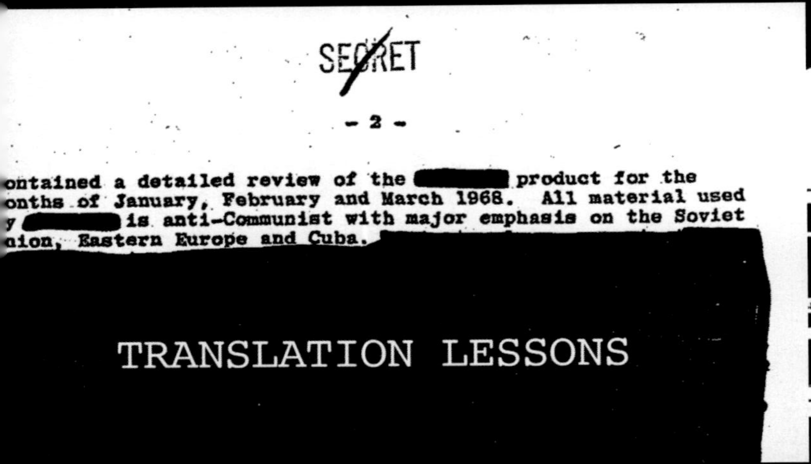

SECRET

- 2 -

ontained a detailed review of the product for the onths of January, February and March 1968. All material used y is anti-Communist with major emphasis on the Soviet nion, Eastern Europe and Cuba.

TRANSLATION LESSONS

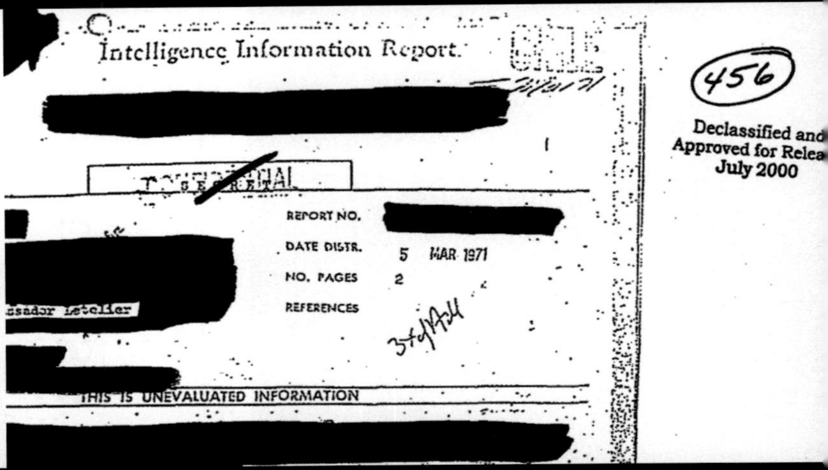

Intelligence Information Report

CONFIDENTIAL

REPORT NO.

DATE DISTR. 5 MAR 1971

NO. PAGES 2

REFERENCES

ssador Letelier

THIS IS UNEVALUATED INFORMATION

456

Declassified and Approved for Relea July 2000

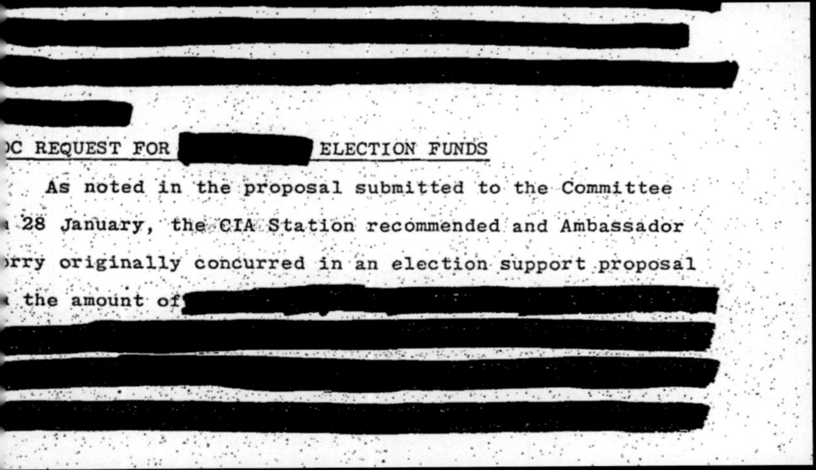

C REQUEST FOR ELECTION FUNDS

As noted in the proposal submitted to the Committee 28 January, the CIA Station recommended and Ambassador rry originally concurred in an election support proposal the amount of

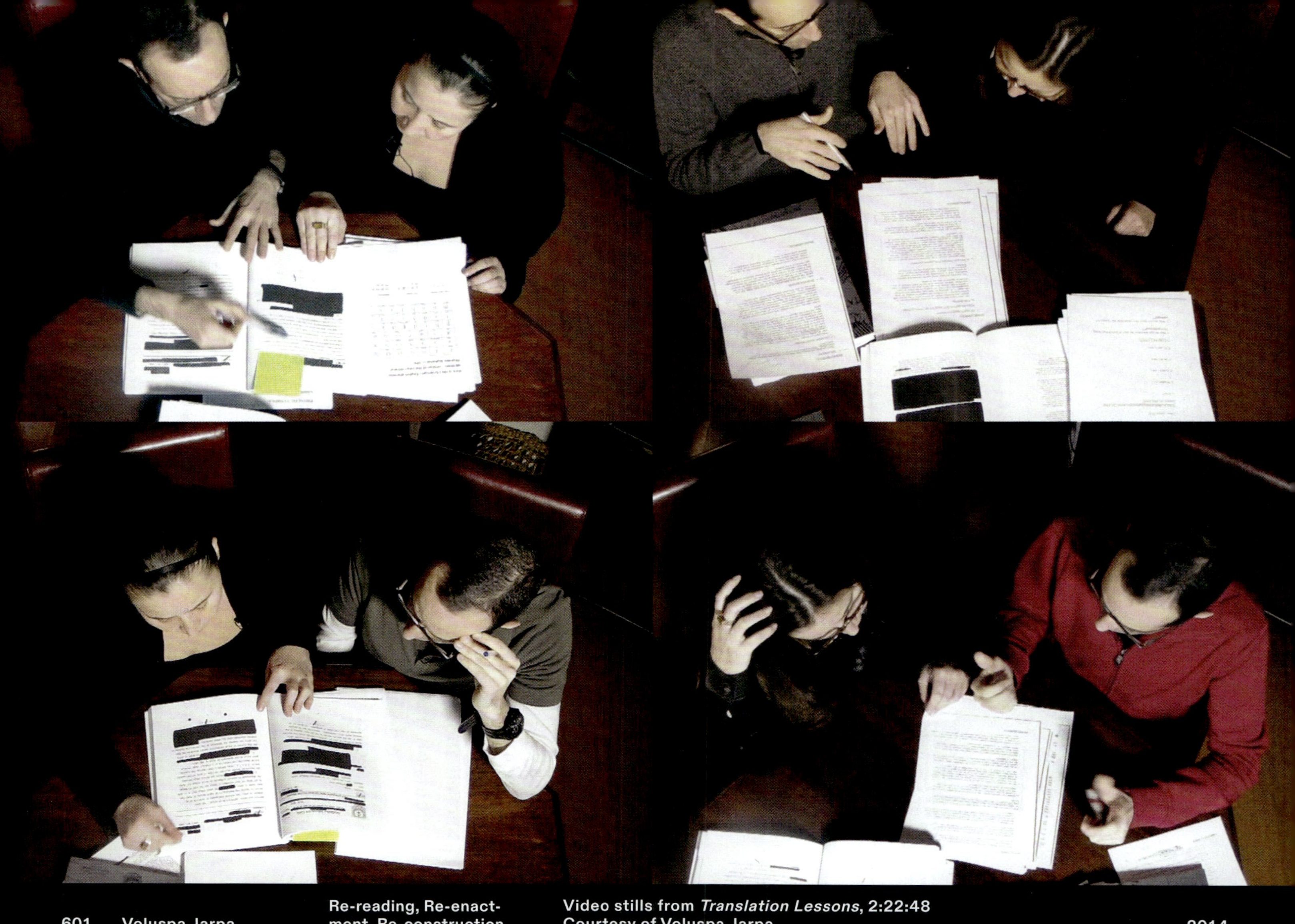

Video stills from *Translation Lessons*, 2:22:48
Courtesy of Voluspa Jarpa

Top Secret

Nedko Solakov

Top Secret, created between December 1989 and February 1990, consists of an index box, filled with a series of cards detailing the artist's youthful collaboration with the Bulgarian state security, which he stopped in 1983.The work caused great controversy when it was first exhibited in the spring of 1990, at the height of the political changes to the long-standing Communist rule. In Bulgaria, the official files still remain closed and for twenty-eight years there were no publicly known documents on the artist's collaboration. It was not until April 2018 that the state documents relating to the involvement of the artist with the state security of the People's Republic of Bulgaria were released. The self-disclosing gesture in this artistic project is still unique in the context of post-Communist Europe, and since its appearance, Top Secret has become an icon of its time.

The forty-minute-long video, which shows the artist rereading the index box's contents, was shot in his studio in Sofia in 2007. In the video, Solakov mistakenly mentions 1976 as the starting year for the Bulgarian secret service. His service period was from 1978 to 1983.

Description written by Van Abbemuseum

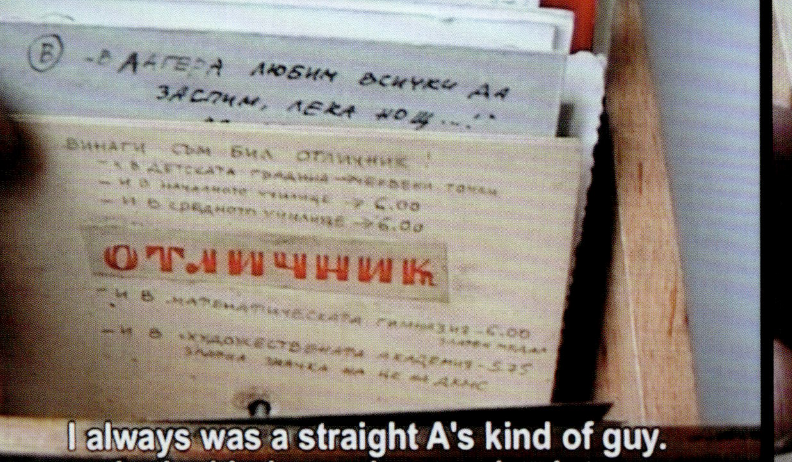

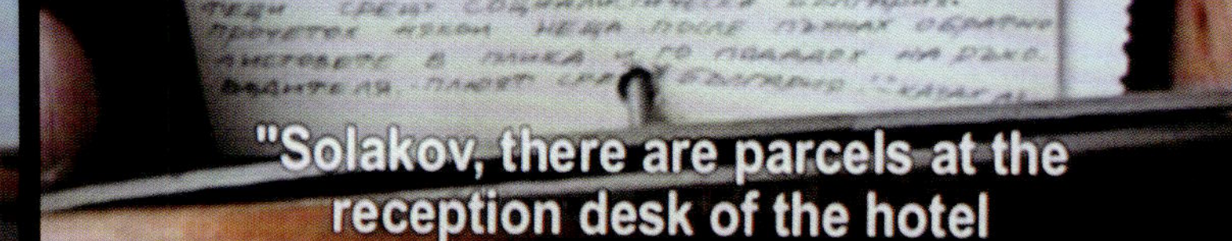

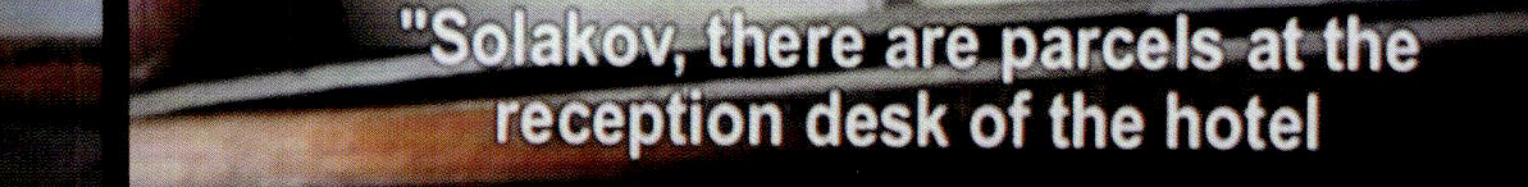

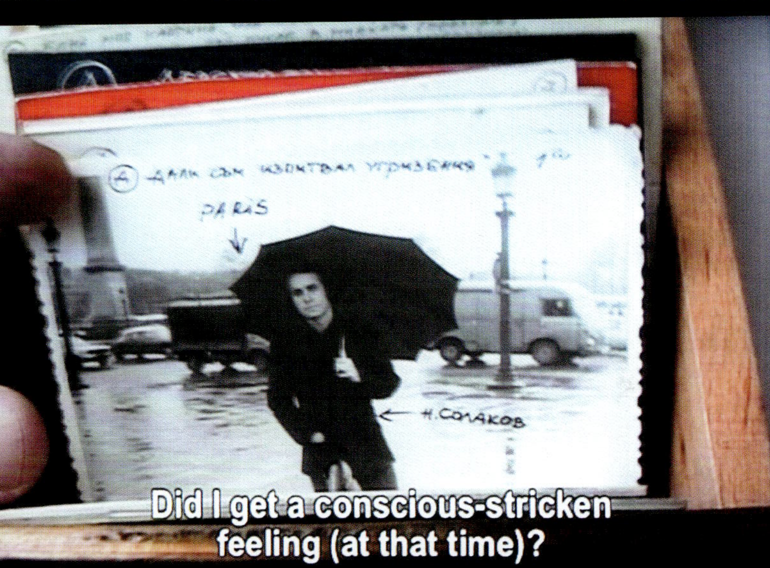

Nedko Solakov — Re-reading, Re-enactment, Re-construction — Three video stills, video on DVD, color, sound, 40:07 min. Courtesy of Van Abbemuseum Collection, Eindhoven — 1989–1990

Csilla Könczei, b. 1963 in Cluj-Napoca, Romania, lives and works in Cluj-Napoca, Romania.

An Abstract Knowledge

Csilla Könczei

In 1993, the artist Csilla Könczei interviewed various people who provided information about their experiences with surveillance by the Romanian secret service, Securitate for her film *An Abstract Knowledge* (*Egy elvont ismeret*). After the fall of communism, they wonder how they can live together with this unknown hostile third party who watched them and took notes on their lives. "We always referred to them as 'comrades' and they had no face." They also had no bodies, people whispered ... and wrote instead of speaking. The first interview partner in the video is the Hungarian poet and writer Géza Szőcs, who was arrested multiple times by the Securitate. In 2012, it was revealed that his own father was a Securitate agent. Szőcs himself was the Hungarian State Secretary for Culture in Viktor Orbán's second government from 2010–2012. In 2016, after the government-initiated suppression of the major left-liberal daily newspaper *Népszabadság*, Szőcs protested against the closing of this particular newspaper's online archive and distanced himself from Orbán's politics. He refers to interaction with the Securitate as a "performance test series"—a series which is again gaining in significance today. **(A)**

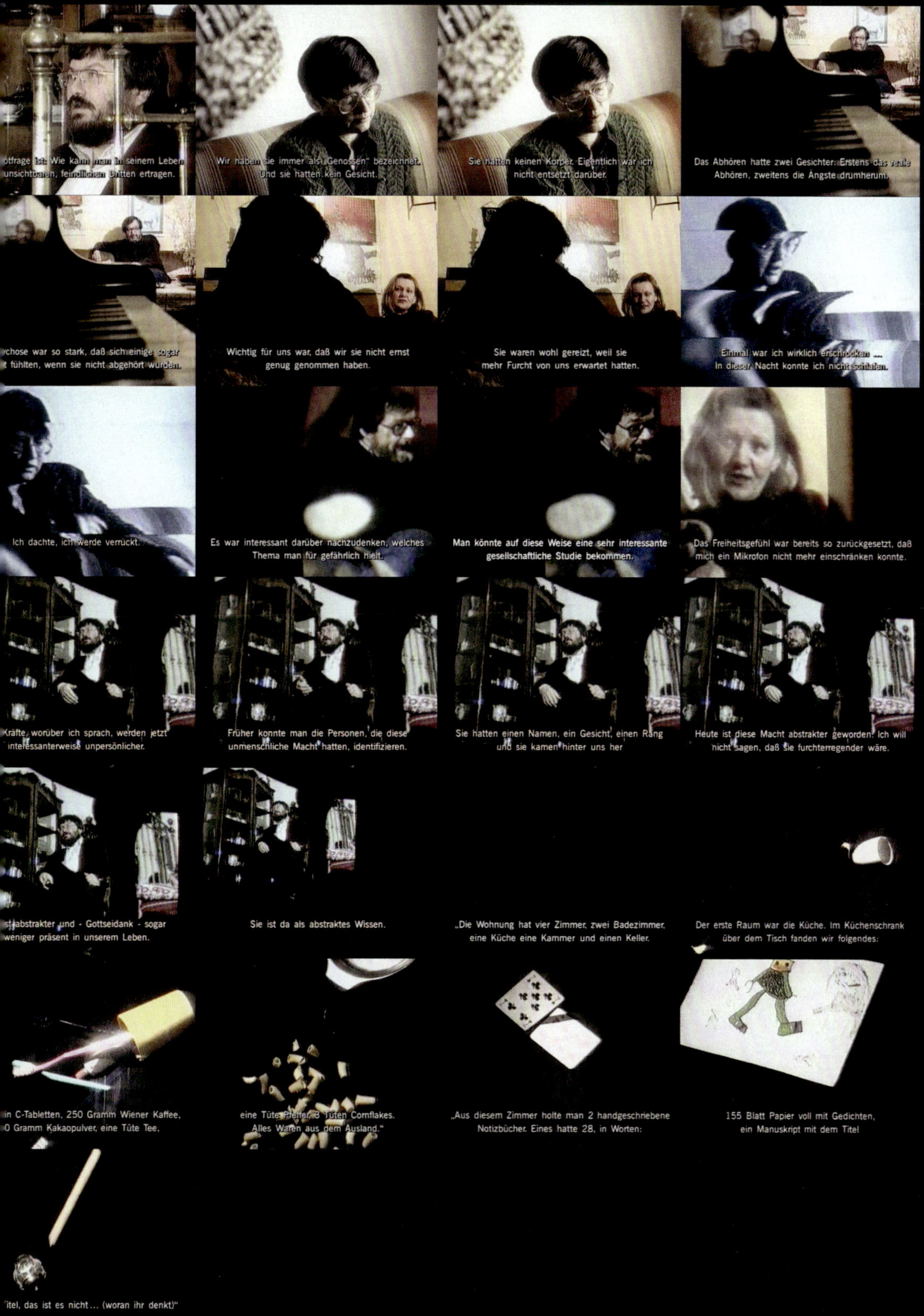

otfrage ist: Wie kann man in seinem Leben
unsichtbaren, feindlichen Dritten ertragen.

Wir haben sie immer als „Genossen" bezeichnet.
Und sie hatten kein Gesicht.

Sie hatten keinen Körper. Eigentlich war ich
nicht entsetzt darüber.

Das Abhören hatte zwei Gesichter: Erstens das reale
Abhören, zweitens die Ängste drumherum.

chose war so stark, daß sich einige sogar
t fühlten, wenn sie nicht abgehört wurden.

Wichtig für uns war, daß wir sie nicht ernst
genug genommen haben.

Sie waren wohl gereizt, weil sie
mehr Furcht von uns erwartet hatten.

Einmal war ich wirklich erschrocken ...
In dieser Nacht konnte ich nicht schlafen.

Ich dachte, ich werde verrückt.

Es war interessant darüber nachzudenken, welches
Thema man für gefährlich hielt.

Man könnte auf diese Weise eine sehr interessante
gesellschaftliche Studie bekommen.

Das Freiheitsgefühl war bereits so zurückgesetzt, daß
mich ein Mikrofon nicht mehr einschränken konnte.

Kräfte, worüber ich sprach, werden jetzt
interessanterweise unpersönlicher.

Früher konnte man die Personen, die diese
unmenschliche Macht hatten, identifizieren.

Sie hatten einen Namen, ein Gesicht, einen Rang
und sie kamen hinter uns her

Heute ist diese Macht abstrakter geworden. Ich will
nicht sagen, daß sie furchterregender wäre.

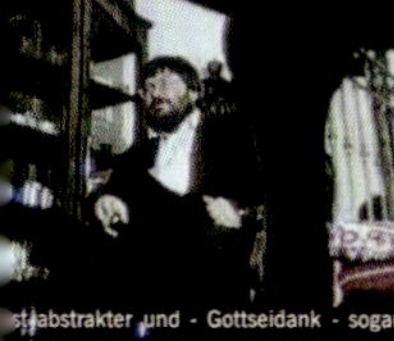

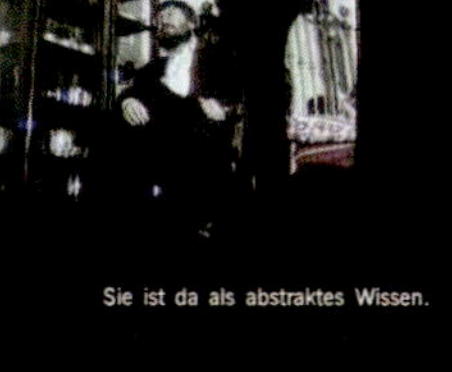

st abstrakter und - Gottseidank - sogar
weniger präsent in unserem Leben.

Sie ist da als abstraktes Wissen.

„Die Wohnung hat vier Zimmer, zwei Badezimmer,
eine Küche eine Kammer und einen Keller.

Der erste Raum war die Küche. Im Küchenschrank
über dem Tisch fanden wir folgendes:

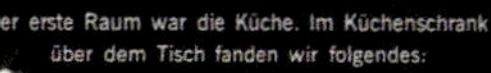

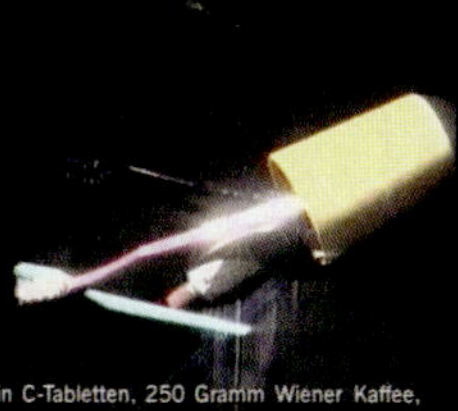

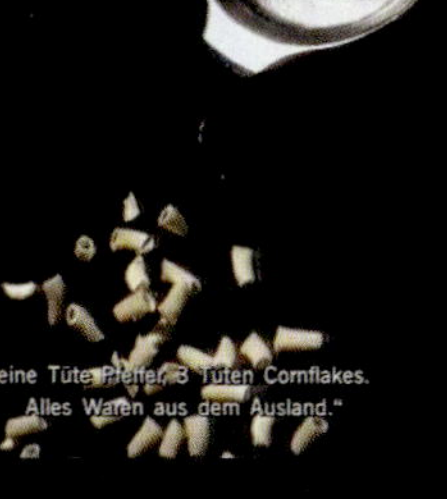

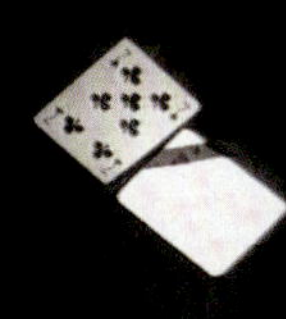

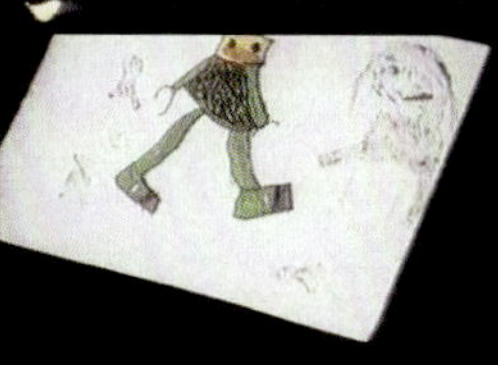

in C-Tabletten, 250 Gramm Wiener Kaffee,
0 Gramm Kakaopulver, eine Tüte Tee,

eine Tüte Pfeffer, 3 Tüten Cornflakes.
Alles Waren aus dem Ausland."

„Aus diesem Zimmer holte man 2 handgeschriebene
Notizbücher. Eines hatte 28, in Worten:

155 Blatt Papier voll mit Gedichten,
ein Manuskript mit dem Titel

itel, das ist es nicht ... (woran ihr denkt)"

Video stills, analog video, Betacam SP (digitized), color, mono, 11:04 min, 1993
Courtesy of Csilla Könczei, ZKM

Re-reading, Re-enactment, Re-construction

Archive-Appropriation

2019

Archive-Appropriation

607

The Survival and Revival of Images

Elisabeth Pichler (EP)

in Conversation with Jens Klein (JK)

For over a decade, Jens Klein, born in Apolda, Germany in 1970, has been engaging in his artwork with the visual legacy of the Stasi. Among the works to emerge from his research in the archive of the Stasi Records Agency (BStU) is *Dog Paths: Index of Conspiratorial Daily Life* (*Hundwege. Index eines konspirativen Alltags*), bringing together the image series *Mailboxes*, *KGA Cableway*, *Walkers*, and *Moped Drivers*. In 2013, Klein added the series *Balloons* to the collection. In 2018, the photo book *Sunset* was published—a photo-essay of locations photographed and archived for border security or in connection with escape attempts, both successful and failed.

Klein's engagement can be placed in a series with other artistic references to this material: in the first years after the opening of the archive, access to Stasi files was granted to certain priority individuals who were entitled to know about them in light of their personal rights. Starting in the early 1990s, we find examples of artists' reactions to confrontation with their own "personal files." Since the late 2000s, a younger generation of artists—as persons "not directly affected," with more distance and a (not always) nuanced perspective—is increasingly engaging with material from the BStU archives. These investigations into visual legacy are often presented as arrangements of images, which first of all "let the images speak for themselves" and only then, in a second step, offer an "interpretive direction" with factual, evaluative, or literary contextual information. The photographer Simon Menner, for example, in *Top Secret: Images from the State Security* Archives (2013), presents photographs where Stasi employees pose for educational materials or are photographed during official occasions and organized leisure activities. In these photos, Menner attempts in a certain sense to make the system transparent in its view of itself. The photographer Arwed Messmer also aims to "turn the pictures themselves into the topic." In *Reenactment MfS* (2014), he brings together photographic documentation connected to failed escape attempts and combines these with his own photographs.

In his works, Jens Klein does not select spectacular or shocking subjects, nor does he look for curiosities. This is demonstrated in his selection of daily activities for *Dog Paths*—people delivering mail, walking their dogs, riding mopeds, or on their way to their small urban garden plots. He leaves us in uncertainty as to why the Stasi was interested in these specific places or the people photographed. In *Sunset* too, the focus is not on individual destinies, but rather, on escape routes into the West. According to Klein, he began his research in the BStU archives with the motivation of "seeing the archive, alongside its function of making transparent structures of control, as an archive of daily life in the GDR."

EP: In your photographic work, you often—and in recent years, almost exclusively—work with photographs which you have not yourself produced. What interests you about photograph "authored by another"?

JK: My work with found material resulted from my interest in history and its contemporary appraisal. Access to historical visual material allows me to connect facts (pictures) from the time in question with my interpretation and thus to create something new. I have never drawn a distinction between my own "authorship" as a photographer and as an artist who works with found material. The emphasis has clearly changed, though. To me, the question occupying me seems more important than the medium I use.

EP: You have been working intensively with material from the BStU archives for more than ten years now. How did you arrive at this interest and how did you land on the idea that there could be material there that you'd like to work with?

JK: Many of my works are concerned with questions that started in Reisdorf, the town where I grew up. When I was a kid, there was a bank robbery in the neighboring town. That was a huge event at the time. Four hundred thousand marks were stolen and there were colored "Wanted" flyers—something relatively rare in the GDR. They were looking for two bank robbers, one with a yellow helmet and one with a red helmet—at least that's how I remember it. It fascinated me that you could rob a bank in the GDR and then go on living anonymously after that: the surveillance system was famously very strict and encompassed both public and private life. I sometimes wondered whether my memory was correct. The memory of these colored helmets and the fact that the bank robbers were never caught. Despite extensive searching, I was never able to find any information about this and turned to the BStU archives. I submitted my first research application in 2006. In the process of searching, there were matches—files on this bank robbery. The original flyer even showed up—with the yellow and red helmets. And there was other material that showed up in this process, which I found just as interesting.

EP: So, your research began with a "comparison" of your own memory with your interest in this specific story?

JK: An interest in this story specifically, but also generally. Legal proceedings for this bank robbery didn't begin until 1996/1997. This GDR criminal case became a criminal case for the Federal Republic of Germany. I am still occupied with this bank robbery—all of the questions still haven't been answered for me. I have done a large amount of research and carried out interviews, and all along I had thoughts about all sorts of things: how did they manage to stay undetected? Did they leave a trail? Were there any tracks? Did they escape with the money maybe? Did the bank robbers leave the country? Which would honestly not make much sense because if you exchanged the money there wouldn't be much left. In any case, I submitted other search requests to the archives and learned about other photo collections: meticulous observations by the Stasi of everyday life in the GDR, which were never planned to be such. But I have been less interested in individual persons or fates than in the general.

EP: The title of your graduate thesis was "On the Attempt to Regain the Past."

JK: The topic of my thesis was the question of the degree to which it is even possible to reconstruct the history of a country that no longer exists on the basis of photographs. What became of this GDR and its inhabitants, this country that I spent a part of my life in? What do we call this area today: the former GDR, the five new states, East Germany? The view into this recent past is full of unclarity; by now there are films, television shows, photo books, and documentaries. There are various ways of interpreting what happened politically. And then there are personal experiences.

EP: I am often confronted with the question of whether artworks like this represent a kind of "aestheticization." In the sense that the aesthetic stimulus or point of entry is important for me as an observer. Not just with photographs but also in observing and interacting with the files themselves. An aesthetics of the files worked with and which work with me and in me. I find the question interesting whether it goes beyond this, whether it becomes complex or multilayered. I ask myself: what exactly might this complexity be? Why do I see one work as complex and multilayered, while I have the feeling that another work remains at a surface level? I think that this biographical connection you bring to the work, or the knowledge of it, plays, on the one hand, a role in my perception of the work and, on the other, really gives me another point of entry into the material.

JK: Using a photograph in an artistic context always implies a certain aestheticization. This question also of course raises the question: *may* we do that? An image is always aesthetic. I look at it and it receives a form; it wouldn't work otherwise. For me, it is more about why we are interested in these images and which questions we want to ask. But to return to your question [of] whether my personal connection gives the work more layers, more complexity: I don't think you need to have been born in the GDR to work with this material as an artist. But it's definitely possible that it brings another dimension to the work. This can be just as much restricting as enriching.

EP: In recent years, we have been seeing an increase in artistic interest in archival materials generally, but also material in the BStU archives specifically. For example, Arwed Messemer (*Reenactment MfS*, 2014) or Simon Menner (*Top Secret*, 2013) have used photographs from these archives for their works. Your approach, or your interest, seems different to me though. How did you proceed with your research, what images interested you and why?

JK: Everyone who researches in the BStU archives has access to the same photographic material. Many of the images you see in the works of Arwed Messmer or Simon Menner were familiar to me from my research. I completely understand the appeal of these images, but for me, other images were more important: the inconspicuous, less spectacular photographs where we can learn something about everyday life in the GDR.

EP: Everyday life also appears in the title of your work *Dog Paths: Index of Conspiratorial Daily Life* alternates between agreement and contrast with what you can see in the photographs. The forms of behavior which were called conspiratorial in Stasi jargon were those which led to concealment of one's own actions, to vigilance, or to deception. I have wondered whether your work ultimately says more about the daily lives of those doing the surveilling than the daily life of those who were surveilled.

JK: The photographs naturally tell us a lot about the everyday life of the people carrying out the surveillance. We notice a lot of dreariness and boredom in the written records accompanying these photos. And the conspiracy is on both sides: those, of course, who are taking pictures in secret and who take possession of the daily lives of the others. But also, the knowledge that there is surveillance and control and that one needs to behave accordingly. I think people can separate that very well. It was kind of schizophrenic; you knew that you were being watched and so behaved accordingly in certain situations or chose not to say things which you knew would be better left unsaid. But there were also moments where that was not the case. In the pictures I selected, people weren't aware that they were being watched—or I presume not, at least. It seems totally banal; nothing is happening that you might think of as suspicious.

EP: I find it notable that you are one of the few artists who conceive of the BStU archives as such, and not only as a "Stasi archive." We are still looking back at an almost thirty year "history of reappraisal."

JK: The archive also tells us a lot about how we interact with history today. The impetus for the occupation of the Stasi offices and the later founding of the BStU was the prevention of file destruction. People wanted to know what was in their files, wanted to access and reclaim their secretly documented lives. And it was also about knowing who those people were who were watching you. The files contained a specific character sketch of the person, and the question arose to what extent that which was written—whether by Stasi employees, colleagues, or even family members—had anything to do with the person and how this person could be recognized in this description by another.

The impetus for the founding of the BStU—"we want to know what's in our files"—and the reclaiming of one's own personal history has further developed. The BStU is presently the largest historical institution in the Federal Republic of Germany—and the history of the GDR is largely read through this archive. The official writing of history thus conceals a part of history—personal experience. The GDR was a dictatorship where the freedom of the individual was not considered something worth protecting. The work of the state security apparatus could damage or destroy the lives of those being surveilled. There was no protection through an independent judiciary. But I wonder whether residents who were not in conflict with the regime could recognize themselves in this way of looking at history. Someone thinks: yeah, okay, but maybe I didn't feel that it was an unjust state; it doesn't match up with my perception, the forty, thirty, or twenty years I spent living there, but this right has been taken away from me. Maybe this person had been at peace or found peace in this country. The official historical narrative is then in conflict with personal experience. Alongside this discrepancy, the question in the 1990s was less about the history of the GDR and more about the question of reunification: how a system is taken over and what possibilities exist for cooperatively shaping this system. These questions definitely did not exist after reunification. Apart from the distinctive pedestrian stoplights (*Ampelmännchen*) and a brand of sparkling wine (*Rotkäppchen*) and certain other consumer food products, not much was considered worth saving. Looking back, there are numerous overlaps with the relationships between colonies and their "mother countries." The work of the transitional trust responsible for privatization (*Treuhandanstalt*) left scars behind. There was also no real GDR identity and the "East German identity" is a product of how this reunification was carried out. And we are still dealing with these consequences today. In this context, engagement with the BStU is also political engagement. And in this sense, it is not just the Stasi archive but the archive of these national agencies.

EP: Your work in this way poses the question of how we look at these pictures today, what we can take away from them.

JK: History does not just take place in the past but is also reflected in how we talk about it in the present day. How we speak about it today, how we look at pictures or evaluate them—that is always today, in the here and now.

Translated from German by Brian Alkire

Mailboxes

Jens Klein

Jens Klein, who has been engaging with photographic materials of the former East German Ministry for State Security for the last ten years, created multiple artistic series from the available visual and serial material—including *Mailboxes* (*Briefkästen*, 2012), *Walkers* (*Spaziergänger*, 2012), *Balloons* (*Ballone*, 2013), and *Sunset* (2018). These are surveillance series based on Klein's research in the BStU. For his presentation of the materials in *Mailboxes*, Klein cuts the photographs' connection to their original context, guiding our attention away from the act of spying and towards that which is captured itself. Jens Klein writes: "In the pictures I selected, people weren't aware that they were being watched—or I presume not, at least. It seems totally banal; nothing is happening that you might think of as suspicious." At the same time, mailboxes were among the most common image tropes of the secret police, intended to show the perfection of their surveillance methods and specifically to point to the spectacular. **(S/K)**

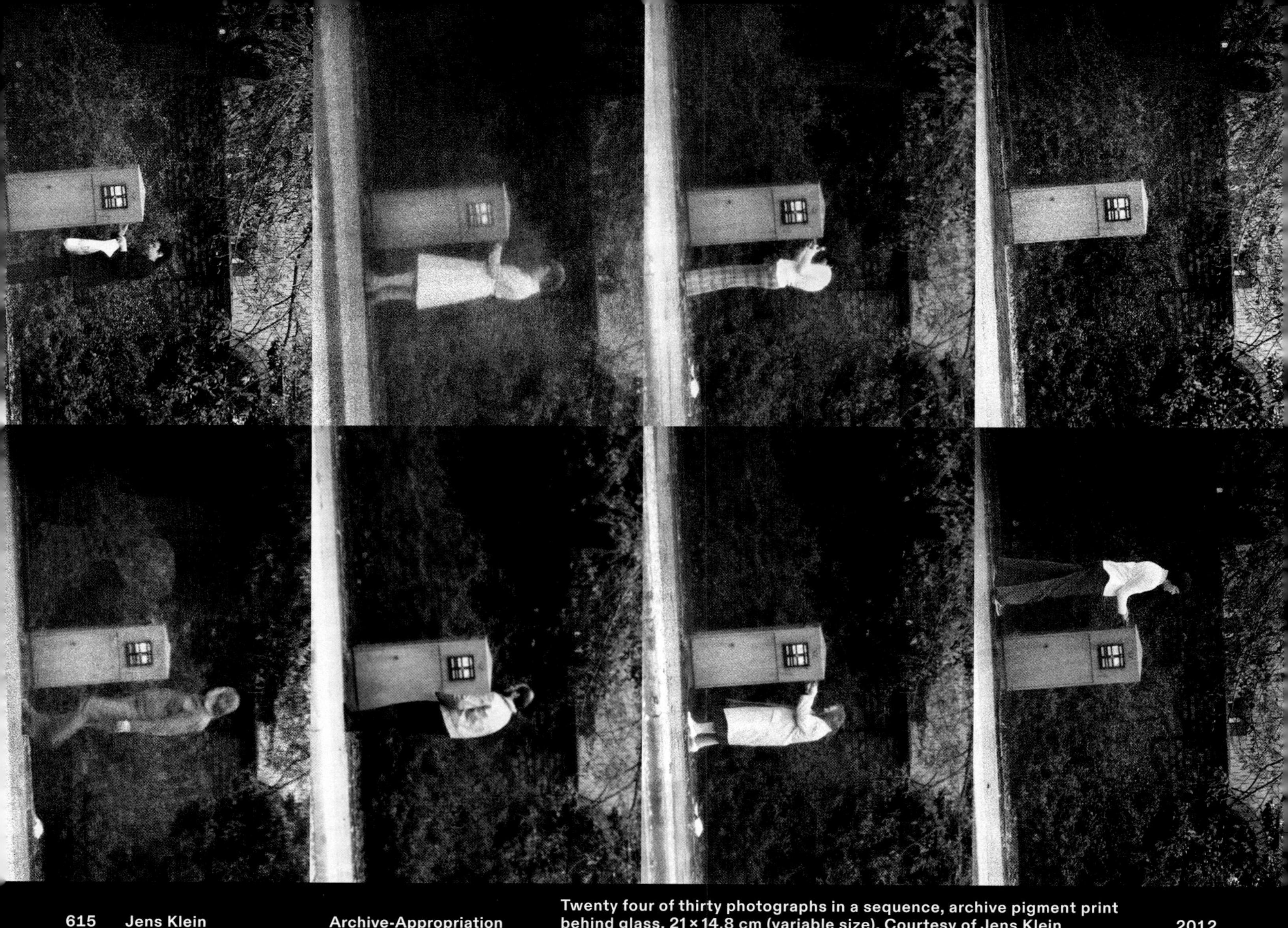

 Jens Klein

Archive-Appropriation

Twenty four of thirty photographs in a sequence, archive pigment print behind glass, 21 × 14.8 cm (variable size), Courtesy of Jens Klein

2012

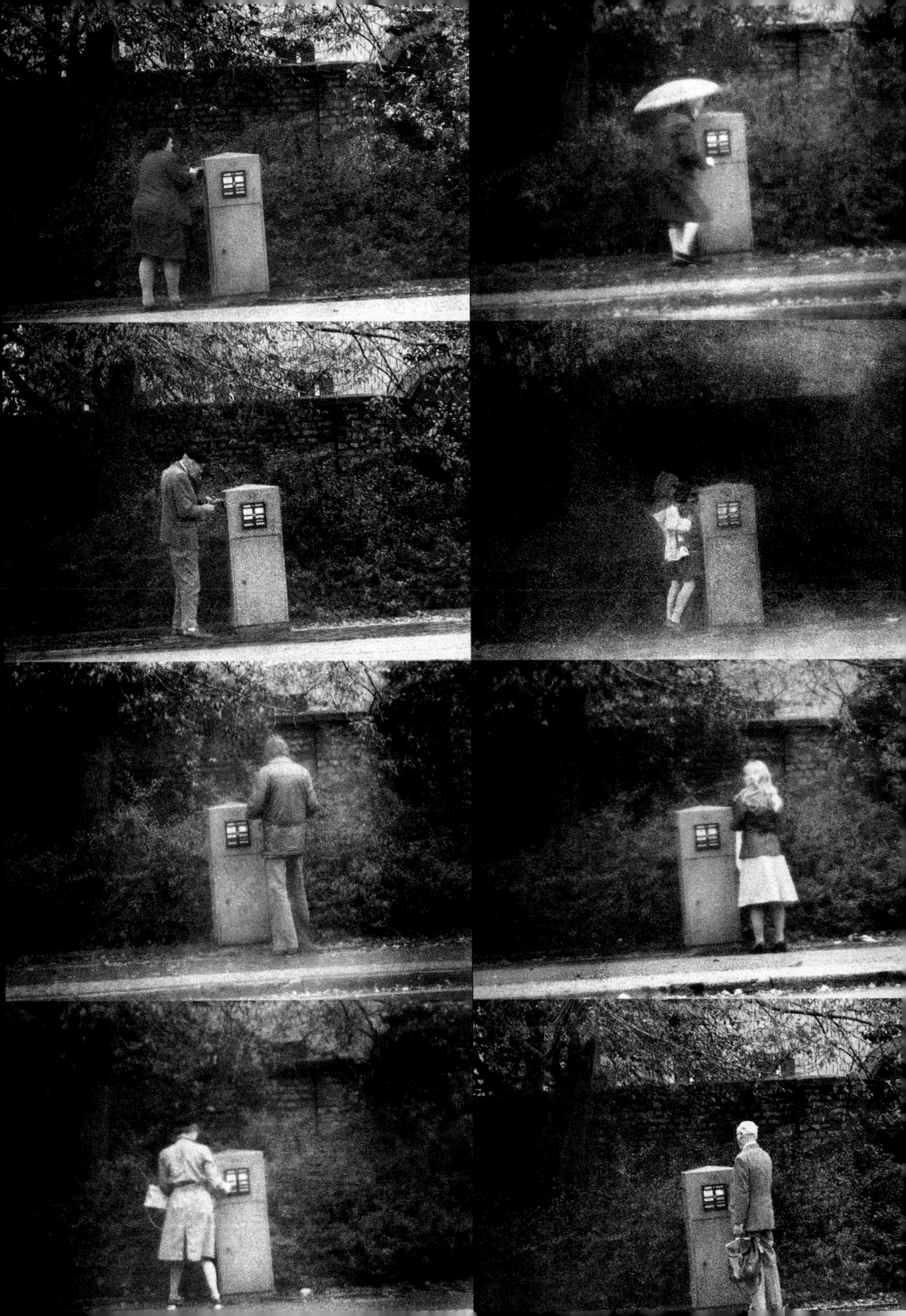

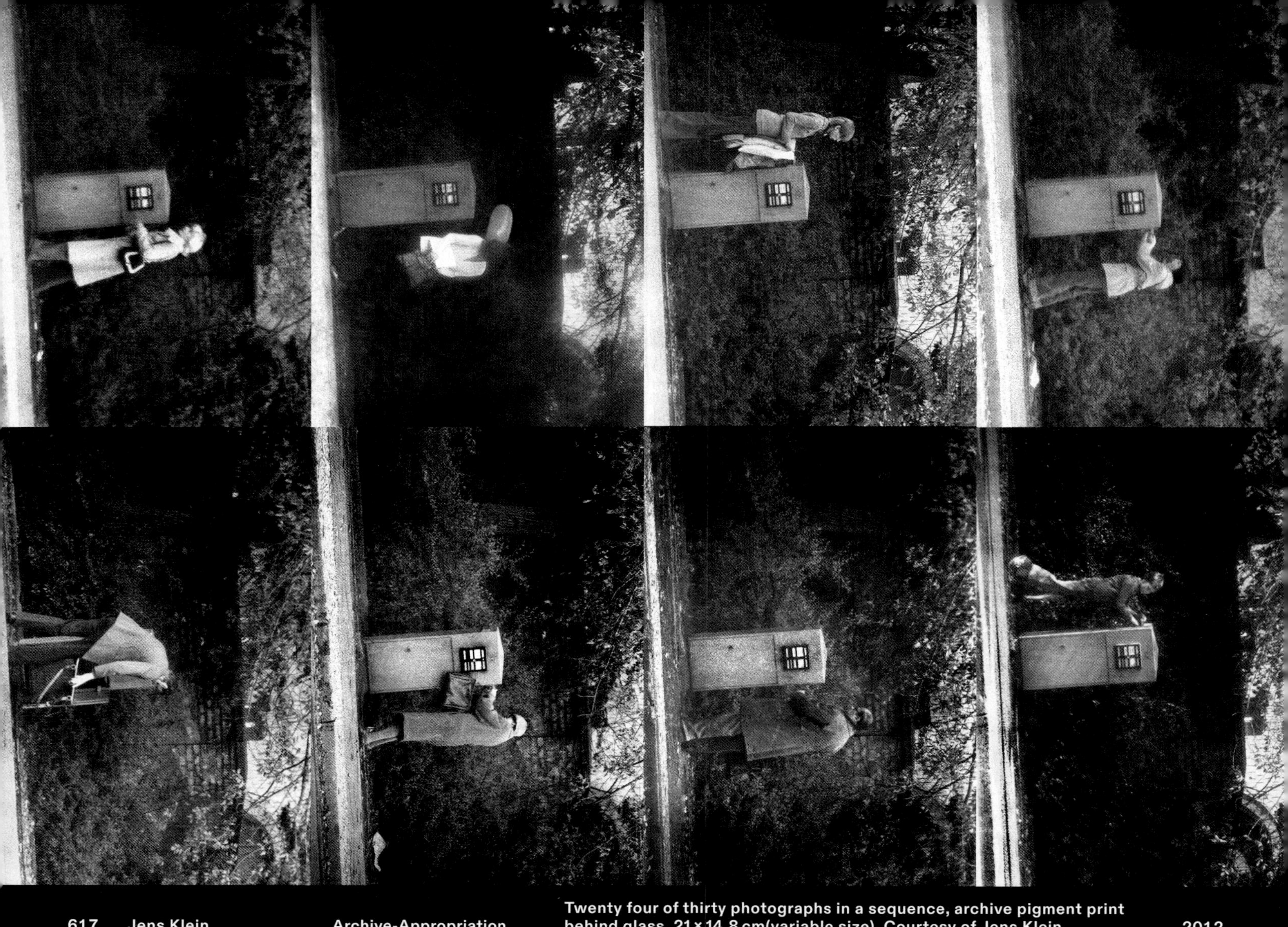

 Jens Klein Archive-Appropriation Twenty four of thirty photographs in a sequence, archive pigment print behind glass, 21 × 14.8 cm(variable size), Courtesy of Jens Klein 2012

Reenactment MfS

Arwed Messmer

"Reenactment" is an imprecise term: it refers in general to the retrospective staging of events with the goal of gaining authentic experiences of the events, how it was or at least could have been. In the context of his research about the development of the Berlin Wall, Arwed Messmer stumbled across photographs and exhibits of the Ministry for State Security (MfS) which were attached to the files about escape attempts and shootings of persons attempting to escape. The border authorities have these "case files" to the MfS for investigation and evaluation and also concealing from family members and the public. Looking at the photographs, we do not immediately know what is reality and what is staged. The Stasi forced captured escapees to crawl back into their smuggler-prepared vehicles, where they were then photographed. This Stasi reenactment was in this way a means of "decomposition." Messmer's reenactment consists of repeating the bureaucratically-preserved testimony; he appropriates the Stasi reenactments as ready-mades. The pressed four-leaf clover was found by the artist in the identification papers of one of the persons shot. The "revisited places" are in turn photos of the present-day condition of places that appear in the files. (A)

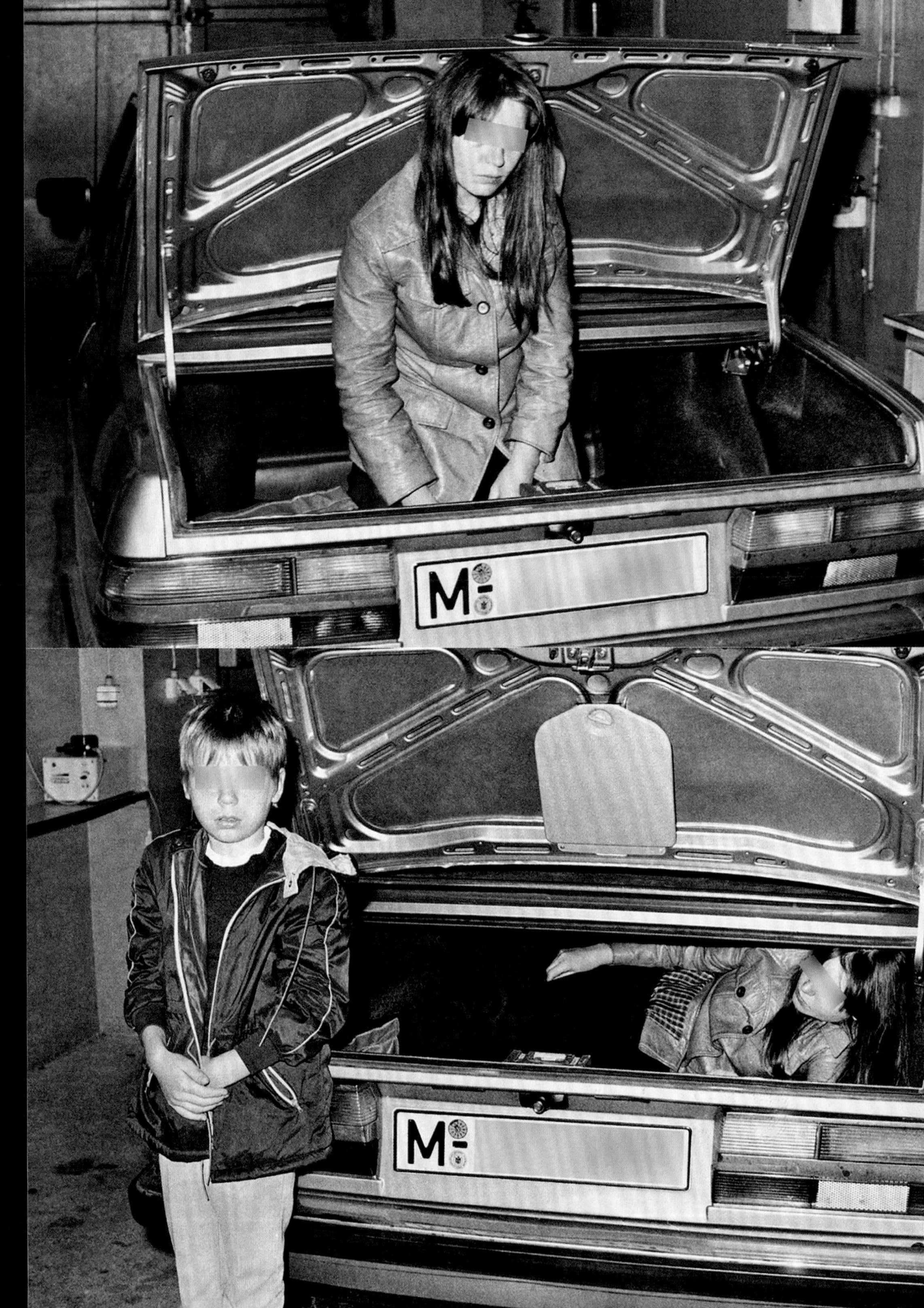
M-
M-

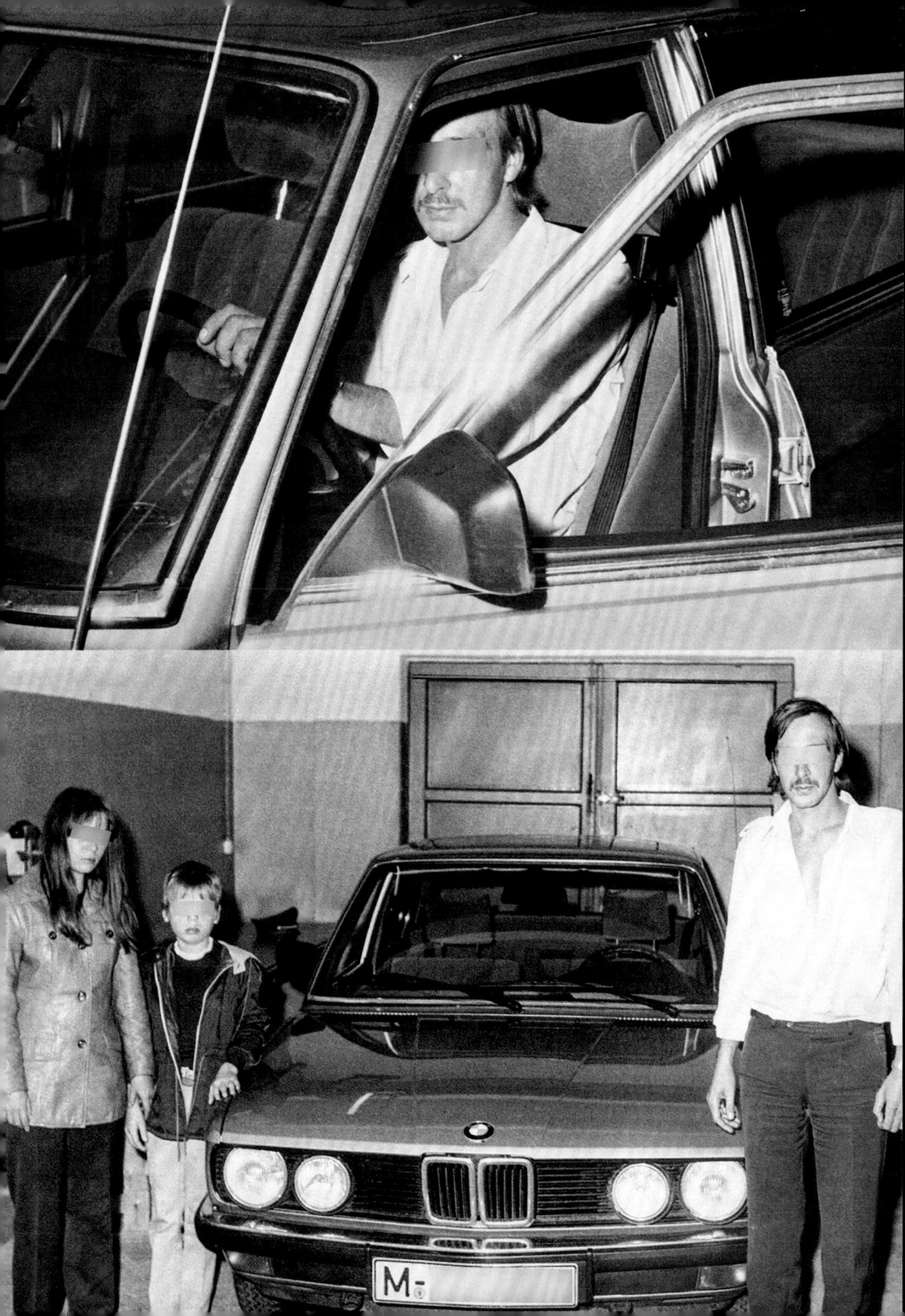

Four tableaus with photographs from the Reenactment MfS series,

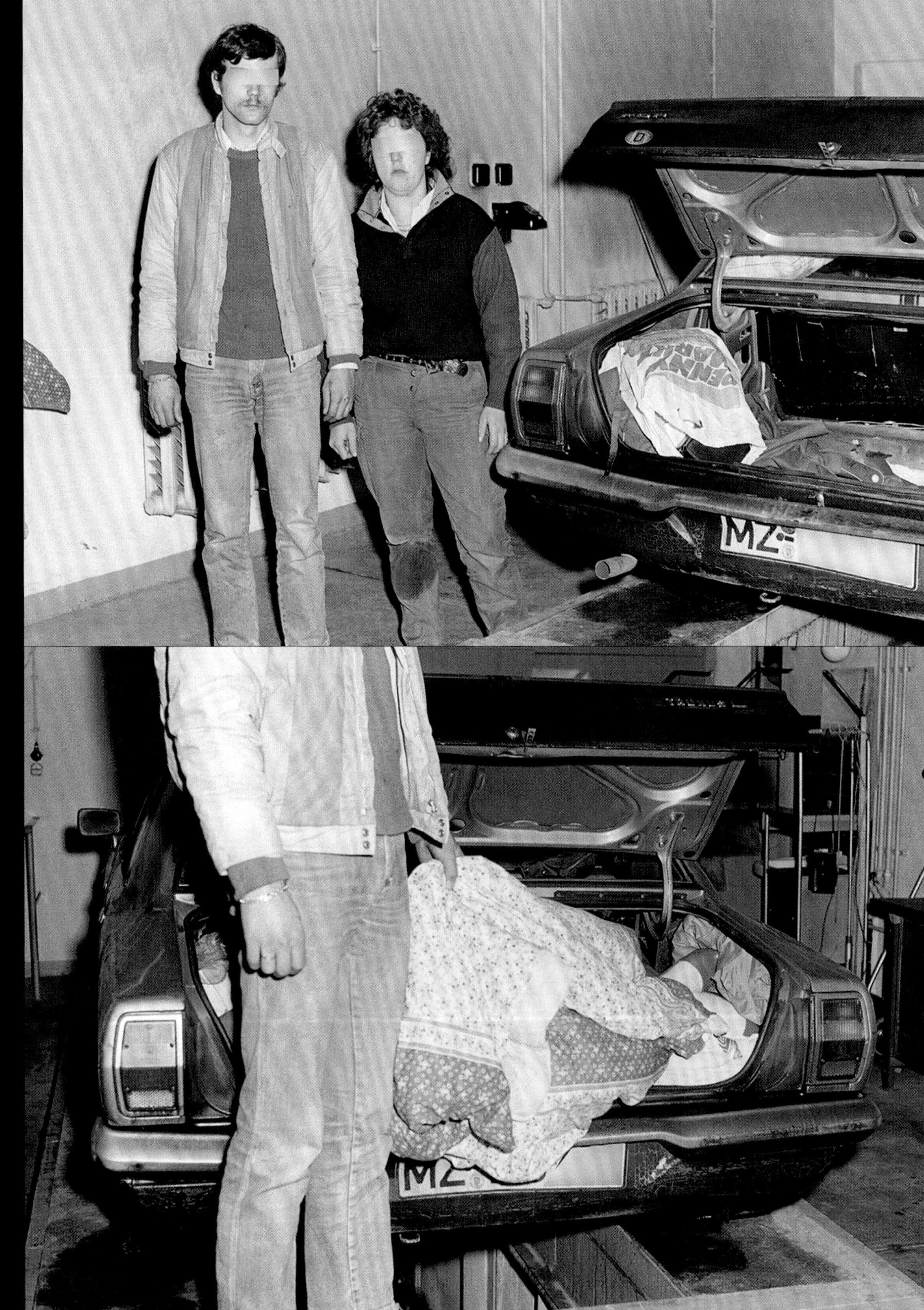
MZ
MZ

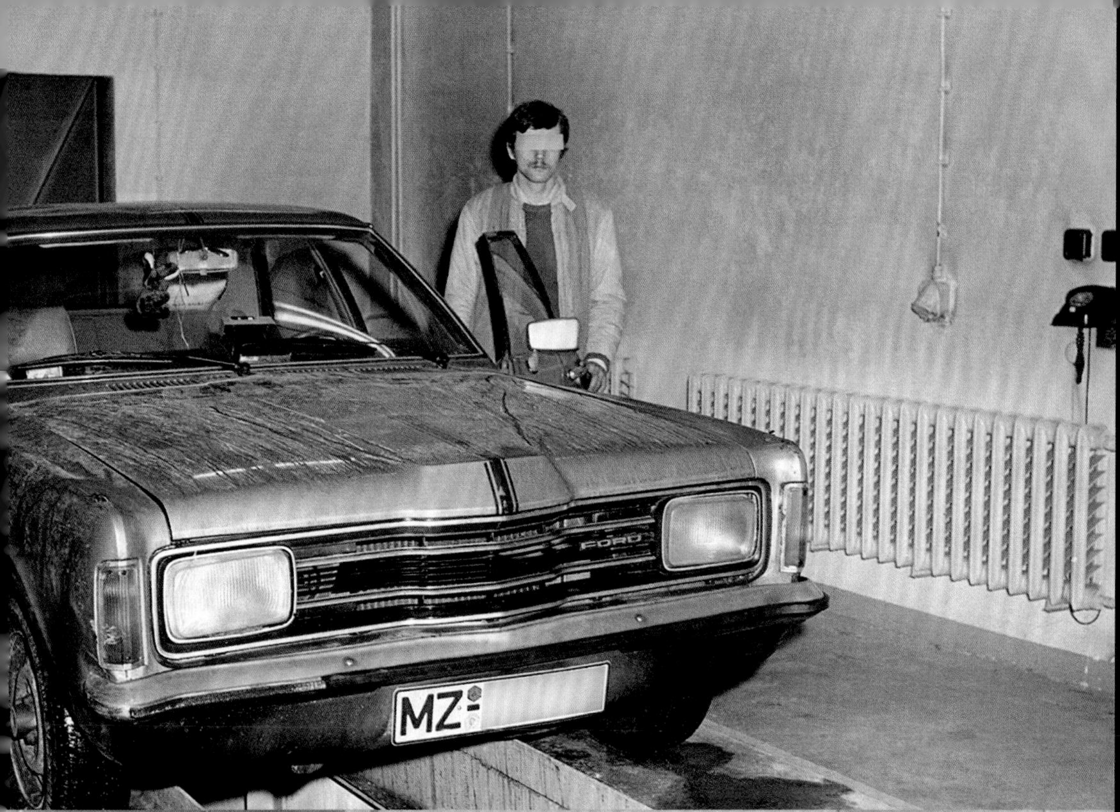

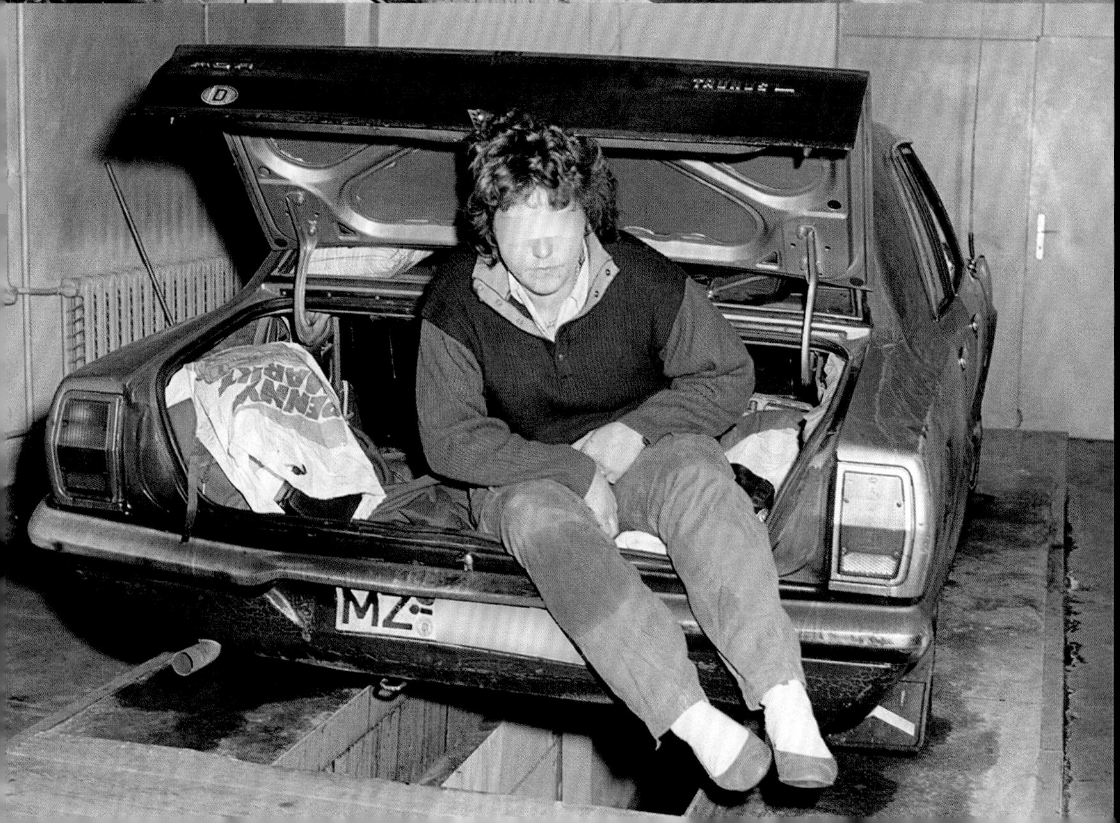

Four tableaus with photographs from the Reenactment MfS series,
Courtesy of Arwed Messmer

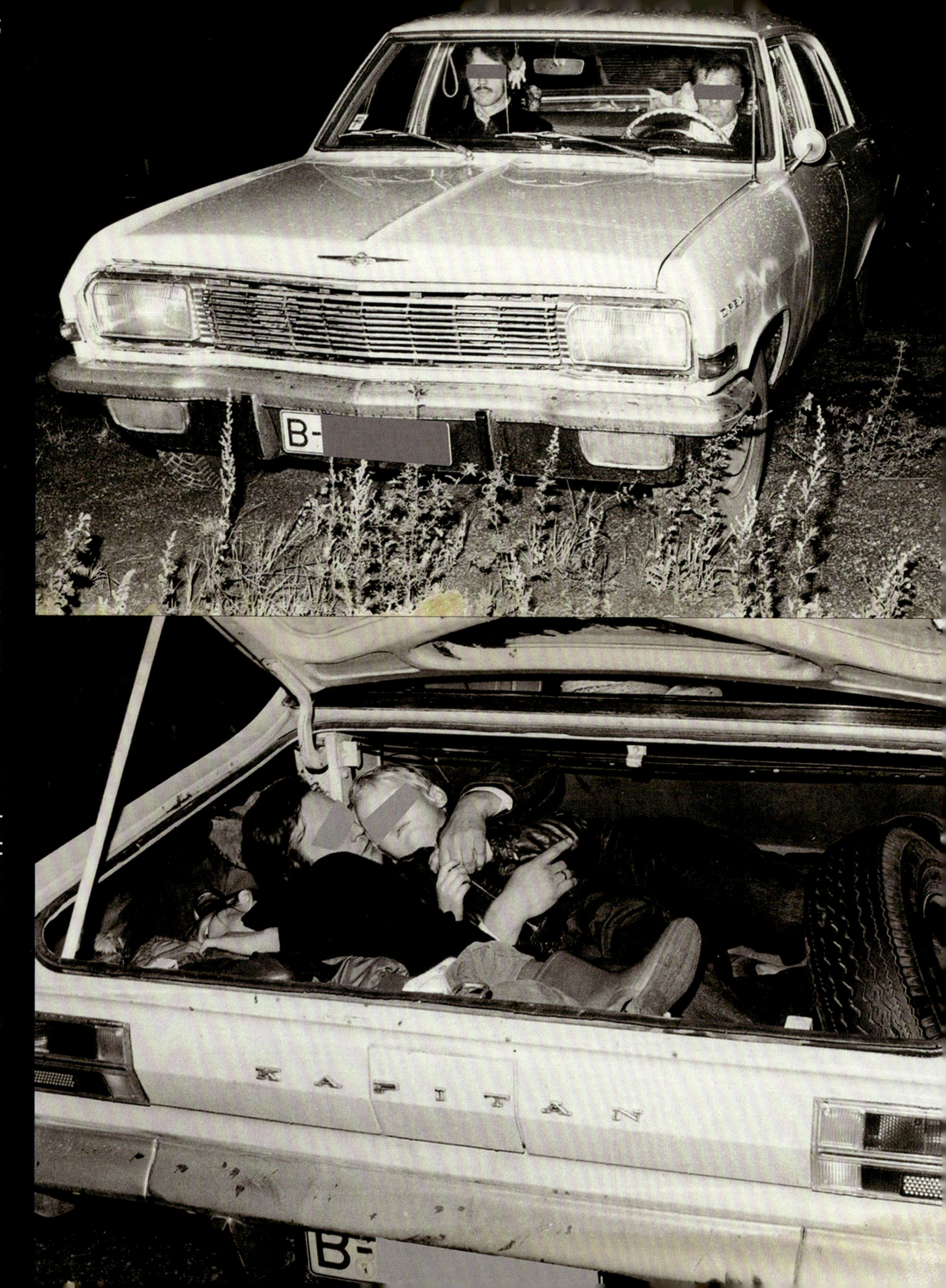
B-
KAPITAN
B-

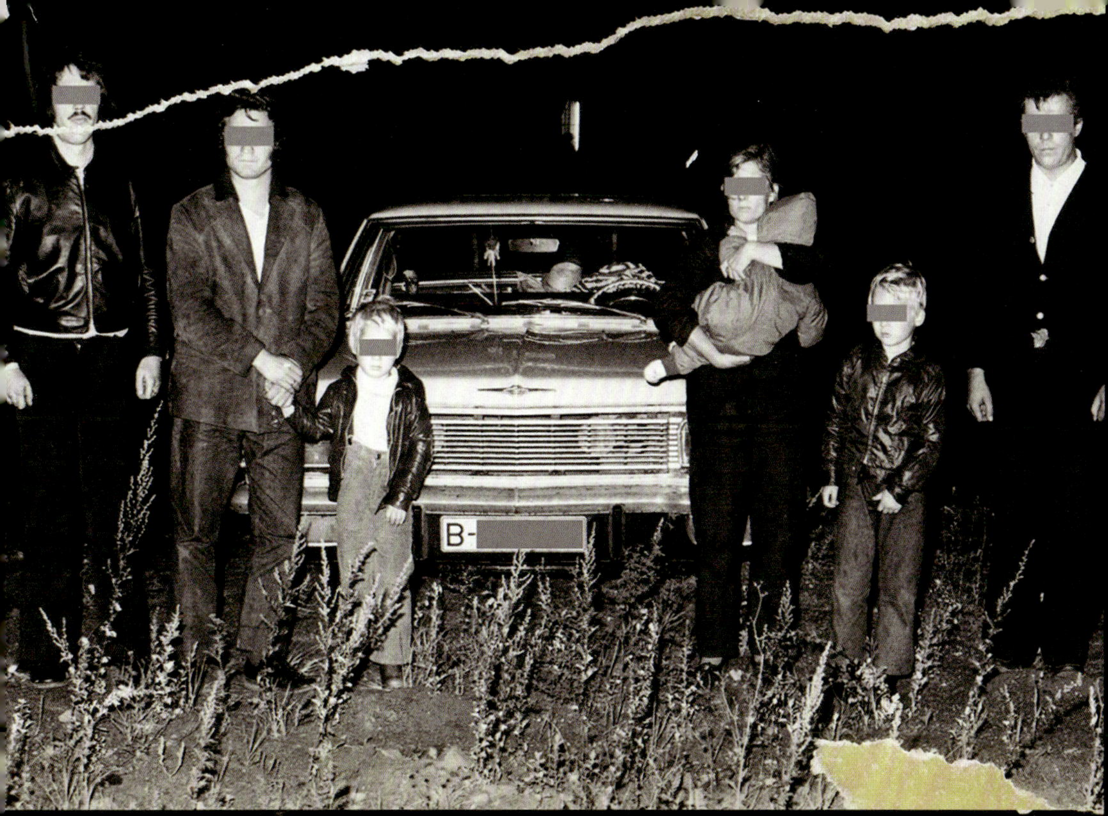

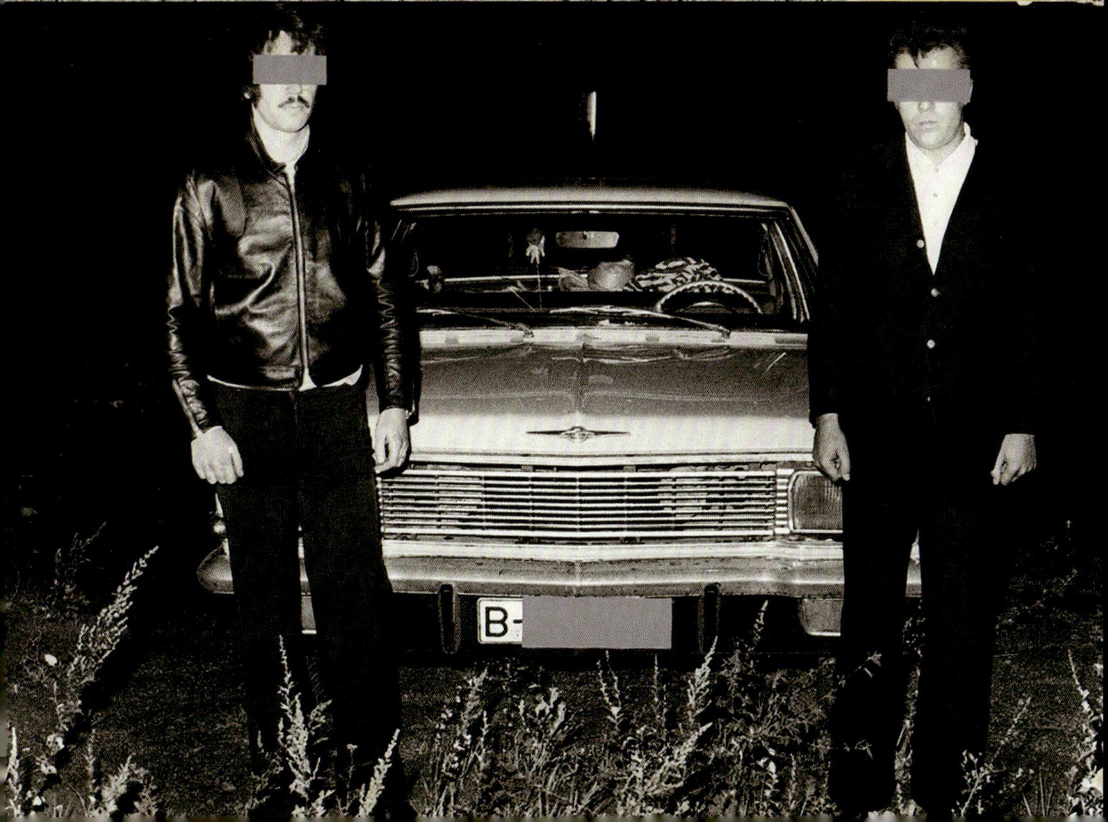

Four tableaus with photographs from the Reenactment MfS series,
Courtesy of Arwed Messmer

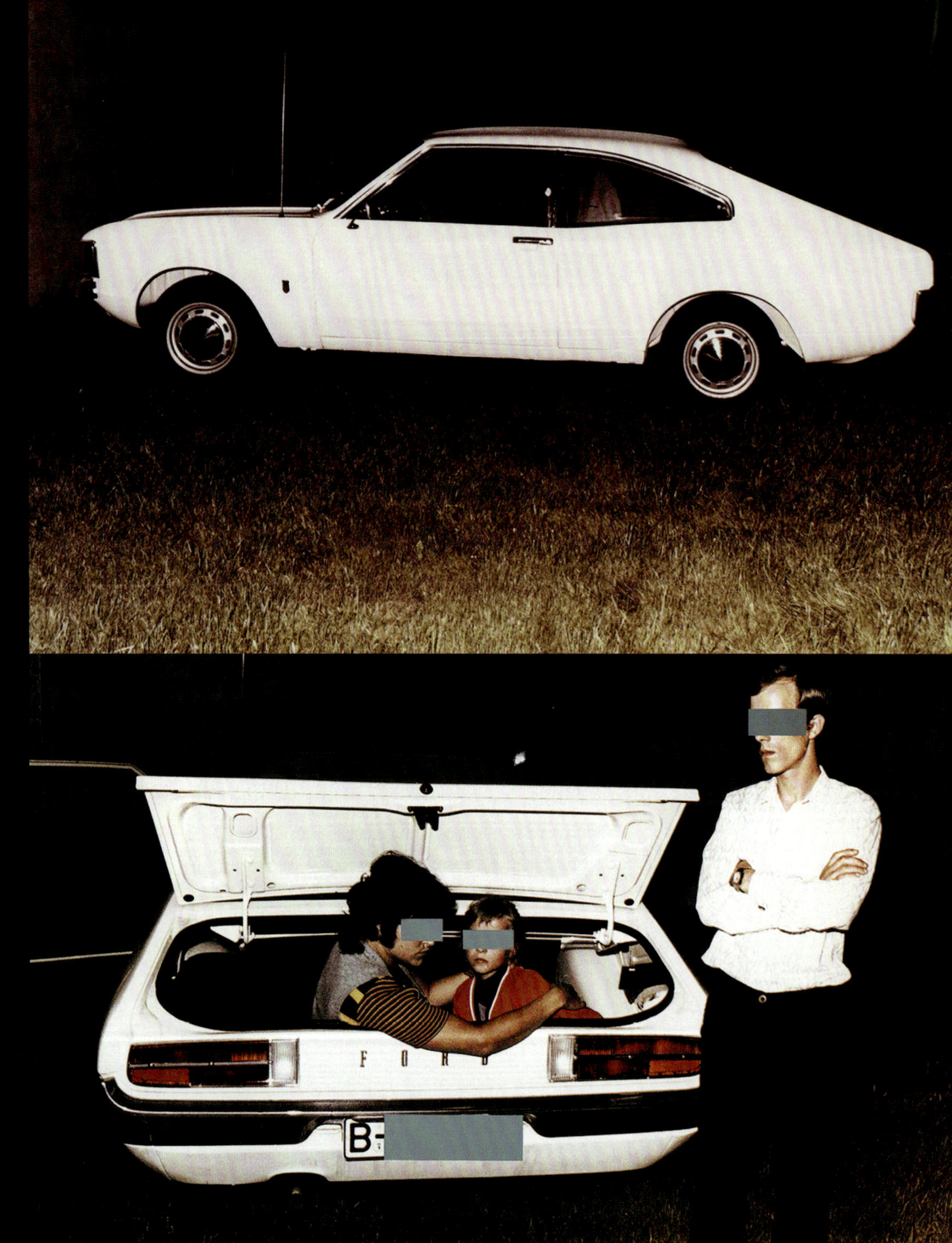

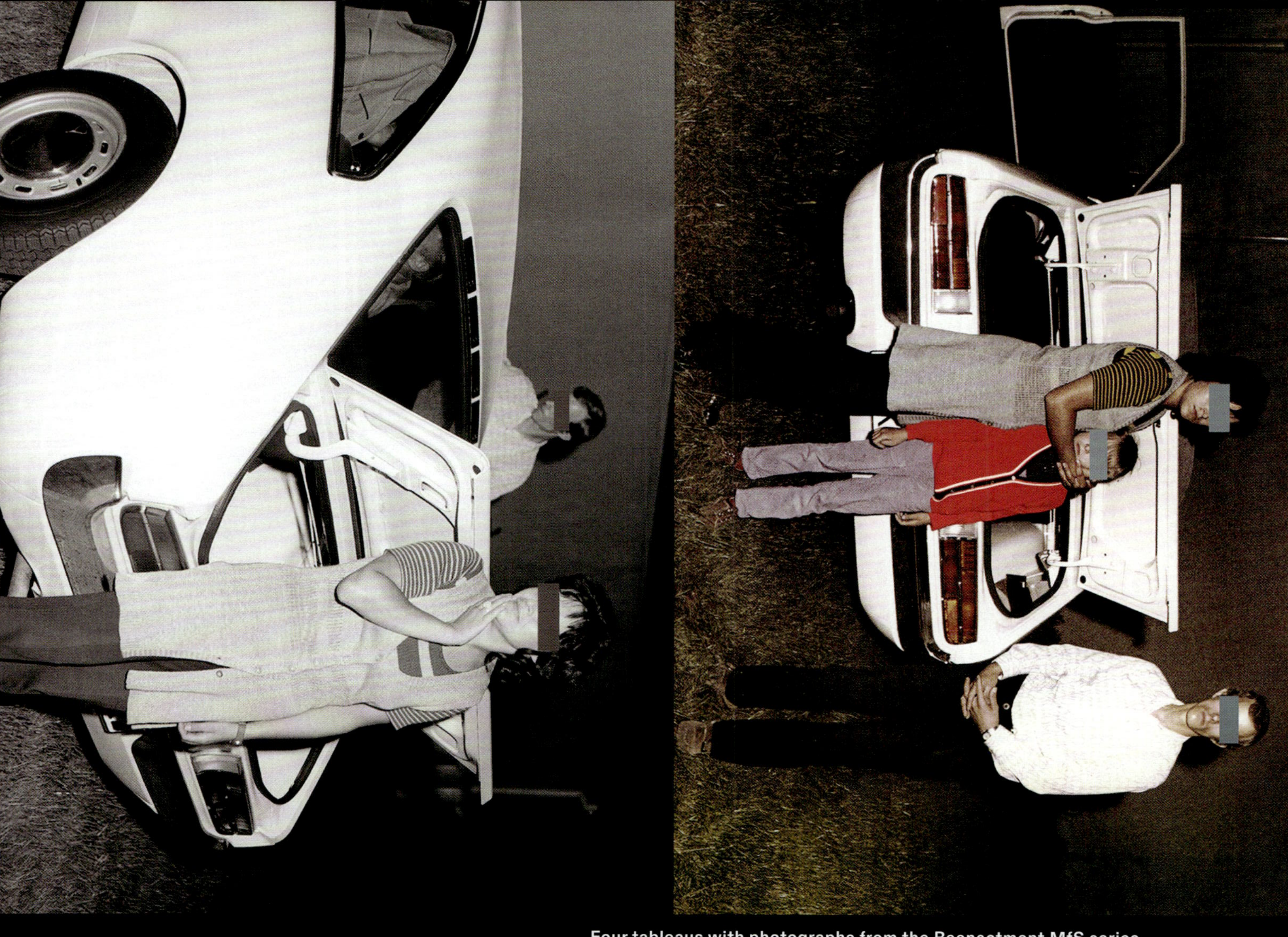

Four tableaus with photographs from the Reenactment MfS series,
Courtesy of Arwed Messmer

2014

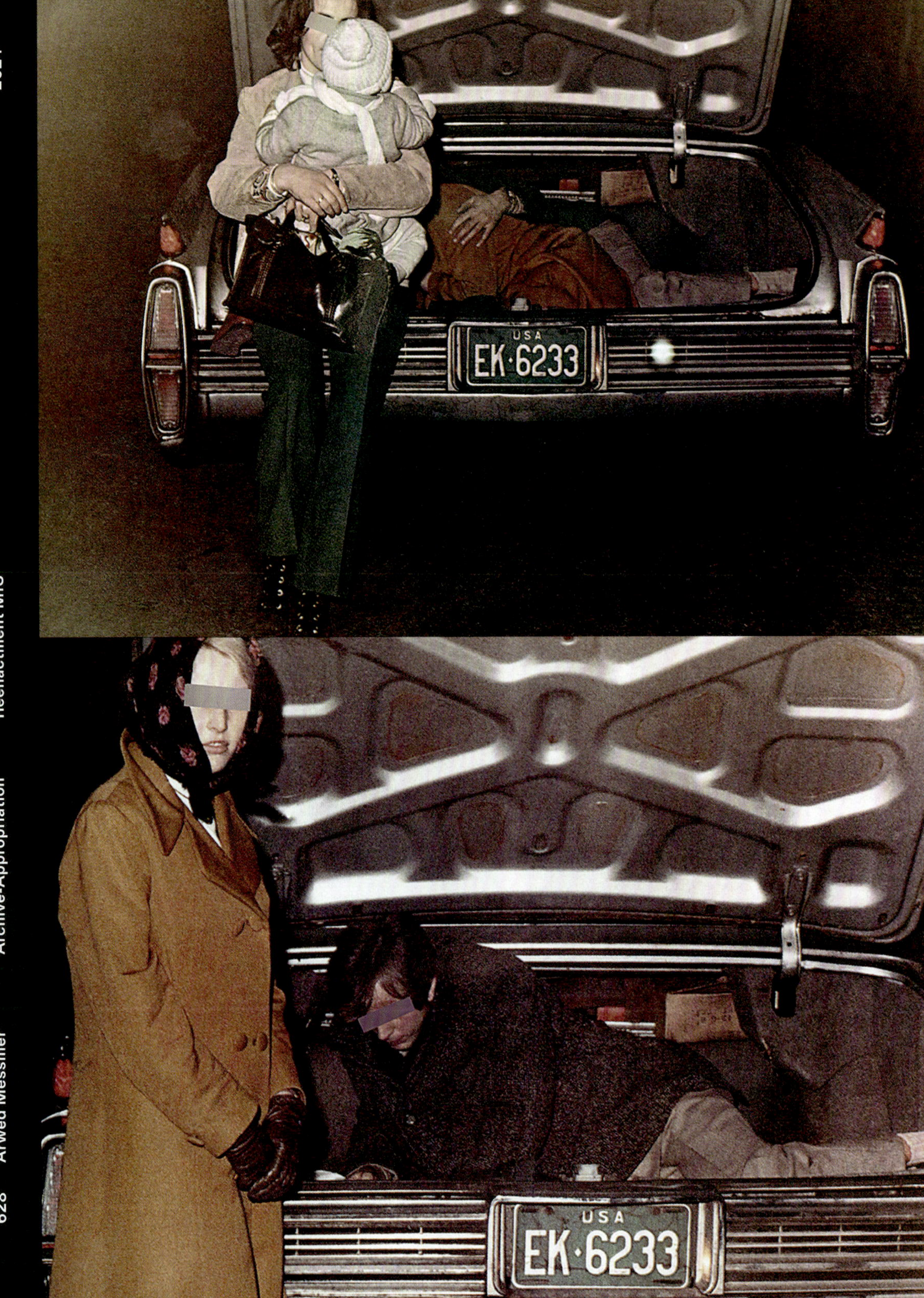
USA
EK·6233
USA
EK·6233

 Archive-Appropriation

Four tableaus with photographs from the Reenactment MfS series, Courtesy of Arwed Messmer

2014

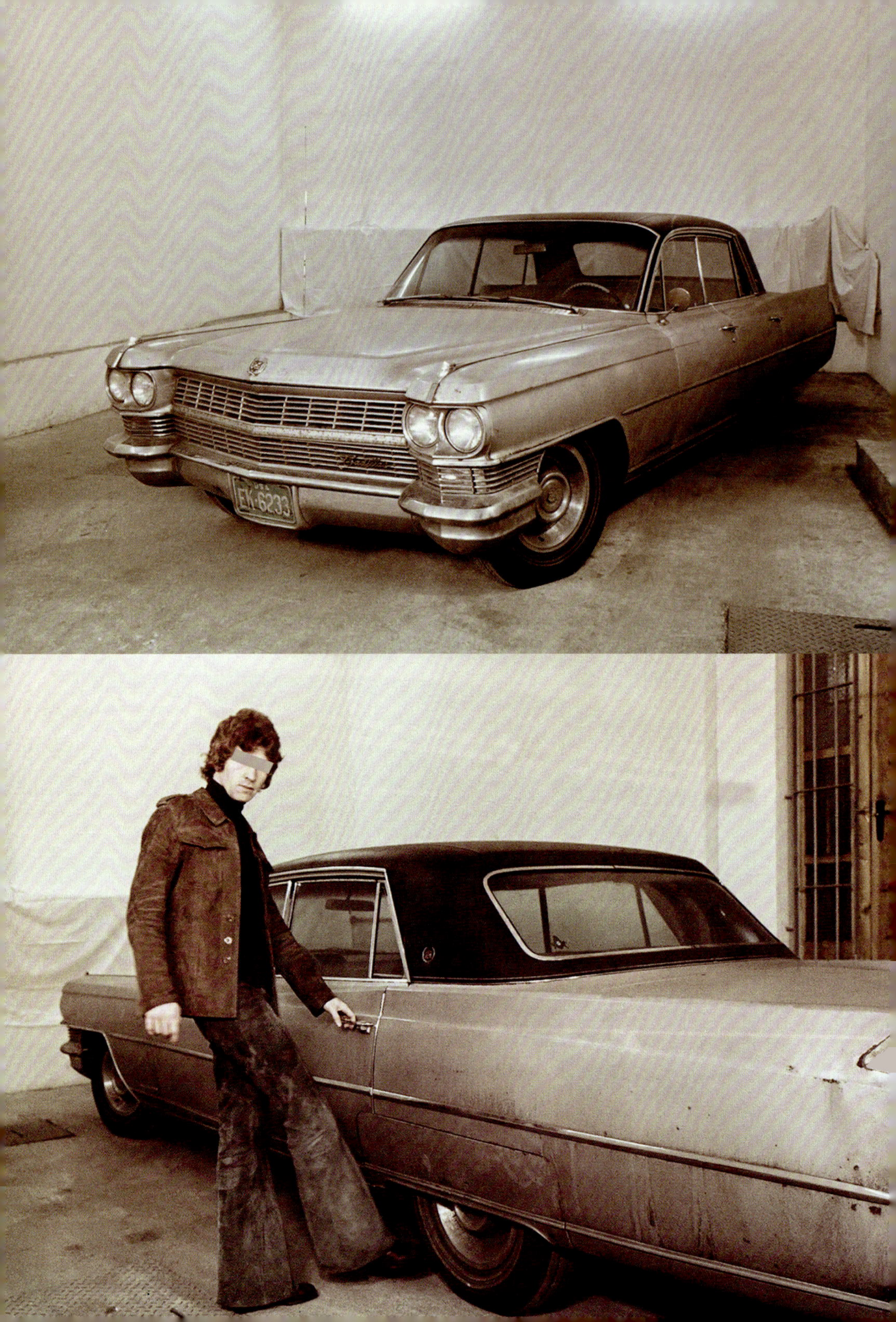
EK·6233

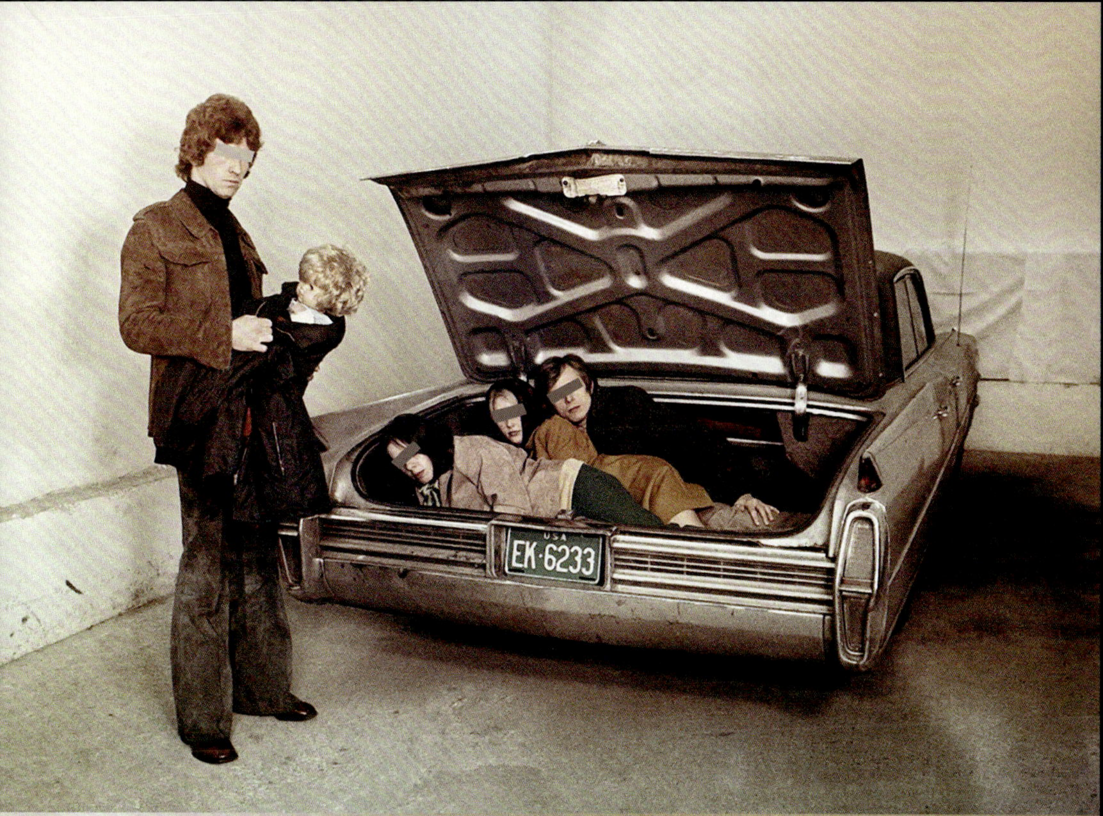

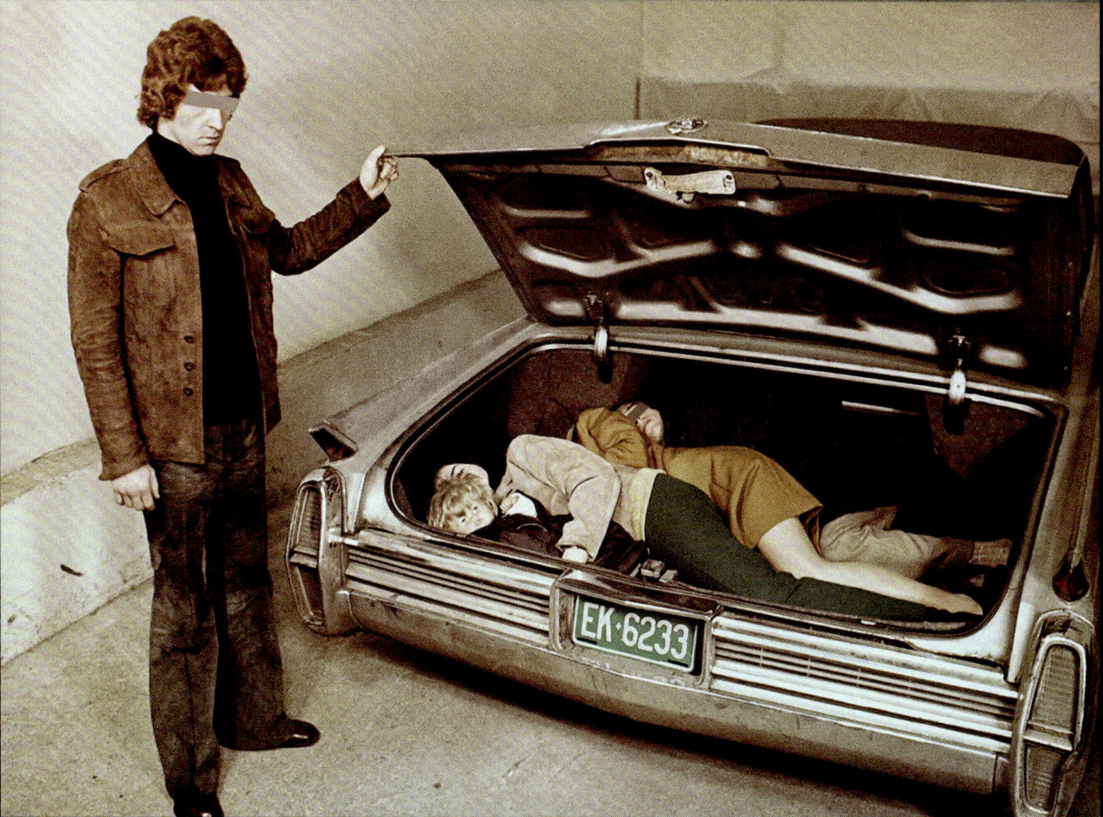

Four tableaus with photographs from the Reenactment MfS series,
Courtesy of Arwed Messmer

2014

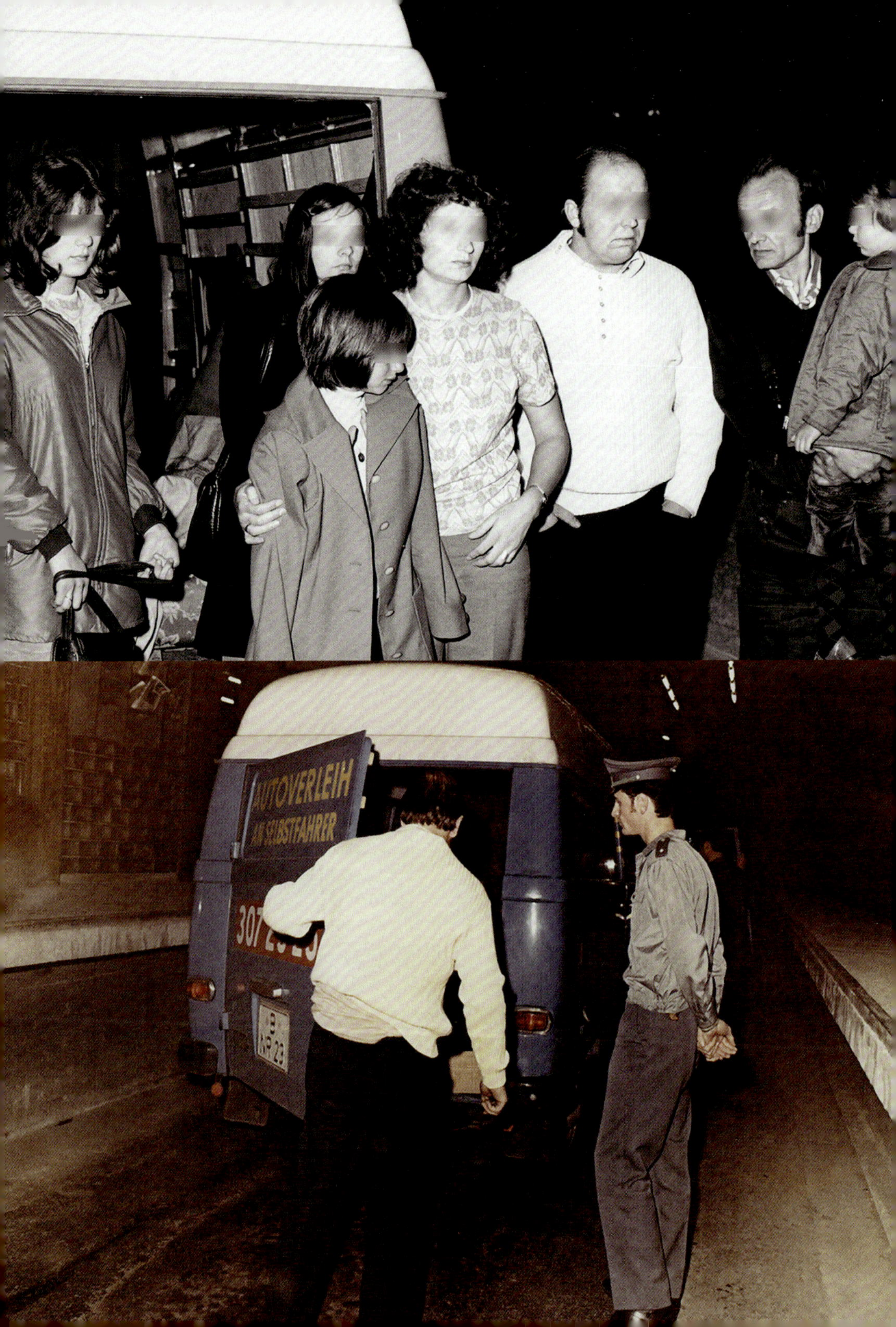
AUTOVERLEIH
AN SELBSTFAHRER

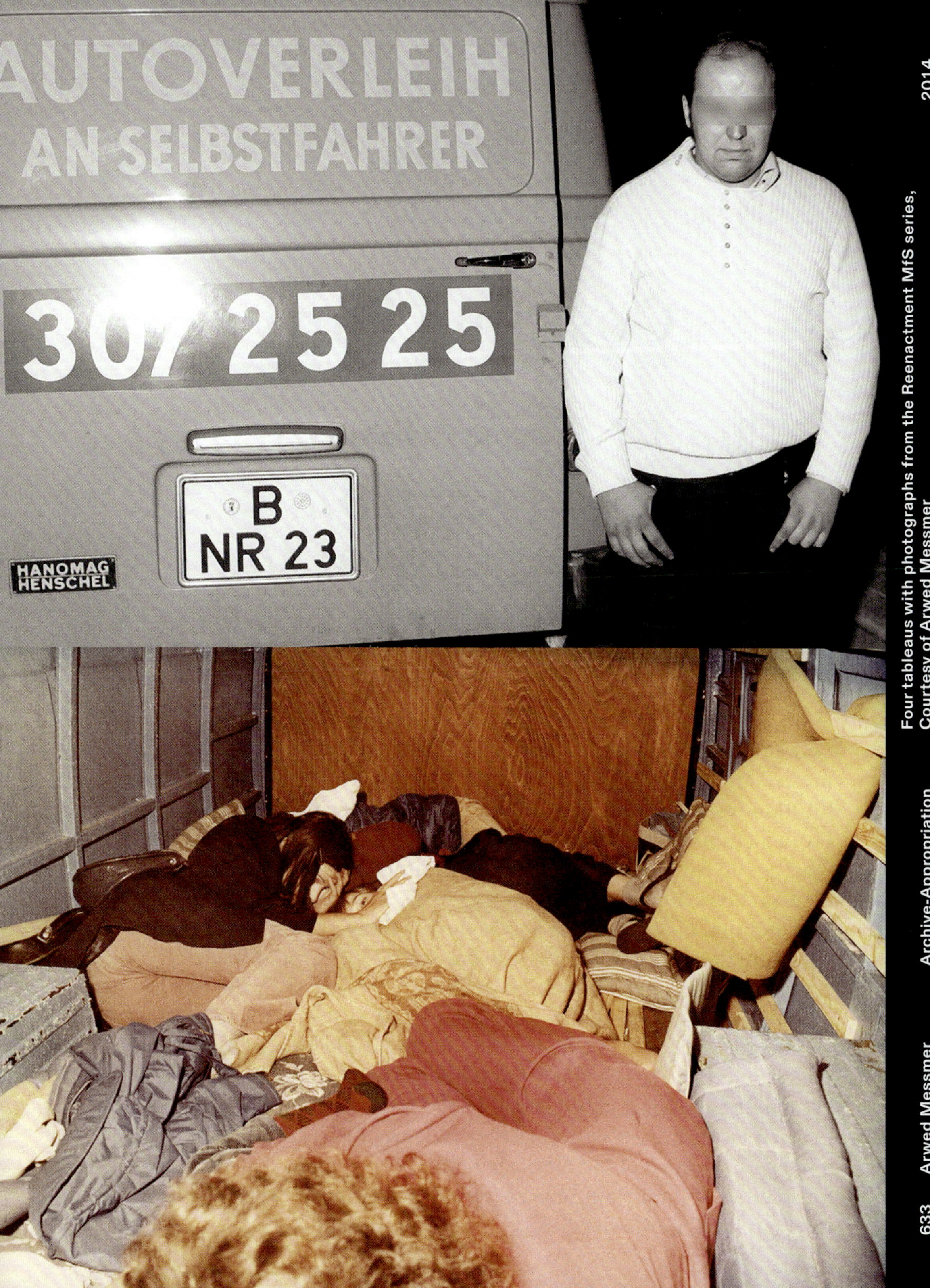

Four tableaus with photographs from the Reenactment MfS series,
Courtesy of Arwed Messmer

How to Give Secret Signals

Costume Party

The 14 Least Important Images from the History of the Bundesnachrichtendienst

Simon Menner

Simon Menner has achieved recognition for his work with photographic material from the Stasi archives. Three series were selected for the exhibition from the Stasi's internal-training materials. The photos in the From a Disguise Seminar series show how one can disguise oneself as a Stasi agent: using wigs, fake noses, and sunglasses. *How to Give Secret Signals* shows how secret messages were communicated from, for example, automobiles. *Costume Party* shows the birthday party of a high-ranking Stasi functionary. The guests—official agents—disguised themselves as representatives of groups which were being observed by the Stasi: peace activists, athletes, and church members. The last series, The 14 Least Important Images from the History of the Bundesnachrichtendienst, makes reference to the blatant imbalance between the East and the West in the reappraisal of history. While most secret service archives in Eastern Europe are now accessible—because the respective states no longer exist—most of the archives in the West remain sealed. These fourteen least important images are all that the artists received from the German Intelligence Service. (A)

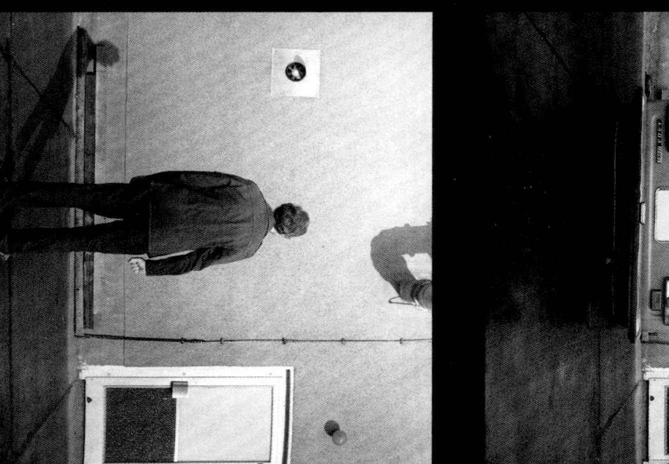

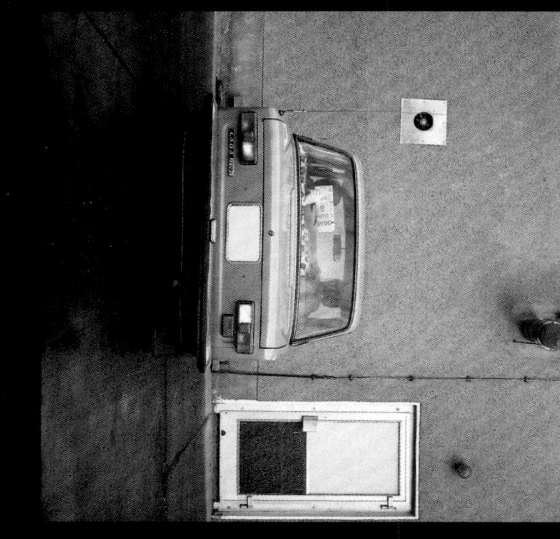

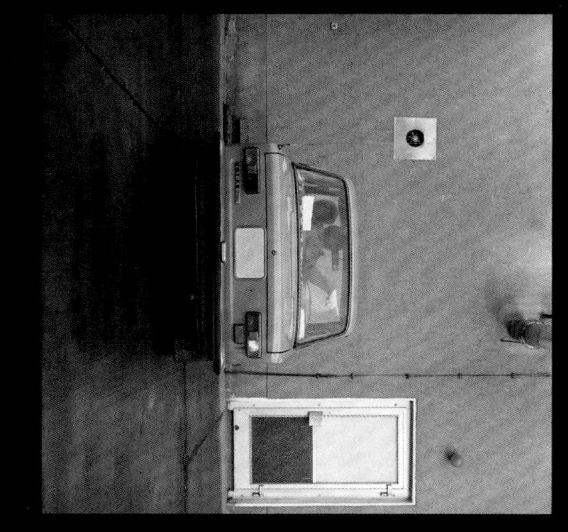

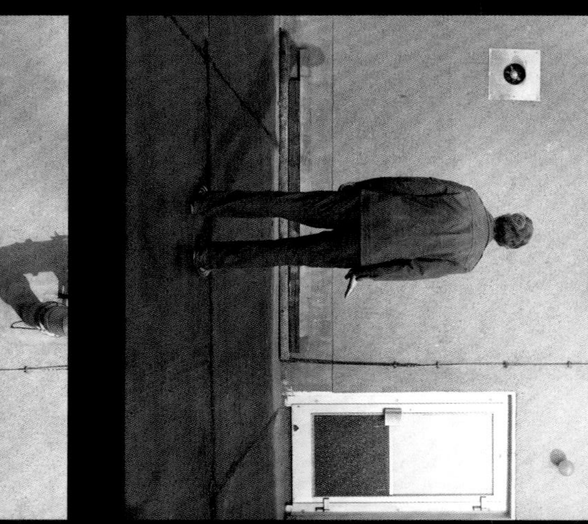

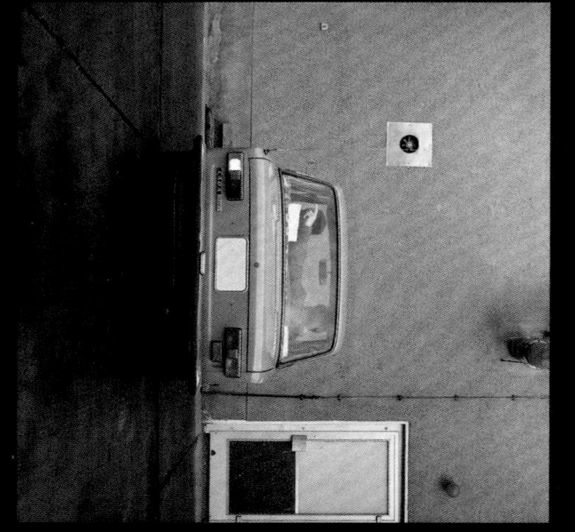

Six photographs from the series "How to Give Secret Signals," each 30 × 30 cm, Courtesy of Simon Menner, BStU 2013

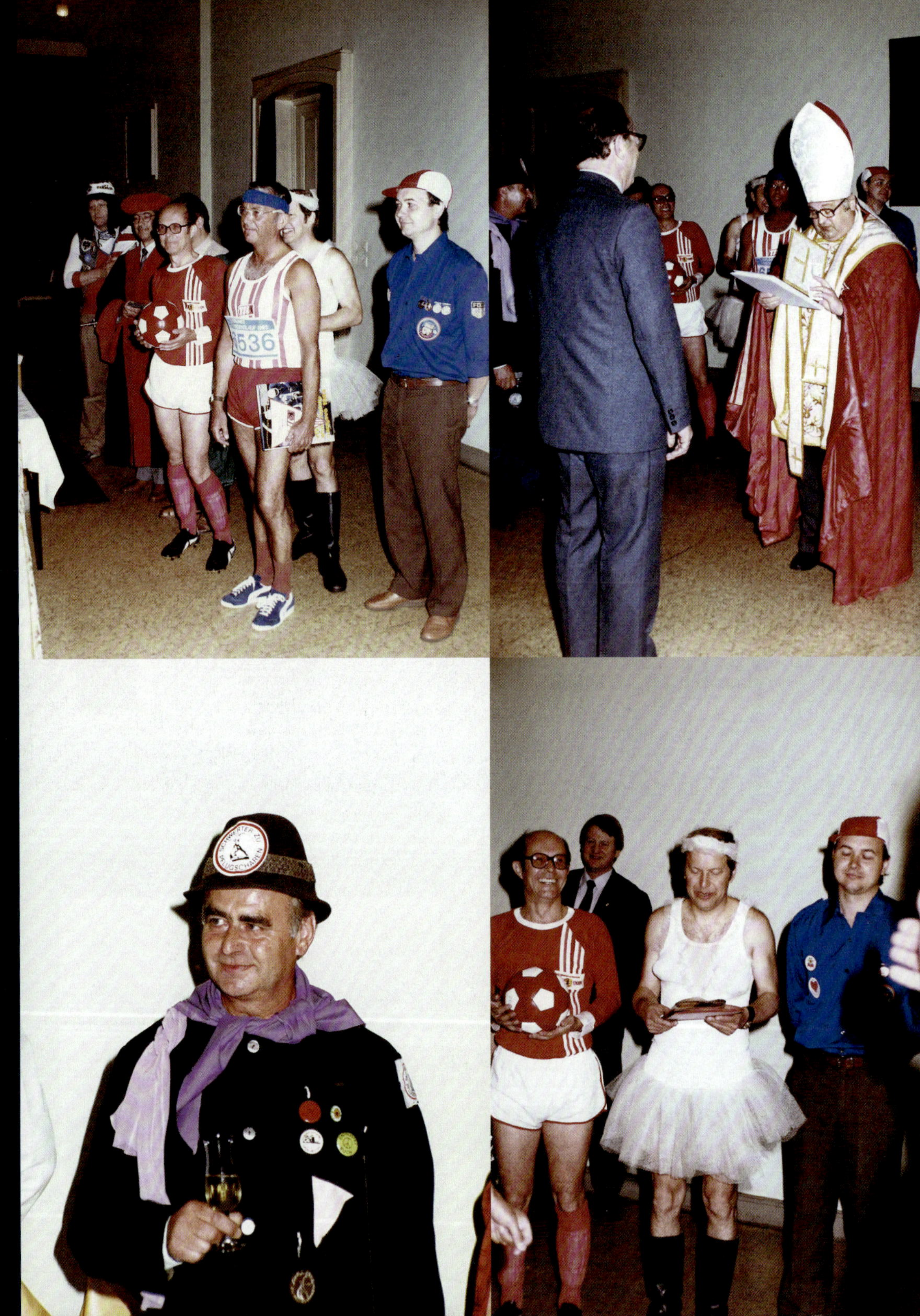
SCHWERTER ZU PFLUGSCHAREN

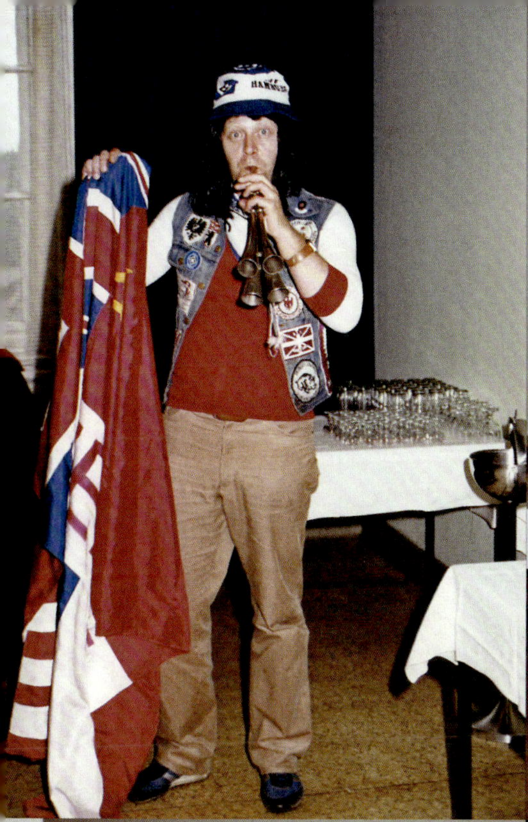

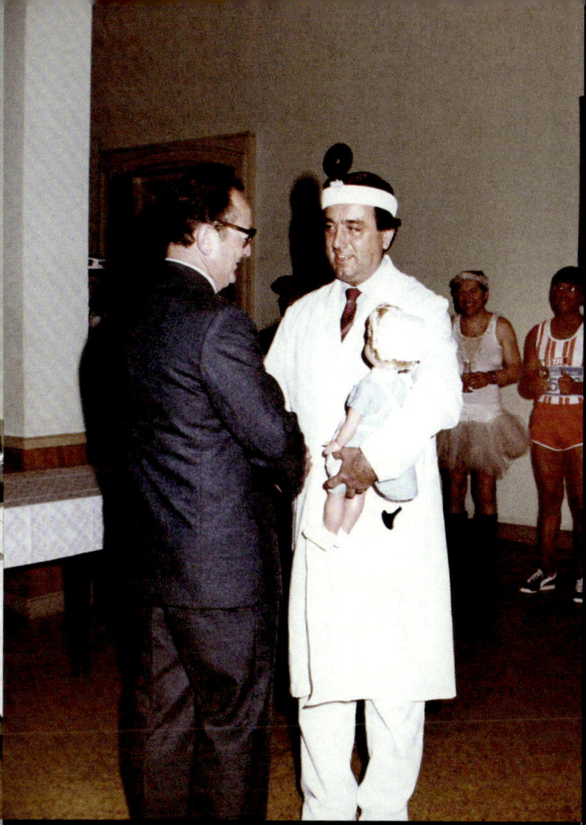

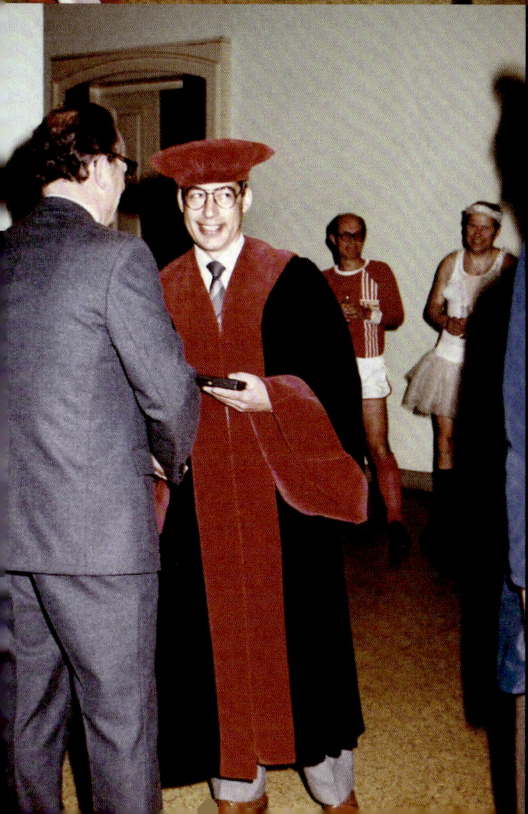

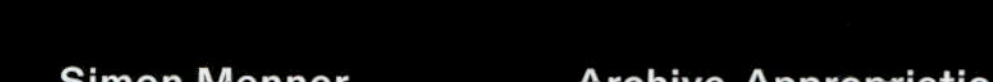

Seven photographs from the series "Costume Party,"
each 21 x 30 cm, of Simon Menner, BStU

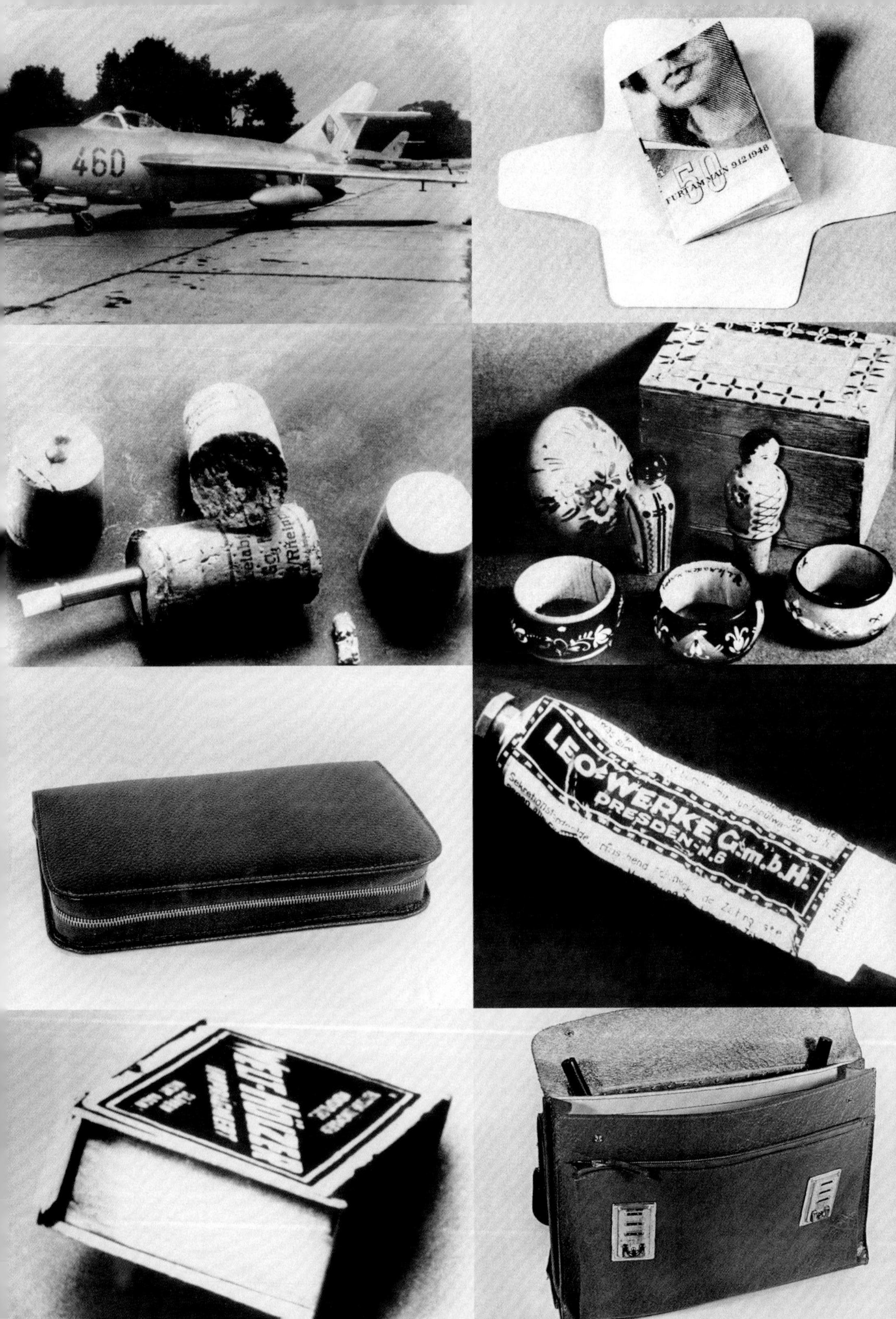
460
FURT AM MAIN 9.12.1948
50
LEO-WERKE G.m.b.H.
DRESDEN-N.6

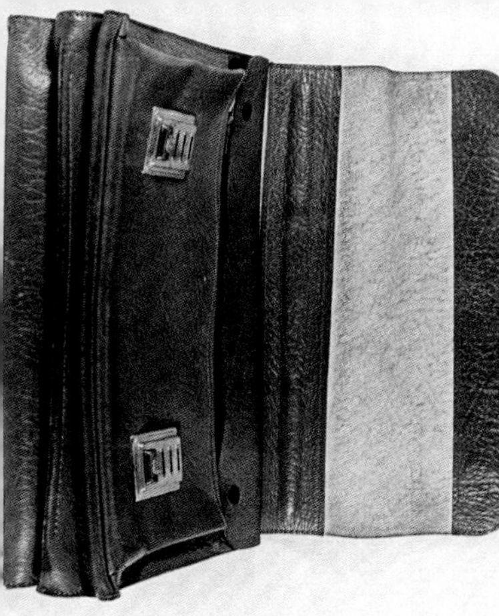

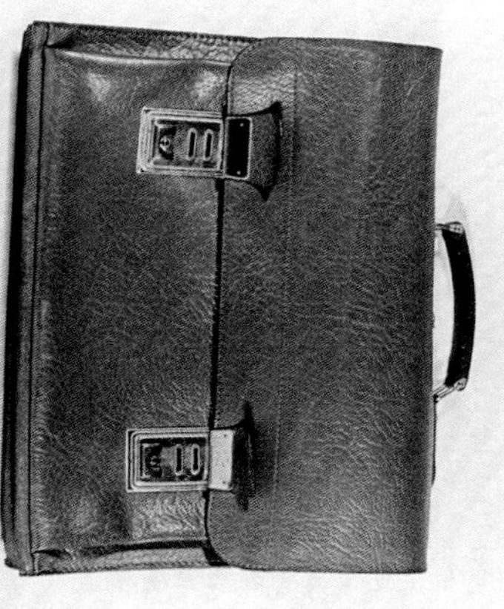

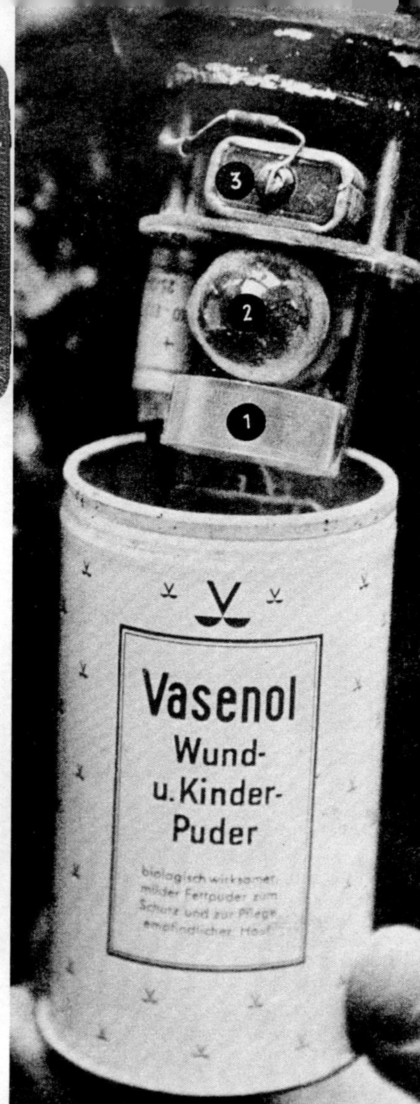

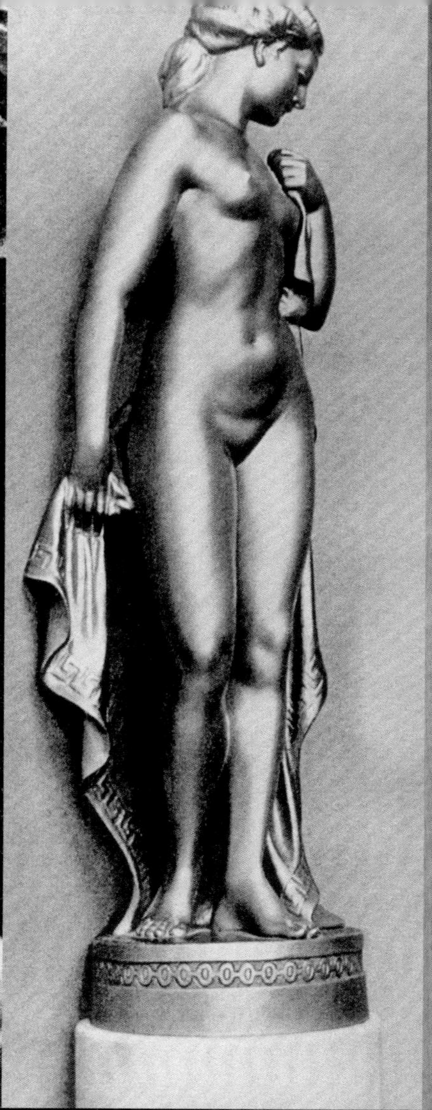

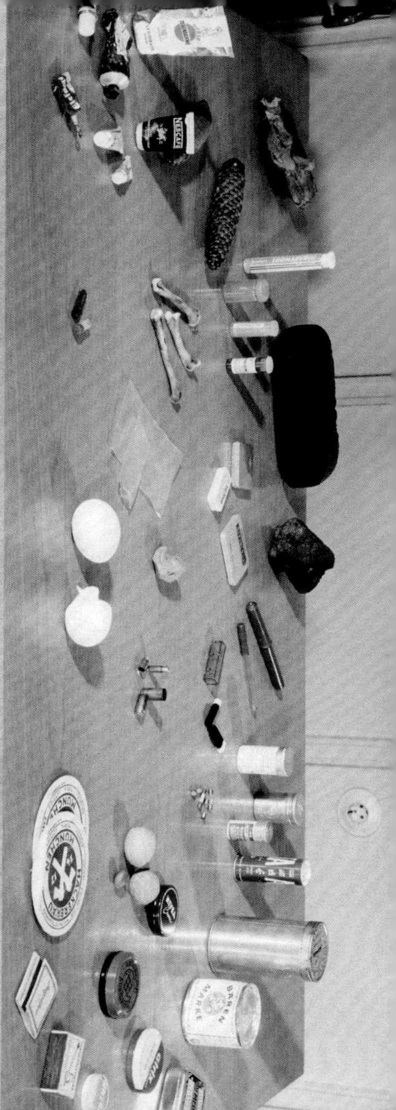

Thirteen photographs, various dimensions,

Tina Bara, b. 1962 in Kleinmachnow, GDR, lives and works in Berlin and Leipzig, Germany.
Alba D'Urbano, b. 1955 in Tivoli/Rome, Italy, lives and works in Berlin and Leipzig, Germany.

Covergirl:

Wasp File (Story Tales)

Tina Bara &
Alba D'Urbano

In 2007, Alba D'Urbano discovered a twenty-five-year-old photograph of her colleague Tina Bara, also a professor at the Academy of Fine Arts Leipzig (HGB), in an exhibition of the Spanish artist Dora Garcia in Leipzig's Galerie für zeitgenössische Kunst (Contemporary Art Gallery). The (anonymous) black-and-white photograph, which is also reproduced on the cover of the exhibition catalogue, shows Tina Bara naked with a black bar over her eyes, together with the line of text reading "BStU-Kopie MfS HA XX/Fo/689 Bild 9." The photo is part of a private black-and-white photo bundle from 1983, which the Stasi confiscated in the context of Operation "Wasps." Dora Garcia uses this material as a ready-made, without, however, researching its origins in detail. "Wasp Files" was the Stasi's code name for the "women for peace" who were engaged in the GDR in the 1980s for demilitarization, disarmament, and peace-oriented child education. The circulation of the "cover girl" is characteristic: originally private souvenir photographs by ambitious amateur photographers (Katja Havemann and Tina Bara), then a document and piece of evidence for state security, then an object of art (Dora Garcia). The artists confront these as violently experienced expropriations by reappropriating the image material and its history as a work of art. (A)

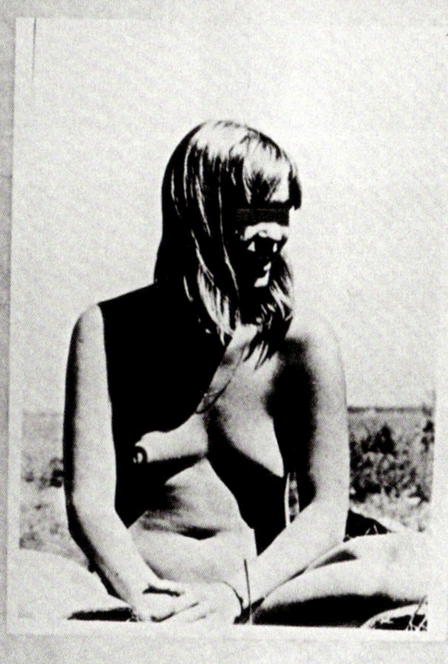

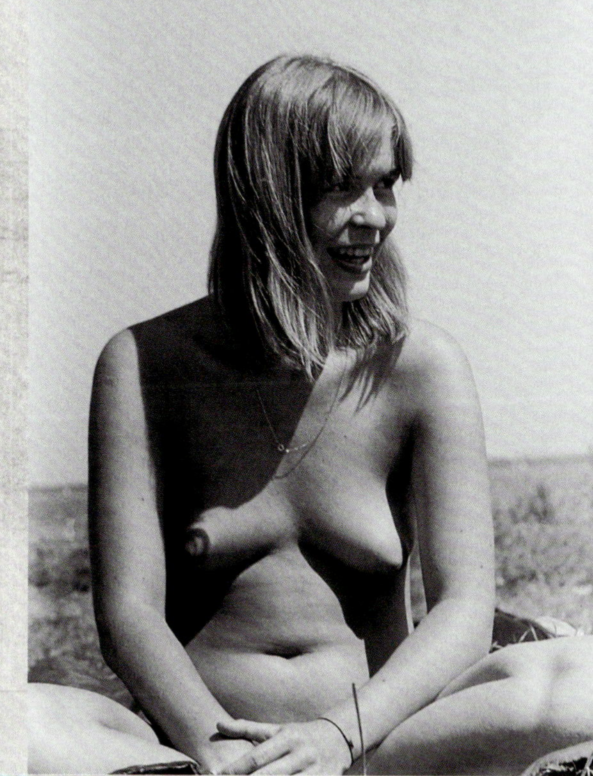

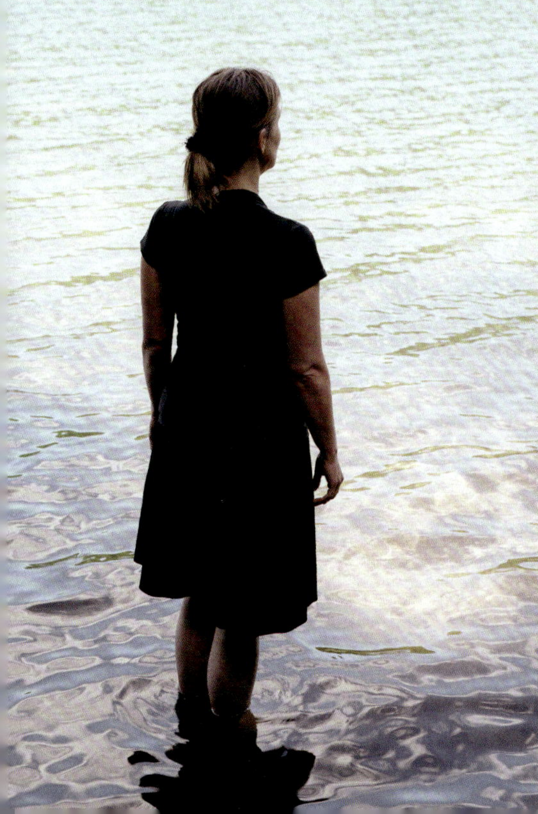

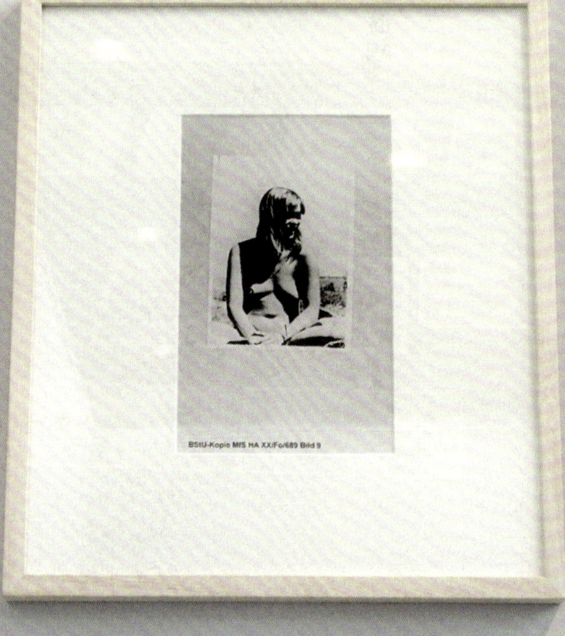

Tina Bara & Alba D'Urbano — Archive Appropriation — Details of the photo wall of sixty-five photographs, various techniques and sizes, text, videostills. Courtesy of Alba D'Urbano, Tina Bara — 2008 2009

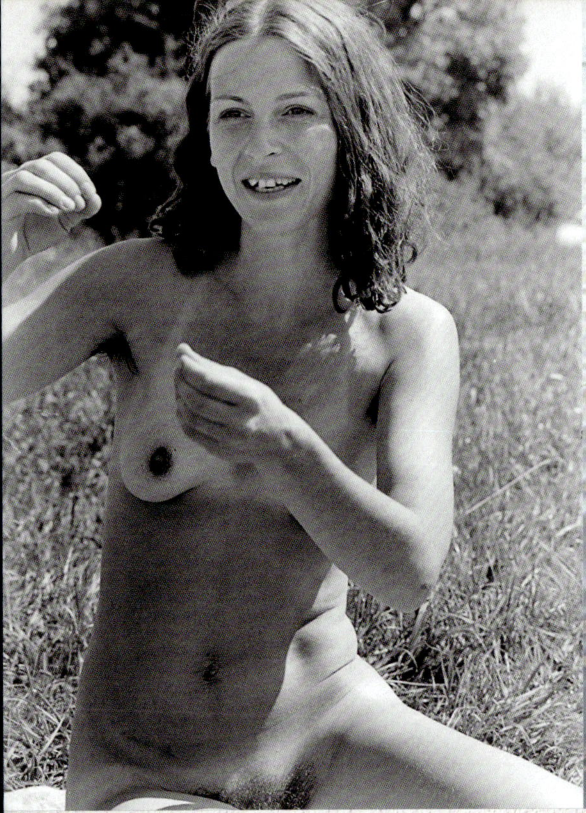

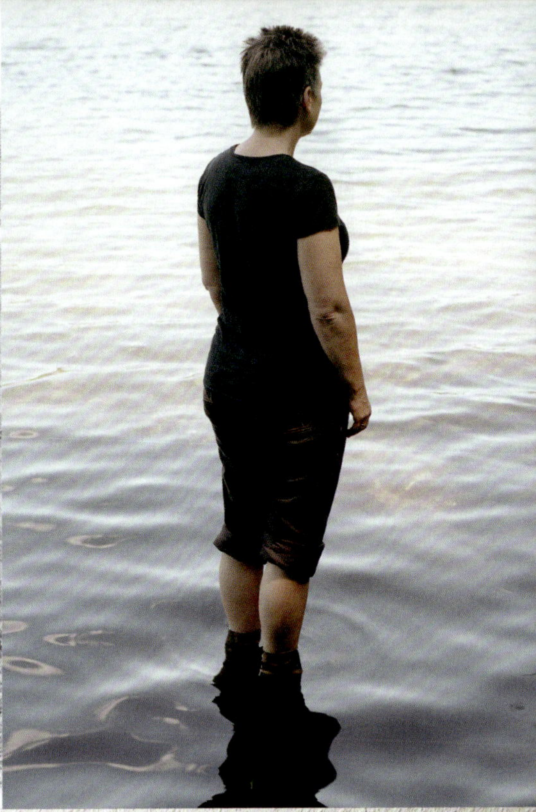

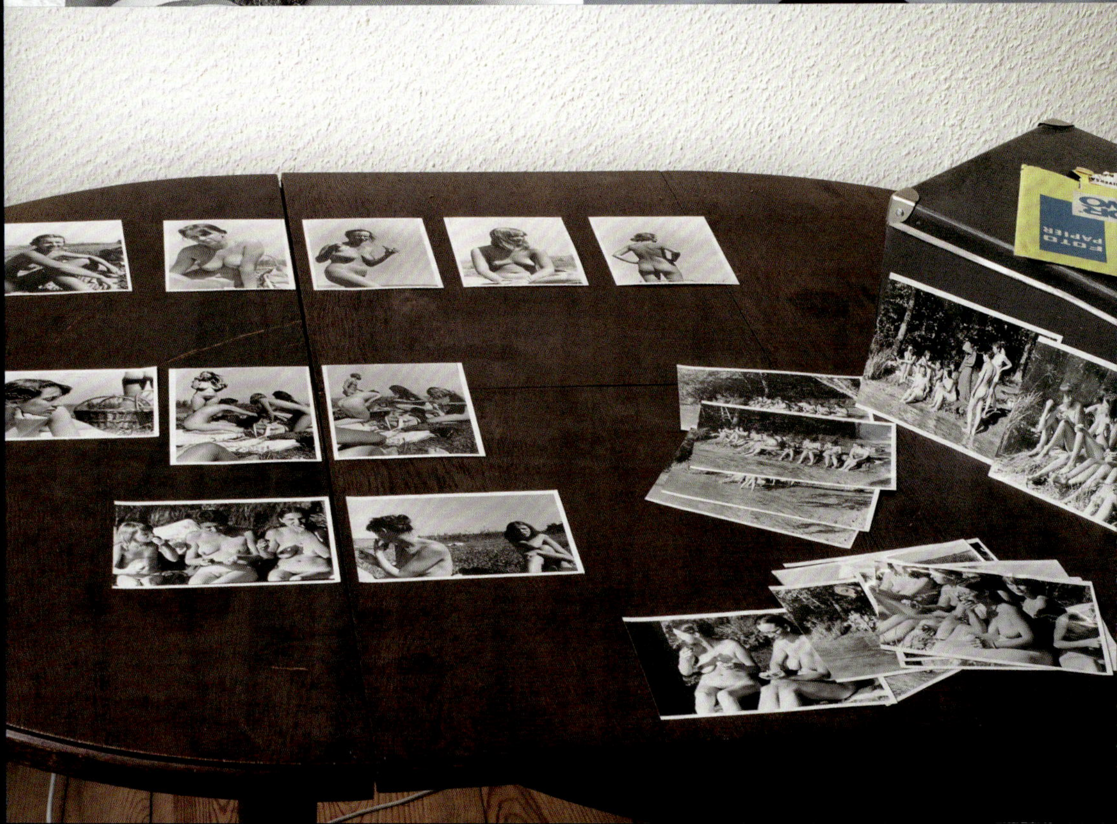

643 Tina Bara & Alba D'Urbano — Archive-Appropriation

Details of the photo wall of sixty-five photographs, various techniques and sizes, text, videostills, Courtesy of Alba D'Urbano, Tina Bara

2008 – 2009

BStU-Kopie MfS HA XX/Fo/689 Bild 8

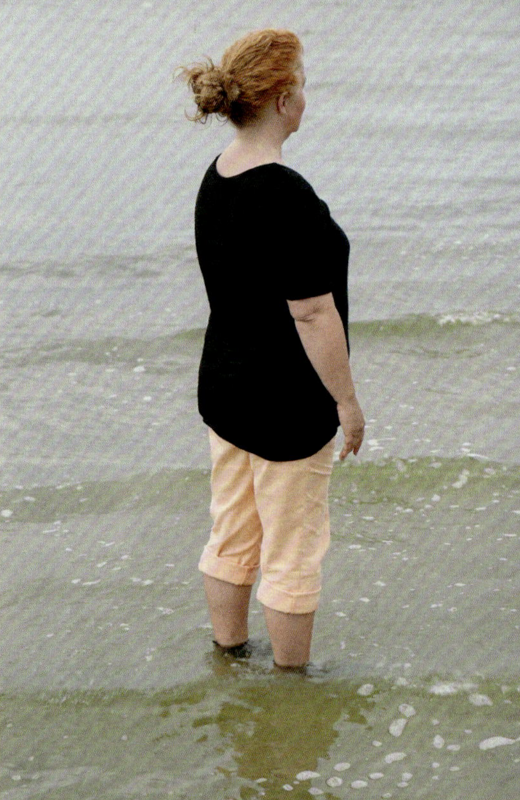

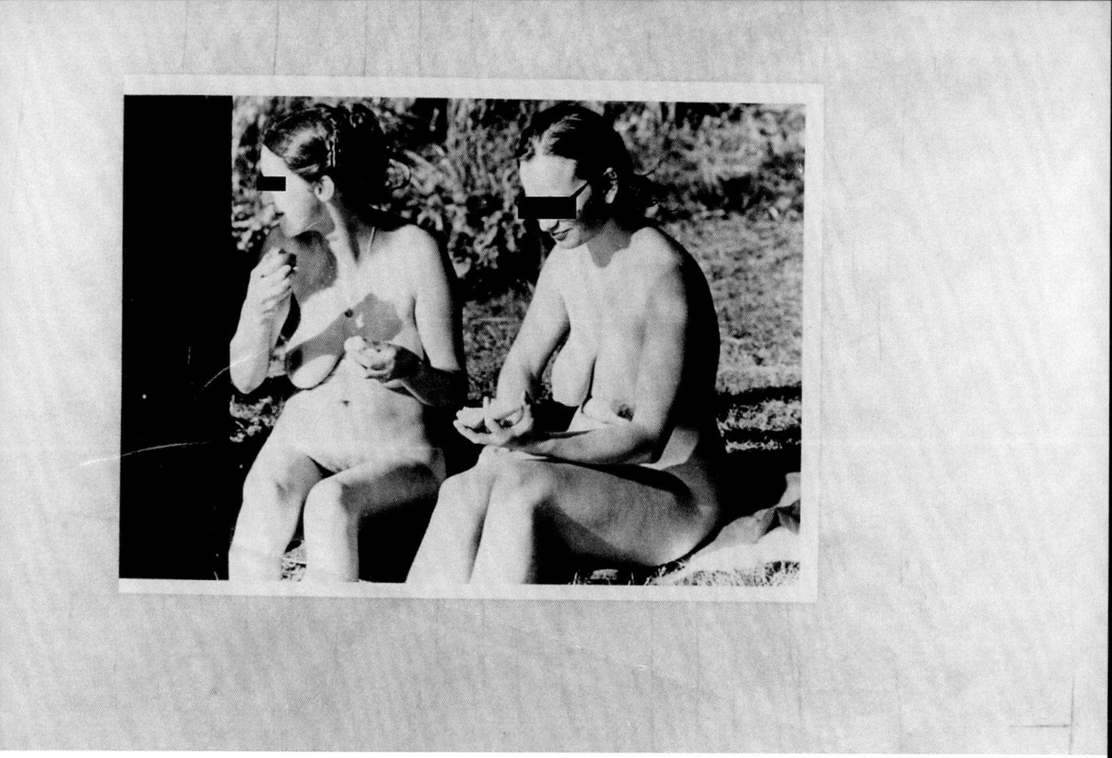

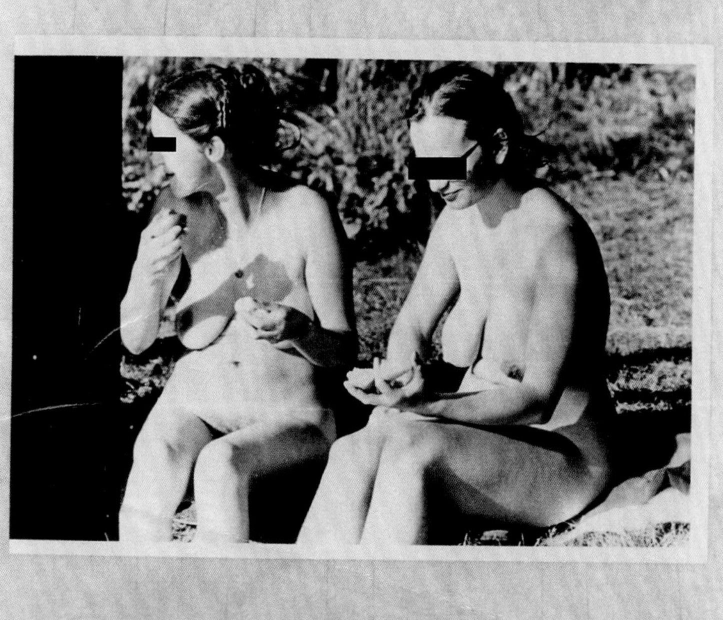

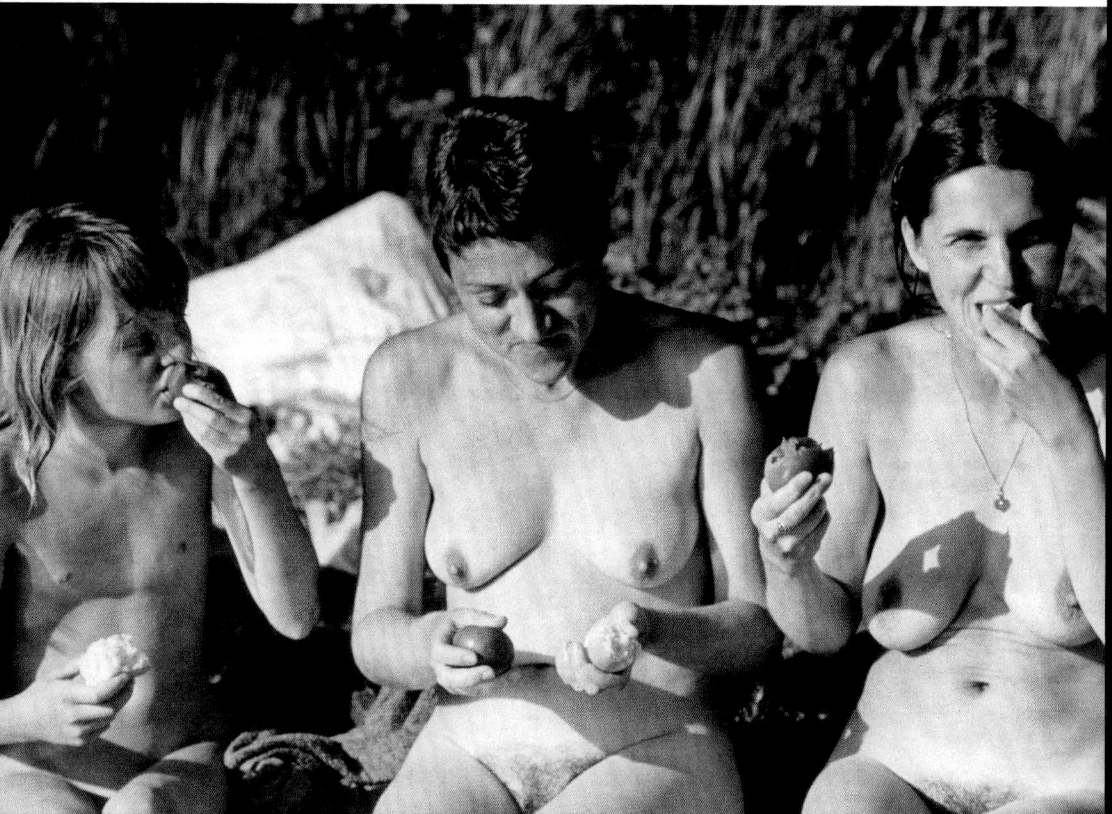

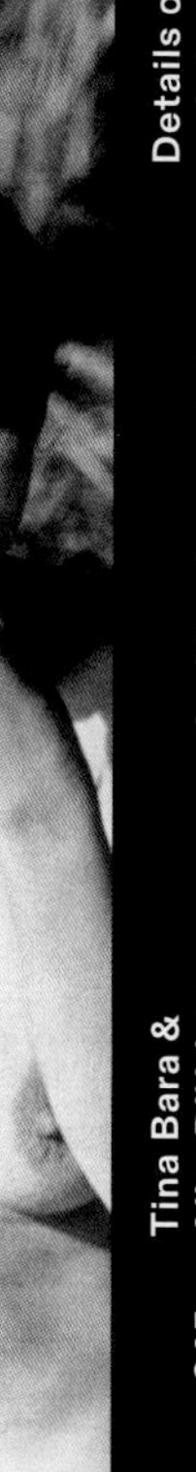

Tina Bara & Alba D'Urbano

Archive-Appropriation

Details of the photo wall of sixty-five photographs, various techniques and sizes, text, videostills, Courtesy of Alba D'Urbano, Tina Bara

2008 – 2009

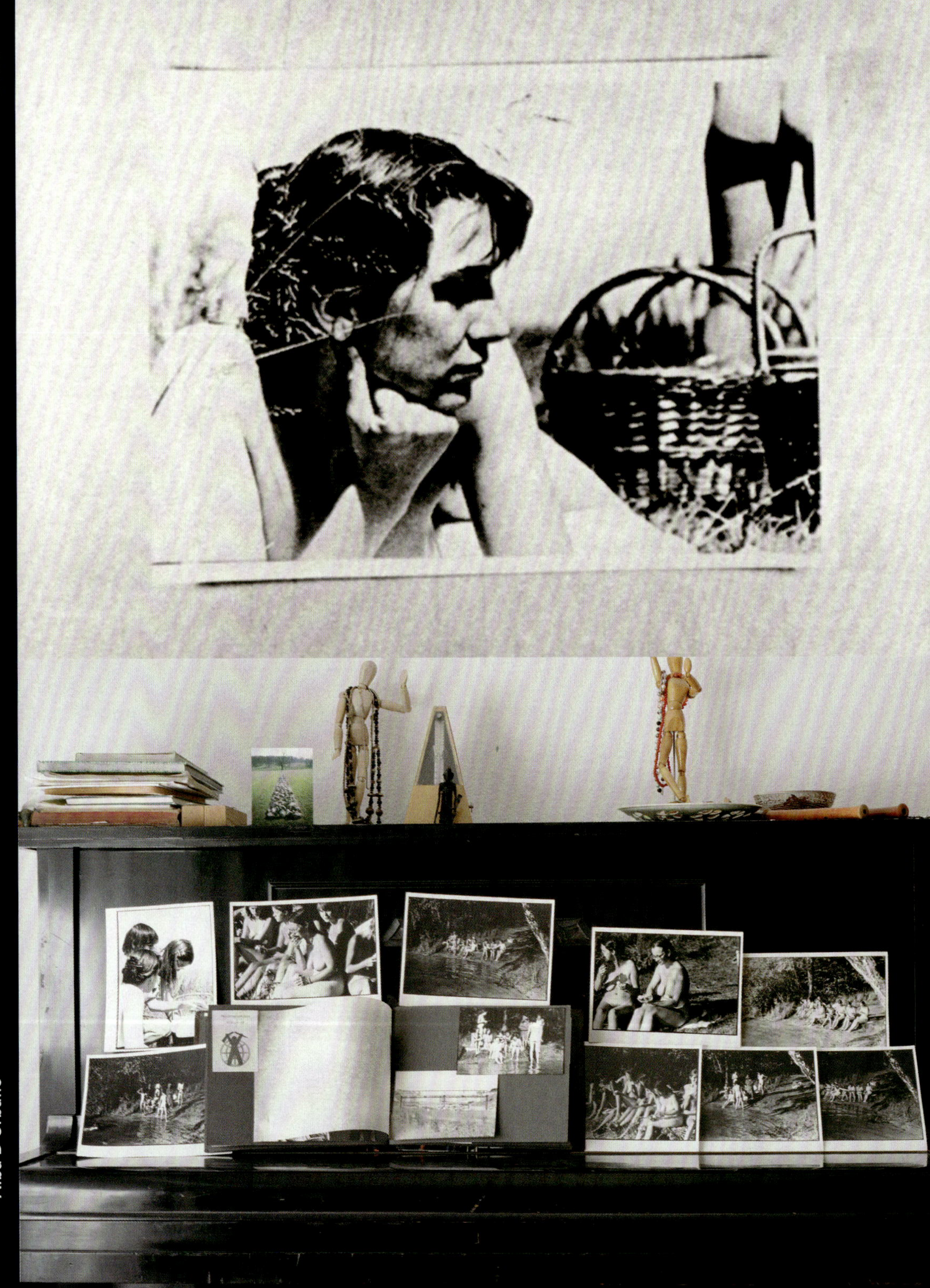

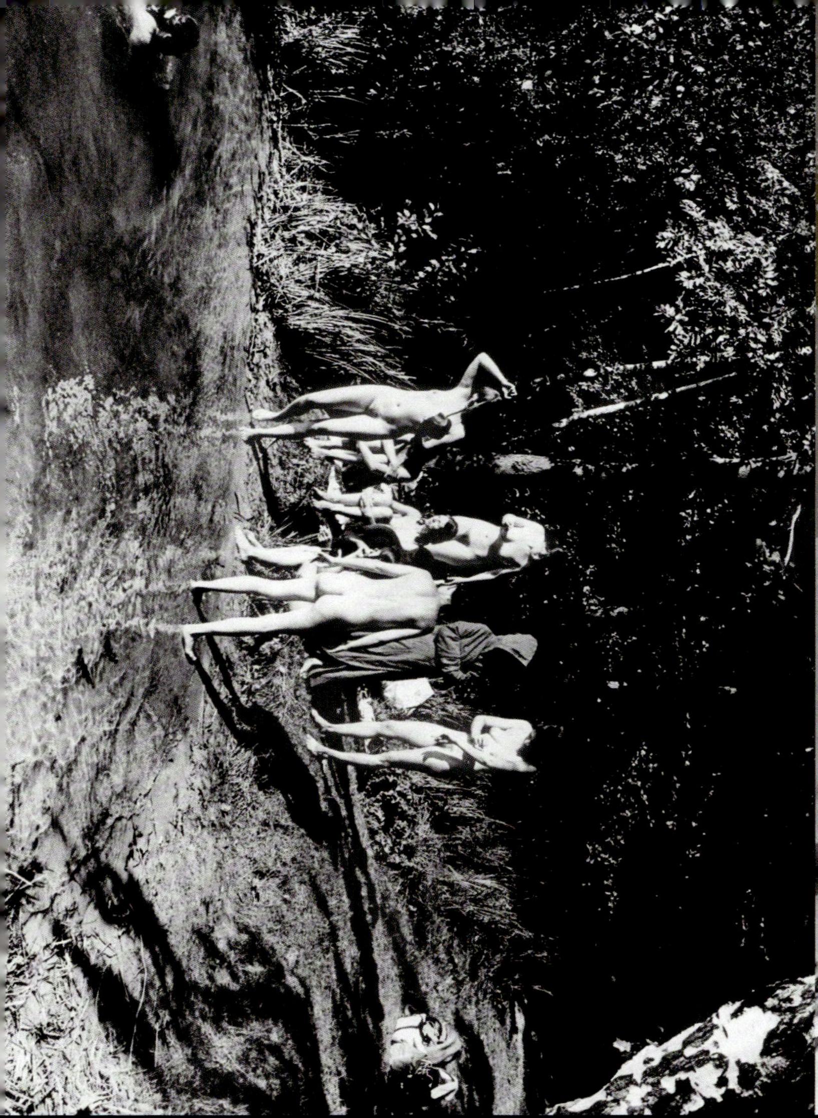

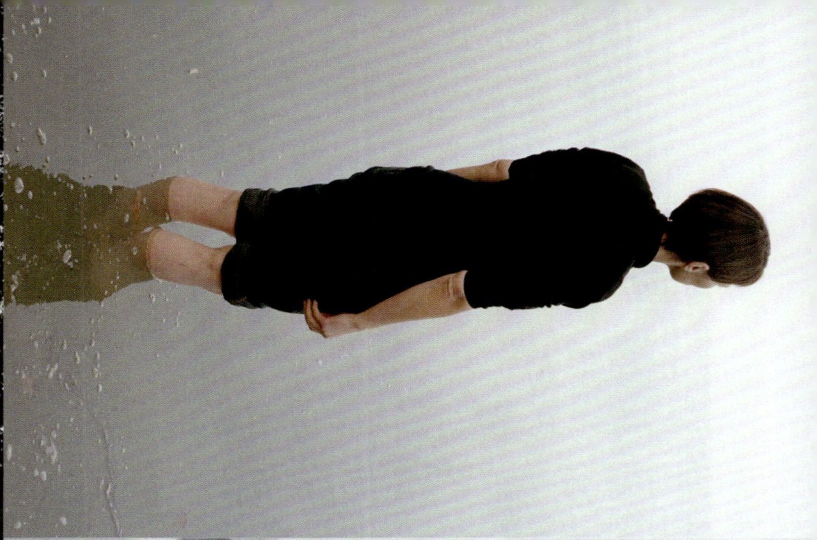

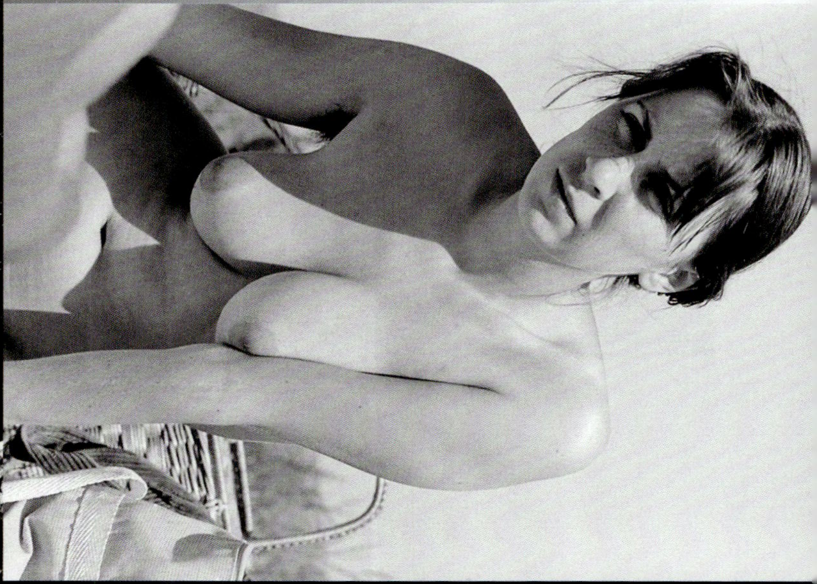

Tina Bara & Alba D'Urbano — Archive-Appropriation

Details of the photo wall of sixty-five photographs, various techniques and sizes, text, videostills. Courtesy of Alba D'Urbano, Tina Bara — 2008–2009

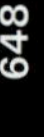

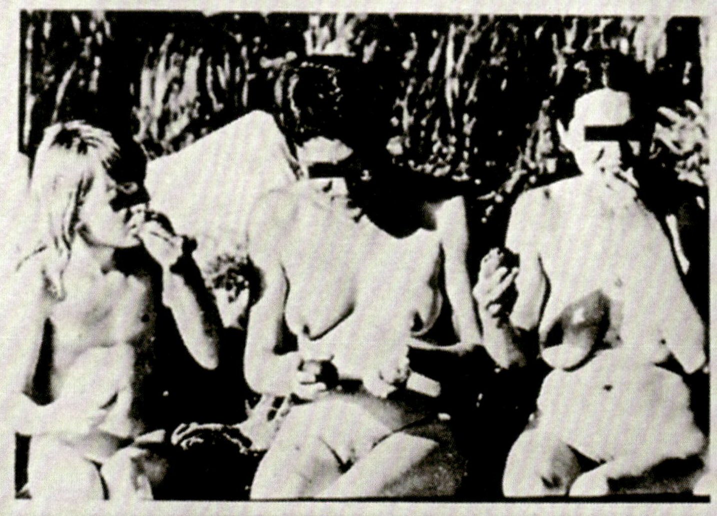

BStU-Kopie MfS HA XX/Fo/689 Bild 5

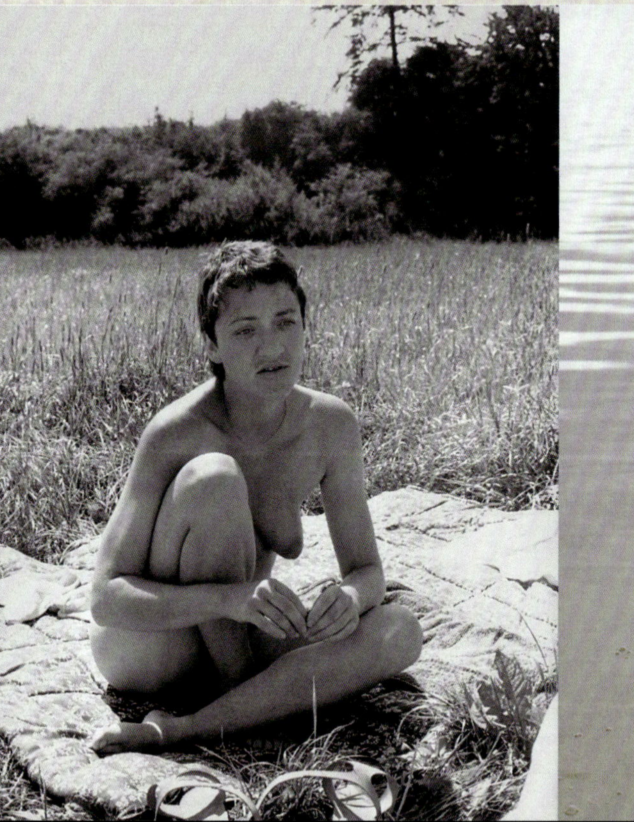

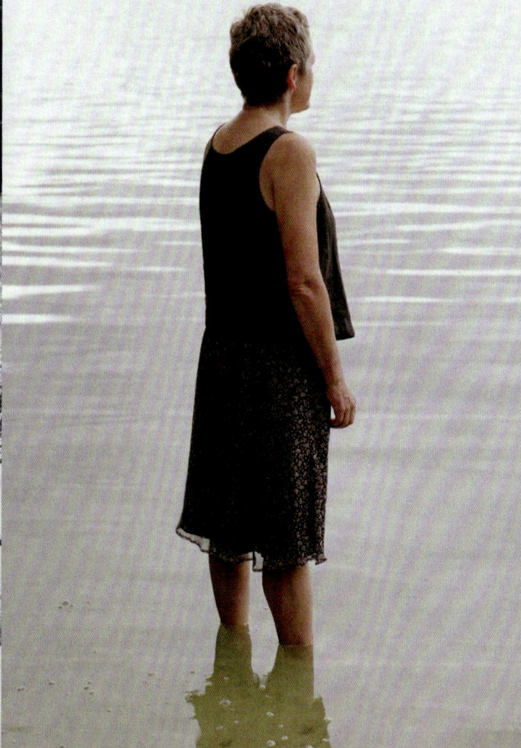

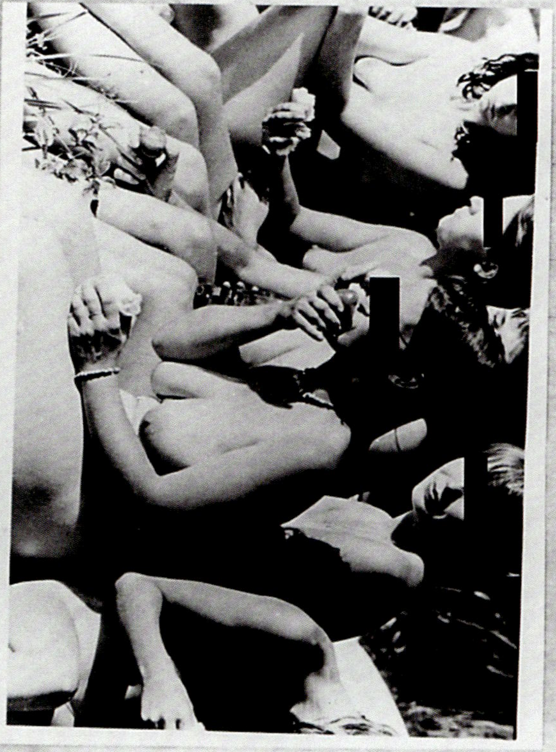

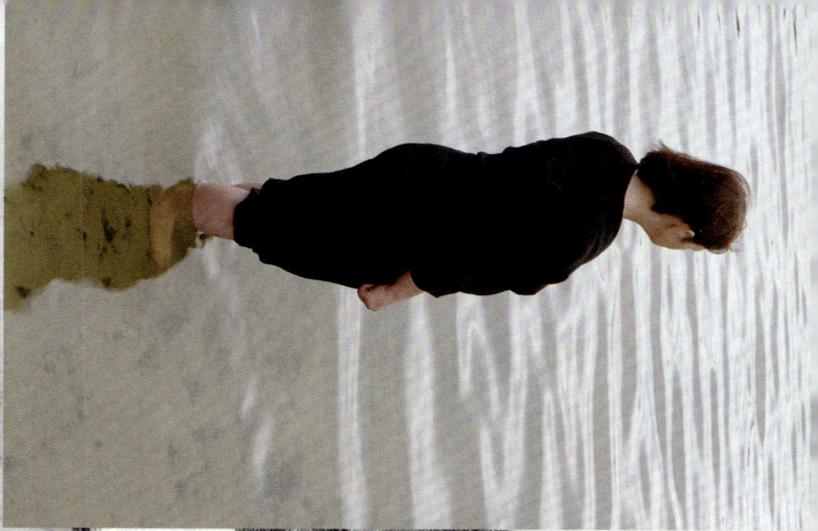

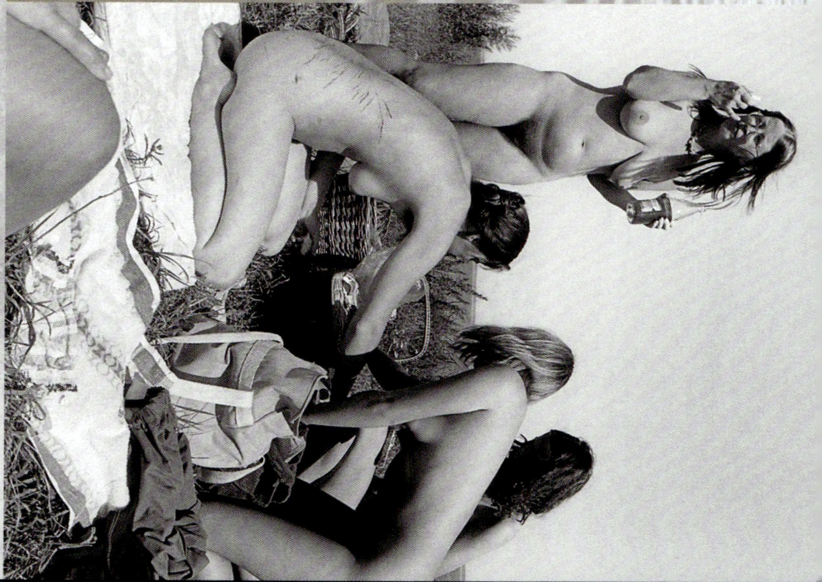

Tina Bara &

Details of the photo wall of sixty-five photographs, various techniques

2008

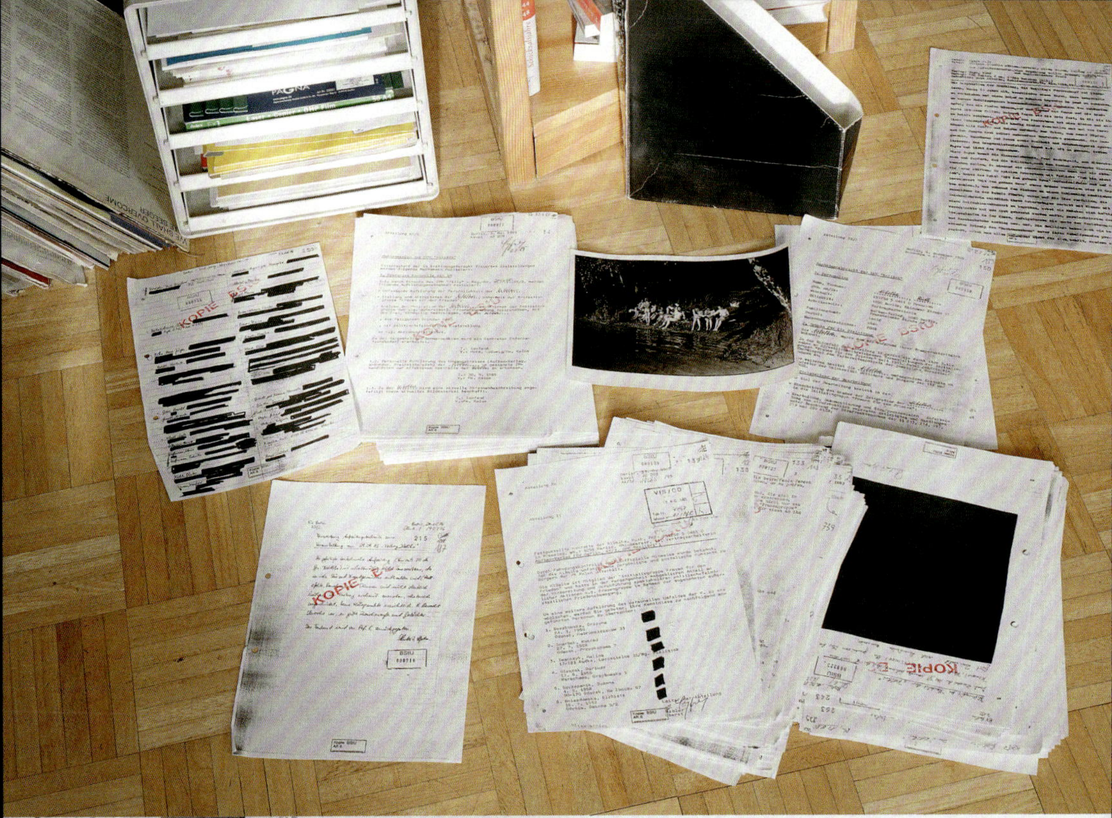

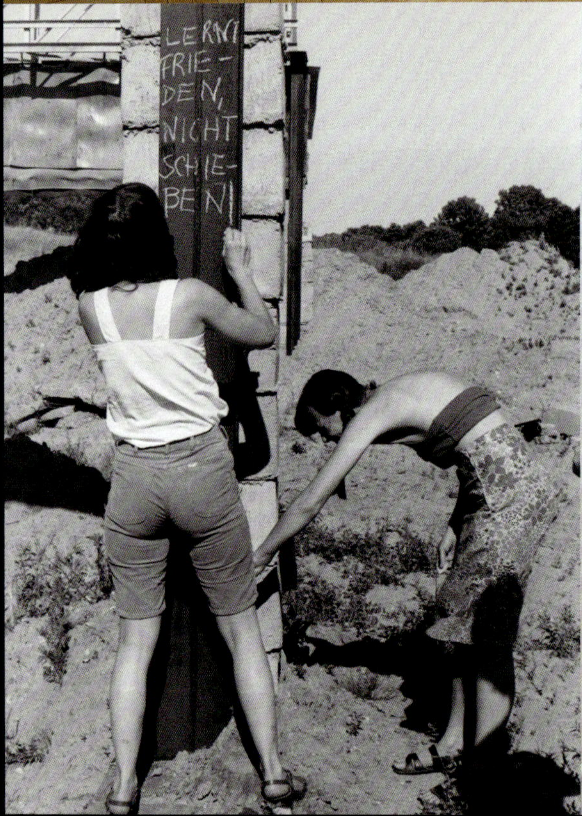

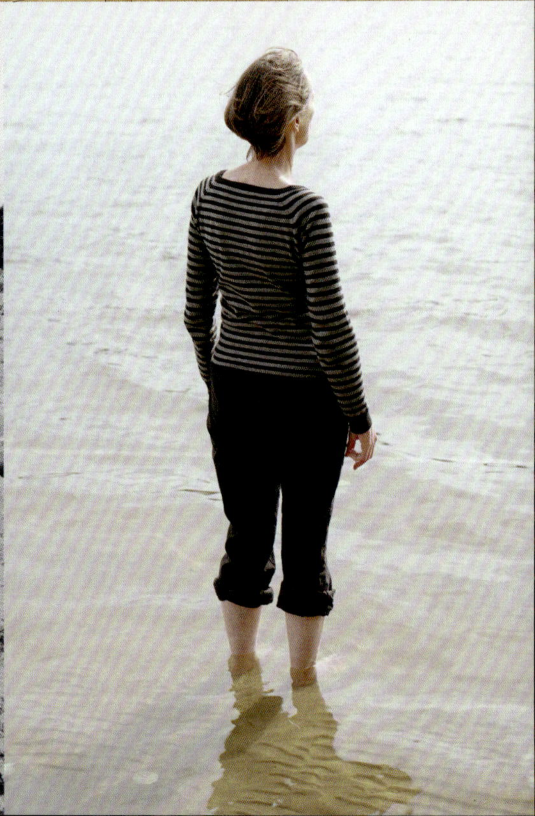

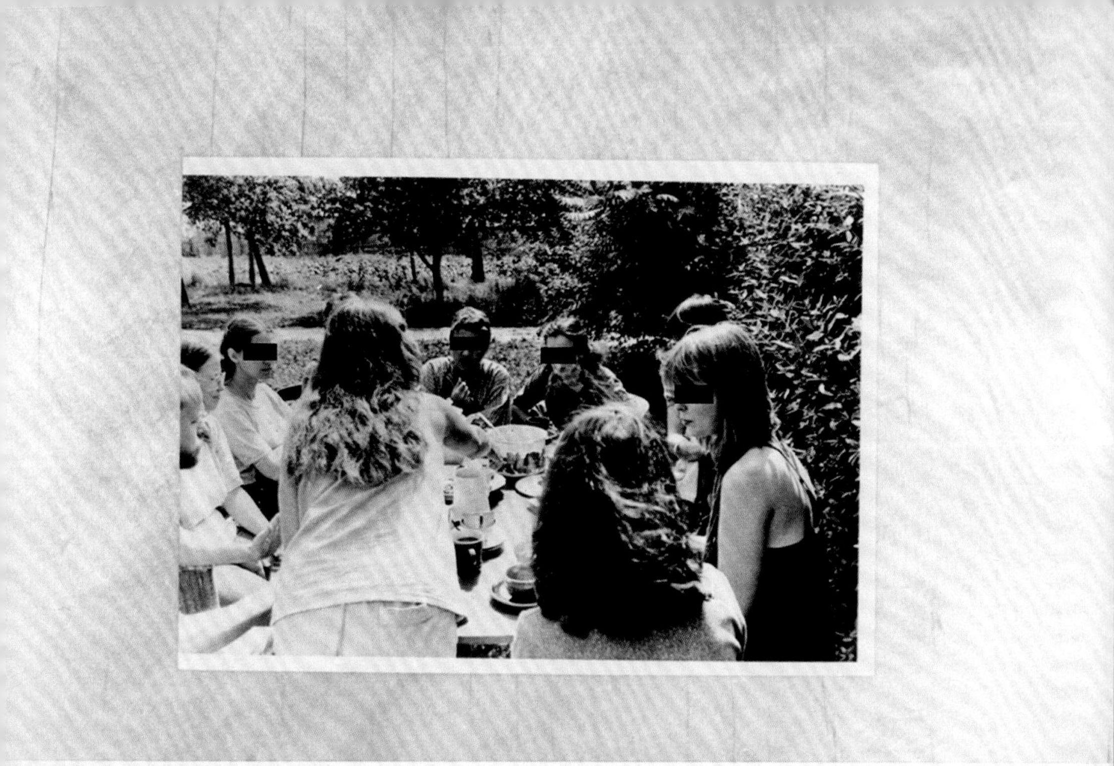

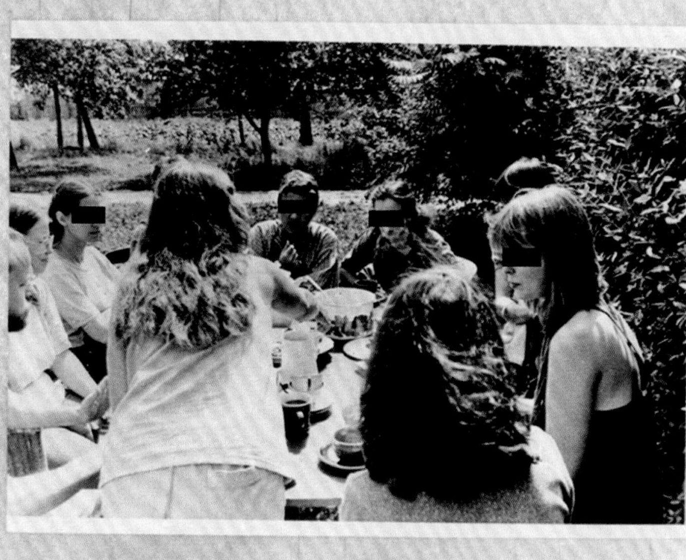

tU-Kopie

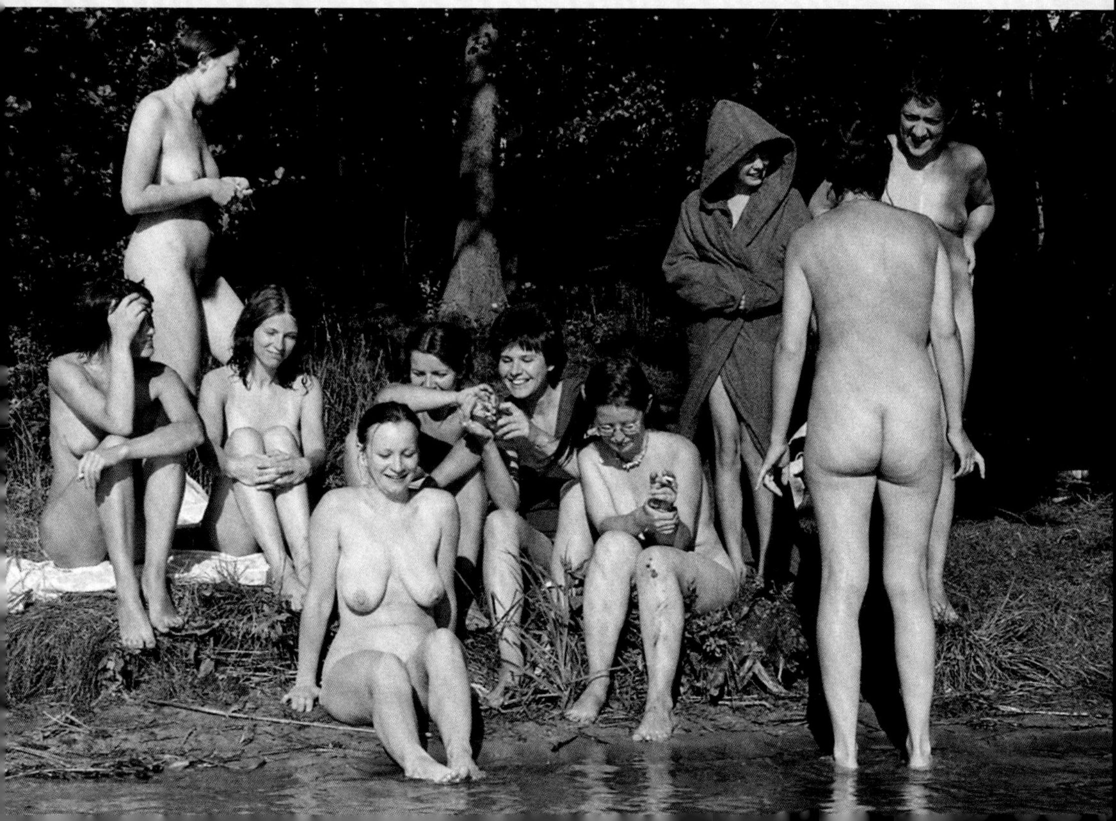

Tina Bara &
Alba D'Urbano

Archive Appropriation

Details of the photo wall of sixty-five photographs, various techniques
and sizes, text, videostills. Courtesy of Alba D'Urbano, Tina Bara

2008
–2009

Annex

Glossary

Adjutant

Term used by Nadezhda Mandelstam in her autobiography to refer to persons who "served two gods at once," who wanted to play a role in the literature and art worlds while simultaneously delivering information to the secret services. The term was discussed at the conference "Stasi, KGB, and Literature" in Moscow in 1993. (See Roginski and Okhotin, "Archivquellen zum Thema KGB und Literatur," in *Stasi, KGB und Literatur. Beiträge und Erfahrungen aus Russland und Deutschland.*)

Agent

Persons, according to the German Office for the Protection of the Constitution (*Verfassungsschutz*), who "are intentionally in contact with a foreign intelligence service and who perform clandestine activities at their command." Different motivations are determinative here, e.g. material or ideological reasons in addition to blackmail. The term is generally not applied to secret police surveillance, although it was repeatedly used in society for informants and collaborators of state security. (https://www.verfassungsschutz.de/de/service/glossar/_lA)

Archive

The following is a list of all archives concerned with the appraisal and research of secret police files:

Germany:	Federal Commissioner for the Records of the State Security Service of the Former German Democratic Republic (*Bundesbeauftragte für die Unterlagen des Staatssicherheitsdienstes der ehemaligen* DDR, BStU), founded 1995
Czech Republic:	Office for the Documentation and Investigation of the Crimes of Communism (ÚSTR, Ústav pro studium totalitních režimů), founded 1996
Hungary:	Historical **Archive** of the Secret Service (ÁBTL, Állambiztonsági Szolgátok Történeti Levéltára), its predecessor Történeti Hivatal (TH), Historical Office, founded in 1996, the ÁBTL founded in 2003
Poland:	Institute for National Memory (IPN, *Instytut Pamięci Narodowej*), founded 1998
Romania:	National Council for the Study of the Securitate **Archives** (CNSAS, *Consiliul Naţional pentru Studierea Arhivelor Securităţii*), founded 2000

Slovakia:	Nation's Memory Institute (UPN, Ústav pamäti národa), founded 2003
Bulgaria:	The Committee for disclosing the documents and announcing affiliation of Bulgarian citizens to the State Security and intelligence services of the Bulgarian National Army; generally referred to as the Dossier Committee (COMDOS), founded 2006.

Since 2013, the Baltic states, Slovenia, and Albania have also joined the consortium. Research is also now possible in Kiev, Ukraine. Furthermore, one can also perform research in the Swiss Federal **Archive**, a collection of files between 1900 and 1990.

In Germany, there is a "right to information" law which, in principle, everyone has vis-à-vis the authorities responsible for protecting the constitution with regard to the personal data stored about them. (https://www.verfassungsschutz.de/de/service/glossar/_lA)

Brother Institutions

Secret services of friendly countries. In East Berlin, for example, there were hidden apartments used for meetings where agents would exchange espionage findings or hold kidnapped emigrants to the West, in order to then hand them over to the respective secret service. Starting in 1955/56, the Stasi took part in multilateral secret service conferences with Eastern Bloc states. By this time, consultations were already taking place between the secret services regarding comprehensive information exchange on persons and facts as well as collaborative espionage against West Germany.

Combination, operative

Methods used in the handling of persons and objects to link various apparently unconnected, legend-related Stasi measures (see **Legend, operative**). They require precisely coordinated actions of unofficial collaborators (IMs), full-time Stasi agents, and in some cases, employees of other institutions in the context of "political-operative collaboration." They serve the purpose of "disorientation," "decomposition," "siphoning," as well as the influence of "handled" persons, the acquisition of information and evidence, and the recruitment and review of IMs. A typical example of this is the exclusion from university studies, from school, or from professional associations. Because the Stasi did not always have IMs available in leadership positions of the respective institutions, exclusions were also accomplished through the influence or spreading of rumors to prominent persons.

Concealment

The Hungarian term (*fátyolozás*) for data and documents which were collected during the course of operations and subsequently "legalized," so that they could continue to be used. The original source needed to be concealed.

Conspiracy

Foundational principle of the Stasi's intelligence and secret police work. It consisted of deploying unofficial forces and other clandestine methods, as well as the concealment of one's own activities, including from other GDR bodies and the SED party apparatus. "Internal conspiracy" is understood as the IM's reporting on him- or herself in the third person. On the basis of internal conspiracy, IMs could also be observed and monitored in the reports of other IMs, as IMs did not always know the identity of other IMs in the same group.

Criminalization

The "use and/or creation of circumstances and conditions which facilitate criminal prosecution" was a "decomposition" measure that attempted to cause dissidents to commit criminal acts in order to then isolate them in prison. In Gabriele Stötzer's files, one can read the following sentence: "In addition, further conditions for criminal prosecution of the person handled in operation 'Toxin,' [named] K., Gabriele, are to be created." We also find the instruction in Operation "Maggot" to "continually check whether indications and evidence of criminal activity and violations of state order can be investigated." (MfS, BV, KMSt, AKG, 3485, Vol.1, BStU 026.)

Chekists

A name for Stasi agents. Chekists (named after the Cheka, the early Soviet secret police apparatus) were understood to be special persons with a "sixth sense" that "allowed them to recognize and detect enemies" (Erich Mielke, 1957). From this ideology emerged the normative model of the "Chekist personality" for the formation and spiritual-moral orientation of Stasi agents as ideological combatants. At the center of this were "deep feelings of hate, revulsion, disinclination, and relentlessness" as the "decisive foundation of passionate and unforgiving struggle against the enemy." In contemporary Russia, former secret service agents who are now active in political leadership positions are called Siloviki, derived from the Russian *sila* (power, strength). Through 1990, a wide variety of ironic names for the secret police and their agents was in circulation:

GDR:	*VEB Horch und Guck* (VEB Listen and Look), *Firma* (the company), *Kombinat* (collective combine), *Verein* (the association), *Freunde von nebenan* (friends next door), *Paul Greifzu* (Paul Grabhold), Memfis (Memphis), *Horch und Greif* (Listen and Grasp), *Freunde mit der Lederjacke* (the friends in the leather jackets).
Soviet Union:	*Kontora/Komitet Glubokovo Bureniya* (deep drilling committee), *kuda nado* (somewhere necessary), *Galina Borisovna* (GB, for KGB analogous to Sofiya Vladimorovna for sovetskaya vlast (Soviet power), *dyadka v sapogakh* (uncle in boots), *stukakhi* (snitches), *perviy otdel* ("Section One), *Komitetchik, chekist, spezi, osobist* (from Osobyj otdel, "Special Section"), *chelovek s Lubyanki* (person from Lubyanka) in Moscow (The headquarters of the KGB are located on Lubyanka street), *chelovek iz bolshova doma* (person from the big house), meaning the government.
Poland:	*psi* (dog) for spies.
Romania:	*Securişti* (custodian of security).
Hungary:	*Vamzer, Hé, Spicli* (spy), *Tégla* (brick), *Besúgó* (snitch).

Decomposition

"Decomposition" was the method of clandestinely combatting persons and groups classified as "hostile-negative" by the Stasi and who were suspected of underground activity. Directive 1/76 on the handling of operative actions defined the goal of decomposition as the preventative hindering of "hostile" actions. This was achieved through the "systematic discrediting of public reputation, authority, and prestige," the "systematic organization of professional and social failures," the "purposeful undermining of convictions," the "creation of mistrust and mutual suspicion," the "creation or use and intensification of rivalries," and the "local and temporal prevention or restriction of mutual relationships." The term was translated directly from the Russian *razlozheniye* into German. In Bulgaria, it was called *razlagane*; in Hungay, *bomlasztas*; and it referred to the "decomposition" of hostile activities outside the legal system. The goal is the "softening" (*fellazítás*) of hostile groups, their ability to act, as well as their internal structure and discipline with complex countermeasures and the dissolution of personal relationships. Partial measures included: denunciation, influencing, isolation, and separation.

"Decomposition" invokes biological semantics. It entails the psychological destruction of opposition members as well as the class enemy (subversion of the enemy). The term was previously used by Lenin to describe the state of capitalism as rotten. The same meaning was used for the opposition and those who were critical of the state. To "decompose" them means to make their decay visible. In this sense, the term describes both a state of affairs and the central measure used by the secret services and state security to destroy the enemy.

Decomposition measures

In Directive 1/76, which marked the beginning of systematic decomposition, the possible measures for disrupting a person of interest are described as follows: "systematic discrediting of public reputation, authority, and prestige" through:

false details and the spreading of rumors about:
adultery
pornographic interests
alcohol abuse
sexual relations with minors
greed for money
neglect of parental duties
betrayal of fellow political campaigners, friends, and acquaintances in interrogations
collaboration with the Stasi
generation of mistrust
summoning persons to state offices
use of anonymous or pseudonymous letters
telephone calls

"systematic organization of professional and social failures with the purpose of undermining the self-confidence of individual persons" through:

denial of educational and career opportunities
expulsion from professional associations, or preventing entry into them
making persons insecure and disciplining them repeatedly through repeated interrogations by police, the Stasi, and superiors in the workplace

In addition, commanding officers liked using the following decomposition measures:

restriction of freedom of movement, meaning:
willfully damaging vehicles

revoking driver's licenses or personal identification documents
destruction of private life, such as:
open round-the-clock surveillance
constant telephone calls
advertising campaigns
secret break-ins and moving household objects around
damaging private property
inventing extramarital relationships
secretly organized alienation of children from parents
creation of conditions for criminal proceedings

The decomposition measures were tailored by the responsible commanding officer to the decomposition target and then sent to higher authorities for review. The basic methods for disrupting a person were developed in the law school (*Juristische Hochschule*) in Potsdam, including in graduate theses. The concrete development and "creative" design were then undertaken by the commanding officer.

Decomposition groups, operative

In these groups, partners of the POZW (*politisch-operatives Zusammenwirken*, "political-operative collaboration") gathered together to actively disrupt events. They were generally university and high school students, teachers, managers at the workplaces of participating dissidents, or even members of local community boards. The behavior required of these groups was orchestrated by anonymous Stasi agents. Their task was to "competently and convincingly explain the politics of the party and government in the realms of peace and defense policy, environmental protection, and human rights." (BStU, ZA, JHS VVS 001-351/86, Bl. 63) This was intended to cause the dissidents' message to get lost in the state-conformant statements of the decomposition group.

Deconspiration

The disclosure of organizations, goals, working methods, and persons who were secretly to be used by the Stasi for operative tasks. Especially significant was the deconspiration of unofficial collaborators. This could be done by the unofficial collaborator him- or herself by intentionally revealing their identity to a third party or unintentionally through a violation of the rules of secrecy. Deconspiration was seen as a major harm to the Stasi and an endangerment of their work. The word "deconspiration" was taken directly from Russian (*dekonspiraciya*) according to the Soviet model and has since come into international use.

Differentiation, political-operative

Differentiation was propagated as a method and working principle within the Ministry for State Security with the intention of gaining as precise a description and categorization as possible of the persons named in the reports, operative person controls, and operative case files. Their attitudes and actions were to be classified according to their "dangerousness" to the system and assigned to specific categories (like indifferent, hostile-negative, etc.).

Discrediting

The "systematic discrediting of public reputation, regard, and prestige on the basis of connected, true, verifiable, and discrediting details and untrue, credible, non-disprovable, and thus equally discrediting details" was a common Stasi decomposition measure (*Das MfS-Lexikon. Begriffe, Personen und Strukturen der Staatssicherheit der DDR*, 390 ff). This was accomplished through the spreading of rumors and false details about a person, the creation of mistrust, the dissemination of anonymous and pseudonymous letters and telephone calls, as well as through issuing summonses to state offices. In the sphere of literature and art, the point was primarily to degrade artistic work. They were discredited as "concoctions," "pamphlets," or as "so-called literature" or "so-called art" (MfS, BV Erfurt AOP "Toxin," Vol. 4, BStU 021). In addition, literary texts or artworks were degraded as "incomprehensible" or "unqualified," and writers and artists were pathologized as mentally ill or categorized as "psychopathic." With Rainer Kurz, e.g. in the operative plan, we read: "evidence should be found that Kurz's prose is bad prose and serves only the goal of agitation and the political-ideological diversion of the enemy" (Marko Martin, "'Geschaffene Machwerke'. Die Sprache der Stasi," in *Text+Kritik, Feinderklärung. Literatur und Staatssicherheitsdienst*, ed. Heinz Ludwig Arnold, Issue 120 [1993], p. 51). In 1985, Russian artist Anatoly Zhigalov was institutionalized in a psychiatric clinic after putting on the action *Golden Subbotnik* (*Zolotoy voskresnik*). (http://conceptualism.letov.ru/TOTART/Anatoly-Zhigalov-avtobiografia.html)

Disinformation

The conscious dissemination of completely or partially contradictory information. The goal of disinformation was to discredit persons, institutions, and political projects in the West, and thus to weaken, isolate, or ruin them. It was also used to influence decisions or to deceive the West about actions or conditions in the East (e.g. political and economic problems, measures against critics of the regime, etc.). In the GDR, it was primarily Department X of Central Department A that was responsible for formulating appropriate content and implementing it in concrete actions (active measures). This term was also derived from the Russian *dezinformaciya* (*deza*); in 1923, the GPU had set up an office of disinformation with the goal of hindering the counterrevolutionary activities of their enemies. In the "Maggot" case, the "decomposition" of the artist group Clara Mosch, false information was spread about multiple members (e.g. rumors about spying activities, affairs) in order to foment conflict.

Disinformation, inner

Vladimir Voinovich's formulation. The Russian writer Voinovich reports of the mendaciousness of his files. Even the small amount of material available shows how informants and agents lied upwards to exaggerate their activities and those of the surveillance subjects in order to build their own "careers" or simply fulfill a quota. "I always knew that it was part of the phenomenon of the Soviet system that the lower-downs lied to the higher-ups, the higher-ups to the lower-downs and that they expected lies from them." (Vladimir Voynovich, *Delo №34840* [Moscow, 1993]).

Diversion, political-ideological (PID)

A central term in the terminology of communist state security services. GDR citizens who expressed dissenting political views with an impact on the public were categorized as "supporters of PID" and accordingly placed under surveillance. PID was considered a prerequisite for the development of organized political opposition. After initial skepticism on the part of the Soviets with regard to this term—where ideological disputes were considered a party matter—the term and its associated operative orientation were later adopted by the other communist secret services. One of the goals was to portray supporters of PID as financed and controlled by the West.

Espionage

Espionage refers to activity in a foreign country which aims at the "communication or delivery of facts, objects, or knowledge" to the home country. (https://www.verfassungsschutz.de/de/service/glossar/_lS)

Fiche

Term for secret service files in Switzerland. In 1990, the so-called "Fiche Scandal" (or "Fiche Affair") took place in Switzerland. In the late 1980s, it was gradually made public that Swiss federal authorities and cantonal police had compiled approximately nine hundred thousand fiches on over approximately seven hundred thousand persons and organizations that were considered suspect: foreign anarchists, Swiss socialists and labor unionists, unwelcome political refugees and foreigners.

Forgery/fake

"Fakes" are active measures of the Stasi which are intended to lead to the discrediting of a person or group and could be understood as disinformation acts on the part of the Stasi. For example, the Friedrichsfeld Peace Circle wanted to release their own publication, the *Friedrichsfeld Fire Alarm*. Before the first edition was even prepared by the Peace Circle, onehundred copies produced by the Stasi appeared in opposition circles in Berlin. But because the bell in the logo was printed backwards, people familiar with the group were able to recognize the forgery (Sandra Pingel-Schliemann, *Zersetzen. Strategie einer Diktatur*, Berlin 2003, p.229). In Operation "Arkade," secret police agents surveilled Jürgen Schweinebraden's Berlin gallery, Arkade, and sent forged invitation cards to those potentially interested in his exhibitions. In doing so, the Stasi discredited the gallerist by having people come on the wrong date. Stasi agents even wrote anti-Stasi poems and passed them off as the work of others. (MfS BV Berlin, AOP 7030/82, Vol.7, BStU 120 ff.)

Full-time agents

Full-time agents were the personnel foundation of the secret police apparatus. They conceived of themselves, as in the Soviet tradition, as "chekists" (see **Chekist**). In a state socialist society, they were part of the state-loyal service class and cultivated an *esprit de corps* of elite "comrades of the first class." The number of full-time agents doubled every decade until the early 1980s. In 1989, there were about 91,000—which means that 1 in every 180 GDR citizens was a full-time Stasi agent.

Gaslighting

A term not used by state security, but which was a typical psychological "decomposition" measure. In psychology, gaslighting is described as a form of manipulating someone's perception to where the victim feels uncertain about their own perceptions. One or more persons, repeatedly and over a long period of time, cause the victim to question reality by morphing the certainty of that reality. This can occur through the denial of truly existing things, behaviors, or events, or less commonly through conscious staging.

The term comes from the title of the 1938 play *Gaslight* by the British dramatist Patrick Hamilton. Hamilton describes the distortion of a victim's perception through the use of repeated, long-term manipulation, as well as a constant questioning and doubting of the victim's reality. While gaslighters are generally individual actors in psychology, the practice of secret services utilizes an entire system of actors guided by the state. It is the state which puts its undesirable citizens into the situation of gaslighting. The manipulation happens, above all, through the denial and simple unbelievability of the practices which state security itself carries out. A typical example can be found in the case files of pediatrician Karin Ritter. Along with the spread of rumors about her, the secret police broke into her apartment: they moved around pictures, shifted flowerpots, and switched out the tea in her tea cans. Apartment break-ins were common among artists. Stötzer writes in her memoirs that "decomposition" entailed both surveillance and breaking into her apartment and stealing her things. (cf.Pingel-Schliemann, *Zersetzen. Strategie einer Diktatur*, 278.)

Handling, operative

Euphemism for all activities and measures of the Stasi's "political-operative work," i.e. the actions of the secret services and secret police relating to persons or fact-finding when the Stasi believed there was evidence of "hostile-negative actions." Handling might include the performance of operative monitoring of persons or an operative case, which led to the creation of a file in the Stasi archives.

Hostile-negative

A "political-operative differentiation" used to characterize a majority of those observed. Persons, activities, or elements who did not align with the ideal socialist image were described as "hostile-negative." It was either decided in the measure plans to transform "hostile-negative" elements into socialist ones, or the persons and groups were "decomposed" and their activities, where possible, thwarted. In the files of artist Gabriele Stötzer, we read: "the hostile-negative attitude of this person, her goal of spreading negative ideas and joining with other hostile-negative persons of like mind, is suited to assist in the organization of a political underground in the GDR" (Gabriele Stötzer, *Stasidada*, typescript). In other secret service languages, there is no direct correspondence to "hostile-negative." In Polish, the term *wroga działalność* (hostile activity) is used.

In the German Office for the Protection of the Constitution, the term "extremist efforts" roughly corresponds to the paradigm of the "enemy within." This includes "activities with the goal of eliminating liberal democracy, preparatory acts, agitation, and acts of violence." In Eastern Europe, it was precisely those acts which took the constitution seriously that were labelled "hostile-negative." Without intending to compare with the techniques of enemy production in dictatorships, abuse can also happen in democracies with regard to the assessment of "extremist efforts," e.g. when political "critics" come under suspicion of extremism, as happened in Germany in 2018 when an investigation was begun into the Center for Political Beauty on suspicion of forming a criminal organization. In Germany, § 129 StGB is considered the "snooping paragraph," through which investigative authorities are authorized to perform mail monitoring, telephone surveillance, long-term observation, the use of **informants** and secret investigators, digital dragnets, and major bugging operations.

Individual procedure

A form of procedure common between 1950 and 1960. At the center of the "operational procedure" was an individual person accused of "hostile activity."

Influencing

An operative method of prevention. Aims at altering the will, the formation of opinions, and the emotions in a "favorable" direction. Influencing is targeted towards politically unstable persons with "unfavorable personality traits" who are inclined towards "negative tendencies."

Informant

A common term in the secret services of both Western and Eastern Europe. The German Federal Intelligence Agency (*Bundesnachrichtendienst*) describes the informant as "a person who in individual cases, or occasionally and voluntarily, offers information about an observation subject to the constitutional defense agencies." (https://www.verfassungsschutz.de/de/service/glossar/_lI) In Hungary and Romania, domestic spies, i.e. those who were called "unofficial collaborators" in the GDR, were called informants. In Robert W. Pringle's *Historical Dictionary of Russian* and Soviet Intelligence, he writes that there were an estimated twenty-two million informants in the Soviet Union during the Second World War; the KGB is alleged to have had ten million until the fall of the Soviet Union (Rowman & Littlefield, 2015). The political police in Switzerland called full-time informants "insiders." They were given code names and generally played the role of leftists (with long hair): "encouraged crimes as *agents provocateurs*, [and] registered dozens to hundreds of sit-in and protest participants" (Frischknecht, Jürg, "Willi von de Bombenpolizei." WOZ 2 [2006]: 619. Accessed June 9, 2019. https://www.woz.ch/.)

Intermediaries (V-Leute), countermen, and information persons

Term of German Federal Intelligence Service (BND) for persons "who are methodically and systematically deployed for the acquisition of information about extremist efforts. They are not employees of the constitutional defense authorities. They are generally paid for their information. The identity of intermediaries is specially protected (see also 'source protection'). The use of intermediaries is an intelligence method/instrument." (https://www.verfassungsschutz.de/de/service/glossar/_lV#v-leute) In contrast, countermen are agents of a foreign intelligence service used for the targeted acquisition of information.

Isolation

A frequently used measure against artists for the "decomposition" of individual groups or groups of friends. The purposes included "isolation in public" or to remove the "influence [of a person] on other artists." (MFS, BV KMSt, AKG, 3485, Vol.1, BStU 021.)

Kidnapping

Defined as the "conveying of persons against their will, and with the use of specific means and methods (violence, threats, deception, narcotics, intoxicants, etc.), from their original residence to another location, state, or region."

In line with this Stasi-specific definition, we can distinguish between three tactical, sometimes combinable, **kidnapping** variants: abductions using physical violence; abductions using narcotics; and **kidnappings** by means of malicious deception. In the 1950s, an increased number of political opponents of the GDR residing in West Germany were kidnapped, sentenced, and imprisoned in the GDR. In 1964, the exiled Czech author Pavel Tigrid, who was the publisher of the exile journal *Svědectví*, was about to be kidnapped by state security at an international PEN congress in Hungary. They were planning to bring him to trial in Prague. However, he was tipped off just in time by the Hungarian secret service and was able to leave for Paris. Nevertheless, in 1966, he was tried in absentia and sentenced to fourteen years in prison.

Kompromat

Proof or evidence of legal or moral misbehavior of a citizen of the GDR. Kompromat was used both in decomposition and the recruitment of unofficial collaborators (IMs). In the latter case, the future IM was blackmailed into collaboration with the Stasi. Because motivational difficulties were expected in such situations, commanding officers rarely used kompromat. In contrast, kompromat was frequently used in decomposition measures, even if it was intentionally staged by the Stasi. The term was taken from Russian, where it is an acronym for *compromising material.*

Legend, operative

Orchestrated fictional facts and guises that triggered desired behaviors in specific persons and/or were intended to put the Stasi in a position to gain certain information. The intelligence background of the person or event, i.e. the informant and the action itself, was to remain hidden. The legend should be believable, based on verifiable facts, and tailored to every individual person to be observed or handled. Depending on the operative goal, there were legends relating to travel, investigations, conversations, and contacts, as well as evasion and retreat backstories. In German intelligence, the legend is the use of "wholly or partially invented or altered biographical data for the purpose of fulfilling the missions of the intelligence services and to protect their agents from third parties. Means of camouflage are used in the legend, particularly cover addresses, cover identification, and cover license plates." (https://www.verfassungs schutz.de/de/service/glossar/_lL)

Liquidation

This term was only used for abstract things like events, possibilities, and subjects, and referred to their "decomposition." In Operation "Arkade," diverse measures were taken to "liquidate the gallery" of Jürgen Schweinebraden, e.g. by means of a power outage which required weeks of repairs afterwards, or the sending of anonymous materials with the goal of defaming the gallery. In Polish files, the liquidation of groups and institutions is interestingly referred to as neutralization (*neutralizacja*), e.g. of the artist group Orange Alternative (*Pomaranczowa Alternatywa*).

Masking

To remain unnoticed during surveillance actions, informants, spies, and agents used the method of masking. In the BStU, one can research how observation bases served as cloakrooms for the storage of professional outfits, wigs, and makeup tools. On the day of deployment, the agents would discreetly dress themselves in a way appropriate to their surroundings, whether as a laborer, forester, or waiter.

Some local Stasi offices used hairstylists and mask-makers as full-time agents for masking measures. "Vehicle masking" referred to Stasi vehicles which received a civilian disguise through private objects, falsified license plates, or imprinted company signs. The term was taken directly from the Russian *maskirovka*, where it still has the same meaning.

Measures, active

Activities of the Stasi in the West that went beyond the collection of information. In the 1950s, this also included kidnappings and assassinations. Later, it mainly concerned the spreading of disinformation, the waging of psychological warfare, and in part, measures to influence political decision-making processes. A spectacular instance was the assassination of Bulgarian exiled author Georgi Markov on September 7, 1978 on the Waterloo Bridge in London. The weapon used was an umbrella. As we now know, the Bulgarian secret service had prepared the tip of the umbrella with a small pellet which was rammed into Markov's right calf by an agent. In the pellet were approximately two hundred micrograms of ricin. In the files, there can be found no term of equivalent significance for domestic actions. They often speak of an operative, political-operative, or disciplinary measure. In the *Historical Dictionary of Russian and Soviet Intelligence,* Robert W. Pringle mentions that contract killing was also called a "wet business" (*mokroye dela*) or "black work" (*chernaya rabota*) (Rowman and Littlefield Publishers, 2015).

Measure Plan

In a measure plan, or action plan, the initial steps were clearly defined and assigned their responsible parties. These measure plans often substantially consisted of "decomposition measures," which were coordinated and planned out by the commanding officer. If the plan was approved by the higher authorities, it was given over to the commanding officer to implement. For example, the measure plan against Hungarian artist Tamás St.Auby plotted to have him admitted to a psychiatric clinic if he did not cease to make happenings.

Methods, Operative

A system of principles and rules gained from experience and scientific knowledge which served to accomplish secret service missions and to effectively implement operative forces and means. The methods were adapted to the specific, actual operative conditions.

Monitoring process

A form of procedure used in the GDR from 1953 to 1960. In monitoring processes, persons were investigated who were considered potentially politically unreliable or hostile, and thus preventatively observed, e.g. former Nazi functionaries, former Social Democrats, participants in the actions of June 17, 1953 as well as persons who had moved from the West. Because the monitoring process gradually declined in significance, the still-existing cases became subject cases in the 1960s.

Network

Hálózat (Hungarian) is a term used internally by Hungarian state security to refer to secret collaborators who were organized as a "network." Also common as a term of self-reference in Romania: *rețea*. (See Verdery, *Secrets and Truth*, 277.)

Observation, operative

"Operative observation" was among the conspiratorial investigative methods generally assigned by the operative service units of the Ministry for State Security and carried out by full-time agents. So-called target persons (also called "observation subjects") were observed for a specific period of time in order to find information about residence locations, connections, work positions, lifestyle habits, and potentially criminal activities. Information from surveillance was entered into personal screening checks, operative case files, and security reviews.

Observer

Stasi agents specially trained in operative surveillance. These were sometimes so-called unknown collaborators or observer-informants (*Inoffizieller Mitarbeiter im besonderen Einsatz*, IME). Observers were trained in secret photography, cartography, personal identification, and vehicle pursuit. They were taught how to move discreetly on foot, in automobiles, and on public transit, as well as how to keep the correct distance from the subject. Sometimes groups of observers were used with different assigned roles. During official or private visits by Western politicians, bodyguards or police officers often functioned as observers.

Operative action (operativer Vorgang, OV)

An operation requiring registration and a general term for individual or group operations which were initiated to enable action against undesirable persons in the framework of secret or sometimes also public investigations. An operation of this kind was opened on the basis of what the Stasi viewed as criminal offenses. It encompassed personal background checks, mission reports, measure plans, and detailed descriptions of the observed person, his or her habits, and milieu. The naming of operative actions was left to the assigned commanding officer, the name often having a relationship to the person being handled. The names often came from the art world, e.g. "autodidact," "paintbrush," "tipper," "interpreter," "silkscreen," "palette," "Schwitters," or "Festő" (painter). Or they were pastiches of the surnames of the observed persons, like "Horgászok" in the case of Péter Halász (whose last name means "fisher"). The operational names were often clearly pejorative and fit into propagandistic enemy schemas, e.g. vermin names for the artist group Clara Mosch ("maggot," "worm") or to emphasize danger, as in the case of Gabriele Stötzer, who was given the operational name "Toxin."

As compared with Russian, this term was slightly adapted, as *delo operativnoy razrabotki* literally means "operation/occasion/matter/dossier of the **operative action**." In Hungarian, the **operative action** was called *O-dosszié* (operative dossier). Similar to the OV is the summary name of collections of personal, group, surveillance, search, object, special event, and monitoring dossiers. The **operative action** pertaining to an individual person was carried out as *személyi dosszié*. In the O-Register (*O-napló*), object files were archived after the conclusion of the action. In Bulgarian, the OV had almost the same name as in Hungary, *operativno delo*. A distinction was also made between personal (*lično delo*) and professional (*rabotno delo*) files. In the Polish files, the Russian origins of the term *sprawa operacyjnego rozpracowania* are palpable, being taken over word for word. The files were named with *kryptonim* and subsequently its code name.

Patronage

Patronage was a decomposition measure in the GDR used on groups of artists to isolate individual group members and thereby bring about the dissolution of the group. By funneling jobs to individual artists, enabling exhibition participation, awarding prizes, grants, and honors, or approving travel to the West, the intention was to both distance the individual artist from other group members and to enable career possibilities in the system. In the artist group Clara Mosch, for example, measures against one member were planned to "cause him, by means of intense political-ideological cultivation, patronage, and appropriate political-op. measures, to distance himself from the activities of persons XX." (MfS, BV, KMSt) 3485, Vol.1, BStU 024. Another form of patronage was undertaken by the Central Intelligence Agency in 1950 with the Berlin-based group "Congress for Cultural Freedom" (CCF), founded in the same year, with the intention of influencing leftist circles through financial injections and pro-American propaganda in the art world. The congress published approximately twenty political magazines, put on events, and organized prize award ceremonies. Abstract Expressionist artists like painters Jackson Pollock and Mark Rothko were given particular support. (See Scott-Smith and. Lerg (ed.), *Campaigning Culture and the Global Cold War: The Journals of the Congress for Cultural Freedom.)*

Performative censorship

Sylvia Sasse's term for state security censorship measures intended to stop art actions and exhibitions by means of performative, theatrical actions. These included breaking water pipes, hindering exhibitions, faking invitation cards for exhibitions, break-ins, and even lavish counterperformances like the Moscow Bulldozer Exhibition on September 15, 1974. Stasi language speaks of "hindering." In Polish and Hungarian files, one finds the term "prevention" in the context of antihappening measures.

"Plainclothes art historians"

Term used by artists to refer to informants and spies who were planted in the art scene. The formulation comes from Russian (*iskusstvovedy v shtatskom*) and was primarily used in the Soviet Union. The artist Sven Gundlach writes for example that "plainclothes art historians" were present disguised as drivers at the Bulldozer Exhibition (Sven Gundlakh. "Vystavka kak aktsiya." *Dekorativnoye iskusstvo* 5: 33).

Preventative surveillance

Society, as well as public, economic, and social institutions, were preventatively surveilled by secret informants and later through unofficial collaborators. The idea was that due to the influence of hostile Western threats, there were dangers to socialism, and thus the GDR, everywhere in society. As a result of the détente policy, the Stasi, keeping in mind their international reputation, increasingly avoided openly repressive measures and replaced them with preventative, clandestine, and manipulative approaches that required significantly more staff resources.

Prioritization

Priorálás (English: "to prioritize") refers to the practice of "searching" for specific topics, keywords, or persons within the archives of state security. It was a daily routine assignment of state security officers and was part of the "ABCs of State Security" (Krisztián Ungváry), which helped to uncover "deconspiration" or supposedly "fictive" recruitments.

Psychology, operative

"Operative psychology" was first offered as a course of study in 1965 at the law school *Juristische Hochschule (*JHS) in Potsdam-Eiche. This was a school specifically transformed for the Stasi. The specialization "Operative Psychology" could be chosen during postgraduate studies. It provided the foundational learning of decomposition measures, interaction with unofficial collaborators, and interrogation of dissidents. Numerous graduate theses discussed practical examples of what such measures or interrogations might look like. Operative psychology with this "goal" was only offered at the JHS in the GDR.

Public and traditional operations

This is a service unit established by the Stasi in 1955. It was responsible for the preparation of exhibitions, print publications, and films for the activities of the Stasi as well as for the placement of such themes in GDR media. Starting in the late 1950s, the Stasi's public operations concentrated on electronic media and film. Particularly successful was the Stasi-inspired 1963 film *For Eyes Only* about the spectacular theft of an index of agents from the Würzburg office of the American military intelligence service MID by the "scout" Horst Hesse.

Questioning

Option permissible under criminal procedural law for officially taking up contact with suspects, witnesses, and other persons before the introduction of investigation proceedings (criminal procedural early review phase) of Eastern European secret police. § 95 StPO/1968 permitted suspects to be "delivered" to questioning ("delivery"). The Stasi sometimes used questioning as a demonstrative measure to intimidate dissidents who themselves could not be subject to investigation proceedings for political reasons. Questioning was also used in decomposition plans to intentionally spread or confirm rumors and to foment distrust in groups. In this book, we have published the questioning of an artist which formally resembles a discussion: the Stasi officers show an interest in the genre of "action art," in the artist's milieu as well as in leverage which they could potentially use against him. In the Soviet Union, there were "prophylactic warnings" and summonses to interviews; between 1967 and 1975, more than one hundred thirty thousand Soviet citizens were summoned to interviews and given warnings. Possible causes of this include the publication of a book, either in samizdat or abroad (Vladimir Voinovich writes about this in his book *Delo №34840*), or also making contact with foreigners. Dissidents report of such summonses in the *Chronicle of Ongoing Events* (*Khronika tekushchikh sobytiy*), the longest-running periodical of the post-Stalin USSR).

Rendezvous

The rendezvous was a secret meeting between a commanding officer or instructor and an unofficial collaborator. The rendezvous was among the "most important methods" of information transfer. It had a number of tasks to fulfill, like personal discussion, the assignment of tasks, and reporting. The training, instruction, qualification, and review of the unofficial collaborator also took place entirely or partially in the rendezvous, which took place, if possible, in a secret apartment. There was the "primary rendezvous," the "pre-rendezvous," and the "visual rendezvous" where the parties signaled to each other, without speaking, whether a primary rendezvous was possible. In his novel, *Revised Version*, Péter Esterházy writes about the rendezvous of his father with state security.

Residentory

A "residentory" (German: **Residentur**) is a "camouflaged intelligence base in an area of operations." A distinction was made between official or semi-official locations (e.g. embassy, commercial delegation). They were respectively referred to as "legal residentories" and illegal, clandestine residentories.

Rumor

Rumors were a popular decomposition measure for isolating persons from a group, from friends, or from family, and for discrediting their public reputation. The truth content of the disseminated rumors was largely undetermined, which made it even more difficult to defend oneself against them. The content was tailored to each individual person, and could concern adultery, pornographic interests, alcohol abuse, sexual relations with minors, greed, betrayal, neglect of parental responsibilities, or even collaboration with the Stasi itself. For example, there was a rumor spread about a potential Stasi informant in the artist group Clara

Mosch. "In the circle of friends and acquaintances, the suspicion should be spread that XX is constantly informing local party and state organs about confidential matters among his group of friends." (MfS, BV, KMSt) 3485, Vol. 1, BStU 022. There were also cases of artists being summoned to "legendary interviews," which were only intended to intensify suspicion that the artist was working with the organs of state.

Security reviews

Procedures for assessing the "security-political" suitability of persons who were to be entrusted with important missions, functions, and authorizations, or to whom authority and/or permissions and approvals were to be assigned. Security reviews and other investigations of persons which took place beneath the level of officially registered operations numbered in the hundreds of thousands annually (1987: approx. four hundred thousand) and were primarily carried out by local Stasi offices. By the end of 1987, an average of one in every two GDR citizens were recorded in the Prevention, Search, and Tip Index of the local Stasi office.

Self-disqualification

Describes the attempt of artists to disqualify themselves in advance from collaboration with state security. The Czech artist Jan Mlčoch avoided collaboration with the secret police by asserting, when offered to become an informant, that he had already announced at work that he had met with an employee of the Interior Ministry. He was thus no longer trustworthy. See Tomáš Pospiszyl, "Look Who's Watching? Photographic Documentation of Happenings and Performances in Czechoslovakia."

Signalization

In Hungary, the term *szignalizáció* refers to a "method which enables the precise assignment of responsibility (prosecution) of persons outside of the context of prevention and criminal proceedings. It is a 'giving a sign' about activities hostile to society for the responsible party, state, social, or economic institutions or authorities" (Béla Révész, *Források a titkosszolgálatok politológiai tanulmányozásához (Sources for the study of the research in politology on secret services)* [Szeged, 2010], 265).

Siphoning (Abschöpfen)

The secret collection of operationally relevant information by the Stasi. Persons could be "siphoned off" by unofficial collaborators. Siphoning also refers to the intentional or unintentional transfer of information from the unofficial collaborator or "social collaborator for security" (*gesellschaftlicher Mitarbeiter für Sicherheit*, GMS) to the commanding officer. One example of this was an "operative measure" against a member of the artist group Clara Mosch, allowing him to travel abroad to the West in order to "siphon" further information, e.g. about art smuggling. (MfS, BV Karl-Marx-Stadt, XIV 73/75, Vol. 5, pp. 6.)

Source

A central category of unofficial collaborator (IM) in Head Office A. "Sources," for the Stasi, were IMs in the West who had access to information about the activities, intentions, resources, and internal structures of "hostile" institutions. These could include political parties, associations, or industrial companies. The German constitutional defense authorities define a source as: "the origin of an item of information. Sources can be persons (e.g. informants) but also media (e.g. internet, printed matter) or other agencies. 'Source protection' is all of those measures which are necessary and appropriate to protect an intelligence source from demasking and its consequences." (https://www.verfassungsschutz.de/de/service/glossar/_lQ)

Surveillance

Surveillance was a central political practice of dictatorships in Eastern Europe. In the case of GDR state security, one speaks not only of a political secret police, but also of surveillance and control organizations. This was not just about the surveillance of people who had already committed crimes, but about the concept of the "preventive surveillance" of citizens and institutions, suggesting that the enemy could be lurking anywhere. In concrete terms, "operative observation" became a conspiratorial investigation method that was intended to pinpoint whereabouts, connections, jobs, and living habits. Training was provided in undercover photography, mapping, personal identification, and chase-driving. Surveillance included both acoustic room surveillance via the wiretapping of systems (telephone surveillance, bugs, etc.), as well as optical and electronic room surveillance through installed vehicles and video cameras, often with the aim of producing kompromat.

Tipper

A category of unofficial collaborator who tipped off the Stasi about persons who might be candidates for unofficial collaboration, particularly in the area of operations. As a rule, this unofficial collaborator had a professional, political, or social position which enabled a corresponding overview. Also used as a term in Hungary, e.g. "tip search" (*tippkutatás*): the first phase of network formation in the search for a person.

Unofficial Collaborator (IM)

Unofficial collaborators (*inoffizielle Mitarbeiter*, IMs) were the "primary instrument" of state security in the GDR for the surveillance of society. Generally acting in secret and of their own accord, they provided information about their professional and private worlds. They worked in every area of GDR society as well as abroad, including in West Germany. In the GDR, they were intended to exhaustively investigate dissenting opinions or even plans to flee to the West and to act accordingly in the interests of state security. With respect to their number, we can identify a similar quantitative development to full-time agents, their number peaking in the late 1970s at around two hundred thousand. In the second half of the 1980s, forty-five hundred to five thousand operations, and about twenty-thousand-person controls, were carried out annually. The Stasi ultimately distinguished between the following subcategories:

Unofficial Collaborator in Special Deployment (*Inoffizieller Mitarbeiter im besonderen Einsatz*, IME)

IMEs were unofficial collaborators who took on special tasks. These could be IMs in "key positions," so-called expert IMs, or those specializing in surveillance and investigation.

– *Unofficial Collaborator for Homeland Defense with Enemy Connections and for the Immediate Handling of Persons Suspected of Hostile Actions (Inoffizieller Mitarbeiter der Abwehr mit Feindverbindung bzw. zur unmittelbaren Bearbeitung im Verdacht der Feindtätigkeit stehender Personen*, IMB*)*

IMBs were particularly important IMs. They enjoyed the confidence of the Stasi, and they also had direct contacts with people classified by the Stasi as hostile.

Unofficial Collaborator for the Assurance of Secrecy and Communication (*Inoffizieller Mitarbeiter zur Sicherung der* Konspiration *und des Verbindungswesens*, IMK) IMKs were indispensable for the secret infrastructure of state security: they made their apartments or rooms available ("secret apartment") as well as their addresses ("cover address") and telephone number ("cover telephone"), or otherwise contributed to the maintenance of secrecy ("other"). The Stasi needed these various categories of IMK to guarantee discreet communication with their informers.

Social Collaborator for Security (*Gesellschaftlicher Mitarbeiter für Sicherheit*, GMS)

GMSs were intended to stand up for "security, order, and lawfulness" and to remain publicly loyal to the state. The "mass vigilance" achieved in this way was intended to hinder the development of "hostile powers" and lighten the burden of IMs and their commanding officers. GMSs were selected and recruited in a similar way to IMs, although confidentiality requirements and file-keeping were more relaxed. GMSs were intended to be used for the direct "handling" of opponents of the regime.

Commanding IM (*Führungs*-IM, FIM)

FIMs managed multiple IMs and/or GMSs to collect incoming information and disseminate the orders of state security. Candidate FIMs were persons who were particularly loyal to the Party (SED) and discreet according to state security.

Upon entering the Stasi, the future IM wrote a letter of motivation, at the end of which he or she specified a new name. This name was freely chosen by the IM, e.g. "Rose," "Kurt," "Rene," "Frank Körner," or "Otto Pfötzner." An IM could also have multiple code names.

In the Hungarian secret service, unofficial collaborators were categorized according to their motivations. Secret agents (Hungarian: *titkos megbízott*, "tmb") acted from political conviction and the informant (*ügynök*) for financial reasons or for other advantages, but also due to blackmail with the help of compromising information in the possession of the secret service. In the Bulgarian secret service, unofficial collaborators were called *špion* or *taen agent* and informants *razuznavč* or *informator*. In the Polish files, the latter were instead called information sources (*źródło informacji*). In the KGB, collaborators were called SEKSOT, the acronym for *sekretnye sotrudniki* or secret collaborators.

Who-knows-who schema (WKW schema, Who's-Who Report)

The WKW schema was a working method for recording and presenting the family, friends, and other relations of a person. It served the purpose of guaranteeing the secrecy and security of IMs, coordinating their deployment, and showing them new deployment possibilities. Graphic representations portray the connections between the IM and other persons, as well as how these other persons were connected themselves. Different colors and symbols were used to portray the different characters of the persons in this system and its connections. It was used primarily in IM files, but also in various operational actions. In the case of the artist group Clara Mosch, IMB "Franziska Platter" was tasked with a who's-who clarification. "MfS, BV Karl-Marx-Stadt, XIV 73/75, Vol.5, pp.9). Sketches were also sometimes created, e.g. of the Gallery Arkade relationship network (MfS BV Berlin, AOP 7030/82, Vol.1, BStU 0153). In the files of Jiří Kolář, there can also be found a list of Kolář's friends and their characteristics in addition to blueprints of his apartment. See Tomáš Pospiszyl, "Look Who's Watching? Photographic Documentation of Happenings and Performances in Czechoslovakia," in this volume.

Compiled by Susanne Wegmann, Kata Krasznahorkai, and Sylvia Sasse
Translated from German by Brian Alkire

The entries originate from various lexicons, primarily from: *Das MfS-Lexikon. Begriffe, Personen und Strukturen der Staatssicherheit der DDR*, 3rd Edition (Berlin, 2016); *The Language of the Secret Services, Appendix* in: Béla Révész, *Források a titkosszolgálatok politológiai tanulmányozásához (Sources for the study of the research in politology on secret services*) (Szeged, 2010).

Index of authors

* The descriptions of the artistic works are by Inke Arns (A), Kata Krasznahorkai (K) and Sylvia Sasse (S).

INKE ARNS, PhD, director and curator of Hartware MedienKunstVerein in Dortmund, Germany (www.hmkv.de). She has worked internationally as an independent curator and theorist specializing in media art, net cultures, and Eastern Europe since 1993. She studied Russian literature, Eastern European studies, political science, and art history in Berlin and Amsterdam (1988–1996). In 2004, she received her PhD from the Humboldt University in Berlin with a thesis focusing on a paradigmatic shift in the way artists reflected the historical avant-garde and the notion of utopia in visual and media art projects of the 1980s and 1990s in (ex-) Yugoslavia and Russia. She has curated many exhibitions at home and abroad—at the Bauhaus Museum Dessau, Museum of Contemporary Art Metelkova Ljubljana, KW Institute for Contemporary Art Berlin, Ujazdów Castle Warsaw, Hartware MedienKunstVerein Dortmund, Haus der Kulturen der Welt Berlin, Muzeum Sztuki in Łódź and BOZAR Centre for Fine Arts Brussels among others—and is the author of numerous articles on media art and net culture. www.inkearns.de

MĂDĂLINA BRAȘOVEANU is an art historian and independent curator, based in Oradea, Romania. She recently received a PhD from the Faculty of Art History and Theory, National University of Arts in Bucharest (Universitatea Națională de Arte), with a thesis on unconventional art practices within artists' collectives in Romania in the 1980s. She researches and writes about art in Romania in socialism, with a focus on artistic micro-communities, conceptual art and archival and exhibition studies. She was recipient of research grants funded by the Getty Foundation, New Europe College, and the Institute for Advanced Studies in Bucharest. She was a member in several research projects funded by the Executive Agency for Higher Education, Research, Development and Innovation Funding (UEFISCDI) for the National Council for Development and Innovation (CNDI). She was assistant curator of the Romanian Participation at the Venice Biennale in 2019.

LILIANA GÓMEZ is a SNSF-professor (Swiss National Science Foundation) at the Institute of Art History at the University of Zurich, where she directs the project "Contested Amnesia and Dissonant Narratives in the

Global South: Post-Conflict in Literature", Art, and Emergent Archives. Recently, she edited *Performing Human Rights: Contested Amnesia and Aesthetic Practices in the Global South* (diaphanes, 2021) and co-edited with Lisa Blackmore *Liquid Ecologies in Latin American and Caribbean Art* (Routledge, 2020). She is the author of *Lo urbano. Teorías culturales y políticas de la ciudad en América Latina* (Pittsburgh, IILI, 2014) and *A Camera in the Laboratory of the Modern. Photographic* Archives *and the Anthropocene* (diaphanes, forthcoming).

HRISTOV HRISTOV is a journalist and researcher. In January 2011, he created an independent, specialized web site dedicated to the former State Security Services entitled desebg.com and to the victims of communism, pametbg.com. Hristo Hristov is the only journalist and researcher to have initiated and won a court proceeding against the Bulgarian state for access to the documents of the former State Security Services during periods of restrictive state policy. The site is in several languages, including English. Among other works, he has published *Kill the Wanderer: The Secret* Archives *of the Bulgarian State Security Services Reveal the Truth about Georgi Markov—Murdered in London by a Poisoned Umbrella*, Sofia 2013.

ILJANA KAMENOVA is a student of Slavic Studies at the University of Zurich. She attended the seminar "Literature and Secret Service" in 2019.

ANNA KRAKUS is an Assistant Professor in the departments of Department of Cross-Cultural and Regional Studies at the University of Copenhagen. She holds a PhD in Comparative Literature from New York University. Her monograph *No End in Sight: Polish Film During Late Socialism* came out with the University of Pittsburgh Press in 2018. Her next project engages with material culture, collections, and files for the former Polish secret police. She has engaged with the secret police files since 2009 when she first undertook a search for Michel Foucault's file from his year in Poland in 1958.

KATA KRASZNAHORKAI is a Berlin-based art historian and curator working at the University of Zurich. During 2014–2019, she was a senior researcher in the European Research Council project titled "Performance Art in Eastern Europe 1950-1990: History and Theory" (www.performanceart.info). Her research focuses on the interrelation between art and state security. Since 1999, parallel to her work as a scholar, Krasznahorkai has been active as a curator for institutions such as the

Ludwig Museum Budapest and the Collegium Hungaricum Berlin. With Sylvia Sasse and Inke Arns, she curated the exhibition "Artists & Agents. Performance art and Secret Services" at the Hartware MedienKunstVerein Dortmund (October 26, 2019 – April 16, 2020). Her monograph *Operative Art History or Who is Afraid of Artists?* will be published by Spector Books in 2021.

ELISABETH PICHLER studied communication design at the University of Applied Sciences in Potsdam and received her master's degree in Cultures of the Curatorial at the Academy of Visual Arts in Leipzig (HGB). Together with Lena von Geyso, she works as a curatorial team called "*Kein Ort, sondern ein Zustand*" ("Not a place, but a condition"), and produces interdisciplinary projects and exhibitions that combine experimental, media-scientific, and artistic approaches. Since October 2016, Elisabeth Pichler has been a scholarship holder at the DFG PhD Program "The Photographic Dispositif" at Braunschweig University of Art (HBK).

TOMÁŠ POSPISZYL is a critic, curator, and art historian. He studied at Charles University in Prague and Bard College in New York. Since 2003, he teaches Art History at the Film and TV School of the Academy of Performing Arts in Prague and since 2012, at the Academy of Fine Arts in Prague. He serves on the board of tranzit.cz, an art initiative in the Czech Republic, for which he prepared exhibitions, lectures, and public programs. Most recently, he worked on the performative exhibition *Július Koller* Archive*: Study Room* in 2012. His publications in English include, among others, the anthology *Primary Documents: A Sourcebook for Eastern and Central European Art since the 1950s*, which he edited together with Laura Hoptman (MIT Press, Museum of Modern Art, New York, 2002).

ŁUKASZ RONDUDA is an art historian and curator specializing in Polish contemporary art and film. He graduated from the Department of Art History at Łódź University in 2001. He currently works on the film collection at the Museum of Modern Art in Warsaw. He is also currently an assistant professor at the School of Social Psychology (Uniwersytet Humanistyczno-społeczny, SWPS) in Warsaw. Ronduda has curated numerous exhibitions, such as *Polish Video Art From the 70s and '80s* (2006), at the Tate Modern in London, and *The Enthusiasts: From Amateur Film Clubs*, a project by the artists Marysia Lewandowska and Neil Cummings. He has published many catalogues and other publications, including *Polish Art of the 70s* (2009) and *1, 2, 3 ... Avant-Gardes*, a volume, co-edited with Florian Zeyfang in 2007.

SYLVIA SASSE is a professor of Slavic Literature Studies at the University of Zurich. She has led different projects on "Performance Art in Eastern Europe 1950–1990. History and Theory" (European Research Council), "Literature and Art on Trial" (Swiss National Science Foundation), theater theory, and theory of literature. She has published numerous books and articles, the last being *Subversive Affirmation: Critique of critique revisited.* In addition, she co-curated the exhibition *Storming of the Winter Palace* with Inke Arns, as well as *Artists & Agents. Performance Art and Secret Services* with Inke Arns and Kata Krasznahorkai at Hartware MedienKunstVerein Dortmund.

TAMÁS SZŐNYEI has been working at the Historical Archives of the Hungarian State Security in Budapest since 2002. Szőnyei has written monographs on new wave music (*Az új hullám évtizede* 1989, 1992). He's also written on the interaction of rock music and literature with the state security based on research into documents of the former secret service: *Nyilván tartottak – Titkos szolgák a magyar rock körül 1960–1990* (*Kept On File—Secret Servants around Rock in Hungary*) and *Titkos írás – Állambiztonsági szolgálat és irodalmi élet 1956–1990* (*Secret Writing—The State Security Services and Literary Life, Volumes 1&2*). Recently, he published a major illustrated catalogue of his collection of Hungarian new wave posters, titled *Pokoli aranykor* (*Infernal Golden Age*, 2017), with a special focus on the interaction between state security and motifs of new wave posters.

ANIKÓ SZŰCS is a Mellon Fellow and Visiting Assistant Professor in Comparative Literature at Haverford College in Philadelphia. She is currently completing her first book, which analyzes contemporary artists' use of state security files in their artworks. She holds a Ph.D. in performance studies from New York University, and an M.A. in theatre studies and dramaturgy from the University of Theatre, Film, and Television of Budapest. She cocurated the exhibition *Revolutionary Voices: Performing Arts in Central & Eastern Europe in the 1980s* at the New York Public Library for the Performing Arts, Lincoln Center, and has published articles in both English and Hungarian.

SUSANNE WEGMANN is a student of Slavic Studies at the University of Zurich. She attended the seminar "Literature and Secret Service" in 2019.

Index of Names

686 Annex 2019